Teaching Reading

A Balanced Approach for Today's Classrooms

Teaching Reading

A Balanced Approach for Today's Classrooms

Pamela J. Farris
Distinguished Teaching Professor
Northern Illinois University

Carol J. Fuhler
Associate Professor
Iowa State University

Maria P. Walther
National Board Certified Teacher, Gwendolyn Brooks Elementary School, Aurora, Illinois

Boston   Burr Ridge, IL   Dubuque, IA   Madison, WI   New York   San Francisco   St. Louis
Bangkok   Bogotá   Caracas   Kuala Lumpur   Lisbon   London   Madrid   Mexico City
Milan   Montreal   New Delhi   Santiago   Seoul   Singapore   Sydney   Taipei   Toronto

TEACHING READING: A BALANCED APPROACH FOR
TODAY'S CLASSROOMS
Published by McGraw-Hill, a business unit of The McGraw-Hill
Companies, Inc. 1221 Avenue of the Americas, New York, NY,
10020. Copyright © 2004, by The McGraw-Hill Companies, Inc. All
rights reserved.
Some ancillaries, including electronic and print components, may
not be available to customers outside the United States.

This book is printed on acid-free paper.

1 2 3 4 5 6 7 8 9 0 DOC/DOC 0 9 8 7 6 5 4 3 2

ISBN 0-07-236070-4

Publisher: *Jane Karpacz*
Developmental editor: *Cara Harvey*
Marketing manager: *Pamela Cooper*
Senior project manager: *Jean Hamilton*
Production supervisor: *Carol Bielski*
Coordinator freelance design: *Gino Cieslik*
Photo research coordinator: *Holly Rudelitsch*
Photo researcher: *Amy Bethea*
Supplement associate: *Kate Boylan*
Media producer: *Lance Gerhart*
Cover design: *Gino Cieslik*
Interior design: *Kay Fulton*
Compositor: *GAC Indianapolis*
Typeface: *10/12 Times Roman*
Printer: *R. R. Donnelley & Sons Company*

Library of Congress Cataloging-in-Publication Data
Farris, Pamela J.
    Teaching reading : a balanced approach for today's classrooms /
Pamela J. Farris, Carol J. Fuhler, Maria P. Walther.— 1st ed.
        p. cm.
    Includes bibliographical references (p.) and index.
    ISBN 0-07-236070-4 (alk. paper)
    1. Reading. 2. Language arts. I. Fuhler, Carol J. II. Walther,
    Maria P. III. Title.
LB1050.F345 2004
372.4—dc21
                                                        2001057906

www.mhhe.com

To the many dedicated teachers in today's classrooms as they day after day nurture and support their students as well as introduce them to the marvels and magic of books. And to my husband, Richard, and our son, Kurtis, who enjoy reaping the knowledge and joy gained through reading.
P.J.F.

To our growing cadre of grandchildren who already know the wonder of books and to their future teachers with the hope that they will strengthen and extend the budding literacy skills of these special young learners.
C.J.F.

To my first and most influential teachers, my parents, Bob and Kay Tausch, who lovingly nurtured my early literacy learning and continue to support my lifelong commitment to strengthen my teaching and positively influence the education profession.
M.P.W.

Pamela J. Farris

Pamela J. Farris is a Distinguished Teaching Professor and former Coordinator of School–University Partnerships at Northern Illinois University. A former elementary teacher and Title I reading coordinator, she has a myriad of experiences in reading and writing instruction. As a professor of undergraduate and graduate literacy courses, Pam works closely with both preservice and in-service teachers. She travels out to visit and assist in classrooms in urban, suburban, and rural settings. A popular, colorful presenter, Pam has presented throughout the United States as well as in Canada, Europe, and Australia. A prolific author, she has published over 170 professional articles in such journals as *Childhood Education, Language Arts, The Reading Teacher, Journal of Reading,* and the *Middle School Journal.* Pam is the author of *Language Arts: Process, Product, and Assessment* (3rd ed.) (2001); *Teaching, Bearing the Torch* (2nd ed.) (1999); and editor of *Elementary and Middle School Social Studies: An Interdisciplinary Approach* (4th ed.) (2004). She is also the author of a children's book, *Young Mouse and Elephant: An African Folktale.* Besides finding time to write in snitches and snatches, she enjoys reading, long walks, horseback riding, music, and gardening. Weekends can usually find her with her husband, Richard, and son, Kurtis, attending a sporting event or music competition.

Carol J. Fuhler

Carol J. Fuhler is a teacher educator and associate professor at Iowa State University. Her past work with sixth through eighth graders in both the learning disabilities classroom and the regular reading program has given her a broad range of experiences and insights into the reading and writing abilities of adolescents. While teaching at Northern Arizona University, Carol was the director of a field-based teacher education program where students earned a dual major in special education and elementary education. With the college classroom housed in the elementary schools, she had a wonderful opportunity to work with a diverse population of elementary children and their teachers on a daily basis. A growing number of grandchildren were too much to resist, and a move was made back to the Midwest where Carol continues to share her love of reading with future elementary education teachers. Her numerous articles on reading and writing have appeared in such journals as *The Reading Teacher, Journal of Reading, Middle School Journal,* and *Social Studies and the Young Learner.* In addition, she has authored two books, *Teaching Geography of North America with Books Kids Love* and *Teaching Reading with Multicultural Books Kids Love.* When not involved in university life, Carol enjoys trying to keep up with the world of children's literature, hiking, antiquing, and sipping a cup of mocha espresso.

Maria P. Walther

Maria P. Walther is a first grade teacher of an inclusion class at Gwendolyn Brooks Elementary School in Aurora, Illinois. She has been spending her days with young learners for the past sixteen years. She was named Illinois Reading Educator of the Year in recognition of her commitment to providing quality reading instruction. While teaching, Maria has continued to further her knowledge about literacy learning and young children. She received her master's degree from Northern Illinois University, then continued studying at NIU to earn her doctorate. Maria graduated with her Ed. D. in Elementary Education in 1998. That year she was awarded the Outstanding Research Award and named Outstanding Young Alumni of the College of Education. Maria recently obtained National Board Certification in the area of Early Childhood Generalist. Maria is committed to spending her days with young children and also spending time sharing her knowledge with teachers. This "double life" keeps her very busy. Maria presents at numerous conferences and workshops at the district, local, state, and national levels. She is constantly researching and creating innovative ideas to share with her colleagues. She has written journal articles and book chapters about early literacy and incorporating children's literature into the curriculum. In addition, Maria teaches reading courses at Aurora University where she helps her students create a "Handbook for Teaching Reading." She has a wonderful husband, Lenny, who is a cartographer at NIU and a die-hard Cubs fan. She and Lenny love spending time with their daughter, Katie, who says that she wants to be a teacher too!

Brief Contents

Contents

PART **III** **Methods for Teaching Reading** **227**

6 **Emergent Literacy: Beginning Reading and Writing** 229

**9   Vocabulary Instruction in a
       Balanced Literacy Program**   377

12 Connecting Reading and Writing: Expository Text 539

Preface

"This school year, let's remember that our goal is to help students become joyfully literate and experience the pleasures and the rewards that most of us associate with learning. May we continue to show, with our selection of activities and materials, that reading is positive, meaningful, and a wise investment of student time and talents." The words of Kathy Jongsma (2002, p. 62), a former teacher and reading consultant, are held dear in the heart of every dedicated elementary and middle school teacher whether we have taught twenty years or are starting our first year of teaching.

Approach of TEACHING READING

The authors of this textbook firmly believe that there is no one best way to teach a child to read or write. Instead, we support the premise that if every child has an excellent literacy teacher who knows how to motivate, guide, and instruct in a wide variety of ways, then every child has the best opportunity to become a lifelong reader and writer. The key here, of course, is an excellent literacy teacher who is adept in the art of balancing motivation, guidance, and appropriate instruction. If our goal as teachers is to prepare one child after another for future success, then we must put our minds together to find the most effective ways to build a literacy foundation from which each child can prosper and grow. As we do so, we must continually seek the latest findings and theories in literacy instruction, digest them in terms of what they mean for our students in our particular classrooms, and then strive to teach what we know in the most accessible ways.

In addition, we must be able to recognize student strengths and needs, understanding how to apply pedagogy to further develop both. Along the way we must collaborate with peers and often make adjustments to prevailing classroom methods so that our teaching is the best it can possibly be for every student. That is a daunting list of "musts," isn't it? But there is one more. Without a doubt, that excellent literacy teacher must also be a lifelong learner.

Teaching Reading: A Balanced Approach for Today's Classrooms was written to address the preceding list of "musts." It is an effort to provide prospective and practiced teachers with the knowledge and skills necessary to make informed decisions about literacy instruction. The text also demonstrates numerous instructional strategies in the form of teaching suggestions and complete lesson plans to apply in the literacy classroom. This book provides the groundwork from which a teacher can begin to form her own philosophy of teaching literacy, armed with sound theory, quality information, and practical, applicable strategies. Combined with an understanding of the diverse students in the classroom, that teacher will have access to the tools necessary to supply balanced literacy instruction.

Integration of Standards

Since meeting the dictates of a set of standards is currently a primary concern of all teachers, the authors have included a wide variety of literacy practices designed to aid teachers in addressing local, state, and national standards—a goal that can be embraced and met. These suggestions grow from two sources—the *Standards for Reading Professionals* and the *IRA/NCTE Standards for the English Language Arts*—and can be adapted as needed. Based upon support from this text, standards become opportunities to improve teaching rather than seemingly impossible hurdles viewed afar with despair.

Core Content

Every textbook has core content—the essential content with which the reader needs to become familiar. The authors believe that informed, knowledgeable teachers are those who are best suited to teach the children of the 21st century. As such, the textbook includes numerous literacy approaches so that as practicing teachers one day, they can adopt, adapt, and utilize particular approaches to best meet the needs of their respective students. Furthermore, they will be able to challenge each reader and writer with a fresh technique or a different way to introduce a strategy. By drawing from a multitude of approaches or strategies, the teachers are attempting to balance instruction, choosing from the best of time-honored practices rather than relying primarily on one method.

Teaching Reading contains the following strands of core content:

A Balanced Approach: Chapter 1, Introduction to Literacy, defines the authors' perception of "balanced reading instruction," and its application is modeled throughout the ensuing chapters.

Standards for Reading Professionals: This set of standards is referenced throughout the textbook to familiarize readers with national standards.

IRA/NCTE National Standards in the English Language Arts: This set of standards is discussed in each chapter along with examples of instructional approaches that teachers use to incorporate them. Teachers can readily transfer these tactics to working with their own local and state standards.

Teaching Diverse Learners: Each chapter addresses the strengths and needs of diverse learners in terms of literacy acquisition. Attention is drawn to how the teacher can make informed instructional decisions in meeting various needs of these students. Information about diverse learning and adapting teaching strategies to meet different needs is integrated throughout the text. A special icon highlights sections that specifically address this material.

Enhancing Literacy Instruction through the Use of Technology: Technology is a potentially powerful educational resource, and thus is addressed throughout the book. Chapters include dedicated technology sections that address technology resources specific to the topic at hand. A special icon highlights the technology sections. Additionally, technology is used to extend the text onto the Online Learning Center at **www.mhhe.com/farrisreading**

and the *Making the Grade CD-ROM* that accompanies the text. See "Supplemental Materials" for a listing of these resources.

Literacy Instruction: Different methods of literacy instruction are addressed through a number of classroom organizational structures including the popular reading workshop, writing workshop, literature circles, guided reading groups, focus groups for specific skill development, grouping by interests, and other appropriate organizational means.

Strategies: The text includes a wealth of teaching strategies to provide examples of how to implement the teaching methods discussed, and to provide resources and ideas to take into the classroom. Additional strategies housed on the Online Learning Center at **www.mhhe.com/farrisreading** are noted in the margins.

Children's Literature: Suggestions of quality children's literature, some old and much new, are included in each chapter along with an annotated bibliography for ease of use. These listings include multicultural children's literature titles reflecting the increasingly diverse faces in the nation's classrooms.

Features for Facilitating and Extending Learning

The text's pedagogical system was developed to facilitate and extend learning.

- **Key Ideas** open each chapter to focus readers on upcoming critical content.
- **Questions to Ponder** are designed to pique the reader's interest, focus one's reading, and encourage reflection upon knowledge gained from the chapter once it is completed through going back and answering the questions.
- **Peering into the Classroom** begins each chapter with a look into a classroom and the lives of teacher and students.
- **Reflection: IRA/NCTE National Standards in the Classroom** connects to *Peering into the Classroom* by encouraging students to analyze how the standards are being implemented by the teachers described in the vignettes. This feature is meant to reassure practicing teachers and novices alike that addressing the standards is not a daunting task. With a little preplanning, standards are easily knit into the existing curriculum.
- **Standards for Reading Professionals** open each chapter as a graphic organizer of what areas of these standards are specifically addressed in the chapter.
- **Teaching Strategies** are provided throughout the text. These numerous, complete, and classroom-tested lesson plans model the use of a literacy instruction strategy. Readers can take a lesson into an appropriate classroom setting, adapt it as needed, and teach it with confidence knowing that it is well-grounded in theory. Overviews of three carefully designed *interdisciplinary units* are provided as well. One unit is appropriate for primary grades, a second is geared toward middle grades, and the last one targets upper-grade readers and writers. Additional teaching strategies

highlighted in the text's margins with an icon are housed on the Online Learning Center at **www.mhhe.com/farrisreading**.

- **Web Links** listed within the text and in the margins can be linked to the Online Learning Center at **www.mhhe.com/farrisreading**.
- **Portfolio Activities** are referenced in the margins. These activities provide suggestions for artifacts you can create for your portfolio. They are housed on the Online Learning Center at **www.mhhe.com/farrisreading**.
- A **Summary** at the end of each chapter highlights critical points throughout the chapter.
- **Chapter Review** lists the student study guide materials available on the Online Learning Center at **www.mhhe.com/farrisreading**.
- **Main Points** lists the principal concepts of the chapter in a clear and concise outline.
- **Key Terms** that are boldfaced within the chapters are listed at the end of the chapter along with a page reference. Reviewing the words will aid readers in recognizing meaningful content, an important step in understanding the concepts to which these vocabulary words are tied.
- **Reflecting and Reviewing** provides thought-provoking questions that encourage readers to think carefully about chapter concepts, return to the chapter to clarify information, and perhaps raise further questions that will prompt additional reading and deepen understanding.
- **Children's Literature** includes a listing of suggested children's books for the particular chapter. A comprehensive, annotated listing of recommended books is included in Appendix A.

A Student-Friendly Text

The features listed above, and the resources you will read about in the "Supplementary Materials" section below, both make this a very student accessible text. Students will appreciate its reader-friendly tone and will also find this text appealing for its strong instructional content. The authors sent the book out for college and university students to read and compare with other elementary methods textbooks. According to one young reviewer, a preservice teacher education major:

"This book is the only methods textbook I couldn't put down. The theory is clearly stated and understandable. And the activities are plentiful and well described. After reading the book, I feel confident that I can successfully teach reading and writing as a new teacher."

Supplemental Materials

For the Student

The student supplements were developed to aid and extend student learning. The following supplements are available:

- *Making the Grade* **CD-ROM:** Packaged for free with new copies of the text, this CD-ROM provides quizzes with feedback for all chapters.
- **Online Learning Center:** Located at **www.mhhe.com/farrisreading,** this site includes a Student Study Guide (with practice quizzes), Online Strategies, Portfolio Activities, Web Links, and additional resources.
- *LitLinks: Activities for Connected Learning in Elementary Classrooms* **by Dena Beeghly and Catherine Prudhoe:** Packaged for free with new copies of the text, this book contains sample lesson plan guidelines for creating literature-centered lessons across the curriculum.

- *Folio*Live: *Folio*Live is an online tool that allows users to create electronic portfolios. Go to **www.foliolive.com** to learn more about this product.

For the Instructor

The following supplements are available to the instructor:[1]

- **Instructor's Manual and Test Bank:** This manual includes information to aid in the preparation of lectures, classroom activities and strategies, authentic assessment ideas and resources. A computerized test bank is available on a dual-platform CD-ROM.
- **Instructor's Resource CD-ROM:** This CD-ROM includes the computerized test bank, PowerPoint slides, and the Instructor's Manual.
- **Instructor's Online Learning Center:** Located at **www.mhhe.com/farrisreading,** this website includes resources for the instructor and PowerPoint slides.
- **PageOut:** This course management tool allows you to create a course website with an interactive syllabus that lets you post content and links, an online gradebook, lecture notes, bookmarks, and even a discussion board where students can discuss course-related topics.

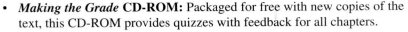

A Final Note to Future Literacy Teachers

In sum, this textbook is aimed at best assisting the reader to understand the basics in developing his or her own philosophy of what constitutes a balanced approach to teaching literacy. Be forewarned, however, because this text alone will not make you a superb literacy teacher any more than reading a "how to" book makes one an accomplished carpenter or gourmet chef. No single book can do that. This text provides you with a strong foundation in literacy. It is your ingenuity, creativity, caring, keen mind, and a lot of practice with a classroom of inquisitive students that will develop you into an excellent literacy teacher. This book is but a starting place. Talk to colleagues, study the basal reader teacher's guides, read current journals, scan quality Internet sites, and learn from other authorities in the field. You need to know up front that

[1]Contact your local McGraw-Hill representative for information on availability and restrictions.

becoming an excellent literacy teacher takes time and practice along with a genuine love for what you do. We cannot emphasize enough that it is the wise, nurturing, well-informed teacher who makes reading and writing enjoyable, relevant, and worthwhile for every student in the classroom. We are pleased to be able to start you on the road toward achieving such a rewarding goal.

Acknowledgments

Books require a host of individuals who devote great care, energy, and attention to their development. This book is built upon the teaching of many, the continuous learning of its writers, and the dreams that it will make a difference for the optimistic, talented teachers-to-be who read it. We have thank-you's aplenty for those who contributed in innumerable ways to bringing this book to completion:

First, we would like to thank our past, present, and future students, who remind us on a daily basis why we entered the teaching profession in the first place! Your wide eyes, smiles, and desire to learn are what keep us motivated. Another acknowledgment must go to the various reviewers who provided sage advice on our chapters through several versions of fine-tuning. A special thanks goes to our final reviewers, who often took the whole book into account as they gave us last-minute pointers. Perspectives from authorities on the outside looking in at our efforts were much appreciated.

Denise B. Binderup, *Western Washington University*
MaryAnne Bonjuklian, *William Paterson University*
Rosemary G. Cameron, *College of St. Rose*
George F. Canney, *University of Idaho*
Beverly E. Cox, *Purdue University*
Kathleen A. Ferrito, *State University of New York College at Cortland*
Kay Floyd, *Tarleton State University*
Dolores Gaunty-Porter, *Chapman University*
Nancy Gibney, *University of Detroit, Mercy*
Diane C. Greene, *Mississippi State University*
Tommy L. Hansen, *University of Nebraska at Kearney*
Allison Hoewisch, *University of Missouri, St. Louis*
Nancy Horton, *University of North Texas*
Janet Kehe, *Upper Iowa University*
Ellen G. Koitz, *Hood College*
Diane L. Lowe, *Framingham State College*
Priscilla Manarino-Leggett, *Fayetteville State University*
Ellen Marcy, *Southeastern Oklahoma State University*
Eugene F. Martin, *Mississippi State University*
Mary C. McMackin, *Lesley College*
William J. Oehlkers, *Rhode Island College*
Scott Popplewell, *Ball State University*

Penny A. Roberts, *California State University, Long Beach*
Leonie M. Rose, *Central Michigan University*
Robert T. Rude, *Rhode Island College*
Sara D. Simonson, *Western Illinois University*
Sandra J. Stone, *Northern Arizona University*
Dorothy R. Troike, *State University of New York College at Cortland*
Kenneth J. Weiss, *Nazareth College of Rochester*

In presenting ideas for the use of the readers of this text, we went to experts to learn what works and are most appreciative of these teachers' willingness to share. This book is filled with ideas from classrooms, ideas that really work with children. Marcie Osmundson, the "Mrs. O" in several classroom visits, is a retired sixth grade teacher extraordinaire. What a legacy she has left in the sixth grade classroom over the years. Her ideas will bear fruit once again as they are transferred from this textbook into your classrooms. An Iowa thanks to Linda Carver and Kyra Wilcox-Conley from Roosevelt Elementary School in Ames, Iowa, for sharing their collaborative ideas with us and with you readers, too. Also, we would like to thank the Tuesday night team: Katherine Phillips, Sue Lambert, and Margie O'Malley. They have spent many a late night together planning, creating, reflecting, and improving our teaching as a result. Your insights, thoughts, and ideas were invaluable in writing this textbook. And huge thanks to Patricia Rieman, for tremendous work in developing the teacher's manual and online center activities, and Donna E. Werderich, for the meticulous proofing of the pages.

A sincere thank-you goes to the publishers who willingly supplied review copies for our consideration. A large number of their superb titles became the focus of our *Teaching Strategies for the Classroom* boxes or are recommended titles to share with children across the grades. Lee and Low Books offered excellent multicultural titles. Candlewick Press and Harcourt Brace contributed titles that worked wonderfully across the genre and the curriculum.

We would also like to thank Jane Karpacz, our publisher, who believed in our ideas; Beth Kaufman, who originally launched the project; and Cara Harvey, our developmental editor, who gave us constant encouragement throughout the writing and reviewing stages. Certainly, Jean Hamilton, project manager, Amy Bethea, photo editor, and Pamela Cooper, marketing manager, greatly added to the creation and success of this book.

Lastly, a heartfelt thanks goes to our families, who experienced the process of writing this book right alongside us, whether they really wanted to or not. To our husbands, a thanks for your infinite patience when we'd disappear for hours (days) at a time and for casting a critical eye over the most recent writing when the manuscript needed it. Without a doubt, this book grew out of the efforts of many people. It is truly a literary labor of love.

Worlds of Words

Writers...
They know all,
they see all,
they do all,
writers.
They can say
'Let there be light!'
and create light,
with a long,
thin
magical wand
that can
make words appear,
disappear
and reappear again,
just like that.
Their best friends
are a pencil
and paper,
with whom they play
every day.
They create a world
of their own.
All this spills
out of their pencils
like water
always spilling
into infinity.
Although
they see everything,
with a beginning,
middle
and end,
like a book,
that is read by,
the reader...

Readers...
They are
the envisioners,
the completers,
the ones who
carry it on.
Readers,
they make
the writer's world
work.
They have to
understand it,
but not completely,
there does
have to be
the wondering.
Without a good reader,
the writer is nothing.
But the reader
needs a writer too,
it's all connected.
And the reader reads,
and wonders,
how
was this writing created,
what was
the writing process?

The Writing Process
And their answer
is in this book,
this writer's world.
Perhaps the reader connects
the writing process
to a garden.
Perhaps they see
the writer's idea
as a seed,
a tiny little seed,
that the writer
cared for
as he would
a real seed.
He had to
work with it,
and let it grow
until it sprouted
into a huge
beautiful
flower,
a huge
beautiful
piece of writing.

Jonathan Atkins, 5th grade
Atkins, J. (2001). Worlds of words. *Language Arts, 78* (5), 449–450.
Used by permission

An Introduction to Teaching Reading

Good Morning!
Today is Tuesday.

"There is no one 'perfect method' for teaching reading to all children. Teachers, policy makers, researchers, and teacher educators need to recognize that the answer is not in the method but in the teacher."

Gerald G. Duffey and James V. Hoffman, respected researchers and educators in the field of reading

Introduction to Literacy

Key Ideas

- A **balanced instructional approach** to literacy education requires that the teacher be knowledgeable about a variety of effective teaching strategies in reading and writing. She must thoughtfully select from them to effectively meet the needs of the increasingly diverse students in her classroom.
- An informed reading teacher bases his philosophy upon a knowledge of the key theories in the field and understands how these theories can be guides when choosing specific instructional strategies.
- *Standards for the English Language Arts* (IRA/NCTE, 1996) and the *Standards for Reading Professionals* (IRA, 1998) describe the literacy process and emphasize various teaching proficiencies that every reading professional should acquire and apply effectively.
- Developing an understanding of the different facets of diversity and how they affect interactions in today's classrooms will facilitate planning appropriate educational opportunities for every learner.
- Technology, with its ever-increasing options, can enhance students' reading and writing proficiencies when it is used in the proper context.

Questions to Ponder

- Why is a balanced reading approach better than a single approach?
- How can an understanding of major learning theories related to literacy education strengthen a teacher's personal approach to literacy instruction?
- What are some general teaching strategies that are useful and help make learning as accessible as possible to learners with varying backgrounds, needs, and abilities?
- How can the changing role of technology improve students' abilities to master reading and writing?

Peering into the Classroom

A New Year, a New Beginning

It is that nervously anticipated first day of school—both for teachers and their students. Alessandra Lopez looks at her fourth grade class of twenty-seven bright-eyed, eager-to-learn students. She faces them with confidence, however, because she is well prepared. In recent weeks, Alessandra has practically lived at the school, reviewing the school district's curriculum, preparing bulletin boards, developing interesting lesson plans, and locating needed instructional materials. By rearranging the desks, chairs, and tables in her classroom, Alessandra managed to squeeze in enough room for a science center complete with the class pet, a hermit crab that her students will later name. Next to the science center is a social studies center with atlases, a globe, and interesting biographies and historical novels. She organized her classroom library so students can easily find and check out books. Quiet areas for literature circles to meet are nearby.

Alessandra also has the supplies and ideas to begin writing workshops and can't wait to help her students write about their own experiences and interests. Four computers are connected to the Internet. Along with a laser printer, this technology team is lined up, ready for action, against the back wall of the classroom. Alessandra has learned how to use a digital camera to take pictures of her students and to import them into a weekly class newspaper. Next week she will pair up students to take turns creating and producing the paper. That newspaper will be welcomed by parents who enjoy staying in touch with the classroom lives of their children.

As part of preparing for this class of learners, Alessandra has devoted a number of hours to finding out about them. In early August, she mailed each of her students a letter introducing herself and her family, including her husband, Hector, and their young son, Rudy. She even included a digital photo of her family and their gray house cat that her son cleverly named "Mouse." Alessandra wrote to her students that she likes to read, play tennis, and garden. In addition, she shared some of her favorite children's authors and books. Most importantly, Alessandra asked her students to write back to her and tell her a little about themselves. Thoughtfully, she included paper and a self-addressed, stamped envelope for them to use in their response. Over the next few weeks the mail carrier delivered some pleasant surprises as most of the students wrote back to their new teacher.

Now that the opening day of school has arrived, Alessandra looks over her class with many new insights. She sees Ramon who is the star player of his soccer team and Jennifer who still grieves for her grandfather. And there's Jake who doesn't like to read and hates to write, even though his letter to her was half a page long. Next to the window is Melissa who dreams of becoming an artist. In front of Melissa is Robert who wants to be an NBA player. Alessandra peers thoughtfully into her students' eyes, hoping to help them meet their dreams, hoping they will come to share her dream—that all of them will love to read and write by the end of the year.

REFLECTION: IRA/NCTE NATIONAL STANDARDS IN THE CLASSROOM

As you become more familiar with the *Standards for the English Language Arts* (IRA/NCTE, 1996), commonly referred to as the national standards for reading and writing, and their importance in structuring quality learning experiences for every learner in the classroom, you will recognize how Alessandra has organized her classroom with those standards in mind. For example, she has made it easy for her fourth graders to access fiction and nonfiction books by carefully organizing her classroom library and by providing an inviting reading area nearby. These efforts support the first standard, which underscores the importance of reading widely. Her science and social studies centers promise tempting opportunities for research into topics of personal interest as advocated by Standard 7. Even her introductory letter to the students at the beginning of the year complete with the thoughtful inclusion of a stamped, self-addressed envelope touches on Standard 12. In this case both she and the students used written language in a personal exchange of information. Then, with an eye to technology, the focus of Standard 8, there are computers, Internet possibilities, and that digital camera. Alessandra's efforts are not unique. In one chapter after another, you will see how naturally classroom teachers intertwine standards with sound, inviting literacy instruction. Look for a complete list of the *Standards for the English Language Arts* as well as the *Standards for Reading Professionals* (IRA, 1998) in the appendix of this book.

INTRODUCTION

Daily life in Alessandra's classroom revolves around creative and engaging literacy activities. Reading and writing permeate the day, sometimes as the focus of an activity, sometimes as instruments for learning and communication across the curriculum. In the process, this young teacher is preparing her students to meet reading and writing **standards**—established goals for literacy. Simply stated, **literacy** entails the ability to read and understand what others have written, along with the ability to write as a means of recording information and for communicating with others. Literacy is not quite that simple, however. Instead, it is a multifaceted concept for it ranges from merely knowing letter–sound relationships on one end of the continuum to critical literacy on the other end, which is the ability to read the world around us (Tiedt, Tiedt, & Tiedt, 2001). It is that level of critical literacy that is the eventual goal for Alessandra's students.

Depending on one's goals in life, literacy demands in today's world are far different than they were in years past. Today, students need to do more than just read. They must be able to take what they read and do something with it—to think critically about it, to problem solve effectively, and to efficiently communicate in various ways. Put another way,

> Critical literacy requires much more than passively absorbing what is on the printed page. It requires attaining a deep understanding of what is read, remembering important information, linking newly learned information to existing schemata, knowing when and where to use that information, using it appropriately in varied contexts in and out of school, and communicating effectively with others. (Graves, Juel, & Graves, 2001, p. 24)

STANDARDS for READING PROFESSIONALS

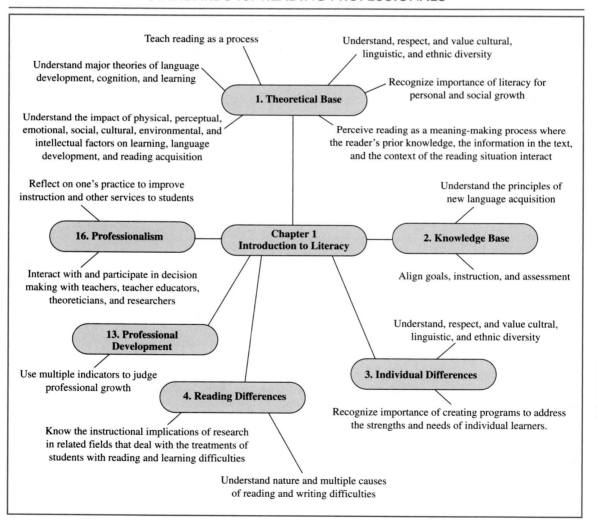

Teach reading as a process

Understand, respect, and value cultural, linguistic, and ethnic diversity

Understand major theories of language development, cognition, and learning

Recognize importance of literacy for personal and social growth

1. Theoretical Base

Understand the impact of physical, perceptual, emotional, social, cultural, environmental, and intellectual factors on learning, language development, and reading acquisition

Perceive reading as a meaning-making process where the reader's prior knowledge, the information in the text, and the context of the reading situation interact

Reflect on one's practice to improve instruction and other services to students

Understand the principles of new language acquisition

16. Professionalism

Chapter 1 Introduction to Literacy

2. Knowledge Base

Interact with and participate in decision making with teachers, teacher educators, theoreticians, and researchers

Align goals, instruction, and assessment

13. Professional Development

Understand, respect, and value cultral, linguistic, and ethnic diversity

Use multiple indicators to judge professional growth

3. Individual Differences

4. Reading Differences

Recognize importance of creating programs to address the strengths and needs of individual learners.

Know the instructional implications of research in related fields that deal with the treatments of students with reading and learning difficulties

Understand nature and multiple causes of reading and writing difficulties

That is a formidable task! Clearly, both reading and writing in their various guises are essential language skills needed by every child who hopes to participate as an informed member of our society. Day in and day out we each encounter reading and writing of many types. Real-world reading includes the names on street signs, words on a menu, written directions to a friend's house, and the names of items on the shelves of a grocery store. Real-world writing involves jotting down items on the grocery list, making a personal "to do" list, sending an e-mail to a friend or class pen pal, or writing down directions to the house of a friend.

In addition, there is the kind of reading that informs or entertains: magazines, books, poetry, newspapers, journals, reports, tables, graphs, schedules, and more (Alvermann, Moon, & Hagood, 1999). Behind each piece of text is the writer who creates it. Most teachers will concur with the authors in *Becoming a Nation of Readers* (Anderson, Hiebert, Scott, & Wilkinson, 1985) when they say that "learning about reading and writing ought to occur in situations where written language serves functions such as to entertain (as in books), to inform (as in instructions on packages), or to direct (as on traffic signs)" (p. 32). In short, the essential literacy skills involved in reading and writing improve when they are applied during relevant learning experiences.

Teaching children how to read and write and to develop and apply literacy strategies so that they can become lifelong learners is the principal goal of every elementary and middle school teacher. Step back and visualize a beginning reader. When that young child first unlocks the pattern of symbols that makes up words and goes on to grasp the meaning of a simple story, a little magic has occurred, hasn't it? As teachers we celebrate such an occasion for we have seen a child join the ranks of readers.

Web Link:
4teachers.org

The child who becomes a willing reader finds his world enriched as he recognizes himself in some of the book characters he encounters. As a listener or a reader, he may empathize with *Owen* (Henkes, 1993), who takes his security blanket along wherever he goes. Another reader may see herself in *Harriet, You'll Drive Me Wild* (Fox, 2000), a story about an energetic child and an exasperated mother. Other readers will empathize with nine-year-old Booker T. Washington, who reveals that *More Than Anything Else* (Bradby, 1995), he wants to learn to read. They may one day chuckle at Ramona's semantic distress over interpreting her teacher's words "Sit here for the present" to mean that she, Ramona, would be receiving a gift. There are additional chuckles in store for readers as they grow up with Beverly Cleary's popular books. Reading and writing taught early and taught well, modeled by authors and by enthusiastic teachers, are truly invitations to a myriad of marvels in the school days ahead.

Certainly, both worlds, real and fictional, are resources for learning the basics of literacy. Book worlds are filled to the brim with fiction and nonfiction reading and opportunities for writing that are either prompted by that reading or extend it in some way. Reading materials of all kinds are meant to enrich and expand the perimeters of each learner's world, but readers must be able to unlock the meaning behind the words to access that richness. In addition, literacy extends beyond books when young writers turn to real-world experiences for materials to use in refining their writing abilities. It is no wonder that the teaching of literacy fundamentals to every child is so imperative, for it is through reading and writing that students are able to succeed in whatever endeavor they choose to pursue in life.

Understanding just how critical these skills can be, a viable question at this point might be, How do I encourage my students to become lifelong readers and writers? In order to foster the motivation that lies at the root of evergrowing literacy skills, teachers must nurture learners on a daily basis. Linda Gambrell (1996) developed a list of six research-based factors related to increased motivation for reading:

1. Teachers model the love of reading;
2. The classroom library is stocked with a wide variety of appealing books;
3. Students have daily opportunities to self-select books to read;
4. Students have daily opportunities to talk with classmates about books;
5. Students are familiar with lots of books; and,
6. Teachers provide the incentives for reading. (p. 23)

According to Gambrell (1996), teachers serve as both models and motivators of reading by creating book-rich classroom cultures that encourage social interactions about books. Such nurturing can be accomplished through various instructional strategies as will be described in the upcoming paragraphs and chapters throughout this textbook.

A BALANCED INSTRUCTIONAL APPROACH

Web Links:
Phonics and Whole Language Learning

Balanced Reading Instruction

The chapter following this introduction takes a historical look at reading, how we once believed it was best taught, how those ideas have changed over time, and how outside forces have influenced ideas about classroom instruction. You will note that the most enduring approach to teaching reading has been packaged in a **basal reading series** format, a carefully designed, developmental set of materials that teachers have relied upon year after year after year. When some teachers were not satisfied with the results of teaching reading using a basal series, you will see how they looked for other options (Zemelman, Daniels, & Hyde, 1998). Others are still looking. Some teachers use children's literature to complement the basal series.

One of the hottest topics in the reading world today continues to be that of achieving some type of "balance" when teaching every child to read (Cassidy & Cassidy, 2002/2003). Unfortunately, what balance means to some is not what it means to others. In this text we take the stance that balance refers to a philosophy of teaching reading. That philosophy is constructed by determining the kinds of knowledge about reading you believe that children in your classroom should attain and then deciding on various ways to teach that knowledge.

When you reach Chapter 3 you will find an overview of a wide variety of methods for teaching children to read and write. The chapter presents a shopping cart of ideas from which a teacher can choose. It says, "Look! You can use this method to do this and that method to do that. Mix them and match them to aid each learner in achieving literacy success." Take a minute and think about what that means. If you select method A, method C, and method D and add a healthy dose of phonics because, based

A well-stocked classroom library with books from every genre is essential at all grade levels. Fiction and nonfiction appeal to readers as do magazines and other printed materials including sports cards, joke books, and cartoons.

upon your assessment, this year's second grade class will thrive on such reading fare, should the second grade teacher across the hall choose exactly the same methods? If you are developing a balanced approach to literacy instruction, your response is, "Probably not." Why? Because each of you is developing your own reading philosophy, honing your beliefs about what methods work best with which children. Understanding that children are unique and one class is quite different from another, you will alter the methods and strategies according to your appraisal of student needs each year (Block, Oakar, & Hurt, 2002; Duffey & Hoffman, 1999). The following chapters will explain how such a philosophy might work, suggest the kinds of knowledge a successful reader and writer might profit from, and demonstrate numerous strategies that could become a part of your teaching repertoire.

It should be apparent to you by now that when using a balanced instructional approach, the focus is not narrowed to include only one method of teaching reading. In fact, classroom teachers must know a wide variety of instructional methods and how to apply them depending on the literacy needs of their students. When they draw on this knowledge and integrate various strategies to best teach this year's students, one could say they are using **differentiated instruction, eclectic teaching,** or a **balanced instructional approach.** While there are a number of different terms for this kind of teaching, this text will consistently refer to a balanced instructional approach or, more simply, a balanced approach.

While it might seem confusing to the novice teacher at first, it is important to recognize that balance is not a standardized product. Because it is tied to one's philosophy of teaching literacy, it will look somewhat different from one classroom to the next. For instance, in Mrs. Mendez's first grade class **literature-based instruction** and **phonics** are not an "either-or" instructional situation because both are an integral part of the classroom day. Children learn the rudiments of phonics, how letters work and sound, within the context of delightful picture books and rollicking poetry. In Mr. Jorgenson's fifth grade classroom, instruction is based on a literature-based basal series for materials and strategies to teach his learners. He changes the pace throughout the year with four or five novels that are read and discussed in literature circles. This gives the students an opportunity to learn from each other as they talk about and respond to an engrossing book (Keene & Zimmerman, 1997; Temple, Martinez, Yokoto, & Naylor, 2001). Often the novels are selected by the students from a collection gathered ahead of time by the teacher. These novels reflect the interests and diversity of class members and are geared to several different reading levels. Later in the year, students spend an extended time independently reading materials of their choice, giving them an opportunity to practice the skills they have learned previously through a number of carefully constructed mini-lessons (Zemelman et al., 1998).

Furthermore, reading strategies might be taught and modeled within the context of a lively picture book and then practiced in related picture books to cement understanding as Miss Lee does. One of her fourth graders' favorite lessons involves learning sequencing skills using the tall tale *John Henry* (Lester, 1994). Then they apply the newly presented skill in small groups while reading a number of other amusing and engaging tall tales (Fuhler, 2000). The fact remains that,

> because research does not support the idea that one size fits all, that one approach will work with all children for all aspects of literacy development for all curricula, a balanced approach must be flexible. Teachers learn to examine all of the alternatives and strive each day to find the best ways to help each child develop as a reader and a writer. (Spiegel, 1999, p. 11)

As teachers, we need to be familiar with several reading strategies as well as model those strategies for our students. Demonstrating out loud how we think as we read helps students develop road maps for their own reading.

The Principles of Balance

OLC

Web Link:
The Reading Wars

Confining one's instruction to one approach would simplify curricular and instructional decision making. But that practice would be based upon the belief that every child can dribble a soccer ball, loves hamburgers with all the works, and keeps his or her bedroom neat and tidy every single day. If children were that homogeneous, then perhaps one method would work in every classroom. It is true that learners have many common characteristics; however, they also differ in a number of important ways. Teachers can honor those similarities and differences through balanced instruction. In Jill Fitzgerald's (1999) words, "A teacher who holds a balanced philosophical view of the reading process makes use of each of the various knowledge sources, that is, teachers, parents, and children learning from one another" (p. 103). Fitzgerald offers three basic principles underlying a balanced instructional approach in literacy:

1. First, the curricular goals of the literacy program drive everything. "The teacher arranges instruction and reading opportunities so that the children can acquire as many kinds of reading knowledge as possible" (pp. 103–104). Included in reading knowledge are such things as an understanding of phonics, word identification strategies, response to what is being read, and affective knowledge including motivation and the desire to read. The knowledge one chooses to teach is always based upon a careful evaluation of each child as a learner (Duffy & Hoffman, 1999).

2. The second principle of a balanced instructional approach is that "instructional methods sometimes considered to be opposites or contrasts are used so that the positive features of each, especially those features not present in the other way of teaching, can permit the fullest array of learning to occur" (p. 104). To illustrate this principle, different kinds of grouping could be used throughout the day, both heterogeneous and homogeneous depending on the skills being taught. At other times, students may be engaged in **discovery or inquiry learning.** It is less teacher-directed and more strongly initiated by the students than when a specific task is taught and modeled by the teacher before students practice and apply their new knowledge as they did with *John Henry* (Lester, 1994) and the tall tales activity. In brief, methods are integrated, the strengths of one building upon strengths of the other, rather than relying upon a singular approach to get a point across.

3. The third principle considers the various kinds of materials that should be used in a classroom to teach reading and writing. Fitzgerald points out that "some knowledge goals, such as love of reading, would most likely be encouraged by reading beautiful, interesting, substantive, and thought-provoking books. Other goals, such as word identification, would likely be best encouraged by reading books with repetitive patterns and highly predictable words. Consequently, a balanced approach teacher may choose a mixture of classic literature books, trade books, easy readers, and predictable books" (p. 104). The use of fine literature is clearly supported in Chapter 10, a primer on children's literature, which also offers practical suggestions for using it to teach reading and writing strategies.

Learning to teach with a balanced instructional approach can be excitingly challenging because there is so much to discover and master. It is not a simple follow-the-recipe method. It may, at times, seem overwhelming to be expected to learn how to teach numerous and varied instructional strategies. However, the classroom teacher who thoughtfully and analytically adopts a balanced approach to reading and writing instruction is similar to the family practitioner in the medical profession—able to meet the needs of nearly all who enter her office. There will be a few students in each classroom who still require the expertise of specialists such as a resource room teacher, reading specialist, or a classroom aide assigned to work with a specific student or group of students, but with effective teaching the majority will advance significantly in their ability to read and write. Spiegel (1999) encourages those who choose a balanced literacy approach when stating that "teachers need to have a firm understanding of a broad range of ways to enhance literacy development and have the wisdom and courage to try different approaches with different learners for different tasks" (p. 11). Finally, Duffy and Hoffman (1999) echo her words when they say, "In fact, no single method or approach has ever proven to be a cure-all" (p. 11), despite often extravagant claims to the contrary.

While the last few pages have focused on approaches to teaching, there is another element that bears comment: the teacher. Good teaching simply cannot be underestimated (Allington, 2002). As recently as a decade ago, researchers believed that what students learned was largely a factor of their family income or parental education. Present research is turning such assumptions upside down. "What schools do matters enormously. And what matters most is good teaching" (Haycock, 2001, p. 10). A recent study by the Boston Public Schools (1998) found that in one academic year, the top third of teachers produced as much as six times the learning growth as the bottom third of teachers. Research indicates that these effects are cumulative and are maintained regardless of race, social class, or prior achievement levels (Sanders & Rivers, 1996). Just imagine the impact that a good teacher with a repertoire of well-selected strategies can have upon a classroom of diverse learners.

Portfolio Activity:
Reflection on Approaches

So important is this element of good teaching that it drew interested researchers to investigate the particular instructional qualities that distinguished highly effective teachers from those who were not (Block, Oakar, & Hurt, 2002). These researchers felt compelled to cull out specific grade level indices of fine literacy teaching. In the process they examined classrooms from preschool through fifth grade. Based upon their findings, they surmised that one impact this information might have is upon pre-service teachers who could make more informed decisions about a grade they might like to teach. Furthermore, current teachers in specific grades can use the information to hone their professional skills. In the process, more of them would achieve the highly effective teacher status. The end result is a win-win situation for both teachers and their students. Read through the summary of expertise in Figure 1.1 (on pages 14–15) to get a general idea of just what it is that makes teachers shine at the different grade levels. You may wish to refer back to the chart periodically as you learn more about quality reading and writing practices in the upcoming chapters.

A LOOK AT EDUCATIONAL THEORY

Theory. It is the origin of what we do in a reading–writing classroom. Whether you decide to use a balanced instructional approach to teaching literacy skills in your classroom or not, you will base your final decision on sound educational theory. It is sound educational theory upon which this textbook is built, and such theory should serve as a foundation in your classroom as well. A well-prepared teacher must have a grasp of past and prevalent theories in order to make the best decisions for learners in her classroom. Those decisions will be the answers to questions like: What will my goals be when teaching literacy? Why will I use one instructional technique over another? Which materials will I select as most effective? How will I assess and evaluate my readers and writers? Is there a best way to arrange the classroom? How will I justify what I am doing when the parents and guardians of my students ask probing questions about classroom practices? All of the answers to such critical questions will emerge from your philosophy of teaching, which will be firmly anchored in relevant theory (DeFord, 1985; Tiedt et al., 2001).

At this point, three decades-old approaches to teaching children to process print and their supportive theories will be addressed. They support some of the methods discussed in the chapters ahead. A number of the theories that you will learn about from chapter to chapter are still popular while others receive less attention these days. As you study the various theories, decide why one appears to have weathered the winds of reading change better than another. The first theories and their related approaches to be examined are the bottom-up approach, the top-down approach, and the interactive approach to teaching reading.

The Bottom-Up Approach

If you think back to your courses in psychology, you will no doubt remember the Russian psychologist Pavlov and the American experimental psychologist B. F. Skinner. Both are noted behaviorists. Behaviorists believe that an individual responds to a particular stimulus and that the response is either strengthened or weakened by reinforcement of some kind. The related theory that grew from their interpretation about the way people learn was translated into an approach to teaching reading called the **bottom-up approach** or the parts-to-whole method. This approach advocated a controlled, sequential way of looking at the reading process in which the stimulus for reading was the print on the page.

Teaching students how to read based upon the bottom-up approach is just as it sounds. Children begin to read at what seems like the bottom of a complex hierarchy of skills, by recognizing the letters of the alphabet, learning the letter names, and understanding their corresponding sounds. Young learners build skill by skill and step by step toward the goal of reading comprehension. Bottom-up advocates believe this approach makes learning easier for children because it breaks complex reading tasks into their basic skills, which can then be mastered one at a time (Carnine, Silbert, & Kameenui, 1990).

If this particular theory undergirds instruction in your classroom, you would assume that the printed text is of primary importance in learning to read. Thus, when a child learns to read, he processes the simplest units that make up a word first, learning letter shapes, names, and sounds. Next, he blends letters together in a left to right sequence to create more complete units. Then words are formed as he studiously sounds out the letters. Words grow into phrases, and eventually a simple sentence is read. So it would continue in a prescribed sequence of steps. In this model, learning is regarded as a one-way process, from the text to the reader, and progress is made one skill at a time. Mistakes are corrected. The texts selected for use would have carefully controlled vocabulary. Text comprehension would be based upon the child's ability to pronounce the words, always moving from the parts to the whole.

Figure 1.1	Summary of expertise of literacy teachers from preschool through Grade 5		
Level	Predominant Role	Motivation	Reteach
Preschool	Guiders (build confidence to discover print in manner like other vocational guides)	Use authentic explorations to ignite query about print; relate learning to home	Hands-on manipulation of letters and words; many input systems in every lesson
Kindergarten	Guardians of children's discoveries about print (cherish students' first attempts)	Use singing, acting out stories, objects, and longer periods of time to reignite interests in literacy	Many adults are in room to support; repeat the literacy experience using the same text and context
Grade 1	Encouragers and supporters (teach literacy all day; answer questions, regardless of how small, immediately)	Vary breadth, rate, and depth of lessons; teach up to 20 different skills in a single hour	Review concepts using varied content, books, methods, and contexts than had been used in the first lesson
Grade 2	Demonstrators (help students climb onto meager or massive prior knowledge by demonstrating literacy processes through masterful think-alouds)	Demonstrate literacy as whole process and how much adults enjoy and value literacy so students can come to value it as well	Conduct personalized, one-to-one conferences; hold students' hands as they find answers to their own questions about literacy
Grade 3	Managers (expert at working with varied groups and multilevel materials simultaneously)	Introduce so many new genres that students fall in love with a specific book; keep literacy interesting	Cultivate new content interest to lift students over obstacles that block their individual learning curves; notice moods
Grade 4	Coaches (stimulate several students individually in different ways during the same lessons)	Move goals up or down the cognitive scale instantly through single instructional sentences	Encourage students to ask questions of themselves; approachable
Grade 5	Adaptors (divide and teach large scopes of knowledge in learnable chunks that stimulate students to want to learn)	Sensitive to and greatly vary the time that they spend teaching one concept from 15 seconds to several days as students' needs warrant	Analyze abilities and challenge students to take a chance to comprehend advanced levels of materials and create sophisticated writings

Source: Block, C. C., Oakar, M., & Hurt, N. (2002). The expertise of literacy teachers: A continuum from preschool to Grade 5. *Reading Research Quarterly, 37* (2), p. 188. Used by permission.

Relate to Students	Classroom Qualities	Lesson Characteristics
Lead students to mimic their speech; class is like a second home with print added	Captivating oral stimuli used daily; relate students' orality to print with smell, taste, and movement	Differ tones, pitches, and body movements to show variability, rhyme, and rhythm of English
Praise correct portions of answers and do not tell them what all was wrong	Print-rich and home-like so children associate positive emotions to print and write notes and messages	Honor and allow for students' individual paces of learning
Praise learning in progress to correct slightest errors positively; teach students to self-regulate	Print-rich space for students to explore resources but unlike prior grades, students use them independently	Teach literacy all day; rapid-paced, play-filled, tell why and how; share in the fun of learning literacy with students
Listen appreciatively and reflectively; stimulate substantive conversations	Classrooms are more relaxed than in younger grades; resources and print are used to challenge students to think deeply; rooms continue to be print-rich	Differentiated and creative so that concepts are taught in ways that students would not have experienced in prior years
Take actions daily to move students toward an internal value for reading; develop independent reading skills and interests	Class is managed so that students read a lot to themselves and one another. Has resources that bridge learning to read and reading to learn	Abstract concepts become concrete with clearly set expectations to get highly effective participation when teacher is not in the group
Identify pupil talents rapidly and lessons focused on these talents; alter pupil attitudes from − to +	Coach pupils and locate resources that enable them to make lifelong decisions from readings; human conditions taught	Set many goals and strategies so students can select their own goals; students assume responsibility to learn alone
In touch with pupil impulse needs; use a sense of humor and think like a fifth grader	Cover vast amounts of material while stimulating students' deep interest in and high levels of understanding of concepts taught	Instill in students a desire to autograph their work with excellence; teach how to organize their thoughts, explore, and learn on their own

Realistically, it is highly unlikely that you will find a classroom today that relies completely on a bottom-up approach because so many additional higher level strategies are needed to understand the words on the page. Unfolding knowledge from the fascinating world of brain research emphasizes how highly effective and adaptable the human brain can be (Jensen, 1998). Under normal circumstances, the brain is efficiently handling a multitude of tasks simultaneously, rather than just one simple task at a time. To acknowledge that ability and to move away from a rather regimented approach, let's take a look at the next theory and resulting approach.

The Top-Down Approach

The **top-down approach,** or whole-to-part model, is a more **holistic** approach to reading. In this case, the reader herself is of primary importance, bringing personal meaning to the reading process from her background of experiences. In this way, she is the catalyst to comprehension, breathing life into seemingly inert words upon the page. Therefore,

> the reading process begins with the highest-level unit possible—meaning in the mind of the reader—and deals with lower-level units, for example words, only to a limited extent. Again, processing operates in a single direction—but in a top-down perspective that view is from the reader to the text (Graves et al., 2001, p. 14).

The theory behind this approach is the Gestalt theory, quite popular in the 1960s. These theorists believed that individuals process stimuli from the whole to its parts as they actively organize and interpret what they see. Because getting a sense of the whole first can influence an understanding of the parts, Gestalt theorists suggested that the whole is actually greater than the sum of the parts. In this model, learning to read is much like learning to speak. Speaking is such a natural process as children gather oral language, immersed in the verbal world around them. To get the meaning of a story, then, students draw on their personal background knowledge collected from the world around them, on their innate ability to use language, and on their expectations of what will happen in the story. In short, the top-down approach is a meaning-driven process rather than print-driven (Reutzel & Cooter, 2000).

If you taught from a top-down model, you might have your class chant or choral read a short poem together, then direct their attention to specific words that rhyme. Once you are comfortable with the fact that the students can read the words, you may or may not look at the pieces of the words that are similar in order to understand why they rhyme, since learning subskills is not the focus in the top-down model. Then, again, you could read through a captivating text like the rhythmic *The Mousery* (Pomerantz, 2000), another opportunity for listeners to delight in rhyming words. The tale would be read several times as listeners savor it in its entirety. Lessons on word recognition could follow at some point, although the main emphasis is more on understanding the story as a whole. If you worry that important skills might not receive the attention they deserve when you focus primarily on a top-down model, there is a more practical approach at your disposal.

The Interactive Approach

Cognitive psychologists who delved into how the brain handles the complex reading process posed a third option. They theorized that it would probably be best to teach reading by drawing from both of the previous approaches to create something better. Thus, the **interactive approach** entered the picture.

When examining the reading process through the lens of the interactive model, you will note that both the reader and the text play critical roles in the reading process. Rumelhart (1980) and his colleagues expostulated that the processing of information is not expressly in one direction or the other. Instead, they believed that a reader grasps the meaning of the text by simultaneously synthesizing information from a number of sources in order to accurately interpret what she is reading. While this process will be examined more closely in Chapter 8 on reading comprehension, the three cueing systems at work in the interactive model are noted in Figure 1.2. The reader draws on knowledge of **graphophonic cues,** recognizing the letters and the

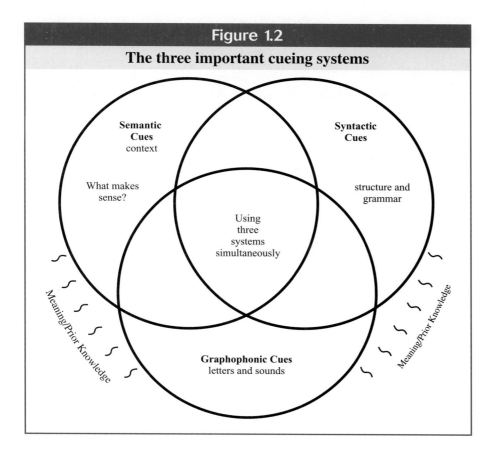

Figure 1.2

The three important cueing systems

Semantic Cues
context

What makes sense?

Syntactic Cues

structure and grammar

Using three systems simultaneously

Meaning/Prior Knowledge

Meaning/Prior Knowledge

Graphophonic Cues
letters and sounds

Creating a secure, comfortable environment where children feel free to interact with peers and their teacher is the job of every classroom teacher.

sounds they make, studies the **syntax,** or the structure of the sentence, and searches for the most appropriate word meanings using **semantic** cues. All the while she is connecting what she reads to prior knowledge and experiences. In this approach, the reader is actively involved in making meaning (Reutzel & Cooter, 2000).

If it is this approach you choose to follow when teaching literacy in your classroom, you would engage in such activities as teaching strategies for decoding words, work on vocabulary development, and model various comprehension strategies as you read aloud to the class. Students would practice these newly acquired skills and strategies as they read in small groups from a basal reader or real books, and then continue to practice new skills on their own. Thus, phonics instruction, word walls, sight words, and reading, reading, reading would make up your day. Another integral part of the reading process would be to activate prior knowledge through thoughtful questioning and engaging hands-on activities. In addition, you would encourage students' thoughtful responses to their reading, perhaps through writing or paired conversations to deepen understanding of what has been read.

Finally, the use of this approach would reflect your belief that both reading and writing are done for genuine reasons because then they will have lasting meaning for every learner (Villaume & Brabham, 2002). Based upon what you have read about developing a philosophy of balancing literacy instruction, you can see that the interactive model suggested by cognitive theorists is still going strong. It advocates the importance of students being actively involved in their own learning, while drawing from what they know to more effectively connect with new knowledge. The interactive model is reinforced through an appealing assortment of learning options in future chapters.

THE RELATIONSHIP BETWEEN READING AND WRITING

The processes involved in reading and writing are so closely related that it is difficult to focus on one in this textbook and ignore the other. Thus, the reading–writing connection will be highlighted in one chapter after another. Particular attention will be devoted to it in both Chapter 11, Connecting Reading and Writing: Narrative and Poetry, and Chapter 12, Connecting Reading and Writing: Expository Text. In those chapters you will find explanations and examples of the two different kinds of reading and the related writing knowledge along with experiences that grow naturally from them. You might keep the following comparisons in mind as you read those chapters.

Pearson and Tierney (1984) depict the close connection between reading and writing in the following way. They describe readers as composers—the same verb that is often assigned to writers. Both readers and writers plan their task (i.e., reading or writing) around a given purpose and consider this purpose as they activate prior knowledge. Readers then read, constructing meaning based upon their purposes and background experiences. Writers, on the other hand, attempt to construct meaning so that the audience, the readers of their work, can understand what they are trying to convey. Writers have a good idea of what they want to present when they write. (See Figure 1.3.)

Figure 1.3

Comparing the reading and writing processes

Reading Process	Writing Process
Prereading	*Prewriting*
• Activate prior knowledge	• Access prior knowledge to aid in writing
Reading	*Writing*
• Construct meaning	• Create meaning
Revisiting Text	*Revising/Editing*
• Change, modify meaning	• Change, modify piece of writing

Consider these additional parallels. Readers read and then may even reread with the meaning sometimes changing or becoming modified as a result (Langer, 1995). Likewise, writers think about what they have written, reread, and use editing and revising as they rewrite. When readers finalize the meaning they have composed, they are finished. When writers complete their final draft, they, too, are finished composing (Cooper, 1997). Both reading and writing involve weaving together critical literacy skills.

Furthermore, reading and writing both touch on different roles according to the materials to be read or written and our purposes for reading or creating them. Rosenblatt (1978) describes these purposes as efferent and aesthetic needs—efferent in that we read and write to gain knowledge and information; aesthetic in that we also read and write for our own pleasure. "The efferent stance pays more attention to the cognitive, the factual, the public, and the quantitative aspects of textual meaning. The aesthetic stance focuses on the affective, the emotional, the private, and the qualitative aspects of personal meaning" (Hancock, 2000, p. 27). Reading and writing are a little like fraternal twins, aren't they? There are many commonalities that tie them together, but they are distinct in their own rights as well.

One way to learn how to pair up lessons in reading and writing is to examine the popular basal reading series (see the sample in Appendix B). As mentioned previously, series by various publishers usually contain leveled textbooks and supportive supplemental materials that are used to teach developmental reading in grades K–8. You will find them in the majority of American classrooms. Connections are frequently made between stories in the student's basal reader and content area subjects like science, social studies, and math. Each basal text contains several different genre of children's literature: traditional tales, fantasy, poetry, realistic fiction, historical fiction, biography, and informational selections. Then, writing activities are used to extend the learning or add a creative twist to selected stories.

Note, too, that a number of the basal lessons can become models for adapting or adjusting instruction by using alternative materials to supplement them. For instance, a skill taught in a basal lesson might be practice sessions within a selection of picture books or the novel a student is reading during independent reading. Natural writing extensions might include journaling in response to what is being read, jotting notes to record information for a report growing out of the current reading lesson, or creating a poem generated by an idea in a basal story. This textbook will build upon what well-designed basal series strive to accomplish, to demonstrate how teachers can help their students use reading and writing as tools of learning throughout the day and across the curriculum (Cunningham & Allington, 2003; Fuhler, 2000; Zemelman et al., 1998).

Research on the best ways to teach reading and writing is plentiful. Driven by the desire to provide opportunities for all children to read and to write effectively, one state after another has adopted specific standards in this area. In an effort to synthesize information from researchers, practitioners, and what various state standards dictate, Zemelman, Daniels, and Hyde (1998) conducted their own research. Their summarized findings in the area of reading and writing appear in Figures 1.4 and 1.5, respectively. You will find that these "Best Practice" suggestions are interwoven throughout this textbook because they mesh smoothly with the concept of balance. In this text we, too, will address the issue of standards that undergird best practices from one state to another. We will begin by taking a look at two sets of standards and discuss how they impact classroom instruction.

THE STANDARDS IN LITERACY INSTRUCTION

Teachers who believe in balanced literacy instruction not only are aware of a variety of alternative reading and writing methodologies but are expected by school district administrators to adhere to local, state, or national standards. In 1996, the National Council of Teachers of English (NCTE) and the International Reading Association (IRA) developed the *Standards for the English Language Arts*. The purpose of these standards was to specify what students in grades K–12 "should know about language and be able to do with language" (p. 1). The English language arts include reading, writing, listening, speaking, viewing, and visually representing. (See standards in-

Figure 1.4

Recommendations on teaching reading

Increase	Decrease
Reading aloud to students	
Time for independent reading	Exclusive emphasis on whole-class or reading-group activities
Children's choice of their own reading materials	Teacher selection of all reading materials for individuals and groups
Exposing children to a wide and rich range of literature	Relying on selection in basal reader
Teacher modeling and discussing his/her own reading processes	Teacher keeping his/her own reading tastes and habits private
Primary instructional emphasis on comprehension	Primary instructional emphasis on reading subskills such as phonics, word analysis, syllabication
Teaching reading as a process: • Use strategies that activate prior knowledge • Help students make and test predictions • Structure help during reading • Provide after-reading applications	Teaching reading as a single, one-step act
Social, collaborative activities with much discussion and interaction	Solitary seatwork
Grouping by interests or book choices	Grouping by reading level
Silent reading followed by discussion	Round-robin oral reading
Teaching skills in the context of whole and meaningful literature	Teaching isolated skills in phonics workbooks or drills
Writing before and after reading	Little or no chance to write
Encouraging invented spelling in children's early writings	Punishing preconventional spelling in students' early writings
Use of reading in content fields (e.g., historical novels in social studies)	Segregation of reading to reading time
Evaluation that focuses on holistic, higher order thinking processes	Evaluation focus on individual, low-level subskills
Measuring success of reading program by students' reading habits, attitudes, and comprehension	Measuring the success of the reading program only by test scores

Source: Reprinted from *Best Practice: New Standards for Teaching and Learning in America's Schools,* Second Edition by Steven Zemelman, Harvey Daniels, and Arthur Hyde (1998). Published by Heinemann, a division of Reed Elsevier Inc., Portsmouth, NH. Used by permission of the publisher.

cluded at end of this textbook.) In addition to the national standards, each state and/or school district has its own respective set of standards and goals for the English language arts. However, most of these local and state standards are aligned with the national goals that serve as their foundation. Thus, in general all teachers have similar

Figure 1.5
Recommendations on teaching writing

Increase	Decrease
Student ownership and responsibility by: • helping students choose their own topics and goals for improvement • using brief teacher-student conferences • teaching students to review their own progress	Teacher control of decision making by: • teacher deciding on all writing topics • suggestions for improvement dictated by teacher • learning objectives determined by teacher alone • instruction given as whole-class activity
Class time spent on writing whole, original pieces through: • establishing real purposes for writing and students' involvement in the task • instruction in and support for all stages of writing process • prewriting, drafting, revising, editing	Time spent on isolated drills on "subskills" of grammar, vocabulary, spelling, paragraphing, penmanship, etc. Writing assignments given briefly, with no context or purpose, completed in one step
Teacher modeling writing—drafting, revising, sharing—as a fellow author and as demonstration of processes	Teacher talks about writing but never writes or shares own work
Learning of grammar and mechanics in context, at the editing stage, and as items are needed	Isolated grammar lessons, given in order determined by textbook, before writing is begun
Writing for real audiences, published for the class and for wider communities	Assignments read only by teacher
Making the classroom a supportive setting for shared learning, using: • active exchange and valuing of students' ideas • collaborative small-group work • conferences and peer critiquing that give responsibility for improvement to authors	Devaluation of students' ideas through: • students viewed as lacking knowledge and language abilities • sense of class as competing individuals • work with fellow students viewed as cheating, disruptive
Writing across the curriculum as a tool for learning	Writing taught only during "language arts" period—i.e., infrequently
Constructive and efficient evaluation that involves: • brief informal oral responses as students work • thorough grading of just a few of student-selected, polished pieces • focus on a few errors at a time • cumulative view of growth and self-evaluation • encouragement of risk taking and honest expression	Evaluation as a negative burden for teacher and student by: • marking all papers heavily for all errors, making teacher a bottleneck • teacher editing paper, and only after completed, rather than student making improvements • grading seen as punitive, focused on errors, not growth

Source: From the *Standards for the English Language Arts* (1996). Copyright © 1996 by the International Reading Association and National Council for Teachers of English. All rights reserved. Reprinted with permission.

guidelines to follow to ensure that every student becomes proficient in the twelve standards of language arts.

As you read this textbook, you will encounter a section entitled, "Peering into the Classroom" at the beginning of each chapter. These vignettes of classroom teachers offer insights into the teaching of reading from the perspective of a balanced instructional approach. Another section follows, "Reflections: IRA/NCTE National Standards in the Classroom." In this segment, the instructional decisions and applications by the teacher in the "Peering into the Classroom" section are analyzed in terms of the *Standards for the English Language Arts* (IRA/NCTE, 1996). The rationale behind these reflections is to reinforce the fact that the standards do not have to add additional hurdles to a teacher's day. You will see one teacher after another thoughtfully integrating them into the typical classroom routine with relative ease.

It is important to distinguish between the two sets of standards highlighted throughout this book. The *Standards for Reading Professionals* (IRA, 1998) are important for all classroom teachers and reading specialists. In addition, near the beginning of each chapter you will find a web of some of these particular standards, alerting you to those that will be addressed specifically within the chapter.

Different from the *IRA/NCTE National Standards for the English Language Arts,* the *Standards for Reading Professionals* emerged from a collaboration between the International Reading Association (IRA) and the National Council for the Accreditation of Teacher Education (NCATE). It is a responsibility of NCATE to accredit various programs in institutions of higher learning. The two organizations worked together to ensure that there are stringent national standards in place for the preparation of teachers across the United States. In short, the standards describe the literacy process and the teaching proficiencies that reading professionals must demonstrate to be effective practitioners (IRA, 1998). As you master the content in each chapter of this book, you will be well on your way to meeting the standards required of a fine literacy professional.

Web Links:
Teaching to
Academic Standards

Teaching to
the Standards

 ## *ADDRESSING DIVERSITY:* CHANGING FACES AND NEEDS IN OUR NATION'S CLASSROOMS

One cannot address the topic of teaching literacy without also examining the topic of diversity in the classroom.

More than ever before classrooms are filled with children who are diverse. Typically some of the children represent culturally diverse backgrounds; others reflect diversity in terms of family makeup. There are students who have traditional two-parent families, while others live with extended families, including grandparents and aunts and uncles. Sometimes children talk of their first family, second family, or third family, as their parents have divorced and remarried, often to mates with children of their own. Furthermore, caregivers may be distant relatives or foster parents.

Aside from the parameters of the family or ethnic origin, a handful of students may be **inclusion** students who have very specific learning needs—identified learning difficulties, low functioning abilities, a physically challenging impairment, or a behavior disorder. Still others may be language delayed, which will impact their ability to read, write, listen, and speak. In fact, the U.S. Department of Education reports that over 10 percent of the school population can be designated as inclusion students or as "at risk" learners (Salisbury & McGregor, 2002). In addition, a large number of students are likely to be **English language learners** (ELLs). The primary language spoken at home is one other than English.

Teaching Strategy:
Creating Classroom
Community

Are you aware that the United States is experiencing the largest wave of immigration since the turn of the 20th century? Immigrants who came here early in that century had their roots primarily in European countries. Today, the newcomers are often from Asia, and Central and South America (Logan, 2000). In looking at classrooms of the past, depending on where one taught, it is safe to say that many teachers have been engaged to some degree with diversity in a broad sense of the word (Nieto, 2000; Sapon-Shevin, 2000–2001). However, the situation is markedly different today.

These changing demographics provide food for thought as teachers plan the most effective educational environments for their evolving classes of learners. Think about the fact that by the year 2020, students of color will make up about 46 percent of the U.S. school-age population; and by 2035, this group will reach the numerical majority of K–12 students (Banks & Banks, in Sapon-Shevin, 2000–2001). As a result, the increasing changes in faces, backgrounds, and abilities of the children in our classrooms will directly affect our choices of strategies and materials with which we choose to teach. In their book, *Children's Books in Children's Hands* (Temple et al., 2001), the authors underscore why the ability to address issues of a wide range of diversity is one that should permeate our teacher education courses and this textbook. Planning for diversity goes beyond faces and families because,

> The United States is a diverse society, and this diversity has many sources. The obvious ways in which both the general and school populations are diverse are gender, culture, ethnic and racial background, language, and physical and mental abilities. Less often acknowledged are differences in social class. All of these differences can affect the ways people see themselves and others. All must be taken into account in forging a working democracy or a harmonious classroom. (p. 83)

Finding ways to meet the instructional needs of such an array of different learners and to prepare them for future productive roles in our democracy can be a formidable task for any teacher. Yet it has to be done. Former Secretary of Education Richard W. Riley emphasized the importance of what happens to every child in our classrooms when he remarked, "How we educate their minds and shape their values now will go a long way to defining the destiny of this nation" (Olson, 2000, p. 31). Here, again, is the rationale for promoting a balanced instructional approach to reading and writing. Armed with an abundance of teaching methods and strategies, and the firm belief that every child has the right to succeed, there is the increased opportunity to meet a myriad of individual needs.

Listening centers are popular with students as they listen to books on tape and follow along with the text. Such centers are widely used with diverse learners, especially English language learners and struggling readers such as this young immigrant from Poland.

Keep in mind the following general guidelines as you prepare to reach and to teach children who fit into the previously discussed descriptors (Allington, 2002; Heilman, Blair, & Rupley, 2002):

- Observe students as they interact in your classroom, noting their learning strengths, styles, differences, and any potential disabilities that may impact their learning.
- Teach to each learner's strengths. Remediate areas of weakness, developing compensatory skills in the process.
- Restructure an assignment to adapt it to the learner.
- Provide appropriate materials to appeal to interest levels and abilities.
- Use direct instruction to ensure understanding.
- Allow enough time for students to read and to write, keeping the focus of classroom instruction and practice on these subjects.
- Monitor understanding carefully and consistently.
- Give directions in a variety of ways—oral, written, visual, and/or auditory—cueing students as necessary.
- Model, model, model. Actively show students how a strategy works instead of just giving an assignment.
- Provide peer buddies as learning partners or tutors.
- Practice inclusion so that every child is involved in classroom activities.

Web Link:
Yahoo! Education

- Evaluate each learner on his or her performance, looking at alternative assessments that support success.
- Be patient and be positive. Remember that every child is a learner and can grow within the structure and support of a thoughtfully run classroom.

The issues of changing demographics and growing diversity are not late-breaking news. Newspapers, journals, and newscasters have been reporting changes within the population of the United States for some time now. Listen to the story some current numbers have to tell (Hodgkinson, 2001):

- About 65 percent of America's population growth in the next two decades will be "minority," with the largest growth reflected by Hispanic and Asian immigrants.
- Ethnic diversity is not evenly distributed across the United States. California, Texas, and Florida continue to reflect rapidly growing culturally diverse communities. Other states that will strongly reflect changing populations are New York, Wyoming, and Alaska (Olson, 2000).
- A discussion of diversity is not complete without addressing the number of children affected by poverty. "Poverty is a universal handicap" (Hodgkinson, p. 9) with 20 percent of children in this country living below the poverty line, a statistic that surprisingly has not changed in fifteen years despite the robust economic period of the 1990s. The economic recession that followed has resulted in fewer jobs and more hardships for low-income families.

Hodgkinson continues by informing readers about where the largest increases in diversity are to occur, namely, around existing large metropolitan areas. He refers to the "inner suburban ring" (p. 8) located at the edge of large cities. This area includes the suburbs of old, but those former homeowners are moving farther away and forming an outer ring of suburbs in the process. The inner ring is the area seeing the greatest increase in changing ethnicities and socioeconomic backgrounds, resulting in a new mix of inhabitants. In all likelihood, these neighborhoods will eventually resemble what it is currently like to teach in the inner city. On the other hand, it appears that the changes in small towns and rural areas will continue to be fairly negligible.

Portfolio Activity:
Student Diversity

What do these demographic changes mean in the classroom? First, the expectation for teachers of today and tomorrow is that they are and will continue to be culturally sensitive and will have the requisite skills for teaching a wide range of students (Nieto, 2000; Sapon-Shevin, 2000–2001; Temple et al., 2001). Next, teachers need to be the leaders who recognize and then act upon what Lynn Olson (2000, p. 31) advocates:

> Americans must prove that demography is not a destiny: that the color of children's skin, where they live, the languages they speak, and the income and educational levels of their parents do not determine the educational opportunities they receive.

As teachers recognize and support the potential of each child, it would be hoped that there would be fewer stories like this one related by Sonia Nieto (2000, p. 1).

> As a young child growing up in Brooklyn, New York, during the 1940s, I experienced firsthand the effects of relative poverty and discrimination. In the schools I attended, a

common perception was that my culture and language were inferior. I spoke only Spanish when I entered first grade, and I was immediately confronted with the arduous task of learning a second language while my developed native language was all but ignored. . . . Equally vivid are memories of some teachers' expectations that my classmates and I would not do well in school because of our language and cultural differences. This explains my fourth-grade teacher's response when mine was the only hand to go up when she asked whether anybody in the class wanted to go to college. "Well, that's okay," she said, "because we always need people to clean toilets."

That kind of insensitivity is simply inexcusable in any classroom. Sadly, similar tales can be echoed and reechoed by many a student from a number of cultural backgrounds based upon years of misunderstandings and deeply seated negative attitudes, and augmented by continued inadequate funding in so many classrooms. Sapon-Shevin (2000–2001) asks how we as educators can develop habits of the mind and heart to respond constructively to diversity, ensuring that injustice and inequality like the true-life story just related become intolerable in our schools. Realistically speaking, that type of change has to happen one person at a time. It is our hope that readers of this textbook will contribute their efforts to changing the tide of intolerance as they provide opportunities to pursue dreams on the wings of strong, pertinent literacy skills.

Suggestions are interwoven throughout this textbook on ways to help students from different backgrounds or with varying learning difficulties to succeed in school. Our track record in this area is not particularly rosy (Nieto, 2000). While cultural differences and multicultural success pose knotty problems for educators, so do different educational handicapping conditions. Certainly this text does not propose to have all of the answers. But we can offer a platform from which to begin. In addition to seeking a helping hand from the bilingual education teacher, reading specialist, or a special education teacher, review the general tips in Figure 1.6 and watch for additional highlighted sections in each chapter.

Often the quality teaching strategies described within the chapter will work well for all learners. Perhaps that strategy may require a little more practice supported by a classroom aide, parent volunteer, or a small group of classmates before it is mastered. Generally, the best advice is that "by using diverse teaching strategies, teachers not only improve their chances of reaching every learner, but also model respect for diversity and help students understand that people are different and learn differently" (Sapon-Shevin, 2000–2001, p. 36). In addition, search the Internet sites suggested throughout the book and ask colleagues for techniques that have worked for them. It cannot be emphasized enough that this book is a strong starting point. You have a lifetime of continuing discoveries ahead if your goal is to make a difference for as many learners as possible.

Web Link:
Curriculum
Educational
Resource

TECHNOLOGY: A GROWING PRESENCE IN LITERACY INSTRUCTION

Bits and bytes. Search engines and websites. Networks and instant messengers. These words could be the beginning of a lesson on vocabulary from the world of

Figure 1.6

Suggestions for making learning a successful experience for all students

- **Become knowledgeable about and respectful of each child's background.** Under the umbrella of Asian or Hispanic, for example, are a number of different ethnic backgrounds. Thus, the wise teacher does not assume that all children within a broad cultural designation are the same.
- **Learn about cultural behaviors.** For instance, if a child does not look you in the eye, do not immediately assume that this is a sign of disrespect. It is often just the opposite. Many Native American children and adults alike in the Hopi and Navajo cultures consider it disrespectful to look you in the eye. Are there other cultures in which this is a taught behavior? Become familiar with them.
- **Children from diverse backgrounds profit from learning in different ways.** For example, with English language learners in particular, try using visual presentations as often as possible. Pictures often translate more easily than verbal directions or explanations when language barriers are present.
- **Celebrate the accomplishments of people of all ethnicities within your classroom and throughout your school.** Use books, posters, guest speakers, videos, and class trips for starters. The message that everyone can succeed can be a powerful motivator.
- **Recognize, support, and honor that children today live in multiple communities,** be it Latino in an urban setting, African American in an inner-city setting, a member of the deaf community, a child identified with some type of disability, or a combination of these and others. Are there accepted norms within these communities with which you should be aware?
- **Implement strategies and activities that apply to Standard 9,** which urges that all "students develop an understanding of and respect for diversity in language use, patterns, and dialects across cultures, ethnic groups, geographic regions, and social roles" (IRA/NCTE, 1996, p. 3).
- **Work with the bilingual education teacher to implement learning opportunities that address Standard 10,** which states that "students whose first language is not English make use of their first language to develop competency in the English language arts and to develop understanding of content across the curriculum" (IRA/NCTE, 1996, p. 3). It is essential that one's native language is not denigrated. It is, in fact, the foundation upon which future learning is built.
- **Move away from a rigid, one method curriculum to a flexible one that includes participation, collaboration, multisensory and cooperative learning** to reach all learners across language barriers and learning boundaries.
- **Involve the family in the child's education,** including parents, guardians, grandparents, older siblings. The family that learns together progresses toward fulfillment together.

Source: Hodgkinson, 2001; IRA/NCTE, 1996; Jensen, 1998; Olson, 2000; Nieto, 2000; Sapon-Shevin, 2000–2001.

computer technology. A realm that was once fantasized in science fiction novels and premiered in state-of-the-art government labs has now invaded the majority of our nation's classrooms. Internet connections shrink distance barriers, placing the world at our fingertips (Means, 2000–2001). The capabilities of the technological domain are awe-inspiring, at least to a novice. It seems this is merely the beginning of opportunities to research a plethora of topics, to refine the art of critical thinking as websites or specific information is carefully scrutinized, or to dialogue through a few keystrokes with students, friends, and educational colleagues around the world. In that light, the 21st century clearly demands that technology be one part of the classroom world, for as Leu (2000, p. 424) remarks,

Today, children need to be prepared for much more than book literacies. The rapid appearance in many of our classrooms of networked information and communication technology (ICT), such as the Internet, requires us to fundamentally redefine our understanding of the literacy curriculum.

Without a doubt, reading and writing using computers as a tool has become as essential as slates, a technological tool of the 1700s and 1800s, were to teachers and their charges in the one-room schools of the past.

Therefore, add to the long list of "musts" that have been discussed thus far in this chapter yet one more, the need to be knowledgeable about technology and its current and potential application to enabling all students access to literacy. Lest you think that is negotiable, note Standard 8 from the *Standards for the English Language Arts* (IRA/NCTE, 1996), which pointedly informs us that students should be able to use a variety of technological and informational resources (e.g., libraries, databases, computer networks, video) to gather and synthesize information and to create and communicate knowledge.

Further reinforcing the need to be technologically literate, the International Reading Association (2002) released a timely position statement entitled "Integrating Literacy and Technology in the Curriculum." The statement shifts one's thinking about the scope of literacy. It reinforces the growing realization that technology can play a critical role in the daily classroom routine. In fact, it is a key component in what is currently considered to be quality reading instruction. Urging teachers to acknowledge and welcome this exciting literacy partner, the position statement recommends the following for teachers:

Web Link:
The International
Reading Association

- Take full advantage of professional development opportunities to build literacy-related technology skills. Read professional publications, check online journals, and investigate electronic mailing lists.

- Integrate technology into the literacy curriculum thoughtfully. Ensure that students become critical consumers of information gleaned via the Internet.

- Explore literacy-related ideas and strategies developed by other teachers that are available at various Internet sites.

- Give every child the opportunity to use and explore technology and to do so safely in your classroom.

Without a doubt, both teachers and their students will embark on a continuous journey of discovery in the ever-evolving process of tying technology and literacy together.

While some of it may not be state-of-the-art equipment, it was predicted that by 2002, far more classrooms in the United States would have computers connected to the Internet than have telephones, televisions, sets of encyclopedias, or comprehensive school libraries. Technology will not replace invaluable print resources, certainly, but will make a variety of them more readily available to a greater number of students. Along with ease of access, however, comes the caution that everything on the Internet is not of equal quality. Critical reading on the part of the teacher and students plus the importance of teacher-previewed sites go hand and hand with responsible access to classroom technology (IRA, 2002). Rather than being intimidating, the riches of technology issue an open invitation to learn from each other and from young students who all too frequently know more about complicated software programs and the Internet than their teachers do. For a wealth of information on

Figure 1.7

Websites:
Computer use in the classroom

Curriculum Educational Resources: This site suggests how valuable the Internet can be in expanding teaching and learning opportunities and offers links to support the suggestions.

4teachers.org: This site is invaluable. Try the tutorials, review tips on protecting children from undesirable sites, and learn ways that learners with diverse needs can profit from technology time among numerous other options.

Yahoo!Education: This site links teachers to popular technology sites and offers tutorials, links, and hints to teachers wanting to broaden their understanding of technology in the classroom.

TRACKSTAR: This site has thousands of reading activities on a multitude of topics. Good for linking with content area assignments in science and social studies.

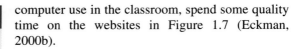

To link to these sites, go to the Web Links area in Chapter 1 of the Online Learning Center at www.mhhe.com/farrisreading.

Web Links:
Children's Literature:
Criticism and Theory

Book Rap

computer use in the classroom, spend some quality time on the websites in Figure 1.7 (Eckman, 2000b).

Building Technological Envisionments

Leu, Karchmer, and Leu (1999) describe the process of adapting to and melding the world of technology and literacy as an "envisionment," an occurrence that takes place when "teachers and children imagine new possibilities for literacy and learning, transform existing technologies to construct this vision, and then share their work with others" (p. 636). Already teachers and their students are turning the Internet into an exchange arena where lessons that really work are shared, opportunities to dialogue are presented, and novices and long-term practitioners profit from innumerable opportunities to learn. Here is a mere sampling of possibilities:

- Books afford the reader an opportunity to change his attitude, rethink his behavior, deal with personal challenges, or examine a social issue in a different way (Rudman, 1995). Sometimes books take on issues that are difficult to address in the classroom, but they are about topics that beg to be discussed. Children's literature instructor Denise Johnson (1999) wanted to present an opportunity for her students to have a reflective conversation with other teachers about complex books like *The Golem* (Wisniewski, 1996) and *Smoky Night* (Bunting, 1994). She turned to an electronic mailing list, Children's Literature: Criticism and Theory (CHILD_LIT), asking if there was another instructor who would be interested in having his or her students interact with her class about complex children's literature (Johnson, 1999). From her query grew a stimulating, reflective electronic dialogue between two classrooms of teachers as they deepened their understanding of books they could eventually use with their own classrooms of learners. Thus, peers interacting with peers via the Internet became a powerful learning experience.

- Students learn from each other as well. Encourage students to expand their thinking as they dialogue about a book they are reading through Book Rap, a site managed by Cherrol McGhee in Queensland, Australia. Here is an opportunity to join in an online variation of the literature circle when students from around the world exchange viewpoints on a shared book (Leu et al., 1999).

- There is a new way to integrate the curriculum. Collaborate globally on an interactive, cross-curricular project, a sure way to heighten motivation and make learning a memorable experience. A central site for teachers wanting to engage in Internet projects is provided by this search engine, which will list numerous potential cooperative learning experiences at the Global School-Net Internet Projects Registry.

- Science takes on new meaning when students work with Hands-On Universe, a program from the University of California—Berkeley's Lawrence Hall of Science. When using this program, students are involved with image processing software that presents images from space via a network of automated telescopes. Terms like "supernova" and "asteroids" rapidly become familiar as students study and research various true-to-life images (Means, 2000–2001).

- Networks and listservers abound providing talk time to teachers and other professionals about irksome problems or offering a place to research, thus continually staying on top of new thinking in the field of education. Never has it been easier to pursue the goal of being a lifelong learner. All you need is the desire, a decent computer with Internet connections, and time to read, respond, and reflect. If you are concerned about issues of bilingualism and diversity, for example, log on to the National Clearinghouse for English Language Acquisition's website.

- Join in a conversation on a network, a group of people tied together by an interest in a particular issue or who are looking for similar information. Being a member allows you to exchange ideas, offer resources, problem-solve, grow professionally, and connect with other colleagues as you learn from someone else's experiences, share yours, and investigate a classroom issue like brain-based learning, early childhood education, integrating technology into your classroom, and so much more (Eckman, 2000a). Several networks are listed in Figure 1.8 for your investigation.

Web Links:
Global School-Net
Internet Projects Registry

National Clearinghouse
for English Language
Acquisition

It appears that the educational applications of quality software and fine Internet sites are far-reaching given adequate equipment and the knowledgeable, enterprising, and creative teacher. Pair up with a colleague to explore Internet options or investigate the potential of various software programs. Invite knowledgeable students to tutor other students, ask for parental assistance if there are parents with expertise to share, and take advantage of workshops and in-service presentations to extend your skills (Brogan, 2000). Exploring the options of technology does not have to be a solitary journey. The preceding tantalizing examples illustrate what Leu (2000, p. 426) had in mind when he wrote about the critical role you will play in the realm of technological literacy:

> The connectivity that characterizes literacy on the Internet permits all of us to learn from one another in ways never before possible. As a result, the more members of the literacy community that enter these worlds, the more insights we can bring to central issues of instructional practice. Even if you are just getting started, you have important information to share with others—questions that get everyone thinking critically about how to best use the new technologies of literacy. In a connected world, good questions are often the most useful information because they prompt thoughtful answers from which others may also benefit.

Expanding Your Technological Horizons

Technology in the form of interactive software and websites packed with information provides an avenue to improving learning opportunities for all learners. Think of the

Figure 1.8

Websites: Literary Resources

A Useful Library Link: Library Spot. This is a superb website for upper elementary and middle school students as it is linked to over 150 major libraries in the United States as well as all of the fifty state libraries and the Library of Congress.

CHILD LIT: This is a mailing list to which one can subscribe if interested in the criticism and theory of children's literature. Presently, librarians, teachers of grades K–12, teacher educators, publishers, authors, illustrators, and parents subscribe.

The Education Index: Click on "subjects" and then select "reading" for a number of informative links addressing reading education. Another option is to click on "lifestyles" and research topics related to a specific age group. "Ask Eric" is also available from this site.

The International Reading Association: This is the website for the International Reading Association (IRA).

The National Council of Teachers of English: Information pertaining to the National Council of Teachers of English can be found at this site (NCTE).

Pathways to School Improvement Resource: This is the Pathways to School Improvement server designed to assist teachers and administrators in providing the latest information regarding instructional practices in grades K–12.

ProTeacher: A wealth of information is provided at this site for K–6 teachers including links to subject areas like Network & Support, Teaching Practices, Classroom Management, Educational Technology, and Reading & Language Arts, to name a few.

Reading Online: Check this online journal regularly for an informative range of articles that educate and entertain. Authorities in the area of literacy are popular authors at this site.

The Teaching Tolerance Project: This particular project was created by the Southern Poverty Law Center in 1991. It provides teachers with free or inexpensive resources that develop students' understanding and respect for others.

Networks to Investigate:

Arts in Education

Brain-Based Education/Learning

Differentiated Instruction

Early Childhood Education

To link to these sites, go to the Web Links area in Chapter 1 of the Online Learning Center at www.mhhe.com/ farrisreading.

 boon it could be for English language learners, students with language processing difficulties, or those with visual impairments when there is an audio component to reading software, for example. Both seeing and hearing the words boost skill acquisition and afford an opportunity for independent practice (Brogan, 2000). In addition, with continuing emphasis on learning that is as real and as related to life as possible, students can connect with experts in the field, can be actively involved in realistic simulations, and receive timely feedback on their work, the latter being a step that is acknowledged to improve learning (Jensen, 1998). Imagine the opportunities for higher level critical thinking and creative, in-depth reading available to a gifted learner via excellent Internet sites.

While many teachers are just trying to catch up with what is currently available, visionaries are moving technology one step further. Even now technology is available that will free the learner from the computer attached to the classroom wall. Wireless

Student assignments involving the use of technology, particularly when using the Internet, must be well planned to use time efficiently.

products like those ever-prevalent, little portable telephones continue to be perfected. Before long, many a student will carry a sensibly priced, handheld computer connected to global networks sized so that it tucks conveniently into their backpacks (Means, 2000–2001). In an age of exploding information and rapidly evolving technology that makes accessing that information increasingly easy, it is truly an exciting time to be an educator. Spend some time visiting and then assessing the value of the following websites as resources in an effort to ensure that you will be the best literacy teacher you can possibly be. Suggestions for both quality software and informative Internet sites that have been reviewed and used by the authors are included in the remaining chapters for your investigation. While some are interspersed throughout the chapters, the majority of the information on related technology will be located for your convenience at the close of each chapter.

WHAT LIES AHEAD: A SKETCH OF UPCOMING CHAPTER CONTENT

What can you expect from the remaining chapters in the textbook? Here is a thumbnail sketch of what lies ahead. In addition to the chapters previously mentioned in this introduction, you will have the opportunity to focus on critical information about literacy skills in Chapter 3, An Overview of Instructional Strategies That Support a Balanced Approach.

Chapter 4, Organizing the Classroom Environment, contains resources and ideas for turning your own classroom into a rich and appealing literacy environment offered by teachers and other authorities in the field. Here, too, is an opportunity to reflect upon which ideas might work with your particular students as you prepare for your first classroom or reevaluate how your current classroom operates. The setting for reading and writing instruction can make teaching and accessing literacy for the future a motivating and engaging pursuit for each and every learner.

Chapter 5, Assessing and Evaluating Literacy Development, will reinforce how assessment and evaluation should drive an effective literacy program. While the ideas and information offered in this chapter could have been integrated into pertinent chapters throughout the book, we felt the strategies and ideas were more easily accessed if separated into their own chapter. Here you will find suggestions for ways to monitor each child's progress in order to better inform your instructional decisions along with techniques for gathering data to review with parents and guardians at conference and report card time.

Chapter 6, Emergent Literacy: Beginning Reading and Writing, provides a firm foundation for building your expertise in teaching literacy to the very young. Skills and strategies critical to phonics instruction are discussed in Chapter 7, A Balanced Approach to Phonics and Word Study. While phonics remains a controversial topic in the reading world, the discussion is currently more about how much phonics instruction is needed rather than whether the skills should be taught at all. In your continuing professional reading you will still find strong supporters of both views.

Comprehension, often noted as the heart of the reading process, is presented in Chapter 8, Reading Comprehension. A number of methods for addressing comprehension are introduced and modeled. They are, by no means, the only ones to use. You must begin with a selection of strategies to polish, however, and those offered for your use are firmly supported by research. The majority of them are applicable across the grades. The study of words comes next. Ideas are formed and conveyed using words, and learning those words is addressed in Chapter 9, Vocabulary Instruction in a Balanced Literacy Program. The importance of teaching students to continually quest for new words and broaden personal vocabularies will be supported in this chapter, and suggestions for making word acquisition a positive, lifelong experience are included.

While numerous reading textbooks provide valuable information about children's literature as a part of the reading curriculum, we felt this topic was so vital that it deserved its own chapter. Thus, Chapter 10, Children's Literature in a Balanced Literacy Program, is presented as an indispensable primer on the topic. If you have already taken an initial course in children's literature, you are the richer for it. Unfortunately, not all education programs require such a course. This primer is offered to briefly introduce the captivating worlds of fiction, nonfiction, and poetry along with their potential for enhancing literacy acquisition as an integral part of a balanced instructional program. This chapter can serve as an invitation to learn more about compelling book literacies or be a timely review of superb books and enticing teaching ideas.

As mentioned previously, the powerful reading–writing connection is discussed in Chapter 11, Connecting Reading and Writing: Narrative and Poetry, and in Chapter 12, Connecting Reading and Writing: Expository Text.

While this textbook is meant to inform and to teach, it is also meant to be used. The teaching strategies presented in each chapter can often be adapted to varying grade levels or learning needs. Each chapter ends with valuable materials to enrich your understanding of the chapter content and to provide additional resources for classroom teaching ideas. Teacher-tested lesson plans model how skills and strategies can be taught. The carefully designed sample interdisciplinary units offer a place to begin, with possibilities to enrich your classroom with engrossing across-the-curriculum learning opportunities. Again, they can be altered to address district curriculum dictates and your individual classrooms of students. It is hoped that you will regard this book as a teaching handbook and return to it as you think and rethink your philosophy of teaching reading as a balanced instructional approach. At another time you may pick this text up as you prepare a lesson for tomorrow's class or use it to spark your own creative lessons.

We are teachers, too, and we understand the magnitude of the job ahead. You face a tremendously exciting career with significant responsibilities. You will become a member of the corps of teachers charged with preparing citizens for the future. We designed this book to support your efforts. Cummins (in Nieto, 2000, p. xiv) makes our joint roles quite clear when he suggests that together we must prepare future adults who:

> know how to access information, who can critically interpret this information to discover what is relevant and useful, and who can work cooperatively across cultural, linguistic, and racial boundaries to solve problems using this information.

While challenging, that is not an impossible charge. The key to success for you and your learners lies in the successful acquisition and application of literacy skills. The tools to get you started are at your fingertips. May you ply them with wisdom, teach them with enthusiasm, and maintain a personal balance by never losing sight of your sense of humor.

Summary

Literacy instruction permeates the classroom day. The skills are crucial inasmuch as reading and writing are needed by every child who hopes to participate as an informed member of our increasingly diverse society. Teachers play essential and critical roles in developing the requisite skills. By becoming familiar with a variety of instructional practices in reading and writing and knowing when to use them, teachers can assist each of their students to gain the necessary high standard of literacy. Wise decisions will be based upon time-tested, educational theory.

Because reading and writing are such closely related processes, it is difficult to talk about one to the exclusion of the other. As a result, in this textbook, reading strategies are emphasized and writing activities, naturally extending from reading experiences, are highlighted as well.

Teachers must keep apprised of students' skills and competencies in reading and writing as they continuously make instructional decisions. This means that students' efforts are regularly assessed and evaluated in light of what they should be learning. In considering how and in what ways students should be learning, teachers can turn to the *Standards for the English Language Arts* (IRA/NCTE, 1996), the *Standards for Reading Professionals* (IRA, 1998), and state-mandated standards. In the process, teachers will be addressing the diversity of the children in their classrooms and broadening the understanding of numerous cultures at the same time as required by those standards. In addition, they will be reminded of the importance of extending literacy into the technological realm. A few of the myriad of technology offerings currently available have been discussed because they promise a rich and varied avenue for both literacy and professional development.

Chapter Review

Go to the Online Learning Center at **www.mhhe.com/farrisreading** to take chapter quizzes, practice with key terms, and review important content.

Main Points

- Literacy goes well beyond simply knowing how to read and to write. Critical literacy involves thinking, decision making, and various ways to communicate.

- Reading and writing are essential language skills needed by every child who hopes to participate as an informed member of both classroom and society.

- Classroom teachers need to know a wide variety of reading and writing instructional methods and apply them depending on the needs of the diverse children in the classroom. This is called a *balanced instructional approach.*

- Learning to teach literacy based upon one's personal philosophy of balance is difficult and challenging because there is so much to discover about the world of reading and writing. Rooting one's decisions in relevant theory will make this a more effective process.

- Early theories that drove reading instruction were the bottom-up approach, the top-down approach, and the integrated approach. Drawing on strengths from the first two, the latter more adequately reflects the complex reading process and is currently more strongly supported.

- A balanced approach to literacy honors the teacher as a decision maker and provides him with the most options to enable students' needs to be met and individual strengths to be further enhanced.

- Both readers and writers plan their task (i.e., reading or writing) around a given purpose and consider this purpose as they activate prior knowledge. Readers then read, constructing meaning based upon their purposes and background experiences. Writers, on the other hand, attempt to construct meaning so that the audience (i.e., the readers of the piece) can understand what they are trying to convey. Writers have a good idea of what they want to present when they begin to write.

- Local, state, and national standards become the guidelines for the teacher to follow to ensure that every student becomes proficient in the twelve areas of language arts.

- Demographics must not become the deciding factor in a child's academic success or failure.

- It is essential to become well-versed in strategies for offering literacy instruction to today's students who reflect diversity in a number of different ways. In the process teachers will be preparing students for their roles as future citizens in a democratic society.

- Reading and writing using the best of technology as a tool to expand teaching and learning options is an exciting option for teachers and learners alike.

- The best literacy instruction occurs when a combination of instructional methods are incorporated by a decisive, well-informed teacher who attempts to meet the needs of all students in the classroom.

Key Terms

balanced instructional approach 9	discovery or inquiry learning 11	holistic 16	phonics 10
basal reading series 8	eclectic teaching 9	inclusion 24	semantics 18
bottom-up approach 13	English language learners 24	interactive approach 17	standards 5
differentiated instruction 9	graphophonic cues 17	literacy 5	syntax 18
		literature-based instruction 10	top-down approach 16

Reflecting and Reviewing

1. It has been said that as teachers we often revert to teaching the way we were taught as children despite the college training we have had in new and possibly more effective ways to educate children. Can you pinpoint several experiences from your years as a student that will positively affect the way you teach your future students? Are there lessons you learned from negative experiences that left you thinking, "I will never do that in my classroom?"

2. Focus now on the issues of diversity that were briefly addressed in this chapter. What personal experiences have you had with diversity in your classrooms as a child? Carefully examine your feelings about teaching children from diverse backgrounds. Do you think these children are coming to your classroom with strengths to share or deficits to remediate? Your honest answers will become a part of your philosophy of teaching literacy skills to each young learner in the succession of students who will pass through your classroom doors.

3. How do you view the role of technology as a tool to teach literacy? Is there anything that worries you about its use? What do you see as the technological strengths of software and/or the Internet? How will the books in your classroom library stack up to technological offerings?

Children's Literature

For annotations of the books listed below, please see Appendix A.

Bradby, Marie. (1995). *More Than Anything Else.* (C. K. Soentpiet, Illus.). New York: Orchard.

Bunting, Eve. (1994). *Smoky Night.* (D. Diaz, Illus.). San Diego, CA: Harcourt.

Fox, Mem. (2000). *Harriet, You'll Drive Me Wild!* (M. Frazee, Illus.). San Diego, CA: Harcourt.

Henkes, Kevin. (1993). *Owen.* New York: Greenwillow.

Lester, Julius. (1994). *John Henry.* (J. Pinkney, Illus.). New York: Dial.

Pomerantz, Charlotte. (2000). *The Mousery.* (K. Cyrus, Illus.). San Diego, CA: Gulliver/ Harcourt Brace.

Wisniewski, David. (1996). *The Golem.* New York: Clarion.

Classroom Teaching Resources

Burgstahler, S., & Utterback, L. (2000). *New kids on the Net.* Boston: Allyn & Bacon.

Fuhler, C. J. (2000). *Teaching reading and writing with multicultural books kids love.* Golden, CO: Fulcrum.

Nieto, Sonia. (2000). *Affirming diversity: The sociopolitical context of multicultural education* (3rd ed.). New York: Longman.

Routman, R. (2003). *Reading essentials.* Portsmouth, NH: Heinemann.

Valmont, W. J. (2003). *Technology for literacy teaching and learning.* Boston: Houghton Mifflin.

"*Literacy is an issue that transcends the mere mastery of reading and writing, one that has deep roots in our national history.*"

Jerome Bruner, leader in curriculum development

CHAPTER 2

The History of Reading and Writing

Key Ideas

- The inventions of paper and the printing press paved the way to a literate society.
- In 1647, the passage of the "Old Deluder Satan Act" in Massachusetts directed the teaching of reading to all children so they might read the scriptures for themselves.
- Children's books began to be published as it became a lucrative business in which publishers could make a profit.
- *McGuffey Readers* were the first basal readers in the United States that were widely used.
- Horace Mann advocated that teachers needed to be trained in **pedagogy** to teach children to read and write.
- World War I set in motion greater emphasis on **standardized reading tests** and instruction.
- A series of basal readers that featured Dick and Jane and their family became extremely popular in the 1940s to 1960s.
- **Linguistic readers** using vocabulary that was based on highly regular sound–symbol, phonic patterns were popular in the 1960s.
- During the first seventy-five years of the 20th century, **reading readiness,** phonics instruction, and standardized testing were stressed in the schools.
- During the 1970s, researchers such as Ken Goodman focused on the **psycholinguistic** view of reading combining a psychological understanding of the process of reading with an understanding of how language works.
- **Emergent literacy** evolved from the study of reading readiness in the 1980s as researchers noted the literacy skills very young children developed from their exposure to environmental print and their early attempts at reading and writing.

- From 1975 to 2000, reading and writing instruction moved from an emphasis on reading basal reader stories and completing worksheets to having students read quality children's literature and write on topics of their own choosing. One aspect of this movement was the **whole language approach** to teaching reading and writing.
- In 1998, the International Reading Association adopted standards for reading professionals that required proficiency in three broad areas: (1) knowledge and beliefs, (2) instruction and assessment, and (3) organizing and enhancing a reading program.
- By 2000, a balanced approach to reading instruction was stressed in order that children learn phonics and comprehension strategies in becoming fluent readers. In addition, the teacher must know when to apply appropriate literacy methods and strategies to best meet students' needs, thereby making critical instructional decisions.
- In 2002, Congress passed the "No Child Left Behind" Act, which mandated that all third through eighth graders be tested annually for reading achievement.

Questions to Ponder

- What historical events have influenced reading and writing instruction?
- How have reading and writing instruction and materials changed over the years?
- How has children's literature changed in the last century?
- How have political events impacted reading and writing instruction?
- What had led to a balanced approach to literacy instruction?
- What are the implications of the "No Child Left Behind Act" for classroom teachers?

Peering into the Classroom

A Perspective from Carol J. Fuhler

It was the age of the "crooners" during my elementary school years in Seattle, Washington. As I moved through the primary grades, Nat King Cole, Perry Como, and Frank Sinatra serenaded listeners with their mellow tones. Judy Garland belted out heart-felt tunes while Louis Armstrong changed the tempo with his popular cool jazz. I was more interested in learning to read than identifying the hit artists during those early grades, however. As I climbed the steep hill to the neighborhood elementary school with my best friend Janet, I was excited about the day ahead and the opportunity to learn to read in the weeks to come.

My reading world consisted of Round Robin Reading. Sitting upon small wooden chairs in a circle, we took turns reading out loud. My new book friends were Dick, Jane, Sally, and Spot who had a rather limited vocabulary compared to today's standards. I memorized sight words and worked my way through primers with wording like,

> Run, Spot.
> Run, run, run.
> Oh, oh, oh.
> Funny, funny Spot. (Scott, Foresman & Co., 1996, p. 10)

Seatwork involved completing countless workbook pages. While I don't have distinct memories of many of my elementary schoolteachers, I can tell you that my first grade teacher, an aged, white-haired woman, absolutely terrified me. I cannot pinpoint why, but the strong worried memory of her still fills my mind today. I don't recall inviting writing centers or cozy reading corners but there was a library and it fast became one of my favorite places in school.

My classroom life included slate blackboards, white chalk, and sometimes helping the teacher by cleaning the erasers outside. The manuscript, and later, cursive alphabet, marched across the top of the chalkboard at the front of the classroom and the best student work was displayed on bulletin boards. Friday spelling tests were a matter of routine. We sat in alphabetical order in rigidly aligned desks that were carved with initials, squiggles, and circles from previous inhabitants. What a different picture and learning environment from classroom worlds of today.

Recess memories include the slap, slap, slap of jump ropes hitting the pavement accompanied by rhymes like "Teddy Bear, Teddy Bear, turn around; Teddy Bear, Teddy Bear, touch the ground. . ." joined by other sounds of students calling, laughing, and enjoying the freedom offered by some unstructured time. Quiet games like playing Jacks with another friend, or joining classmates for a ball game called Four Square, made recess much too short. In general, school days flew by, and all too soon I would be on my way back down that Seattle hill before I knew it, sharing highlights of the day with my best friend.

School years sped by, the music changed dramatically, and so did the cities as I completed the bulk of my schooling in Denver and my senior year in a small Illinois town. I read my way through basal after basal, and I still haunted the library enjoying the Bobbsey twins, traveling with Mary Poppins, tickled with Mr. Popper's penguins, and sleuthing with Nancy Drew. While the time to read has greatly diminished during my professional years, I still manage to eke out time to savor a new children's book or escape into the world of an adult novel. Seeds planted early in life through the days with Dick and Jane have blossomed into a personal love of reading that I delight in sharing whenever possible. How fortunate young readers are these days with the bounty of reading materials from textbook to tradebook with which they can master the skills necessary in learning to read.

A Perspective from Pamela J. Farris

Elvis, Brenda Lee, and the Supremes belted out rock and roll tunes over the school bus radio as I, a six-year old wearing a brand new red plaid dress, began first grade in a small Midwestern rural school. There, with blue hair and a flowered dress behind an oak desk centered in the front of the classroom, sat Mrs. Hayman, the first and second grade teacher. Only three elementary teachers were in the school as each taught two grades. There was no kindergarten as this rural school district lacked the funds to provide it. One got to know the teachers REALLY well whether you wanted to or not. And you already knew all of the kids in your class. After all, it was a teeny tiny town with one speed limit sign—15 miles per hour—and no stop signs. There were three girls and six boys in my first grade class, a perfect number for a baseball team.

Four rows of oak desks with empty ink wells and intricate black cast iron flowered legs were attached to runners on the floor. They ran perpendicular to the front chalkboard. Tiny wooden chairs lined the back of the classroom near the cloakroom door. A poster of eight different colored hens with words labeled beneath each—white, black, red, green, yellow, orange, brown, and blue—sat on the chalkboard railing. The pencil sharpener nearby would only sharpen pencils the size of Lincoln logs. Enormous windows on the south wall peered out to the surrounding cornfields over monstrous looking silver radiators that hissed and popped during the cold winter months. More promising was the classroom's north wall that held the treasure trove of the classroom—two shelves of well-worn children's books, the complete extent of the library for first and second graders.

A slight Southern breeze blew in through the windows and I inhaled deeply. My senses took everything in—the sweet smells of newly polished floors, old textbooks, pencil shavings, and new leather shoes; the touch of carvings on my newly assigned wooden desk, the sleekness of new crayons, and drips of perspiration running down the back of my neck; the taste of cold milk on a warm afternoon; listening to every word my teacher spoke; and seeing my own name on my textbooks, words on the chalkboard, and two whole rows of yet to be read books sitting on a shelf only a few feet away. To this six-year-old, the world was perfect.

We learned to read from a phonics-based program. Each page had the story at the top and phonics activities across the bottom. After reading short stories about Jim, Dot, and their black cocker spaniel dog, Tag, we marked short a's and long o's and crossed out silent e's. Nowhere in any of the books was Tag ever referred to as a cocker spaniel—that didn't fit with the controlled vocabulary of the phonics series. We were encouraged to read the books in the classroom library. The teacher even set up a contest as to who would read the most books during the year. The winner was Sally, my best friend. I came in second. Kirby was third. My good friend Billy didn't read many books that year. Throughout the year he had always colored with a red crayon. At the end of the year, he wasn't promoted to second grade with the rest of us. At the time, I wished he had colored with blue and green and orange and yellow so he wouldn't be kept back in first grade.

While we were encouraged to read, writing was merely copying down something the teacher had written on the chalkboard. Usually these were thank you letters to parents for treats or get-well notes to ill classmates.

Mrs. Hayman read aloud to us every day. Usually she picked an adventure series about the Bobbsey Twins, two sets of fraternal boy–girl twins from a wealthy family who lived in the city and had both a maid and a driver–caretaker. At Halloween, she read poetry by a Hoosier poet, James Whitcomb Riley, including my favorite, "The Raggety Man." Shivers still run up my spine as I recall her voice dramatically reading "and the goblins will git you if you don't watch out" from "Little Orphant Annie." As a six-year-old, those words hauntingly floated around in my head, lingering as a reminder that I should always "wash the dishes up" and be alert "when the wind goes wahooooo wahoooooo!"

Second through sixth grade years brought more freedom to write as we wrote stories and various forms of poetry. What joy to write down a humorous story or poem to share with classmates! The upper grades also brought more basal readers with folktales and plays as well as stories about children my age. On the meagerly filled library shelves, I discovered biographies and read and reread about Babe Ruth sleeping with his pitching arm in a laundry hammock as he rode the train from one major league game to another, the struggles of Helen Keller to overcome her disabilities, the varied life of Davy Crockett, frontiersman, member of U.S. Congress, and defender of the Alamo, and the adventures of Kit Carson as he strode across the western plains and Rocky Mountains.

Elementary school was one of the greatest events of my life as I learned to read, discovering a most pleasurable, informing, and entertaining lifelong activity. And writing became a passion almost as essential as breathing.

A Perspective from Maria P. Walther

It was Parent Night at George F. Nixon Elementary School. My sister and I stayed home and listened to our babysitter's favorite bands—the Beatles, Beach Boys, and the Temptations—while our mom and dad went to meet with our teachers and learn about the school's curriculum. As my mom mingled with the other parents in my first grade classroom, she noticed a bulletin board.

Approaching it, she saw a familiar paper with a detailed drawing of our family. Below the picture, in my very best first grade spelling and handwriting, I had carefully written a story about my family including the following line: "My father is an electrishun [electrician]. My mother is nothing." That story has been retold in a humorous tone numerous times in our family over the years. In reality, it was the farthest thing from the truth. My first grade teacher, Miss Engelhardt, knew it was not true because when I arrived at her classroom door on the first day of school, I was ready to learn. It was my mom who provided me with *everything* I needed to know in order to learn how to read and write.

I grew up in Westchester, Illinois, a small suburb near the city of Chicago. Just a quick trip on the CTA subway, my father's employer, found us in the city with much to discover. We went to all the wonderful museums and the two area zoos. My mom and her friends began what is now known as "Mom's Day Out"—day trips taken with their children to expose them to the rich experiences necessary to be successful in school. My sister and I along with neighborhood friends performed plays in the basement, painted on long rolls of paper stretched down the driveway, found out how cornmeal was made at Graue Mill, and went to children's plays at a theater-in-the-round. Such endless experiences gave me a rich foundation that I took with me to first grade.

Miss Engelhardt, my teacher, was young and enthusiastic and I loved every minute of first grade. Her energy and passion for learning inspired me to be a teacher. In her colorful, inviting classroom, Miss Engelhardt taught us to read using the reformed i/t/a (Initial Teaching Alphabet) alphabet. The i/t/a/ alphabet had different symbols for each of the vowel sounds. It was somewhat like learning to read using the pronunciation guide of a dictionary. We learned the characters of the i/t/a alphabet and then used them to build words. We read these words in readers that were written in the special alphabet. We also did a lot of writing. We had a whole school newspaper called the "Knight's News" that published pieces written by students and teachers. I still have the copy of the one issue that includes my famous first grade family report!

As I moved through the grades I spent third, fourth, and fifth grades in an environment the teachers named "Skylab." We spent those three years with the same teachers, my favorite being Mrs. Krauklis. She also was an inspiration. By then we were using a traditional basal reading program, but nothing about my education was traditional. The teachers were innovative and used approaches that would still be considered appropriate today—making me and my classmates most fortunate students. We signed contracts for our large projects (similar to meeting the requirements of today's rubrics), did a limited amount of worksheets, and a lot of writing. When we were studying the regions of the United States, Mrs. Krauklis challenged us to do a report for each of the fifty states. Those of us who completed the fifty reports were treated to dinner at her house—a moment still recalled fondly by this former student. Reading and writing continued to be a part of my life both in school and at home. I spent many hours with Laura Ingalls Wilder traveling across the prairie and giggling with my friends about the insights we learned about life from Judy Blume's (1970) books including the highly controversial *Are You There God, It's Me Margaret?*

As I look back at the way I learned how to read and write, it is the experiences I had that had the greatest impact. I was fortunate to have a rich, meaningful literacy background both in school and at home. These valuable experiences translated into a love of learning that has continued throughout my life. Educators today have the enormous responsibility to create memorable literacy events for their students.

Your Perspective of Literacy

You may have grown up at a time when whole language was in vogue—the belief that reading should be relevant and meaningful to children with more emphasis on comprehension and a lighter touch on phonics. Or you may have attended schools that stressed phonics and being able to figure out unfamiliar words by "sounding them out." Lots of writing may have been part of the assignments you completed throughout elementary and secondary school with the teachers pointing out the need to develop the writing process by jotting down your ideas first and them polishing and smoothing them later. Regardless of how you learned to read and write to become an excellent literacy teacher, you need to understand a variety of instructional approaches to use with your students. Then you can delight in the successes your students encounter. Or, to paraphrase a popular song, "Who let the readers out? You! You! Who let the writers out? You! You!"

REFLECTION: IRA/NCTE NATIONAL STANDARDS IN THE CLASSROOM

Much like song trends, so too are there instructional trends in literacy. While Dick and Jane no longer romp through the basal readers, basal readers still are very much a part of reading instruction. Phonics, shunned by many educators in the 1980s, has resurfaced and is taught in nearly every first grade classroom in the country. The Initial Teaching Alphabet as an instructional strategy has fallen to the wayside, probably collecting dust on some forgotten bookshelf.

Today's educators understand that there is no one best method or strategy to teach reading and writing skills—there are many, many ways. Good teachers know a wide variety of strategies and apply them as their students need them. Educators are also aware of the need for standards for both students and themselves. By setting and meeting high expectations for themselves, they are serving to set and achieve high expectations for their students.

INTRODUCTION

Portfolio Activity:
One-Room Schoolhouse

Whether an individual is successful in life or not is largely dependent upon that person's ability to read and write. Reality dictates that if you are illiterate, you are likely doomed to be in the lower class of society and forced to do manual labor to earn a wage. With few exceptions, the better paying jobs or higher status positions go to the literate members of our society. This is as true today as it has been throughout history.

The history of reading and writing is referred to as literacy history. Unlike the history of countries, the history of literacy has failed to become a popular avenue for writers or researchers. Few professional articles deal with the history of reading and writing. But how reading and writing are taught in our schools continues to be controversial. While we look forward to new literacy instructional ideas and the plethora

STANDARDS for READING PROFESSIONALS

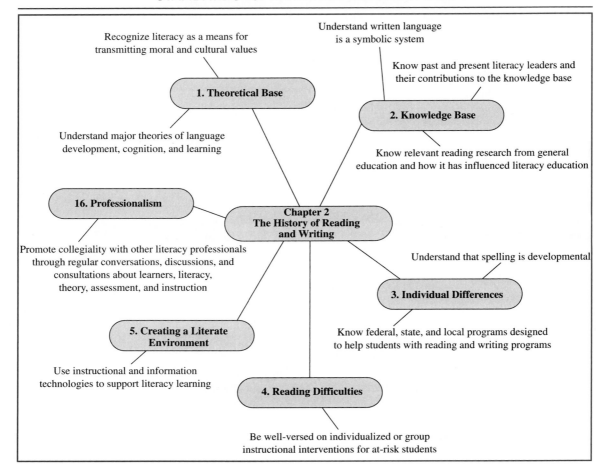

Recognize literacy as a means for transmitting moral and cultural values

Understand written language is a symbolic system

1. Theoretical Base

Know past and present literacy leaders and their contributions to the knowledge base

2. Knowledge Base

Understand major theories of language development, cognition, and learning

Know relevant reading research from general education and how it has influenced literacy education

16. Professionalism

**Chapter 2
The History of Reading
and Writing**

Promote collegiality with other literacy professionals through regular conversations, discussions, and consultations about learners, literacy, theory, assessment, and instruction

Understand that spelling is developmental

3. Individual Differences

5. Creating a Literate Environment

Know federal, state, and local programs designed to help students with reading and writing programs

Use instructional and information technologies to support literacy learning

4. Reading Difficulties

Be well-versed on individualized or group instructional interventions for at-risk students of technological innovations related to literacy, we still need to assimilate the insight of the present and integrate the richness of our past (Stahl & King, 2001). Thus, each of us as teachers needs to be knowledgeable of instructional practices from the past as well as those currently used.

Like the study of history itself, the study of literacy history has changed over the years. History includes narratives of the common individual; likewise, individual case studies of the typical student are acceptable practices in reading and writing. Literacy history teaches us what not to do. It offers teachers practical knowledge in three different ways: (1) it lays down the background of reading and writing and provides a new lens for us to look through; (2) since historical events are part of a time and place, such events are affected by factors that preceded them and, in turn, affect what comes afterward; and, (3) like all history, literacy history is charged with emotion, and our knowledge of it allows for a sense of continuity to develop among individuals (Moore, Monaghan, & Hartman, 1997). Hard to imagine people fervently arguing about reading? Heated discussions about literacy take place everywhere: the faculty lounge in elementary schools, along poolside while the kids are learning to float and dog paddle, in grocery and discount retail store aisles, and even on the floor of Congress. Literacy and how it is taught evoke emotion and passion just as reading a good book does for a reader.

As we begin the 21st century, let us reflect on the roots of literacy instruction that have brought us where we are today. As we do so, consider how we were taught to read and how that relates to current instructional practices.

EARLY INFLUENCES UPON CHILDREN'S READING AND WRITING

Reading was once left to the upper class, scribes, and educated children. And to be educated, one had to be born into wealth and position. Back then boys were given greater education than girls for it was believed that education was wasted upon females who would marry and have children. By the mid-20th century, many parents still refused to fund their daughters' college educations because they believed they would marry and "settle down raising a family." Until inventions that enhanced literacy access for everyone, only a small number of the population, largely male, learned to read and write. (See Figure 2.1.)

Important Inventions

Figure 2.1
Early reading and writing developments
Sumerians and Egyptians—Original writing in the form of signs and symbols
Chinese—Invented paper, then a means to mass-produce it
Gutenburg—German printer who invented movable type
Caxton—Printed the first book in English on a movable type printing press
Hornbook—A tool for learning the ABCs in early classrooms

Historians believe that writing was invented by the Sumerians and the Egyptians at about the same time, roughly 3500 B.C. In various locations throughout the world symbols representing words have been found on walls of caves indicating that our ancestors desired to communicate with others, including people not immediately present. Signs and symbols were left on trees, rocks, and caves to signify that someone had already passed that way, the hunting was good in the area, or to proclaim a significant event such as the birth of a child or the loss of a loved one. Thus began our quest to read and write.

Carving symbols into wood or stone was extremely time consuming. And carrying around the final version of the writing was an equally arduous task. You probably think your backpack of books is heavy, but imagine toting wood and stone filled with symbols around all day, every day. When the Chinese invented paper using fibrous materials such as bark, hemp, or silk, a major accomplishment occurred for literacy. Writing could now be easily carried from place to place.

The Chinese weren't finished with improving on the media used for literacy as they were to make a much more significant breakthrough. In 105 B.C., Cai Lun, head of the Chinese imperial workshops, created an efficient means of mass-producing paper (Cotterell, 1994). This invention led to literacy slowly spreading throughout the world. It was not until the Moors brought the art of papermaking to Spain in about 1150 A.D. that Europeans had ready access to this important material. Before then, "the literary heritage of Europe consisted of the oral tradition and parchment manuscripts laboriously handwritten by monks and scribes" (Norton, 1999). Books were expensive, valued possessions of the wealthy class or religious groups. Even children of nobility were rarely permitted to touch books. Their tutors would read to them or dictate while the children wrote on slates.

Paper combined with perhaps the greatest technological advancement in reading, the invention of the movable type press, were what led to literacy for all—rich and poor, adults and children. Johann Gutenburg, a German printer, created a movable type press in about 1436. Word of the miraculous press spread throughout Europe. Upon learning of Gutenburg's printing press, an Englishman named William Caxton visited Germany where he learned the art of printing in Cologne. In 1475, Caxton printed the first book in English, *The Recuyell of the Historyes of Troye*. A year later, in 1476, Caxton brought his press to England where he went on to print over 100 books.

The invention of the movable type press was important for three significant reasons. Books became less expensive, making way for lower classes to become literate. Spelling became uniform. And, for the first time, books written solely for children were printed. Caxton's first book for children was *Caxton's Book of*

Hornbooks were used to teach the alphabet and scriptures from the Bible.

Curtesye, targeted at young minds to move them toward virtuous activities (comb your hair, clean your ears, don't quarrel with dogs, don't chatter, and don't blow on your food) (Norton, 1999). Such reading was encouraged by adults, but was undoubtedly quite boring for children. Later Caxton printed Sir Thomas Malory's *Le Morte d'Arthur (The Death of Arthur),* the story of the adventures of King Arthur and his knights of the Round Table, clearly more compelling reading for youngsters than learning about courtesy and minding one's manners.

Around 1550, small wooden paddles similar to miniature ping-pong paddles covered with a sheet of hammered cow's horn appeared. These "hornbooks" were used to teach the alphabet and the Lord's Prayer or other scriptures. This was the alphabetic method of reading instruction in which children learned the names of letters followed by learning how to spell syllables and then memorized passages of content, particularly Biblical passages. The alphabetic method of reading instruction prevailed until the 1790s (Smith, 1965). Only a few hornbooks have been preserved as most were destroyed or worn out when children discovered they could be used to bat pebbles back and forth—gnipping and gnopping across the wooden desks.

Early Education Laws

In 1642, the first education law was enacted in the New World in Massachusetts. Although territorial schools were in existence in and around what is now St. Augustine, Florida, the Massachusetts law was the first to require parents to educate their children. In 1647 another law was passed in Massachusetts, the "Old Deluder Satan Act." Like the 1642 law, this law was strongly supported by the "Puritans, who believed it was critical that everyone be able to read the Bible and interpret its meaning" (Farris, 1999, p. 125). The Old Deluder Satan Act suggested that Satan, or the devil, would not want children to learn how to read because he would "keepe men from the knowledge of Scriptures" (Shurtleff, 1853). Thus with these two laws, Massachusetts led the way for its children to become literate in the New World.

Web Link:
Old Deluder Satan Act

Early Instructional Materials

In 1690, *The New England Primer* was printed with woodcut illustrations. It included the alphabet, the catechism, hymns, and prayers. Children were to read it and reread it until they had memorized the entire book, word for word. The *Primer,* as it was known, became the most widely read schoolbook in America where it was used for over 100 years to teach reading. Between 1700 and 1850 over 3 million copies of *The New England Primer* were sold, making it the widest used textbook of that extended historical period.

The New England Primer began with several pages devoted to the alphabet in capital and lower case letters, lists of two-letter syllables beginning with ab, ac, ad, . . . then eb, ec, ed, . . . and so on, for each vowel and on through the alphabet. These were followed by lists of one-syllable words, and then two-syllable words followed by lists of three-, four-, and five-syllable words. Most of the words were of a moral and religious character. The next portion of the *Primer* was the woodcuts illustrating each letter in the alphabet along with two- or three-line rhymed verses. The text of reading matter was devoted to moral lessons for children as well as the Lord's Prayer, the Apostle's Creed, and the Ten Commandments (Butts & Cremin, 1953). Children were expected to memorize the entire book, a task today's students would find incredulous.

In the typical elementary school in the 18th century, boys sat on benches separate from the girls. They were taught to read and write from *The New England Primer* and the Bible. School opened with a psalm or hymn and prayers. "The smallest children began with spelling and were put into spelling class. Spelling and pronunciation of words were practiced in groups so the slow learner could profit from the oral works of others. When the beginners had learned to spell and to read, they were advanced" (Butts & Cremin, 1953, p. 121). Students then read from the Bible, newspapers, and letters.

The Roots of Children's Literature

While *The New England Primer* was becoming the prominent reading instructional book in America, books for children gained acceptance in England. In 1744, a London businessman named John Newbery noticed that Mother Goose rhymes were popular with young children. Newbery opened a shop where he sold medicines and children's books, a rather unusual combination but still a successful venture meeting the medicinal requirements of all and literary needs of children. In 1765, Newbery published *The Renowned History of Little Goodie Two Shoes,* the story of an orphan girl, Margery Meanwell, who is taken in by a virtuous clergyman and his wife. Later Margery learns to read and then goes from house to house teaching other children to read as well (Cullinan & Galda, 1998). Because of his efforts to publish books especially for children, the Newbery Award for the most distinguished contribution to children's literature in the United States is named for John Newbery.

Readin', 'Ritin', and 'Rithmetic

At the time of the Revolutionary War, illiteracy was commonplace. In the rural agrarian areas, children learned the practical affairs of life from their parents. Fathers taught their sons farming, carpentry, and harness mending while mothers instructed their daughters in the finer points of cooking and sewing. School was limited to teaching the 3 R's—reading, writing, and arithmetic—with the primary goal being able to read and interpret the Bible and newspapers as well as do everyday math. This practical approach to the 3 R's meant that letter writing was an instructional necessity along with how to keep household accounts in ledgers. After the Revolutionary War, government documents were used as reading material. Indeed, one of the first jobs of President Andrew Jackson as a boy was to read aloud the Declaration of Independence in the square of the small town in which he lived.

THE COMMON SCHOOL MOVEMENT

During the late 1700s and the 1800s as the frontier expanded, so too did interest in education. Many political leaders such as Thomas Jefferson and educators such as

Horace Mann believed that free public education would strengthen America. This period became known as the **Common School Movement.** As the country stretched westward as part of the Northwest Territory, Congress established that a portion of land was to be set aside in each township to provide a location for a public school. Thus began the "little red schoolhouse," one-room, mostly wooden, schools designed to serve children in grades 1–12, although many children dropped out of school after attending only a few grades. Schools were located in small towns or out in the countryside of each township where students would sometimes walk several miles to attend. Those children whose families were fortunate enough to own a pony or horse, rode or drove a buggy or farm wagon to school.

During the Common School period, Noah Webster wrote two books that became landmarks in literacy. In 1783, Webster wrote the *Grammatical Institute of the English Language,* which contained three parts. The first part was published as the *American Spelling Book* but soon became known to all as "the blue backed speller." This book helped standardize American spelling and introduced phonics to reading instruction in the United States (Smith, 1965/1986/2002). By 1850 the population of the United States was under 23 million, but incredibly about 1 million copies of the blue backed speller were sold annually. Indeed, its popularity led Webster to push for the first national copyright law. A strong love of language and its correct use led Webster to write *The American Dictionary of the English Language* which is still being revised and published.

Spelling had always been taught as part of reading. But by the mid-1800s, spelling began to be considered as a separate subject largely due to the popularity of Webster's blue backed speller. Spelling correctly became a fad for both students and teachers. Spelling bees became so popular that in rural communities, they became a major social event with people traveling great distances on horseback or by horse and buggy just to attend.

The evolution of the teaching of writing was comparable to that of reading and spelling. Schools in colonial America lacked chalkboards and an ample supply of paper. Quill pens used for writing were made from feathers with ends whittled with knives. Ink was stored in small containers called wells. Writing instruction was largely rote copying and imitation. Children weren't taught that writing involved developing and connecting ideas so that the reader would be able to understand the message as is commonly accepted practice today.

Unlike Europeans, during the 1800s, colonial Americans held teachers in little respect. They were poorly trained with extremely low salaries. In addition to instructional duties, teachers were expected to serve as the school's janitor, and, in some instances, assisting with burying the dead of the community (Mayer, 1960). During the Common School Movement, however, European schools influenced American education. In 1806, Joseph Neef, a follower of Johann Pestalozzi, came to the United States where he proposed a rich variety of experiences for elementary children that would draw out individual personalities. Neef believed that reading, spelling, and writing should revolve around the child's everyday life (Butts & Cremin, 1953). Neef's beliefs about learning and teaching would be one of a number of theoretical bases that influenced **pedagogy** in American schools. His beliefs and those of

Americans Francis Parker and John Dewey were the foundation upon which the whole language movement was founded over 160 years later in the 1970s.

The 1800s produced probably the greatest supporter of education in the United States, Horace Mann. A lawyer and member of the state legislature, Mann was appointed the first secretary of education of Massachusetts in 1837. Wielding an incredible amount of influence on the Common School Movement, Mann brought forth an impassioned plea for improving education for all children. Through his annual reports, Mann helped revolutionize education. Mann believed that "(1) education should be universal, regardless of economic status; (2) education should be free; (3) education should be dependent upon carefully trained teachers; and (4) education should train both men *and* women" (Farris, 1999, p. 132). Not afraid of controversy, Mann convinced wealthy businessmen that educating all children would benefit themselves because educated workers would make fewer mistakes and be more efficient. In a time when taxes for schools was very unpopular, Mann remained persistent in urging free public education for all. In addition, Mann advocated that women made better teachers of children during their early school years because he believed women were more caring and insightful than men. Mann's views were highly criticized as the preponderance of teachers at that time were males. Very few women in Mann's day were permitted to be educated. Most fathers supported educating their sons but viewed a similar education for daughters as a waste of money as they would only end up married and having children. Mann advocated that every child, regardless of social class, be taught to read and write.

The Common School Movement of the 19th and early 20th centuries provided both educational and social opportunities for many children. Others were not so fortunate. Consider that slave children were seldom taught to read or write. Indeed punishment for a slave who taught another slave to read was usually the amputation of his or her thumbs. A slave without thumbs was useless and served as a warning to others. Likewise, educational developments for Hispanic and Native American children during the same period were also not on the same level as those for Anglo-Americans as they were first educated in church schools, then secular public schools.

Spanish-speaking Hispanic children in what later became the southwestern and western United States were usually taught separately from Anglo-American children. Reading and writing materials were often few or inadequate for the number of students. Compounding the situation, materials were typically not in Spanish, the students' first language, but written in Latin, if religious text, or English.

While African American, Hispanic, and Native American children were suffering from cultural clash, large groups of Asians began arriving on the West Coast. The 1840s brought many Chinese, who were mostly poor and uneducated, fulfilling the need for cheap labor. The late 1890s and early 1900s brought Filipinos to the West Coast and Japanese to Hawaii. School segregation was commonplace in California with Asian students not being permitted to attend public schools with Anglo-American children.

Thus, the Common School Movement advanced public education by promoting education for all children and better training for teachers. However, many cultural groups—African Americans, Asians, Hispanics, and Native Americans—were not privy to many of the educational advancements during the 1800s and early 1900s. (See Figure 2.2.)

Phonics and Whole Word Methods of Reading Instruction

The mid-1800s saw reading instruction change from phonics to the "word method" in which children learned to read and memorize entire words instead of analyzing words according to their sounds. Ever since the word method was introduced, there has been a controversy in reading as to whether a phonetic approach or a whole word approach is the best method of early reading instruction (Smith, 1965/1986/2002).

> ### Figure 2.2
> ### Literary influences from the Common School Movement (19th and early 20th centuries)
>
> - Leaders like Thomas Jefferson championed free public education
> - Birth of the one-room schoolhouse
> - Noah Webster's *American Spelling Book* ("blue backed speller")
> - Spelling bees
> - Pestalozzi and Neef proposed rich experiences for children
> - Horace Mann proposed universal education for all children, boys and girls, delivered by well-trained teachers

In the mid- to late 1800s, over half the elementary school day was devoted to the teaching of reading, writing, and spelling. During this period, reading instruction moved from rote memorization to concern for having the student understand the material read. Textbooks contained material that interested children. The vast majority of children in the mid- to late 1800s learned to read from a basal reading program created by William Holmes McGuffey, who gathered stories and poems from a variety of sources. He tried to include reading selections based on the values of honesty, perseverance, kindness, courage, gratitude, reverence, industriousness, and patriotism. Such works were placed into a series of graded readers called *McGuffey Readers* along with phonics and cursive handwriting exercises. Here is an example of a lesson of the *First McGuffey Eclectic Reader:*

Web Link:
The New McGuffey Fourth Reader

> See my dear, old grandma in her easy-chair! How gray her hair is! She wears glasses when she reads.
>
> She is always kind, and takes such good care of me that I like to do what she tells me.
>
> When she says, "Robert, will you get me a drink?" I run as fast as I can to get it for her. Then she says, "Thank you, my boy."
>
> Would you not love a dear, good grandma, who is so kind? And would you not do all you could to please her?

McGuffey included selections from authors of his day such as Henry Ward Beecher, father of Harriet Beecher Stowe, and works of writers from the past, including Shakespeare. Since there were few pieces that were copyrighted, McGuffey used any stories and poems he thought appropriate. The *McGuffey Readers* are considered to be "the great textbook of American middle-class values" (Mosier, 1947, p. 123). For his efforts, McGuffey earned a grand total of $500 for his reading series. The idea of a basal reading program to cover the entire elementary, and now middle school, grades has continued and is the most widely used reading instructional material package available today.

20TH-CENTURY INFLUENCES ON LITERACY

During the 20th century, more research was conducted on the teaching of reading than any other subject. And yet, we still can not specifically say how the brain converts symbols into meaning. We do know it seeks out patterns over rules. Certainly there were many changes in reading and writing instruction during the past 100 years as we moved from teaching phonics, reading, and writing rules to having students learn processes and become aware of language patterns.

The Impact of Scientific Study

By the end of the 19th century, readers and spellers still referred to God and Christianity. The beginning of the 20th century brought about major changes in education as scientists began researching physiology, neurology, genetics, and heredity. Albert Binet in France began to test for intelligence in children, creating a scale of normal mental ages for children of various chronological ages. Meanwhile, in Russia, Ivan Pavlov developed a theory of conditioned reflexes as being fundamental to learning based on his research with dogs. Whenever he fed the dogs, he would ring a bell. After doing this for a period of time, the dogs would salivate at the sound of the bell whether or not food was present. Other researchers included Wilhelm Max Wundt in Leipzig, who examined sense perception, and Francis Galton, who studied hereditary factors.

Reading research was increasingly being conducted in the United States. The first study of the amount of time students spent reading was done in the 1890s by the president of Harvard University, Charles W. Eliot (1898). His findings indicated that reading and English language instruction made up 37 percent of the school day, but the total time students actually spent reading in grades 1 through 6 was only 46 hours. As a result, Eliot went on to found Harvard classics, a program that promoted elementary and secondary students' reading of quality literature. Harvard classics is still a very popular program and is used by many schools throughout the country.

Early reading research also included findings on how fast individuals could read. Consider one such study in which it was discovered that good readers could read up to twice as fast silently as orally (Huey, 1908). Huey advocated, "We have surely come to the place where we need to know just what the child normally does when he reads, in order to plan a natural and economic method of learning to read" (p. 9). However, over the next 50 years, few reading researchers considered case studies, looking at how individual children learned to read (Birnbaum, Emig, & Fisher, 2003). Later researchers focused on eye movement and reading comprehension. William S. Gray (1938) pointed out that the problems with reading comprehension were difficult to pinpoint by research. Even by the 1950s there were few studies conducted on comprehension.

Perhaps the greatest influence on reading instruction was E. L. Thorndike's research on the stimulus–response theory. According to Thorndike, when connections are pleasurable, the result is satisfying to the student. When connections are not pleasurable, the result is annoying to the student. Thus, motivation came to be considered a factor in teaching reading. Another of Thorndike's findings was the concept of readiness. Thorndike stated that when the action system is ready to act, satisfaction will follow action, but failure to act will result in annoyance. This could be interpreted that children should be taught to read when they are developmentally ready in the reading realm. **Reading readiness** was championed by William S. Gray and between 1925 and 1935 became widely accepted (Smith, 1965/1986/2002). American schools began administering reading readiness tests to five-year-olds to determine whether they were at a stage in which formal reading instruction should begin. Likewise, **standardized reading tests** became part of the annual assessment programs for most school districts to ascertain the reading achievement of students at the various grade levels.

Web Links:
Reading Readiness
Components and
Tips for Parents

Emergent Literacy:
A Synthesis of Research

Reading Readiness and Emergent Literacy

Initial reading instruction for young children consisted of reading readiness during which the child was to learn the alphabet and how to distinguish between sounds. Pictures of common objects and their beginning and ending sounds were part of reading readiness worksheets and workbooks. Phonics was introduced as sound–symbol relationships. Students were expected to identify letter–sound relationships and write them as part of fill-in-the-blank written exercises. **Linguistic readers** were basal reading programs with controlled vocabulary that used words with frequently found phonics patterns such as cat, bat, sat, hat, and mat.

Publishers of reading books began printing reading readiness books that introduced students to letters and sound–symbol relationships as well as words. The next book for young beginning readers was the **preprimer,** a small softbound book containing a limited number of stories based on one theme. Preprimers were introduced to children at the beginning of first grade. The number of words in each preprimer was limited and controlled with specific phonics skills being introduced. Later, workbook pages or worksheets accompanied the stories. After reading three or so such preprimers, children moved to the **primer,** a larger collection of stories. Traditionally, at the beginning of the second semester of first grade, the students began the **first reader,** a hardback basal reader. This approach continued through the 1970s when the theory of emergent literacy began influencing reading and writing instruction. Before children learn to read, they experiment with scribbling and writing. In a similar fashion, young children hold up a picture book and, in a singsong manner, pretend to read as they use intonation to "convey" the meaning of the printed word. And, of course, the first word almost all children want to learn to write is their own name.

Manuscript Handwriting

During the 1920s, handwriting was also receiving attention. In 1922, Marjorie Wise came from England to Columbia University in New York and gave a presentation on a new form of handwriting called "manuscript." Thus, the roaring 20s gave us bathtub gin, raccoon coats, flappers, the crash of '29, and the introduction of **manuscript handwriting** for primary students. Heretofore, the beginning of the 20th century brought about major changes in education. The sticks and circles of manuscript handwriting, sometimes referred to as "print," were found to be easier for young writers to form as the strokes required less fine motor control. The straight and slanted lines along with circles were more natural movements for young children to make. Since manuscript handwriting was quite similar to that of the print found in books, kindergarten and first grade teachers were quick to adopt manuscript as a new form of handwriting. Indeed many teachers still refer to manuscript handwriting as "print."

Teacher Preparation

Accompanying research in education at the beginning of the century were changes in the preparation of elementary teachers. Unlike the early Greek culture where those "who taught children to read and write were treated with great disdain and contempt" (Mathews, 1966, p. 9), teaching became a respectable field for young people to enter in early 20th-century America. State certification standards had been raised across the country from merely completing twelve years of schooling and passing a written examination to having successfully completed a minimum of two years of college before being pronounced qualified to teach. State normal schools that had been established during the Common School Movement now reexamined how reading, spelling, and writing were instructed. More effective methods were adopted. For instance, simple words that children saw over and over as beginning readers were presented as sight words, often written on strips of tagboard. Students were expected to memorize the sight words and to recall them "on sight."

Classrooms in the early 1900s were often crowded, particularly in urban areas. Slate chalkboards were used to present lessons instead of using paper and pencil or computer programs as we use today.

When the United States became involved in World War I, the draft brought men from a variety of backgrounds into the military. The Army began using written tests to determine aptitude. A substantial portion of recruits were found to be illiterate. Many had only a few years of formal schooling. For the first time, illiteracy received national attention. Despite increased schooling of the populace, illiteracy still was a major problem during World War II as over 1 million men were not accepted for military service because they could not read or write. Many who were accepted had only meager literacy skills. Some dictated letters home to their more literate comrades.

In the 1920s, the stimulus–response theory was criticized by Gestalt psychologists. They believed that an individual sees a whole pattern (Gestalt) and changes his behavior accordingly. Thus reading instruction moved from drill and practice of phonics and rote memorization to whole word and whole sentence instruction. The education pendulum was swinging back to where the roots of reading and writing instruction had been in the 1600s and 1700s prior to the blue backed speller's introduction.

In the years following World War I through the 1930s, schools and the teaching of reading and writing were criticized. One group thought that traditional instruction was best with students doing drill and practice, phonics, and memorizing. Learning was to be from books. Many citizens who held strong religious, disciplinary, and/or scholarly beliefs supported such traditional views. Another group supported a progressive approach to education that expanded the role of the 3 R's by adding art, music, and physical education. This group argued that learning was best when the learner was actively involved, thereby advocating hands-on experiences. Letting children progress at their own individual rate of development was another aspect of education supported by this group. The education pendulum began swinging at a faster rate as schools adopted first one practice before abandoning it to move to another, different approach to reading. Likewise, teacher education programs changed. Some advocated a pure phonics approach such as the Initial Teaching Alphabet (i/t/a), which encouraged teaching children to read by using diacritical markings commonly found in dictionaries. Other programs stressed individualized reading in which every child self-selected and read trade books independently and engaged in small group work only when skills were taught by the teacher.

The presence of basal readers grew during this period as publishers were quick to make profits on the expanding baby boomers entering school. Most basal readers included stories accompanied by workbooks and worksheets with related skills.

From the 1960s through the 1980s, the "emphasis of instruction within this time period was on decoding, vocabulary knowledge, and the ability to demonstrate that main ideas or important information could be identified after reading vocabulary-controlled texts often created specifically for use in instruction and assessment" (Raphael & Hiebert, 1996, p. 3). The term "developmental reading" arose as research by such individuals as Jerome Bruner (1977) and Jean Piaget (1973) indicated that students learned at different rates and should be taught when they were ready to learn to read. Developmental reading is the teaching of reading to elementary and middle school students, and **remedial reading** instruction occurs whenever a student lags behind or has difficulty learning in a developmental reading program.

By the 1980s, a new definition of reading was emerging that emphasized the reader's construction of meaning. "Reading is the process of constructing meaning through the dynamic interaction among the reader, the text, and the context of the reading situation" (Wixson & Peters, 1984, p. 4). This change in definition resulted in having teachers become more familiar with children's literature as "authentic full-length texts" became the instructional materials. In addition, teachers were to assist students to become more aware of when and why certain reading strategies would be most appropriate to use with what kind of text (Raphael & Hiebert, 1996). Thus, reading comprehension strategies were stressed as "schemata" became a prevalent term inside the classroom.

The 1980s brought about cries for increased standards for teachers and those entering teacher education programs. New standardized tests were adopted by teacher preparation programs to weed out candidates lacking mathematical and/or literacy proficiencies. Large school districts adopted their own testing of current teachers and new applicants.

Things had changed little in the 1990s as individual states revised certification standards for teachers. In the battle of the "reading wars" of phonics versus comprehension (Lemann, 1997) as the primary focus of instruction, the call came out for balance. "Probably this is because both phonics advocates and those who favor a more holistic approach consider balanced reading instruction as a compromise position" (Cassidy & Wenrich, 1998/1999, p. 402). Suddenly every elementary teacher needed to be quite familiar with phonics instruction as well as comprehension strategies.

Advancements in Children's Literature

Children's literature was made accessible to lower income families largely through public libraries and the publication of Golden Books, an imprint of Simon and Schuster, in 1942 during WWII. Frustrated that they could not afford to buy children's books for their own children, a group of doctoral students at Teachers College, Columbia University in New York City, began writing inexpensive books. The result was the creation of an American institution. Not only could parents afford to buy the Golden Books, but they were readily available for purchase at grocery and drugstores. The most popular Golden Book is also the best-selling children's book ever, *The Poky Little Puppy* by Janet Sebring Lowery (1942).

From 1940 to 1973, Ursula Nordstrom made her mark on children's literature as an editor of children's books at Harper publishers. When challenged by a noted children's librarian as to "what qualified her, a nonlibrarian, nonteacher, nonparent, and noncollege graduate to publish children's books, Nordstrom just as pointedly replied, 'Well, I am a former child, and I haven't forgotten a thing'" (Marcus, 1998, p. xxii). Nor have readers forgotten Ursula Nordstrom. Maurice Sendak was a window dresser in New York when Nordstrom discovered him. She combined the writings of Else Holmelund Minarik with Sendak's illustrations. The result was *Little Bear* (Minarik, 1957), the first book of the I Can Read Books, an essentially new genre of children's literature. These books were designed for beginning readers to read on their own without assistance. Nordstrom also edited such books as *Charlotte's Web* (White, 1952), *Goodnight Moon* (Brown, 1947), *Where the Wild Things Are* (Sendak, 1963), *Harriet the Spy* (Fitzhugh, 1964), *The Giving Tree* (Silverstein, 1964), *Bedtime for Frances* (Hoban, 1960), and *Julie of the Wolves* (George, 1972). Nordstrom was described as the "single most creative force for innovation in children's book publishing in the United States during the twentieth century. A high-strung, voluble, tartly witty woman, Nordstrom brought devotion and verve to the quest for originality and honesty in books for young people, a readership she believed had long been ill served by sentimental illusions and false pieties of their elders" (Marcus, 1998, xvii). Many books edited by Nordstrom continue to be strong sellers.

The popularity of paperback books and their availability to children via book clubs made it possible for most children to possess their own libraries. Such inexpensive selections of children's literature also made it possible for teachers to develop their own classroom libraries to share quality literature with their students.

Basal Readers During the Cold War Period

In 1947, Scott, Foresman, and Company published a series of basal readers designed to relate to children and reflect the current family values of the period. By the 1950s, Scott Foresman had emerged as the dominant basal reading series with its sequence of stories about Dick and Jane and their younger sister, Sally. Spot and Puff, the family's dog and cat, became household names known across America. If the *McGuffey*

Readers reflected the middle-class values of the 19th century, the Dick and Jane readers did likewise for the 20th century. Father went to work each day while Mother stayed home in their suburban house. Workbooks and worksheets that accompanied the stories in the basals became popular instructional ancillaries—sight word cards, pocket charts, and ditto sheets. Other publishers used the same format and found a ready market as teachers relied on such instructional materials.

Phonics: The Great Debate

In the 1950s, there was a return to basics with the 3 R's being once again stressed. Part of this was fear, an element of the Cold War. With the former U.S.S.R.'s successful launch of Sputnik in 1957, many Americans were afraid that U.S. schools were preparing pampered students who could not read or write adequately. Once again the controversy as to whether the phonetic approach was superior to the whole word method raged. In 1955, Rudolf Flesch, a newspaper reporter, wrote a book entitled *Why Johnny Can't Read.* Flesch contended that beginning reading needed to be taught by the phonics approach. The discussion lingered into the 1960s when Jeanne Chall, a Harvard educator, wrote a book challenging Flesch's view. Chall's (1967) book was entitled *Learning to Read: The Great Debate.* In it, Chall presented research findings as to what was known and what wasn't known about how children learn to read. In 1967, Bond and Dykstra published "The First Grade Studies" which compared phonics and the whole word approach for beginning reading instruction. They concluded that neither method was clearly superior.

A Boom in Children's Literature

During this period there emerged a tremendous growth in children's literature. In 1952, E. B. White's beloved and timeless *Charlotte's Web* was published. The following year came *Little House on the Prairie* (Wilder, 1953). Picture books were suddenly popular as the baby boom continued. In 1957, Dr. Seuss's incomparable *Cat in the Hat* debuted. Max and his monsters let the rumpus begin in *Where the Wild Things Are* (Sendak, 1963). Patterned books in which the lines were repetitive and predictable became in vogue including *Brown Bear, Brown Bear, What Do You See?* (Martin, 1964) and *The Very Hungry Caterpillar* (Carle, 1969), both classics that still sell several thousand copies each year.

Books about minorities and their culture were also being published for children. Ezra Jack Keats' (1962) *The Snowy Day* portrayed a young black child enjoying the first snow of winter. *The Snowy Day* won the Caldecott Award in 1963 for the best illustrated picture book. Over a decade later, in 1975, the Caldecott Award was presented to Gerald McDermott (1974) for his Native American folktale, *Arrow to the Sun.* In 1976, an African folktale won the Caldecott Award, *Why Mosquitoes Buzz in People's Ears* retold by Verna Aardema (1975) and illustrated by Leo and Diane Dillon. Awards for books by African American or Latino/Latina authors and/or illustrators began gaining prominence first with the Coretta Scott King Award in 1970 and later with the Pura Belpé and the Americas awards. Henceforth multiculturalism would be represented in children's literature at all levels with children's authors and illustrators from all cultures being encouraged to write about their own cultures.

The 1960s and 1970s: The Open Classroom Movement

During the 1960s the open classroom movement took place. There was an emphasis on individualized instruction in which each student progressed at her own rate of reading development. If there were twenty-five students in a class, they could have been reading twenty-five different books or stories in a basal reader series. Some school districts still used grouping by ability—"Redbirds, Bluebirds, and Crows" depending on the students' reading abilities. Because students usually sat in a circle and took turns reading out loud, this became known as "round robin reading." According to Jeanne Chall (1967, p. 212), teachers who follow the basal reading program are "virtually enslaved to the program."

In 1964, President Lyndon Johnson put forth his proposed Great Society in which all citizens were to have equal rights. Blacks were guaranteed the right to vote and use all public facilities equally with whites. Probably the greatest impact the Great Society had upon reading and writing was the passage by Congress in 1965 of the Elementary and Secondary Education Act (ESEA), which gave federal funds to public schools, largely to fund compensatory education programs. This law established Title I, which funded remedial reading and math programs in public schools that had large numbers of students from impoverished families. **Head Start,** which targeted four- and five-year-olds from low-income families and expanded their emotional, language, physical, and life experiences in order to improve their later performance in school, was also created as part of this law.

Web Link:
The National
Head Start
Association

The 1960s also found the first attempt by basal reading publishers to include minorities. Initially, illustrations were the only noticeable representation of minorities. Some publishers put brown ink on what had been white characters in previous editions. In fact, one publisher rushed a basal reader to the presses with one major error—the face of the policeman had been darkened to a mahogany but his hands were still white as they were in the earlier edition.

The openness of society during the 1960s and 1970s resulted in topics that were formerly considered taboo for children becoming themes of children's literature. Judy Blume found success in *Are You There God? It's Me, Margaret* (Blume, 1970), in which a girl encounters puberty, and *Tales of a Fourth Grade Nothing* (Blume, 1972), which examined family relationships. Death and friendship were encompassed in Katherine Paterson's (1976) Newbery Award winning *Bridge to Terabithia. The Great Gilly Hopkins* (Paterson, 1978) examined the hopes and fears of a feisty foster child.

Psycholinguistic and Socialistic Views of Reading

Believing that children's interactive relationship between cognition and language was crucial, Jean Piaget (1973) found that children explore their surroundings—interpreting and giving meaning to what they experience. In short, language reflects thought, according to Piaget.

Another researcher who considered children to be active participants in their own learning was a Russian psychologist named Lev S. Vygotsky (1962, 1978). Unlike Piaget, Vygotsky wrote that language actually stimulates cognitive development as

In the 1950s, a typical classroom looked like this one—highly structured and organized. Three reading groups were common—"blue birds, red birds, and black birds." Begun in the early 1960s, the open classroom movement allowed for more individualized instruction in reading. Students were no longer grouped by ability but worked at their own pace of learning.

young children learn to regulate their own problem-solving abilities by talking them out. If you watch young children, they routinely voice their thinking as they attempt to resolve a problem, albeit putting together a puzzle or figuring out how to run a toy truck around the edge of the sandbox. The next step occurs when children begin internalizing language. At this point, language becomes a means to an end as they discover that language can be used by them to achieve their own goals.

During the 1960s and 1970s, **psycholinguistic** study of reading was led by the findings of Ken Goodman (1973). Researching reading as a language process, Goodman considered a linguistic approach to viewing how children read. Reading is an active, not passive activity. As such, Goodman believed that readers continually anticipate meaning and sample text for informational clues based upon their own expectations. Reading was thus a kind of "psycholinguistic guessing game." When the reader guesses wrong, a miscue occurs (Goodman, 1973). This is because the reader is combining information from three different aspects of written language: *graphophonemic,* or the regularity of sound–symbol relationships; *syntactic,* or the word order of sentences; and, s*emantic,* or the meaning the language conveys based upon the reader's own background knowledge, experiences, conceptual understandings, and values.

As a child read passages aloud, Goodman marked down everything the child said. Soon Goodman discovered that sometimes what the child said wasn't the exact text, but the meaning did not change. For instance when a young child read "train" for "toy," the meaning stayed intact. At other times, a child might substitute a word that was grammatically correct but did not hold the same meaning, such as "ride" for "run." When the child substitutes "a" for "the," it signifies that the child knows that an article precedes a noun.

Goodman (1965) coined the term "miscue analysis" for how readers make sense of the printed page. Two basic assumptions underlie this theory: (1) miscues are never random, and (2) unexpected responses result from the same process as expected responses (Brown, Goodman, & Marek, 1996, p. vi). According to Goodman (1973), a miscue in reading occurs when the expected response and the observed response are not the same. Cues can be visual, that is, the word may look like the word in the text (e.g., *though* for *thorough*); semantic, that is, the word may hold similar or the same meaning as the word in the text (e.g., *book* for *binder*); or syntactic, that is, a word commonly found in a particular word order (e.g., Rachel drove the *car* [for the word *van*] home.) Miscue analysis procedures led to teaching students reading strategies. Wixson (1979) noted that several factors influence a child's reading including difficulty of text, the reader's ability, and language development. Thus, miscue analysis may not be the most appropriate assessment measure for diverse populations.

Like the psycholinguists, sociolinguists (1975) began looking at thinking and language and how they were related. According to Michael Halliday (1975), language is what makes us uniquely human as we use it in the personal, social, and academic aspects of our daily lives. For instance, we communicate differently in intimate settings with loved ones than we do in ritual settings such as weddings and courtrooms. Another sociolinguist, Frank Smith (1978, p. 640) believes that "the uses to which language is put lie at the heart of language comprehension and learning." Furthermore, he (Smith, 1989) asserts that the degree to which teachers are emotionally involved in what they are teaching is conveyed to the students. A teacher who is bored with the subject or topic being taught is not interesting. Thus, teachers need to demonstrate how literacy plays an important role in their own lives to meet their own emotional and functional needs.

Spelling and Writing Research

Like much of the 20th century, most of the research funding in education was devoted to studying reading. At the elementary level in the years between 1955 and 1972, $3,000 was spent on reading research studies for every $1 spent on writing research. Indeed, researching how children learn to write was rarely the focus. Over two-thirds of the writing studies during this period were primarily concerned with how the classroom teacher taught writing to students (Graves, 1981).

In 1971, during a research study on phonics, Charles Read made a discovery that changed how we teach both writing and spelling. Read found that preschool children tended to "invent" the spellings of words they use in their writing. Read also found that such inventions were predictable and not random. Consonant sounds were used

Stages of Spelling of Children		Table 2.1
Emergent Stage PWR (dump) (Pre-K to middle 1st grade) • Corresponds to emergent reading and writing	Random string of letters (usually capital) used to represent a word	
Letter Name–Alphabetic Stage LK (like) (K to middle 2nd grade) • Corresponds to beginning reading and writing	1 to 3 consonants used to represent a word	
Within Word Pattern Stage bote (boat) (Grade 1 to middle 4th grade) • Corresponds to transitional reading and writing	Letters used closely resemble sounds contained in a word	
Syllables and Affixes Stage plesur (pleasure)	Vowels in every syllable	
Derivational Relations appointmint (appointment)	Spelling of base word is generally accurate; now adding derivational endings	

consistently. Additional research by Gentry (1981) and Henderson (1985) found that children move through five temporary stages of spelling. These stages of spelling include emergent, letter name–alphabetic, within word pattern, syllables and affixes, and derivational relations (Bear, Invernizzi, Templeton, & Johnston, 2000), and they are outlined in Table 2.1. The idea of **emergent literacy** for beginning readers and writers evolved.

While invented or temporary spelling, as it is now called, was being studied, so too was writing. Donald Murray (1968) studied successful novelists and authors such as John Steinbeck to learn how they wrote. Murray found that writing was a process of stages. First the author engages in prewriting, or rehearsal. In this stage the author thinks about the topic, asks herself questions about what she already knows about the topic and what she wants to know, brainstorms as to where additional information can be gathered and then gathers it, and so on. The next stage is writing. Here the author puts pencil to paper or sits at the keyboard and writes. During the writing stage, the author concentrates on getting her ideas down on paper. Mechanics such as grammar, punctuation, and spelling are secondary as they can be corrected or added later. The third stage is revising. Here the writer adds, deletes, or moves things around. This stage is followed by the editing stage where the piece is polished and rewritten. The last stage is publishing, or sharing with others. In the 1970s, Donald Graves (1983), a graduate student of Murray's, decided to research how first graders wrote. Graves found that first graders followed the same writing process: rehearsal, writing, revision, editing, and publishing. This resulted in writing instruction for children being taught by stressing the writing process rather than the final product, which had prevailed for over 100 years. Writing research by Graves and others pointed out that writing is very much a social practice "that not only celebrates the lives and experiences of the people who engage in its process but also acknowledges the importance of the actual writing the process itself produces" (Blake, 2001, p. 436).

Writing research also changed reading methodology as teachers were encouraged to integrate writing in supporting reading instruction (Au, Mason, & Scheu, 1995). Strong proponents of writing encouraged teachers to have children write in content areas to promote greater understanding of informational text (Atwell, 1998; Graves, 1989). Beginning in 1995, reading methods textbooks began addressing how writing instruction supports the teaching of reading as students learn strategies that are useful in both of these language arts (Au, Mason, & Scheu, 1995).

The Whole Language Movement

Web Links:

The Whole Language Approach

Whole Language Umbrella

With Graves' discovery that first graders followed the same writing process as professional writers, writing instruction at the elementary level came to be based on the process rather than the product approach. At the same time comprehension of the whole story was stressed over breaking words down into pieces. This holistic approach was based on constructivism in which students learn from firsthand experiences as they "construct" and expand their knowledge base. In reading and writing it became known as the **whole language approach.**

One of the leaders of the whole language movement in the United States was Ken Goodman (1986, p. 26) who writes, "Whole language is firmly supported by four humanistic-scientific pillars. It has a strong theory of learning, a theory of language, a basic view of teaching and the role of teachers, and a language-centered view of the curriculum." Whole language involved using real, relevant materials with students as they are given choices as to what they would read or discuss.

Created in New Zealand and Australia by noted educators such as Andrea Butler (1984), Brian Cambourne (1984), Marie Clay (1979), Don Holdaway (1980), and Jan Turbill (1984), the whole language approach spread to the United States and Canada, resulting in children's literature and process writing moving to the forefront of reading and writing instruction. Leaders of the movement in North America included Ken and Yetta Goodman (1989), Frank Smith (1988), and Dorothy Watson (1989). Publishers of basal readers changed from a behavioristic approach to address this holistic approach, which focused on having children read quality children's literature and write daily in journals. According to Fuhler (1990, p. 312) these new basal readers

> reflect a concerted effort to include recognized children's authors, a variety of literary genre, excerpts, and complete stories from award winning books to entice children to read. Depending on the publisher, there is increased emphasis on process writing, thought-provoking questions, and techniques to teach effective reading strategies as well as a decreased emphasis on skills in the middle to upper grades.

The whole language movement of the 1970s and 1980s was accompanied by a surge in children's literature purchases by schools for classroom use and library holdings. Teachers began using thematic units in which a topic entailing several concepts was used to teach reading and writing along with other subject areas such as art, math, music, physical education, science, and social studies. For instance, a thematic

The whole language movement encouraged student discussion of quality children's and young adult literature.

unit on frontier life might have the entire class reading *Sarah, Plain and Tall* (MacLachlan, 1985), learning to square dance in physical education, and singing folktales of the period such as "Old Dan Tucker." Picture books became popular for reading and writing instruction in kindergarten through eighth grade. Russell Freedman's (1989) *Lincoln: A Photobiography* a book for older readers won the Newbery Award in 1990. Other popular picture books to be published during this time included *Jumanji* (Van Allsburg, 1981), *Owl Moon* (Yolen, 1987), and *The True Story of the Three Little Pigs as Told by A. Wolf* (Scieszka, 1989). A flood of chapter books ensued in the 1980s including *Dear Mr. Henshaw* (Cleary, 1983), *Hatchet* (Paulsen, 1987), and *Number the Stars* (Lowry, 1989).

The 1980s and 1990s: Cries for Educational Reform

The early 1980s found many criticisms raised about the quality of public schooling. In 1985 came the publication of *Becoming a Nation of Readers: The Report of the Commission on Reading* (Anderson, Hiebert, Scott, & Wilkinson, 1985). The report criticized how reading and writing were taught in the schools. It also emphasized the vital role of parents in their children's learning to read and write. Here is a list of the findings, many of which are still appropriate today:

Parents should read to preschool children and informally teach them about reading and writing.

Parents should support school-aged children's continued growth as readers.

Preschool and kindergarten reading readiness programs should focus on reading, writing, and oral language.

Teachers should maintain classrooms that are both stimulating and disciplined.

Teachers of beginning reading should present well-designed phonics instruction.

Reading primers should be interesting, comprehensible, and give children opportunities to apply phonics.

Teachers should devote more time to comprehension instruction.

Children should spend less time completing workbooks and skill sheets.

Children should spend more time in independent reading.

Children should spend more time writing.

Textbooks should contain adequate explanations of important concepts.

Schools should cultivate an ethos that supports reading.

Schools should maintain well-stocked and managed libraries.

Schools should introduce more comprehensive assessments of reading and writing.

Schools should attract and hold more able teachers.

Teacher education programs should be lengthened and improved in quality.

Schools should provide for the continuing professional development of teachers (Anderson et al., 1985, 117–120).

Discussions evolved among educators as to what type of reading and writing instruction was appropriate: direct instruction or guided instruction. In direct instruction, the teacher clearly specifies the concept in her instruction. In guided instruction, the teacher nudges the students to discover the concept on their own, a constructivist approach to learning. In addition, independent reading and writing were advocated as part of reading and writing workshops during language arts instruction.

The 1980s and 1990s brought computers into the classroom. Software programs such as Accelerated Reader (Advantage Learning Systems, 2000) and Reading Counts (Scholastic, 2001) permitted students in grades K–12 to self-test their reading comprehension of primarily narrative literature. Such programs were reminiscent of the SRA reading program introduced in the 1950s, which consisted of a box of cards with stories or informational text that students read independently and then checked their comprehension on a self-test.

By the end of the 1980s and 1990s, several children's literature publishers had merged while others ceased to exist. Many small bookstores were forced out of business. Large booksellers began to exert influence as to what should be published based solely on predicted sales. Before an editor of a children's book would offer a contract to an author for a specific manuscript, for example, the editor would first have to obtain the approval of a major book chain as well as a commitment for purchase of a specified number of books. Because some publishers of children's books are owned by media giants who produce films, pressure is sometimes exerted on authors of historical books for children to literally change the course of history so that it reflects the screenplay and not historical facts. For instance, authors of books about *Amistad,* the story of a slave ship that was taken over when the slaves escaped, were pressured by the movie studio to include nonfactual material (Myers, 1997).

The arrival of J. K. Rowling's Harry Potter series jolted the publishing world. *The New York Times* was so taken with the strong sales of the Potter series of books that, in 2000, it created a best-sellers list solely for children's books. Rowling's (2000) *Harry Potter and the Goblet of Fire* sold over 2.3 million copies during the first week it was available in the United States, an incredible feat heretofore unheard of in children's literature. Subsequent films continue to fuel the series' popularity.

As authenticity in children's literature and assessment became important, the need for teachers to become aware of curriculum development and teacher research arose. According to Taffy Raphael (1999, p. 49), "when we're doing research, instead of just doing a product (like a curriculum or activity idea), we're going back after we've done it and we're really looking at what the kids gained from it or how we could build on it." "Teachers who strike an inquiring stance construct *teaching* as a professional activity and *teachers* as thoughtful, reflective, and powerful agents of change" (Murphy & Dudley-Marling, 1999, p. 8). Whether teacher research in solving literacy and other curricular problems will continue as a movement will largely depend upon how it is viewed by educational reforms and the media at large.

Teaching Strategy:
Quadraramas

Media such as newspapers, news magazines, and television continued to probe and examine reading instruction in the 1990s. Upon receiving several complaints from constituents, some members of Congress pressed for an examination of how reading was being taught in our nation's schools. In 1990, Marilyn Adams released a report of her federally funded study comparing phonics and whole language as reading instruction techniques. Adams' report, entitled *Beginning to Read: Thinking and Learning about Print,* concluded that beginning reading "programs for all children, good and poor readers alike, should strive to maintain an appropriate balance between phonics activities and the reading and appreciation of informative and engaging texts" (p. 125). This coined the phrase "balanced reading instruction." Adams' findings were interpreted as meaning that "while phonics knowledge is essential for children's success with reading and writing, children must also be taught to read for purpose and meaning" (Morrow & Tracey, 1997, p. 645). The publication of *Phonics They Use* by Patricia Cunningham (2000), now in its third edition, found a ready audience as many teachers were convinced that phonics instruction had been lacking in the reading curriculum. Rather than teaching students phonics rules, now the trend was to teach letter patterns (i.e., at, ang, ick, oat) that commonly appeared in English since the brain seeks patterns rather than rules as we think.

By the mid-1990s, most teachers had moved to supplement basal readers with children's literature through classroom libraries. Some teachers avoided using basals completely, choosing to use quality children's literature and class or group discussions of the text.

ADDRESSING DIVERSITY: ENGLISH LANGUAGE LEARNERS

There have been several influxes of immigrants from non-English-speaking countries throughout the history of the United States. Irish fled Ireland during the Potato Famine of the mid-1800s. Scandinavians sought a new life with better farmland that Minnesota and Wisconsin offered. Leaving behind their homeland of Prussia, later known as Germany, Germans and Jews avoided World War I and II. Over the past fifty years, many Eastern Europeans, like their Cuban counterparts during the revolution in Cuba in the late 1950s, fled communist regimes. The end of the Vietnam Conflict resulted in numerous Indochinese (Vietnamese, Mong, Cambodian, Laotian, and Thai) immigrants fleeing their homeland for the safety and opportunities the United States offered. Likewise many Central Americans and Mexicans have sought a better life in America.

The Bilingual Education Act of 1968, later Title VII of the Elementary and Secondary Education Act (ESEA), provided a new source of funding for the education of Hispanic and Native American and other limited English-proficient students. Bilingual education programs were created to provide instruction in the student's native language as well as in English. Despite the increased fiscal resources, bilingual programs in the mid-1970s had produced only mediocre results. Later a Supreme Court ruling, *Lau v. Nichols* (1974), resulted in defining the legal responsibilities of schools serving limited English-proficient students. The 1974 Equal Educational Opportunities Act gave legislative backing to the *Lau* decision. Schools now had to provide such students with instruction in their native, or first, language.

By the late 1990s, the influx of immigrants, especially those who spoke Spanish, resulted in numerous research studies about second language acquisition. Educators began to look for language acquisition patterns and similarities. Children who were younger than age six were considered to be still acquiring oral language in their first or native language; those between the ages of seven and thirteen were considered to be acquiring reading and writing skills in their first language. Current research suggests that those children who are picking up a second language (i.e., English) have been found to develop their English reading skills more rapidly if they already know how to read in their first language. In addition, it takes between one and three years for most children to attain basic interpersonal, conversational skills in a second language but between five and seven years to develop cognitive academic proficiency in a second language (Carrier, 2001).

By the end of the 20th century, bilingual education programs had many problems, the greatest being a lack of qualified teachers who were proficient in reading and writing in both English and the native language of their students. Thus bilingual education was denounced as being inefficient. Some states, including Arizona and California, replaced these programs with English immersion programs.

"Although many linguists agree that the many varieties of English spoken by diverse groups in our society are cohesive, logical, highly structured linguistic systems in their own right, negative values have often been associated with many varieties of English used by diverse members of our society at large. In most cases, nonacademic varieties of

English are seen as inferior to their mainstream academic English counterparts. Clearly, with the demographic changes that are occurring in our country, Americans will need to realign their attitudes concerning language use with the realities of the changing population" (Ball & Farr, 2003, p. 435).

Language connections, particularly between English and Spanish, began to take on increased importance as children transitioned from Spanish to English. When considering vocabulary, the emphasis was placed on true cognates, words that are in both English and Spanish that have the same meaning (i.e., special/especial; ranch/ranchero; fiesta/fiesta). Word order was found to be somewhat similar in English and Spanish; however, adjectives follow nouns in Spanish but precede nouns in English. While English has several contractions, only a few exist in Spanish.

Teachers need to be aware that Spanish has five vowel sounds (a, e, i, o, and u) while English has between eleven and seventeen, depending on regional dialect. English also has numerous consonant sounds that aren't present in Spanish (d, g, j, ll, r, rr, v, x, y, and z). Thus, first language Spanish speakers may not be able to perceive or discriminate many of these sounds resulting in substitution of Spanish sounds by children (i.e. 'b' sound for the 'v' as in *Thank you berry much.*). Other sound differences noted include the lack of 'ing' suffix in Spanish and no initial 'sh' consonant cluster or 'dg' consonant cluster.

National and State Standards: A Call for Best Practices

The mid-1990s brought cries of concern over lack of standards at the national and state levels. Businesses were burdened by having to teach new hires how to read, write, and perform simple mathematical problems. Members of Congress and state legislatures called for increased standards for schools before funding would be granted. Then President Bill Clinton insisted that each state develop academic standards and implement accompanying assessment plans before federal funding would be granted. Each state developed reading and writing achievement tests to be given to students at different grade levels. Major professional education groups such as the Association for Childhood Education International (ACEI), the International Reading Association (IRA), the National Council of Teachers of Mathematics (NCTM), the National Council of Teachers of English (NCTE), and the National Council of Social Studies (NCSS), developed standards for their respective content areas with IRA and NCTE developing the English Language Arts standards.

In 1998, the International Reading Association (IRA) adopted standards in which it believes all teachers should be proficient. Three broad categories addressed the *Standards for Reading Professionals*:

1. *Knowledge and Beliefs About Reading,* which includes understanding theories of reading development, individual differences, the nature of reading difficulties, and principles of assessment.

2. *Instruction and Assessment,* which includes being able to create instructional environments; to teach word identification, phonemic awareness, letter–sound correspondence, vocabulary skills, strategies for comprehension

and the construction of meaning, and study strategies; and to assess student performance and progress.

3. *Organizing and Enhancing a Reading Program,* which includes abilities to communicate information about reading to various groups, to develop literacy curricula, to participate in or conduct research, to collaborate or supervise other literacy practitioners, to communicate assessment results, and to engage in professional activities (IRA, 1998, p. 2).

The above standards are those you and your teaching colleagues will be expected to hold competence in. The specific literacy instructional competencies are listed at the end of this book.

With national and state standards in place, school districts sought out pedagogical practices that were most effective in meeting the newly adopted standards. Teachers were asked to put into effect instructional practices that best aided literacy acquisition of students based upon the nature of reading and writing along with how children learn to read and write. Linda B. Gambrell and Susan Anders Mazzoni (1999) summarized the principles of best practice of literacy instruction based upon research findings (see Figure 2.3).

When George W. Bush became president in 2001, there was a call for increased testing of students, such as was previously implemented in Texas where he had served as governor. Bush called for objective tests, that is, tests consisting of true-

---

Figure 2.3

Research-based best practices

1. Teach reading for authentic meaning-making literacy experiences: for pleasure, to be informed, and to perform a task.
2. Use high-quality literature.
3. Integrate a comprehensive word study/phonics program into reading/writing instruction.
4. Use multiple texts that link and expand concepts.
5. Balance teacher- and student-led discussions.
6. Build a whole class community that emphasizes important concepts and builds background knowledge.
7. Work with students in small groups while other students read and write about what they have read.
8. Give students plenty of time to read in class.
9. Give students direct instruction in decoding and comprehension strategies that promote independent reading. Balance direct instruction, guided instruction, and independent learning.
10. Use a variety of assessment techniques to inform instruction.

Source: Reprinted with permission from *Best Practices in Literary Instruction* by Linda Gambrell and Susan Anders Mazzoni, Guilford Press (1999).

false and multiple choice items, to be administered annually throughout the nation to all students in grades 3–12.

CURRENT PRACTICE: A BALANCED APPROACH TO LITERACY INSTRUCTION

By the end of the 20th century, whole language had faded in popularity as states such as California that had adopted it had vast declines in student reading achievement scores. Today most American schools use a developmentally grounded, basal reader program with leveled books called basal readers in grades K–8. Such basal readers contain several different genre of children's literature: traditional tales, fantasy, poetry, realistic fiction, historical fiction, biography, and informational selections. A teacher's instructional manual, a student's workbook, and other accompanying materials make up the remainder of the basal reader program. Children's literature supplements the literacy program and content area reading as students are encouraged to engage in independent reading. In addition, most teachers of early grade students include phonics instruction. Writing is taught as a process approach in which students are encouraged to think about and discuss their topic as well as gather information, put down a draft of their ideas, revise and edit, and then produce a final, polished version as their final writing product.

Teachers work collaboratively to develop and implement curriculum that meets local, state, and national standards.

The new cry for the millennium was "best practices" (see Figure 2.3). Interdisciplinary instruction in which reading and writing were taught along with another subject such as science or social studies was encouraged. And phonics would be integrated into reading and writing instruction for young readers and writers. This has been called the "balanced approach," or differentiated instruction approach, in that a variety of different instructional approaches are used to meet the needs of students in a diverse classroom.

In the words of Jerry L. Johns and Laurie Elish-Piper (1997):

> Rightly or wrongly, test scores appear to have contributed to the call for balance. In California, for example, declining reading scores on the National Assessment of Educational Progress and state reports were considered by a Reading Task Force. . . . One of the recommendations of the task forced focused on a balanced reading program that would combine skill development with literature and language-rich activities (p. xiii).

In short, teachers who use a balanced approach to literacy instruction call on a variety of instructional approaches strategies, those supported as best practices. The result is an eclectic teaching methodology. There is no one right approach to teaching reading and writing. It is up to the teacher to be familiar with several different instructional methods and strategies and apply them to meet individual students' needs. (See Figure 2.4).

Figure 2.4
Methods of reading instruction

Early 1800s	Phonics method—sound and symbol relationships
Mid-1800s	Word method—read and memorize entire words
Mid to late 1800s	Basal readers first introduced (*McGuffey Readers*)— stories and skills lesson
1920s	Reading readiness
1930s–1940s	Standardized reading tests
	Drill and practice instruction in reading and writing
1950s	Basal readers with stories about family life; workbooks and worksheets accompanied each story
1960s–1980s	Emphasis on decoding and vocabulary acquisition; finding the main idea
	"Developmental reading" term coined to indicate children learn to read at different rates and should be taught when they are ready to learn
1980s	Reading is a meaning constructing process involving the text, the reader, and context of reading situation; whole language and comprehension stressed; quality children's literature promoted
1990s	Phonics reemerges as critical reading instructional strategy
2000s	Balanced instruction (comprehension + phonics + writing) in literacy
2002	Increased emphasis on standardized testing

"No Child Left Behind" Act

In 2002, President George W. Bush signed into law the "No Child Left Behind" Act, a new version of the Elementary and Secondary Education Act (ESEA). This $26.5 billion federal education law was the most extensive educational reform bill in over thirty years, resulting in a 25 to 30 percent increase in federal aid to poor schools. The primary focus of the bill is accountability with public school students in grades 3 through 8 being tested beginning with the 2005–2006 school year by their state in the areas of reading and math. In addition, each school district must report the scores of diverse populations in an attempt to improve reading and math achievement of minority students. Phonics instruction for emergent and beginning readers is also promoted in the bill. Students in the elementary grades are to receive an hour and a half to two hours of daily uninterrupted reading instruction. Within twelve years of the passage of the ESEA revision, students must achieve 100 percent academic proficiency in reading as defined by the state in which they live.

Portfolio Activity:
No Child Left Behind

Summary

Reading instruction in the United States initially relied upon letter–name recognition. The publication of the "blue backed speller" by Noah Webster in 1793 led to the introduction of phonics as part of beginning reading instruction. By the mid-1800s, the whole word approach became popular. Since that time there has been much discussion and research as to which approach is superior.

Writing instruction was used to teach children how to write letters and keep ledgers of the family's accounts. Later students were to write on topics provided by the teacher. In the 1970s, writing was viewed as a process of rehearsal, writing (called drafting), revising, editing, and publishing, or sharing.

Children's literature advanced when it was found to be a profitable venture. Thanks to talented authors and dedicated editors, the quality of children's books continued to improve. During the 1990s, the publication of children's books became increasingly viewed by large publishers as a means to make money for their companies and stockholders, overshadowing the literary tradition of developing the best books for children to read and enjoy.

By the year 2000, phonics had once again regained popularity. At the turn of the century, teachers turned to "best practices" as identified by research findings in teaching reading and writing to meet the newly imposed standards in English language arts. In order to meet the needs of all students, teachers began using a balanced approach to teaching reading and writing as they attempted to differentiate instruction based upon student needs.

The "No Child Left Behind" Act was signed by President George W. Bush in 2002. It was the most extensive educational reform bill passed by Congress in over thirty years. The major focus of the bill was to improve reading and math scores with increased accountability.

Chapter Review

Go to the Online Learning Center at **www.mhhe.com/farrisreading** to take chapter quizzes, practice with key terms, and review important content.

Main Points

- The history of reading and writing is referred to as literacy history.

- Reading was once left to the upper class, scribes, and educated children.

- In 1690, *The New England Primer* was printed. It included the alphabet, the catechism, hymns, and prayers. Children were to read it and reread it until they had memorized the entire book, word for word.

- In the 1600s to 1700s, writing instruction was largely rote copying and imitation.

- During the Common School Movement, European schools influenced American education.

- Wielding an incredible amount of influence on the Common School movement in the mid-1800s, Horace Mann brought forth an impassioned plea for improving education for all children.

- The mid-1800s saw reading instruction change from phonics to the "word method" in which children learned to read and memorize entire words instead of analyzing words according to their sounds.

- During the mid-1800s, William Holmes McGuffey included texts based on the values of honesty, perseverance, kindness, courage, gratitude, reverence, industriousness, and patriotism in a series of graded readers called *McGuffey Readers* along with phonics and cursive handwriting exercises.

- The beginning of the 20th century brought about major changes in education as intelligence and achievement tests were developed and used to make judgments about academic ability of students.

- During the mid-1900s, the term "reading readiness" evolved to describe a young child's "readiness" to learn to read. By the 1980s, reading readiness had been replaced by emergent literacy.

- From the 1940s through today, there have been numerous advancements in the publication of children's literature making it readily accessible to all children.

- During the 1960s and 1970s, researchers Jean Piaget and Lev Vygotsky's works were noted as they separately studied the interactive relationship between cognition and language in children.

- During the 1960s and 1970s, the psycho-linguistic study of reading was led by the findings of Ken Goodman, who believed that reading is an active not passive activity, as was thought previously.

- The debate about phonics instruction has been long-standing in America and is still a major issue in reading instruction on the national scene.

- By the 1950s, Scott Foresman emerged as the dominant basal reading series with its sequence of stories about Dick and Jane and their younger sister, Sally, along with Spot and Puff, the family's pets.

- In 1971, Charles Read found that preschool children tended to "invent" the spellings of words they use in their writing. Read also found that such inventions were predictable and not random.

- The popularity and low cost of paperback books and their availability to children via book clubs made it possible for most children to possess their own libraries.

- In the 1970s Donald Graves discovered that first graders followed the same writing process as adult writers: rehearsal, writing, revision, editing, and publishing. Graves' research resulted in writing instruction at the elementary level being based on the process rather than the product approach.

- The whole language approach became popular in the 1970s as it involved using real, relevant materials, with the students given choices as to what they would read or discuss.

- The early 1980s found many criticisms raised about the quality of public schooling. In 1985, came the publication of *Becoming a Nation of Readers: The Report of the Commission on Reading* (Anderson, Hiebert, Scott, & Wilkinson, 1985). The report criticized how reading and writing were taught in the schools.

- The middle 1990s brought cries of concern over lack of standards at the national and state levels. State legislatures and the U.S. Congress pushed for new standards in reading and writing as well as other content areas.

- By the 1990s, the pressure to increase test scores resulted in research considering the best practices in literacy instruction.

- In 1998, the International Reading Association developed standards for reading teachers. These standards addressed knowledge and beliefs about reading, instruction and assessment, and organizing and enhancing a reading program.

- By 2000, literacy instruction called for a balanced approach to teaching reading and writing, infusing phonics in grades K–2. The teacher's judgment of determining students' needs as well as her expertise in a wide variety of literacy methods and strategies have become the focus of reading and writing instruction.

- The "No Child Left Behind" Act (2002) emphasized improved reading achievement for all students.

Key Terms

Common School Movement	53	preprimer	57
emergent literacy	65	primer	57
first reader	57	psycholinguistic	63
Head Start	62	reading readiness	57
linguistic reader	57	remedial reading	59
manuscript handwriting	57	standardized reading test	57
pedagogy	53	whole language approach	66

Reflecting and Reviewing

1. Think back to how you learned to read. Was phonics instruction a part of it? Did you read stories from a basal reader? Write down your recollections of how you learned to read and write.

2. Ask your parents or grandparents what they remember about learning to read and write. Compare their experiences with your own. How are they alike? In what ways do they differ?

3. What were your favorite books to read during free reading time? Do you still read the same genre(s) when you have the opportunity?

4. Think about the teachers you had from kindergarten through middle school. Does a particular one stand out because of the teaching methods used? What were the strengths of that particular teacher in regard to teaching reading and writing?

5. Consider the past 100 years of reading and writing instruction. What changes have occurred? What makes balanced literacy instruction so appealing?

Children's Literature

For annotations of the books listed below, please see Appendix A.

Aardema, Verna. (1975). *Why Mosquitoes Buzz in People's Ears.* (L. & D. Dillon, Illus.). New York: Dial.

Blume, Judy. (1970). *Are You There God? It's Me, Margaret.* New York: Bradbury.

———. (1972). *Tales of a Fourth-Grade Nothing.* New York: Dial.

Brown, Margaret Wise. (1947). *Goodnight Moon.* (C. Hurd, Illus.). New York: Harper and Row.

Carle, Eric. (1969). *The Very Hungry Caterpillar.* New York: Philomel.

Cleary, B. (1983). *Dear Mr. Henshaw.* (P. O. Zelinsky, Illus.). New York: Morrow.

Dr. Seuss. (1957). *The Cat in the Hat.* New York: Random House.

Fitzhugh, Louise. (1964). *Harriet the Spy.* New York: Harper and Row.

Freedman, Russell. (1989). *Lincoln: A Photobiography.* New York: Clarion.

George, Jean Craighead. (1972). *Julie of the Wolves.* (J. Schoenherr, Illus.). New York: Harper & Row.

Hoban, Russell. (1960). *Bedtime for Frances.* New York: Harper and Row.

Keats, Ezra Jack. (1962). *The Snowy Day.* New York: Viking.

Lowrey, Janet Sebring. (1942). *The Poky Little Puppy.* (G. Tenggren, Illus.). New York: Golden Books/Simon & Schuster.

Lowry, Lois. (1989). *Number the Stars.* Boston: Houghton Mifflin.

MacLachlan, Patricia. (1985). *Sarah, Plain and Tall.* New York: HarperCollins.

Martin, Bill, Jr. (1964). *Brown Bear, Brown Bear, What Do You See?* (E. Carle, Illus.). New York: Holt.

McDermott, Gerald. (1974). *Arrow to the Sun.* New York: Viking.

Minarik, Else Holmelund. (1957). *Little Bear* (M. Sendak, Illus.). New York: Harper and Row.

Paterson, Katherine. (1976). *Bridge to Terabithia.* New York: HarperCollins.

———. (1978). *The Great Gilly Hopkins.* New York: HarperCollins.

Rowling, J. K. (2000). *Harry Potter and the Goblet of Fire.* New York: Scholastic.

Scieszka, Jon. (1989). *The True Story of the Three Little Pigs as Told by A. Wolf.* (L. Smith, Illus.). New York: Viking.

Sendak, Maurice. (1963). *Where the Wild Things Are.* New York: Harper & Row.

Silverstein, Shel. (1964). *The Giving Tree.* New York: Harper & Row.

Smith, N. B. (1965/1986/2002). *American Reading Instruction,* Newark, DE: International Reading Association.

Van Allsburg, Chris. (1981). *Jumanji.* Boston: Houghton Mifflin.

White, E. B. (1952). *Charlotte's Web.* (G. Williams, Illus.). New York: HarperCollins.

Wilder, Laura Ingalls. (1953). *Little House on the Prairie.* (G. Williams, Illus.). New York: HarperCollins.

Yolen, Jane. (1987). *Owl Moon.* (J. Schoenherr, Illus.). New York: Putnam.

Planning for Instruction

"It has been repeatedly established that the best instruction results when combinations of methods are orchestrated by a teacher who decides what to do in light of children's needs."

Gerald G. Duffey and James V. Hoffman, professors of reading

An Overview of Instructional Strategies That Support a Balanced Approach

Key Ideas

- The learning environment a teacher and her students create provides a place filled with materials and opportunities to help children learn and practice their literacy skills.

- An educator using a balanced approach is a wise consumer of instructional materials, a thoughtful decision maker who is able to choose the most effective teaching strategies, and an expert observer of each and every one of her students.

- There are a multitude of resources available to teachers of reading and writing.

- A working knowledge of the different types of materials enables the caring teacher to select the appropriate resources to fulfill the instructional purpose and meet the needs of her students.

- Along with selecting the perfect materials, teachers choose instructional approaches that match their goals and their learners.

- Understanding the meaning of the written word is the ultimate goal of reading.

- Most successful readers and writers possess **phonological awareness, phonemic awareness,** the **alphabetic principle,** and have a working knowledge of **phonics.** Teachers develop these skills by showing children how words work.

- Word study activities support students as they learn **high-frequency words,** attend to spelling patterns, and discover the meaning of vocabulary words.
- In a balanced approach, reading and writing go hand in hand.
- Classrooms today are filled with diversity. In a balanced literacy classroom, diversity is celebrated and, through a myriad of teaching approaches, the needs of diverse learners are addressed.
- It is crucial that teachers and students make connections with parents and with the community.
- Technology enhances reading and writing instruction.

Questions to Ponder

- How does the learning environment Ms. Kay creates, in *Peering into the Classroom,* encourage her students to learn and practice their literacy skills?
- What are the different types of texts and how do they support reading development?
- What are the various instructional approaches available to teachers who are planning literacy lessons?
- How is comprehension addressed in a balanced program?
- How can teachers help students develop an understanding of the complexities of written words?
- What are the different types of writing students will experience in a balanced literacy classroom?
- How does a balanced approach to instruction encourage teachers to celebrate diversity in the classroom?
- How does technology enhance reading and writing instruction?

Peering into the Classroom

Good Morning!

"Good morning, Ms. Kay!" a bright-eyed boy shouts as he bounces into the room. "Good morning, Jamal, how are you today?" wonders his teacher. "I'm fine. Guess what? I got a new dog last night," Jamal replies excitedly. "Wow, you can write about that in your journal," encourages Ms. Kay. So begins another day in

Ms. Kay's first grade classroom. As the rest of the children enter the room, they, too, greet their teacher, get organized, and begin writing in their daily journal. Ms. Kay circulates as they are writing and gently reminds individual students to apply the skills they are learning during their daily literacy lessons. "This is the end of a sentence; what are you missing?" she asks. "Oops! That's a word wall word. Did you spell it correctly?" It is obvious that Ms. Kay knows each student in her classroom and is able to adjust her "on-the-spot" teaching suggestions accordingly. She's an expert "kid watcher."

Once students finish writing in their journals, they join Ms. Kay on the carpet and begin their daily routine. Together Ms. Kay and her students compose a morning message and Ms. Kay carefully writes it on the chalkboard, thinking aloud as she writes each word. While writing the message, Ms. Kay purposely misspells words and forgets a few punctuation marks. The children delight in finding and correcting their teacher's errors. As soon as the morning message is edited, the group chorally chants a poem together and searches for all the rhyming words. Ms. Kay then shares the story *Boo to a Goose* (Fox, 1998). The youngsters screech with laughter at the words, "I'd skip across *town* with my pants hanging *down,* but I wouldn't say 'Boo!' to a goose." "Read it again!" they beg. As Ms. Kay enthusiastically rereads the story, the boys and girls eagerly join in.

After story time, the students sit in a circle and carefully listen as a few of their peers share what they wrote in their daily journal. The youngsters complete their morning routine by moving back to their desks to work on practicing the new words for the word wall.

As one looks around Ms. Kay's classroom, there is evidence of literacy learning filling every space. Brightly painted bookshelves line the walls holding hundreds of children's books for the students to read and enjoy. There is a writing center filled with the necessary tools to write and illustrate stories, poems, and letters. The walls are covered with word lists, brainstorming charts, facts, sentences, and stories—all created during literacy lessons.

In their book, *Classrooms That Work: They Can All Read and Write,* Patricia Cunningham and Richard Allington (2002) describe three components to a literacy environment: "models, materials and time" (p. 29). They believe that teachers, other adults, and older children should model reading and writing. This translates to a classroom stocked with authentic literacy tools and a daily schedule that offers large blocks of time for uninterrupted reading and writing. A brief glimpse into Ms. Kay's classroom shows that the efficient use of models, materials, and time is crucial to creating a literacy environment. Ms. Kay *models* editing and other aspects of the writing process for her students through the use of the morning message. She provides them with a variety of *materials* for reading and writing. Most importantly, Ms. Kay gives her youngsters *time* to practice their skills on a daily basis by writing and sharing their journals, singing and chanting poems, and enjoying and discussing stories together.

REFLECTION: IRA/NCTE NATIONAL STANDARDS IN THE CLASSROOM

What is Ms. Kay doing in her classroom that reflects a firm understanding of the *Standards for the English Language Arts* created by the International Reading Association and the National Council of Teachers of English (1996), and what would this activity look like in an intermediate grade classroom? Using a variety of materials and teaching strategies, Ms. Kay creates a literacy community where students can "participate as knowledgeable, reflective, creative and critical members" (Standard 11). She teaches her students how to apply their knowledge of the conventions of language by asking them to help her edit the morning message (Standard 6). In an upper grade classroom the knowledge of conventions is addressed in a similar manner during an "interactive edit" activity (Fountas & Pinnell, 2001). During this five-minute activity, the class works together on a large piece of chart paper, the overhead projector, or individual papers to edit a sentence or two, dictated by the teacher, for conventions and then discusses the reasons for corrections as a group.

Ms. Kay also encourages her students to write and share their journals because she knows how important it is for young learners to acquire a wide range of writing strategies to help them communicate with various audiences for different purposes (Standard 5). When students grow as writers, they will begin to use writing as a tool for understanding their reading. A reading response journal where students record their thoughts, questions, and reflections (Fountas & Pinnell, 2001) will help intermediate grade teachers meet this same goal. This brief glimpse into Ms. Kay's classroom provides a prelude to the wealth of knowledge a teacher must possess to create an effective, balanced reading program.

INTRODUCTION

The purpose of this chapter is to offer you, the reader, "the big picture" by introducing the spectrum of strategies that support a balanced approach to teaching. The authors offer this shopping cart of strategies to teachers who are going to choose a balanced approach because, as Dixie Lee Spiegel (1999) shares,

> A balanced approach is a decision-making approach through which a teacher makes thoughtful decisions each day about the best way to help each child become a better reader and writer. A balanced approach requires and enables a teacher to reflect on what he or she is doing and to modify instruction daily based on the needs of each individual learner. The modifications are drawn from a broad repertoire of strategies and a sound understanding of children, learning and the theoretical bases of these strategies. (p. 13)

If you are going to be a thoughtful decision maker in your classroom, then you must be well-versed in the approaches contained in this chapter. Each of the teaching techniques highlighted here is more fully explored later in the textbook. It is our hope that this chapter will provide a framework upon which you can attach the knowledge you gain from reading this textbook. When studying a new topic, one gains deeper meaning if they view the whole before focusing on the parts. Think of it as the picture on the box of a puzzle. Here are all the pieces and how they fit together to create a balanced program. In Chapters 4 through 12 we will open the box and look at the individual pieces with a better understanding of the magnificent picture they create. That is why

STANDARDS for READING PROFESSIONALS

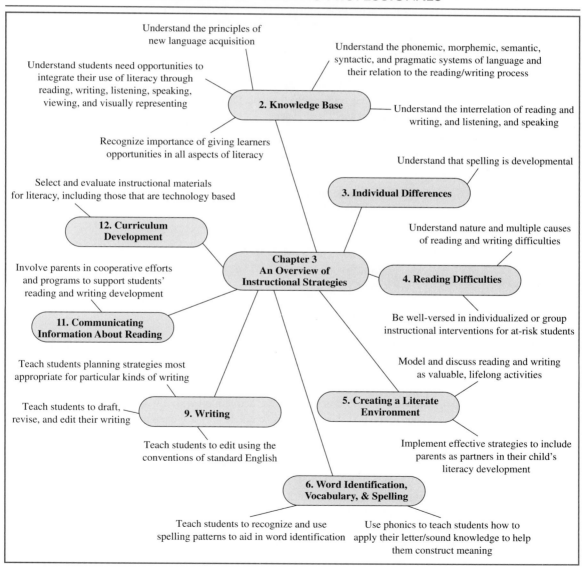

Figure 3.1

Three broad categories of knowledge about reading and writing

Local Knowledge

Reading
Phonological awareness
Ability to read sight words
Knowledge of some orthographic patterns to decode words
Use of a variety of word identification strategies
Understanding of word meanings

Writing
Developmental spelling
Ability to spell sight words
Knowledge of some orthographic patterns to encode words
Use of a variety of spelling strategies
Understanding of word meanings

Global Knowledge

Reading
Understanding, interpretation, and response to reading
Strategies that enable understanding and response
An awareness of strategic use

Writing
Strategies for effective writing
An awareness of writing techniques

Affective Knowledge

Reading and Writing
Feelings, positive attitudes, motivation, and desire to read and write

Source: Adapted from Fitzgerald, J. (1999). What is this thing called balance? *The Reading Teacher,*
53 (2), 100–107.

we believe it is important that you are acquainted with a wide variety of strategies and then, later in the text, discover how to effectively use each technique.

Let's begin our preview of instructional materials and approaches by looking at the types of knowledge we would like our literacy learners to possess. In Fitzgerald's (1999) article she shares three broad categories of knowledge about reading that are equally important for literacy learners. These categories of knowledge can also be applied to writing (see Figure 3.1).

This chapter will introduce several instructional strategies that teachers, using a balanced approach, can capitalize on to create a classroom where students cultivate all three kinds of reading and writing knowledge (Fitzgerald, 1999). Later chapters

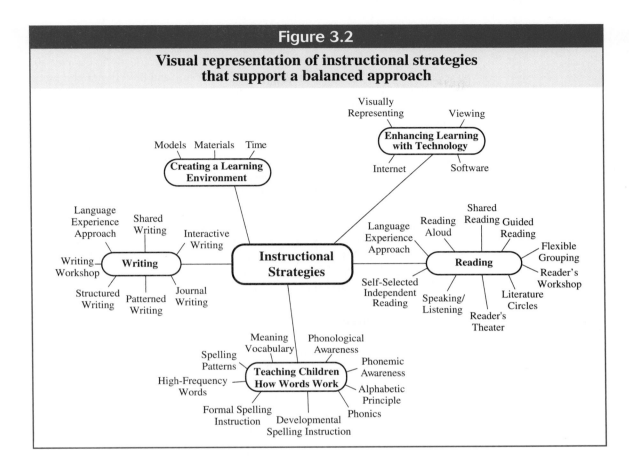

Figure 3.2

Visual representation of instructional strategies that support a balanced approach

will go into more details. See Figure 3.2 for a visual representation of the teaching techniques. These methods address the six English language arts that are outlined in the *Standards for the English Language Arts* (IRA/NCTE, 1996): reading, writing, speaking, listening, viewing, and visually representing. The following pages include *brief* descriptions of materials and the teaching techniques for reading and writing that are put into action in balanced literacy classrooms to share the exciting world of learning with students.

MATERIALS THAT SUPPORT A BALANCED APPROACH

The stories educators use to teach reading and inspire writing come from a variety of sources. "Beauty and diversity in the landscape of literature can generate fresh ideas in the minds of readers as balanced reading programs include a rich range of literature and a textbook-trade book blend that permeates the entire school day" (Burke, 1999, p. 57). Carefully chosen materials that match curricular goals and students' needs are a must in a balanced program. Throughout this book and specifically in Chapter 10, you will discover a wealth of ideas for sharing the beauty and diversity of children's literature with your students. As you build your classroom library, you want to choose beautiful, high-quality books and also books that represent diversity. The following four guidelines for selecting quality multicultural literature will be useful in choosing books that represent the diverse cultures of your students and the world at large.

1. Gather collections of books about a specific race or ethnic group that portray them in a wide range of occupations, educational backgrounds, living conditions, and lifestyles to avoid stereotyping and offer positive images about that specific group. Each book should be culturally accurate and depict issues in ways that reflect the beliefs and values of that culture.

2. Avoid stereotyping by choosing literature that portrays varieties of a particular culture or ethnic group. Select literature rich in cultural details that enhance the story. Look for books that avoid implying that specific occupations, recreational pastimes, family organizational structure, or values are unique to a race or ethnic group.

3. Check that literature is free from derogatory terms for particular racial groups unless the terms are essential to a conflict or used in historical context. Find books that include authentic dialogue and relationships. When a book uses another language, such as Spanish, words do not need to be translated if the context of the sentence defines it.

4. Choose books that include members of a "minority" group for a purpose. These characters should be unique individuals whose lives are rooted in their culture. (Huck, Hepler, Hickman, & Kiefer, 2004; Yokota, 1993)

The following section describes the different sources of stories and furnishes a sampling of how teachers use these tales to broaden a learner's local, global, and affective knowledge of reading and writing.

Published Reading Series

Many schools across the country still use a published reading series as one component of their literacy program. These published reading series are often referred to as basal readers. There are two main types of basal readers that teachers today may encounter as they enter their first classroom: controlled vocabulary basals and literature anthology basals.

The Controlled Vocabulary Basal Reader

Recall the history of basal readers that was outlined in Chapter 2. The definition of a basal reader has evolved over time. In the past, the basal reader was characterized as "a sequenced package of materials that used repetition as a key tool for creating new associations in the learner. Inherent in the sequencing of material was the concept that reading could be built up from words to sentences and from sentences to texts"

(Murphy, 1991, p. 202). This definition applies to the controlled vocabulary basal, which was created to teach reading using the bottom-up method described in Chapter 1. In a controlled vocabulary basal, the preprimer and primer texts are written according to formulas. A set number of **high-frequency words** are introduced at each level, then repeated a certain amount of times in each story and throughout each book. Typically, the very first story in a preprimer basal text consisted of ten to fifteen words repeated in various ways. The result often reads something like this, "I can go. Can you go? No, I can not go. I can help you. You can not help. I can not go."

The publishers of basal readers expanded this definition in response to the trends in literacy education. The basal readers of the late 1980s included an increase in quality children's literature, more writing used in teaching beginning reading, and less emphasis on phonics (Teale, 1995). In the early 1990s, a new wave of basal readers appeared in elementary classrooms. These basals became literature-based and made a leap from a controlled vocabulary, leveled approach to arranging stories in a literature anthology approach. William Teale (1995) describes this change as "the most profound change of our lifetime in first grade basal materials, and perhaps the most profound change of the century" (p. 121).

Literature Anthology Basals

The new **literature anthology basals** consist of selections that are directly taken from trade books and most often remain in their original format. "Because these selections were not created exclusively for a textbook publisher, the vocabulary, syntax, and illustrations usually appear in their original format, eliminating the former common practice of rewriting a story to control vocabulary" (DeSotell, 1998, p. 8). As you examine the stories in your basal text you will want to refer to the guidelines for selecting quality multicultural literature outlined on page 88. It is essential that the literature you share with children represent the rich diversity of their society. If the basal text you are using has selections that you believe do not meet the guidelines, bring it to the attention of your principal so that you can develop a plan for including more diverse selections.

The teacher's guides that accompany basal readers have also evolved. The teacher's guide that accompanied the *McGuffey Readers* included "brief messages to teachers in the preface or brief statements in the students' texts. Current teacher's guides have become complete separate texts—many with 200 pages plus" (Nastase & Corbett, 1998, p. 52). With this deluge of information, knowledgeable professionals are challenged to select the most meaningful and appropriate activities for their learners.

The current literature anthology basals have both pros and cons for teachers and for students. The inclusion of popular trade book stories makes the literature anthology basal more appealing to young readers, and they are excited to read stories they can find at their local library. Another plus is that the appealing stories offer abundant opportunities for written response. The extensive teacher's manual provides a multitude of instructional activities to teach reading skills and strategies and to extend and respond to the story in writing. Unfortunately, the vast amount of information is often daunting to a novice. Daunting, yes, but not unmanageable. As you continue to read this textbook and begin to develop your philosophy of a balanced approach, you will be better prepared to pick and choose activities that effectively meet the needs of your learners.

In the early grades, the use of pattern stories and repetitive text makes it easier for students to "memorize" the pattern of the story and feel like a successful reader. In Macmillan/McGraw-Hill's *Spotlight on Literacy* series (1997), children begin on the road to reading by enjoying the simple, repetitive story *Rain* (Kalan, 1978). "Rain on the green grass. Rain on the black road. Rain on the red car. Rain on the orange flowers" (pp. 12–15). Each page of the text contains a picture of the item described in words. The strong text-to-picture match in *Rain* supports a budding reader and often leads to early success which is the key. But for many readers, especially those who are struggling, this early success often diminishes when the stories shift from a patterned story to a standard story format and less support is present. As the readers progress through the grades, one story in the anthology may be unreadable for those who are struggling and yet perfect for the average reader. The next story is accessible for the below grade level readers, but much too simple for the average student. "The sequence of stories is sometimes uneven in difficulty; for example, a relatively easy text can be followed by one that demands a large leap in reading ability" (Fountas & Pinnell, 1999, p. 23). This poses a challenge for teachers. This challenge is best met by using a balanced approach and supplementing the literature anthology basal with other resources such as trade books that represent a variety of genres and diverse cultures, poetry and songs, texts created during language experience approach lessons, big books, leveled books for guided reading, text sets for literature circles, children's magazines, and the basic materials for writing.

Children's Literature: Enticing Readers and Inspiring Writers

Portfolio Activity:
Annotated Bibliography

The world of children's literature is constantly growing with over 8,000 children's books published each year. As a result, there exists a collection of superb books for readers of all ages. The possibilities for using these books are endless. (You will find a useful guide to the world of children's literature in Chapter 10.) Children's literature is first used for reading aloud "new favorites" and rereading "old favorites" to students of all ages. "A key goal of the read-aloud is to extend children's involvement with books, with the teacher rereading old favorites as well as new titles on topics and genres that challenge children's thinking" (Hiebert & Raphael, 1998, p. 97).

After a sidewalk field trip to observe trees, a resourceful kindergarten teacher shares the classic Caldecott winning book *A Tree Is Nice* (Udry, 1956). As the first snow gently falls outside the window, the class meets the snow-loving Wilson Bentley in the picture book biography *Snowflake Bentley* (Martin, 1998). Older students spend an enlightening week getting to know Bud Caldwell, an orphan during the Great Depression in *Bud, Not Buddy* (Curtis, 1999). An enterprising teacher can find a book for almost every occasion or topic of study. (For a list of suggested read-aloud books organized by grade level see Chapter 4.)

A spectrum of children's books in a classroom is crucial not only for reading aloud but also for self-selected reading time. A primary classroom should have books and other texts in every corner: big books, small books, student-made books, pattern books, nursery rhyme books, multicultural books, Dr. Seuss books, science books, sports books, social studies books, pet books, short chapter books, long chapter books, books by favorite authors, and children's magazines! If you find yourself teaching in an intermediate or middle school classroom, the collection of books will include books to read aloud for literature study, various types of poetry anthologies, reference and informational books, series books, books that have received awards (see Appendix C for lists of award-winning books), leveled books, collections of short stories, journals, magazines, and newspapers (Fountas & Pinnell, 2001). "The world of children's books has expanded enormously in the last decade. There is something for everyone out there. We believe that a child who does not like to read is *a child who has not found the right book*" (Cunningham, Hall, & Sigmon, 1999, p. 23).

Books are a supreme vehicle to model literary elements such as characters, setting, and theme. After reading *Big Anthony: His Story* (dePaola, 1998), second grade students formulate a clear picture of the main character, foolish Big Anthony, Strega Nona's sidekick who never pays attention. The first snow always brings delight. Why not extend that delight by discussing the lovely setting in the book *Snow* (Shulevitz, 1998)? Older readers explore the theme of searching for what is truly meaningful in life while reading the book *Brian's Return* (Paulsen, 1999). Teaching literary elements through fine literature makes learning an exciting and memorable experience.

Carefully selected literature is also a boon to teachers who are introducing skills in a meaningful context or teaching young writers the techniques used by experienced authors. The colorful adjectives in *The Napping House* (Wood, 1984) will inspire young readers and writers to try more descriptive words in their own writing. Well-written children's books are excellent models for young writers. Beginning in kindergarten, teachers can model for students how to read like a writer. They can show budding writers how authors employ the elements or traits of good writing. In her book *Creating Writers through 6-Trait Assessment and Instruction* (2000), Vicki Spandel identifies six traits that make writing work: ideas, organization, voice, word choice, sentence fluency, and conventions. As you choose books to add to your read-aloud fare, look for books that have clear ideas with interesting details, an engaging and easy-to-follow organization, a strong voice, vivid word choice, fluent sentences, and a good use of the conventions of writing. Finally, quality children's literature serves as a springboard for a variety of student responses, including visual representation, poetry, drama, song, and art.

Teaching Strategy:
Introducing Students to the Traits of Good Writing

Poetry and Song

The rhyme, rhythm, and cadence of poetry entice children to read and listen to the beauty of our English language. Poems can be silly, funny, serious, or sad. There are poems written about almost any topic. Children can relive the joys of doing something new through the poems of Lilian Moore (1995) in *I Never Did That Before*. The humorous poetry collection *Laugh-Eteria* (Florian, 1999) will have students in stitches. Science enthusiasts will discover much in Lee Bennett Hopkins' (1999) collection entitled *Spectacular Science: A Book of Poems*. One of the many fine multicultural samplings is *Meet Danitra Brown* (Grimes, 1994), which offers readers a thought-provoking glimpse into a young African American child's life. Other poets

Students reread "old favorite" poems in their song and poem book.

that tickle the funny bone and have entertained readers for years are Jack Prelutsky and Shel Silverstein.

For teachers of young learners, poetry, songs, rhymes, and chants are engaging and entertaining texts. When teachers read, sing, and talk about the language in these materials with their students, they help to strengthen phonological awareness, phonemic awareness, and phonics skills. Poetry is "a vehicle for helping children better understand the sound structure of their language" (Opitz, 2000, p. 104).

For older learners, the use of poetry can help to "deepen students' personal responses and interpretations of literature" (Strickland & Strickland, 1997, p. 210). Dorothy and Michael Strickland (1997) suggest a three-step model for sharing and responding to poetry with children. First, students are immersed in the poem. They begin by listening, then join in by chanting, clapping, and commenting on the aspects of the poem that appeal to them. Second, students explore and respond to the poems in a variety of ways. Finally, students experiment with creating their own poetic pieces either orally or in writing. This teaching sequence "offers students many opportunities to become more aware of the writer's craft and the characteristics of various poetic forms" (p. 203).

Texts Created During Language Experience Approach Lessons

The **language experience approach** (LEA) is a tried and true method to literacy instruction. In 1963, Sylvia Ashton Warner documented the use of the approach with Maori children from New Zealand. At about the same time, scholars from the United States, including Roach Van Allen, Russell G. Stauffer, and Jeanette Veatch, were advocating the approach and conducting extensive research in LEA classrooms. "The

LEA philosophy is based on several related theories: how people learn, how people read, and how others can help. At the intersection of these theories are notions about what makes learning easy" (Rasinski & Padak, 2001, p. 121).

Teaching Strategy for the Classroom

AN ACTIVITY FOR WRITING CINQUAIN POETRY

DEFINITION OF CINQUAIN

A cinquain is a 5-line poem containing 22 syllables in a 2—4—6—8—2 syllable pattern. Cinquains usually describe something, but they can also tell a story.

You *can* allow children to bend the guidelines a bit if needed—the message of the poem is more important than adhering to the formula.

CINQUAIN MINI-LESSON:

1. Share the story—*Take Me Out to the Ballgame* by Jack Norworth.
2. Have students close their eyes and picture themselves at a ball game. What do you see there? What do you smell? What do you hear? What do you taste?
3. Record students' responses on a group "senses cluster."
4. Create a group cinquain about baseball on chart paper.

Figure A	Senses cluster

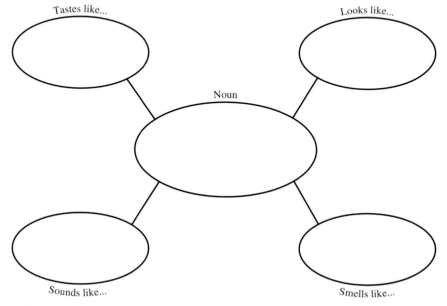

This senses cluster helps students organize their ideas before writing their own cinquain poem.

CREATING INDIVIDUAL CINQUAINS

5. Students will pick their own topic and create their own senses cluster.
6. Students will take ideas from the senses cluster to create their own cinquain using format included.

Figure B	Cinquain poem format

_____
Title

_____
One noun (person, place, thing) (2 syllables)

_____
Two words describing the noun (4 syllables)

_____
Three action words ending with -ing (6 syllables)

_____
Four words that express feelings or observations about the noun
(8 syllables)

_____
Two syllables that rename/describe the noun (2 syllables)

Let's take a moment to examine the philosophy that supports the use of LEA. First, what makes learning easy? Learning is easy when you are actively involved, the content is relevant and interesting, you have a positive attitude, and you are motivated and successful (Hall, 1985). How do people read? Stauffer (1969) characterized reading as a mental process similar to thinking. To read and comprehend, children have to think and reason when they read. "Meaning is the important thing—not saying the words. Reading is a thinking process not a parroting process" (p. 186). Finally, how can we, as teachers, use LEA to help our students? Children young and old delight in telling tales about their experiences. Teachers must capitalize on this desire to share. When using LEA, students are given ownership in classroom activities because the teacher helps them create a text that is based on their own personal thoughts, ideas, and language (Veatch, 1986). Now that you have an understanding of the philosophy, let's find out how a teacher puts this teaching strategy to work in her classroom to create texts for reading.

In their book *From Phonics to Fluency* (2001), Tim Rasinski and Nancy Padak detail the following six steps for obtaining dictated LEA texts from groups of students:

1. Provide a common experience for students. The possibilities are endless: Field trips, school events, a favorite book read aloud, science experiments, or social studies topics.

2. Initiate an in-depth discussion about the experience. Guide, don't lead, the discussion so that all students get opportunities to express their thoughts, opinions, and feelings about the experience.

3. After a thorough discussion, begin to take dictation. When taking dictation remember these important tips: "Use print that is large enough for the whole group to read. Space words clearly. Say the words as you write them. Use standard spelling and adhere to capitalization and punctuation rules. Don't edit text in any other way, though. Record students' language exactly as expressed" (p. 122).

4. When your dictated text is complete, read it aloud. Encourage your students to read it silently as well. Make any changes that children suggest. Then ask the class to decide on a title.

5. To build fluency, read and reread the dictation a number of times.

6. Create individual copies for each student.

Later in the chapter we will see this process in action in a second grade classroom.

Big Books for Shared Reading

The concept of a **big book** came from New Zealand's Don Holdaway (1980), who observed the interaction between parents and children reading together and encouraged teachers to re-create this experience in their classrooms. When a caregiver and a child read a bedtime story, they can both see and touch the text. In order for this to happen in the classroom, the text has to be large, clearly written, and in plain sight for the entire group. Also, because the opportunities to touch the text are not as frequent as during the lap reading experience, it is essential that students have time to interact with the text during the rest of the day (Fisher & Fisher Medvic, 2000).

Before publishers began creating big books, teachers and their students did it themselves. This is an economical way to begin a shared reading collection. To create the enlarged texts, teachers write stories on large pages as their students dictate or retell experiences. Illustrated by the students, these large pages are then made into books. Children relish the opportunity to read their stories over and over. "Publishers were quick to latch on to this idea and started publishing big books of some of their stories, thereby negating half the value of the child's input in both retelling and illustrating" (Huck, 1996, p. 27). Today's commercial big books are written and illustrated by many popular children's book authors. Such books provide a wonderful way to share stories and teach reading strategies to the entire class. Some suggestions for selecting appropriate big books for shared reading lessons are included in Figure 3.3. Other enlarged texts for shared reading include charts with songs, poems, and chants. These may be either commercially prepared or teacher made.

Figure 3.3

Criteria for selecting big books for shared reading

Choose books that:

- Control the amount of print on the page and the location of that print.
- Are repetitive with small variations reinforced by the illustrations.
- Have large boldfaced type and ample space between each word.
- Have engaging illustrations that support the text.
- Are from different genres: fiction, nonfiction, plays, and poetry.

Source: Fisher, B., & Fisher Medvic, E. (2000). *Perspectives on shared reading: Planning and practice.* Portsmouth, NH: Heinemann.

Leveled Books for Guided Reading Lessons

Books for guided reading lessons are leveled according to the supports and challenges they offer young readers who are learning strategies for independent reading. Different leveling systems have been used for many years. As discussed earlier, basal readers are leveled by word difficulty. The early levels are labeled: Readiness, Preprimer 1, Preprimer 2, Preprimer 3, Primer, and Grade One. "Many reading programs are organized by stages or phases in the acquisition of reading" (Fountas & Pinnell, 1999) such as Early, Emergent, Transitional, and Self-Extending. (For a complete explanation of these stages see Chapter 6.) The tutorial program Reading Recovery developed by Marie Clay (1993) has its own leveling system that includes a very fine text gradient ordered from 1 through 20. In their book *Matching Books to Readers: Using Leveled Books in Guided Reading, K–3* (1999), Irene Fountas and Gay Su Pinnell developed a text gradient that includes sixteen levels (A through P), which encompass kindergarten through third grade. In their 2001 publication, *Guiding Readers and Writers Grades 3–6: Teaching Comprehension, Genre, and Content Literacy,* the authors extended the text gradient to accommodate readers in grades 3 through 6 and now has levels ranging from A through Z. Some factors that Irene Fountas and Gay So Pinnell (1996, p. 114) considered when creating their levels were:

Teaching Strategy:
Getting Started with
Book Leveling

1. Length.
2. Size and layout of print.
3. Vocabulary and concepts.
4. Language structure.
5. Text structure and genre.
6. Predictability and pattern of language.
7. Illustration support.

Fountas and Pinnell also suggest ways for teachers to work together in a school or district to level their current materials. Leveled books assist teachers in providing small group reading instruction at each student's specific level.

Text Sets for Literature Circles

As students grow as readers, it is important that they have the opportunity to participate in literature discussion groups or literature circles. In order for this to occur, the teacher needs to collect **text sets** of six to eight books of the same title. Teachers should select texts that elicit conversation, are at various levels, and explore different genre. (For an example of a third grade text set see p. 104.) Once the texts are selected, students choose the book they want to read. Students then form a small group based on their book choice. The group, with guidance from the teacher, designs a schedule for reading, reflecting, and discussing. Each day children read the assigned portion of text and make notes to prepare for the discussion. To support struggling readers, teachers often pair up students for reading or provide a tape-recorded version of the text. The teacher's role during discussion is to facilitate and observe the learning. After the book is finished, students may share their insights and excitement about the book with the class—a great way to get other students interested in reading the book.

Paper, Pencils, and Much More

Stop for a moment and think about all of the materials we discussed thus far: basal readers, children's literature, poems and songs, language experience approach texts, big books, leveled books, and text sets. What else do we need in the classroom to help learners express the thoughts and ideas they gain from reading these texts and relating them to their personal experiences using their own written words? The answer seems obvious—a piece of paper and a pencil! But just as we discovered with print resources in a balanced literacy classroom, there are different materials designed for different writing tasks. We will divide these writing resources into two categories: writing materials for teachers and writing materials for students.

Writing Materials for Teachers

Earlier in the chapter you learned the importance of using quality literature as a model for good writing. You, as the teacher, also have to be willing to model your own writing for your young learners. Effective writing teachers model writing each day for their students. In Ms. Kay's classroom, she and her class created a daily morning message. As she wrote the message, she verbalized her thinking. This is one approach to teaching writing that gives students a glimpse into the mind of an experienced writer. Other approaches include the language experience approach, shared writing, and interactive writing. Teachers using these approaches need certain materials at their fingertips. Anytime you model writing for your learners or compose a piece together, you must ensure that all children can clearly see the text.

Some classrooms have ample chalkboard or dry erase board space making an easy-to-use place to write enlarged texts together. One disadvantage to writing a text on the board is that it is not permanent. Many teachers prefer to use a large tablet of chart paper when they are writing a text that they want to display or revisit. This large chart paper is available at any teacher supply store and comes in many varieties. Another appealing option is the overhead projector. Writing on an overhead transparency, the teacher can face her students and write using her normal size of handwriting, making it quicker and easier. The text is projected on the screen for all to see. By photocopying the transparency, the text can also be easily reproduced for each child in the class. Finally, a little later in the chapter you will meet Ms. Wang. She uses her classroom computer hooked to the LCD panel to create a language experience story with her students. Afterward, she prints copies via a laser printer. If you are fortunate enough to teach in a school that has this type of technology, this is a wonderful alternative. As we introduce different approaches to teaching writing later in the chapter, think about which of these materials you would choose to use in your classroom.

Writing Materials for Students

After you have modeled a writing skill or strategy, children need ample time and appropriate materials to practice. Students from kindergarten through middle school should have frequent opportunities to practice the craft of writing in a journal. Journals serve different purposes at different times, in different classrooms. You will learn more about the types of and purposes for journals later in this chapter.

Along with journals, children need a variety of papers and writing tools in the classroom. Just as the classroom library is filled with books of all sizes, shapes, colors, and kind, so should be the classroom writing center. An inviting writing center serves the same purpose as an inviting classroom library—it encourages youngsters to practice, practice, practice. (You will learn how to create a well-stocked writing center in Chapter 6.) In a balanced literacy classroom students should be surrounded by materials that will entice them to read and inspire them to write.

INSTRUCTIONAL APPROACHES TO TEACH READING

Now that you are familiar with the various types of materials you may encounter in a classroom, the next step is to gain some beginning knowledge of the varied instructional approaches that utilize these resources. This is imperative for a teacher who is using a balanced approach because this teacher "values multiple ways of learning and arranges her or his reading program to incorporate diverse instructional techniques and settings" (Fitzgerald, 1999, p. 103).

One goal of reading instruction is to assist students in becoming **strategic readers.** The qualities that strategic readers possess are illustrated in Figure 3.4. These readers possess the skills necessary to efficiently read and thoroughly comprehend text. Regardless of the instructional approach, teachers should be constantly modeling and instructing students in the essential elements of reading.

Two main categories of reading strategies include comprehension strategies and methods for tackling unknown words. Rachel Brown, Pamela Beard El-Dinary, and Michael Pressley (1996) refer to this type of reading instruction as "transactional strategies instruction (TSI)" (p. 177). The comprehension techniques included in these lessons are (a) predicting upcoming events, (b) verifying predictions, (c) visualizing story content, (d) summarizing the story, (e) making connections to background knowledge, and (f) monitoring understanding. The methods for tackling unknown words involve (a) skipping the word and continuing to read, (b) using picture and word clues, and (c) rereading the portion of text with the unknown word (Brown et al., 1996). There are a variety of instructional approaches teachers can take advantage of to help students become independent readers by developing their comprehension and word recognition abilities. These approaches include the language experience approach (LEA), reading aloud, shared reading, guided reading, flexible grouping, self-selected independent reading and reading workshop, literature circles, reader's theater, and listening instruction.

Figure 3.4

Characteristics of strategic readers

The strategic reader:

1. Analyzes—Understands how various kinds of texts and different reading goals require particular strategies.
2. Discriminates—Identifies the reading task and sets a purpose for reading (reading to study for a test versus reading for pleasure).
3. Plans—Chooses appropriate strategies for reading situations: relates new knowledge to prior knowledge, summarizes, questions, clarifies, and predicts.
4. Monitors comprehension—Knows comprehension is occurring and knows what is being comprehended.
5. Regulates—Knows how to repair/fix up comprehension.
6. Develops a positive attitude toward reading.

Source: Cook, 1986; Paris, Lipson, & Wixson, 1983.

The Language Experience Approach

Earlier in the chapter you learned the philosophy and six steps to creating a language experience text. Let's visit a classroom to see this process in action. A number of students in Ms. Wang's second grade class celebrate Chinese New Year. Because of this, the rest of the students were interested and excited to learn more about this special holiday event. Ms. Wang contacted a few parents of Chinese descent who would be willing to share information about their family's customs and traditions with the class. She also incorporated Chinese folk tales into her literacy lessons, reading, among others, Margaret Mahy's version of *The Seven Chinese Brothers* (1990) with its carefully researched watercolor illustrations. She included Lily Toy Hong's *Two of Everything* (1993) into her math lesson. This lighthearted tale about a couple who find a magical pot that duplicates everything clearly illustrates the concept of multiplication.

After a wonderful presentation by the parents complete with a videotape of a Chinese New Year parade, the students sat together on a rug to discuss the event. The class talked about the information they learned and asked their peers more questions. Some shared their disappointment in never having the opportunity to participate in the celebration, others their excitement of having their parents be part of their classroom that day. As the discussion slowed, Ms. Wang sat down at her computer, which was projected on the large classroom screen through an LCD panel, and began to take dictation. The finished piece read:

Chinese New Year
Written by 2-W

We learned all about Chinese New Year today. Mrs. Luo taught us how to use chopsticks to eat rice. It was tricky! Mr. Song brought in a video of The Lion Dance. We practiced with a real lion. We would need a lot more practice before we could do it in a parade. We all wish we could celebrate Chinese New Year.

After rereading the text a few times, Ms. Wang printed out a copy for each student. Each student carefully illustrated his or her copy of the text, then added it to the collection of language experience texts in a three-ring notebook they stored in their desks. This notebook is used often during literacy lessons for rereading and teacher-directed lessons about the conventions of print. Ms. Wang closed the lesson by reading the nonfiction piece *Lion Dancer: Ernie Wan's Chinese New Year* (1990) by Kate Waters and Madeline Slovenz-Low. The class enjoyed comparing what they had written to what was written in the book.

Reading Aloud

The power and benefits of **reading aloud** to children have been thoroughly documented in the educational literature as far back as 1908, when E. B. Huey stated in his textbook on reading that "the secret of it all lies in parents reading aloud to and with the child" (p. 332). Reading aloud fosters a child's affective knowledge about reading. (For a list of the many values of reading aloud see Chapter 6.) Kindergarten students delight in the rhymes as Miss Bindergarten and her class prepare for a new year in *Miss Bindergarten Gets Ready for Kindergarten* (Slate, 1996), while older students will be on the edge of their seat as their teacher reads the latest Harry Potter fantasy by J. K. Rowling. Teachers often forget the power of reading aloud to older students. The experts (Huck, Hepler, Hickman, & Kiefer, 2004) remind us that daily stories in the middle grades and middle school are essential. Reading aloud to older students helps improve their comprehension and increase their vocabulary and

Reading aloud should take place in classrooms on a regular basis.

knowledge base. "Primarily, however, the read aloud time will cause children to want to read. Once children have heard a good book read aloud, they can hardly wait to savor it again. Reading aloud thus generates further interest in books. Good oral reading should develop a taste for fine literature" (pp. 575–576). Reading aloud should take place in classrooms on a regular basis. In Nancy Atwell's (1987) words, "It is a mistake for educators to regard reading aloud as mere entertainment, that it is essential to reader growth. Hearing good literature brings it to life, fills that classroom with an author's words, and provides kids one more avenue for loving books" (p. 208). A natural extension of the read-aloud concept is shared reading.

Shared Reading

A community of learners interacting with a text and with each other is one of the goals of **shared reading.** Bobbi Fisher and her daughter Emily Fisher Medvic (2000) paint an inspiring picture of shared reading:

> A daily shared reading time in primary classrooms supports the foundations of literacy teaching and learning for all children. It continues to build on the literacy started at home with the bedtime story, and it helps children develop a love of learning as they learn about literacy and learn to read. It involves rigorous teaching and learning, and provides models for extending these literary experiences to practice and sharing times throughout the day. It also promotes community and builds self-esteem. (p. 3)

In an interview with Barbara Park (1982), Don Holdaway describes the three phases of a shared book experience. Phase one includes the introduction of the book for the shared enjoyment of reading. Some predicting about meaning and vocabulary should take place during this phase, but it should not overshadow the sheer enjoyment of the book. Repeated readings constitute the second phase. This is a time when "the strategies of reading are taught and exemplified within a deeply meaningful context" (p. 816). In the final phase, the children are given ample opportunity to reread the text independently and complete related follow-up activities. Shared reading supports the diverse learners in a classroom because it "is a noncompetitive time when children of different abilities and experiences learn from and with each other" (Fisher & Fisher Medvic, 2000, p. 3). (For a complete shared reading lesson plan see the Teaching Strategy for the Classroom box.)

Teaching Strategy for the Classroom

SHARED READING LESSON PLAN: THE CHICK AND THE DUCKLING

I. OBJECTIVES

The students will:

- Interact with the book and with each other by discussing the pictures and events in the story.
- Observe the concepts of print demonstrated by the teacher.

- Identify words and word parts to develop a concept of a word.
- Form a beginning knowledge of quotation marks.

II. MATERIALS

- A song: "Six Little Ducks" written on chart paper or sentence strips for the pocket chart.
- A short poem.
- A familiar text: *A Duck in a Truck* (1999) by Jez Alborough.
- A new text: big book of *The Chick and the Duckling* (1972) by Mirra Ginsburg.
- Sticky notes to cover words in big book.
- A pointer.
- Masks of different sizes to highlight words.
- Chick and Duckling puppets (made from paper and ice cream sticks) for each student.

III. INSTRUCTIONAL APPROACH

A. Motivator

- Sing the song "Six Little Ducks" together, encouraging the children to use motions to act it out.
- Chant the short poem. Have students point out features of the poem by using different size masks to highlight words and word parts.

B. Teacher/Student Interaction

- Introduce and read the big book.
- Begin by writing the title, *The Chick and the Duckling,* on the board. Ask the students to predict what they think the story is about. Next, display the cover and elicit more predictions.
- As you read the story, encourage children to make predictions about events. Also, place sticky notes on key words to develop the strategy of using the picture clues. For example, you may want to cover the word "butterfly" in the sentence, "'I caught a butterfly,' said the Duckling," and have the students use the picture clues to help them predict the covered word.
- Reread the big book:
  1. After the first reading is completed, it is important that you go back and reread the story straight through. Ask the students to point out something they noticed in the initial reading that they are going to search for in the subsequent reading (Fisher & Fisher Medvic, 2000).
  2. To develop a beginning knowledge of quotation marks, divide the class in half and reread the story while students act out the Chick and Duckling parts.

C. Gatekeeping

- At the conclusion of the readings and rereading, the class can work together to fill out the simple story map illustrated in Figure A.

IV. EXTENSIONS

To extend the students' knowledge of chicks and ducklings and help them with the comprehension strategy comparing and contrasting, the class can create a Venn diagram comparing Chicks and Ducklings.

Figure A	**Primary story map**

Title:	Characters:	Setting:	Words:

Beginning:	Middle:	End:

V. ADAPTATIONS/MODIFICATIONS FOR DIVERSE LEARNERS

One way to adapt shared reading for students with diverse needs is to create a small group shared reading activity (Koskinen et al., 1999):

Step 1: Choose a book for a small group based on the group's instructional needs.

Step 2: Introduce the book by looking at the cover, giving a brief overview, and asking the students to predict what might happen in the story.

Step 3: Read the book aloud to students, pointing to the words as you read.

Step 4: Reread the book orally together.

Step 5: Have students reread the story in pairs to develop fluency. Place the book in a designated spot for later rereading.

Guided Reading

Educators of budding readers have the enormous responsibility to steer those readers toward independence. Irene Fountas and Gay Su Pinnell (1996) describe **guided reading** as a small group lesson where the teacher encourages the readers to utilize strategies that will enable them to read and comprehend increasingly more challenging texts. The ultimate goal of guided reading is to equip learners with the independent reading strategies necessary to be successful readers.

In guided reading:

1. A teacher works with a small group.
2. Children in the group are similar in their development of a reading process and are able to read at about the same level of text.
3. Teachers introduce the stories and assist children's reading in ways that help to develop independent reading strategies.
4. Each child reads the whole text.
5. The emphasis is on reading increasingly challenging books over time.
6. Children are grouped and regrouped in a dynamic process that involves ongoing observation and assessment. (Fountas & Pinnell, 1996, p. 4)

(A complete guided reading lesson plan is included in Chapter 6.) A guided reading lesson is one reason to group students for instruction. Teachers also form flexible groups for other instructional purposes.

Flexible Grouping

Flexible grouping allows the teacher to form instructional groups for a variety of reasons. Fifth grade partners reading *Joyful Noise* (Fleischman, 1988), a Newbery award-winning book of poems designed for two voices, is one type of group. Another group might consist of a first grade teacher and her students working in a skill group to find the rhyming words in *A-Hunting We Will Go* (Kellogg, 1998). Second grade students may form groups based on student choice when reading their favorite Henry and Mudge book by Cynthia Rylant. Michael Opitz (1999) suggests the following teaching strategies for flexible grouping:

1. *Cooperative Reading Activity (CRA)*—This technique is most often used for content area reading. First, the teacher divides the text into manageable chunks. Next, he assigns each group a portion of the text to read and discuss. After reading, each group reports to their classmates the information they gleaned from the text.
2. *Cut-Apart*—The cut-apart activity provides an opportunity for the entire class to orally read either a sentence or paragraph from a story or poem. The teacher divides a story or poem into sections and assigns each section to a student or group to read orally. Students practice, and then the class reads the entire story aloud. This tactic enables all students to succeed, builds listening comprehension, and increases fluency.
3. *Genre Study/Text Sets*—This strategy provides all students in the classroom an opportunity to read books in the same literature genre or about the same curricular topic and contribute to class discussions and projects regardless of their reading level. In a third grade classroom where students are studying biographies of famous women, the struggling readers could read *A Girl Named Helen Keller* (Lundell, 1995), while the average readers read *A Picture Book of Amelia Earhart* (Adler, 1998), and the advanced readers read *Minty: The Story of Harriet Tubman* (Schroeder, 1996). After reading these

inspiring biographies, the students engage in discussions and activities related to these famous women.

4. *Single Title, Varied Mode*—Another method to offer the same reading experience for all readers is to provide different modes for experiencing the same text. Students can read the same text either independently, collaboratively, or using a tape-recorded version.

Self-Selected Reading and Reading Workshop

The research on the importance of self-selected independent reading by the students is clear. The more words that pass in front of a reader's eyes, the greater the opportunity for that child to become a better reader (Allington, 1977). A study that focused on independent reading (Anderson, Wilson, & Fielding, 1988) found that a child's reading skills improve significantly if they read independently for at least ten minutes per day or one hour per week. This research is the foundation upon which reader's workshop/self-selected reading time is based.

Reading workshop/self-selected reading time is designed to accomplish two goals. The daily time spent engaged with text helps to build a classroom community of readers and to increase the students' awareness and use of effective reading strategies. "**Self-selected independent reading** is that part of a balanced literacy program during which children get to choose what they want to read and to what parts of reading they want to respond. Opportunities are provided for children to share and respond to what is read. Teachers hold individual conferences with children about their

Self-selected reading time in a first grade classroom.

books" (Cunningham, Hall, & Sigmon, 1999, p. 21). The following is a sample of a ninety-minute **reading workshop** format for intermediate-grade students:

> 20–30 minutes: Reading strategy mini-lesson
>
> 10–15 minutes: Sustained silent reading
>
> 30–40 minutes: Independent reading/conferences
>
> 15 minutes: Sharing reading

The teacher would begin the reading workshop by presenting a mini-lesson to model and demonstrate a specific reading strategy or give explicit instruction of a comprehension strategy. This lesson is followed by a period of sustained silent reading. During this time students self-select literature that interests them and use the strategies they are learning to read independently at their own pace. Following the sustained silent reading, students continue to read independently and conference with each other or with their teacher. During these brief conferences students discuss their current book and their use of reading strategies. Finally, the teacher brings the class together to share what they are reading.

For primary students a half-hour time block may be more appropriate with five to ten minutes for teacher read-aloud, fifteen to twenty minutes for independent reading and conferencing, and five to ten minutes for sharing. In her article, Kathleen Jonson (1998) outlines nine classroom practices that will enhance the independent reading program:

1. Schedule a daily time for independent reading. Increase the duration of reading time according to the students' development.
2. Equip the classroom with an assortment of reading materials. The classroom library should include books from different genre and cultures on a variety of topics and books and materials made by students.
3. Provide emergent readers with short, predictable pattern stories and other simple decodable texts to increase their confidence and reading ability.
4. Promote books to students by doing book talks.
5. Encourage students to reread "old favorites." Marie Clay (1991) found that rereading a text after several days or even weeks is a very good strategy for young readers.
6. Teach children how to pick appropriate books. (See Teaching Strategy for the Classroom box.)
7. Visit the school library on a regular basis.
8. Begin home reading programs, so students also have a chance to read independently at home.
9. Monitor and assess students' progress in reading.

Teachers choose to call this time of day many things: S.S.R. (sustained silent reading, D.E.A.R. (drop everything and read), R.A.B.B.I.T. (read a book because it's terrific), and many more. Whatever the name, it is a crucially important component to a balanced literacy program.

Teaching Strategy for the Classroom

AN ACTIVITY FOR SELECTING "BARGAIN" BOOKS

When children are self-selecting literature for independent reading, teach them how to carefully select a "bargain" book by doing the following:

1. Work together with the entire class to make a reference chart. Begin by saying, "When we go shopping at the store, we look for items that are a bargain. That means we get the most for our money. When items are too expensive, we cannot afford them; and when they are too cheap, they are often not well-made." Have the students share their own shopping experiences and times they and their parents have searched for a bargain.
2. Ask the students to tell you characteristics of a book that would be too expensive, too cheap, and a bargain. Depending on the grade level, some may include:

TOO EXPENSIVE

The book is long.
The print is small.
I can only read a few words on each page.
I have never heard this book read aloud.
There are not many pictures.

A BARGAIN

I can read *almost* every word on the page.
My teacher has read this book to me before.
I can read this book during guided reading.
I know a lot about the topic.

TOO CHEAP

The book is short.
The print is big.
I have read this book over and over before.
I know every word in the book.

3. Call children over to the classroom library in small groups and explain that you are going to help them to become good book shoppers. Help them use the chart to select books at their level to read independently. Some teachers like to have students store these books in a plastic bag, which they call their book "shopping bag."

Literature Circles/Literature Discussion Groups

Literature circles provide an opportunity for readers to construct meaning together in a social context. The groups for literature circles are formed "to explore and understand the texts and the potentials within the texts" (Gilles, Dickinson, McBride, &

Vandover, 1994, p. 499). The teacher begins by sharing an intriguing passage from the book to pique students' interests. Students are then given time to read and respond to the text on a personal level. Then, in a relaxed discussion setting, they can predict, verify, clarify, and challenge their interpretations. During this "grand conversation," the teacher's role is to serve as a model, a facilitator, and a guide. (Literature circles will be more fully explained in Chapter 8.)

Reader's Theater

Reader's theater is any oral presentation where two or more students dramatize a text by reading aloud from a script. "The readers have the task of using reading rate, intonation, and emphasis on the meaning-bearing cadences of language to make the print come alive" (Hoyt, 1992, p. 582). Teachers have the option of choosing from the many published scripts available, or they can engage youngsters in creating their own scripts. In many stories there are only a few main characters; therefore, not all students are able to participate. To alleviate this dilemma, teachers assign students to work together in groups to choral read certain sections of the script. To support the actors' efforts during reader's theater, follow the suggestions given by first grade teacher Barbara Ryan Larkin (2001). Begin by choosing a script or story with several characters and a fast-moving plot. Next, read the story aloud to help students grasp vocabulary words. Following the oral reading, chorally read the entire script with your class to familiarize the students with the parts. Another option, if a script is not available, is to prepare an overhead transparency of the story and then create the script as a whole class. Divide students into small groups to play each character's part and teach them how to highlight their character's words in the script. The most important step is to allow ample time for children to practice, practice, practice! Once students have practiced, they will be anxious to perform. Begin with short performances and try to perform for an audience whenever possible. Once stories are dramatized, the scripts and any props make an appealing addition to the fine arts center. Reader's theater is an "authentic way of motivating children, developing fluency, and building comprehension through repeated reading" (Larkin, 2001, p. 481). (A complete reader's theater script is included in Chapter 10.)

Speaking and Listening

The instructional approaches discussed thus far from reading aloud to reader's theater all depend on the students' using effective listening strategies. Effective listening is crucial to learning. This belief is shared by Rebecca Brent and Patricia Anderson (1993), who outline a method of **listening instruction.** First, teachers model the use of good listening skills during both class discussions and one-on-one conference. Second, they teach lessons about specific listening skills. Finally, they provide numerous opportunities for students to practice effective listening.

One way to do this is by having students give presentations. Students as young as first grade benefit from numerous opportunities to stand up in front of the class and give a prepared presentation. If students are given multiple opportunities to present, from first grade through eighth grade, imagine how well-prepared they will be for speech class in high school. First grade students at Gwendolyn Brooks Elementary School celebrate the winter holidays in various ways. As a part of this celebration their teachers have developed a speaking activity that honors each student's specific customs and traditions. Each first grader prepares a three-minute presentation (based on the form that appears in Figure 3.5) complete with a visual aid to share with the class that explains how they celebrate the winter holidays with their family. The class learns about Kwanzaa, Hanukkah, Christmas, and Eid, just to name a few. Those students who do not celebrate a winter holiday share their adventures in the snow and during special family activities.

Figure 3.5

Winter holiday report form

Name _____

My Holiday Customs

During the Winter Holidays my family and I celebrate _____

_____

_____

We always _____

_____

_____

We visit _____

_____

_____

We like to eat _____

_____

_____

Feel free to change these sentences as needed.

INSTRUCTIONAL APPROACHES TO TEACH CHILDREN HOW WORDS WORK

One way to develop a child's local knowledge about reading is through the use of various instructional approaches that highlight phonological awareness, phonemic awareness, phonics, and word study.

Phonological Awareness

Prior to coming to school young children are developing their **phonological awareness.** Children demonstrate their growing phonological awareness in many ways. For instance, they love to hear poems and rhyming songs and begin to hear the rhymes; they invent nonsense names by substituting one sound for another; they divide long words into syllables or clap each syllable in a phrase; they notice when words they hear begin with the same sound (Burns, Griffin, & Snow, 1999). Parents, caregivers, and early childhood educators enhance a child's awareness of spoken words and their meanings by exposing them to simple games, nursery rhymes, and rhythmic activities.

Phonemic Awareness

Phonemic awareness is a young child's understanding that the words they *hear* are made up of a series of individual sounds (Yopp, 1992). Phonemic awareness is not the same as phonics! Phonemic awareness is the knowledge of the separate sounds in *spoken words,* and phonics is the relationship between letters and sounds in *written words.* "Phonemic awareness is an important precursor to success in reading" (Stahl, 1992, p. 621). Children who have phonemic awareness can do the tasks listed in Figure 3.6.

Many studies have shown the importance of phonemic awareness in early reading success. Marilyn Adams (1990) found that the top two characteristics of prereaders that best predicted their success or failure in learning to read were the knowledge of letters and phonemic awareness. In order to benefit from formal reading instruction, young children must have a certain level of phonemic awareness. Studies show that phonemic awareness can be successfully taught to young children. Three ways to help develop phonemic awareness in young children are:

Figure 3.6

Phonemic awareness tasks

1. Rhyme: Do these words rhyme:

cat	hat	(yes)
hill	mail	(no)
run	ran	(no)

2. Blend isolated sounds together to form a word: What word do you say/hear when we put these sounds together?

a-t	(at)
h-o-t	(hot)
sh-i-p	(ship)

3. Tell how many sounds can be heard in a word: How many sounds do you hear in these words?

it	(2)
cook	(3)
hit	(3)

4. Isolate phonemes in a given word:
   What is the first sound you say/hear in red? (/r/)
   What is the last sound you say/hear in pencil? (/l/)

5. Segment spoken words into their constituent sounds: What sounds do you hear in these words?
   cat (/c/-/a/-/t/)
   it (/i/-/t/)

6. Substitute sounds in spoken words
   What word would you hear if you changed the /h/ in hop to /m/? (mop)

7. Delete a sound from a spoken word
   What word would you hear if we left the /s/ off the beginning of slap? (lap)

1. Expose children to books, songs, poems, nursery rhymes, and chants that play with the sounds of language (Burns, Griffin, & Snow, 1999).
2. Provide explicit instruction in phonemic awareness tasks (Adams, 1990).
3. Engage children in extensive writing experiences and allow for invented spelling (Clay, 1998; Cunningham, 1990; Snow, Burns, & Griffin, 1998).

The Alphabetic Principle

The **alphabetic principle** is the child's ability to link sounds to the written letters. It is defined by Burns, Griffin, and Snow (1999) as,

> A writing system design principle that associates units from the limited set of phonemes of oral language with units from the limited set of letters of the alphabet, yielding a highly productive alphabetic writing system. Knowledge of the alphabetic principle is awareness that written words are composed of letters that are intentionally and conventionally related to phonemic segments of the words of oral language. (p. 147)

The principle is crucial to early reading instruction, as Marilyn Adams (1990) states: "Very early in the course of instruction, one wants students to understand that all twenty-six of those strange little symbols that comprise the alphabet are worth learning and discriminating one from the other because each stands for one of the sounds that occurs in spoken words" (p. 245). One simple way to help foster the alphabet principle in young learners is by reading and discussing alphabet books. Also, after sharing a poem with the children a teacher can challenge them to find all the words in the poem that begin with a specified letter. Teachers can create a word study center where children compare letters and visually differentiate among letters using magnetic letters, block letters, letters on tiles, letters cut out of cardboard, and many more. (A description of a word study center appears in Chapter 6.)

Phonics

In her book *Beginning to Read,* Marilyn Adams (1990) defines the *word* **phonics** as "a system of teaching reading that builds on the alphabetic principle, a system of which a central component is the teaching of correspondences between letters or groups of letters and their pronunciations" (p. 50). But Adams goes on to say that defining phonics *instruction* is much more difficult. Phonics instruction has been an area of debate for decades. (For a complete history of phonics instruction see Chapter 7.) The most current controversy exists between those who believe in a systematic, intensive approach to phonics teaching and proponents of holistically oriented approaches.

Explicit Code or Skills Emphasis Phonics

Explicit phonics teaching is "the systematic, sequential presentation of phonics skills using isolated, direct instructional strategies" (Morrow & Tracey, 1997, p. 646). In an explicit phonics lesson children learn about parts of a word and then build toward whole words (Strickland, 1998). An explicit code or skill emphasis lesson might consist of a first grade teacher introducing the digraph /th/ by showing students a number of pictures of /th/ items and writing the corresponding words on the board. The children would then be instructed to return to their seats to complete a worksheet where they had to circle words that begin with the /th/ sound.

Embedded Code or Meaning Emphasis Phonics: Reading- and Writing-Based Phonics

Embedded phonics teaching occurs in the context of real texts. A meaning emphasis phonics lesson would:

1. Begin with the skill in the context of a story, poem, or rhyme.
2. Move to word play that includes blending.
3. Apply the skill in the context of a new selection.

In their study of classroom teachers' use of phonics instruction, Lesley Mandel Morrow and Diane Tracey (1997) refer to this type of instruction as "contextual instruction," which:

> includes learning within meaningful and functional contexts. Incidents of such instruction can happen spontaneously when the teacher or child points out a phonic element. Contextual instruction can occur in activities such as the **morning message,** language experience charts, storybook reading, or anytime when the teacher or child notices phonic elements within the texts and discusses them as they arise. (p. 646)

Phonics: A Balanced Approach

Educators who want to impart a balanced approach to teaching phonics should consider the following thoughts of Dorothy Strickland (1998):

1. Instruction is systematic when it is thoughtfully planned, proceeds in an orderly fashion, and attends to the needs of all learners.
2. The intensity of instruction will vary based on the ongoing assessments of the students' needs.
3. "Instruction should be engaging and rich with meaning, yet grounded in curricular expectations that are visible to teachers, parents, students and concerned others" (p. 53).
4. "Instructional techniques that help children understand and make use of the alphabetic code should be applied with those that guide students in reading comprehension, thoughtful response to literature and the effective use of the writing process" (p. 53).

Developmental Spelling Instruction

Teaching students how to spell using sound–letter correspondences is an important component of a balanced literacy curriculum. As Patricia Cunningham (2000) points out, "Encouraging invented spelling is one of the main ways teachers have of helping children develop their understanding of how phonemes make up words" (p. 36).

Children progress through developmental stages in their spelling (see Table 2.1, Stages of Spelling of Children, in Chapter 2). By analyzing students' writing samples from journals and other written pieces teachers must determine the stage the child is at and what type of spelling instruction would be most appropriate. (Spelling development will be more fully explored in Chapter 7.)

Word Study

Word study is an important component of a balanced literacy curriculum. Helping children both young and old understand how words work will boost their reading and writing ability. Children must learn to use a variety of strategies to solve words in both their reading and writing. As students develop from kindergarten to middle school, it is the teacher's job to demonstrate how to orchestrate the available strategies. Irene Fountas and Gay Su Pinnell (2001) describe five strategies for solving words in both reading and writing:

1. Sound (phonetic strategies): Thinking about the sounds of words.
2. Look (visual strategies): Thinking about the way words look.
3. Meaning (morphemic strategies): Thinking about what words mean.
4. Connections (linking strategies): Using what you know about one word to figure out a new word.
5. Inquiry (research strategies): Using reference materials (lists, charts, dictionary, thesaurus, computer programs) to learn about words.

The knowledge of these five strategies will help guide you as you choose word study activities in your classroom. It is important to address all five, even for upper elementary and middle school students, because "the strategies readers and writers use to make sense of words are interrelated. Becoming literate means learning the 'inner workings' of language, both oral and written" (Fountas & Pinnell, 2001, p. 372).

High-Frequency Words

Patricia Cunningham (2000) states two noteworthy reasons why students should *not* decode or invent-spell high-frequency words:

1. "When children at an early age learn to recognize and automatically spell the most frequently occurring words, all their attention is freed to decoding and spelling less-frequent words and, more important, for processing meaning" (p. 54).
2. Most high-frequency words are not pronounced or spelled in predictable ways (i.e., the, which, people, through). Many of them cannot be decoded, and if you invent the spelling, you will invent it wrong.

In the early grades, the **word wall** assists students who are developmental spellers to move toward conventional spelling by teaching them commonly misspelled words. (For teaching suggestions related to the word wall see Chapter 7.)

Spelling Patterns: Learning to Use Phonograms

The study of spelling patterns, also known as word families, makes sense because "38 **phonograms** with added beginning consonants can make 654 different one-syllable words" (Fry, 1998, p. 621). These **rimes** will also be helpful for finding familiar chunks in multisyllabic words during reading (Bear, Invernizzi, Templeton, & Johnson, 2000). (For a complete list of phonograms see Chapter 7.)

Moving Beyond Developmental Spelling Instruction

As students become more proficient at using sound–letter relationships to spell, teachers must begin to engage students in activities that teach word study strategies. Some of these activities include making words, word sorts, word searches, crossword puzzles, and other spelling methods. (These strategies will be more fully explored in Chapter 7.)

Meaning Vocabulary

Pause for a moment and think about the vocabulary you have encountered in this chapter. You may have stopped along the way to ponder a word or phrase: "Guided reading, I know I've heard that term before, what exactly does it mean?" or "Phonemic awareness, is that the same as phonics?" Vocabulary words are the key to reading. To really know a word one must be able to:

1. Read it in a variety of contexts, grasping its meaning each time.
2. Understand how the context of a word affects the meaning.
3. Realize the connotations or implied meanings of a word when it is used a certain way.
4. Use a word metaphorically, if appropriate. (Fountas & Pinnell, 2001, p. 375)

It is our job as teachers to provide instruction that will deepen students' understanding of words. In their study, Steven Stahl and Marilyn Fairbanks (1986) found that vocabulary instruction increased students' word knowledge and their reading comprehension. They also found that activities where children were given both information about the word's definitions and examples of the word's usages resulted in the largest gains. Vocabulary acquisition is a complex process and cannot be left to chance alone. You will find many superb vocabulary strengthening ideas in Chapter 9.

INSTRUCTIONAL APPROACHES TO TEACH WRITING

A balanced approach to teaching reading includes an equal emphasis on the teaching of writing. Dixie Lee Spiegel (1999) imparts that "literacy is not just reading. It includes writing. Any literacy program that attends only to reading and ignores the reciprocal relationships between reading and writing development cannot by definition be a balanced approach" (p. 11). Effective writing teachers include the following "best practices" in their daily routine (Zemelman, Daniels, & Hyde, 1993):

1. Encourage student ownership and responsibility by helping them choose their own topics, set their own goals, and review their own progress.
2. Spend class time on prewriting, drafting, revising/editing, and sharing whole, original pieces.
3. Model the stages of writing for their students.
4. Teach grammar and mechanics in context during the editing stage.
5. Write for real audiences and purposes.
6. Write across the curriculum as a tool for learning.
7. Use constructive and efficient evaluation.

As you read this section, you will become familiar with the various instructional techniques used to teach the craft of writing.

The Language Experience Approach

Teachers using the language experience approach in a balanced literacy classroom quickly discover that it is not only an approach to teaching reading but an effective method for teaching young writers. "By writing for children, you free them to express meaning in oral language without having to concern themselves with the mechanics involved in written language. In language experience, you are demonstrating the writing process, sometimes making comments about the construction of text" (McCarrier, Fountas, & Pinnell, 2000, p. 21).

The language experience approach is also a very effective strategy for diverse learners who do not yet possess the fine motor skills to control a pencil but are able to tell a story. The students can verbally tell their stories to the teacher or a volunteer, and that person can write their ideas down for them.

Shared Writing

Shared writing closely resembles the language experience approach, but differs in one aspect. In shared writing the teacher and students write collaboratively. This process, developed by Moira McKenzie (1985), encourages students and their teachers to write responses to children's literature selections, an event the class experienced, or a science or social studies topic. Shared writing assists young literacy learners in making the connection between oral and written language, encourages them to pay increased attention to the sounds in words and to spelling patterns, and helps them develop writing skills in a meaningful context (Fountas & Pinnell, 1996).

Interactive Writing

"**Interactive writing** provides opportunities for teachers to engage in instruction precisely at the point of student need" (Button, Johnson, & Furgerson, 1996, p. 447). The teacher and the children write using a "shared pen," which involves the children in the writing (Fountas & Pinnell, 1996). During an interactive writing experience the teacher and students work together to create a piece of writing. The topic can range from recording the experience the class had on a field trip to writing a report about a famous American. While composing, the teacher selects individual students to come up and assist her with writing letters, words, or phrases depending on their ability.

Journal Writing

An advocate of the use of journals is Regie Routman (1991), who believes that personal **journal writing** has the following benefits for students and their teachers:

1. Promotes fluency in writing.
2. Promotes fluency in reading.
3. Encourages risk taking.
4. Provides opportunities for reflection.
5. Validates personal experiences and feelings.
6. Provides a safe, private place to write.
7. Promotes thinking and makes it visible.
8. Promotes development of written language conventions.
9. Provides a vehicle for evaluation.
10. Provides a record. (pp. 199–200)

A journal is a place for the students to record their thoughts and ideas in writing. In the early grades a child's journal contains mainly drawings with a few words or simple sentences that tell about the drawing. As children grow as writers, their journal entries become more complex. Teachers use different materials for their students' journals. In the primary grades, children often write on blank sheets of paper or primary writing paper stapled together with a construction paper cover and back. Intermediate grade children may use a spiral notebook or composition book. Young writers can record their daily adventures, reactions to a book, or results of a science experiment in their journal. The list in Figure 3.7 includes different types of journals and their purposes.

There are many books available that model journaling for young writers. In an appealing picture book, *Mississippi Mud: Three Prairie Journals* (Turner, 1997), Lonnie, Amanda, and Caleb share their journey via their journals. In *The Great Green Notebook of Katie Roberts* (Hest, 1998), twelve-year-old Katie shares her thoughts about the world in her journal entries. For middle school readers, *Jazmin's Notebook* (Grimes, 1998), where Jazmin

---

Figure 3.7

Different types of journals and their purposes

Daily Journal—This journal is a place for students to record their own thoughts, ideas, and feelings. This journal can either be kept private or shared with others.

Weekend Journal—A spiral notebook that is written in each Monday, this journal provides the student and the teacher with a yearlong record of the child's progress as a writer.

Reader's Response Journal or Literature Log—This journal is used to respond in writing to a story a child is reading. It is an excellent way for students to prepare for discussions in literature circles.

Learning Log—Children write in this journal after an experience in science, social studies, math, or other content area classes. It provides a place to record facts, reflect on learning, and formulate questions to improve understanding.

Dialogue Journal—In this journal the student and a peer, teacher, or parent write back and forth to clarify thoughts about a book they are reading.

fills her notebook with her thoughts and dreams, provides an excellent model for students. Journal writing allows children to reflect and respond to events and activities in writing. It helps students find and develop their personal voice.

Patterned Writing

Patterned writing helps students add the structure of the English language to their written work. This type of writing is described by Robert and Marlene McCracken (1995) as "merely standard sentence speech patterns of oral English; we use them to elicit thinking, to develop oral syntax and rhythm, and to make recording ideas possible for beginning writers in grade one" (p. 134). Patterned writing is a way to teach children the structures of writing useful frame sentences. "Our language includes grammar and sentence structure which are both important in communicating effectively with others. We must share with our students the many structures in English language, and provide them with the structures needed to write both narrative and expository works. They must learn the difference between these two forms and be able to write in both forms" (Walther, 1994, p. 21).

Teachers use both narrative and expository writing frames in the classroom. A writing frame is simply a sentence or group of sentences with words missing. The children copy the sentences and fill in the missing words using ideas from a chart created when the class brainstorms. Students use frame sentences in a reading journal to do rewrites based on the language patterns in the stories they are reading. Frame sentences are also used in learning logs that relate to science and social studies lessons. Patterned writing is just one piece to the writing puzzle. Patterns support writers as they develop. Teachers who use frame sentences often find that the same sentence patterns end up in the child's independent writing pieces. The exclusive use of frame sentences is not recommended; they are a beginning support, and their use should decrease as the year progresses and the students' writing skills improve. The repeated practice with frame sentences helps guide children toward becoming independent writers.

Structured Writing

Structured writing lessons provide opportunities for students to write on a specific topic or prompt. This type of writing prepares students for the essay exams often found on state tests and during other similar writing situations. The goal of these writing lessons is to help students prepare a piece that has a focus, is organized, provides specific details, and utilizes a strong voice. Structured writing lessons should include narrative, persuasive, and expository forms (Burger, Chapman, & Christiansen, 1998). During a structured writing lesson, students in a primary classroom may learn the components of a narrative text (characters, setting, problem, and solution). The teacher's mini-lessons would focus on the components as children compose a narrative story about their favorite birthday party. Students in an intermediate classroom may learn how to write an expository piece and pen a report about the Civil War. During structured writing activities, the teacher is choosing the topic or prompt, while during writing workshop this responsibility is shifted to the child.

Writing Workshop

Writing workshop is a way to implement the process of writing for children (Atwell, 1987; Calkins, 1994; Graves, 1983, 1994). Children in a writing workshop classroom write on self-selected topics while the teacher serves as a facilitator or guide. The children learn, through teacher modeling, reading well-written pieces, and focused mini-lessons, the writing process. They experience the process as they prewrite, write, revise, edit, publish, and share their writing. The classroom becomes a community of writers where children learn the craft of writing by writing. (Chapters 6 and 11 discuss the writing workshop in greater detail.)

ADDRESSING DIVERSITY: DIVERSE LEARNERS

Web Link:
IDEA the Law

Language Links

Classrooms across the country are becoming more diverse. The inclusion of special needs students in regular classrooms, the increase of English language learners, the ethnic diversity of our communities, and the wide variety of home experiences that children have prior to attending school are all factors in the makeup of today's classrooms. Utilizing a balanced approach "empowers teachers to select what is right for the ever-changing environment of their classrooms, teachers can be confident that they can come close to meeting the needs of each child" (Spiegel, 1999, p. 13). While each student has his/her own individual learning style and needs, it is important for educators to become familiar with the characteristics of students with special needs in order to modify the curriculum to support the students. Children in a classroom may be academically/cognitively diverse, culturally diverse, or physically diverse. There is also a growing population of children with behavioral disorders. To effectively teach those children, the teacher will have to adapt the current curriculum to meet their needs. In order to modify and adapt the curriculum, the teacher must be flexible. "This flexibility helps to ensure that each child receives a developmentally appropriate education because he or she is viewed as an individual, not as a third grader or an earth science student or someone who is learning disabled" (Spiegel, 1999, p. 13).

A Brief History of Inclusion

In a moment you will visit Kingsway School, a school where students with special needs are included in the regular classroom. Take a moment to reflect on your early educational experiences. How were students with special needs serviced when you were in school? Were students taught in a self-contained classroom? Were students with disabilities occasionally mainstreamed into your classes or were special needs students a part of your classroom community? A brief history of inclusion will provide a framework for understanding the structure of Kingsway School. In the early years of compulsory education at-risk students and students with disabilities either stayed at home or were segregated in self-contained special education classrooms, special schools, or institutions. In the 1954 case *Brown v. The Board of Education,* the Supreme Court ruled that separate but equal is unconstitutional, laying the groundwork for the end of segregation of students—first by race and next by disability (Henley, Ramsey, & Algozzine, 2002). Another important outcome of the civil rights movement that prevents discrimination against individuals with disabilities is Section 504 of the Vocational Rehabilitation Act of 1973. This law prevents the discrimination against all individuals with disabilities in programs that receive federal funding, as do all public schools. Through Section 504, some students not eligible for services through special education may be entitled to accommodations to help them in school.

The next major change in how students with disabilities are taught came about as a result of the 1975 passage by the U.S. Congress of PL 94-142, the Education for All Handicapped Children Act. This landmark federal legislation mandated a free, appropriate education for children with disabilities aged three to twenty-one within the least restrictive environment. For many students the least restrictive environment is a general education classroom. To ensure that instructional services are tailored to meet the child's needs this law provides for the development of an individualized education plan (IEP). An IEP is prepared annually by the school personnel and includes a statement of the student's current level of functioning, annual goals for educational performance, and short-term educational objectives that are defined in measurable terms. It also specifies who is responsible for delivering services, how long they will last, where they will be provided, and how progress will be evaluated. PL 94-142 has

Utilizing a balanced approach helps all children achieve success.

been referred to as the "first compulsory special education law," and the changes we see in special education today are a direct response to its provisions (Ysseldyke, Algozzine, & Thurlow, 2000).

In 1990, two laws further impacted special education services. First, President George H. W. Bush signed a civil rights law based on the Vocational Rehabilitation Act of 1973 called the Americans with Disabilities Act (ADA). This law protects all individuals with disabilities and requires that public buildings be accessible to people with disabilities. Also in 1990, PL 94-142 was renamed the Individuals with Disabilities Education Act (IDEA). In 1997, President Bill Clinton signed a law to amend IDEA adding a number of new provisions. It recognized that since most students were spending a majority of their time in general education classrooms, the classroom teacher should be a member of the team that writes the child's individualized education plan (IEP). To provide an education in the least restrictive environment many students with disabilities are included in general education classrooms. In order for inclusion to be successful, appropriate supports such as collaboration among school personnel, effective use of instructional aides, appropriate physical and technical accommodations, and

Web Links:

National Information Center for Children and Youth with Disabilities

Internet Resources for Special Children

Portfolio Activity:
Modifications

ongoing staff development must be in place. Research indicates that a successfully implemented and maintained inclusive environment with planning, cooperation, preparation, and collaboration by all involved can impact successfully both students with disabilities and their classroom peers (Richey & Wheeler, 2000).

Peering into a Full Inclusion School

Kingsway School is a full inclusion school. The special needs children are assigned to a regular classroom. Each classroom teacher is responsible for making sure the goals on that child's individualized education plan (IEP) are met. Many of the students also have a full-time teaching assistant to support their needs. The building also has a support facilitator, the case manager for all of the inclusion students. The support facilitator guides the teachers and their assistants in making curricular modifications and keeping records of the child's progress on the IEP.

This year there are a number of special needs students attending Kingsway School who are included in the regular classroom. In first grade we meet Roy who has fetal alcohol syndrome (FAS). Fetal alcohol syndrome occurs when the mother drinks alcohol during the first months of her pregnancy. A child with FAS might be born with learning difficulties, organs that do not function properly, or weak muscles. Brianna, a second grade student, has cerebral palsy (CP). Cerebral palsy is caused by damage to the brain and results in many different disabilities. It usually causes a lack of muscle control and coordination. Many people with CP cannot walk or talk. Brianna moves about in a motorized wheelchair and has limited verbal skills. In addition to the adapted lessons she receives in the classroom, she meets with a speech and language pathologist to improve her communication skills. Maria is in third grade. She is bilingual and gifted. Fortunately for Maria the teachers at Kingsway School realized that, although Maria was still developing her ability to communicate in English, she was one of the brightest students in the class. Her classroom teacher, the bilingual teacher, and the gifted teacher collaborate on a regular basis to create a learning environment for Maria where she is engaged in authentic learning experiences that allow her to choose different activities to match her learning style. In fourth grade, Juan has dyslexia. Dyslexic children experience difficulties reading, writing, or talking because their brains perceive things in a much different manner. Juan's teacher knows how important it is to help this child maintain his enthusiasm and confidence about reading. He is always looking for ways to assist Juan with reading. Audio taped books helped Juan with his reading of content area materials. After determining his students' interests, Juan's teacher found enticing books at Juan's instructional level and worked with him to guide him to successfully read them. Finally, in fifth grade we meet Andrew who has Down's syndrome, a condition caused by a chromosome irregularity. Andrew has the physical characteristics that are common to a child with Down's syndrome. He is small and stocky with small hands and feet. He has a flat facial profile and slanted eyes (Shore, 1998). Andrew has weak muscles, heart problems, hearing loss, and needs speech therapy to help him speak clearly. Despite the daily challenges that Andrew faces, he is a cheerful and upbeat student who is able to participate in many of the class activities with minor modifications.

Along with the special needs students, there are also a number of children at Kingsway School that have attention deficit disorder (ADD) and attention deficit hyperactivity disorder (ADHD). Children with ADD and ADHD have difficulty paying attention and concentrating. Children with ADHD also are hyperactive and have trouble sitting still. Both ADD and ADHD can be hereditary. Each of these students will need adaptations and modifications in order to be successful in the regular classroom. Specific strategies for supporting students with ADD/ADHD are found in Chapter 4.

For some students the modification may be minimal, and for other students an alternative activity may be necessary. The following planning strategy called IN-CLUDE (Friend & Bursuck, 2001) is designed to help teachers meet the challenge:

I—Identify classroom environmental, curricular, and instructional demands.

N—Note the student's learning styles and needs.

C—Check for areas of potential success.

L—Look for potential problem areas.

U—Use the information gathered to brainstorm instructional adaptations.

D—Decide which adaptations to implement.

E—Evaluate the student's progress.

(See Figure 3.8 on page 122 for websites to assist parents and teachers of diverse learners.)

THE HOME/SCHOOL CONNECTION

It is vitally important that teachers foster strong home–school connections. Parents are a valuable knowledge source for teachers using a balanced approach. Teachers can begin by communicating with parents on a weekly basis through a classroom newsletter. This newsletter can be written by the teacher with help from his students or, in the upper grades, by the students themselves. Another great way to get parents involved is by inviting them to assist in the classroom. For those parents who are working or are uneasy about coming to the school, an evening event where the children are the focus is often an appealing alternative. For example, teachers can organize a family reading night where parents come to school with their youngsters (who are wearing their pajamas) and read books together. (For more examples and ideas for parent involvement see Chapter 4.)

Web Links:
SERI Parents' and Educators' Resources

Disability Connection— Mac Access

TECHNOLOGY: LEARNING ENHANCEMENTS

The *Standards for the English Language Arts* (1996) have broadened the definition of literacy to include visual language. A visually literate person possesses the ability to be an "active, critical and creative user . . . of the visual language of film and television, commercial and political advertising, photography and more" (p. 5). Teachers must look for ways to enhance their lessons to include technology because technology is a powerful tool for getting work done. When educators thoughtfully integrate

To link to these sites, go to the Web Links area in Chapter 3 of the Online Learning Center at www.mhhe.com/ farrisreading.

Figure 3.8

Websites for parents and teachers of diverse learners

SERI Parents and Educator's Resources
   A site with links to resources for parents and teachers.
National Information Center for Children and Youth with Disabilities
   A national information and referral center that offers information on disabilities and disability-related issues for families, educators, and other professionals.
Parents Helping Parents
   Parent organization with information on diverse learners.
Family Village
   Website with many resources on disabilities.
IDEA the Law
   A site with links to resources for parents and teachers about the Individuals with Disabilities Education Act.
Internet Resources for Special Children
   A site offering extensive resources on special education.
Disability Connection—MacAccess
   A wealth of information about adaptive technology available on the Web. Both shareware and freeware resources are highlighted.
SPEDTECH - L
   This is a mailing list that discusses integration of technology and special education.
Source: Burns, Griffin, & Snow, 1999. *Starting out right.* Baltimore: National Academy Press.

various technology resources into their balanced literacy program, they are providing their students with firsthand experiences that demonstrate the versatility of technological tools. It is important that teachers view technology as a tool to enhance learning rather than the delivery system (Bitter & Pierson, 2002). With this view teachers evaluate hardware, software, and online resources to determine if these tools will assist them in meeting their instructional goals and provide meaningful opportunities for children to develop, practice, and extend their literacy skills. Once this evaluation is complete, they develop appropriate activities. The development of these activities should be guided by both the IRA/NCTE *Standards for the English Language Arts* (1996) and the NETS *Standards for Schools* (1999). Teachers have such a wide variety of technological tools and resources available to them. (See Figure 3.9 for technology resources and teaching ideas.) They can enhance and extend their lessons using the many activity-based CD-ROMS available. (Guidelines for evaluating software are found in Figure 3.10.) Students and teachers can create presentations using such hypermedia programs as KidPix, PowerPoint, or Hyperstudio. The Internet is a powerful tool that can assist the school community with an unlimited array of activities. (Guidelines for reviewing educational websites are found in Figure 3.11.) Technology available to teachers and students continues to grow at such an amazing rate that teachers must be committed to discovering new possibilities that will enhance their teaching and the learning of their

Figure 3.9

Technology resources and teaching ideas

Hardware

Computer

Utilized in schools to execute software programs that enhance learning and increase productivity.

Printer

Teachers and students print hard copies of documents created in software programs listed below.

Scanner

Teachers and students scan in photographs, pictures, and maps to enhance a variety of documents.

Presentation Equipment (large screen monitor, LCD panel, or classroom television connected to a computer)

Students create advertisements about their favorite book and present them to the class.

Digital Camera

Photograph events on a field trip. Print out pictures, have students write a caption for each picture to create a class memory book.

Video Camcorder

Record middle school students presenting various reader's theater scripts of popular children's books. Make a library of videotapes for the elementary school students.

Audiotape Player/Cassette Tapes

Tape record young children singing or chanting their favorite poems. Place the cassette tape and copies of poems in the listening center.

Overhead Projector/Overhead Transparency Film

Use overhead to model and think aloud while you write.

Software

Productivity Software (word processor, database, spreadsheet)

Students use word processors to compose, revise, and edit pieces of writing.

A database is helpful when organizing research data for an expository report in science and social studies.

Many teachers use spreadsheets to maintain student records and grade reports.

Drill and Practice/Instructional Game Software

Young readers practice matching letters and sounds.

Writing Software

Students compose a narrative story complete with illustrations.

Reference Software (encyclopedia, dictionary, thesaurus)

Students use these tools while researching topics of interest.

Multimedia Presentation Software (PowerPoint, Hyperstudio)

Fifth grade students can work in a cooperative group to create a presentation about the book they read and discussed in their literature circle group.

Interactive Books

These books assist struggling readers and ESL students by reading the text to the students and offering many opportunities for the child to interact with the story and pictures.

Online Resources

Internet

Students research their family history/cultural background for an autobiography.

E-mail

Students interview experts about a content area topic and share their discoveries with their peers.

---

students. Activities that introduce learners to technology and the important role it plays in today's society are included in the Teaching Strategy for the Classroom box. Technological advancements continue to assist us in our teaching.

Figure 3.10

Guidelines for evaluating educational software

There are abundant software titles available to educators. The following list of questions will help you make knowledgeable decisions about the software you utilize in your classroom or school:

Documentation and Supplementary Materials

- Does the software program have stated educational objectives?
- Do the installation directions, teacher's guides, and student workbooks make the program easier and more effective to use?

Program Content

- Does the program content match the stated objectives?
- Does the instruction presented reflect current research?
- Does the program allow for a variety of learners?
- Is the content up-to-date and free from errors and unwanted stereotypes?

Presentation

- Is the content developed logically, with meaningful examples and illustrations?
- Is the presentation clear and displayed with enough variety to keep your students interested?

Effectiveness

- Does this instructional tool lead to student learning or would a nontechnical teaching strategy meet your goals and students' needs more effectively?
- Do students appear to grasp the concepts covered in the program following its use?
- Are they able to apply what they have learned to other situations?
- Are they interested in the topic/concept presented?

Audience Appeal and Suitability

- Does the content meet the needs of your learners?
- Does it hold their interest?
- Will they be able to read and respond as needed?

Practice/Assessment Feedback

- Does the assessment and practice provided in the program match the objectives and instruction?

Ease of Use

- How easy is it to work through the program?
- Are there directions and a "help" screen available from every screen?
- Are the directions and "help" items easy to understand?
- Do students have control over their own speed and can they navigate where they want to go?

User Interface and Media Quality

- Do the graphics, audio, video, and animations combine to create a virtual learning environment?
- Do these elements heighten student interest and promote instruction or are they merely decorative?
- Do the media elements utilize the latest technology and function without technical problems?

Source: Bitter, G., & Pierson, M. (2002). *Using technology in the classroom.* Boston: Allyn and Bacon.

Figure 3.11

Guidelines for evaluating educational websites

There are abundant websites available to educators. The following list of questions will help you make knowledgeable decisions about the websites you utilize in your classroom or school:

Documentation and Credibility

- Are the name, contact information, and credentials of the site author clearly stated?
- Is the date of latest site revision indicated?
- Is new information highlighted?
- Is the site free to users?
- Can you access the site without providing a name?

Content

- Does the site title represent the content?
- Are the purpose and goals clearly stated?
- Can the site content be used for a variety of learning styles and intelligences?
- Does the site have links to other relevant sites?
- Is the information current and accurate?
- Is the content free from stereotypes and biases?

Audience Appeal and Suitability

- Is the general appearance of the site appealing to your students?
- Is the language developmentally appropriate for your students?
- Are the text and graphics appropriate for your students?
- Is the content of the linked sites appropriate for your students?

Ease of Use, Navigation, and Accessibility

- Can your students navigate through site without difficulty?
- Are help features and site maps available and easy to access?
- Is the information well organized?
- Are links to the home page included on each succeeding page?
- Are links to other sites relevant and do they work properly?
- Is the site accessible to learners with disabilities?

User Interface and Design

- Are navigation options clearly marked and self-explanatory?
- Are spelling, grammar, and punctuation correct?
- Is the text clear and font suitable for your students?
- Is the site free from advertising or is the advertising inconspicuous?

Source: Bitter, G., & Pierson, M. (2002). *Using technology in the classroom*. Boston: Allyn and Bacon.

Teaching Strategy for the Classroom

INTRODUCING STUDENTS TO TECHNOLOGY

ACTIVITY 1

Objective: To emphasize the importance of technology in the workplace.

- Brainstorm a list of the different kinds of workers in your community.
- Assign each student in your class a worker and have them research how this worker uses technology in his or her workplace.

- Have each student draw a picture (primary grades) or write a short report about the use of technology in the workplace.
- If possible, invite community workers to school to do a presentation on the types of technology they use.

ACTIVITY 2

Objective: To introduce students to computer-related vocabulary and the devices found both inside and outside computers.

- Collect various items related to computer technology: floppy disk, circuit board, CD-ROM, CPU, mouse, hard drive, etc. (Ask a local computer store if they have any obsolete computers that you could take apart.)
- Make cards with the names of the items.
- Have students match the cards to the corresponding item. (This would make a great center activity.)
- When students have finished with the activity, the parts and names make an interesting bulletin board display.

Summary

Effective teachers like Ms. Kay create learning environments filled with materials and abundant opportunities to help students learn and practice their literacy skills. Educators who subscribe to a balanced approach are knowledgeable about the different types of materials they can use with their students and how to utilize these materials in a variety of innovative ways. Having an arsenal of effective instructional approaches is important for both the novice and experienced teacher. These approaches should focus on developing students' comprehension of the written word. Students also need to understand how words work. They should have developed phonological awareness and the alphabetic principle in the early grades and have a working knowledge of phonics. Students who are involved in daily word study activities will have a better understanding of high-frequency words, spelling patterns, and vocabulary words. In a balanced classroom, reading and writing go hand in hand. Teachers use a variety of techniques to develop competent writers. As the classroom populations become more diverse, it is critically important that all learners be exposed to a wide variety of materials, experiences, and instructional strategies to develop their lifelong literacy skills. "Ultimately, instruction must be informed by how children learn and how they can be best taught. Achieving informed balance is an ongoing endeavor that requires knowledge, time, and thoughtfulness" (Strickland, 1998, p. 52).

Chapter Review

Go to the Online Learning Center at **www.mhhe.com/farrisreading** to take chapter quizzes, practice with key terms, and review important content.

Main Points

- Knowledgeable educators select materials that match the curricular goals and learners' needs.

- A controlled vocabulary basal reader is written according to a formula, and each story contains a large percentage of high-frequency words.

- A literature anthology basal includes selections taken directly from trade books.

- The possibilities for using children's literature in a balanced reading program are endless.

- Students learn from, and enjoy, poetry and songs.

- Big books offer teachers a way to re-create the lap reading experiences young children had with their parents.

- Leveled books are a must for teachers who want to do guided reading.

- Teachers collect text sets for students to read, respond to, and discuss during literature circles.

- Reading aloud is an enjoyable and beneficial daily ritual.

- Shared reading helps students learn about literacy and learn to read.

- Teachers nudge students toward independent reading as they meet with small groups for guided reading.

- Teachers form flexible groups to meet diverse students' needs.

- During self-selected reading time students hone their newly acquired reading strategies.

- Literature circles provide an arena for students to gain deeper meaning from the text through social interaction.

- Students dramatize a tale by reading a script during reader's theater.

- Effective listening is crucial to learning.

- Students who possess phonological awareness enjoy hearing and playing with language.

- Phonemic awareness is the awareness of sounds in spoken words.

- When children can link sounds to the written letters, they understand the alphabetical principle.

- Phonics is a system of teaching that shows youngsters how words work.

- Two main types of phonics teaching are explicit code or skills emphasis phonics and embedded code or meaning emphasis phonics.

- Teachers should balance the types of phonics instruction they utilize in their classrooms.

- Developmental spelling instruction is an important component in a balanced literacy classroom.

- Students must learn how to read and spell high-frequency words.

- Children who know common spelling patterns can spell a multitude of words.

- Teachers must encourage students to develop their reading and writing vocabularies.

- Reading and writing go hand in hand.

- Recording students' thoughts and ideas in their own words is called the language experience approach.
- Teachers and students write collaboratively during shared writing.
- Sharing the pen is a key feature of interactive writing.
- Journal writing offers students a venue for reflecting and responding to events and activities.
- Patterned writing offers young authors the support of language patterns.
- Structured writing lessons help students learn the characteristics of narrative, persuasive, and expository pieces.
- Children learn about and experience the writing process during writing workshop.
- Utilizing a balanced approach helps teachers meet the needs of diverse learners.
- Teachers must make every effort to build strong ties between home and school.
- Technology enhances reading and writing lessons.

Key Terms

alphabetic principle	111	phonics	111
big book	95	phonograms	114
flexible grouping	104	phonological awareness	110
guided reading	103	reader's theater	108
high-frequency words	89	reading aloud	100
interactive writing	115	reading workshop	106
journal writing	116	rime	114
language experience approach	92	self-selected independent reading	105
listening instruction	108	shared reading	101
literature anthology basal	89	shared writing	115
literature circles	107	strategic reader	98
morning message	112	structured writing	117
patterned writing	117	text sets	96
phonemic awareness	110	word wall	113
		writing workshop	118

Reflecting and Reviewing

1. What strategies did Ms. Kay use in her first grade classroom? Do you think any of these strategies would work in a third, fifth, or eighth grade class?
2. What do you remember about the way you learned phonics? Is it similar to or different than the type of phonics instruction that is included in a balanced approach?
3. It is obvious after reading this chapter that to effectively teach using a balanced approach you must be familiar with a wealth of information. What will you do as a classroom teacher to keep yourself informed?

Children's Literature

For annotations of the books listed below, please see Appendix A.

Adler, David. (1998). *A Picture Book of Amelia Earhart.* New York: Holiday House.

Alborough, Jez. (1999). *The Duck in the Truck.* New York: HarperCollins.

Curtis, Christopher Paul. (1999). *Bud, Not Buddy.* New York: Delacorte.

dePaola, Tomie. (1998). *Big Anthony: His Story.* New York: G. P. Putnam's.

Fleischman, Paul. (1988). *Joyful Noise.* (E. Beddows, Illus.). New York: HarperCollins.

Florian, Douglas. (1999). *Laugh-Eteria.* San Diego, CA: Harcourt.

Fox, Mem. (1998). *Boo to a Goose.* (D. Miller, Illus.). New York: Dial Books.

Ginsburg, Mirra. (1972). *The Chick and the Duckling.* (J. Aruego & A. Dewey, Illus.). New York: Macmillan.

Grimes, Nikki. (1994). *Meet Danitra Brown.* (F. Cooper, Illus.). New York: Morrow.

————. (1998). *Jazmin's Notebook.* New York: Dial.

Hest, Amy. (1998). *The Great Green Notebook of Katie Roberts.* (S. Lamut, Illus.). New York: Candlewick.

Hong, Lily Toy. (1993). *Two of Everything.* New York: Whitman.

Hopkins, Lee Bennett. (1999). *Spectacular Science: A Book of Poems.* (V. Halstead, Illus.). New York: Simon & Schuster.

Kalan, Robert. (1978). *Rain.* (D. Crews, Illus.). New York: Greenwillow.

Kellogg, Steven. (1998). *A-hunting We Will Go!* New York: Greenwillow.

Lundell, Margo. (1995). *A Girl Named Helen Keller.* New York: Scholastic.

Mahy, Margaret. (1990). *The Seven Chinese Brothers.* (M. & J. Tseng, Illus.). New York: Scholastic.

Martin, Jacqueline Briggs. (1998). *Snowflake Bentley.* Boston: Houghton Mifflin.

Moore, Lilian. (1995). *I Never Did That Before* (L. Hoban, Illus.). New York: Antheneum/Simon & Schuster.

Norworth, Jack. (1999). *Take Me Out to the Ballgame.* New York: Aladdin.

Paulsen, G. (1999). *Brian's Return.* New York: Delacorte.

Schroeder, Alan. (1996). *Minty: The Story of Harriet Tubman.* (J. Pinkney, Illus.). New York: Dial.

Shulevitz, Uri. (1998). *Snow.* New York: Farrar Straus Giroux.

Slate, Joseph. (1996). *Miss Bindergarten Gets Ready for Kindergarten.* (A. Wolff, Illus.). New York: Dutton.

Turner, Ann. (1997). *Mississippi Mud: Three Prairie Journals.* (R. J. Blake, Illus.). New York: HarperCollins.

Udry, Janice May. (1956). *A Tree Is Nice.* (M. Simont, Illus.). New York: HarperCollins.

Waters, Kate, & Slovenz-Low, Madeline. (1990). *Lion Dancer: Ernie Wan's Chinese New Year.* (H. Cooper, Illus.). New York: Scholastic.

Wood, Audrey. (1984). *The Napping House.* (D. Wood, Illus.). New York: Harcourt Brace.

Classroom Teaching Resources

Blair-Larsen, S. M., & Williams, K. A. (Eds.). (1999). *The balanced reading program.* Newark, DE: International Reading Association.

Cunningham, P. M., & Allington, R. L. (2002). *Classrooms that work: They can all read and write,* 3rd ed. Boston: Allyn & Bacon.

————. Hall, D. P., & Sigmon, C. M. (1999). *The teacher's guide to the four blocks.* Greensboro, NC: Carson-Dellosa Publishing Company.

McIntyre, E., & Pressley, M. (Eds.). (1996). *Balanced instruction: Strategies and skills in whole language.* Norwood, MA: Christopher Gordon.

Routman, R. (1999). *Conversations: Strategies for teaching, learning and evaluating.* Portsmouth, NH: Heinemann.

Strickland, D. S. (1998). *Teaching phonics today: A primer for educators.* Newark, DE: International Reading Association.

"*The organization and look of our rooms, the materials we use, and the way we structure the day send a powerful message to children and parents about our attitudes toward teaching and our expectations for our children.*"

Sharon Taberski, teacher at the Manhattan New School in New York City and educational consultant throughout the United States and in Canada

CHAPTER 4

Organizing the Classroom Environment

Key Ideas

- When carefully orchestrated, the physical environment of a classroom invites learners to read and write in authentic and meaningful ways.
- Knowledgeable teachers select materials that support learners as they strive toward meeting the goals outlined in the national standards, the state's English language arts standards, and the local curriculum.
- In primary classrooms, some teachers choose to create literacy centers to engage the rest of the class while they are working with small groups of students.
- An educator in a balanced literacy classroom assumes many roles.
- Teachers and students collaborate to build a strong community of literacy learners.
- Accomplished teachers are acquainted with the range of learners with special needs they may find in their classrooms.
- Effective teachers use a variety of techniques to manage a classroom of students with diverse learning needs.
- Organization and classroom management are keys to an optimal learning environment.
- Well-designed lessons, based on standards and clear objectives, guide teachers in delivering a coherent curriculum.
- Resourceful educators reach beyond the classroom to make connections with parents and other professionals and also to expand their knowledge about teaching.

- The world of instructional technology grows each day. Teachers need to become acquainted with software programs and websites before sharing them with their students.

Questions to Ponder

- What questions should teachers ask themselves when they are setting up their classrooms?
- What is the one material every well-stocked classroom needs?
- How do educators create meaningful literacy centers?
- What are the roles of an effective teacher?
- What are the key principles to classroom management?
- How can teachers address the needs of diverse learners in the classroom?
- How are engaging lessons designed?
- How do teachers reach beyond their classroom walls to make connections with parents and other professionals?
- What role does technology play in a balanced reading program?

Peering into the Classroom

Ready or Not, Here They Come!

The classroom was hot and stuffy after being closed all summer. Thirty desks and chairs were stacked in one corner, boxes of books and supplies in another. After a few hectic months of filling out applications, sending résumés, visiting schools, and participating in interviews, Katherine had finally landed her first teaching job. All through college she had dreamed of this day, and now here she was, standing in her very own classroom two weeks before classes were scheduled to begin. Katherine spent the entire day in new teacher orientation meetings learning about the school district's balanced literacy curriculum. Meetings were also scheduled to introduce the novice teachers to the math, science, and social studies programs. Earlier that week Katherine met with her new teaching teammates. They all seemed very helpful and, since they had been teaching for many years, already had their classrooms all set up and ready to go. Walking into them was almost too overwhelming for Katherine, and she was taken aback by the amount of work to be accomplished before her students arrived.

A heavy box filled with the district's language arts curriculum and a booklet containing the state learning standards dropped to the floor as Katherine took in every detail of her new classroom. It was basically a square room with three windows and built-in bookshelves spanning the west wall, a long chalkboard and two small bulletin boards filling the north and south walls, and a row of coat hooks lining the east wall. Exhausted after the long day of meetings, Katherine sat at her new desk and thought, "How am I supposed to turn this empty room into a welcoming place where children want to learn? Where do I begin? The time is running short; the kids are coming soon. How do I prioritize? How can I possibly get it all done?" As tears welled up in her eyes, she remembered her old college reading textbook, the one with the chapter about classroom management. Katherine pondered softly aloud to herself, "Maybe I should dig that out tonight; it might give me a few ideas about where to start . . ."

REFLECTION: IRA/NCTE NATIONAL STANDARDS IN THE CLASSROOM

Katherine's experience is not unique; many novice teachers find themselves in her shoes. The first years of teaching can be challenging and a bit overwhelming. But with the many challenges comes the reward of watching children blossom before your eyes. College courses and textbooks like this one provide a knowledge base about the content of literacy lessons. But the deepest learning about teaching comes from the practical experience of teaching in a classroom day after day after day. Educators quickly discover that there are so many different demands pulling them in all directions. Teachers must find a common vision, which becomes a target to aim all the teaching and learning. Standards supply this vision. Whether you are teaching in a small rural school district or find yourself teaching in the inner city, the national *Standards for the English Language Arts* (IRA/NCTE, 1996) and *Standards for Reading Professionals* (IRA, 1998) offer a vivid picture of what is expected on a national basis.

As you read the beginning chapters in this textbook, you met teachers in their classrooms working toward that common vision. Remember Alessandra Lopez, who began the year by writing to her students to open the lines of communication. Think back to the rich classroom environment created by Ms. Kay for her fortunate primary students. Ms. Kay's on-the-spot teaching inched students along the path to independent learning. As you continue reading, you will encounter many other teachers who share a common vision. Discover a kindergarten teacher, Mr. Clyde, who has a multifaceted room filled with abundant opportunities for his students to grow as literacy learners. Travel to Bristol Elementary School and view exemplary phonics lessons taking place in the classrooms. Listen in as the sixth graders in Mrs. O's class engage in a Human Bingo activity that enriches and extends their vocabularies. Join Miss Coleman's students and their engaging discussion about the novel *Hatchet* and

Ramon and Miss Bartelone reading and responding to books that they enjoy. By peering into these classrooms you will catch a glimpse of the standards in action. The words of the standards are the guiding vision for these teachers, who create memorable literacy experiences for their students. These experiences are an invitation to find the joy in reading and writing so that these valuable activities will become lifelong pleasures, not just in-school assignments.

STANDARDS for READING PROFESSIONALS

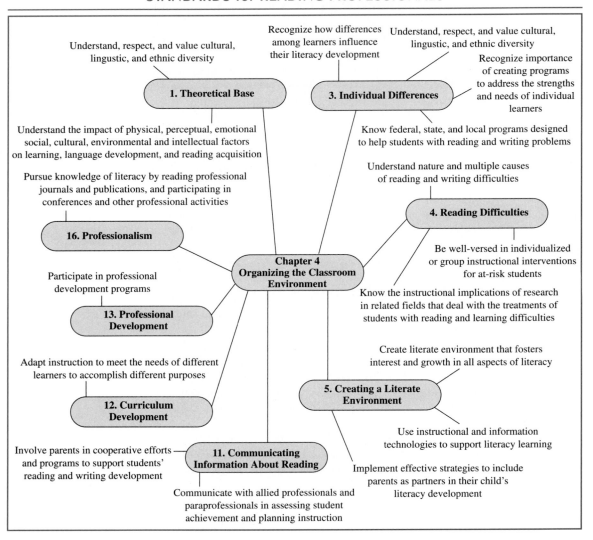

Understand, respect, and value cultural, lingustic, and ethnic diversity

Recognize how differences among learners influence their literacy development

Understand, respect, and value cultural, lingustic, and ethnic diversity

1. Theoretical Base

3. Individual Differences

Recognize importance of creating programs to address the strengths and needs of individual learners

Understand the impact of physical, perceptual, emotional social, cultural, environmental and intellectual factors on learning, language development, and reading acquisition

Know federal, state, and local programs designed to help students with reading and writing problems

Pursue knowledge of literacy by reading professional journals and publications, and participating in conferences and other professional activities

Understand nature and multiple causes of reading and writing difficulties

4. Reading Difficulties

16. Professionalism

Be well-versed in individualized or group instructional interventions for at-risk students

Chapter 4 Organizing the Classroom Environment

Participate in professional development programs

Know the instructional implications of research in related fields that deal with the treatments of students with reading and learning difficulties

13. Professional Development

Create literate environment that fosters interest and growth in all aspects of literacy

Adapt instruction to meet the needs of different learners to accomplish different purposes

5. Creating a Literate Environment

12. Curriculum Development

Use instructional and information technologies to support literacy learning

Involve parents in cooperative efforts and programs to support students' reading and writing development

11. Communicating Information About Reading

Implement effective strategies to include parents as partners in their child's literacy development

Communicate with allied professionals and paraprofessionals in assessing student achievement and planning instruction

INTRODUCTION

The environment of a classroom sets the stage for learning. An attractive, well-planned classroom design coupled with the actions of a caring, knowledgeable teacher make a critical difference in the education of children. This chapter is a "user's guide" for the methods presented in this text. It provides the reader with an action plan for creating the underlying structure that forms the foundation of a balanced literacy classroom. You will learn ways to design the physical environment of the classroom for optimal student engagement. Students will be engaged in a classroom where they feel welcome and have a sense of belonging. An inviting classroom is a comfortable place where the routines and spaces provide a structure for productive learning experiences (Fountas & Pinnell, 2001). The "nuts and bolts" of designing literacy centers will also be discussed. To effectively use the approaches shared in this text, teachers must work with their students to create a community of learners. The second section of the chapter focuses on the creation of this community and includes a description of the teacher's role and tips for fostering a productive social environment. It also delves into the issues related to educating diverse learners in a balanced literacy classroom. Next, we will share helpful strategies for planning for instruction, including a look at the role technology plays in a balanced literacy classroom. The final portion of the chapter examines the notion that educators must reach out beyond the walls of the classroom. This includes making connections with parents and other professionals. Also, to grow as educators, teachers seek out new knowledge and ideas through membership in professional organizations, reading educational books and journals, networking with other teachers, and reflecting on and, if necessary, adjusting their current practices. Demanding? Yes. Impossible? No, especially when you use a carefully devised plan such as the one that follows.

THE PHYSICAL ENVIRONMENT

When teachers are preparing to set up their classrooms, they begin by assessing the space and materials with which they have to work. Some classrooms are spacious and have interesting nooks and crannies, while others are simply a small square room like Katherine's first classroom. Some have lots of windows and abundant storage space, while others have few or no windows or very little storage. Whether a teacher is fortunate enough to find herself in a large classroom or finds herself working in a room the size of a walk-in closet, there are things she can do with the physical environment to make it an inviting place to grow and learn.

Selecting Materials

Depending on the district or school in which you begin teaching, the curriculum and the supporting materials will vary. Many districts have adopted materials to support their curriculum such as literature anthology basals to guide the reading instruction, while others have book rooms filled with leveled books that teachers use during their guided reading lessons. Still others use a traditional controlled vocabulary basal

A well-stocked classroom library is the heart of a balanced literacy classroom.

program as the foundation of their reading instruction. Your first job is to find out what kind of materials your school is currently using and also what their district curriculum espouses. It is crucial to locate and become familiar with a copy of the learning goals for your state and any other information pertaining to the design of the curriculum. A copy of the state goals should be kept handy for future reference. Based on this knowledge you can begin collecting the additional materials and supplies you will need. A well-stocked classroom library is the heart of a balanced literacy classroom.

Books, Books, Books

Regardless of which type of instructional program the school district is using, teachers must begin collecting a classroom library to support and extend the lessons they are teaching. A rich classroom library should contain at least seven books per child (International Reading Association, 2000). Many beginning teachers use books from the school library or local library to enhance their current collection. Some may have purchased books from garage sales. Those beginning teachers who purchased paperbacks from book clubs, made available through methods courses, may have an excellent start on their classroom libraries. In the beginning-of-the-year letter home, encourage parents to contribute a book to the classroom library. Either hard cover or paperback, it can be read and enjoyed and then become a permanent part of the classroom library. Little by little your library will grow.

If you find yourself in a classroom where most books in your classroom library are in English and the children you are teaching speak another language, consider the tactic that second grade teacher Danny Brassell used (1999) to create in the students' words "nuestra biblioteca." The second graders in this class created a library of books themselves. They made books about their families, friends, and their neighborhoods. They authored classroom newspapers and comic strips. The library grew in leaps and bounds and so did the students' attitude about reading. As Danny shares, "For many students our classroom library was their first opportunity to have a wide exposure to books in Spanish. Our classroom library not only improved students' reading but their attitudes toward their own culture as well" (p. 651). In addition to the wide range of literature included in this textbook, Figure 4.1 provides lists of some "musts" for classroom libraries in grades K–1, 2–3, 4–5, 6–8. This is a good place to browse and get ideas for books to add to your growing collection.

Gathering Supplies

Each school and school district has a different way to supply teachers with the supporting materials that they need to run a classroom. By supporting materials we mean the items needed to arrange and house the books and other literacy supplies. Some teachers receive a certain amount of money allocated from the school budget to order their supplies from a school supply catalog, while others are given a purchase order to shop at a local school supply store. Sometimes the school's parent–teacher organization will give each teacher funds to spend on additional classroom supplies. Unfortunately, many teachers find themselves in a school where budgets are tight and supplies are low. Finding out how your school budget works is an important step in gathering the "extras" you will need to do many of the activities in this book and to organize and display the items in your classroom. One key to organizing supplies and materials is to place each item in a clearly marked container that fits neatly into a clearly marked space. When on a limited budget, creative teachers find uses for ordinary "around the house" items to help them arrange their classroom supplies. Here are just a few ideas to get you started:

- Old soup cans covered with bright contact paper transform into colorful pencil holders.
- Old typewriters (manual or electric) make a great addition to a writing center.
- Shoeboxes become useful containers for all different supplies.
- Plastic butter dishes, deli and yogurt containers, flavored coffee boxes, and the like, can hold game pieces, magnetic letters, crayons, and other small objects.

Garage sales and flea markets are great places to find treasures for your classroom. Also, it is extremely beneficial to enlist the help of willing parents to gather additional supplies. In your newsletter add a section that lists the items needed for classroom activities and projects. Many parents are more than willing to donate an item or two to their child's class. If your school or district has a "supply list" that they send home at the beginning of each year, ask if you can add some "basic classroom supplies" to that list like resealable bags of various sizes, paper towels, paper and envelopes for the writing center, and the like. Finally, local businesses are often willing to donate small items for classroom use or even computers that are outdated for commercial use but

Figure 4.1

Classroom library suggestions

Grades K through 1

Aardema, Verna. (1975). *Why Mosquitoes Buzz in People's Ears: A West African Tale.* (L. & D. Dillon, Illus.). Scholastic.

Ada, Alma Flora. (2000). *Frog Friend.* (L. Lohstoeter, Illus.). Scholastic.

Ahlberg, Janet. (1986). *The Jolly Postman.* Little, Brown.

Aliki. (1982). *We Are Best Friends.* Greenwillow.

Allard, Harry. (1977). *Miss Nelson Is Missing!* (J. Marshall, Illus.). Houghton Mifflin.

Aylesworth, Jim. (1992). *Old Black Fly.* (S. Gammell, Illus.). Holt.

———. (1998). *The Gingerbread Man.* (B. McClintock, Illus.). Scholastic.

Bang, Molly. (1999). *When Sophie Gets Angry—Really, Really Angry.* Blue Sky Press.

Baylor, Byrd. (1974). *Everybody Needs a Rock.* (P. Parnall, Illus.). Scribner.

Brett, Jan. (1989). *The Mitten.* Putnam.

———. (2000). *Hedgie's Surprise.* Putnam.

Briggs, Raymond. (1978). *The Snowman.* Random House.

Brown, Marc. (1976). *Arthur's Nose.* Little, Brown.

Brown, Margaret Wise. (1947). *Goodnight, Moon.* (Clement Hurd, Illus.). Harper & Row.

Bruss, Deborah. (2001). *Book! Book! Book!* (T. Beeke, Illus.). Arthur A. Levine.

Burton, Virginia Lee. (1942). *The Little House.* Scholastic.

Calmenson, Stephanie. (1998). *The Teeny Tiny Teacher.* Scholastic.

Cannon, Janell. (1993). *Stellaluna.* Harcourt.

Carle, Eric. (1969). *The Very Hungry Caterpillar.* Philomel.

———. (1971). *Do You Want to Be My Friend?* Harper.

———. (2000). *Dream Snow.* Philomel.

Carlson, Nancy. (1990). *I Like Me.* Puffin.

Cherry, Lynne. (1990). *The Great Kapok Tree: A Tale of the Amazon Rain Forest.* Harcourt.

Christelow, Eileen. (1989). *Five Little Monkeys Jumping on the Bed.* Clarion.

Coles, Robert. (1995). *The Story of Ruby Bridges.* Scholastic.

Cowley, Joy. (1999). *The Red-Eyed Tree Frog.* (N. Bishop, Photo.). Scholastic.

Crews, Donald. (1978). *Freight Train.* Greenwillow.

Cronin, Doreen. (2000). *Click, Clack, Moo: Cows That Type.* (B. Lewin, Illus.). Simon & Schuster.

de Paola, Tomie. (1975). *Strega Nona.* Prentice Hall.

Dorros, Arthur. (1991). *Abuela.* (E. Kleven, Illus.). Dutton.

Edwards, Pamela Duncan. (1997). *Barefoot: Escape on the Underground Railroad.* HarperCollins.

Ehlert, Lois. (1989). *Color Zoo.* Lippincott.

Fleming, Denise. (1994). *Barnyard Banter.* Holt.

Fox, Mem. (1986). *Hattie and the Fox.* Bradbury.

Gibbons, Gail. (2000). *Apples.* Holiday House.

Ginsburg, Mirra. (1972). *The Chick and the Duckling.* Macmillan.

Goble, Paul. (1978). *The Girl Who Loved Wild Horses.* Bradbury Press.

Hall, Zoe. (2000). *Fall Leaves Fall.* (S. Halpern, Illus.). Scholastic.

Henkes, Kevin. (1996). *Lilly's Purple Plastic Purse.* Greenwillow.

———. (2000). *Wemberly Worried.* Greenwillow.

Hindley, Judy. (2002). *Do Like a Duck Does.* (I. Bates, Illus.). Candlewick.

Hoffman, Mary. (1991). *Amazing Grace.* (C. Binch, Illus.). Dial.

Houston, Gloria. (1992). *My Great-Aunt Arizona.* (S. Condie Lamb, Illus.). HarperCollins.

Hutchins, Pat. (1967). *Rosie's Walk.* Macmillan.

Keats, Ezra Jack. (1962). *The Snowy Day.* Scholastic.

Kellogg, Steven. (1971). *Can I Keep Him?* Dial.

———. (1988). *Johnny Appleseed.* Morrow.

———. (2000). *The Missing Mitten Mystery.* Dial.

Kraus, Robert. (1971). *Leo the Late Bloomer.* (J. Aruego, Illus.). Prentice.

Lionni, Leo. (1968). *Swimmy.* Pantheon.

Luthardt, Kevin. (2001). *Mine.* Atheneum.

Figure 4.1

(continued)

Grades K through 1 (concluded)

Marshall, James. (1972). *George and Martha.* Houghton Mifflin.

Martin, Bill. (1967). *Brown Bear, Brown Bear, What Do You See?* Holt.

———. (1989). *Chicka Chicka Boom Boom.* Simon & Schuster.

———. (1999). *A Beasty Story.* (S. Kellogg, Illus.). Harcourt.

Marzollo, Jean. (1993). *Happy Birthday, Martin Luther King.* (B. Pinkey, Illus.). Scholastic.

Mayer, Mercer. (1968). *There's a Nightmare in My Closet.* Dial.

McCloskey, Robert. (1941). *Make Way for Ducklings.* Viking.

McCully, Emily Arnold. (1992*). Mirette on the High Wire.* Scholastic.

Numeroff, Laura Joffe. (1985). *If You Give a Mouse a Cookie.* Harper.

———. (2000). *If You Take a Mouse to the Movies.* Laura Geringer Book.

Pfister, Marcus. (1992). *The Rainbow Fish.* North-South.

Polacco, Patricia. (1990). *Thunder Cake.* Philomel.

———. (1993). *The Bee Tree.* Philomel.

Rathmann, Peggy. (1995). *Officer Buckle and Gloria.* Putnam.

Rohmann, Eric. (2002). *My Friend Rabbit.* Millbrook.

Rylant, Cynthia. (1985). *The Relatives Came.* Scholastic.

———. (2000). *In November.* (J. Kastner, Illus.). Harcourt.

Sendak, Maurice. (1963). *Where the Wild Things Are.* Harper.

Shannon, David. (1998). *No, David!* Scholastic/Blue Sky.

Shaw, Charles Green. (1947). *It Looked Like Spilt Milk.* HarperCollins.

Shaw, Nancy. (1986). *Sheep in a Jeep.* Houghton.

Shulevitz, Uri. (1998). *Snow.* Farrar.

Simmons, Jane. (1998). *Come Along, Daisy!* Little, Brown.

Slate, Joseph. (1996). *Miss Bindergarten Gets Ready for Kindergarten.* Dutton.

Steig, William. (1998). *Pete's a Pizza.* HarperCollins.

Taback, Simms. (1997). *There Was an Old Lady Who Swallowed a Fly.* Viking.

———. (1999). *Joseph Had a Little Overcoat.* Viking.

Tafuri, Nancy. (1984). *Have You Seen My Duckling?* Greenwillow.

Van Allsburg, Chris. (1985). *The Polar Express.* Houghton.

Viorst, Judith. (1972). *Alexander and the Terrible, Horrible, No Good, Very Bad Day.* Macmillan.

Waber, Bernard. (1972). *Ira Sleeps Over.* Houghton Mifflin.

Williams, Linda. (1986). *The Little Old Lady Who Was Not Afraid of Anything.* Crowell.

Wood, Audrey. (1984). *The Napping House.* (D. Wood, Illus.). Harcourt Brace.

Wood, Audrey. (2000). *Jubal's Wish.* Blue Sky Press.

Grades 2 through 3

Ackerman, Karen. (1988). *Song and Dance Man.* (S. Gammell, Illus.). Knopf.

Adler, David. (1993). *Cam Jansen and the Chocolate Fudge Mystery.* Puffin.

———. (1992). *A Picture Book of Harriet Tubman.* Holiday.

Anno, Masaichiro (Mitsumasa). (1983). *Anno's Mysterious Multiplying Jar.* Philomel.

Arnosky, Jim. (2000). *All about Turtles.* Scholastic.

———. (2002). *Watching Desert Wildlife.* National Geographic.

Barrett, Judi. (1978). *Cloudy with a Chance of Meatballs.* Atheneum.

Bang, Molly. (1985). *The Paper Crane.* Greenwillow.

Blume, Judy. (1971). *Freckle Juice.* Dell.

Figure 4.1

(continued)

Grades 2 through 3 (concluded)

Borden, Louise. (2000). *A. Lincoln and Me.* (T. Lewin, Illus.). Scholastic.

Bulla, Clyde Robert. (1987). *The Chalk Box Kid.* Random House.

Bunting, Eve. (1991). *Fly Away Home.* (R. Himler, Illus.). Clarion.

Byars, Betsy Cromer. (1996). *My Brother, Ant.* Puffin.

Cheney, Lynn. (2002). *A Patriotic Primer.* Simon & Schuster.

Cherry, Lynne. (1992). *A River Ran Wild.* Harcourt.

Cohen, Barbara. (1983). *Molly's Pilgrim.* Bantam, Doubleday, Dell.

Cole, Joanna. (1989). *Magic School Bus* series. Scholastic.

Cooney, Barbara. (1982). *Miss Rumphius.* Viking.

Demi. (1990). *The Empty Pot.* Holt.

de Paola, Tomie. (1999). *26 Fairmont Avenue.* Putnam.

Dorros, Arthur. (1987). *Ant Cities.* HarperCollins.

Falconer, Ian. (2000). *Olivia.* Atheneum.

Fritz, Jean. (1969). *George Washington's Breakfast.* Coward.

Gardiner, John Reynolds. (1980). *Stone Fox.* Harper.

George, Jean Craighead. *Arctic Son.* (1997). Hyperion.

Gibbons, Gail. (1992). *Recycle.* Little, Brown.

Hausman, Gerald. (1994) *Turtle Island ABC: A Gathering of Native American Symbols.* Harper.

Heller, Ruth. (1981). *Chickens Aren't the Only Ones.* Scholastic.

Howe, James. (1999). *Horace and Morris but Mostly Dolores.* (A. Walrod, Illus.). Atheneum.

Hutchins, Pat. (1986). *The Doorbell Rang.* Scholastic.

Jenkins, Martin. (1999). *The Emperor's Egg.* (J. Chapman, Illus.). Candlewick.

Johnston, Tony. (1994). *Amber on the Mountain.* Dial Books.

King-Smith, Dick. (1997). *A Mouse Called Wolf.* Crown.

Kinsey-Warnock, Natalie. (1989). *The Canada Geese Quilt.* Dell.

Krull, Kathleen. (2003). *Harvesting Hope: The Story of Cesar Chavez.* (Y. Morales, Illus.). Harcourt.

Lowery, Linda. (1987). *Martin Luther King Day.* Carolrhoda Books.

———. (1999). *Aunt Clara Brown: Official Pioneer.* (J. L. Porter, Illus.). Carolrhoda.

Lundell, Margo. (1995). *A Girl Named Helen Keller.* Scholastic.

MacLachlan, Patricia. (1996). *Sarah, Plain and Tall.* Scholastic.

Martin, Rafe. (1992). *The Rough-Face Girl.* Putnam.

McKissack, Pat. (1994). *Christmas in the Big House, Christmas in the Quarters.* (F. McKissack, Illus.). Scholastic.

Pallotta, Jerry. (1991). *The Dinosaur Alphabet Book.* Children's Press.

Parish, Peggy. (1983). *Amelia Bedelia.* Harper & Row.

Peet, Bill. (1996). *The Wump World.* Scholastic.

Pilkey, Dav. (1992). *Dragon's Fat Cat.* Orchard.

Rhodda, Emily. (2001). *Rowan of Rin series.* Apple.

Rylant, Cynthia. (1997). *Poppleton Everyday.* Scholastic.

Schroeder, Alan. (1996). *Minty: A Story of Young Harriet Tubman.* Dial.

Scieszka, Jon. (1989). *The True Story of the Three Little Pigs.* Puffin.

Shannon, George. (1996). *Tomorrow's Alphabet.* Greenwillow.

Sharmat, Marjorie Weinman. (1998). *Nate the Great and Me: The Case of the Fleeing Fang.* (M. Simont, Illus.). Delacorte.

Siebert, Diane. (1989). *Heartland.* Harper Trophy.

Silverstein, Shel. (1964). *The Giving Tree.* Harper & Row.

Sis, Peter. (1991). *Follow the Dream: The Story of Christopher Columbus.* Knopf.

Turner, Ann Warren. (1992). *Katie's Trunk.* Macmillan.

White, E. B. (1952). *Charlotte's Web.* Harper & Row.

Wick, Walter. (1997). *A Drop of Water: A Book of Science and Wonder.* Scholastic.

Winter, Jeanette. (1988). *Follow the Drinking Gourd.* Knopf.

Yolen, Jane. (1992). *Encounter.* Harcourt.

Figure 4.1

(continued)

Grades 4 through 5

Ackerman, Karen. (1994). *Night Crossing.* Knopf.

Arnosky, Jim. (2002). *Field Trips.* HarperCollins.

Avi. (1995). *Poppy.* Orchard Books.

———. (2002). *Crispin: The Cross of Lead.* Hyperion Press.

Babbitt, Natalie. (1975). *Tuck Everlasting.* Farrar.

Banks, Lynne R. (1980). *Indian in the Cupboard.* Doubleday.

Blume, Judy. (1972). *Tales of a Fourth Grade Nothing.* Dell.

Blumenthal, Deborah. (2001). *Aunt Clare's Yellow Beehive Hair.* (M. Grandpre, Illus.). Dial.

Bridges, Ruby. (1999). *Through My Eyes.* Scholastic.

Brooks, Bruce. (1990). *Everywhere.* HarperCollins.

Bruchac, Joseph. (2001). *Sacajawea.* Scholastic.

Cleary, Beverly. (1991). *Strider.* Morrow.

———. (1996). *Dear Mr. Henshaw.* Morrow.

———. (1999). *Ramona's World.* Morrow.

Clements, Andrew. (2001). *School Story.* (B. Selznick, Illus.). Simon & Schuster.

Coerr, Eleanor. (1977). *Sadako and the Thousand Paper Cranes.* Putnam.

Curtis, Christopher Paul. (1999). *Bud, Not Buddy.* Delacorte.

Dahl, Roald. (1961). *James and the Giant Peach: A Children's Story.* Knopf.

Danzinger, Paula. (1974). *The Cat Ate My Gymsuit.* Delacorte.

Erdrich, Louise. (1999). *The Birchbark House.* Hyperion.

Freedman, Russell. (1987). *Lincoln: A Photobiography.* Clarion.

George, Jean Craighead. (1959). *My Side of the Mountain.* Dutton.

Giff, Patricia Reilly. (1997). *Lily's Crossing.* Delacorte.

Hahn, Mary Downing. (1986). *Wait Till Helen Comes.* Clarion.

———. (2001). *Anna on the Farm.* Clarion.

Holt, Kimberly Willis. (2001). *Dancing in the Cadillac Light.* Putnam.

Howe, Deborah. (1979). *Bunnicula: A Rabbit Tail of Mystery.* (James Howe, Illus.). Avon.

Joosse, Barbara. (2001). *Ghost Wings.* (G. Potter, Illus.). Chronicle.

Kinsey-Warnock, Natalie. (1991). *The Night the Bells Rang.* Cobblehill.

Konigsburg, E. L. (1967). *From the Mixed-Up Files of Mrs. Basil E. Frankweiler.* Atheneum.

Lewis, C. S. (1994). *The Lion the Witch and the Wardrobe.* Harper.

Lowry, Lois. (1989). *Number the Stars.* Houghton Mifflin.

McSwigan, Marie. (1942). *Snow Treasure.* Scholastic.

Naylor, Phyllis Reynolds. (1991). *Shiloh.* Macmillan.

O'Dell, Scott. (1990). *The Island of the Blue Dolphins.* Houghton Mifflin.

Paterson, Katherine. (1977). *Bridge to Terabithia.* Harper.

Paulsen, Gary. (1987). *Hatchet.* Bradbury Press.

Polacco, Patricia. (1994). *Pink and Say.* Philomel.

Raskin, Ellen. (1978). *The Westing Game.* Dutton.

Reeder, Carolyn. (1989). *Shades of Gray.* Macmillan.

Rowling, J. K. (1997). *Harry Potter and the Sorcerer's Stone.* Arthur A. Levine.

Ruckman, Ivy. (1984). *Night of the Twisters.* Crowell.

Sciezska, Jon. (1997). *Math Curse.* (L. Smith, Illus.). Viking.

Tchana, Katrin. (2000). *The Serpent Slayer and Other Stories of Strong Women.* Little Brown.

Wilder, Laura Ingalls. (1953). *Little House on the Prairie.* Harper & Row.

Winthrop, Elizabeth. (1985). *The Castle in the Attic.* Holiday House.

Grades 6 through 8

Ackerman, Karen. (1991). *The Leaves in October.* Atheneum.

Adams, Richard. (1972). *Watership Down.* Macmillan.

Almond, David. (1998). *Skellig.* Dell Yearling.

Figure 4.1

(continued)

Grades 6 through 8 (continued)

Anderson, Janet. S. (1997). *Going Through the Gate.* Dutton.

Angelou, Maya. (1969). *I Know Why the Caged Bird Sings.* Bantam.

Anonymous. (1971). *Go Ask Alice.* Prentice Hall.

Armstrong, Jennifer. (1992). *Steal Away.* Orchard.

Asimov, Isaac. (1966). *Fantastic Voyage.* Bantam Books.

Auel, Jean M. (1985). *The Mammoth Hunters.* Bantam Books.

Barron, T. A. (1990). *Heartlight.* Philomel.

Bauer, Joan. (2000). *Hope Was Here.* Putnam.

Burnford, Sheila Every. (1961). *The Incredible Journey.* Little, Brown.

Campbell, Eric. (1991). *The Place of Lions.* Harcourt.

Clements, Andrew. (1996). *Frindle.* Simon & Schuster.

Collier, James Lincoln. (1994). *With Every Drop of Blood.* Delacorte.

Conrad, Pam. (1985). *Prairie Songs.* Harper & Row.

Cottonwood, Joe. (1995). *Quake!* Scholastic.

Creech, Sharon. (1990). *Absolutely Normal Chaos.* Harper Trophy.

Curtis, Christopher Paul. (1995). *The Watsons Go to Birmingham—1963.* Delacorte.

Deuker, Carl. (1993). *Heart of a Champion.* Joy Street Books.

Fenner, Carol. (1995). *Yolanda's Genius.* M. K. McElderry Books.

Forbes, Esther. (1971). *Johnny Tremain.* Houghton Mifflin.

Fox, Paula. (1984). *One-Eyed Cat.* Dell.

Freedman, Russell. (1997). *Out of Darkness: The Story of Louis Braille.* Clarion.

Grimes, Nikki. (1998). *Jazmin's Notebook.* Dial.

Haddix, Margaret Peterson. (1995). *Running Out of Time.* Simon & Schuster.

———. (1998). *Among the Hidden.* Aladdin.

———. (2001). *Among the Imposters.* Aladdin.

Hahn, Mary Downing. (1994). *Time for Andrew: A Ghost Story.* Clarion.

Henderson, Aileen. (1995). *The Summer of the Bonepile Monster.* Milkweed.

Hesse, Karen. (1994). *Phoenix Rising.* Holt.

———. (1997). *Out of the Dust.* Scholastic.

Hickam, Homer H. (1999). *Rocket Boys.* Delacorte.

Hobbs, Will. (1993). *Beardance.* Maxwell Macmillan.

———. (1996). *Far North.* Morrow.

Hughes, Monica. (1990). *Invitation to the Game.* Simon & Schuster.

Hunt, Irene. (1970). *No Promises in the Wind.* Grosset & Dunlap.

Janeczko, Paul. (2001). *A Poke in the Eye: A Collection of Concrete Poems.* Candlewick.

Korman, Gordon. (1992). *The Twinkie Squad.* Scholastic.

———. (1993). *The Toilet Paper Tigers.* Scholastic.

Levine, Gail Carson. (1997). *Ella Enchanted.* HarperCollins.

———. (1999). *Dave at Night.* HarperCollins.

Lowry, Lois. (1993). *The Giver.* Bantam Doubleday Dell.

———. (1995). *Anastasia, Absolutely.* Houghton Mifflin.

MacLachlan, Patricia. (1993). *Baby.* Delacorte.

Mead, Alice. (1995). *Junebug.* Farrar.

Meyer, Carolyn. (1993). *White Lilacs.* Harcourt.

Myers, Edward. (1994). *Climb or Die.* Hyperion.

Naidoo, Beverly. (1997). *No Turning Back: A Novel of South Africa.* HarperCollins.

Naylor, Phyllis Reynolds. (1994). *The Fear Place.* Maxwell Macmillan.

———. (1996). *Shiloh Season.* Atheneum.

———. (2000). *Jade Green: A Ghost Story.* Maxwell Macmillan.

Nixon, Joan Lowery. (1993). *The Name of the Game Was Murder.* Delacorte.

North, Sterling. (1963). *Rascal.* Scholastic.

Park, Linda. (2001). *A Single Shard.* Clarion.

Paterson, Katherine. (1978). *The Great Gilly Hopkins.* Harper & Row.

Figure 4.1

(concluded)

Grades 6 through 8 (concluded)

Patneaude, David. (1993). *Someone Was Watching*. A. Whitman.

Paulsen, Gary. (1987). *Hatchet*. Trumpet.

———. (1990). *Woodsong*. Scholastic.

———. (1990). *Canyons*. Delacorte.

Philbrick, W. Rodman. (1993). *Freak the Mighty*. Scholastic.

Randle, Kristen D. (1995). *The Only Alien of the Planet*. Scholastic.

Raskin, Ellen. (1978). *The Westing Game*. Dutton.

Rinaldi, Ann. (1993). *In My Father's House*. Scholastic.

Robinson, Barbara. (1994). *The Best School Year Ever*. HarperCollins.

Sachar, Louis. (1998). *Holes*. Farrar, Straus & Giroux.

Saldana, Jerry. (1990). *The Jumping Tree*. Delacorte.

Spinelli, Jerry. (1990). *Maniac Magee*. Scholastic.

———. (2001). *Loser*. Laura Geringer Books.

Taylor, Mildred D. (1995). *The Well: David's Story*. Dial.

Wisler, G. Clifton. (1991). *Red Cap*. Lodestar Books.

Woodruff, Elvira. (1994). *Magnificent Mummy Maker*. Scholastic.

fine for student use. Acquiring the materials and supplies for your classroom is an important part of arranging the physical environment. And don't forget to drop a thank-you note to each of the donors. You want the goodwill you have established to continue throughout the year.

Arranging the Room

When we revisit the quote at the beginning of the chapter, Sharon Taberski reminds us that the look of the classroom sends a powerful message to all who walk through the door. She extends that idea when she explains, "When we create classroom environments that are attractive, comfortable, and purposeful, providing materials that support our work with children, structuring our time to support our goals, then we'll surely reap the results of our efforts" (Taberski, 2000, p. 33). Included in this section are two classroom maps and a guided tour of each room to help illuminate the purposes behind the design. The following list of questions provides a framework for developing a classroom design:

1. Is there a meeting space where students can comfortably sit and listen?
2. How will the desks and tables be arranged?
3. Are materials easy to locate and return?
4. Are students going to manage their own supplies or will group supplies be provided?
5. Is there a classroom library filled with books from all genres and cultures and a wide variety of other print materials?
6. Are books well organized and clearly displayed? Is there a system for book checkout?
7. Are there quiet spaces for independent reading, writing, and listening?

8. Is there a well-stocked writing center?

9. Is there a designated space to meet with small groups or conference with individuals?

10. If parent volunteers are working in the classroom, is there a comfortable spot for them to sit and work?

11. Are all areas clearly labeled with guidelines and expectations?

Primary Map and Tour

Web Link:
Research References
for Emergent Literacy/
Beginning Reading

Welcome to Mrs. Lambert's first grade classroom. Just seeing the map in Figure 4.2 is not enough; it is important to understand why Mrs. Lambert set up her classroom the way she did and what purpose each area serves. Let's accompany Mrs. Lambert as she leads us on a tour around her classroom. We begin in the writing center, which has cans filled with different colorful pens and pencils, a variety of colors and types of paper, and other interesting things including a mailbox and a magnetic board filled with letters. "I've lowered this large rectangular table so that my students can sit on the floor and work here. This provides more space by eliminating the need for chairs. Oftentimes I'll sit here with them and have on-the-spot conferences during writing workshop."

As we walk across the front of her room, we pass the listening center and a basket labeled "Poetry Center" filled with supplies. We arrive at the heart of the primary classroom, the meeting area. "This space is our meeting area. This is where we gather every morning to read a story, chant a poem or sing a song, and do the shared writing of the morning message." Notice how the meeting space is large enough for all the students to sit comfortably. Mrs. Lambert has placed a colorful rug on the floor for her students to sit on, an easel to hold the books she is reading, a pocket chart on a stand to display the poems and songs, an overhead projector on a low cart that she uses during her writing workshop mini-lessons, and a short director's chair with the words "Sharing Chair" painted on the back.

The tour continues around to the back of the room where we pass by the reading center and the parent helper table. As we turn the corner, there is a kidney-shaped table surrounded by eight stools where the students sit for small group reading lessons. "The stools take up less space than chairs and tuck neatly under the table when we are finished using them," the teacher pointed out. "Space saving is the key."

The classroom is filled with print that is appropriate and interesting to first graders. There is a word wall filled with the high-frequency words that her students used to misspell in their writing, as well as charts with different graphic organizers that Mrs. Lambert and her students created during their science and social studies lessons. Every space of Mrs. Lambert's classroom is carefully designed to meet the diverse needs of her students.

Intermediate/Middle School Map and Tour

"Welcome. My name is Mr. Augustino, and I am going to show you around my fifth grade classroom. Let's begin in my favorite area, the reading area. I found this couch at a garage sale and the lamps and rugs are from the local thrift store. The students love sitting here and reading their novels in preparation for literature circles." (See

Figure 4.2

Primary classroom map

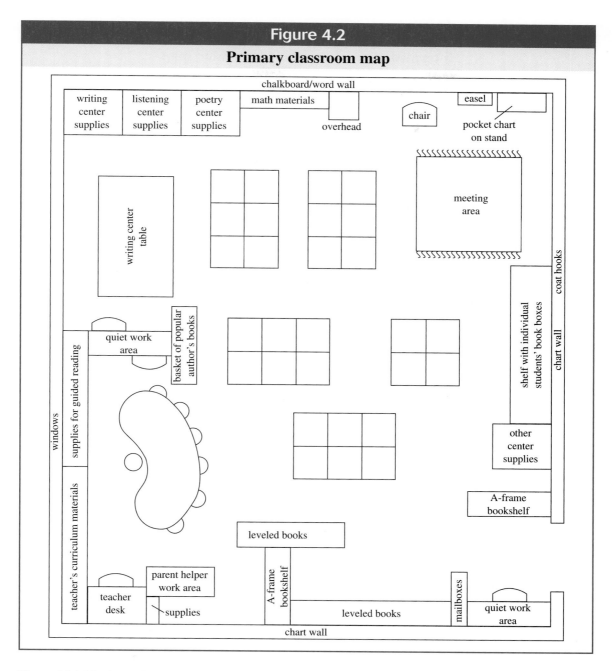

Figure 4.3.) Mr. Augustino uses Fountas and Pinnell's (2001) "turn taking system" to ensure every student gets a comfy place to read once a week. To implement this system write each reading space (couch, pillow, bean bag chair) on a long piece of paper

Figure 4.3

Intermediate/middle school classroom map

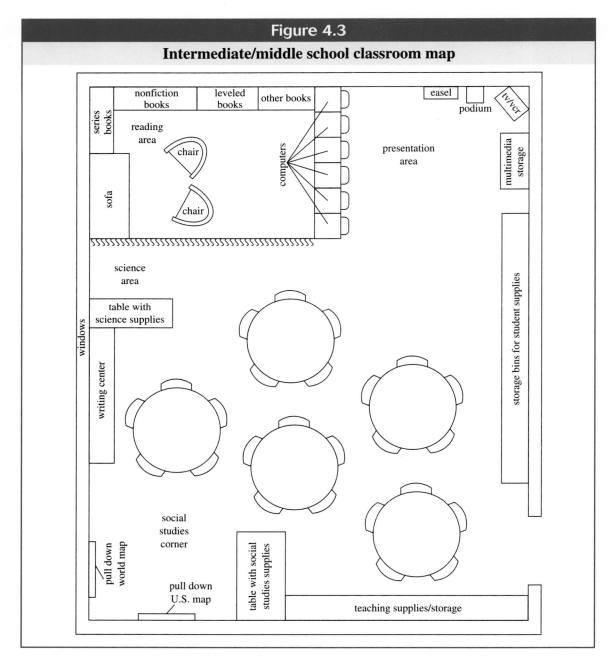

and each child's name on a clothespin. Each day children move their clothespins, in order, to a new spot; this makes selecting a reading space quick and easy. We notice the surrounding shelves are filled with books from all genres, allowing all students' interests to be fulfilled. Titles selected for a new round of literature circles catch our interest, and we stop to take a peek. The theme is strong characters across cultures, and the offerings are enticing: *Bud Not Buddy* (Curtis, 1999), *The Birchbark House* (Erdrich, 1999), *Jazmin's Notebook* (Grimes, 1998), *Our Only May Amelia* (Holm, 1999), and *Dragon's Gate* (Yep, 1993).

"Over in this corner is the presentation area. I borrowed this old music stand from the band director and brought the karaoke machine from home because my daughter no longer uses it. In this area students give their presentations using a variety of media." The students in Mr. Augustino's class have been trained in using the VCR camera, the digital camera, the scanner, and the appropriate computer programs like PowerPoint and HyperStudio to create multimedia presentations. "As part of the school supply list my students bring in a VCR tape, a cassette tape, and five CD-ROMs or floppy disks to record their presentations throughout the year."

"This is the science area where students do activities related to our current science theme. We are studying the human body now." As we glance around, we see posters of the body and a microscope and slides with different germs and other interesting specimens to examine. An exercise chart, where students are recording their daily exercise, is posted next to the food pyramid. Next to the science area is the social studies corner. "You'll notice the social studies corner is stocked with maps, atlases, a globe, and other resources for students to use when they are researching different topics. You can see that I do not have a teacher's desk, just these round tables around the room, where I meet with small groups or individuals for reading and writing conferences."

As we look around Mr. Augustino's classroom, we see that most of the print hanging on the walls is generated by the students as they read and write to learn about topics that interest them. It is a bustling place when the students are present, and each area of the room is clearly labeled with its purpose and guidelines for the students to follow while they are working there.

Creating Literacy Centers

If a teacher wants to have blocks of time to meet with small groups for focused reading lessons like guided reading, she must plan activities that will engage the other students while she is working with a small group. This idea is echoed by Fountas and Pinnell (1996) when they state, "All other class members must be engaged in meaningful literacy. They must be able to function without teacher assistance, maintaining and managing their own learning. It will not be productive (or even efficient) for children to be doing busy work like coloring or fill-in-the-blank worksheets" (p. 53). To manage these types of activities many teachers choose to use literacy centers. The following section includes some ideas for literacy centers.

The reading center is a quiet, comfortable area where children go to enjoy good books. The center might have a small carpet, pillows, and a lamp. The books are organized and displayed in a kid-friendly way. For young children, it is much easier for them to choose books if they can see the cover. By placing books in baskets, along a chalk rail, or on an easel, they are able to look at the covers when they are choosing books. For older students, displaying some of the books with the spine facing out is appropriate, but you still want to have spaces to display books so they can see the covers. Spinning racks are very good for display as they take up little space and make the covers, with their attractive illustrations, visible. After all, it is the cover of the book that grabs the reader's attention.

Students listen to their favorite stories on cassette tapes in the listening center. Many teachers choose to use a cassette tape player with individual headphones for the listening center. Unfortunately, the headphone cords are easily tangled and children usually need assistance to untangle them. To avoid this problem there are two other options. First, the children can listen to the tape recorder with the volume low enough not to disturb the other students. The second option is to locate a small amount of money to purchase individual tape players with their own headsets from a local discount store. These are fairly inexpensive ($10 or less) and allow the students to listen to books on tape anywhere in the room. This is especially important in smaller classrooms where there is not enough space for each center and even a little noise can be quite distracting.

Children love the poetry center. It is a place where they reread and interact with the poems the class has been practicing during their shared reading lessons. Some teachers put each poem on an overhead transparency and place their overhead projector close enough to the floor so that the students can sit around it. Children enjoy using different kinds of small pointers and other tools to track the print in the poems. Small colored overhead tiles (usually used for math lessons) are also placed in the center so that students can highlight words they know, word wall words, words that begin with a certain letter, or anything else they want to focus on while they are reading the poem. Teachers also make a paper copy of each poem, which students then store in their own three-ring binder of poetry. Reading the poems in the binder is also something students can do in the poetry center.

For upper elementary grade children the poetry center might include a growing collection of magnetic words for creating magnetic poetry and five or six cookie sheets, which provide a creative work space. Once students have created a poem on the cookie sheet, they simply write their final creation on a 5 × 8 index card. These cards are added to a growing collection on a nearby bulletin board or slipped into a photo album with plastic sleeves. Including a collection of poetry anthologies will inspire their poetry writing.

Primary teachers spend large amounts of time to ensure that their classroom is a print-rich environment. Due to the busy schedules of the day, students are often not given time to read all the print in the room. The "read the room" center provides a focused time to read and learn from the print resources available in the classroom. When in this center, students use different types of long pointers to track the print they are reading. Pointers are simply made by affixing a colorful eraser on the top of a wooden dowel rod. Yardsticks and rulers also make great pointers. To increase motivation, some teachers also provide students with different size, shapes, and colors of sunglasses to use while perusing the print in the room. Also, students may use clipboards to record different words that they find around the room.

The fine arts center provides students with opportunities to dramatize the stories they are reading and to respond to a familiar literature selection in other artistic ways. The supplies in the center might include different types of puppets, reader's theater

Teaching Strategy:
Scavenger Hunts

The teacher needs to demonstrate for students how to use a software program.

scripts like the one provided in Chapter 10, art supplies, and directions to make different projects like dioramas, mobiles, and collages.

In the computer center students use the different software programs to enhance their literacy lessons. Many appropriate programs are highlighted in this textbook. Teachers also post a student-friendly website for investigation during the week. Depending on the number of computers in the classroom, teachers must generate specific guidelines for computer use. Who is in control of the mouse? How long does each child get to spend at the computer? When do you print out work? Can students take their disks home to do work? Which websites are appropriate for classroom use?

Once the teacher has created and designed the centers, she must teach the rules and the routines to her students. This is a crucial part of classroom management. At the beginning of the year the teacher plans time each day to introduce a literacy center and model the use of the materials in it. Once she has introduced a few centers, she divides the children into their work groups and monitors their activities while they are using the centers. The teacher continues this routine, by introducing one or two centers each day, then allowing the children to work in the center while she models, monitors, and guides them. After each center time, the teacher takes a few minutes to "debrief" the students and discuss the good behaviors she observed. The teacher should not plan on meeting with small groups until she is confident that the class knows how to independently use the centers in an appropriate manner. The time invested at the beginning of the year will pay off handsomely later, when students can work on their own without disturbing the teacher while she is working with small groups.

THE SOCIAL ENVIRONMENT

The social environment of your classroom is created day by day as you and your students get to know each other. Think of your classroom as a home and the students in it as a family. What are the characteristics of a happy family? What creates a nurturing home environment?

To begin with, people in a family care about and respect one another; this care and respect is modeled by the parents. In a classroom it is your job to model care and respect for your students by treating each child as a capable, unique individual. Secondly, in a caring family people work together to accomplish goals; the same is true for a classroom. With carefully designed large and small group activities you can demonstrate for students how important it is to help each other when they are reading and writing. When you encourage students to work together to peer edit a writing workshop piece or discuss a novel during a literature circle, you are helping to create a collaborative classroom environment. Next, family members respect each other's differences, strengths, and weaknesses. They celebrate accomplishments and rally around a member who is having a bad day. Children in a classroom need the same kind of encouragement and support to feel a sense of belonging. Finally, when a child in a family is having severe behavior or learning problems, parents often seek outside help. That same help may be available to you in your school community with social workers, psychologists, reading resource teachers, speech and language pathologists, learning disabilities resource teachers, nurses, and the school principal there to help. Of course, there will be good days and bad days. As you continue reading this chapter, you will become familiar with the characteristics of learners with special needs, learn more about your role as a teacher, discover a sampling of strategies to assist diverse learners, and find out how to reach out for assistance to colleagues, parents, and other organizations to help make every day a good day. Let's begin by getting acquainted with the variety of diverse learners who have special needs.

ADDRESSING DIVERSITY: LEARNERS WITH SPECIAL NEEDS

In Chapter 3 you visited Kingsway School. The teachers at that school have learned how to modify their literacy curriculum to successfully include learners with special needs into their general education classrooms. Today it is most unusual to have a classroom without a child with special learning needs. Usually there are two or three, or even more, students who need additional instructional assistance. Our role as the teacher is to create a respectful, inclusive social environment where *all* students are encouraged and expected to grow and learn.

Students Who Are Struggling Readers and Writers

Schools across the country face the challenge of educating students who struggle with literacy skills. In your classroom you will also face that challenge. Who are the struggling readers and writers? In their book *Schools That Work: Where All Children*

Read and Write (2002), Richard Allington and Patricia Cunningham answer that question by discussing three factors that affect students' success in school: poverty, parents' education, and gender. Children who grow up in poverty are often at-risk for school failure. The environmental factors related to living in "poverty contribute to mild mental retardation by limiting access to experiences that lay the foundation for educational achievement and good health" (Henley, Ramsey, & Algozzine, 2002, p. 58). To help a child of poverty succeed in a balanced literacy classroom a caring teacher creates ways to support the child in school.

Jeanne Chall and her associates at Harvard University conducted a study to determine what instructional techniques were effective in supporting struggling, low-income intermediate grade readers. The findings summarized by Chall and Mary E. Curtis (2003) show that the students who made at least one full year's growth in reading achievement from one school year to the next benefited from the following instructional techniques:

- Reading instruction was provided on or above the child's current reading level (not below);
- Instruction was given in comprehension of texts in reading, social studies, science, health, and other content areas;
- Meaning vocabulary was stressed during content area reading instruction as well as during reading language arts;
- Diverse materials were provided on a wide variety of reading levels, some of which challenged even the best readers;
- Frequent field trips and other activities were conducted to expose students to new experiences and new vocabulary and to help build up background knowledge for reading about the unfamiliar;
- Homework was assigned in reading that included workbooks in the earlier grades, and reading of trade books and content area materials in the later grades; and
- The children's parents were in direct personal contact with their teachers (p. 417).

In addition to these techniques, supplying the child with reading material to take home on a daily basis is a must. For more ideas consult with your district or school social worker.

"Parental educational attainment is related to the success children experience in school" (Cunningham & Allington, 2002, p. 3). Schools and teachers expect parents to be involved in their child's education. Unfortunately, not all parents have the same beliefs. Although we know that parents are important in a child's school career, we must not penalize those students who do not get parental support. Look for other ways to support the child in your school community. Seek out peer tutors, cross-age partners, or a volunteer from the community to listen to the child read, help him or her complete homework, or prepare for tests.

When we look at the factor of gender, we find that "boys, more often than girls, are retained in grade, placed in remedial classes, identified as having learning disabilities, and suspended from school" (Allington & Cunningham, 2002, p. 6). Again, we must adjust our teaching methods to match the learning styles of the boys in our class by increasing active, hands-on activities. Instead of choral reading a poem or song, act it out. To spice up a retelling, have students perform a puppet show. Provide children with opportunities to build, create, and experiment as they learn to read and write.

Each individual student in your classroom will come to you with strengths and weaknesses; it is your responsibility to become knowledgeable in the area of reading and writing development and skilled in assessment and intervention techniques. The information in this textbook will help you get started. Throughout this text you will find practical, helpful strategies for assisting students who may struggle to learn to read and write.

Students with Sensory Impairments

Students with visual or hearing impairments may experience difficulties acquiring literacy skills. Because seeing and hearing are vital to school learning, these students benefit from responsive teachers who collaborate with support personnel to make adaptations and provide appropriate learning tools to increase their students' abilities to learn. A list of assistive technology tools appears in Figure 4.4.

Visually Impaired Students. Most students who are visually impaired have limited ability to see but are not blind. A visually impaired student may need adapted reading material in Braille, large print, or audiotape format. In addition, some visually impaired learners may use magnifying lenses and bright light or hold material close or at a certain angle to help them read. If a student is having trouble tracking print while reading, you may consider supplying a pointer or highlighting tape. For young learners you can model the use of these items during a shared reading lesson. A computer with a text enlarger and/or a speech synthesizer attached to a standard word processing program will aid students in completing written tasks. Each visually impaired child has unique learning needs and will need specific modifications. Collaboration with the vision itinerant specialist or other knowledgeable professionals in your school community is a must.

The following general adaptations may be helpful: When arranging the physical environment of your classroom, ensure that there are clear open spaces to move from place to place. Try to reduce the glare from lighting or reflection such as bright sunlight on snow outside classroom windows. Consider assigning a visually impaired child a responsible partner at the beginning of the year to help orient them to the physical arrangement of the class and school. When presenting written information to the class, use a white board with a black marker instead of a chalkboard to increase visual clarity. Keep whiteboard space uncluttered and erased clean so there are no phantom marks to distract the learner. Model for students the importance of speaking clearly and giving clear directions. Get in the habit of addressing students by name so that the visually impaired child will begin to recognize his or her classmates' voices.

Hearing Impaired Students. A hearing impaired child has a limited ability or an inability to receive auditory information, which, in turn, interferes with his or her learning. Hearing impaired students may wear a hearing aid or use an FM system (teacher wears microphone and student wears receiver) to amplify sound. Both of these adaptive devices amplify all of the sounds in the room, not just the voices, so it

Figure 4.4   Assistive technology tools

What Is Assistive Technology (AT)?

- Refers to items, pieces of equipment, or products used to increase, maintain, or improve the capabilities of individuals with disabilities.
- These items are often categorized according to their level of complexity.

Examples of low- and high-technology solutions for reading and writing follow:

Activity	Low-Technology Solutions	High-Technology Solutions
Reading		
• Holding book	• Nonslip mat • Book holder	• Electronic version of book on computer
• Turning pages	• Rubber finger • Universal cuff with pencil and eraser • Head/mouth stick	• Electric page turner
• Reading words	• Reading glasses • Magnifying glass • Enlarged print • Slant board • Ruler to read line by line • Cardboard "jig" to isolate words (*"jig" is a card with a rectangle cut out to read word by word*)	• Enlarged computer monitor • Book on tape • Software that "reads out loud" • Reading pen • Language master with books
Writing		
• Holding pencil	• Built-up pencil • Larger writing instruments • Weighted pen or pencil • Head or mouth stick to hold instrument	• Orthotics • Prosthetics • Word processor • Laptop computer
• Keyboarding	• Keyboard mitt with isolated fingers • Keyboard overlay • Head or mouth stick	• Voice recognition software • Scanning software • Alternative keyboards (*expanding or miniature*) • Word prediction software • Spell check • Cassette recorder • Augmentative communications devices
• Using paper	• Templates • Color-coded or texture-line paper • Tape paper to desk • Clipboard	• Augmentative communications devices • Word processor

Adapted from: Van Laarhoven, T., Munk, D., Bosma, J., & Rouse, J. (June 2002). "Assistive Technology for Individuals with Learning Disabilities." Paper presented at Partnership Conference, Northern Illinois University, DeKalb, IL.

is important to reduce extraneous noise. One of a hearing impaired child's greatest literacy difficulties is learning the vocabulary and nuances of the English language. When introducing new vocabulary use a variety of modalities to increase understanding. For hearing impaired emergent readers, the language experience approach, where the child's dictated stories become his or her reading material, is often a more effective path to reading success than phonics. Some hearing impaired students will use speech reading (watching others' lips, mouths, and expressions) or require an interpreter. When you or your students are sharing oral information, make sure that you are facing the hearing impaired student, enunciating clearly, using sufficient volume, and staying in the same location. Also, use a variety of visual and tactile aids to give directions or explain concepts. If the hearing impaired child is using sign language to communicate, you may want to invite a deaf education teacher into your classroom to help you and your students learn some basic signs.

Students with Communication Disorders

Web Link:
Speech Therapy
Activities

Children with communication disorders have difficulties with speech and/or language that interfere with their communication (Friend & Bursuck, 2001). Two of the most common speech problems are articulation and stuttering. Articulation is the inability to pronounce sounds correctly at and after the developmentally appropriate age, and stuttering is where a child involuntarily repeats a sound or word disrupting speech fluency. Choral reading of poetry, chants, rhymes, and raps helps students build oral language fluency in a nonthreatening way. Also, adapting reader's theater scripts so that students read in small groups instead of individually will help to build a child's fluency and self-confidence.

Students with language problems have trouble with receptive and expressive language. Learners who struggle with receptive language may not understand questions, may have difficulty following directions, and are unable to retain verbally presented information. Students with expressive language difficulties are unable to communicate their thoughts clearly because their spoken language includes incorrect grammar, limited use of vocabulary, and frequent hesitations (Friend & Bursuck, 2001). Children with receptive language difficulties often have trouble with reading comprehension. These students benefit from a strategy developed by Linda Hoyt called "frontloading." Before reading a text teachers engage learners in hands-on activities to teach the concepts and content that will later be presented in the text. You will find more powerful prereading activities in Chapter 8. Your school's speech-language pathologist is a knowledgeable resource person who can provide a wealth of activities to boost the skills of a child with communication disorders. (See additional ideas in the Managing a Diverse Classroom section.)

Students with Mild Mental Retardation

It is as difficult to describe a child with mild mental retardation as it is to characterize any individual student in your classroom. "Students with mild mental retardation demonstrate specific learning problems in mental processing, social adaptation, and perception. However, students with mild mental retardation show a great deal of variability in learning characteristics, and generalization about their abilities or disabilities can lead to stereotypes and negative teacher expectations" (Henley, Ramsey, & Algozzine, 2002, p. 87). As stressed throughout this section, before adapting a lesson it is essential to know the individual child's needs. Some powerful reading strategies for students with mild mental retardation are also effective with all learners. They include helping students connect books and related activities to real-life experiences. During read-alouds and independent reading time invite your students to make connections to the ideas presented in the books. To model this strategy think aloud as you read texts and make comments like, "This story reminds me of something that happened to me yesterday (or a plot in another book, or a world event)." To strengthen comprehension, teach students how to use story maps or other graphic organizers to retell stories or summarize nonfiction texts. Model for students how to monitor their comprehension by self-questioning during reading. For example, while reading a nonfiction text use sticky notes to mark new information you learned and jot down questions you have about the topic. Provide students with frequent, meaningful opportunities to practice these strategies. And then give positive feedback for their efforts.

Students with Specific Learning Disabilities

The characteristics of children with specific learning disabilities are as unique as the individual students who possess the traits. In 1977 the U.S. Office of Education developed functional criteria for determining whether a child has a learning disability. Through a variety of assessment measures the school's multidisciplinary team must determine that a child is not achieving commensurate with his or her age or ability in one or more of the following areas: oral expression, listening comprehension, written expression, basic reading skill, reading comprehension, mathematical calculation, or mathematical reasoning. Students whose discrepancy between ability and achievement is due primary to a visual, hearing, or motor handicap, mental retardation, emotional disturbance, or environmental, cultural, or economic disadvantage cannot be identified as having a learning disability. It is important for teachers to match their instructional strategies to the learning styles of their individual students.

Students with Behavioral and Emotional Disorders

When children have long-term extensive unacceptable behavior problems that occur in a number of different settings, these are considered to be behavioral and emotional disorders. Such children may strike out aggressively either verbally and/or physically attacking peers or those in authority such as teachers and parents. They may be destructive. Others may withdraw and be silent, exhibit anxiety whenever change in routine occurs, or feel unduly pressured at everyday events. Such behavior disrupts learning not only for the child, but for others in the classroom as well. As teachers, we must become familiar with the student's behavior patterns—both acceptable and unacceptable—and deal with the outbursts in a calm manner. Establishing a predictable daily routine where the child is given choice in at least some parts of the day is helpful. To increase a child's desire to participate and improve their literacy skills, select reading and writing activities that the student enjoys. You can determine this by collecting anecdotal records pertaining to the child's interests; you will learn more about these in the next chapter.

Students with ADD/ADHD

A child with an **attention deficit disorder (ADD)** has difficulty sustaining attention and in some cases is impulsive. When children are also hyperactive, that is when the disorder becomes labeled **attention deficit hyperactivity disorder (ADHD)**. As a teacher what kind of characteristics are you going to be looking for? The diagnostic criteria for an attention deficit are defined in the American Psychiatric Association's *Diagnostic and Statistical Manual* of *Mental Disorders* (DSM-IV) (1994) and appear in Figure 4.5.

The criteria are divided into two categories: inattention and hyperactivity-impulsivity. When looking at these criteria it is important to note that in order to be diagnosed the symptoms had to be present before the age of seven, must occur in two or more settings, and must interfere with a child's social or academic functioning. A diagnosis for ADHD should only be made after ruling out other factors related to medical, emotional, or environmental variables that could cause similar symptoms. Therefore,

Figure 4.5

Diagnostic criteria for attention deficit hyperactivity disorder

Characteristics of Inattention

1. Often fails to pay close attention to details, makes careless mistakes.
2. Often has difficulty sustaining attention in tasks or play activities.
3. Often does not seem to listen when spoken to.
4. Often has difficulty following through on instructions and finishing schoolwork (not due to oppositional behavior or failure to understand directions).
5. Often has difficulty organizing tasks and activities.
6. Often avoids, dislikes, or is reluctant to engage in tasks that require sustained mental effort (such as schoolwork or homework).
7. Often loses things necessary for tasks (e.g., toys, school assignments, pencils, or books).
8. Is often easily distracted by extraneous stimuli.

Characteristics of Hyperactivity

1. Often fidgets with hands or feet or squirms in seat.
2. Often leaves seat in classroom.
3. Often runs about or climbs excessively in situations where inappropriate.
4. Often has difficulty playing or engaging in leisure activities quietly.
5. Is often "on the go" or often acts as if "driven by a motor."
6. Often talks excessively.

Characteristics of Impulsivity

1. Often blurts out answers.
2. Often has difficulty awaiting turn.
3. Often interrupts or intrudes on others.

Source: Adapted from American Psychiatric Association. (1994). *Diagnostic and statistical manual of mental disorders* (4th ed.). Washington, DC: Author.

physicians, psychologists, educators, and parents work together to conduct a multifaceted evaluation of the child including medical studies, psychological and educational testing, speech and language assessment, neurological evaluation, and behavioral rating scales completed by the teacher and parent. Some students who are diagnosed will begin taking medication and others will not. There are two types of medication prescribed for students with attentional deficits: stimulants (such as Ritalin) and antidepressants (often given to teenagers who are fighting depression along with learning and attentional issues) (Fielding, 1999). Whether a child in your classroom is diagnosed and on medication or not, you will still have to find effective ways to manage the student's behavior on a daily basis. Elizabeth Fielding (1999) offers a list of suggestions that appear in the Teaching Strategy for the Classroom box later in the chapter.

Students Who Are Gifted and Talented

In your classroom you will not only find children who need modifications to meet curricular expectations but will also find students who have extraordinary abilities and skills. In the 1988 Gifted and Talented Students Act (PL 100-297) the federal government defines gifted students as those who possess demonstrated or potential high-performance capability in intellectual, creative, specific academic and leadership areas, or the performing and visual arts. You will note that their definition includes not only a child with a high IQ, or academic achievement, but those students who excel in other areas. When working with gifted and talented youngsters you need to cultivate and value all areas of intelligence. It is helpful to refer to Howard Gardner's Multiple Intelligences Model (1993). Gardner recommends that teachers use activities that require one or more intelligences to develop and enhance the creative and cognitive strengths of the students. The following list gives a teaching idea for each type of intelligence.

- **Linguistic intelligence:** Respond to a text you are reading by writing a poem.
- **Musical intelligence:** Compose and perform a song about a character from a book.
- **Logical-mathematical intelligence:** At the end of the year, survey your classmates about their top ten books. Tally, graph, and present your results.
- **Spatial intelligence:** Draw a map of the character's journey throughout a book.
- **Bodily/kinesthetic:** Play charades with book titles and favorite characters.
- **Interpersonal:** Work in a small group to present a reader's theater performance.
- **Intrapersonal:** Read silently and independently and respond to your book in a personal reading log.
- **Naturalistic:** After reading books about animals, make a chart to classify the different types of animals.
- **Spiritualistic:** After reading a book about friendship, list what makes a good friend.

By offering all of your students multiple opportunities to engage in a range of literacy learning experiences you will be able to begin to see which of your students have extraordinary talents. It is important to remember that gifted students come from all walks of life. Consider the thought-provoking words that follow.

One does not need to speak English in order to be gifted or academically talented. Gifted children are found in poor ethnic neighborhoods in Chicago and Los Angeles, in the projects of New York and Miami, and in new immigrant populations found in West Palm Beach and San Francisco. Gifted children are found in the trailer parks and homeless shelters. They are found in rural America and in migrant camps. They are in every school these students attend, and it should be noted that the increase of "students of color" has not been matched by increases in gifted education services that meet their needs. Only now are we paying attention to these children. (Castellano & Diaz, 2002, p. 96)

An observant teacher is one who is searching for the giftedness in all of her students.

English Language Learners

Another rapidly growing population in the nation's classrooms is made up of students whose first language is not English, commonly referred to as English language learners (ELLs). It is estimated that 22 percent of the school-age population live in homes where a language other than English is spoken on a regular basis (Crawford, 1997). Roughly 4 million children between the ages of five and seventeen live in homes where Spanish is the spoken language (Garcia, 2000). Nearly one-fourth of all public school classroom teachers speak some Spanish words or sentences during the school day (Farris, 1999). In addition, growing populations of Asian-speaking children challenge teachers who never had the option to learn related languages as part of their education. In other areas of the United States, Native American children are part of the classroom family. Faced primarily with English-speaking teachers and the bulk of their learning materials in the same language, school days for such students must be daunting indeed. The knowledge Sarah Hudelson, Leslie Poynor, and Paula Wolfe (2003, p. 429) gained from examining case studies guide elementary teachers as they attempt to nurture children's second language development. These informed educators suggest that teachers:

1. Create an environment that both acknowledges and respects the language and literacy development of the child's home and community;
2. Provide multiple opportunities for language interactions that include oral and written experiences with both the teacher and classmates;
3. Observe children's language interactions and plan instructional activities that reflect the reality of the idiosyncratic nature of literacy development in children; and
4. Allow and value the use of the first language in the language and development of the second language.

Later in the chapter you will find more ways to support **English language learners.**

Accomplished Teachers

The International Reading Association's position statement entitled "Excellent Reading Teachers" (2000) suggests that excellent reading teachers possess the characteristics of good teachers in general. Therefore, when looking at the role of the teacher, we will begin by examining what makes a high-quality teacher, then focus on the specific characteristics of an excellent reading teacher. The National Board for Professional Teaching Standards (2001) outlines five core propositions in their policy statement "What Teachers Should Know and Be Able to Do:"

1. Teachers are committed to students and their learning. They are dedicated to making knowledge accessible to all students, celebrating individual differences, and modifying lessons to meet students' needs.

2. Teachers know the subjects they teach and how to teach those subjects to their students. They understand the subject they are teaching and appreciate how that subject is created, organized, linked to other disciplines, and applied in real-world settings.

3. Teachers are responsible for managing and monitoring student learning. Accomplished teachers command a range of generic instructional techniques, know when each is appropriate, and can implement them as needed. They use multiple methods for measuring individual students' growth.

4. Teachers think systematically about their practice and learn from experience. They carefully examine their practice, seek to expand their repertoire, deepen their knowledge, sharpen their judgment, and adapt their teaching to new findings, ideas, and theories.

5. Teachers are members of learning communities. They collaborate with other professionals, parents, and the community for the students' benefit. (National Board for Professional Teaching Standards, 2001)

The characteristics described above are those that all educators should possess. Let's extend those now and look specifically at the characteristics of the reading teacher. In January 2000, the International Reading Association adopted the position statement entitled "Excellent Reading Teachers." This statement details six research-based critical qualities of knowledge and practice for teachers of reading:

1. They understand reading and writing development, and believe all children can learn to read and write.

2. They continually assess children's individual progress and relate reading instruction to the children's previous experiences.

3. They know a variety of ways to teach reading, when to use each method, and how to combine the methods into an effective instructional program.

4. They offer a variety of materials and texts for children to read.

5. They use flexible grouping strategies to tailor instruction to individual students.

6. They are good reading "coaches" (that is, they provide help strategically).

Although these are characteristics of an excellent reading teacher, the first quality underscores what the authors of this textbook stress over and over: reading and writing go hand in hand in a balanced literacy classroom. The rest of the six qualities also reemphasize the importance of the ongoing and varied assessment measures as described in the next chapter and the wide range of instructional methods and materials that you will learn about. In addition, the authors wholeheartedly support the notion that excellent teachers are wise and capable decision makers, mixing and matching strategies to enhance every child as a learner.

BUILDING A COMMUNITY OF LEARNERS

Earlier in the chapter we discussed four tenets that serve as the building blocks of the social foundation of a classroom:

1. Model care and respect.
2. Demonstrate how to work together to accomplish goals.
3. Respect each other's differences, strengths, and weaknesses.
4. Seek outside help for students with severe learning and/or behavior difficulties.

On top of this social foundation, a community of learners is built. A successful learning community must teach, support, and challenge each member in that community. Recall the three principles of balanced instruction in Chapter 1. A thriving learning community is created when (a) teachers know their curricular goals and the needs of their students, (b) they thoughtfully integrate methods that match the goals and needs of their students, and (c) they use a wide variety of materials. Earlier in this chapter you learned how to acquire materials to support the curriculum. As the chapter continues, we will discuss ways to meet a diverse student's needs and also tactics for planning instruction to meet curricular goals.

Classroom Management: Meeting the Needs of All Students

To best meet the needs of all the students who enter your classroom, you have to know how to manage a classroom filled with students with different backgrounds, personalities, and learning needs. The following section will provide some insights into the world of classroom management.

The key principles of classroom management are establishing a reliable routine, communicating clear rules and expectations, and being firm, fair, and consistent when dealing with students. It is important as you think about your first few days of teaching that you try to establish a routine as quickly as possible. Students should know where to hand in homework, where to put notes for you, and how to move from one activity to the next (called "transitioning"). A consistent routine is a lifesaver in a classroom. Children thrive on routine and function much better when they know what to expect. Remember the morning message you learned about in Chapter 3? This powerful activity is a marvelous way to begin a daily routine. After the morning message, it is helpful if you review the day's schedule; this will eliminate questions throughout the day like "Do we have P.E. today?" and "When will it be time for lunch?"

This organizational format is easily adapted for middle grade learners. An advanced organizer for their day is written in a select spot on the chalkboard where students will learn to look for it day after day. Announcements, scheduled class times for content area lessons, and the day's specials are duly noted. If something exciting or unusual is to occur, it might be highlighted as a "News Flash" or some other catchy title. Many students thrive on routine. Life in a classroom has fewer bumps and hitches when students are not surprised by what lies ahead.

Once you have decided on your daily routine, it is important to think about the classroom management plan that you want to employ. Many schools have building-wide discipline plans or grade level specific plans that you will need to know. If this is not the case, then you will need to create your own plan. A small number of rules, usually three or four, clearly stated, is a good place to start. Some teachers choose to just have one rule that covers it all like "Do not disturb the learning of others." It is important to ask students for their input when creating classroom rules. They also need to know what consequences will occur if they choose not to follow the guidelines you have established. This is where parent communication is a must. It is important that those challenging students who are having severe discipline problems be dealt with on an individual basis with regular communication between home and school. Later in the chapter we will take a closer look at strategies for managing students with diverse learning needs.

Managing a Diverse Classroom

Integrated throughout this text you will discover examples of how to modify lessons for learners with diverse needs. It is important to remember that *all* learners benefit from the activities that take place in a balanced literacy classroom. That thought is echoed by Kathryn Au (1997), "Students have the best opportunity to gain experience with the application and orchestration of skills and strategies when they engage in the full processes of reading and writing. That is why authentic literacy activities—reading and writing that is real and meaningful—are central to a successful classroom literacy program, especially for students with diverse backgrounds" (p. 188). In addition to providing students with a well-managed classroom and a balanced curriculum, teachers must know how to modify their management plan and instruction to support students with diverse learning needs.

Classroom management is a major concern of both beginning and experienced teachers. How does one know what is an appropriate reaction to an inappropriate behavior? Should a child with an attention deficit disorder (ADD), or an attention deficit hyperactivity disorder (ADHD), be excused completely for his or her behavior? What are appropriate expectations for the behavior and literacy learning of a student with diverse learning needs? Because each child is unique, this is an area with no easy answers. First and foremost, you must get to know each individual child in addition to his or her family culture and background, academic strengths and weaknesses, and ability to interact socially with others. When you know each student's needs, then you can begin to modify the literacy curriculum to meet their needs. The next section will give you some useful strategies to add to your repertoire.

Struggling Readers

After reviewing six effective research-based reading programs, Ann Duffy-Hester (1999) offers teachers the following ten principles for developing an effective classroom program for struggling readers. Notice as you read through these principles that we have indicated the chapters in this text where you will find the information you need to create this kind of program.

1. Your reading program should be balanced, drawing on multiple theoretical perspectives. (See Chapters 1 and 2.)
2. Every component of the reading program should have a practical and theoretical justification. (See Chapters 1 and 2.)
3. Explicit teaching of word identification, comprehension, and vocabulary strategies may take place in conjunction with authentic reading and writing activities. (See Chapters 7, 8, and 9.)
4. Each day you should read aloud from a variety of genres and provide time for students to read at their instructional and independent levels. (See Chapters 6, 8, and 10.)
5. Your reading instruction should be guided by meaningful reading assessments. (See Chapter 5.)
6. You must become a thoughtful decision maker, using your practical, personal, and theoretical knowledge to inform reading instruction. (Chapters 1, 2, and 3.)
7. Encourage your administrators to provide staff development opportunities that include opportunities to reflect on your current practice. (Chapter 4.)
8. Your reading program should be based on multiple goals for student success, goals as diverse as enhancing voluntary reading, discussion, genre knowledge, and other goals beyond improved test scores. (All chapters.)
9. Provide multiple contexts for student learning and multiple types of tasks. (All chapters.)
10. Design your reading program to support the reading growth of all children, both struggling and nonstruggling readers. (All chapters.)

Students with Communication Disorders

Keep in mind the following four strategies when working with students who have a speech and/or language problem:

1. **Create an accepting social environment:** You set the tone of your classroom. It is important to model tolerance and patience with all learners. Children should feel free to communicate without worrying about making mistakes. When students make a communication error, it is better to model the correct pronunciation or sentence structure for them than to simply correct their mistake. Also, to help children who stutter, allow plenty of time for them to speak, do not interrupt them or supply words, and praise their successful efforts to communicate clearly as you do with your other students.
2. **Encourage listening and teach listening skills:** To teach effective listening begin by modeling what good listeners do. When you are listening to your students, maintain eye contact, lean in to hear them, and acknowledge their thoughts and ideas with a nod or a comment. Before you begin speaking, give

a verbal or visual signal to indicate to your students that you want them to listen. Make oral material easier to understand by sharing information in short segments and using visual aids, graphic organizers, movement, and/or music to engage your learners.

3. **Use modeling to expand students' language:** When students are retelling a story and say "Arthur is funny," you can model a more detailed sentence by replying "Yes, Arthur is funny and he is very smart, too."

4. **Provide meaningful contexts for students to practice speech and language skills:** Throughout this text there are countless ways to engage students in meaningful activities that will build their communication skills (Friend & Bursuck, 1999).

Teaching Strategy for the Classroom

SUGGESTIONS FOR ASSISTING STUDENTS WITH ADHD IN THE CLASSROOM

1. Keep directions simple to facilitate comprehension.
2. Gain eye contact to help children focus before receiving information.
3. Present information in a variety of modes. Write and say directions or show pictures for young learners.
4. Begin and end your lesson by clearly stating key ideas.
5. Allow for more review and reinforcement.
6. Allow more time for tests or the taking of untimed tests.
7. Be consistent and structured. These are two important factors that lead to optimum classroom functioning for these students.
8. Keep distractions to a minimum.
9. Allow older students to tape-record lectures and to take tests orally into a tape recorder.
10. Have the student explain how he learns.
11. Find the strengths. Help students realize and capitalize on what they do well inside and outside the classroom. This will reinforce self-esteem.
12. Uncover and address any weaknesses. Remember, ADHD is often accompanied by other learning disabilities. Be sure these disabilities are also uncovered so that they can be remediated.

Source: Adapted from Fielding, 1999, pp. 17–18.

Students with ADD/ADHD

Other than medication and the suggestions found in the Teaching Strategy in the Classroom box, there are two modification strategies that have been used with ADHD children. One approach is **behavior modification.** The basic premise of this approach is that positive behaviors gain positive reinforcement and negative behaviors receive no reinforcement. When the child does something positive, she may be rewarded by the teacher with stickers or a choice of free time activity. Negative reactions are ignored. For instance, when Erin remembered to do her homework and brought it to school to turn it in, the teacher gave her two stickers. Once Erin collects ten stickers, she gets extra computer time.

A second approach to use with ADHD students is called **cognitive behavior therapy.** Sometimes controversial, cognitive behavior therapy requires the student to "learn to internally reward and support themselves in desired classroom behaviors" (Fielding, 1999, p. 14). The four steps in cognitive behavior therapy are (a) identify the problem, (b) explore strategies to use, (c) review consequences for appropriate and inappropriate behavior, and (d) choose a strategy and implement it. One strategy might be to use small reminder cards taped to a student's desk: Did I turn in my lunch money? Did I write my name on my paper? Did I finish my homework for reading? writing? math? The student is encouraged to give himself self-praise when it is deserved, silently saying "Awesome Job!" or "You're the Best!"

Students with attentional difficulties are not the only students you may encounter who have behavioral difficulties. Unfortunately, there is no magic solution to dealing with children who disrupt the learning in a classroom. As we stated earlier, the keys to classroom management are a reliable routine, clearly stated rules and expectations, and a consistent and fair manner when addressing problems.

English Language Learners

If you are an English-dominant teacher and you find yourself in a multicultural context, LeAnn Putney, Yiqiang Wu, and Joan Wink (1999) offer the following ten-item "What I Can Do" list:

1. I will not make judgments about the students based on any test (language or psychological) that is not in the language of the students.
2. I will not label. If English is the language of the classroom, and the students are not yet able to learn English, I will find help. I will not make assumptions about "language difficulties" for bilingual students who are in the process of acquiring English.
3. I will encourage all students to speak in their own language.
4. I will respect the culture of each student by encouraging students to share and to write about their families and traditions.
5. I will post assignments in multiple languages all around my classroom.
6. I will invite the students' parents to the classroom to read and to share with us.
7. I will hang signs around the school in the languages of the students.
8. I will encourage all students to speak and to learn in their primary language.
9. I will invite community members to my class.
10. And, most importantly, I will provide books in the languages of the students. (pp. 14–15)

Harold Hodgkinson (2000/2001), the director of the Center for Demographic Policy, adds the following tips for teachers who are working with students from diverse cultures in their classroom.

1. If a student's record shows that he or she is "Hispanic," take time to find out what country the student's family is from, what language is used in the home, and how proficient the family members are at speaking English and reading in their native language.

2. If a child will not look you in the eye, do not call attention to it. When you have an opportunity, speak to the child in private about their reasons. Some Hispanic and Native American children are taught that it is rude to look the teacher in the eye.

3. Help those students and teachers who are new to the area get settled and feel at home.

4. If you have a lot of diversity in your classroom, use a variety of visual presentations. Pictures often convey meaning when words do not.

5. Communicate to your students that you value all children and you expect them all to do their best.

Along with the previous tips shared, we know that most English language learners (ELLs) find learning easier in a structured setting (Burden & Williams, 1998). Thus, the classroom teacher may establish certain classroom routines beginning the first day of school that are expected of everyone: students, teacher, and teacher aides. This provides security for all students as the element of surprise is eliminated. Then, gradually, structures may be modified to accommodate all learners.

Ideally, teachers meet and talk with parents and caregivers of all the students at the beginning of the school year. Remember to ask the parents what mode of communication they prefer. This is particularly important for children whose parents may speak another language or are unable to read due to literacy difficulties. Sending a letter or note home may not suffice as the parent may not respond or may be unable to read English. However, some parents may prefer notes because they may have a friend, neighbor, or co-worker who is willing to read and translate for them. In some cases there needs to be direct communication, either face to face with a translator present or via the telephone with a translator on a third phone (Farris, 2001). Later in the chapter there is a more complete list of strategies the classroom teacher can use to help communicate with family members.

Web Link:
Babel Fish Prompts'
Online Translator

It is understandable that an English language learner may become discouraged and frustrated. Imagine moving to a foreign country and not knowing a single word. Often such children will put their heads down on their desks as it becomes too difficult to interpret what the teacher is saying in English. This situation will change with time, practice, patience, and appropriate instruction. As second language learners begin to become proficient in English, **codeswitching** will occur. This is the use of two languages together. For example, two boys whose primary language is Spanish may be talking about a football game. Their conversation may be in Spanish with English football terms interspersed (i.e., blitz, interception, touchdown) (Farris, 2001). This type of communication will require active listening and quick processing on the part of a non-Spanish-speaking teacher or classmate.

In this section we have addressed numerous ways to assist an English language learner in feeling a part of the learning community. As we end our discussion, we would like to offer a list of ways to modify instruction for ELLs. The instructional suggestions for second language learners described in the Teaching Strategy for the Classroom box are designed to be general suggestions for new teachers to follow.

Teaching Strategy for the Classroom

INSTRUCTIONAL SUGGESTIONS FOR ENGLISH LANGUAGE LEARNERS (ELLs)

- Establish routines and structure.
- Use direct instruction.
- Label things in the classroom in both languages and use a picture. When it is time to leave the classroom for special classes, lunch, or recess, hold up a sign labeling the event in the two languages.
- Monitor progress frequently.
- Keep a list of vocabulary mastered; periodically tape-record and date classroom conversations.
- Allow for oral interaction between students during learning activities.
- Demonstrate whenever possible as you say the words as well as use body language to teach verbal concepts.
- Find a staff member or another student who speaks the student's first language to engage in conversations to lessen feelings of isolation.
- Provide books with parallel language, that is, English and Chinese, English and Spanish.
- Read to the student as often as you can.
- Use computer software that visually and orally presents the student's first language and English.
- Model acceptance of another language for your class by picking up and using words of the student's first language.
- Use a lot of repetition. Break down large tasks into smaller tasks.

These suggestions along with continued support and encouragement will help English language learners.

PLANNING FOR INSTRUCTION

Remember Katherine, the teacher who just landed her first teaching job? What did she do the next morning after rereading her old college reading methods textbook? Well, she began to organize the physical environment of her classroom. She moved desks and boxes and scoured garage sales for books and other interesting items to add to her room. As the first day approached, she thought a lot about how she would create the social environment of her classroom and she also began planning for instruction. She set goals for herself and her students, she sketched a long range plan with the help of her experienced teammates, and then she began thinking about her daily schedule and individual lesson plans. She knew her schedule would change many times before the end of the year, but she also remembered how important it was to establish a daily routine. Katherine also took an afternoon to meet with the Library

Media Center director in her school to find out what kind of technology and books were available. As you continue reading, you will learn about the steps Katherine followed as she planned engaging instruction for her students.

Setting Goals

It is critical that, as teachers, we set goals not only for our students but for ourselves. Many schools and school districts have an established mission or vision statement and accompanying goals. Just as goals for the students should be reasonable and attainable, our professional goals should be too. When creating a balanced literacy environment one cannot expect to be an expert at everything the first year, the fifth year, or even the fifteenth year. Outstanding teachers evolve year after year. They set specific, attainable goals and strive to achieve them. They do not try to set up centers for guided reading, create a hands-on science program, and replace their math textbook with teacher-created lessons all in one year. They select one element of their curriculum at a time and fine-tune it, taking time to reflect and discuss their difficulties and successes with supportive colleagues.

With these thoughts in mind, how do teachers set goals for their students? First, just as the teachers we met in this text did, they begin with the national standards as the overarching vision. Next, they examine the state or local standards. Finally, educators let the school district's specific curricular goals guide their goal setting. It is important to ask yourself, "What do you want your students to know and be able to do by the time they leave your classroom?" These are your goals; post them somewhere in your classroom and refer to them often. Use your goals as a gauge to measure the effectiveness of each lesson you deliver. Let them help you to weigh the benefits of activities that you may see others in your school doing. For example, is it more effective for students to write an alphabet book when they are studying the letters or to color a worksheet with each letter on it? Will you reach your goals if children make a craft project after reading each story or if they respond to their reading through writing, drama, and presentations? Along with setting curricular goals, it is also important to make a long range plan.

Long Range Planning

Long range planning is difficult, but necessary. The days and weeks in a school year pass very quickly. There are school holidays, assemblies, field trips, special projects, state and local testing, fire drills, snow days, teacher in-service days, and many other events that creep into your instructional time. In many school districts a five-day school week is a rarity. Teachers must take time to look at their entire year and sketch out a flexible plan. When will you teach the interdisciplinary unit about insects or heroes? When will you do literature circles? What will your focus be during writing workshop? Effective teachers know that much of what you do in your classroom will depend on your students and their needs. By having a long range plan, you have the opportunity to schedule meaningful field trips and guest speakers, arrange for sharing materials with others in the building, and allow for integration of your teaching into other areas of the curriculum. For example, if the music teacher knows you are focusing on rhyming words, she can include a few rhyming songs during her class.

Or if the art teacher knows you are studying geometry in math, he can include geometric designs in a project. Figure 4.6 shows an example of a long range plan for a first grade curriculum.

Lesson Planning

You have read a variety of specific lesson plans that used slightly different formats to demonstrate the unique ways teachers plan for instruction. The following components are the basic parts of an effective lesson plan:

I. Objectives: What is the purpose of the lesson? What do you want the students to know and be able to do when you are finished? What is the main concept you are trying to teach?

II. Materials: List all the materials you will need to teach the lesson.

III. Instructional Approach

    A. Motivator: How are you going to engage the students' attention? Remember to link the new material to prior learning.

    B. Teacher/Student Interaction: What are you going to do and in what order? What kinds of questions will you ask? What will the students be doing? Remember to give clear directions and model the procedures you want students to follow. Also, don't forget to tell students what to do when they are finished.

    C. Gatekeeping: Bring the lesson to a close. Check for understanding. Think of a clever transition to the next activity.

IV. Extensions: How can you extend this lesson into other areas of the curriculum or other lessons?

V. Adaptations/Modifications for Diverse Learners: How can this lesson be modified for a below grade level student, an above grade level student, or one with diverse learning needs?

Samples of Daily Schedules

Earlier in this chapter we discussed the importance of long range planning and all of the interruptions that occur in schools. When planning your daily schedule the same principles apply. Often you have to work around the lunch schedule; the schedule of special classes like art, music, and P.E.; and other schedules arranged by the school. Federal law requires 1½ to 2 hours of uninterrupted literacy time. Many schools encourage teachers to collaborate to create a workable schedule for all. In Figures 4.7 and 4.8 you will see an example of a primary schedule and an intermediate schedule to give you an idea of how to organize and plan your day.

TECHNOLOGY: ENHANCING LEARNING

Technology has long been viewed as an important key to improving education. A national teacher survey found that 96 percent of the respondents favored an

Figure 4.6		Long range plan					
	MATH	**LANGUAGE ARTS**	**SPELLING**	**SCIENCE**	**HEALTH**	**SOCIAL STUDIES**	**OTHER**
SEPTEMBER	SORTING GEOMETRY PATTERN CHPT. 1, 2, 9	Rain Chick and Duckling I am an Apple "Darrell Morris"	BEGINNING SOUNDS: M, S, F, B, T, C, A, R, L, P	AIR AND WEATHER	HEALTHY BODY		RESPECT
OCTOBER	PATTERN NUMERAL WRITING COUNTING	Down by the Bay My Friends Monday Morn. Whose Baby? * Dolch 1 * Lena	BEGINNING SOUNDS: O, D, G, N, W, I, H, J, K, V, U, Y	AIR AND WEATHER		COLUMBUS DECISION MAKING	FIRE PREVENTION OCTOBER ANIMALS COOPERATION
NOVEMBER	CONCEPT OF ADDITION CHPT. 3	Everything Grows Titch Book Clubs	BEGINNING SOUNDS: Q, Z, X, E, SHORT VOWEL:A			FIRST AMERICANS	RESPON-SIBILITY
DECEMBER	ADDITION STRATEGIES CHPT. 5&6	I Need a Lunchbox Holiday Reports * Dolch 2	SHORT VOWELS: A, I	THE SOLAR SYSTEM		HOLIDAY CUSTOMS AROUND THE WORLD	SERVICE
JANUARY	ADDITION STRATEGIES CONCEPTS OF SUBTRACT. CHPT. 4	Hattie Chicken Lick. Rex & Lilly *Reindeer *Darrell Morris *Bojabi Tree	SHORT VOWELS: O, E, U			FAMOUS AMERICANS: M L King GEOGRAPHY	GOAL SETTING
FEBRUARY	PLACE VALUE SUBTRACT. STRATEGIES CHPT. 8	GBE Turnip Nursery Rhymes Tarts *Live Teddy Bear	LONG VOWELS DIGRAPHS			FAMOUS AMERICANS: LINCOLN & WASHINGTON	100 DAY HONESTY
MARCH	REVIEW ADD. AND SUB. CHPT. 15 & 10	Gunnywolf Book Clubs *The Giant *Dolch 3	DIGRAPHS, BLENDS: BL, GL, PL	EARTH AND ROCKS			TREES SELF-ESTEEM
APRIL	MEASURE-MENT MONEY CHPT. 7 & 13	Henry/Mudge Trek/Sophie Jimmy Lee *The Kittens	BLENDS: CL, SL, FL, GR, TR, BR, DR, CR, FR, SK/SC, SM SN, SP, ST,	EARTH DAY INSECTS			HUMANITY
MAY	TIME EXTENDING NUMBER IDEAS CHPT. 14 & 18	Rattlesnake Fortunately Letter to Amy Mr. Rabbit Guinea Pigs *Darrell Morris	LONG VOWEL PATTERNS AND ENDINGS	INSECTS			PERSEVER-ANCE

Figure 4.7

Primary schedule

	Monday	Tuesday	Wednesday	Thursday	Friday
8:50–9:05	Students begin arriving, Work on daily journal				
9:05–9:20	Attendence, Pledge, Journal Writing				
9:20–9:35	Shared Writing/Morning Message, Review Schedule				
9:35–9:50	Poem, Story, Calendar				
9:50–10:30	Guided Reading & Centers	Thinking Journal/ Math	10:05–10:30 P.E.	Guided Reading & Centers	Guided Reading & Centers
10:30–10:45	RECESS/SNACK				
10:45–11:30	Writing Workshop	Writing Workshop	Writing Workshop	Writing Workshop	Thinking Journal/ Math
11:30–12:15	Literature Study	Literature Study	Literature Study	Thinking Journal/ Math	Literature Study
12:15–12:45	Word Study	Guided Reading & Centers	Word Study	Word Study or Computer Lab	Word Study
12:50–1:25	LUNCH/RECESS				
1:35–2:00	ART	MUSIC	Story/ D.E.A.R.	Story/ D.E.A.R.	Story/ D.E.A.R.
2:00–2:25	ART	P.E.	Thinking Journal/ Math	Science/ Social Studies	Science/ Social Studies
2:25–2:55	Story/ D.E.A.R.	Story/ D.E.A.R.	2:20–2:50 Mrs. Wood	2:25–2:50 P.E.	Science/ Social Studies
2:55–3:20	3:00–3:20 Book Buddies	Science/ Social Studies	Science/ Social Studies	Science/ Social Studies	2:50–3:15 MUSIC
3:20–3:30	PREPARE FOR DISMISSAL				

increased use of technology, particularly computers, to improve education in the United States (Feistritzer, 1996). Technology's vast appeal is attributed to three factors: (1) the desire to prepare students in an increasingly technological workforce, (2) the potential for computers to provide a vehicle for self-directed learning, and (3) the perception that computer use in the classroom will increase productivity (Cuban, 1993). The Apple Classroom of Tomorrow research project, which began in 1987, found that when technology is integrated throughout the curriculum, the benefits are many. Some are included in the list that follows:

Figure 4.8

Intermediate schedule

5th Grade Schedule

	8:50–9:15	9:15–9:40	9:40–10:05	10:05–11:10	11:10–12:10	12:10–12:20	12:25–1:00	1:00–1:15	1:15–2:00	2:00–2:45	2:45–3:20	3:20–3:30
Mon.	Opening	Gym	Spelling	Reading	Math	DEAR	Lunch	Wash-room	Science	Science	Writing	Closing
Tues.	Opening	Gym	Spelling	Reading	Math	DEAR	Lunch	Wash-room	Science	Science	Writing	Closing
Wed.	Opening	Gym	Spelling	Reading	Math	DEAR	Lunch	Wash-room	Science	Science	Writing	Closing
Thurs.	Opening	Gym	Spelling	Reading	Math	DEAR	Lunch	Wash-room	Science	Science	Writing	Closing
Fri.	Opening	Gym	Spelling	Reading	Math	DEAR	Lunch	Wash-room	Science	Science	Writing	Closing

1. Computers actively encourage children to work together and work harder.
2. Students' behavior changes for the better when they are immersed in a constructivist and collaborative learning environment where technology is freely available.
3. Students take responsibility for their own learning, becoming more resourceful and gaining a respect for their learning and other students.
4. Academic results improve.
5. Students write more effectively and finish whole units of study far more quickly. (*Apple Education News,* 1997, pp. 1–3)

As you have seen, uses of the computer can be as simple as drill and practice exercises such as those found in developing phonics skills in *Phonics Voyage* (Oxendine, 1999), *Reader Rabbit* (The Learning Company, 2002). Emergent readers enjoy interactive software such as The Learning Company's Dr. Seuss' (1999) *Green Eggs and Ham* and *Cat in the Hat* (2000). With this program, the story is read to the child. The child can elect to highlight various aspects of the illustrations to see animation occur. A plus of these types of programs is that most offer the text in English, Spanish, and sometimes other languages—all on the same computer disk (CD).

Higher level thinking skills are encouraged and promoted when software programs present simulations and applications of knowledge and skills (Latham, 1999). *Storybook Weaver Deluxe* students explore the writing process. Children create their own storybooks by selecting from hundreds of illustrations and writing their own story to accompany the pictures. Microsoft's successful adaptation of Joanna Cole's *The Magic School Bus* series (Scholastic, 1996) has resulted in students' gaining and applying scientific information via the computer. In *The Magic School Bus Explores Inside the Earth* (Microsoft, 1996), geological facts are presented with narration, sound, video, and animation. Students can perform four experiments and develop their expository writing skills as they complete six reports. Informational material and problem-solving activities are also available with the Dorling Kindersley software series. Science and social studies software includes *The New Way Things Work* (Dorling Kindersley, 2000), and *Eyewitness World Atlas* (Dorling Kindersley, 1999).

Informational programs such as *Leonardo the Inventor* (Softkey, 1995) enable middle childhood and middle school students to engage in interdisciplinary learning as they view the media presentation of Leonardo da Vinci's incredible inventions. This can be coupled with use of the Internet to view da Vinci's artwork. Popular encyclopedia software includes *Compton's Multimedia Encyclopedia* (Compton, 2000) and Microsoft's (2003) *Encarta. Encarta* permits students to not only view encyclopedia entries, often accompanied by sound and narration, but click on to websites on the Internet related to the topic of interest.

As you read through this textbook, you found numerous software programs, websites, and suggestions for including technology in your balanced reading program. A few books to help steer you in the right direction include:

Burgstahler, S., & Utterback, L. (2000). *New kids on the net: Internet activities in elementary language arts.* Needham Heights, MA: Allyn & Bacon.

Meers, T. B. (1999). *101 best web sites for kids.* Lincolnwood, IL: Publications International.

Wepner, S. B., Valmont, W., & Thurlow, R. (Eds.). (2000). *Linking literacy and technology: A guide for K–8 classrooms.* Newark, DE: International Reading Association.

REACHING BEYOND THE CLASSROOM

From the moment you walk into your classroom in the morning until the moment your last student waves good-bye, you are completely focused on teaching the lessons, managing the behavior, taking care of the record-keeping tasks and paperwork, and adhering to the schedule you created. This hectic day often leaves teachers with little time to reflect on their teaching and renew themselves as professionals. It is vitally important, especially in your first years of teaching, that you connect with people other than your students. Often taking the time to call a parent of a difficult child may give you insights into managing that child's behavior. Chatting with some colleagues after school may help you to adjust a lesson that has been troubling you. Reading an article in a professional journal or attending a professional meeting is a great way to gain new knowledge that will boost your professional energy level and help you grow as an educator.

Parent Involvement

Parents and caregivers are your partners in the education of their children at every grade level. Our role as a teacher is not only to educate our students but to educate and inform those who care for our students. There are a multitude of ways to open the lines of communication between home and school and form strong relationships. Let's take a few moments to look at some of the creative and innovative ways teachers share information with parents.

As a teacher you know how important it is to have the support of the family of your students. Some parents may have the desire to support your efforts but find it difficult due to their lack of literacy knowledge. If you find that this is the case, you may have to modify your communication tactics, just as you would modify your teaching tactics for a diverse learner. Susan Bohler (1996) and her colleagues offer the following suggestions for supporting parents who have difficulty with literacy:

1. **Conduct parent evenings.** To encourage all parents to attend a school event make sure you schedule it at a convenient time for all, provide child care during the meeting, and deliver information in an enjoyable and easy to understand way. Parent evenings can focus on how to encourage a child's literacy development through everyday activities like making dinner (reading

Teaching Strategy:
Mystery Reader

Web Links:
Parents Helping Parents

Family Village

Portfolio Activity:
Parent Evening

Having samples of the student's work organized in a folder saves time during a parent-teacher conference. Such samples demonstrate the student's literacy progress.

recipes, cans, boxes), grocery store shopping, playing games, and visiting the local library on a weekly basis.

2. **Make cassette tapes** to accompany the literature you are reading in the classroom. Send home the book, tape, and a small tape recorder so that the family can enjoy listening to the story together. Enlist the help of school personnel such as the secretary, custodian, playground and lunchroom monitors, principal, and other support personnel to help you make the tapes.

3. **Use simple or alternative means of communicating with parents** such as making a phone call instead of sending home a note.

4. **Schedule home visits.** Visiting a child's home is often less threatening than asking the parent to come in to school. Bring a bag of activities with you to help demonstrate the different ways you can develop literacy through play. Mary Louise Ginejko, a middle school teacher in an inner-city school, goes to all her students' homes and meets their families prior to the beginning of the school year. During her visit, she conveys to the parents or caregivers her genuine interest in and concern for their child. In addition, she presents a bit of her teaching philosophy and explains her expectations of students on a level her listeners can understand. In so doing, she is gaining the trust of both the students and their parents and caregivers.

5. **Create a classroom lending library.** Videotape some literacy lessons and let parents check them out. Also make books, cassette tapes, and videotapes available for checkout.

6. **Send home magazine packs.**

7. **Send home copies of familiar nursery rhymes and songs.**

8. **Make the parent aware of community programs.**

9. **Suggest that your district create a homework hotline.**

Phone Conversations

Many conversations with parents occur over the telephone. It is a good idea for teachers to keep an accurate record of these conversations for future reference. One way to do this is by making a phone log. A phone log contains a booklet with a page for each student on which you list the pertinent information. See Figure 4.9 for a sample page.

Positive Postcards

When a student learns a new reading strategy, has read a certain number of books, or does something else wonderful that her parents should know about, a positive postcard is a great way to communicate this information to parents. A teacher can purchase these postcards at the local teacher supply store or create them herself. Then she simply jots a quick note to the family and drops it in the mail.

Newsletters

Another effective form of communication is a weekly or monthly newsletter. A newsletter is helpful for parents to keep them informed of what is going on in the classroom each day. A clearly written newsletter offers parents a common language

Figure 4.9

Sample phone log page

Name:
Address:
Home Phone Number:
Birthdate:

Mother's Name: _____   Place of Employment: _____
Phone: _____

Father's Name: _____   Place of Employment: _____
Phone: _____

Date	Initiated By	Concerns	Outcome

when talking to their child about the school day. It facilitates a more focused conversation, when a parent can say, "I read in your newsletter that you are learning about different versions of Cinderella; which is your favorite?" And it helps eliminate the common answer to "What did you do in school today?" "Oh, nothing." A newsletter

Figure 4.10

Primary newsletter (Grade 1)

1-W's Newsletter
1-11-01

Happy New Year!! I hope you all had a relaxing winter break. I bet you are wondering what we have been doing for the past 7 days!! As you can see from your child's folder, we have been very busy . . .

Math: We continue to study addition strategies in math. The strategies we have covered thus far are Zero Facts, Counting on, Doubles, Making a 10, and Doubles + 1 or Number Neighbors (1+2, 3+4, 4+5, 5+6, 6+7, 8+9, etc.). Next week we will learn how to add three numbers. Also, Mrs. Riemer checked your child on their facts to 10. The recording sheet is enclosed in the Thursday folder. Please practice the circled facts with your child. We continue to practice at school when we do the "Flash Card Challenge." Ask your child about this enjoyable activity.

Spelling Through Phonics: The short vowels are still the focus of our spelling lessons. We have studied the short a and i. We are currently working on the short o sound. We are learning about spelling patterns or word families. These common patterns help us read and spell many other words. For example, if you can spell/read "bat," you can spell/read: "cat, mat, fat, hat," and so on. Our new word wall words this week are: will, get, some, come, here.

Guided Reading/Centers: During center time I have been individually assessing each child for 2nd quarter report cards. I have checked the 2nd quarter sight words (recording sheet enclosed) and read a story with your child to determine his/her reading level, see which reading strategies he/she is using, and how well he/she can retell/comprehend a story he/she has read. I will share these results in the 2nd quarter comment card. As always, please feel free to call after report cards if you have any questions or concerns.

Literature Study: We have spent the last two weeks reading a funny story called *Hattie and the Fox*. We love listening to the song that goes with it. We wrote in our reading journal about what the story reminded us of and talked about quotation marks. We are also making a mural of our own version of the story.

Science and Social Studies: We finished studying the nine planets this week. Enjoy sharing your child's planet book—it was a lot of hard work!!!!! Also, we learned many interesting facts about Dr. Martin Luther King, Jr. We used those facts to create the book in your child's folder and also a class biography of this amazing man. We enjoyed reading a book about Ruby Bridges. There is an *excellent* Disney video about Ruby Bridges available at Blockbuster. If you get the opportunity to rent it, I think you and your child will enjoy watching it together. I had a chance to see her speak this fall; she is a truly amazing woman and was a brave young girl—we can all learn a lot from her. She has also written a children's book—it is excellent.

also provides a place to remind students and parents about upcoming events and assignments and eliminates the need for extra notes going home. Some teachers write their newsletter on their own (see Figure 4.10); others do it in a shared writing format with the children providing the content. Many upper grade teachers shift the responsibility of a newsletter to their students with a different group of students each month during the year creating the newsletter (see Figure 4.11).

Weekly Folders

In a balanced literacy classroom students are not doing worksheets or workbook pages. Many of the activities they are engaged in take more than one day to complete.

Figure 4.11

Intermediate newsletter (Grade 4)

News Notes from 4-M
June 2002

FROM MRS. M

Time flies when you are having fun! I can't believe it is the end of our year already. I feel a mixture of sadness and relief that the school year is almost over. I will miss my 4-M students and I send them off with my best wishes and all the wisdom I can stuff into these last few days. Thanks to all my parents - you have been great communicators and I was thankful for your assistance and insight.

Here is your homework for the summer: READ! READ! READ!, have fun, sing, whistle, dance, help out around the house, draw pictures, write stories, eat Popsicles, stay up late at least once to gaze at the stars, be kind and be careful!

See you in August!

STUDENT NEWS:

Tests

We have had many tests this year, including math tests, spelling tests, and social studies tests. Right now we had a social studies test on dairy farming and soon we will have a math test. Some tests are fun and some tests aren't.
H. W.

Math

In math we are learning average, which is where you find the average of a few numbers. Some of the other things we've learned this year are long division, two-digit multiplication, and many other things. Math is fun!
W. K.

Camp Edwards

Camp Edwards was a lot of fun. Some of the things we learned will help us in the future.
J. T.

Some of my favorite activities were rocks, row boating, tie-dyeing and many more. I think everybody had a lot of fun! I wish we could go again.
M. C.

Science

In science we learned about owls. We dissected owl pellets to see what the owl ate. Some interesting facts we learned about owls are their eyes are the size of ours, they can fly silently, and they can turn their head almost all the way around.
K. W.

In Our Opinion:

Fourth grade is fun but it goes by fast so use your time well.
S. E.

Fourth grade was exciting, fun, and an educational experience because we went many places and learned many things.
K.W.

Fourth grade is different than any other grade.
J. E.

Fourth grade is amazing experiences that no other school could give.
R. G.

Fourth grade was the greatest year of my life!
L. A.

Fourth grade is wonderful! There are great activities like going to Camp Ed., making a T. V. show, and dissecting owl pellets. The food was great but watch out for that homework.
M. K.

Also, when children are composing in writing workshop, recording their thoughts in journals and reading response logs, and discussing texts in literature circles, they are engaged in less visible learning. Parents are not able to see daily examples of their child's learning progress. One way to assist parents in tracking their child's progress and communicating with them about their child is by using a Thursday folder. A Thursday folder is simply a two-pocket folder with the word "keep" written on one pocket and the word "return" written on the other. Each Wednesday, the teacher or the

	Figure 4.12		
	Thursday folder comment sheet		
Date	**Teacher Comments**	**Parent Signature**	**Parent Comments**

Portfolio Activity:
Thursday Folder

students take samples of their work and place them in the appropriate pocket. For example, if the student has written many interesting entries in a reading log, the teacher can place that in the return side so that the parents can share it with their child on Thursday night. It is returned to school on Friday so the student can continue her work. The reason the folder goes home on Thursday is to eliminate the chance that it might get lost over the weekend. To encourage ongoing dialogue with parents on a regular basis there is a comment sheet in each folder (see Figure 4.12) for teacher comments and parents' questions or comments.

This ongoing, weekly communication between home and school is time-consuming at first, but eventually it alleviates the need for a lot of extra note writing. For example, if the parents have a question that they do not need an immediate answer to, they will wait and write it in the Thursday folder. Also, the teacher can keep parents updated on their child's progress. In the upper grades a space for student comments would also be appropriate. The contents on the return side and the comment sheet are returned to school on Friday. (A note communicating this system to parents is provided in Figure 4.13.)

Narrative Comments

What items did your parents save from your elementary school years? Do you have any old report cards or papers that contain a teacher's written comment? Think about that for a moment. The narrative comments you write on a child's report card or as part of their portfolio have an everlasting impact. With that in mind narrative comments should be carefully written. Susan Schafer, author of the book *Writing Effective Report Card Comments* (1997), offers the following quick tips for writing narrative comments:

Figure 4.13

Thursday folder note

Dear First Grade Parents,

This is your child's THURSDAY FOLDER. It will be coming home on Thursday filled with your child's weekly work. This MIGHT include spelling work, math pages, booklets related to our current theme, homework, and/or any other daily work collected during the week. Note that the folder has two sides: a "return side" for items that must be sent back to school and a "keep side" for items to keep at home.

Also included in the folder is a section for teacher comments and parent comments. I will *periodically* be using the teacher comment section to inform you specifically about your child's academic and social progress in first grade. Please feel free to use the parent comment section to share any questions, comments, or insights about your child that you feel I should know to more effectively meet his/her needs. Please note: As this is a weekly form of communication, I will not be responding to your questions until the next week, unless it is an urgent matter that requires immediate attention.

Please take time each Thursday to carefully review your child's work with him/her. This is an excellent way to keep track of your child's progress in first grade. Discuss with your child the strengths and weaknesses of his work. Remember to focus on your child's strengths.

YOUR CHILD'S THURSDAY FOLDER MUST BE RETURNED TO SCHOOL ON FRIDAY with your signature and any comments. This will ensure effective communication between home and school.

Your support is greatly appreciated!

Dr. Maria Walther

1. Start with something positive.
2. Provide encouragement.
3. Address both academic and social areas. Be specific and use a lot of detail and concrete examples.
4. Include helpful strategies that parents can use at home.
5. Make comments objective and personal. Highlight a unique aspect of each child.
6. Record observable behavior.
7. Attach work samples.
8. Use simple, common language that parents can understand. Avoid educational jargon.

The comments that you write should help to build a child's confidence and improve learning.

Parent Library

A parent library is an important section of the school library. School librarians should work closely with the teachers and the parent–teacher organization to identify the needs of parents and stock the library accordingly. If your school does not have a parent library or resource center, you may want to begin a small parent library of your own. When you come across resources, articles, and other documents that may be helpful for your parents, collect them in a file folder, binder, or box. Inform parents that these resources are available for them to check out at their convenience. Some teachers create documents based on the needs of their students. In the Teaching Strategy for the Classroom box you will find a note a first grade teacher wrote for parents who were struggling to get their children to read books. How could you adapt this idea for your middle grade readers?

Teaching Strategy for the Classroom

COMMUNICATING WITH PARENTS OF RELUCTANT FIRST GRADE READERS

1. *Follow your child's interests.* Many first graders love science books. There are a number of great science series written at a first grade level: *Rookie Read about Science* books published by Children's Press, *Let's Read and Find Out Science Books,* and *The Magic School Bus Series,* which includes books and videos.

*2. *Find riddle and joke books.* First graders like elephant jokes, gross punch lines, and jokes that make adults groan. Let them read their jokes aloud to you and try to catch you on the riddles while you're doing the dishes.

3. *Establish a family D.E.A.R. (Drop Everything and Read Time).* Set aside a time each evening or morning where the whole family sits and reads for five to ten minutes. It is important that children see adults reading too!!

4. *Subscribe to a children's magazine.* Some excellent magazines include *Ranger Rick, ZooBooks, Highlights for Children, Sports Illustrated for Kids.*

5. *Get your child hooked on a series.* You can read the first book of the series to your child, then let them read the rest on their own.

Chapter Books Series:
Henry and Mudge by Cynthia Rylant
Cam Jansen by David Adler
Nate the Great by Marjorie Weinman Sharmat
Frog and Toad by Arnold Lobel

Picture Book Series:
George and Martha by James Marshall
The *Cut Ups* by James Marshall
The *Arthur* Books by Marc Brown
The *Pinkerton* Books by Steven Kellogg

*6. *Find an interactive book.* Some books allow the reader to make choices about the next section to read such as *Choose Your Own Adventure* books. Let your child read his/her chosen path to you, then you read your choice to him/her.

*7. *Read to a younger child.* Ask your first grader to read to a younger child regularly. This additional practice improves their reading fluency and helps them see the joy in sharing books with others.

8. *Visit the library regularly.* This will help you to find out what kind of books your child enjoys, and it is a great family outing that promotes the importance of reading. Also, while you're there, talk to the librarians. They are excellent resource people who are aware and willing to share the new and exciting books that are available.

9. *Don't forget poetry books.* First graders love the funny poems written by Shel Silverstein and Jack Prelutsky.

* These ideas came from an excellent resource for helping children from preschool through age twelve enjoy both reading and writing: Cullinan, B. (1992). *Read to me: Raising kids who love to read.* New York: Scholastic.

Classroom Website

Many school districts and individual schools have websites. An extension of this is to create a classroom website. The website could contain general information about the classroom, including a daily schedule and notes about upcoming special events and projects. Teachers could post their classroom newsletter. Students also contribute to the website by posting projects or reports. It is important to remember that any time you are going to use a photograph or child's name for public display, you must obtain parental permission.

Working with Other Professionals

The other teachers in your building or district are one of your best resources. Take time to ask questions and solicit advice from those who seem willing to help. If a new professional book comes out that you want to read, form a study group to read and discuss the book. Some books to get you started are listed in Figure 4.14. Find other teachers who have a similar philosophy of teaching and meet on a regular basis to discuss curricular plans. Working with other professionals is one way to expand your knowledge and expertise about teaching.

Your growth as a professional does not end when you get your first teaching job. Exemplary teachers are always

Teachers work together to create an interdisciplinary instructional unit.

Figure 4.14

Professional resources

For the Novice Primary Teacher

Burns, S., Griffin, P., & Snow, C. (1999). *Starting out right: A guide to promoting children's reading success.* Washington, DC: National Academy Press.

Cunningham, P. M., Hall, D. P., & Sigmon, C. M. (1999). *The teacher's guide to the four blocks.* Greensboro, NC: Carson-Dellosa Publishing Company.

Fisher, B., & Fisher Medvic, E. (2000). *Perspectives on shared reading: Planning and practice.* Portsmouth, NH: Heinemann.

Fountas, I. C., & Pinnell, G. S. (1996). *Guided reading: Good first teaching for all children.* Portsmouth, NH: Heinemann.

————. (1999). *Matching books to readers: Using leveled books in guided reading, K–3.* Portsmouth, NH: Heinemann.

Opitz, M. (2000*). Rhymes and reasons: Literature and language play for phonological awareness.* Portsmouth, NH: Heinemann.

Perlmutter, J., & Burrell, L. (2001). *The first weeks of school: Laying a quality foundation.* Portsmouth, NH: Heinemann.

Routman, R. (2003). *Reading essentials.* Portsmouth, NH: Heinemann.

Yopp, R. H., & Yopp, H. K. (2001). *Literature-based reading activities* (3rd ed.). Boston: Allyn and Bacon.

For the Novice Intermediate Teacher

Atwell, N. (2000). *In the middle.* (2nd ed.) Portsmouth, NH: Heinemann.

Calkins, L. M. (2001). *The art of teaching reading.* New York: Addison Wesley Longman.

Daniels, H. (1994). *Literature circles: Voice and choice in the student centered classroom.* York, ME: Stenhouse.

Fountas, I. C., & Pinnell, G. S. (2001). *Guiding readers and writers grades 3–6: Teaching comprehension, genre, and content literacy.* Portsmouth, NH: Heinemann.

Fuhler, C. J. (2000). *Teaching reading with multicultural books kids love.* Golden, CO: Fulcrum.

Harvey, S., & Goudvis, A. (2000). *Strategies that work: Teaching comprehension to enhance understanding.* York, ME: Stenhouse.

Keene, E. O., & Zimmerman, S. (1997). *Mosaic of thought.* Dubuque, IA: Kendall/Hunt.

Morretta, T. M., & Ambrosini, M. (2000). *Practical approaches for teaching reading and writing in middle schools.* Newark, DE: International Reading Association.

Wood, K. D., & Dickinson, T. S. (2000). *Promoting literacy in grades 4–9.* Boston: Allyn & Bacon.

looking for ways to improve their instruction. They continue to take college courses, read professional books and journals, and join professional organizations. Figure 4.15 lists professional journals and organizations that you may be interested in subscribing to or joining. Make becoming a lifelong learner a personal and professional goal, and take deliberate steps year after year to reach that goal.

Figure 4.15

Professional journals and organizations

Professional Journals

Book Links
American Library Association
50 E. Huron Street
Chicago, IL 60611

This journal contains information about new books. The columns focus on the use of children's literature with students and provide background information about authors and books.

Journal of Adolescent and Adult Literacy
International Reading Association
800 Barksdale Road, P. O. Box 8139
Newark, DE 19714-8139

This journal is appropriate for teachers in the intermediate grades and above.

Language Arts
National Council of Teachers of English
1111 Kenyon Road
Urbana, IL 61801

This journal covers the language arts from preschool through grade 6. Each issue includes an article on current research in the language arts plus a list of children's books.

The New Advocate
Christopher-Gordon Publishers
480 Washington Street
Norwood, MA 02062

This quarterly journal provides in-depth information about children's literature, including articles and book reviews.

Reading Horizons
Reading Center and Clinic
Western Michigan University
Kalamazoo, MI 49008

Published five times a year, this outstanding journal contains a bevy of articles that link theory and practice and is reasonably priced.

The Reading Teacher
International Reading Association
800 Barksdale Road, P. O. Box 8139
Newark, DE 19714-8139

This is a popular journal for elementary teachers. It is filled with articles about current trends in language arts, sections on children's literature, and many practical ideas.

WEB (Wonderfully Exciting Books)
Martha L. King Center for Language
   and Literacy
The Ohio State University
Columbus, OH 43210

Recently published children's books and their role in the classroom are the focus of this journal.

Professional Organizations

International Reading Association
National Council of Teachers of English

Your local reading council
Your state reading council

Summary

In the beginning of this chapter you met Katherine, a novice teacher like yourself who is just beginning to get her feet wet. As you continued you read about all the components that fit together to make a successful, engaging literacy learning environment for all students. A lot of thought goes into the physical environment of the classrooms. Teachers gather materials and supplies and carefully design the physical arrangement to reflect their instructional goals. During guided reading, some teachers create literacy centers for their learners. In order to create an inclusive and supportive social environment teachers must be acquainted with the students with special needs that they may be teaching. Accomplished teachers are thoughtful decision makers who reflect on their teaching and strive to find ways to improve their knowledge and skills. The key principles to classroom management are establishing a reliable routine, communicating clear rules and expectations, and being firm, fair, and consistent when dealing with students. When planning for instruction, it is crucial to set clear, attainable goals and strive to meet them. Effective teachers utilize a variety of methods to reach beyond the classroom walls to impact student learning. Finally, technology is a helpful teaching tool to utilize time efficiently.

Chapter Review

Go to the Online Learning Center at **www.mhhe.com/farrisreading** to take chapter quizzes, practice with key terms, and review important content.

Main Points

- A well-designed physical environment invites children to engage in meaningful literacy activities.

- Teachers must locate supplementary materials to enhance their lessons.

- A well-stocked classroom library is a must.

- The look of a classroom sends a powerful message to all who walk through the door.

- In order to successfully meet with small groups, teachers must carefully plan activities to engage the rest of the class. Creating literacy centers is one way to achieve this goal.

- The social environment of a classroom mirrors a well-functioning family.

- The role of the teacher is to be a wise and capable decision maker who mixes and matches strategies to meet the needs of each learner.

- A well-managed classroom is a must for meaningful learning to take place.

- All learners benefit from the activities that take place in a balanced literacy classroom.

- Teachers must learn how to manage students with diverse behavioral needs.

- Working with diverse students is challenging and rewarding, and there are a number of strategies to help teachers meet the challenge.

- It is important to set goals and create a long range plan for the year.

- An effective lesson plan has specific components.

- Technology can enhance teaching and learning in many ways.

Key Terms

attention deficit disorder (ADD) 156	codeswitching 165
attention deficit hyperactivity disorder (ADHD) 156	cognitive behavior therapy 164
behavior modification 163	English language learners 158

Reflecting and Reviewing

1. Imagine that you were just hired for your first teaching job. You have a month to prepare for your students. Describe your plan of action: What will you do first, next, last? How will you prioritize?

2. In this chapter you visited and viewed maps of two classrooms. Design your dream classroom. What will it look like? What materials, supplies, and furniture will it contain?

3. You read about a variety of ways to communicate with parents. Which ways appealed to you? Which would you like to try? Have you heard or read about other parent communication tactics to add to the list?

Children's Literature

For annotations of the books listed below, please see Appendix A.

Curtis, Christopher Paul. (1999). *Bud, Not Buddy.* New York: Delacorte.

Erdrich, Louise. (1999). *The Birchbark House.* New York: Hyperion.

Holm, Jennifer. (1999). *Our Only May Amelia.* New York: HarperCollins.

Paulsen, Gary. (1987). *Hatchet.* New York: Macmillan.

Yep, Laurence. (1993). *Dragon's Gate.* New York: HarperCollins.

Classroom Teaching Resources

Freeman, D. E., & Freeman, Y. S. (2001). *Between worlds: Access to second language acquisition* (2nd ed.). Portsmouth, NH: Heinemann.

Graves, D. H. (2001). *The energy to teach.* Portsmouth, NH: Heinemann.

Risko, V J., & Bromley, K. (Eds.). (2001). *Collaboration for diverse learners: Viewpoints and practices.* Newark, DE: International Reading Association.

Software

Cat in the Hat. (2000). The Learning Company.

Compton's Multimedia Encyclopedia. (2000). Compton's.

Encarta. 2003. (2003). Microsoft.

Eyewitness World Atlas. (1999). Dorling Kindersley.

Green Eggs and Ham. (1999). The Learning Company.

Leonardo the Inventor. (1995). Softkey.

The Magic School Bus Explores Inside the Earth. (1996). Microsoft.

My First Amazing World Explorer. (1996). Dorling Kindersley.

Phonics Voyage. (1999). Arrow Education.

Reader Rabbit. (2002). The Learning Company.

Storybook Weaver Deluxe. (1994). MECC.

The New Way Things Work. (2000). Dorling Kindersley.

"What teachers need are assessment instruments that measure worthwhile skills or important bodies of knowledge. Then teachers need to show the world that they can instruct children so that those children make striking pre-instruction to post-instruction progress."

W. James Popham, noted assessment and evaluation expert

CHAPTER 5

Assessing and Evaluating Literacy Development

Key Ideas

- Teaching requires that **assessment** be used to monitor student progress in meeting instructional goals and benchmarks as well as effectiveness of instructional strategies.
- Assessment approaches should include ways for students to monitor their own progress.
- The best way to assess and evaluate student progress is to use a combination of **alternative assessment** tools such as artifacts, portfolios, rubrics, and standardized tests.
- Assessment and **evaluation** involve **formative** and **summative** measures.
- There are several alternatives to paper and pencil tests. These include use of **rubrics, anecdotal records, checklists, running records,** and more.

Questions to Ponder

- What type of assessment is appropriate for measuring the standards for the English language arts?
- What are **standardized tests** and what role do they play in teaching reading and writing?
- What is **authentic assessment** and what is its role in reading and writing instruction?
- What are **informal testing measures** and how can they aid instruction?
- How are **rubrics** developed and used?

Peering into the Classroom

Professional Development Day

To open the new year, the school district had hired a time management expert for the first teacher orientation meeting. She shared insights on how teachers could be more efficient in their instruction and in completing the myriad of paperwork associated with the job. To drive home a point, the consultant brought out a clear one-gallon glass jar and announced, "Time for a quiz." Then she brought out about a dozen fist-sized rocks and carefully placed them one at a time inside the jar. When the jar was filled to the top, she asked the teachers "Is this jar full?"

"Yes," came the general response from the crowd with only a couple of teachers voicing a negative.

"Really?" asked the consultant as she reached under the table for a container of pea gravel. She poured the gravel into the gallon jar, shaking the jar from time to time to get even more gravel inside. The consultant then asked, "Is the jar full now?"

"No," came the reply from the curious teachers.

The consultant smiled and said, "You're getting it." Then she took a small bucket of sand and poured it into the gallon jar. "Is it full now?" she asked.

"No!" shouted the teachers.

"Good," said the consultant as she reached below the table for a pitcher of water that she then poured into the gallon jar until it reached the brim. The consultant then asked, "What is the point of this illustration?"

One eager teacher said, "No matter how busy the school day is, you can always fit more into it."

"That's probably true, but it's not the point of this illustration." The consultant paused and then went on. "The first thing that went into the jar were the big rocks, then smaller rocks, then sand, and finally the water. As teachers we have to focus on the big rocks, the goals for our students to reach. Next we need to focus on the pebbles or the objectives. Then we choose the sand, or skills and strategies for learning. Finally, comes the water that immerses all the sand, pebbles, and rocks. Water represents the application of all the students have learned. And the jar represents the assessment process, as we, as teachers, continually peer inside our students to make certain they are attaining the goals, objectives, skills, and learning strategies, and are applying them in their everyday lives."

This simple illustration helps us as teachers from straying from the curriculum. We have to keep the "big rocks" and "pebbles" constantly in the foreground of our teaching. They are the road maps to where we want to go. During the instructional process we add the "sand" and encourage students to immerse themselves in the "water" as they read and write for a variety of purposes. And we're constantly observing, evaluating, and assessing our students' strengths and needs.

REFLECTION: IRA/NCTE NATIONAL STANDARDS IN THE CLASSROOM

Assessment is the gatekeeping we do to monitor our students' progress. No doubt about it, assessment continues to take on a greater role in how and what we teach. National and state education funding appears to be headed toward school performance on standards based tests. Teachers find themselves painted into a corner with no way out. Either students score better on state and national achievement tests or the principal or central administration may scrutinize your teaching. Never before has so much pressure been placed on the shoulders of teachers for students to have high test scores. And to complicate things further, each state has its own assessment measures.

As assessment becomes increasingly more important, it must be kept in proper perspective. According to Ann M. Courtney and Theresa L. Abodeeb (2001), "teachers have a central role in the assessment of literacy. They are responsible for the structure of the literacy events and assessment practices in their classroom. They have the responsibility of determining what is important for students to know" (p. 2). In turn, we need to share such information with those who work with each student, such as special education teachers and paraprofessionals as well as parents. To carry this burden, knowledgeable teachers turn to the standards to guide their way.

INTRODUCTION

Assessment is an important component of the instructional process. Simply put, assessment is the act of gathering data in order to better understand the strengths and weaknesses of a student's learning as it relates to the goals of the school district and state. In other words, assessment is the gauging of the progress a student makes in reading and writing. **Evaluation** is the act of using assessment results or data to make informed decisions about future instruction. Assessment can include tests, student work, interviews, teacher observations, and other kinds of approaches.

Standards and assessment have been given a tremendous amount of attention in recent years as the quality of America's schools continues to be debated. As teachers, we need to align our teaching with national, state, and local standards and assess our students in meeting those goals. Instruction is adjusted based upon assessment results. **Alternative,** or authentic, **assessment** has evolved out of the need for more accurate assessment of what students can do. "Teachers are in a better position to know and learn about an individual's development than outsiders. They are with the student over time and across a variety of learning situations. As a result they become aware of the subtle changes and nuances of learning within and across individuals" (Tierney, 1998, p. 377).

The purpose of the learning situation determines the different forms and times for assessment (Alleman & Brophy, 1999). When students are engaged in a reading activity, our observation as teachers may be the most appropriate assessment tool. To determine how third graders in one school district comprehend as compared to other third graders throughout the nation, a **standardized reading test** would be more suitable.

STANDARDS for READING PROFESSIONALS

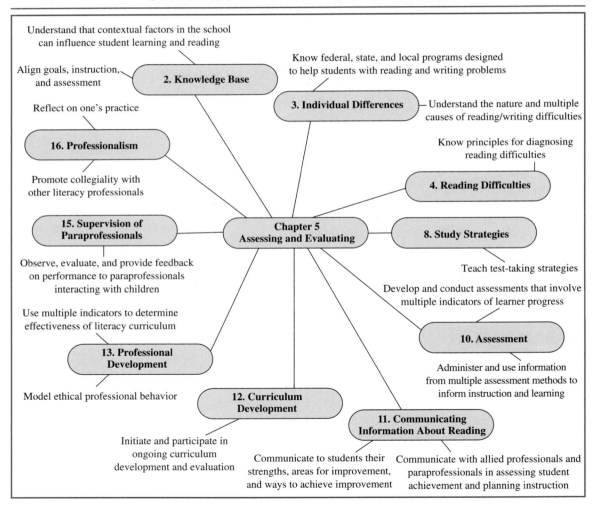

Understand that contextual factors in the school can influence student learning and reading

Align goals, instruction, and assessment

Reflect on one's practice

2. Knowledge Base

Know federal, state, and local programs designed to help students with reading and writing problems

3. Individual Differences — Understand the nature and multiple causes of reading/writing difficulties

16. Professionalism

Promote collegiality with other literacy professionals

Know principles for diagnosing reading difficulties

4. Reading Difficulties

15. Supervision of Paraprofessionals

Observe, evaluate, and provide feedback on performance to paraprofessionals interacting with children

Use multiple indicators to determine effectiveness of literacy curriculum

Chapter 5 Assessing and Evaluating

8. Study Strategies

Teach test-taking strategies

Develop and conduct assessments that involve multiple indicators of learner progress

10. Assessment

13. Professional Development

Model ethical professional behavior

12. Curriculum Development

Administer and use information from multiple assessment methods to inform instruction and learning

11. Communicating Information About Reading

Initiate and participate in ongoing curriculum development and evaluation

Communicate to students their strengths, areas for improvement, and ways to achieve improvement

Communicate with allied professionals and paraprofessionals in assessing student achievement and planning instruction

In order to use assessment measures effectively, we must understand basic learning principles. Here are three that relate closely to assessment and evaluation.

1. *Learning isn't a direct, linear upward line.* Like their physical growth, children's learning takes place in spurts. Sometimes learning plateaus occur. Students can experience regression, particularly if they are under stress or pressure such as an unstable home life.

2. *Learning is affected by motivation, effort, and self-esteem.* Students who aren't enthusiastic about reading and writing are less likely to do well in their literacy development than those peers who just can't wait to read another book or write a story. Students need relevant learning tasks to motivate them to devote their attention and energy to the task. Lack of effort and low self-esteem can hinder student progress in literacy. Confident readers and writers often achieve beyond a teacher's expectations or projected expectations of a standardized test battery.

3. *Learning processes and goals should accommodate student diversity.* A class of twenty-eight students will have twenty-eight individuals with different interests, backgrounds, and desires. The typical classroom has students with a variety of cultures with varying instructional needs. Inclusion and second language students are also a part of such a classroom. Students need to learn to work together as a community of learners. As the teacher, you need to provide them with a variety of choices of how learning goals can be accomplished.

Assessment is important as it provides clues to the instructional needs of students and to how we modify our teaching to meet those needs. In some cases, special reading and writing programs available in the school, such as Title I, may be of assistance to students. Research has found that how well readers control the reading process—that is, using graphophonic, semantic, and syntactic language clues as they sample, predict, confirm, and integrate—is indicative of their reading ability. Effective readers process language well, whereas ineffective readers either do not or cannot process printed language as well (Martens, Goodman, & Flurkey, 1995; Rhodes & Dudley-Marling, 1996). By determining a student's strengths and needs, we can better utilize instructional methods to meet the child's needs.

BALANCED ASSESSMENT

Assessment has different purposes. As classroom teachers, we may view daily, ongoing assessment as a means for finding information about making instructional decisions regarding the reading and writing development of students. From their perspective, students may use assessment to identify their own strengths and weaknesses and to reflect on how they might improve in specific areas. Such ongoing assessment is called **formative assessment.** Parents may consider assessment as a means of comparing their children's performance with that of other students. From yet another perspective, school administrators may consider assessment as an indicator of whether students, teachers, and schools are successful. Lastly, community members

Web Link:
Focus on Reading
Assessment

and state leaders may view assessment as a way to gauge whether the schools are accountable and effective (Farr, 1992). Comparing annual reading test results by schools is **summative assessment.**

One thing is quite clear. More formative assessment in the classroom with accompanying feedback to students is needed. Over 250 research studies involving formative evaluation were examined by Paul Black and Dylan Wiliam (l998), who concluded that self-assessment by students is a critical factor in improving achievement. Black and William (1998) state:

> Self-assessment by pupils is in fact *an essential component of formative assessment.* When anyone is trying to learn, feedback about the effort has three elements: redefinition of the *desired goal,* evidence about *present position,* and some understanding of a *way to close the gap between the two.* All three must be understood to some degree by anyone before he or she can take action to improve learning. (p. 141)

When students are informed in advance of expected achievement targets and are provided with description feedback that offers specific suggestions and insights as to how to improve their performance, then achievement improves. Likewise, instruction must be adjusted based on the results of classroom achievement.

Whether or not tests should lead or follow the curriculum is a debate that continues. Certainly, standardized achievement tests do determine to some extent what is taught in the classroom (Farr & Beck, 2003).

Formative assessment for learning makes for more confident students who, in turn, take greater risks as they attempt new things. They grasp what it is like to be, to a greater degree (than with standardized tests and summative assessment), in charge of their own learning and thus are more motivated.

Assessment and evaluation rely largely upon standards, benchmarks, standardized testing, and authentic assessment. As teachers we need to use these as guides to aid us in determining our students' strengths and needs in regard to the standards for our grade level so we can plan the appropriate instructional activities. The following sections elaborate on these.

STANDARDS FOR READING AND WRITING

Each state has established standards for reading and writing. For each grade level, specific goals have been set for students to attain. For second graders, a state standard might be to read independently, while fourth graders are expected to read aloud with fluency. Seventh graders may be expected to write expository information in a clear and informative manner. These are broad standards, or **benchmarks,** that we need to keep in mind when planning our daily lessons for our students.

Teachers, like students, are given standards to achieve such as the *Standards for Reading Professionals* (IRA, 1998). These standards have been broken down by topic and included in the chapters of this book with the complete list at the end of the book. We are expected to be proficient in many instructional areas in order to best serve the needs of our students and meet community, state, and national expectations.

> "When students are not accurate or fluent in dealing with print, then these skills must be addressed in order for reading to improve. When students are proficient with print but de-

ficient in reading comprehension, then instruction in word meanings, background knowledge, text structures, or strategies for comprehension may be necessary for improvement" (Chall & Curtis, 2003, p. 417).

It is only through assessment of students' strengths and needs in language and literacy, viewed in the context of their literacy development, that appropriate instructional decisions can be made in the teaching of reading and writing (Curtis & Longo, 1998; Roswell & Chall, 1994).

Global Standards for the Entire Curriculum

Four global standards have been found to lead to measurable improvement on a variety of state assessment measures (reading, math, science, social studies, writing, etc.) while still allowing teachers to be creative in meeting the needs of all students in the community (Strong, Silver, & Perrini, 2001). These are:

Web Link:
The Nation's Report Card

1. **Rigor**—being able to read and understand powerful and challenging texts and the ideas that animate them.
2. **Thought**—being able to acquire the disciplines of learning: collecting and organizing information; speaking and writing effectively; mastering the ability to do inquiry and problem-solve; and being able to reflect on one's own learning.
3. **Diversity**—being able to understand one's own strengths and needs, learning styles, multiple intelligences, and cultural heritage as well as working with others who are different from themselves.
4. **Authenticity**—being able to apply what is learned inside the classroom to situations in everyday life as a member of a community. (Strong, Silver, & Perrini, 2001, pp. 1–2)

Rigor requires that we stretch and challenge our students. Reading aloud chapter and nonfiction books to children in the primary grades or having fifth graders recreate Shakespeare's *A Midsummer Night's Dream* causes students to think and perceive ideas differently. Using primary documents for middle school social studies to convey the history of your town, World War II, or the impact of the tragic events of 9-11 adds rigor to the curriculum. Such constant exposure to difficult text as a reader or listener, with accompanying interaction with peers, enables students to develop not only their thinking ability but their self-confidence as learners. The more rigorous the curriculum, the better students perform on achievement tests. Research shows that "good readers are better students in every subject area" (Brozo, 2002, p. 12).

The second global standard identified by Strong, Silver, and Perrini (2001) is thought. Students need to have a clearly defined purpose for the tasks they are assigned as well as pursue the purpose under conditions of uncertainty. As such, our students need to acquire expertise in the disciplines of thinking so they can manage uncertainty. Knowledge acquisition, inquiry, problem solving, communication, and reflection are all tools our students need. One of the best ways to motivate student learning and have students internalize their new learning is through the use of interesting books (Guthrie, Alao, & Rinehart, 1997).

Diversity, the third global standard, recognizes the differences among children. As teachers we want all of our students to reach their full potential. We do this by varying our teaching strategies, assessment measures, and content to support our students in their learning. This is referred to as differentiated instruction. While quality is stressed in the curriculum, we permit students to make choices in how objectives and goals are met.

The last global standard is authenticity, or making classroom learning relevant to the world of our students. This involves the kinds of work people do in society, sources of information, the acquisition of useful communication (listening, speaking, reading, writing, viewing, and visually representing), and problem-based learning. A well-planned career day with visitors representing a wide span of professions is an example of an authentic learning experience.

Creating Grade-Level Benchmarks

Web Link:
Early Reading
Assessment Tools

Teachers need to create goals for student learning for each particular grade, commonly referred to as grade-level benchmarks. Such benchmarks represent what the typical student at that grade level will achieve by the end of the school year. Most school districts require that grade-level benchmarks be derived from state standards. As such, the standards serve as a banner for the school to achieve and exceed rather than a template to be followed and criteria to be met.

Three benchmarks for kindergarten might be:

> The students know and can form all the letters (upper- and lowercase manuscript) of the alphabet.
> The students will know initial consonant sounds.
> The students can identify rhyming words.

Examples of benchmarks that teachers at the first grade level might set are:

Portfolio Activity:
State Standards

> Students will know 100 sight words.
> Students will be able to read independently and comprehend simple chapter books.
> Students will write in complete sentences using capital letters at the beginning and periods, question marks, or exclamation points at the end.

Examples of benchmarks that teachers at the sixth grade level might set are:

> Students will be able to comprehend and critically evaluate fiction.
> Students will read during free time in school and outside of school.
> Students will be able to write narrative, expository, persuasive, and poetic pieces.

Five or six benchmarks are sufficient for each grade level so both teachers and students will be able to remember them all and keep the assessment process manageable. Writing the benchmarks on a small chart that is placed in a noticeable but not dominating location in the classroom serves to set the navigational guide for the school year.

STANDARDIZED TESTING

Think how many times you've filled in bubbles of standardized, timed reading, math, or intelligence tests as part of your educational experience. Today's students are being asked to take even more such tests. Standardized testing developed early in the 1900s as paper and pencil tests that could be administered quickly to large masses of people. When the United States became involved in World War I, such tests were used to screen soldiers who had been drafted from various parts of the country. Many of these men had limited formal schooling, and a substantial number were illiterate.

Standardized tests are paper and pencil tests with true-false, multiple choice, or matching items. The tests are based on behavioral objectives with the results of a single test determining the evaluation. Rather than viewing how a student considers a problem and thereby gaining insight into the child's thinking processes, the final result or product is all that is considered. Teachers rarely have input as to which standardized tests are used. Generally, standardized tests are given once a year in grades 2 through 8 to determine reading comprehension, vocabulary, grammar, spelling, math concepts, math computation, science, social studies, and reference skills.

Standardized tests are timed tests in which the teacher reads the directions word for word so that the students are following the same specific directions as all other students taking the tests in other classrooms throughout the school district and the country. The teacher cannot assist the students during the test, and students must remain in the room until the predetermined time has expired.

As teachers, we are very much aware that standardized testing does not have the same effect on all of our students. Some students are eager to get to school on the day when the Iowa Tests of Basic Skills or the state achievement tests are given because they can show their "stuff." These students know in advance that they will perform well because of their previous personal history with such measures. Other students dread such tests because of a history of personal failure. As Richard J. Stiggins (2002, p. 761) writes, "Some come to slay the dragon, while others expect to be devoured by it."

Criterion Referenced Tests

Criterion referenced tests are exams that have set standards upon which the test items have been developed. If you have a driver's license, then you've taken a criterion reference test. Recall that the driver's exam includes such items as identification of traffic signs and knowing basic laws such as speed rates in a school zone or on the interstate highway. Each respective state's motor vehicle handbook contains all of the information that the test is based upon. The goal of criterion referenced tests in this case is to screen out those drivers who would make our streets and highways unsafe for other motorists and pedestrians. It is possible for a driver to score 100 percent correct on the test items. Criterion tests are useful in other situations as well. Can the five-year-old identify the different kinds of animals found on a farm or colors of crayons in a box of eight crayons? Such tests can be useful even at much higher learning levels. Can the medical student locate and identify specified body parts or, given the symptoms, identify the illness? If not, you probably would opt not to have that individual as your surgeon during an emergency appendectomy.

Norm Referenced Tests

Scores of standardized tests have been normed throughout the United States by the testing company. These are referred to as **norm referenced tests.** To norm a test, hundreds of students throughout all the regions of the country at the same grade level and time of year are given the test. The number of items correct is computed with the results presented in percentiles. By design, half of the students taking the test will score above the 50th percentile and half will score below it. For instance, Brittany scored at the 68th percentile in vocabulary on her fourth grade standardized test. This means that for every 100 students at the same grade level throughout the country, Brittany scored better than 67 but lower than 32.

The most accurate way to utilize standardized test results is by an entire class, school, or school district. For instance, a class that scores at the 42nd percentile on reading comprehension compared with 56th percentile for the school district as a whole at the same grade level needs additional work in comprehension. Perhaps the students aren't applying reading strategies effectively. Or they don't engage in reading as a leisure time activity. Or they don't have a sufficient amount of instructional time in reading. Or maybe the class has a large number of English language learners. Or the teacher doesn't teach effectively. In reality all of these possibilities could be true or all could be false. Most likely it is a combination of factors.

Item Analysis

The results of the standardized tests need to be interpreted if they are to aid instruction. In order to find out more precisely how a class, school, or school district performed, an **item analysis** is done. Teachers look at the group's performance by teaching objectives. For instance, being able to sequence events is a comprehension skill. By considering the breakdown by test items that relate to sequencing, teachers can determine the group's strengths or weaknesses in this particular area. To aid instructional decision making, the results of the standardized tests need to be interpreted.

Individual student standardized norm-referenced test results should always be carefully thought about by the teacher. "Norm-referenced test results do not offer the teacher much guidance on students' specific strengths or instructional needs. At best, they provide some independent confirmation for teachers' judgments. At worst, in particular for the low-performing students, they become the basis for labeling and tracking students, and fail to reveal much about the full range of reader abilities" (Hoffman, Au, Harrison, Paris, Pearson, Santa, Silver, & Valencia, 1999, p. 249).

Preparing Students for Taking Standardized Tests

Some teachers attempt to "teach to the test." In other words, they cover content that is on the test. Tests represent a particular set of knowledge or skills. For instance, a twenty-item math test on addition of two-digit numbers represents the skill of being able to add two-digit numbers. If the test is to examine vocabulary knowledge, having students memorize vocabulary to inflate their scores is inappropriate and a waste of valuable instructional time. However, having students read a wide variety of genre of children's literature and find interesting words to share with the class will yield enhanced vocabulary scores and, likely, increased reading comprehension scores as well. Teaching to the test may be either item teaching or curriculum teaching. Teaching that is focused directly on having students perform well on specific items or items that are similar is item teaching. The instruction is based on having students practice either the same items they will encounter on the test or others that have quite similar structure and content. Such instruction is a type of cheating. However, curriculum teaching is a kind of teaching to the test that is appropriate in that teachers direct their instruction toward a definite body of content knowledge or a particular set of cognitive skills represented by a specified test. In curriculum teaching, teachers target instruction at content that is represented on the test rather than at test items. With this approach, students' mastery of the knowledge or skills on which the test items are based is increased, resulting in higher test scores overall (Popham, 2001).

If a teacher is in a school district that strongly encourages high test scores, the teacher may divert her attention from instructing all the students in the class. Rather, she focuses "on those who are in need of attention and who have the potential to be brought up to passing levels" (Hoffman, et al., 1999, p. 251). Therefore, average to above-average students are neglected.

The best approach for teachers is to adapt instructional practices that will assist students in taking standardized tests. Part of this strategy would be the curriculum-teaching approach along with set practices that will assist students in their test-taking abilities. For instance, some students need to develop confidence in their ability to perform well on such tests. Others need to be reminded not to rush through items and to find key words in questions, and so on. So guided, students can develop strategies for dealing with difficult texts including:

- Asking another student or a parent to read sections of the text aloud to you
- Reading short portions of the text and then pausing to tell yourself about something that you have just read
- When reading a narrative text, rereading it with exaggerated expression to give the characters life
- Rereading the text while keeping your finger under the words as you read them so you will stay focused
- Questioning yourself after reading a paragraph, saying silently to yourself, "This is mainly about _____"
- Noticing key facts and statistics so you can return to the same place in the text later if you need that specific information
- Writing key words or concepts on sticky notes to mark specific sections of the text
- Reading a variety of genre including game rules, magazines, newspapers, and the like, so that you will be comfortable reading different types of text (Calkins, Montgomery, Santmans, & Falk, 1998)

Encourage students to reread textual material as well as to read and then go back over the same passage to skim for information. These techniques should be part of your instructional practice. For instance, a teacher asked her young charges which state Abraham Lincoln was from. Several students raised their hands. She called on Ramon who replied, "Illinois." The teacher then said, "Show me how you knew it was Illinois. Where in the book does it tell you?" In this instance, the teacher is demonstrating the need to locate information, a reference skill that will be used time and time again. Students must not get the impression that one reads a text only once. As the teacher, you need to model reading and rereading to find specific information. And, keep in mind, modeling appropriate learning behavior must be done repeatedly in different contexts if all students are to acquire this skill.

Standardized tests require a substantial amount of stamina and patience by students. It is helpful for them to be able to stay engaged in reading for the same length of time as the longest subtest of the standardized test they will be taking. This can be done by moving to increasingly longer periods for free reading, often called Sustained Silent Reading (SSR), Sustained Quiet Uninterrupted Individualized Reading Time (SQUIRT), Drop Everything and Read (DEAR), or Read a Book Because It's Terrific (RABBIT). At the beginning of the school year, students may only be able to sit for five or ten minutes during SSR. This time should be increased a few minutes each week until the students can stay engrossed in the book they have selected for the duration of what would be the equivalent time of the longest subtest.

Having students practice taking timed tests with similar formats is helpful, including using "bubble" answer sheets. This aids students in becoming more familiar

Preparing students to take standardized achievement tests by giving similar structured exams (i.e., using bubble answer sheets for a science test, setting time limits) helps ease student tension and improve performance.

with the testing situation. If the tests are to be given in a room other than the regular classroom, it is advisable to take the students down to that room a couple of times so that they will feel comfortable later during the testing situation. You might select a two- or three-day lesson that you could teach in the testing room. By doing this, not only will the students get used to the surrounding environment, but you will also have the opportunity to note any unique acoustical problems that you will need to eliminate or reduce in reading the test directions to the students.

State Assessment Measures

As mentioned earlier in this chapter, states have developed their own assessment measures for both reading and writing based on their respective state standards. Such tests are relatively new to the assessment horizon. In 1972, only one state had such tests. Eighteen years later every state had a test measuring reading. By 2000, every state had a test measuring writing as well. Most states administer the tests to certain grade levels each year. For example, the third, fifth, eighth, and eleventh grade levels in a state may be given reading and writing tests.

State assessment tests are similar to standardized tests in many ways. For instance, the tests are timed and are divided into sections. The state tests are standardized and normed; however, the standardization and norming is usually conducted only within the state where it is administered. The state tests are designed to assess the state goals and objectives in reading and writing. Most state departments of education also set benchmarks, or levels of learning, for reading and writing for the various grades. For instance, one benchmark may be proficiency in phonics by the end of third grade. You and your colleagues should be aware of benchmarks and address classroom instruction accordingly. Preparing lesson and unit plans with state grade level benchmarks and objectives in mind is critical if students are to perform well on the state tests. So important are the benchmarks and objectives that some states require teachers to know both benchmarks and objectives, being able to apply instructional strategies accordingly as part of teacher certification.

Many states provide school, class, and individual student test results. Some states use this information to fund schools or to even take control of poorer scoring school districts. Individual student scores are becoming high stakes in that unless certain minimum scores are attained, the student cannot graduate from high school.

AUTHENTIC ASSESSMENT

Have you kept a writing portfolio or a journal of the books you've read for a class? If so, your teacher was using authentic assessment, another gatekeeping device. In recent years, **authentic assessment** has become increasingly important in teaching reading and writing as it is the continuous assessment of ongoing work embedded in classroom contexts. Authentic assessment is based on the premise that teachers "who are in contact with the children daily and who understand how local circumstances enable and constrain learning are in the best position to offer . . . reliable, useful, and learning-centered assessments of student work" (Gallagher, 2000, p. 506). Authentic

Web Link:
Performance and
Portfolio Assessment for
Language Minority
Students

assessment includes student work (journals, writing, speaking, portfolios, projects, reading records), teacher observations (**anecdotal records,** checklists, notes), and information from teacher/student conferences (Cambourne & Turbill, 1990; Leslie & Jett-Simpson, 1997).

Developing alternative assessment tools requires that some basic principles be followed. Here are six principles to guide us in creating alternative, authentic measures (Alleman & Brophy, 1999):

- Assessment is considered an integral part of the curriculum and instruction process.
- Assessment is viewed as a thread that is woven into the curriculum, beginning before instruction and occurring at junctures throughout in an effort to monitor, assess, revise, and expand what is being taught and learned.
- A comprehensive assessment plan should be goal oriented, appropriate in level of difficulty, feasible, and cost effective.
- Assessment should benefit the learner (promote self-reflection and self-regulation) and inform teaching practices.
- Assessment results should be documented to "track" resources and develop learning profiles. (p. 16)

These guidelines are beneficial as we develop authentic assessment measures for reading and writing.

Portfolio Activity:
Internet Inquiry

Anecdotal Records

Anecdotal records are observations of students taken by the teacher as the students work. Such notes provide the teacher with insights on how students go through a learning process to develop a product such as a piece of writing or the answer to a comprehension question about an expository text. By taking such anecdotal records, you are able to make decisions as to how to assist a student in the learning process or even how the learning process might be restructured to better support the student's learning strategies and development as a reader and writer.

Anecdotal records are open ended. As the teacher, you may elect to include specific, rich details of the student as the student engages in literacy processes. Different situations may cause you to record diverse details that, when analyzed, may shed additional light on a child's learning. For example, Richard, a second grader, loved to tell jokes and stories, but he didn't enjoy chapter books. Week after week, his teacher noticed that his library selections were always nonfiction, informational books. Using this information from her anecdotal records about Richard, she sought out chapter books that contained short chapters with lots of humor for him to read during free reading time. To some extent, what you record depends upon your teaching, your students, and the context of the activity in which the student is engaged.

The content of anecdotal records needs to be written in a manner that will be useful. Thorndike and Hagen (1977) suggest three guidelines for the content of anecdotal records in the classroom:

1. Describe a specific event or product.
2. Report rather than evaluate or interpret.
3. Relate the material to other facts that are known about the child.

In classrooms where students are encouraged to be responsible and independent as readers and writers, teachers find more time to take anecdotal records. In classrooms where reading and writing are highly teacher directed, teachers have less time for recording such information. Despite being a labor-intensive process, anecdotal records provide valuable information. You must decide how and what your student expectations and teaching style will be and then determine the degree to which you'll incorporate anecdotal records as part of your assessment plan.

Each of us needs to discover what works best to record information about our students. Some teachers rely upon a clipboard that they tote around during different times of the day. The clipboard can be used in a variety of ways. It may contain five pages, each divided into thirds, with a different student's name in each 1/3 of the page so that the entire class is included. The teacher writes notes throughout the week, indicating each student's strengths, weaknesses, and so forth. At the end of the week, the information is then recorded on the computer and stored on a hard drive or disk with a separate file for each student. Both the contents of the clipboard and the computer cannot be accessible to students. Another way to use the clipboard is to have a page divided into four sections (one section for each week of the month) for each student. This can be bulky if there are twenty-five to thirty students in the class, but it does enable the teacher to see progress over time, a particularly helpful approach during a unit study. Some teachers use sticky notes with the date and names of the students to be observed written on them. Other teachers carry around a thin photo album using 4 by 6 index cards with the student's name written on the bottom line of the card. The index cards are taped in staggered fashion down the plastic photo slipcovers. When a student's card is filled, it is slid into a plastic photo slipcover and a new one taped in its place. When the teacher wants to write an anecdotal entry, she merely finds the student's name on the bottom of the card, flips up the cards taped above it, and begins writing.

There are a number of different things we need to look for to jot down as we create our student anecdotal records. Here are some suggestions as to what you may want to look for and record:

- Engagement in reading and writing
- What affects engagement in reading and writing
- What aspects of text student attends to
- Interactions with others during reading and writing
- Interactions with materials
- Insightful or interesting things students say
- Hypotheses students are trying out in reading and writing
- Misconceptions students have
- Changes students make in writing
- How students use text before, during, and after reading

- How a lesson affects a student's reading and writing
- Comparisons between what students say and what they do
- How, where, and with whom students work
- What are students' interests
- How students generate and solve problems in reading and writing
- Ideas for reading and writing lessons and materials
- How one reading and writing event relates to another
- How students use a variety of resources in reading and writing (Rhodes & Nathenson-Mejia, 1999, p. 86)

After the anecdotal records have been recorded, they must be carefully analyzed. This includes making inferences about your students' reading and writing based on the observations you made. It also includes identifying patterns of behavior, such as the teacher discovering reading habits and interests. Anecdotal records may also be used to identify strengths and needs in students' reading and writing.

As part of the analysis of anecdotal records, the teacher must formulate questions. For example, what was the effect of a mini-lesson on details on Antoine's descriptive writing? How did Sheryl and Tainia interact when they rewrote the story as a play? Does Jessica ever demonstrate leadership skills in any activity other than reading buddies? In what ways can the lessons be adapted to meet Jason's needs?

Anecdotal records are quick glimpses of stories of your students. These notes assess not only your students' reading and writing development but also your own teaching.

Book Logs

Having students write down the titles and authors of the books along with the date they read them provides valuable information. Known as book logs, the titles give the teacher a clue as to the particular genre, or kind of books, the student prefers whether it is historical fiction, fantasy, informational books, and so on. Authors give a clue as to the quality of the text being read. Award-winning authors tend to produce high-quality books. Some authors tend to produce enjoyable, quick read books. Both kinds of books are acceptable in the classroom, but they share different information in assessment.

Dating the log's entries helps you determine how quickly the student gets through a book. If a fourth grader takes a month to read a seventy-five-page book, it's doubtful that he was able to follow along with the story. A shorter, easier book might be suggested for future reading. By the second semester of first grade, students should be able to read a picture book in a day and a chapter book in three days. Granted these are easy picture books such as *The Carrot Seed* (Krauss, 1958) or chapter books such as Arnold Lobel's *Frog and Toad* and Cynthia Rylant's *Henry and Mudge* series. Calkins (2001) believes that fourth graders should read twenty-five books the caliber of Beverly Cleary's *Ramona* and Roald Dahl's *Matilda* during a school year. By upper elementary and middle school, students in Calkins' view should be reading a book a week, if not more.

Artifacts of Reading and Writing

Most of what we want to know about children's reading is invisible. "How they process print, what meaning-making strategies they use, their personal connections, or their confidence is not readily obvious. Thus, it is up to the assessment tools to make the invisible visible" (Barrentine, 1999, p. 4). With writing we have more clues, but still much is invisible. The way to make such intangibles tangible is to use artifacts of daily reading and writing. Samples of student work such as a dated weekly journal in which students write one day each week, learning logs, and literature response journals are excellent daily or weekly artifacts. Story reflections, illustrations, character maps, and Venn diagrams (Yopp & Yopp, 1996) are other good reading artifacts. Story maps, written drafts through completed pieces, and graphic organizers among other instructional techniques can be used as writing artifacts.

Portfolios

Portfolios developed out of the idea that to show one's work and development, an artist presents an array of the different kinds of work he created. As such portfolios reflect the breadth and depth of the artist's command of his craft. The work contained in a portfolio is then shared with the owner's critics or with patrons of the arts. In reading and writing, portfolios are used in a similar fashion—to demonstrate the student's progress and growth as a reader and writer. The portfolio approach has great intuitive appeal in reading and writing assessment as "it resonates with our desire to capture and capitalize on the best each student has to offer; it encourages us to use many different ways to evaluate learning; and it has an integrity and validity that no other type of assessment offers" (Valencia, 1999, p. 113).

There are different forms of portfolios used in reading and writing. *Show portfolios* include only a few select samples of the student's efforts. These samples are usually selected by the student with input from her teacher. *Working portfolios* include a broad sampling of the student's work. Working portfolios are used to guide and organize daily instruction (Farr, 1992). Portfolios may also include both teacher and student observations as well as informal assessment techniques such as checklists (Cambourne & Turbill, 1990; Goodman, 1991). *Diagnostic portfolios* provide a complete student profile as these portfolios include running records, book log reflections, journals, writing logs, retelling outlines, goal reflections by the student and the teacher, reading and writing interest inventories, and other informal assessments (Courtney & Abodeeb, 2001). Student work can be scanned and saved on CD-ROMs as a digital portfolio.

Farr (1992) believes that "the portfolio is the flagship of performance assessment" (p. 13). Farr goes on to write that

> a successful portfolio approach to assessment must revolve around regular and frequent attention to the portfolio by the student and the teacher. It does minimal good just to store a student's papers in a big folder and let them gather dust for lengthy periods of time. Papers must be added frequently; others can be weeded out in an ongoing rearrangement and selection process; most importantly, the whole process should involve frequent self-analysis by the students and regular conversations between the teacher and the student. (p. 13)

Teachers need to plan for the portfolio and then manage it. It is important to give some thought so you are *selective* about the contents, making certain that what is included reflects the broad goals of instruction. For instance, goals might include "understanding the author's message, learning new information from expository texts, summarizing the plot of a story, using word identification skills flexibly to construct meaning, reading fluently, or exhibiting an interest and desire to read" (Valencia, 1999, p. 115). If the instructional goals are not clearly stated and specified, the portfolio loses its focus and becomes little more than a collection of work.

A second aspect is the need to think about what can be done instructionally to assist students in reaching those instructional goals. How do activities and assignments fit into the picture? For example, a story map can be used to assess students' plot knowledge after they read a story or book. It can also be used to measure students' knowledge of story structure.

Keep in mind that the portfolio belongs to the student. Thus, students need to have some voice in what goes in or what is removed from the portfolio. The portfolio is not a collection of work. Rather it is an ever changing array of the student's work. It includes drafts of writing through the finished product. It includes reflections on books and articles read. Lists of books attempted, that is, books the student started to read but did not finish, as well as those completed are included. Skill lists and checklists are part of the portfolio. The contents of a portfolio can be organized in two layers: (a) the actual evidence, or raw data, and (b) the summary sheet or organizing framework that synthesizes information in the portfolio (Valencia, 1999). A compilation of student work and progress notes by both the teacher and the student goes in the first layer. The summary sheet is helpful in conferencing with the student and in parent-student-teacher conferencing.

Managing the contents of a portfolio is crucial. Some students need to learn how to stay organized and others may seem to never be organized, always losing papers. Having color-coded folders for each subject along with a daily assignment folder can aid such students. Just getting into the practice of putting things back in the same place will help some students become more efficient in filing away their work.

Flexibility is a major asset of the portfolio; however, it is also a drawback. To be effective, portfolio evaluation must be consistent and reliable to avoid inequity across students and schools. Teachers in a school and school district need to discuss the goals and priorities for instruction and assessment. The more artifacts collected, the greater the consistency in evaluation. Two levels of assessment evidence are needed in order to make certain of consistency—required evidence and supporting evidence. Required evidence permits us to look across students as well as within each student. This includes particular tasks or activities, checklists, or projects selected from a predetermined list. All of these need to be tied to identified goals and are included in the portfolios of all students at a particular grade level. The content can be somewhat structured (i.e., a writing log for science or math) or somewhat unstructured (i.e., the student selects a piece of writing to go into the portfolio each month or records an oral reading sample and dates it for each grading period). This kind of information is good to have to share with school administrators.

Supporting evidence is additional evidence that is not a part of every student's portfolio, such as a copy of a letter a student wrote to an author or politician, an il-

Sitting down with students individually on a quarterly basis to discuss their current goals and set new ones is very important, particularly at the intermediate and middle school grade levels. Students are then held responsible for their own learning.

lustration of a prediction of the ending of a mystery, a semantic map on a social studies chapter, and the like. Supporting evidence is important in that it builds "the complete picture of the student's literacy abilities because it adds the depth and variety typically missing in traditional assessments" (Valencia, 1999, p. 116).

The teacher and student should meet at least once each grading period to discuss the portfolio. At that time, pieces can be added to the portfolio while others are removed. In addition, this is a perfect time to set goals for the upcoming grading period. During this meeting, you and the student review and reflect upon how much the student has developed as a reader and writer during the past few weeks as well as since the school year began. Point out the effort put forth by the student and the work accomplished.

Rubrics

Rubrics became popular in recent years with the advent of authentic assessment. Two types of rubrics are commonly used: scoring and checklist. For scoring rubrics, students are given a rubric that states precisely the number of points each portion of the assignment is worth before they begin to attempt the assignment. An example is presented in Figure 5.1. Rubrics may be in a matrix format (see websites listed in this section.)

Rubrics can be easily made for an assignment or activity by going to one of two websites www.rubistar.4teachers.com or www.teach-ology.com and typing in the objective(s) for the task to be completed. The website then will develop the accompanying rubric. These rubrics can then be saved for future reference to save valuable time. The rubric should be shared with the students, discussing each requirement as

Figure 5.1

Scoring rubric for expository report

Possible Points	Points Earned	Criteria
5 points	____	Chooses topic on schedule
10 points	____	Follows guidelines for research
10 points	____	Completes rough draft
5 points	____	Self-proofs and gets peer to proof
15 points	____	Final draft uses student's own words, is neat, and is written to the student's ability
Total points possible = 45 points		Total points earned = _____

Figure 5.2

Checklist rubric for literature response journal

Criteria	Always	Most of the Time	Rarely	Comments
1. Book is on assigned topic				
2. Daily entries				
3. Entries relate to plot				
4. Entries relate to characters				
5. Entries are thoughtful, reflective				

specified. Some teachers post the rubric for major assignments in a prominent classroom location as well as providing copies to students.

Using a checklist format for rubrics results in quicker evaluation by the teacher. Like the scoring rubric, criteria are established and presented to the students prior to their starting the assignment. Above is an example of a checklist rubric (Figure 5.2):

Applying Rubrics in the Classroom: The Fish Bowl

The Fish Bowl was designed as a means to assess student understanding of a book. Upper elementary and middle school students become accountable for their independent reading by reading aloud, asking a question, and answering a question in front of their peers (Katz & Kuby, 2001). The books may be those used for free reading time. Claudia Anne Katz and Sue Ann Kuby, both eighth grade teachers, have students read selections of their own choosing and then prepare a presentation for a small group of students. Each student reads aloud a self-selected passage (no longer than half a page in length) that was practiced earlier. This aids in developing reading fluency. The student also writes a twenty- to twenty-five word summary of the book. This serves as the opening for their presentation, so the student must strive to "hook" the audience by making the summary interesting.

Since formulating thoughtful, higher level questions requires some skill, Katz and Kuby model this behavior for their classes and provide additional instruction. The questions are posed from the audience.

Students along with the teacher can create a checklist rubric for grading the Fish Bowl activity. Included in the rubric should be summary, read aloud/fluency, explanation of passage selected for read aloud, and ability to answer questions. Before students prepare for the Fish Bowl, they should be given a list of questions along with the rubric so they will know what is expected of them. Questions might include:

What problem is posed in the story?

How do the characters try to solve the problem?

What else might solve the problem?

What is the most interesting thing about this book?

What did you discover that you didn't know before you read this book?

What does the author do well or not do well in this book?

What lesson does the author want you to learn from this book?

Describe one of the characters so your audience would recognize him or her.

The Fish Bowl works well with eight or twelve students. If you have diverse learners, try eight students to start out, with you serving as a model the first time. Have the four students who are presenting sit in windmill fashion, chairs angled so students 1 and 3 are back to back and students 2 and 4 are back to back. Then have student 5 sit facing student 1, student 6 facing student 2, and so forth, on the perimeter of the windmill. Student 1 begins the presentation by giving the title and author of his book and then reading the summary he has written. The summary should provide a broad overview of the book as well as whet the appetite of the listeners. If the summary is weak, it demonstrates that student 1 has a poor understanding of the book. Next, student 1 reads the passage that has been selected. The passage might be an exciting part of the plot, a good description of the way the main character feels, or an interesting writing style utilized by the author. After reading the passage aloud, student 1 explains why the passage was selected and then fields questions from students 5 through 8 (or 5 through 12, depending on how many students are involved in the Fish Bowl), who are seated in the outer circle around the windmill. It takes about an hour to do a Fish Bowl for four students at the middle school level, less time for students at the intermediate level.

Web Links:
Creating Rubrics

Teach-nology

Checklist rubrics are, in effect, a modification of the scoring rubric and anecdotal records. They are effective measures that do require more time for the teacher to review when considering instructional approaches. However, they provide more insight as to the student's strengths and needs than scoring rubrics. Again, you must determine what your goals are and how each type fits into your instructional and assessment needs.

Rubrics are good assessment measures for reading and writing projects such as this autobiographical project.

INFORMAL TESTING MEASURES

Web Link:
Ericae.net

Informal testing measures are used by teachers at the beginning of and at different times during the school year to determine students' reading and writing abilities. Included in this category are running records, informal reading inventories (IRIs), holistic evaluation of writing, and spelling assessment. These are described below.

Running Records

During an informal reading inventory (IRI), the student reads leveled passages and answers comprehension questions as the teacher notes miscues. A variation of the IRI for emergent and beginning readers is another observational procedure called **running records.** Developed by Clay (1985), running records guide our teaching by evaluating students' strengths and needs during reading. The running record requires the teacher to jot down whether the children are self-monitoring their reading, if the reading material is appropriate, and what strategies the students are using to identify unknown words. In Clay's (2000, p. 3) view, "running records provide an assessment of *text reading,* and are designed to be taken as a child reads orally from any text. The successful early reader brings his speech to bear on the interpretation of print. His vocabulary, sentence patterns, and pronunciation of words provide indispensable clues for recognizing printed words." As teachers, we look for patterns in each child's errors. Based on the type of errors made, we can then discover what cues they are using and those they need to develop and apply.

In running records, the teacher collects data about the student during the regular classroom reading activities in which the student reads aloud. Using a sheet of lined paper, the teacher makes a check mark for each word that the child says correctly in a line of text. A perfect score would equal the same number of check marks as words in the line (not sentence). If the student inserts a word or substitutes another word, those words are written down. For an omitted word, the teacher draws a short line to indicate the word was skipped. If the student corrects his or her own error, the teacher writes "sc" for self-correction. The scoring guide for running records is outlined below:

Teaching Strategy:
Assessing Fluency

Correct word	check mark
Insertion	word child says
Omission	———
Substitution	word child says in lieu of correct word
Self-correction	sc

Cueing systems used by the student can be determined through the use of running records. For instance, if a child says the word "gave" for "handed," the meaning remains the same. However, if a child substitutes "says" for "said," it is a grammatical difference. The meaning is essentially the same, but the teacher will know to work on verb tense as part of the child's language development.

For first and second grade teachers, the task of keeping running records is relatively easy as students tend to read more slowly than upper grade students. The font size of the print is larger, and the textual material is less complicated. Running records do not interrupt the flow of reading lessons nor do they require special preparation on the teacher's part. Running records, like IRIs, can be translated into independent, instructional, and frustration reading levels (see Figure 5.3 for examples of running scripted and unscripted records).

Reading Levels for Running Records and IRIs

Independent Level. At this level, the student reads fluently with excellent comprehension and high interest. This level is also called the *recreational level* as students can read freely on their own without any assistance (recognizes 95 percent of the words with 90 percent comprehension).

Instructional Level. At this level, the student progresses in developing reading competency under the teacher's guidance. Reading material needs to challenge the student but not be too difficult as to cause discouragement. This level is also called the *teaching level* (recognizes 90 percent of the words with 75 percent comprehension).

Frustration Level. At this level, the student is unable to pronounce many of the words or is unable to comprehend the material adequately. There is often word-by-word reading. The frustration level is also the lowest level at which

Figure 5.3

Example of running records

Running records may be scripted or unscripted. A scripted running record requires that the teacher have a written copy of the text to use as a scoring sheet. An unscripted running record does not require a copy of the text, only a piece of paper and pencil.

Examples of Scoring a Scripted Text as a Running Record:

Correct:	✓ ✓ ✓ ✓ ✓ ✓ The paper was easy to fold.
Insertion:	✓ ✓ ✓ ✓ ✓ up ✓ Shading his eyes, he looked ∧ skyward.
Omission:	✓ ✓ ✓ ✓ The boy threw the ~~paper~~ ✓ ✓ ✓ ✓ airplane into the sky.
Substitution:	✓ ✓ ✓ loamed ✓ ✓ ✓ Thick, blue haze ~~loomed~~ over the city.
Self-correction:	✓ ✓ sc ✓ ✓ ✓ ✓ The boy coughed as he ran to
(not counted as error)	✓ ✓ ✓ ✓ ✓ ✓ where the paper airplane landed.

Examples of Unscripted Scoring of the Above Text

Number of words in each line
1. (6)
2. (6)
3. (5)
4. (4)
5. (7)
6. (7)
7. (6)

In scoring the running record, total the number of words in the passage (43). Next, total the number of errors made by the child (3). Subtract the number of errors (3) from the total number of words in the passage (43) and divide by the total number of words (43). The answer is 93 percent. This percentage is the number of words the child read correctly. A score of 93 percent means the child is reading at his/her instructional reading level.

the reader is able to understand. The text is too difficult to engage the reader sufficiently for instructional purposes (recognizes less than 90 percent of the words and 50 percent or less comprehension).

Listening Capacity Level (IRIs only). Unlike the other three levels, this level is determined by the child being read to by the teacher or aide. The teacher is seeking to determine the greatest level at which the student can comprehend material that is read aloud. Sometimes this is called the *potential level* because this would be the highest level the student could read fluently if there were no comprehension or pronunciation problems (comprehension level is 75 percent).

The teacher would then classify the errors as insertions, omissions, and substitutions to gain more insight as to the student's reading difficulties. In short, running records are taken to capture progress "from the time a child tries to retell a story from the pictures in a book until the reader has become a silent reader" (Clay, 2000, p. 4). Ideally, the student's path of progress will indicate that the increasing challenges of progressively more difficult textual reading material are being met.

Diverse learners may possess pronunciation differences that should not be counted as errors. For instance, an African American child may say "asx" for "asked," "wif" for "with," or "poo" for "pool." Such pronunciations are not uncommon in Ebonics or Black English. A native Spanish speaking child may have difficulty pronouncing the English language sounds of v, j, z, sh, ng, and zh (as in measure) because these are not common sounds in their first language. Dialects also should not be a factor in the coding. In certain parts of the country, the words "pin" and "pen" are pronounced the same way as are the words "are" and "our." These should not count as errors.

Using Retellings to Assess Comprehension

As students move from emergent readers to being independent readers, assessment measures are needed in addition to those already mentioned in the chapter. Retelling stories can give the teacher insights as to a student's comprehension and understanding of text. Taberski (2000) uses retellings along with running records to determine the reading progress of young readers. She has her students individually retell stories as she takes notes. After the retelling is completed, she then uses these guidelines in assessing each child's comprehension.

Guidelines in Using Retellings to Assess Young Children's Comprehension

When a child understands what he's read, he may indicate this by:

- Summarizing what happened in the story or informational book
- Using the book's illustrations to support what he's saying
- Referring to the text to back up what he's saying
- Giving examples
- Appearing confident and at ease
- Spontaneously giving information about the story or text
- Responding emotionally to the text: he may say he loves or hates the text, laugh and smile, or express sadness at how it made him feel
- Making connections between the book and other books or experiences he's had himself

When a child doesn't understand what he's read, he may indicate this by:

- Giving a lot of details, particularly giving quite specific information regarding the first two or three pages (often the only part he may understand)

- Showing an overdependence upon the illustrations to tell what happened
- Referring to the text either too much or not at all
- Giving no examples from the text
- Appearing uncomfortable, trapped, and wiggling a lot. He may hesitate a great deal and insert numerous "ums"
- Relying on teacher's prompts to get through the retelling, often looking to the teacher in a pleading way for help
- Not responding emotionally to the text
- Making no connection between the text and other books or experiences he has had himself

(Adapted from Sharon Taberski, 2000)

The accuracy of the child's retelling should be measured. If a student is reading a text independently and has a retelling accuracy rate below 95 percent, one can assume the difficulty lies with the child not knowing enough words. Thus, much effort is devoted by the child in trying to discover what the words are and little concentration is left to direct toward getting the meaning of what he is reading. When the accuracy rate is 95 percent or higher, and the child doesn't understand what is read, the text is probably too difficult for the child (Taberski, 2000). It could be too long or have a more complex plot, characters, problems, settings, and events than the child is used to reading. Reading such text may be too labored for the child to gather understanding and comprehension during the reading process. In particular, second language learners who lack a rich oral English vocabulary are placed at a disadvantage when they encounter this type of text.

Informal Reading Inventory

Informal reading inventories (IRIs) have been used for decades to find the proper fit of the book to the child. IRIs are especially helpful in differentiated instruction. The teacher estimates the student's reading level and selects a level, or even two levels, below that point. The student then reads aloud a word list at that selected level. This continues until the student fails to read aloud 90 percent of the word list. Next, the student reads aloud short passages from graded material as the teacher marks any errors on a scoring sheet. Next the teacher administers comprehension questions based on the passage and records those responses. The student then reads aloud the next reading level passage and answers the comprehension questions. This continues until the textual material is too difficult for the student. At that point, the oral reading portion of the test is halted and the teacher reads aloud the next reading level passage and asks the accompanying comprehension questions. This continues until the student performs poorly on the listening test. Later, the teacher determines the student's reading level and assigns books that are somewhat challenging but not too troublesome for the student. Any comprehension or word identification problems are noted by the teacher for use in future instructional plans.

Reading levels can be determined for each student by individually administering an IRI. An example of the coding system commonly found in most IRIs is in Figure 5.4.

Figure 5.4

Coding system for informal reading inventory (IRI)

1. *Omission.* A word, phrase, or sentence is failed to be read out loud by the student. *Code = circle the omitted word(s)*

   Example: John dropped his (library) book. He never noticed until he arrived home.

2. *Substitution.* A word is substituted for another word or words. *Code = Draw a line through the word in the text and write the substituted word above it.*

   Example: Alice ran as gracefully as a ~~gazelle~~. (*giraffe* written above)

3. *Mispronunciation.* The word is pronounced incorrectly. *Draw a line through the word in the text and write the phonetic version the child pronounced above it.*

   Example: James ran to the ~~creek~~. (*crik* written above)

4. *Insertion.* A word (or words) is inserted into the passage. *Mark with a caret (^) to show where the word is inserted and write the word above the caret.*

   Example: The big dog licked its ^paw. (*hurt* written above)

5. *Repetition.* A word or phrase is repeated. *Underline portion of the text that is repeated.*

   Example: The kite <u>was caught</u> in the tree.

6. *Reversal.* The order of a word (or words) is transposed. *Use a curved line ⁀ (the proof mark for transposition) over and under the word(s) transposed.*

   Example: The large giant was taller/than us.

7. *Pronunciation.* A word (or words) is pronounced by the examiner for the student. *Put the letter "P" over the word pronounced.*

   Example: The judge declared the man innocent. (*P* over "declared")

8. *Self-correction.* The student successfully corrects the error without assistance. *Put a "C" inside a circle and draw a line under the portion the student self-corrected.*

   Example: Balloons <u>flew</u> off into the sky. (Ⓒ above "flew")

9. *Unsuccessful correction.* The student tries to correct the error but fails to do so. *Put "UC" inside a circle and draw a line under the portion of text the student attempted to correct. Record each attempt. 1. (word(s) used) 2. (word(s) used).*

   Example: Marty <u>tried</u> to find the lost toy boat. (UC above "tried")

10. *Abandoned correct form.* The word(s) is read correctly but then the student abandons the form to use a different response. *Put "AC" in a circle above the word and draw a line where the student abandoned the correct text. Write the different response above the correct word(s).*

    Example: The girl thought the ocean was <u>amazing to see</u>. (AC *cold and deep* above)

There are a number of commercially prepared IRIs that are available in English such as the *Classroom Reading Inventory* (Silvaroli & Wheelock, 2004) and the *Flynt/Cooter Reading Inventory for the Classroom* (Flynt & Cooter, 1995). Some have also been translated into other languages such as Spanish, for example, the *Basic Reading Inventory* (Johns, 2000). Typically, at least two forms of the IRI are contained in the same manual so that the teacher may administer an IRI twice to the same student to aid in measuring reading and/or listening achievement.

A drawback to informal reading inventories is that they must be conducted on a one-to-one basis with the student and teacher. Therefore, they are quite time consuming. Hence, some experienced teachers use informal reading inventories during the school year only with those students who seem to have difficulty with word identification or comprehension strategies.

DIVERSE LEARNERS AND ASSESSMENT

Good readers and writers tend to share a number of characteristics, including how they are viewed by teachers. Allington (2001) has studied struggling readers as well as good readers and has come up with a set of characteristics regarding each type of reader:

Struggling readers are more likely to:

- Be reading materials that are difficult for them
- Be asked by the teacher to read aloud
- Be interrupted by the teacher when they miscall a word
- Be interrupted by the teacher more quickly than an average or good reader
- Pause at a word and wait for the teacher to prompt
- Be told by the teacher to sound out a word

In comparison, good readers are more likely to:

- Be reading materials of appropriate difficulty
- Be asked by the teacher to read silently
- Be expected to self-monitor and self-correct
- Be interrupted by the teacher only after a wait period or at the end of a sentence
- Be asked by the teacher to reread or cross-check when interrupted

Similar occurrences take place during writing as well. Struggling writers are more likely to:

- Be given suggestions to improve their writing
- Be expected to do less variety of writing
- Be expected to do less self-checking, revising, and editing

Good writers are more likely to:

- Be expected to write in all genres
- Be asked questions by the teacher in order to improve the piece of writing
- Be expected to do self-checking, revising, and editing

Gender is an issue in teaching reading and writing. Consider the following statistics: Boys are:

- Three to five times more likely than girls to be placed in school programs for reading or learning problems (National Center for Education Statistics, 2000)
- About 50 percent more likely to be retained a grade than girls (Kleinfeld, 1999)
- Among the over 80 percent of the children and adolescents identified with attention deficit disorder (ADD) and attention deficit hyperactivity disorder (ADHD) (American Psychiatric Association, 1994)

Girls are:

- As a group, better achievers on standardized reading achievement tests in elementary school than their male counterparts (Pottorff, Phelps-Zientarsky, & Slovera, 1996)
- Found to be less than 20 percent of the children and adolescents identified with attention deficit disorder (ADD) and attention deficit hyperactivity disorder (ADHD) (American Psychiatric Association, 1994)
- More likely to finish high school than boys (despite the possibility of teenage pregnancy, only 45 percent of all dropouts are female) (National Center for Educational Statistics, 1998)

As we take this information into consideration, we realize we need to be proactive with our struggling readers and writers as they need to engage in more literacy activities. Such students also need additional direct instruction and modeling by us. More structured assignments in both reading and writing provide them with the guidance they need until they develop command of the skills or strategies being taught. Struggling readers and writers may need more time to develop a response to a question.

Individual Educational Plans (IEPs)

As stated earlier in Chapter 4, most classrooms have inclusion students who have **individual educational plans (IEPs)**. Such plans state the student's current level of performance along with a goal for the school year and a time line. A team of the classroom teacher, special education teacher, school psychologist, building principal, speech therapist, and other support personnel work collaboratively to develop challenging yet realistic instructional objectives for the student. Each objective has evaluation criteria and a time schedule such as daily, weekly, and so forth. Figure 5.5 contains an IEP for an inclusion student.

As teachers, we should set and expect realistic expectations for all readers and writers as we challenge them and provide the necessary instructional support and resources they require.

TECHNOLOGY AND READING ASSESSMENT

Web Link:
Rhodes to Reading

Reading software that measures comprehension is used in many classrooms to assist teachers in gathering assessment data. Such programs as *Accelerated*

Figure 5.5

Literacy individual educational plan (IEP)

CURRENT PERFORMANCE LEVEL: Student is able to identify 24 out of 26 letters of the alphabet with verbal cues. She experiences difficulty, however, with the letter-sound concept. Student has also been recently introduced to rhyming, but has not yet mastered this concept.

ANNUAL GOAL: Given a CVC word with the vowel provided, Student will identify 1 of the 2 consonant sounds in the word on 7 out of 10 opportunities across 9 consecutive weeks.

IMPLEMENTATION DATE: 1–21–2003   IMPLEMENTATION BY: SUPPORT STAFF

INSTRUCTIONAL OBJECTIVE	EVALUATION CRITERIA SCHEDULE	DATE REVIEWED WITH RESULTS
When given orally presented, randomly selected individual consonant sounds, Student will say the letter of the alphabet that represents the sound in 17 out of 21 consonant sounds presented across 3 consecutive weeks.	Daily Work Progress Monitoring Informal Assessments Quarterly	
When presented with individual, randomly selected consonant letter names accompanied with visual representation of the letter, Student will orally produce the letter sound of 17 out of 21 consonant sounds across 3 consecutive weeks.	Daily Work Progress Monitoring Informal Assessments Quarterly	
Given a word, Student will state a word that rhymes with the word given on 4 out of 5 trials across 3 consecutive weeks.	Daily Work Progress Monitoring Informal Assessments Quarterly	

Reader (Institute for Academic Excellence, 1998) and Scholastic's *Reading Counts!* (www.readingcounts.com) enable students to independently be tested for comprehension of children's literature apart from the traditional basal reader program. Typically such software programs rely heavily on testing students' recall of information presented within the book. Unfortunately, application of knowledge gained as well as critical or higher level thinking skills are not measured to any extent. Each student's score is monitored by the software program, which keeps track of progress throughout the school year.

Both *Accelerated Reader* and *Reading Counts!* have over 20,000 books categorized by reading difficulty so that teachers can better assist students in finding appropriate reading material at their independent reading level. A special feature of *Reading Counts!* is the Book Expert search option, which allows teachers to locate books on topics within a specified reading difficulty range. Scholastic offers a special awards program that accompanies *Reading Counts!* For a modest cost of roughly a dollar per book when twelve copies are purchased, schools can provide books as rewards for students who complete a specified amount of reading.

A Web-based management system called *Book Adventure* is a free source for teachers and students. Over 10,000 books are organized into forty interest categories. Books can be located by interest, author, title, and grade level difficulty. End of the book quizzes are generated from a test item bank making each test unique, unlike the tests for *Accelerated Reader* and *Reading Counts!* which are set forms. *Accelerated Reading, Reading Counts!* and *Book Adventure* do not offer instructional assistance for readers.

To locate books that match well with a child's reading level go to www.reading a-z.com or www.leveledbooks.com and these websites will give lists of appropriate books. Different genre of books are included to meet student interests.

Web Links:
Reading A–Z

Leveled Books

READABILITY FORMULAS

Readability formulas have been around since the 1950s. The *Dale-Chall Readability Formula* (1995) was one of the first and has been recently revised. Best used for reading material that is at the fifth grade level and higher, the *Dale-Chall Readability Formula* gives an estimated level of difficulty. The Microsoft Word word-processing program offers an easy to use readability measure based on the *Flesch-Kincaid Formula.* To use it, simply go to the "Grammar" feature under "Preferences" and click the mouse on "Document Statistics." Then either type or scan in the text to be measured to get an estimate of the level of reading difficulty. Another scale is the *Fry Readability Scale,* perhaps the simplest to use. The *Fry* requires that you count the number of sentences and words and then use a graph or scale to find the passage's readability level (Figure 5.6).

HOLISTIC EVALUATION OF WRITING

Writing ability can be a challenge for teachers to evaluate at the beginning of the school year. Holistic evaluation of writing enables a teacher to get an overall picture of the students' writing abilities rather than attempting to find out all of the writing skills students possess. Holistic evaluation is best used when three teachers at the same grade level cooperate to evaluate their students' writing proficiencies. The teachers first agree on a topic for the students to write about, such as "My Favorite Holiday." Then the teachers write on the topic for the same amount of time they plan to allow their students (i.e. twenty-five minutes for a second grade class; forty minutes for a fifth or sixth grade class). If the teachers find they can adequately address the topic in the amount of time established, they then give the topic to their students. If more time is needed, the time limit is increased for the students. If the topic proves to be too difficult, the teachers brainstorm for another topic. The teachers then create a ten-item rubric (content and writing conventions, such as grammar, handwriting, spelling, punctuation) to evaluate the students. An example of a holistic evaluation form follows (see Figure 5.7 on page 222).

Figure 5.6

Fry Readability Graph

Graph for Estimating Readability—Extended

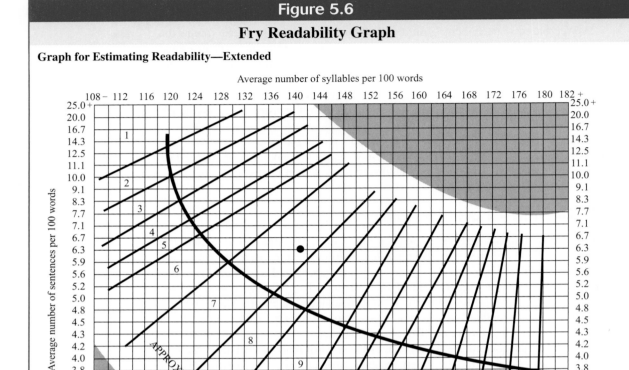

Students are given code numbers so that the teachers can't readily identify their work. For instance, students in Mrs. Crandell's class are assigned numbers between 1 and 30, in Mr. Johnson's class numbers are between 31 and 60, and in Miss Santini's class numbers are between 61 and 90.

The teachers administer the writing assignment under the allocated time restraint they previously agreed upon. After the students leave for the day, the three teachers gather the papers and meet to evaluate them. Initially, ten papers are taken randomly from the stack of ninety papers. The teachers then individually rate each of the papers. No more than one minute is devoted to each student's paper. After each teacher has evaluated all ten papers, the teachers then compare their scores. There shouldn't be more than three points' difference between the three teachers (scorers) for any one student's paper. Any significant discrepancies are discussed. When the

Expanded Directions for Working the Readability Graph

1. Randomly select three sample passages and count out exactly 100 words each, beginning with the beginning of a sentence. Do count proper nouns, initializations, and numerals.

2. Count the number of sentences in the 100 words, estimating length of the fraction of the last sentence to the nearest one-tenth.

3. Count the total number of syllables in the 100-word passage. If you don't have a hand counter available, an easy way is to simply put a mark above every syllable over one in each word, then when you get to the end of the passage, count the number of marks and add 100. Small calculators can also be used as counters by pushing numeral 1, then pushing the + sign for each word or syllable when counting.

4. Enter graph with *average* sentence length and *average* number of syllables; plot dot where the two lines intersect. The area where the dot is plotted will give you the approximate grade level.

5. If a great deal of variability is found in syllable count or sentence count, putting more samples into the average is desirable.

6. A word is defined as a group of symbols with a space on either side; thus, *Joe, IRA, 1945,* and *&* are each one word.

7. A syllable is defined as a phonetic symbol. Generally, there are as many syllables as vowel sounds. For example, *stopped* is one syllable and *wanted* is two syllables. When counting syllables for numerals and initializations, count one syllable for each symbol. For example, *1945* is four syllables, *IRA* is three syllables, and *&* is one syllable.

Source: From *Elementary Reading Instruction,* by E.B. Fry (New York: McGraw-Hill, 1997). Reprinted by permission of McGraw-Hill Companies, Inc.

scoring issue has been resolved, it is written down on the rubric for the criterion. For instance, if a student used only short, simple vocabulary words, that would be a 2 in word choice as compared with the student who used three interesting, colorful words and was assigned a 4 for word choice.

After the rubric has been developed for the ten randomly selected papers, the remaining eighty papers are evaluated individually by all three teachers. The teachers then analyze their own students' scores to examine individual students' strengths and weaknesses in writing. In addition, each criterion is averaged and noted so that the teacher will know the strengths and weaknesses of the class. For example, if Mrs. Crandell's class scored an average of 3.7 on quality of ideas but only 2.3 on organization, she will address one of her first mini-lessons to teaching her students how to organize their writing.

Figure 5.7
Holistic evaluation of writing

Date: _____   Student Number _____

Type: Narrative   Final Score _____
       Expository
       Persuasive

Content	High		Average		Low/Not Present
1. Quality of ideas	5	4	3	2	1
2. Organization	5	4	3	2	1
3. Word choice	5	4	3	2	1
4. Sentence fluency	5	4	3	2	1
5. Support of ideas	5	4	3	2	1

Writing Conventions

	High		Average		Low/Not Present
6. Voice	5	4	3	2	1
7. Grammar/usage	5	4	3	2	1
8. Spelling	5	4	3	2	1
9. Punctuation/ Capitalization	5	4	3	2	1
10. Handwriting	5	4	3	2	1

Source: Adapted from P. J. Farris, *Language arts: Process, product, and assessment,* 3rd ed., published by McGraw-Hill, 2001. Used by permission.

Typically, holistic evaluation of writing occurs three times over the year. With this schedule, the teacher can better ascertain the students' acquisition and development of writing skills. Such practice can help students with timed state tests.

Spelling

During the past thirty years, spelling has received a great amount of attention. In 1971, Read discovered that preschool children tend to "invent" the spellings of words they use in their writing. Furthermore, Read concluded that such invented spellings were predictable and not random. This became known as "invented spelling" or "temporary spelling." While researchers concentrated on the spellings of preschoolers and students in the early grades, little attention has been devoted to conventional spelling and accompanied teaching methods for upper elementary and middle school students. "Children who are not yet at the correct stage of spelling development—that is, students who do not spell approximately 90 percent of spelling words correctly and whose errors are not mostly at the transitional level—do not benefit from formal spelling instruction" (Tompkins, 2000, p. 341).

To determine students' spelling ability, a teacher may make a simple spelling inventory. For first and second graders, select about 20 three- to five-letter words with different initial and final consonant sounds (i.e., man and bat) and long and short vowels (i.e., gate and fin). For third grade and higher, taking five words from each level of a graded spelling series will suffice. The important thing to remember is to start with easy words and go up. Hence, begin with easy second grade words when administering such a test to third grade students, then move on to third grade words. If you have a diverse classroom, start with first grade words. At the higher levels, start two or three grade levels below. For example, for a seventh grade test, begin with fourth grade words and go up in difficulty from there.

In analyzing the test results, look for patterns. Does the child write "pre" for "per"? "Becuz" for "because"? Or "shun" for "tion"? Such clues will give you insight as to what spelling errors need to be resolved as part of your teaching.

Another spelling assessment measure that is effective is the spelling sentence test. At the beginning of the school year, select or create a sentence that has words with common spelling patterns. During the first week of school, read the sentence out loud for the students to write. Date the sample and collect. Then three months later repeat the process using the same sentence. Do it again three months later. This gives a baseline for spelling instruction as well as a demonstration of the growth of the student during the school year.

Here are two sample sentences:

For a second grade class:

The blue truck stopped in back of the department store.

For a fifth grade class:

In February, we conduct science experiments inside but we take notes of the changing environment outside.

Such periodic spelling assessments can be very informative to the teacher and to students as well. Caution needs to be taken that the students don't memorize the sentence and use it to study for the reexaminations later in the year.

Summary

Teachers need to be aware of the various ways to assess students' literacy development. Finding the appropriate assessment measure and applying it can yield results that, when analyzed, can be used to modify instruction. All forms of assessment—standardized tests, authentic assessment, and informal testing measures—play an important role in the curriculum process. The key is to select the appropriate measure and analyze the results in consideration of instructional methods. By doing so, the teacher will be more efficient and effective in assisting students in their literacy learning.

Chapter Review

Go to the Online Learning Center at **www.mhhe.com/farrisreading** to take chapter quizzes, practice with key terms, and review important content.

Main Points

- The purpose of the learning situation determines the different forms and times for assessment.

- Assessment is the act of gathering data in order to better understand the strengths and weaknesses of a student's progress in reading and writing.

- Evaluation is the act of using assessment results or data to make informed decisions about future instruction.

- Benchmarks are measures the typical student should attain.

- Assessment can include tests, student work, interviews, teacher observations, and other kinds of approaches.

- Learning isn't a direct, linear upward line.

- Learning is affected by motivation, effort, and self-esteem.

- Learning varies according to student diversity.

- States have developed their own assessment measures for both reading and writing based on their respective state standards.

- Standardized tests are based on behavioral objectives with the results of a single test determining the evaluation.

- Anecdotal records are observations of students taken by the teacher as the students work.

- Samples of student work, such as a dated weekly journal in which students write one day each week, learning logs, and literature response journals, are excellent daily or weekly artifacts for reading and writing assessment.

- In reading and writing, portfolios are used to demonstrate a student's progress and growth as a reader and writer.

- A rubric states the criteria for which an assignment will be evaluated. Scoring rubrics state precisely the number of points each portion of the assignment is worth before the students begin to attempt the assignment. A checklist rubric results in quicker evaluation by the teacher. Like the scoring rubric, criteria are established and presented to the students prior to their starting the assignment.

- Informal reading inventories (IRIs) are used to find the proper fit of the book, usually a basal reader, to the child.

- The running record requires the teacher to jot down whether the children are self-monitoring their reading, if the reading material is appropriate, and what strategies the students are using to identify unknown words.

- Holistic evaluation of writing enables a teacher to get an overall picture of the students' writing abilities rather than attempting to find out all of the writing skills students possess.

- Invented or temporary spellings are predictable and not random.

Key Terms

Reflecting and Reviewing

1. How can assessment be balanced?
2. In what ways can I assist my students in performing better on state and national standardized tests?
3. What types of authentic assessment fit best with my teaching style and the grade level I teach?
4. How can I incorporate the results of my student assessment into my instruction to meet state benchmarks for achievement?
5. What kinds of assessment can I use to help me be both more effective and more efficient as a teacher in meeting student needs and the school district goals?

Classroom Teaching Resources

Flynt, E. S., & Cooter, R. B. Jr. (1995). *Flynt/Cooter reading inventory for the classroom.* Scottsdale, AZ: Gorsuch Scarisbrick Publishers.

Johns, J. (2000). *Basic reading inventory.* Dubuque, IA: Kendall-Hunt.

———. (2000). *Basic reading inventory: Spanish version.* Dubuque, IA: Kendall-Hunt.

Sivaroli, N. (2004). *Classroom reading inventory (CRI),* 10th ed. Boston: McGraw-Hill.

Tompkins, G. E. (2000). *Teaching writing: Balancing process and product,* (3rd ed). Upper Saddle River, NJ: Prentice Hall.

Software

Advantage Learning Systems. (2000). *Accelerated reader.* Wisconsin Rapids, WI: Advantage Learning Systems.

Scholastic. (2000). *Book counts!* New York: Scholastic.

Methods for Teaching Reading

"*To begin on the lifelong journey that the tools of reading and writing permit, young children need to participate with literacy in meaningful ways.*"

Elfrieda Hiebert and Taffy Raphael, experts in the area of reading

Emergent Literacy: Beginning Reading and Writing

Key Ideas

- **Emergent literacy** is the development of activities and behaviors related to written language that begins early in a child's life and continues until the child reaches the stage of conventional literacy.

- The International Reading Association (IRA) and The National Association for the Education of Young Children's (NAEYC) joint position statement *Learning to Read and Write: **Developmentally Appropriate Practices** for Young Children* (1998) is highlighted and used as a springboard for the chapter content.

- From birth to preschool, children go through identifiable stages as their oral language develops. Oral language is the foundation for reading and writing.

- The teaching approaches discussed in the chapter can be adapted in many ways to meet the needs of diverse learners.

- Reading aloud is an entertaining activity that is crucial to the development of an emergent reader and writer.

- Children learn the concepts of print by noticing surrounding environmental print, engaging in **literacy play centers,** and interacting with text in meaningful ways.

- Emergent readers need the support of teaching techniques like **shared reading** and **guided reading** to develop literacy skills.

- Self-selected independent reading is an important literacy event in primary classrooms.

- Budding writers use temporary spelling to communicate their ideas.

- The five types of writing children in primary classrooms do are **shared writing, interactive writing, patterned writing,** guided writing or **writing workshop,** and independent writing. Each type of writing offers students a different level of support.
- The daily use of shared reading and writing experiences like the morning message is a powerful way to reinforce the skills of emergent readers and writers.
- Technology enhances the learning of young children.

Questions to Ponder

- What is the definition of emergent literacy?
- According to the IRA/NAEYC position statement: What are effective ways in which parents and family members encourage a preschooler's reading and writing growth? How do first grade teachers foster the literacy development of their students?
- In what kind of environment does oral language flourish?
- How do young readers develop? What can parents and educators do to promote this development?
- How do children learn concepts of print?
- How do shared and guided reading lessons support children's literacy growth?
- What are the benefits of encouraging young writers to use their own temporary spellings?
- What kinds of writing experiences inspire young children as they compose pieces?
- Why is the morning message such a powerful instructional tool?

Peering into the Classroom

Animals, Animals

Mr. Clyde's kindergarten classroom radiates with enthusiasm. It is a bright, colorful, and inviting place that hums with activity. During the month of April, the room becomes an environment for the study of animals. A pocket chart with each child's name and a picture of their favorite creature hangs on the wall next to the word study center. The creative arts center is decorated with posters and pictures from author/illustrator Eric Carle's many books with animal themes. The creative drama center has animal masks, ears, tails, and other props to act out animal stories. Near the listening center, there is a basket filled with books and cassette tapes including *Brown Bear, Brown Bear, What Do You* See? (Martin, 1964) and *Wiggle Waggle* (London, 1999). Mr. Clyde's classroom is home to a writing center stocked with a wealth of writing tools. His literacy play centers usually reflect the ongoing theme and currently include a pet shop and a veterinarian's office complete with pictures and X rays of cats, dogs, and hamsters for the children to explore. Baskets of books fill the shelves, housing texts at varying levels ranging from wordless picture books to simple pattern books. Lively charts with nursery rhymes and songs dot the walls. At the beginning of the year Mr. Clyde and his students labeled all the items in the room; these functional labels are now part of the print-rich classroom environment.

Portfolio Activity:
Classroom Floorplan

During this particular April morning, Mr. Clyde is working with a small group of students in a guided reading lesson. The focus of the lesson is teaching the children to use picture clues and beginning sounds to figure out unknown words. Mr. Clyde has selected a simple book that has a clear picture–word correspondence to help support the readers as they apply the strategy they are learning. While Mr. Clyde and his group read, there is another small group of children at the word study center. They are sorting animal pictures by their beginning sounds, a skill Mr. Clyde has been focusing on during their literacy lessons. In the creative drama center children are putting on a play of *Hattie and the Fox* (Fox, 1986), the story they read during their shared reading lesson. Across the room, the pet shop is humming with excitement as children use their imagination to buy, sell, and care for pets. Others are using the computer program *Sammy's Science House* (Edmark, 1995) to explore animal habitats. Mr. Clyde's kindergarten classroom is a shining example of the plentiful opportunities for learning that occur in the primary grades. It is important to note at this point that many of the literacy skills that Mr. Clyde's students currently possess began to develop long before they arrived at his door (Snow, Burns, & Griffin, 1998). In this chapter the development of a young literacy learner will unfold before your eyes. The importance of a developmentally appropriate curriculum is highlighted along with the crucial role parents, caregivers, early childhood professionals, and primary grade teachers play in the development of a young reader and writer.

REFLECTION: IRA/NCTE NATIONAL STANDARDS IN THE CLASSROOM

Peering into Mr. Clyde's classroom affords us the opportunity to see a primary teacher using approaches that are endorsed by the national *Standards for the English Language Arts* (1996). Standard 1 reminds teachers to expose students to a wide range of carefully selected print and nonprint texts. When selecting texts teachers should consider the following criteria:

1. Relevance to students' interests and other readings.

2. Relevance for students' roles in society and the workplace.

3. Literary quality.

4. Balance and variety in form, style, and content.

5. Complexity of texts. Students need texts that challenge and provoke them and simpler texts that promote fluency. (IRA/NCTE, 1996, p. 28)

Mr. Clyde knows each of the students and carefully selects books that invite them to read. One way he does this is by stocking his room with books related to his animal theme. Young children are fascinated with the animal world and pour over books that detail the actions of animals. In his literacy play centers, Mr. Clyde places print and nonprint text that familiarizes his students with the inner workings of a pet shop and veterinarian office. The quality of literature is reflected in his choices of well-known, award-winning authors like Eric Carle and Bill Martin, Jr. Mr. Clyde also takes great care to offer his young students a variety of print materials, ranging from pocket charts on the wall to small books in their hands, to entice them to read. He knows that when he and his students engage in activities that encourage them to think and talk about the story, they will acquire new vocabulary, develop print awareness, and play with and analyze the sounds of language (Neuman & Celano, 2001). Finally, Mr. Clyde arranges some of his books in baskets according to their reading level so that children find some texts that challenge them and others that are a perfect fit.

INTRODUCTION

Web Link:
Teaching PreK–8:
The Professional
Ideabook for Teachers

The experiences that a child has as he is growing up dramatically shape who he is and how he will learn. As early as 1938, John Dewey stated that "everything depends upon the *quality* of the experience which is had" (p. 27). More recently in an introduction to the book *Read to Me: Raising Kids Who Love to Read* (Cullinan, 1992), Jim Trelease writes, "Young impressionable minds are very much like fuzzy socks. The wider and richer the fields of experience we bring them through, the more ideas and skills will stick to them and eventually grow" (p. 2). It is the awesome responsibility of educators to accompany young learners through those wider and richer fields of experiences as they take their first eager steps on the pathway to lifelong learning.

WHAT IS EMERGENT LITERACY?

The term **emergent literacy** was coined by Marie Clay (1966) in her doctoral dissertation. The concept of emergent literacy creates a new view of early reading and writing and "represents a relatively recent way of thinking about the reading and writing development of young children" (Strickland & Morrow, 1988, p. 70). Before the 1980s many early childhood educators subscribed to the **reading readiness** view. Proponents of reading readiness believed either that children's readiness was a result of maturation or that appropriate instructional experiences would foster or boost readiness. In classrooms where teachers believed that maturation was the key to reading readiness, students were tested to determine their mental age, and reading instruction was only offered when students had reached the required stage of development. Others who thought that readiness resulted from educational experiences developed reading readiness programs that consisted of a variety of workbook activities to develop a child's visual and auditory discrimination, letter recognition, and knowledge of letter sounds (Teale & Yokota, 2000).

Fortunately, early literacy is no longer viewed as a discrete set of skills to be mastered, but as a process that involves real literature and purposeful writing. From the time they are born, children are developing concepts about language and about print. "All forms of literacy (reading, writing, speaking, and listening) interact with each

STANDARDS for READING PROFESSIONALS

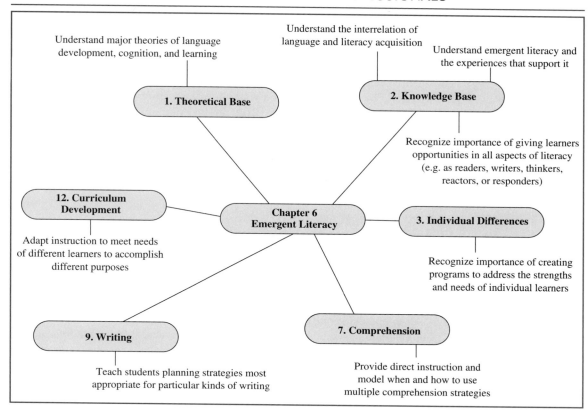

Understand major theories of language development, cognition, and learning

Understand the interrelation of language and literacy acquisition

Understand emergent literacy and the experiences that support it

1. Theoretical Base

2. Knowledge Base

Recognize importance of giving learners opportunities in all aspects of literacy (e.g. as readers, writers, thinkers, reactors, or responders)

12. Curriculum Development

Chapter 6 Emergent Literacy

3. Individual Differences

Adapt instruction to meet needs of different learners to accomplish different purposes

Recognize importance of creating programs to address the strengths and needs of individual learners

9. Writing

7. Comprehension

Teach students planning strategies most appropriate for particular kinds of writing

Provide direct instruction and model when and how to use multiple comprehension strategies

Figure 6.1

Emergent literacy perspective

The emergent literacy perspective:

- Focuses on early *literacy* development, not *reading* readiness, because reading, writing, and oral language develop simultaneously rather than sequentially.
- Does not focus on readiness, but on ongoing literacy growth.
- Understands that children's literacy development occurs at different rates and that young children take a variety of paths to conventional reading and writing.
- Is multidimensional.
- Assumes literacy develops naturally and occurs in the child's home and school environments.
- Endorses purposeful reading and writing activities because children learn written language through active engagement with their world, not by completing workbook pages.

Source: Teale, W. H., & Yokota, J. (2000). Beginning reading and writing: Perspectives on instruction. In D. S. Strickland & L. M. Morrow (Eds.), *Beginning reading and writing* (pp. 3–21). New York: Teachers College Press.

Portfolio Activity:
Narrative Description

other. There is a strong relationship between them, and each influences the others during its development. The concept of emergent literacy assumes the development of literacy as a continuum that begins at birth and continues through life" (Johns, Lenski, & Elish-Piper, 1999, p. 5). In order to most adequately meet the needs of emergent learners, teachers must design programs and create activities that reflect a knowledge of the development of a young literacy learner (see Figure 6.1). As you look at Figure 6.1, think about Mr. Clyde's classroom: did the activities you saw in his classroom reflect an emergent literacy perspective? This perspective is the key to providing young children with the spectrum of literacy concepts and strategies they will need to get a jump start in reading and writing. As you continue reading this chapter, you will discover how to provide a sturdy foundation for young learners through the use of an emergent literacy approach.

DEVELOPMENTALLY APPROPRIATE PRACTICES

Web Links:
International Reading Association

NAEYC

The International Reading Association (IRA) and the National Association for the Education of Young Children (NAEYC) (1998) worked together to create a document entitled *Learning to Read and Write: Developmentally Appropriate Practices for Young Children*. In this research-based position statement a continuum of children's development is outlined (see Figure 6.2).

This continuum is a superb resource for teachers because it summarizes the actions of children, teachers, and caregivers at each stage of growth. As the chapter progresses, you will discover how to implement **developmentally appropriate practices** in your classroom and how to apply the research and suggestions in this position statement to encourage the growth of emerging readers and writers. In this document, a child's

Figure 6.2

Continuum of children's development in early reading and writing

Phase 1: Awareness and exploration
(goals for preschool)

Children explore their environment and build the foundations for learning to read and write.

Children can

- enjoy listening to and discussing storybooks
- understand that print carries a message
- engage in reading and writing attempts
- identify labels and signs in their environment
- participate in rhyming games
- identify some letters and make some letter–sound matches
- use known letters or approximations of letters to represent written language (especially meaningful words like their name and phrases such as "I love you")

What teachers do

- share books with children, including Big Books, and model reading behaviors
- talk about letters by name and sounds
- establish a literacy-rich environment
- reread favorite stories
- engage children in language games
- promote literacy-related play activities
- encourage children to experiment with writing

What parents and family members can do

- talk with children, engage them in conversation, give names of things, show interest in what a child says
- read and reread stories with predictable texts to children
- encourage children to recount experiences and describe ideas and events that are important to them
- visit the library regularly
- provide opportunities for children to draw and print, using markers, crayons, and pencils

Phase 2: Experimental reading and writing
(goals for kindergarten)

Children develop basic concepts of print and begin to engage in and experiment with reading and writing.

Kindergartners can

- enjoy being read to and themselves retell simple narrative stories or informational texts
- use descriptive language to explain and explore
- recognize letters and letter–sound matches
- show familiarity with rhyming and beginning sounds
- understand left-to-right and top-to-bottom orientation and familiar concepts of print
- match spoken words with written ones
- begin to write letters of the alphabet and some high-frequency words

What teachers do

- encourage children to talk about reading and writing experiences
- provide many opportunities for children to explore and identify sound–symbol relationships in meaningful contexts
- help children to segment spoken words into individual sounds and blend the sounds into whole words (for example, by slowly writing a word and saying its sound)
- frequently read interesting and conceptually rich stories to children
- provide daily opportunities for children to write
- help children build a sight vocabulary
- create a literacy-rich environment for children to engage independently in reading and writing

What parents and family members can do

- daily read and reread narrative and informational stories to children
- encourage children's attempts at reading and writing
- allow children to participate in activities that involve writing and reading (for example, cooking, making grocery lists)
- play games that involve specific directions (such as "Simon Says")
- have conversations with children during mealtimes and throughout the day

Figure 6.2

(continued)

Phase 3: Early reading and writing (goals for first grade)

Children begin to read simple stories and can write about a topic that is meaningful to them.

First graders can

- read and retell familiar stories
- use strategies (rereading, predicting, questioning, contextualizing) when comprehension breaks down
- use reading and writing for various purposes on their own initiative
- orally read with reasonable fluency
- use letter–sound associations, word parts, and context to identify new words
- identify an increasing number of words by sight
- sound out and represent all substantial sounds in spelling a word
- write about topics that are personally meaningful
- attempt to use some punctuation and capitalization

What teachers do

- support the development of vocabulary by reading daily to the children, transcribing their language, and selecting materials that expand children's knowledge and language development
- model strategies and provide practice for identifying unknown words
- give children opportunities for independent reading and writing practice
- read, write, and discuss a range of different text types (poems, informational books)
- introduce new words and teach strategies for learning to spell new words
- demonstrate and model strategies to use when comprehension breaks down
- help children build lists of commonly used words from their writing

What parents and family members can do

- talk about favorite storybooks
- read to children and encourage them to read to you
- suggest that children write to friends and relatives
- bring to a parent–teacher conference evidence of what your child can do in writing and reading
- encourage children to share what they have learned about their writing and reading

Phase 4: Transitional reading and writing (goals for second grade)

Children begin to read more fluently and write various text forms using simple and more complex sentences.

Second graders can

- read with greater fluency
- use strategies more efficiently (rereading, questioning, and so on) when comprehension breaks down
- use word identification strategies appropriately and automatically when encountering unknown words
- identify an increasing number of words by sight
- write about a range of topics to suit different audiences
- use common letter patterns and critical features to spell words
- punctuate simple sentences correctly and proofread their own work
- spend time reading daily and use reading to research topics

What teachers do

- create a climate that fosters analytic, evaluative, and reflective thinking
- teach children to write in multiple forms (stories, information, poems)
- ensure that children read a range of texts for a variety of purposes
- teach revising, editing, and proofreading skills
- teach strategies for spelling new and difficult words
- model enjoyment of reading

What parents and family members can do

- continue to read to children and encourage them to read to you
- engage children in activities that require reading and writing
- become involved in school activities
- show children your interest in their learning by displaying their written work
- visit the library regularly
- support your child's specific hobby or interest with reading materials and references

Figure 6.2

(concluded)

Phase 5: Independent and productive reading and writing (goals for third grade)

Children continue to extend and refine their reading and writing to suit varying purposes and audiences.

Third graders can

- read fluently and enjoy reading
- use a range of strategies when drawing meaning from the text
- use word identification strategies appropriately and automatically when encountering unknown words
- recognize and discuss elements of different text structures
- make critical connections between texts
- write expressively in many different forms (stories, poems, reports)
- use a rich variety of vocabulary and sentences appropriate to text forms
- revise and edit their own writing during and after composing
- spell words correctly in final writing drafts

What teachers do

- provide opportunities daily for children to read, examine, and critically evaluate narrative and expository texts
- continue to create a climate that fosters critical reading and personal response
- teach children to examine ideas in texts
- encourage children to use writing as a tool for thinking and learning
- extend children's knowledge of the correct use of writing conventions
- emphasize the importance of correct spelling in finished written products
- create a climate that engages all children as a community of literacy learners

What parents and family members can do

- continue to support children's learning and interest by visiting the library and bookstores with them
- find ways to highlight children's progress in reading and writing
- stay in regular contact with your child's teachers about activities and progress in reading and writing
- encourage children to use and enjoy print for many purposes (such as recipes, directions, games, and sports)
- build a love of language in all its forms and engage children in conversation

Source: *Continuum from Learning to Read and Write: Developmentally Appropriate Practices for Young Children.* (1998). A joint position statement of the International Reading Association and National Association for the Education of Young Children. Copyright 1998. All rights reserved. *The Reading Teacher,* Vol. 52, No. 2, October 1998.

progression in early reading and writing is divided into five phases (see Figure 6.3). These phases are "intended to be illustrative, not exhaustive. Children at any grade level will function at a variety of phases along the reading/writing continuum" (IRA/NAEYC, 1998, p. 200). The first phase on the continuum is awareness and exploration. It is during this phase that a child's oral language begins to develop.

ORAL LANGUAGE DEVELOPMENT

Language is the basis for communication and a vehicle for reflecting on and understanding the world. Noted linguist Noam Chomsky believes that "a language can be acquired, in all of its richness and complexity because the child basically already knows it as part of its biological endowment" (Putnam, 1994/1995, p. 33). As a child grows, his language ability grows with him. Chomsky's biological view of oral language development does not fully account for the role that socialization plays in language

Web Link:
Language Links

Figure 6.3

Summary of the five phases on the reading and writing continuum

Awareness and exploration	Preschool	Children explore their environment and build the foundations for learning to read and write.
Experimental reading and writing	Kindergarten	Children develop basic concepts of print and begin to engage in and experiment with reading and writing.
Early reading and writing	First grade	Children begin to read simple stories and can write about a topic that is meaningful.
Transitional reading and writing	Second grade	Children begin to read more fluently and write various text forms using simple and more complex sentences.
Independent and productive reading and writing	Third grade	Children continue to extend and refine their reading and writing to suit varying purposes and audiences.

Source: IRA/NAEYC Joint Position Statement: Learning to Read and Write: Developmentally Appropriate Practices for Young Children, adopted 1998.

growth. Russian psychologist Lev Vygotsky views language as a meaning making process and believes that "meaning is a social and cultural phenomenon and all construction of meaning is a social process" (Halliday, 1994, p. 70). Vygotsky proposes that children's cognitive abilities increase when they engage in meaningful interactions with parents, teachers, skilled peers, or other members of society. M. A. K. Halliday (1994) suggests that it is the child who initiates language and that caring elders track and reply, letting the youngster set the pace.

At birth, a newborn has the ability to produce a variety of sounds: cooing, crying, gurgling, murmuring, and other noises. In just two short weeks an infant can recognize his mother or caregiver's voice. By the third week of life, babies respond to human voices with sucking, gurgling, and other pleasurable expressions. The purpose of an infant's early communication is to attract attention from the caregivers in his environment. These sounds are not understandable to adults, but excited parents and relatives quickly acknowledge and enthusiastically encourage the infant's budding speech. Between one and two months of age, infants begin making "human" noises called "cooing." Next, between three and six months babies start to babble. When they babble, they repeat consonant–vowel combinations like na-na-na or ga-ga-ga. As infants grow, their speech becomes more refined.

At approximately six to nine months, infants begin to understand their first words. **Receptive vocabulary** refers to the words an individual understands. Infants first begin to understand simple directions, such as "wave bye-bye" between nine to twelve months. Around their first birthday, toddlers say their first word. A child's first words are usually nouns or names: juice, dada, doggie, or horsie. Each of these first words is

Figure 6.4
Development of vocalization

Crying	Birth
Cooing, crying	1–2 months
Babbling, cooing, crying	3–6 months
First words	8–14 months
First sentences (telegraphic speech)	18–24 months
Simple syntactic structures	3–4 years
Speech sounds correctly pronounced	4–8 years
Most semantic distinctions understood	9–11 years

Source: From *Language Arts: Process, Product, and Assessment,* 3e (2001), by Pamela J. Farris. McGraw-Hill Companies. Reproduced with permission of The McGraw-Hill Companies.

referred to as a **holophrase,** because one word represents a complete sentence. After producing their first word, youngsters rapidly develop their vocabulary acquiring about fifty words during the next six months. Children's receptive vocabulary also expands rapidly, from twelve words on their first birthday to more than three hundred words by their second birthday. During this time, children begin to put words together to convey their thoughts. These two-word utterances are termed **"telegraphic speech"** because they sound like the language used in telegrams (Brown & Fraser, 1963).

Expanding on his telegraphic speech, the child continues to develop his vocabulary and sentence length. "The child's sentences grow in length and complexity from two to three to four or more words, on average over the remainder of the preschool period" (Snow, Burns, & Griffin, 1998, p. 48). The grammar, or **syntax,** of a five-year-old begins to mirror that of an adult and uses a wide range of grammatical forms. A child at that age can usually carry on a clear conversation with an adult. By the age of four, a child understands all of the sounds in a language, but he may be eight years old before he is able to articulate the sounds correctly (see Figure 6.4).

A young child's spoken language develops in leaps and bounds. By the time he arrives at the classroom door, he has an enormous supply of oral language knowledge at the tip of his tongue. This knowledge is the foundation for reading and writing; therefore, teachers must follow the path started by parents and enthusiastically encourage a child's oral language growth by creating situations that require young learners to communicate in spoken words. Engaging students in discussions before, during, and after a read-aloud story is one simple way to expand children's speaking vocabularies. Other activities include:

1. Encouraging students to retell and act out their favorite stories using props and small toys.

2. Giving students unstructured time to converse with their peers in the classroom and on the playground.

3. Providing stuffed animals or puppets for students to talk behind. This is especially helpful for shy children.

As teachers interact with their young students and listen to them talk, they informally assess four components of a child's oral language: (a) articulation, (b) language production, (c) conversation, and (d) self-confidence. Teachers who want to formally assess their young students' oral language abilities will find the chart in Figure 6.5 helpful.

☞ DIVERSE LEARNERS AND EMERGENT LITERACY

Addressing the needs of all learners in a classroom is an ongoing challenge, but it is the "teachers' responsibility to recognize and value all children's rich and varied potentials for learning and to provide appropriate educational opportunities to nurture them" (*Standards for the English Language Arts*, 1996, p. 8).

What do you as the teacher need to do in order to provide appropriate educational opportunities to nurture emergent readers who are struggling to learn to read and write? Richard Allington (2002) identifies six common factors that are present in exemplary elementary classrooms. He dubs these factors the six Ts: time, texts, teaching, talk, tasks, and testing. He points out that each of these important factors has positive effects on the diverse range of learners in any classroom. Effective teachers plan ample *time* for students to engage in meaningful reading and writing activities. Struggling emergent readers will not become better readers by completing comprehension worksheets; they need time to practice, practice, practice. All readers need a steady diet of *texts* that they can accurately read with fluency and good comprehension. In Chapter 3 you learned about leveled texts for guided reading; later in this chapter you will see how to put leveled books in the hands of students and nudge them along the path to proficient reading. Accomplished teachers actively *teach* their students. They regularly and explicitly model the thinking strategies that good readers and writers employ. Encouraging students to *talk* to you and to other students will help to improve their oral language development and their understanding of texts. Teachers guide this purposeful talk by asking open-ended questions and encouraging students to discuss ideas, concepts, strategies, and responses. Designing *tasks* where students are engaged for longer periods of time and are given some choices leads to increased student ownership. Finally, effective teachers assess student work and *tests* based more on effort and improvement than on achievement (Allington, 2002).

When teaching reading in a primary classroom it is important to remember that each child will be at a different stage of reading development and each child will learn how to read in a different way, using different strategies. Children who are strong auditory learners with a solid grasp of letter–sound concepts may rely more on phonics to help them sound out words, while students who are visual learners may memorize sight words and learn to read that way. By providing young learners with time to practice reading and writing while engaged in meaningful tasks, and by stocking your classroom with a variety of texts and explicitly modeling strategies for learning to read, you can reach all different learners. The National Reading Panel's (2000) report reviewed a large body of research in reading instruction in the critical early grades (K–3) and identified methods in five areas of reading instruction that consistently

Figure 6.5

Language development of the emergent literacy child

Name   Teacher

Age: Grade: Date:

	Always	Sometimes	Never
Speaks clearly without misarticulations or stuttering (i.e., stuttering, articulation disorders)			
Pronounces consonant sounds correctly			
Pronounces consonant blends correctly			
Pronounces consonant digraphs correctly			
Pronounces short vowels correctly			
Pronounces long vowels correctly			
Pronounces diphthongs correctly			
Can successfully use one-word sentences			
Can successfully use two-word sentences			
Can successfully use three or more word sentences			
Can identify words that rhyme			
Can identify familiar environmental sounds			
When engaged in a conversation with adults, can understand their language and respond			
When engaged in a conversation with another child, can understand the language and respond			
Can follow oral directions			
Has a good vocabulary			
Uses a variety of sentence patterns (syntactical/ grammatical structures)			
Can be understood by adults			
Can be understood by other children			
Enjoys talking with adults			
Enjoys talking with other children			
Teacher comments:			

Source: From *Language Arts: Process, Product, and Assessment,* 3e (2001), by Pamela J. Farris. McGraw-Hill Companies. Reproduced with permission of The McGraw-Hill Companies.

Figure 6.6

Research-based early reading instruction

Phonemic awareness instruction is most effective when:
- Children are taught to manipulate phonemes using alphabet letters.
- Instruction focuses on only one or two rather than several types of phoneme manipulating. (See Chapter 7.)

Phonics instruction is most effective when:
- The program or plan of instruction is systematic and includes a carefully selected set of letter–sound relationships organized into logical sequence with precise directions for teachers.
- Students have ample opportunities to apply their phonics knowledge to meaningful reading of words, sentences, and stories.
- The program begins in kindergarten or first grade. (See Chapter 7.)

Fluency instruction is most effective when:
- It is developed by hearing models of fluent reading.
- Students engage in repeated oral reading. (See this chapter.)

Vocabulary instruction is most effective when:
- Students engage daily in oral language, listen to adults read to them, and read widely on their own.
- Students are explicitly taught both individual words and word learning strategies. (See Chapter 9.)

Text comprehension instruction is most effective when:
- Students are taught comprehension strategies.
- Strategies are taught through explicit instruction and cooperative learning.
- Teachers help readers use strategies flexibly and in combination. (See Chapter 8.)

Source: Adapted from National Reading Panel 2000 Report, *Teaching Children to Read.*

relate to reading success. These five areas and the research-based findings are high-lighted in Figure 6.6. Add these effective instructional approaches to your personal arsenal of strategies to bolster the learning of all students in your classroom.

THE DEVELOPMENT OF A READER

The joy of being a primary grade teacher is assisting as a child's reading skills develop. There is nothing more satisfying than watching a youngster, who entered your classroom unable to read, leave your classroom with a book under her arm and enough beginning knowledge about the world to question, read, and discover the wonders that await her between the covers of that book.

The Language Experience Approach

As we continue to think about beginning readers and how they develop, recall the important role oral language plays in building a strong foundation for learning to read.

Figure 6.7

Benefits of reading aloud

Fountas and Pinnell (1996) list many values in reading aloud to children. This thoroughly enjoyable practice:

1. Involves children in reading for enjoyment.
2. Demonstrates reading for a purpose.
3. Develops a sense of story.
4. Increases vocabulary.
5. Expands linguistic repertoire.
6. Creates a community of readers through enjoyment and shared knowledge.
7. Establishes known texts to use as a basis for writing and other activities through rereading. (p. 22)

Teachers who use the language experience approach (LEA) capitalize on their students' wealth of oral language. Remember Mrs. Wang and her students in Chapter 3? Together they wrote about a shared experience. This dictated story is a familiar text that students can read and reread (Rasinski & Padak, 2001).

LEA texts provide other literacy opportunities. A lengthy dictated text can be cut apart, pasted on individual pages, and illustrated to create a book. Teachers use these texts to demonstrate the concepts of print. For example, when you are writing down a child's words, it is important to say each word while it is being written. This demonstrates for youngsters that even though oral language is a steady stream of speech sounds, when we write the words down, they are separated by spaces. To extend this learning, students can circle or underline words in the text (Rasinski & Padak, 2001).

Reading Aloud

When you watch the expressions on the faces of young children caught up in a wonderful read-aloud, you know without question that this is time well spent. In an ideal world all children would come to school with a rich background of read-aloud experiences. Unfortunately, that is not the case. Despite the fact that the benefits of reading aloud are many (see Figure 6.7) and the materials needed are few, many children come to school having limited experiences with the printed word. Today many parents and children are choosing television, computers, and video games over the simple pleasure of sharing a good book. If a child is read to thirty to forty-five minutes each day from the time he is six weeks old, he will enter first grade with "1,000 to 1,700 hours of storybook reading—one on one with his face in the books" (Adams, 1990, p. 85). As educators, we know that "the single most important activity for building [these] understandings and skills essential for reading success appears to be reading aloud to children" (IRA/NAEYC, 1998, p. 198). It is our responsibility to be read-aloud advocates in our communities by reminding our family, friends, and neighbors that the few minutes spent reading with a child *every day* can make an enormous difference in their literacy skills for the rest of their lives.

It is important that young children are surrounded by books that they can touch and read.

The Family's Role

From the day a baby is born the family has an enormous responsibility. Along with the guarantee that their child is fed, clothed, healthy, and happy, they should make their home a stimulating environment where a child will grow and learn. Parents today take great time and care in decorating their baby's room; unfortunately, many do not spend as much time collecting books to read to their new infant.

Consider this scenario: Even before Katie was born, her parents joined a children's book club. By the time Katie arrived, there was a well-stocked bookshelf in her room. There were **concept books** to teach letters, numbers, and colors, board books for Katie to handle herself, and even bathtub books! When she was a baby, Katie would sit on her parents' laps and eagerly listen to stories. As Katie grew older, she and her parents would chant their favorite part, carefully look at the pictures, and talk about the events in the story. This "interactive lap reading" became part of their nightly ritual and something that was never skipped. When Katie went with her parents to a restaurant or to the doctor's office, she brought her own bag brimming with books filled with lively tales to help her pass the time. At her day care center her favorite place was the reading corner where she spent hours looking at books. Along with the book experiences that Katie and her parents enjoyed, they also limited the amount of television that she watched. They believed that time was too precious to spend it in front of a TV. Katie's parents prepared materials to read to their daughter, set aside time to read and discuss them, and modeled reading as an enjoyable and entertaining activity that can take place anywhere.

Through her research Dolores Durkin (1966, 1974–75) found that children who entered kindergarten and were already reading possessed a common characteristic—they came from literacy rich home environments. Their homes were like Katie's, filled with books. In addition to books, literacy rich homes have a variety of writing materials for young children to use like crayons, pencils, markers, and paper. Children in these homes typically have a special place set aside where they can do literacy related activities. It is crucial that we communicate the importance of a literacy rich home to the parents of our students. Teachers can do this through the use of newsletters, brochures, and evening programs designed to educate parents on the important role they play in their child's literacy development. Not only does the home environment affect a child, but the interactions that children have with their parents while engaged in literacy activities also have a profound impact. Diane Tracey (2000) gives the following advice to parents who are reading with their children:

Web Link:
The Smarter Kids Foundation

1. Get your children to talk!
2. Help your children understand the story.
3. Praise your children.
4. Relate the book to your life.
5. Ask your children good questions during storybook reading.
6. Wait for answers.
7. With younger children, point to words when you read.
8. With older children, take turns reading.
9. Choose books carefully.
10. Have fun! (pp. 50–51)

Taking this concerted effort to foster literacy into the classroom, the teacher has the same responsibilities. He should prepare engaging materials, make time to read a variety of carefully chosen books, and share the joy of reading with his students day after day after day.

The Teacher's Role

Because of its importance in building future reading and writing skills, the process of reading aloud should get center-stage focus in primary classrooms.

To select material to read to students, teachers need to become familiar with the myriad of books available. There are numerous bibliographies and other excellent resources to help educators and parents select books to read aloud to young children. However, a more enjoyable way to discover great books is to take an afternoon to visit the local library or bookstore, pull some books off the shelf and read!

Another important point is that teachers should make time each day to read to their students from a variety of good books reflecting different genre (IRA/NCTE *Standards for the English Language Arts,* 1996; Zemelman, Daniels, & Hyde, 1998). Reading aloud should not be limited to one story after lunch. A great way to kick off every day is with a delightful story. This tale can be related to the theme the class is studying and can set the stage for the entire day of learning. Stories make terrific

Web Link:
The American Library Association

Resources for Locating
Read-Aloud Books

transitions from one activity to the next. Also, consider ending each day by gathering together to read a favorite story. Kindergartners should actively listen to at least one to two books each day, and first graders should hear at least two to four pieces of literature daily (*Reading & Writing Grade by Grade*, 1999).

To acquaint students with math concepts, grab one of the many entertaining math concept books. For very young children, concept books are their first exposure to nonfiction (Huck, Hepler, Hickman, & Kiefer, 2004). During a math lesson you might introduce the concept of one-to-one correspondence to your students using Cathryn Falwell's (1993) colorful book *Feast for Ten*. Older children can learn about counting and the Swahili language in the book *Moja Means One* (Feelings, 1974). If you are looking for a superb series of math picture books, Stuart Murphy has authored a leveled set of math books that explain ideas ranging from counting with *Every Buddy Counts* (1997) to division in *Divide and Ride* (1997). Each text includes teaching ideas to extend the concepts in the book.

Using a simple nonfiction book as a motivator for a science lesson fills young minds with background knowledge about the concepts they will explore during the lesson. Some authors specialize in fact-filled science texts for young readers. They include Jim Arnosky with his endearing character Crinkleroot, who loves to guide readers as they explore wild places in *Crinkleroot's Guide to Knowing Butterflies* (1996) and *Crinkleroot's Guide to Walking in Wild Places* (1990). Gail Gibbons' well-written and clearly illustrated books also introduce science concepts to young learners. Gibbons' books include *Apples* (2000), *From Seed to Plant* (1991), *The Moon Book* (1997), *Planet Earth/Inside Out* (1995), *Recycle* (1992). and *Spiders* (1993). Along with picture books that feature science topics, some publishers have compiled a series of science books that are appropriate to use as read-alouds for young learners. These series include:

> First Discovery Books: Scholastic
>
> Hello Reader! Science Books: Scholastic Inc.
>
> Let's-Read-and-Find-Out Science Series: HarperCollins Publishers
>
> Rookie Read-About Science Series: Children's Press

Teachers use books during their social studies lessons to introduce their students to famous people in history like *Johnny Appleseed* (Kellogg, 1988) and *Ruby Bridges* (Coles, 1995). Books can widen a young student's world by exposing them to the different aspects of geography. Junior geographers will discover their global address in the simply written *Me on the Map* (Sweeny, 1996) or look at geographical areas from the perspectives of animals in *As a Crow Flies: A First Book of Maps* (Hartman, 1991). Students can also learn about different cultures as they travel with *Madlenka* (Sis, 2000) around her diverse neighborhood. "The use of stories in social studies is a powerful way to engage students' interest and provide readers with opportunities to develop personal understandings" (Walther, 2001, p. 218).

Poetry is another type of text that enhances any read-aloud program. Poems are available on most any topic. "Poetry is meant to be heard. Its rhythm and cadences and its rhyme, if any, make it a natural vehicle for introducing children to print"

Figure 6.8
Poetry collections for young learners

Carlstrom, Nancy White. (1990). *It's About Time, Jesse Bear and Other Rhymes.* New York: Macmillan Publishing Company.
Rhymes tell about Jesse Bear's daily activities.

Dragonwagon, Cresent. (1997). *Alligators and Others All Year Long: A Book of Months* (J. Aruego & A. Dewey, Illus.). New York: Aladdin.
The animals in this text celebrate each month of the year.

Florian, Douglas. (1999). *Laugh-Eteria.* San Diego: Harcourt.
More than 150 humorous poems that address a wide range of topics.

Hoberman, Mary Ann. (1998). *The Llama Who Had No Pajama: 100 Favorite Poems* (B. Fraser, Illus.). San Diego: Bowdner Press/Harcourt Brace.
The best of Hoberman's poetry is enhanced by detailed illustrations.

Hopkins, Lee Bennett (Compiler). (1998). *Climb into My Lap: First Poems to Read Together* (K. Brown, Illus.). New York: Simon & Schuster.
A vast collection of read-aloud poems enhanced by watercolor illustrations.

Hopkins, Lee Bennett. (1995). *Good Rhymes, Good Times.* New York: HarperCollins.
A collection of original poems that range in topic from sounds in the city to seasons of the year.

Newcome, Zita (2002). *Head, Shoulders, Knees, and Toes and Other Action Rhymes.* Cambridge, MA: Candlewick.
Action and motion rhymes that help children with body parts and movement.

Numeroff, Laura J. (1999). *Sometimes I Wonder If Poodles Like Noodles.* (T. Bowers, Illus.). New York: Simon & Schuster.
An illustrated collection of humorous verses about a child's day-to-day activities.

Yolen, Jane (Collector). (1995). *Alphabestiary: Animal Poems from A to Z* (A. Eitzer, Illus.). Honedale, PA: Wordsong/Boyds Mills.
Seventy-one short and lively poems about animals. Includes poems by William Blake and Aileen Fisher.

(McCracken & McCracken, 1986, p. 102). Some excellent collections of poetry for young children are highlighted in Figure 6.8.

 ## *SUPPORTED READING: TECHNOLOGY AND TUTORS*

Reading aloud to children opens a world of literature for them. There are various ways for a teacher to enhance and adapt the read-aloud experience to meet the diverse needs of the learners in his classroom.

Cassette Tapes and CD-ROM Books

Many popular children's books are available on cassette tape. These tapes are helpful for students who are having difficulty independently reading the text and for English language learners. Teachers buy commercially prepared tapes or can record the stories themselves. There are a number of benefits to self-recording the text: (a) the teacher is able to read the story at a slower pace, making it easier for students to follow along; (b) while reading the text, the teacher pauses to remind students to point to words, look at picture clues, and self-monitor while reading; (c) the teacher also has the option of stopping as he reads to ask comprehension questions; (d) the teacher can highlight the concepts and strategies that the class is currently working on; and (e) the children love hearing a familiar voice on tape. Cassette tapes and books are placed in a listening center for children to listen to and enjoy.

Another technological aid to reading aloud is the CD-ROM book. CD-ROM books engage readers with text in a different format. The multimedia presentation makes stories come to life and entertains students with a fluent, expressive text narration and animated story characters who dance, sing, and move across the computer screen (Labbo, 2000). One company that has a large number of CD-ROM books available is Broderbund. This company's Living Books series includes such popular titles as *Arthur's Teacher Trouble, The Tortoise and the Hare*, and *Little Monster at School*. Living Books have an option for the reader to listen to the book in either English, Spanish, or Japanese. In her article, Linda Labbo (2000) suggests that teachers working with young children must be clear about their expectations for computer use. She offers a list of twelve developmentally appropriate activities for students to do with CD-ROM books in a computer center. These activities are included in the Teaching Strategy for the Classroom box.

Cross-Age Tutors and Community Members

The use of cross-age tutors is beneficial for all learners and is an effective way to assist those students who speak languages other than English. Primary teachers can locate upper grade students in their building who speak the same language as their students and pair them up to read and discuss books together.

Community members are another valuable asset to the school. Many schools today form school–business partnerships with local businesses. These partnerships allow students greater opportunities to interact with working members of society. Schools set up programs where employees from local businesses spend their lunch hour, once a week, in classrooms tutoring a student who is in need of help.

At-Home Reading Programs

A program that is designed to build a strong connection between home and school is the "Three for the Road" backpack program (Richgels & Wold, 1998). This program was created to help the family reinforce and practice literacy skills at home using a carefully prepared backpack full of materials. To begin this program a teacher selects books from a variety of genre and difficulty levels. Next, he categorizes the books according to genre and sorts books in each genre according to ease of reading. "'Three for the Road' users will find books at three levels of challenge in each backpack. Average readers in target classrooms will find the easiest book to be a 'breeze' . . . the book at the in-between level to be 'just right' . . . and the third book to be 'a challenge'" (p. 21). It is important that a teacher selects books that meet the needs of the learners in his classroom.

Teaching Strategy for the Classroom

DEVELOPMENTALLY APPROPRIATE CD-ROM BOOK ACTIVITIES

COMPREHENSION AND FLUENCY ACTIVITIES

1. Begin by listening to the story.
2. Read along with the book.
3. Echo read the story.
4. Read it first, then listen.
5. Use the text as a reader's theater script.

WORD STUDY ACTIVITIES

6. Look for letters or words you know.
7. Find words that have the same sounds.
8. Find rhyming words.

RESPONDING TO THE STORY

9. Read along with a copy of the book.
10. Explain how one screen connects to other screens.
11. Tell how the special effects enhance the story.
12. Tell about stories that are the same.

In order for students to get the full benefit of these activities, teachers must model the activities for students, locate mentors who will sit beside the students as they interact with the book, and finally develop a manageable computer use schedule.

An alternative to the "Three for the Road" activity is to create leveled backpacks specifically geared toward readers at different stages. A teacher can create backpacks for emergent, early, transitional, and self-extending readers. Once the books are selected and organized, the teacher prepares support materials. "Each 'Three for the Road' backpack contains a letter to parents, a response journal, writing and drawing materials, hand puppets, a lost and found tag, and a checklist of the backpack's contents" (Richgels & Wold, 1998, p.22). Finally, the teacher designs a workable schedule so that all students have an opportunity to take the backpack home during the school year and, upon its return, share their family literacy experiences with the class. One option would be to create three such backpacks, each with different books and materials, so that students in the classroom would have greater access. Before sending the backpack home it is imperative that teachers model the appropriate use of the materials in the backpack for the students and parents.

Developing Concepts of Print

Children are intrigued by the world of print around them, which makes meeting the following goal a pleasurable experience for teacher, parent, and the learner alike: "A central goal during these preschool years is to enhance children's exposure to and concepts about print" (IRA/NAEYC, 1998, p. 199). Children need to know the following **print concepts:** directional movement, one-to-one matching of spoken words to printed words, and book conventions (Clay, 2000). There are a variety of ways to achieve this goal in the primary classroom. They include using **big books** as an instructional tool to model and demonstrate how print works, creating a print-rich environment, and providing opportunities for students to interact with print in the classroom.

By using a big book teachers introduce and reinforce many concepts of print. Let's go back to Mr. Clyde's classroom to find out how he helped his kindergartners understand the concepts of print. One strategy Mr. Clyde employs is shared reading. To begin a **shared reading** lesson with the big book *Things I Like* (Browne, 1996), Mr. Clyde shows his young readers the cover and back of the book. The class talks about the title page and dedication page. As he reads the text and his children join in, Mr. Clyde carefully points to each word to demonstrate left to right progression and the concept of a word. With every shared reading lesson important print concepts are taught and reinforced. During the repeated readings of the big book, Mr. Clyde points out punctuation marks, discusses how to do a return sweep when there are two lines of print on the page, and highlights letters, words, the spaces between words, word parts, and sentences.

Teaching Strategy:
Posting Word Walls in
Limited Spaces

Creating a print-rich environment and encouraging students to read the words in their world is another way to teach print concepts. A print-rich classroom helps children understand what letters and words look like, learn that words convey meaning, learn that all things have names and that words are used to name things, and connect words to the items they name. At the beginning of the year Mr. Clyde worked with the class to label the objects in the room. Labeling objects in the class is very helpful for students learning English as a second language. Directions for centers and other daily activities are clearly written and posted at the children's eye level. Teachers also add colorful pictures to these directions to assist learners who are not yet reading. Clearly labeling students' supplies and daily work will give them multiple opportunities to see and read their name. A creative way to help students learn each other's names is to post their photos at eye level along with a caption about themselves that they dictate to you. Asking children to bring in words from cereal boxes, fast-food containers, and other places in their environment that they can read and posting these words on a bulletin board entitled "Words We Can Read" is another excellent way to encourage students to pay attention to print. Children are surrounded by words outside their classroom. It just makes sense to surround them with words inside the classroom, too.

To assess an emergent reader's concept of print, educational psychologist Marie Clay (2000) developed the concepts of print task as one component of a six-part survey to systematically observe students' progress in kindergarten and first grade. To give the assessment, an adult reads a predesigned text to a child while asking the child specific questions that they answer by showing, not telling. During the session the child demonstrates understanding or lack of understanding of directionality, letters/words, and punctuation. An adapted version of Clay's test appears in Figure 6.9.

Figure 6.9

Concepts of print

Title of Book _____

Directions: Using the book that you have selected, give the following prompts to encourage the child to interact with it. Read the story aloud as you proceed. Place a ✓ next to each item answered correctly.

Prompt	Response (✓ = correct)	Print Concept
1. Hand the child the book upside down, spine first, saying something like: "Show me the front of this book." Then read the title to the child.		layout of book
2. Say: "I would like to begin reading the story, but I need your help. Please open the book and point to the exact spot where I should begin reading."		print conveys message
3. Stay on the same page and say: "Point to where I need to start reading."		directionality: where to begin
4. Say: "Point to where I should go after I start reading."		directionality: left-to-right progression
5. Say: "Point to where I go next." Read the pair of pages.		directionality: return sweep
6. Turn the page and say: "Point to where I should begin reading on this page. Now point to where I should end." Read the page.		terminology: beginning and end
7. Turn the page and say: "Point to the bottom of this page. Point to the top of it. Now point to the middle of it." Read the page.		terminology: top, bottom, middle
8. Using the same page, say: "Point to one letter."		terminology: letter
9. Again using the same page, say: "Point to one word."		terminology: word
10. Turn the page. Make sure that this page contains words that have corresponding upper- and lowercase letters. Read the pages. Then point to a capital letter and say: "Point to a little letter that is like this one."		matching lower- to uppercase letters
11. Turn the page and say: "Let's read these pages together. I'll read and you point." Read the pages.		speech to match print
12. Finish reading the book. Then turn back to a page that has the punctuation marks you want to assess. Point to the punctuation mark and say: "What is this? What is it for?"		punctuation: period, question mark, quotation marks

Literacy Play Centers

The kindergartners in Mr. Clyde's classroom had opportunities during the day to participate in **literacy play centers.** His classroom environment included a creative drama center, a listening center, a writing center, a reader center, the pet shop, and the veterinarian's office. These centers encourage an emergent reader's literacy development because they give students a chance to read and write "in realistic ways for reasons they understand; in other words, instruction is placed in a context meaningful to the learner" (Johns, Lenski, & Elish-Piper, 1999, p. 5). The following tips will help the novice when creating centers that encourage sociodramatic play:

1. Prepare the environment by making sure each center has the necessary literacy props. Each area should appeal to students' interests and include appropriate books and writing materials. For example, the creative drama center in Mr. Clyde's classroom includes the props to act out stories, books with animal stories, cards with yarn attached to write the character's name, blank paper and clip boards for writing scripts, and construction paper to create scenery. A cash register, tickets, and play money also reside in the center for students to use when they are ready to sell tickets to their performance.
2. Allow plenty of time for children to create scripts and scenarios.
3. Encourage and model rehearsals of story retellings. Be an actor yourself, demonstrating for students ways in which dramatization takes shape.
4. Foster students' involvement in dramatizations that involve print. For example, the pet shop would be stocked with pet name tags, price stickers, paper to write "for sale" signs, and a variety of books about pets. (Burns, Griffin, & Snow, 1999)

Other literacy play centers include the block area stocked with signs and labels for students' creations and paper to record "blueprints" of their structures; the puzzle/manipulative area with legos and large sheets of paper for students to create maps of the cities in which their buildings reside; a natural science area with books about the topic being studied, magnifying glasses, and posters (Goldhaber, Lipson, Sortino, & Daniels, 1996).

Shared Reading

As described in Chapter 3, shared reading is a powerful instructional approach for young learners. During shared reading lessons teachers build on their students' previous experiences with text and choose books that are good language models. This technique expands a child's vocabulary, supports those students who are on the verge of reading, and familiarizes students with texts that will eventually become resources for reading and writing. While sharing enlarged texts, teachers model phrased, fluent reading, draw attention to print concepts, and study words and word features in a meaningful context (Fountas & Pinnell, 1996). A simple formula to guide the development of a shared reading experience follows (Fisher & Fisher Medvic, 2000):

Step 1: Select a text that is suitable for shared reading. The best stories for young learners have an engaging story line, have pictures that support the text, and, most importantly, have rhyme, rhythm, and repetition.

Step 2: Begin your shared reading lesson with a familiar song or two. While you are singing the songs, you may want to stop to discuss the content of the texts, point out interesting words, explore phonetic elements, or add actions or movements to act out the song.

Step 3: Reread some old familiar books that are in big book format. These books include ones that the children request, books that tie in with the current theme, or a book that is a good example of a convention of print or phonic element you want to stress. If you are going to introduce a new text, then you may only reread one old favorite so that the children are still attentive and eager to learn.

Step 4: Introduce the new story. Show the cover and discuss the title, author, illustrator, and cover illustration. Model prediction for your students. For example, you might say, "From the title I can tell. . . ." or "When I look at this illustration I think the story might be about . . . " Continue to encourage your students to predict and confirm their predictions as you read through the text.

Step 5: Read the story. The first time through, concentrate on enjoying the story and capturing the interest of the students.

Step 6: Reread the story. Use this opportunity to teach preselected strategies.

Step 7: Independently read the text. Place small copies of the text in the reading center for students to enjoy.

Shared reading lessons offer support for children learning English as a second language and for students with articulation and stuttering difficulties because they can join in with the group and read the text with the support of many repeated readings.

To extend the shared reading lesson and build your struggling readers' fluency try a research-based method called assisted reading (Stahl & Kuhn, 2002). Assisted reading is a strategy that helps emergent readers make the transition from the labored, word-by-word reading that takes place as they engage in purposeful decoding to the fluent, expressive reading that most students develop by third grade. After you have completed the steps listed above and determined the text was at the child's instructional level, enlist the help of an older student, a parent, or community member. The pair rereads the text simultaneously so that the more skilled reader is scaffolding fluent reading for the less skilled reader. The child can continue to build fluency by rereading the text with a tape recording and taking it home to read to a family member.

To extend shared reading lessons for your advanced readers collect related books and reading materials from a variety of genres. Encourage your advanced readers to select an appealing text at their reading level, read it, and prepare a short book review for the class. Post the book reviews on a bulletin board entitled "Critics Corner."

Guided Reading

Students in a primary classroom will all be at different stages of reading development. These stages are outlined in Figure 6.10. One way to address the different

Figure 6. 10

Stages of reading development

Emergent Readers	Early Readers

Description

Emergent Readers

- use mostly information from pictures
- may attend to and use some features of print
- may notice how print is used
- may know some words
- use the introduced language pattern of books
- respond to texts by linking meaning with their own experiences
- are beginning to make links between their own oral language and print

Early Readers

- rely less on pictures and use more information from the print
- have increasing control of early reading strategies
- know several frequently used words automatically
- read using more than one source of information
- read familiar texts with phrasing and fluency
- exhibit behaviors indicating strategies such as monitoring, searching, cross-checking, and self-correction

Age & Grade Range

Emergent Readers

Approximately age 2 to 7
Preschool to early grade 1

Early Readers

Approximately age 5 to 7
Kindergarten to grade 1

What might guided reading be like?

Emergent Readers

Reading will be moving from shared to guided reading. The teacher prompts children to use pictures and to use language. The focus is on early strategies such as one-to-one matching and directionality.

Early Readers

After the introduction, children independently read the whole book, solving difficulties with little help.

What might the introduction be like?

Emergent Readers

The introduction:

- is rich, providing children with language and patterns of the book
- may draw attention to frequently used words
- covers the whole book
- as a transition from shared reading, may include a complete reading by the teacher, with children joining in, before children read on their own

Early Readers

The introduction:

- ranges from fully covering the book to just providing a brief overview before reading
- focuses on particular words by locating them
- introduces unfamiliar language structures
- provides a strong support for meaning

Development is unique and complex, so these provide only a broad frame for observing changing patterns.

Transitional Readers

Description

- have full control of early strategies
- use multiple sources of information while reading for meaning
- integrate the use of cues
- have a large core of frequently used words
- notice pictures but rely very little on pictures to read the text
- for the most part, read fluently with phrasing
- read longer, more complex texts

Age & Grade Range

Approximately age 5 to 7
Kindergarten to grade 2

What might guided reading be like?

Each child reads the whole text independently after the introduction. Often, children can read the whole text with just a summary overview. Teachers continue to provide a fuller introduction when a text with new features is introduced.

What might the introduction be like?

The introduction:

- may involve brief support that enables independent reading of the text
- may include less detail but continues to provide a good framework for reading
- familiarizes readers with new concepts, particular vocabulary words, and unusual language structures
- assures that students are tuned in to the meaning of the selection

Self-Extending Readers

Description

- use all sources of information flexibly
- solve problems in an independent way
- read with phrasing and fluency
- extend their understanding by reading a wide range of texts for different purposes
- read for meaning, solving problems in an independent way
- continue to learn from reading
- read much longer, more complex texts
- read a variety of genre

Age & Grade Range

Approximately age 6 to 9
Grades 1 to 3

What might guided reading be like?

Children read the whole text independently with a brief overview or provocative introduction. New text features are carefully introduced. They may come together to discuss particular aspects of text (like characters or setting) at appropriate breaks in the reading (for example, of chapter books), they may extend reading in responsive ways.

What might the introduction be like?

The introduction:

- may be provocative in terms of arousing interest or questions in the reader's mind
- may be geared to helping children notice aspects of text or understand the structure of different genres
- may build an understanding of the importance of previewing a text before reading
- has the goal of enabling children to introduce books to themselves

Source: Reprinted by permission from *Guided Reading: Good First Teaching for All Children*. By Irene Fountas and Gay Su Pinnell. Copyright ©1996 by Irene Fountas and Gay Su Pinnell. Published by Heinemann, a division of Reed Elsevier Inc., Portsmouth, NH.

learning needs is through **guided reading** lessons. Guided reading lessons are small group lessons that the teacher conducts while the rest of the class is engaged in an alternate activity. A large classroom with twenty-five to thirty children may have five or six groups. For a description of the management of literacy centers during guided reading see Chapter 4. Guided reading lessons are not lengthy and do not require many additional materials, just the children, the books, and a knowledgeable teacher. Successful lessons occur when the teacher knows each and every student in his class and also knows the texts so that he can carefully match his students to the appropriate text. Students are grouped based on their ability and on which reading strategies they need to practice.

During the lesson, effective reading strategies are directly and systematically taught through the text. The teacher begins by choosing his purpose for meeting with the small group. For example, Mr. Clyde was meeting with his group to help them learn the strategy of using picture clues to tackle unknown words. He selected a text that matches this purpose and is interesting, manageable in length, and appropriate in difficulty. A thorough, but brief, book introduction begins each lesson to "interest the children in the story, relate it to their experience, and provide a frame of meaning that will support problem solving" (Fountas & Pinnell, 1996, p. 8). In a conversational manner, he introduces the title and author and gives an overview of the text. He assists the readers in making connections to their experiences. The teacher then "'debugs' the book for the children by directing their attention to new text features they will need to use as readers. . . . The teacher would rarely read the book to the children first: the goal is for them to read it themselves" (Fountas & Pinnell, p. 8).

These children are reading books they have chosen from the classroom library.

During reading, young students read the texts silently or in a whisper voice. The teacher moves from student to student to listen and observe as they read. After the children read the text, the group may have a brief discussion or the teacher may return to part of the text to reinforce the development of a certain strategy; but because this is meant to be a short, focused reading lesson, the "after reading" activities are brief. Routinely, the teacher asks one student to stay behind so that he can take a running record of their reading behaviors (see Chapter 5). For a sample guided reading lesson see Figure 6.11.

Independent Reading for Young Children

As children learn about concepts of print through read-aloud stories and learn reading strategies during shared and guided reading, it is crucial that they have time to practice what they are learning by independently reading books chosen from the classroom library. Recall the Teaching Strategy for the Classroom box in Chapter 3, An Activity for Selecting "Bargain" Books. This strategy and others like it are essential as you assist your less skilled readers in book selection during self-selected reading time. All readers reap the greatest benefits toward increased fluency and independent reading development by reading interesting and manageable texts each day. Keep in mind that students should be able to read the words of the text with 95 percent accuracy and easily comprehend the story (Worthy & Broaddus, 2002). The challenge then is to find appealing books at the reading levels of your students. Enlist the help of your school librarian, local librarian, or reading resource teachers to locate appropriate materials for your struggling readers.

Teachers may also find that some of their students are advanced readers, and they must incorporate ways to challenge these youngsters and advance their reading and comprehension skills. One way to do this is by teaching the students how to respond to their independent reading in a reading log. Again, it is important to help the student select a book at his reading level, then guide the student as he reads the text. When the student is finished reading, he responds to one of the questions on the reading log sheet. (See Teaching Strategy for the Classroom box: A Reading Log.)

Teaching Strategy for the Classroom

A READING LOG

1. Choose a book.
2. Write down the title, author, and the number of pages in the book.
3. Carefully read the book.
4. Write a response to one of the following ideas:
   a. My favorite part of the book was _____ because . . .
   b. My favorite character was _____ because . . .
   c. I thought it was funny/sad when _____ because . . .
   d. This book reminded me of when I _____ because . . .

    e. This book reminded me of the book _____ because . . .

    f. A different ending would be . . .

    g. Would you recommend this book to a friend? Why or why not?

    h. Write a letter to your teacher, your family, or a friend about the book.

5. Turn Reading Log in to your teacher.

6. Conference with her about the book.

7. Start over !!! Happy reading!!

The reading center is a space where children can go to read and explore books. Teachers organize their book collections in numerous ways. Some teachers arrange their literature alphabetically by author, while others prefer to sort them by topic, theme, or genre. Still others level their books according to an established criteria. See Chapter 3 for a description of leveled books. An important aspect of book organization is teaching the children how to select the books they want to read and where to return them when they are done. Some teachers affix a colored dot sticker, available at discount retailers and office supply stores, to each book to identify genre or level and place them on shelves, in plastic milk crates, or in smaller bins featuring the same colored dot.

Teachers acquire books for their classroom library from various sources. The school or local library is one valuable resource. In most cases the children's librarians are knowledgeable about their collections and willing to assist a novice teacher in selecting engaging material for young readers. Garage sales are another wonderful opportunity to find some treasures. Ordering from book club companies such as Scholastic, Troll, Trumpet, or Carnival is helpful when building a class library collection. Many book clubs offer paperback editions of popular book titles at reasonable prices. When students order books from these sources, teachers earn bonus points, which they use to increase the volume of reading material in their classroom. Another inventive alternative is to have parents donate a paperback book to the class on their child's birthday. The teacher can honor the child by placing her name and birth date on a special bookplate in the inside cover and share the book with the class. A much healthier alternative than a chocolate cupcake! For those children unable to donate a book, the teacher could supply a book or ask the Parent Teacher Organization in the school to donate some books.

THE DEVELOPMENT OF A WRITER

Emergent writers are slowly figuring out that the words they say can be written down and that those written words can be read by themselves and others (McCarrier, Pinnell, & Fountas, 2000). Teachers can help these young scribes by supporting them as they develop their own temporary spelling system and by immersing them in a variety of writing activities.

Figure 6.11

Guided reading lesson plan: *I Went Walking* by Sue Williams

Story Summary: This colorful story tells the tale of a boy who goes on a walk and meets many animals along the way. The animals follow him to create a parade. The refrain of the story is, "I went walking. What did you see?"

I. OBJECTIVES

The students will:

Learn how to use the pictures to support their reading.

The strategy that I am going to work on during this lesson is using picture clues to support reading, and I selected this text because on each page the picture clearly illustrates the animal the boy meets.

II. MATERIALS

Four to six copies of the book *I Went Walking*

III. INSTRUCTIONAL APPROACH

A. Motivator

Conduct a thorough book introduction.

Cover/title page

T: Today we are going to read a story by Sue Williams called *I Went Walking*. It is about a little boy who went on a walk. Have any of you gone walking?

T: Let's go on a picture walk and see what happens to the boy in *I Went Walking*.

Pages 2-3

T: What is the boy doing in the picture? Where is he going? Do you see anything hidden in the basket?

Continue the book introduction in this manner, focusing on the pictures and how they help to tell the story. In this book you may want to point out the color words, since each animal is described using a color: brown horse, red cow, green duck.

B. Teacher/Student interaction

Students independently read text in a quiet voice. Move from child to child, listening to them read. As you listen, observe your students to see if they are using the strategy you introduced. When you notice a child applying the strategy, point it out and congratulate the child. Assist any students with problem solving, if needed. This is also a good time to take notes about the strategy use of individual readers (Fountas & Pinnell, 1996).

C. Gatekeeping

After reading, discuss the story with your students; have them share their ideas and feelings. You may want to return to the text for one or two teaching points, sharing with children what you observed while they were reading.

IV. EXTENSIONS

Have children work in small groups or with a partner to think of animals they might see at the zoo and the colors of these animals. Ask the students to draw a picture of one of these zoo animals. Students can label the picture using the frame sentence, I saw a _____ looking at me.

V. ADAPTATIONS/MODIFICATIONS FOR DIVERSE LEARNERS

To adapt this lesson for diverse learners you would simply make sure that the text you selected for the group was at their level and, through your book introduction, provide enough support so that they will be successful when reading.

The Importance of Temporary Spelling

Young children need ample opportunity to write throughout the day. Writing enhances a child's reading development because writing develops concepts of print, letter and word knowledge, and phonological awareness (Cunningham, 2000; Snow, Burns, & Griffin, 1998). Students in early childhood and primary classrooms are not yet ready to write conventionally; teachers and parents must encourage their spelling approximations and guide them toward conventional spelling. To support their spelling approximations teachers should (Richgels, 1989):

1. *Observe and reinforce.* Watch and listen while students read and write. If students know many of the letters of the alphabet and are interested in words, they are ready for you to point out letters and words in the room that will help them with their writing.

2. *Treat budding writers as you treat budding speakers.* Do not criticize or correct an emerging writer who is using a spelling system that is different from yours.

3. *Encourage children to stretch out words and spell themselves.* Instead of spelling words for them say, "I think you can stretch out that word yourself and write down the sounds that you hear."

4. *Do shared writing lessons.* Model writing about things you want to tell your students. Show them how you stretch out words; use the environmental print in the room and other strategies to spell words when you write.

5. *Celebrate approximations.* When children use the letters CR to spell car say, "That's good first grade spelling—I can read that!" Do not say, "That is good, but it is not right. It should be C-A-R."

The Stages of Spelling Development

As introduced in Chapter 2, children go through five stages of spelling development. A child at each stage has different learning needs, which the teacher addresses in various ways. The following is a description of a student's spelling behavior at each stage (Bear, Invernizzi, Templeton, & Johnson, 2000):

Stage 1: Emergent Spelling (Pre-K to Middle of 1st Grade)

Children at this stage pretend to write. They create large scribbles that look more like drawings. They often tell a story while they draw. At the beginning of this stage, there is no order to the marks they put on the page. Later, they begin to use letters and develop directionality. Toward the end of this stage children begin to write down letters they know at the beginning of words and also enjoy writing familiar words like mom, cat, dog, and love over and over again.

> **Suggested teaching activity for students at this stage:** Teach children to recognize and write the letters of the alphabet and play with sounds in words.

Stage 2: Letter Name–Alphabetic Spelling (K to Middle of 2nd Grade)

For children at this stage writing is a slow, labor-intensive process. They spell each word sound by sound. They begin by spelling the first sound in syllables, then the first and last sound. By the middle of this stage, writers start to use a vowel in each syllable, and then proceed to spell short vowel patterns conventionally.

> **Suggested teaching activity for students at this stage:** Create simple picture cards that represent words with different beginning sounds; have students sort cards according to beginning sound.

Stage 3: Within Word Pattern Spelling (Grade 1 to Middle of 4th Grade)

This stage is characterized by students who are becoming more fluent writers. They begin to look at the vowels within syllables and examine long vowel patterns. The beginning of this stage is reached when children can correctly spell most single-syllable short vowel words and use consonant blends and digraphs correctly.

> **Suggested teaching activity for students at this stage:** Have students conduct word hunts for specific spelling patterns that the child has learned. Ask the child to look through a text he has recently read and record all the words that follow a certain pattern.

Stage 4: Syllables and Affixes (Grades 3 to 8)

In the preceding stages students focused on single-syllable words and patterns. During this stage they look at polysyllabic words. They are learning how to double consonants when adding word endings.

> **Suggested teaching activity for students at this stage:** Introduce your students to the basics of sorting and comparing words. Create a list of activities that your students can do with a prepared list of words:

1. Choose five list words and circle each base word.
2. Make the appropriate words on your list plural.
3. Circle any prefixes.
4. Underline any suffixes.
5. Classify words.

Stage 5: Derivational Relations (Grades 5 to 12)

Students who reach this stage are spelling most words correctly. Teachers in the upper grades help students learn about the history of words and their derivations.

> **Suggested teaching activity for students at this stage:** Collect words in a notebook to examine, in detail, during word study time.

THE ROAD TO INDEPENDENT WRITING

To develop competent, enthusiastic, and independent writers teachers immerse students in a reading/writing classroom and guide students through different writing experiences to teach them the craft of writing. Effective teachers have high expectations for their students and communicate these expectations through individual interactions with children. They provide students with the tools and skills needed to become a writer and endless opportunities for children to write for a variety of purposes. Teachers and students engage in different types of writing activities including shared writing, interactive writing, guided writing (writing workshop), and independent writing.

Shared Writing

Ideas for **shared writing** lessons come from various places. Earlier in the chapter the importance of reading aloud was discussed. These daily encounters with text furnish young writers with the rich language of experienced authors. Books with repetitive language patterns serve as superb launches for a class rewrite of a story. Exposure to a variety of genres and also to multiple works by the same author gives students models for various types of writing. Shared writing offers teachers the opportunity to model and demonstrate how writing works. While the teacher and the students work together to compose books, stories, letters, and charts, the teacher uses opportunities to focus on letters, words, and sounds. Shared writing lessons show children that they can record their ideas in written language, and these pieces become a resource for the classroom. One popular use of shared writing is composing a morning message. A detailed description of this activity is included at the end of this chapter.

Interactive Writing

Interactive writing supports children as they learn about the writing process. It is an instructional approach where a teacher literally shares the pen with a group of children. The teacher and students collaboratively compose and construct a written text for an authentic purpose. The ideas for these texts usually come from shared experiences. The texts created during the interactive writing sessions are either published for the class library or displayed in the room for students to reread and refer to later in the year. During an interdisciplinary instructional unit on insects (see Figure 6.12), Ms. O'Malley, a first grade teacher, and her students work together using a shared pen to create an "Insect Encyclopedia." The essential elements of interactive writing (McCarrier, Pinnell, & Fountas, 2000, p. 73) listed below help to orchestrate the lesson:

1. Providing a foundation of active learning experiences.
2. Talking before writing to establish a purpose.
3. Composing the text.
4. Constructing the text using a shared pen.
5. Rereading, revising, and proofreading the text.
6. Revisiting the text to encourage word solving.
7. Summarizing the learning.
8. Extending the learning

To begin, Ms. O'Malley provides her students with background information for the writing and engages children's interest through active learning experiences. Throughout the unit she shares a wide range of texts about insects including fiction, nonfiction, poetry, and songs. The junior entomologists are also observing insect life

Figure 6.12

An Interdisciplinary Instructional Unit for Primary Grade Students: Going Buggy

Math
• Introduce the concept of time by reading *The Grouchy Ladybug* by Eric Carle.
• After reading *Inch by Inch* by Leo Lionni, have students use paper inchworms to measure objects in the room.

Language Arts
• Do a shared writing lesson based on the poem "I Like Bugs" by Margaret Wise Brown. Work with your students to rewrite the poem about a favorite bug.
• Encourage students to prepare short oral presentations about their favorite insects.
• Create a class alphabet book of insects

Reading
• Do a shared reading of the big book *The Very Hungry Caterpillar* by Eric Carle.
• Stock your reading center with the titles listed below.
• Do a readers theater performance of *The Grouchy Ladybug.*

Social Studies
• Make a poster comparing an ant city to a people city.
• Invite an entomologist to visit the classroom and share information about his occupation.

Related Arts
• Create a diagram showing the life cycle of a butterfly.
• Using red paint have students create a scene with "fingerprint" ladybugs.
• Create a bug habitat using an old pop bottle.
• Sing and do actions for the following songs: "The Ants Go Marching," "The Itsy Bitsy Spider."
• Read the song picture book *Hey Little Ant* by Phillip & Hannah Hoose.

Going Buggy

Read Other Books
• *Old Black Fly* (Aylesworth, 1992)
• *Buzz! A Book about Insects* (Berger, 2000)
• *I Like Bugs* (Brown, 1999)
• *The Butterfly House* (Bunting, 1999)
• *The Grouchy Ladybug* (Carle, 1977)
• *The Very Hungry Caterpillar* (Carle, 1987)
• *Buz* (Egielski, 1995)
• *Inside an Ant Colony* (Fowler, 1998)
• *Spiders* (Gibbons, 1993)
• *Inch by Inch* (Lionni, 1962)
• *Insects Are My Life* (McDonald, 1995)
• *The Bee Tree* (Polacco, 1993)
• *Bugs, Beetles and Butterflies* (Ziefert, 1998)

Science
• Observe the life cycle of a butterfly. Record observations in a science journal.
• Collect and observe backyard bugs.
• Use a Venn diagram to compare insects and spiders.

Idea Extensions:

An Insect Museum
• Students create 3-dimensional insect models using clay, pipe cleaners, and construction paper. Display in school for all to see.

Small Group Research Report
• In small groups, with teacher assistance, research and write an expository piece about an insect of choice.

cycles and doing other activities to learn more about bugs. This wealth of knowledge is an essential building block for a successful interactive writing experience.

To begin the actual interactive writing lesson, Ms. O'Malley gathers her class around an easel or chalkboard where a piece of chart paper is posted at the child's eye level. She has a basket of supplies for both writing and fixing up text (markers, address labels, correcting tape, white out, etc.). Ms. O'Malley and her students discuss the purpose for their writing. They talk about making one page for their encyclopedia each day until they have written about all the insects they studied. This book will be a fact-filled big book for future reference.

Next, the class brainstorms the items they want to include on their page: (a) where the insect lives, (b) what it looks like, (c) what it eats, and (d) other interesting facts. Then the writing begins with Ms. O'Malley and her students alternating to complete the text. She chooses children to help, based on their ability to write a sound/letter, word, or phrase. For example, if Tawnia is having difficulty recognizing the letters of the alphabet but she knows that her name starts with "T," Ms. O'Malley asks her to come up and write the letter "T" as often as possible. During the writing, it is also important to model using the references in the room like alphabet/picture charts, name charts, word family charts, and the word wall to help with spelling unknown words. Because this is a first grade class, the text is brief and to the point. Ms. O'Malley knows that her students have short attention spans, and she wants to have time to reread, revisit, and proofread the completed text. While they are rereading, one of the students notices that the word "the" is on the word wall and another spots the rhyming words tree and bee. Ms. O'Malley applauds her students for these observations and focuses on a few other words that she wants her students to notice. The class completes this lesson by comparing their text to other texts they have read during the unit. They save the page to add to their final Insect Encyclopedia.

Patterned Writing

Patterned writing is one way to guide writers in the use of the structures of the English language. The word "structures" comes from the work of Robert and Marlene McCracken (1995). They believe that children must know "how to write the structures of the English language; that is, how to connect words into sentences, paragraphs, and stories" (p. 133). They suggest starting with the simplest structure: a list. Children can make lists about any topic. Young writers can compose a list of things that are red or a list of animals that lay eggs.

The second type of structure is called a frame sentence. According to the McCrackens (1995) frame sentences are standard sentence speech patterns of oral English that are used to elicit thinking, to develop oral syntax and rhythm, and to make recording of ideas possible for beginning writers. Some sample frame sentences include:

> A _____ is red.
> A _____ is red.
> A _____ is red.
> But a _____ is not red.

In Mr. Clyde's kindergarten class children used a frame sentence to write about their favorite animal. Remember the pocket chart filled with animal names and the students' pictures? After Mr. Clyde and his students created that chart, each child got their own page with the words "My favorite animal is _____." printed on it. The children wrote the name or drew a picture of their favorite animal in the blank. After writing their page, each child had the opportunity to share their piece with the class. Then Mr. Clyde bound the pages together to create a class book entitled *Our Favorite Animals.* Throughout the year, the children have the opportunity to take the book home to share with their family. Teachers also use the patterns from literature as a resource for frame sentences. It is important to note that the use of patterned writing is a temporary support as children travel down the road toward independent writing. Teachers must be careful not to overuse frame sentences and to allow children to express their own thoughts and ideas in many different ways. Other ideas for frame sentences are included in Figure 6.13.

Guided Writing: Writing Workshop in the Primary Grades

During **writing workshop,** "the children are constructing their individual pieces of writing with teacher (and eventually peer) guidance, assistance, and feedback" (Fountas & Pinnell, 1996, p. 35). Because young children depend on routines, a predictable daily schedule is important to the success of writing workshop. In the primary grades, the schedule may look like this:

5–15 minutes:	Modeling/mini-lessons
20–30 minutes:	Writing/conferencing
5–15 minutes:	Sharing

Obviously the times will vary from day to day and also change as the year progresses. Early in first grade a writing workshop session may last thirty minutes, but as the children become more skilled at writing, the time may increase to forty-five minutes. During writing workshop the budding authors progress through the stages of writing, but not all at the same time. The stages are (a) prewriting, (b) drafting, (c) revising, (d) editing, and (e) publishing/sharing.

Prewriting

During the prewriting phase children explore topics. They think about ideas that they know and care about. Teachers may want to begin a prewriting mini-lesson (for other mini-lesson ideas see the following Teaching Strategy for the Classroom boxes) by sharing the story by Marc Brown (1996) called *Arthur Writes a Story.* This story is also available on a video cassette from Random House (1997). In this book Arthur is given an assignment to write a story and is having trouble thinking of a topic. He tries many imaginary topics but finally settles on something he has experienced—getting his new dog Pal. This is an important lesson for young writers: they will be most successful if they begin by writing about something with which they are familiar. Once the idea of topics has been introduced, the students can brainstorm a list of topics.

First grade teacher Mary Dolan uses the "Bright Ideas" web in Figure 6.14 to give her writers a place to record their ideas for stories. For young learners, it is sometimes helpful to send a list home for parents to help with (since they know the experiences their child has had).

Teaching Strategy for the Classroom

GOOD IDEAS FOR MINI-LESSONS

MINI-LESSONS

Mini-lessons are short, focused lessons introducing or reinforcing different writing skills or techniques. Mini-lessons are teacher directed with student participation. The teacher thinks aloud as he writes, explaining what he is doing and why. The content of these lessons is based on teacher observation of student writing needs. The lessons are about ten minutes long and focus on one strategy at a time.

GOOD IDEAS FOR MINI-LESSONS

- Actual class procedure during writing workshop.
- Rules for writing workshop made by teacher and students.
- Teacher models his own writing using "think-alouds."
- Working together with the class on shared writing.
- Read aloud a book, any book! Books are excellent writing models (ex. "hook" sentences).
- Teacher models journal writing in his own journal.
- Teacher models the steps of the writing process.
- Teacher discusses the words authors use (publish, illustrate, edit, topic, dedicate).
- Structured writing lessons on letter writing, narrative writing, expository writing, and persuasive writing.
- Grammar and usage.
- Capital letters.
- Punctuation marks.
- How to choose a topic.
- How to stay on topic.
- How to use a story web.
- Adding details.
- How to add to or change a story.
- Conferencing.

Source: Adapted from Cunningham, Hall, & Sigmon (1999). *The teacher's guide to the four blocks.* Greensboro, NC: Carson Dellosa.

Once children have topics, they need to organize their ideas. Some teachers provide students with story maps or a story web. Others simply ask children to draw a picture of their story's beginning, middle, and end. These prewriting activities help a child organize his thoughts before putting them down on paper.

Figure 6.13

Frame sentences

Simple frames for the beginning of the year:

I like _____.

I can _____.

I have _____.

When learning about colors:

A _____ is red.

A _____ is red.

A _____ is red.

But a _____ is not red.

Teaching rhyme and rhythm:

_____ here,

_____ there,

_____, _____ everywhere!

When comparing two animals (great when used with Venn diagram):

Use when reading *The Chick and the Duckling* by Mirra Ginsburg

Chicks _____.

Ducks _____.

They both _____.

When studying place/directional words:

On the farm I would see . . .

_____ near the _____.

_____ in the _____.

_____ on the _____.

Teaching number words and days of the week:

I saw one _____ on Monday.

I saw two _____ on Tuesday.

I saw three _____ on Wednesday.

During Halloween (can be used with many units, just replace ghosts with planets, leprechauns, other animals, etc.)

Ghosts are _____ and _____.

They can _____ and _____.

Ghosts move _____ and _____.

The best thing about ghosts is that

they are _____!!

When studying Native Americans:

The _____ Indian tribe

lived _____.

Their homes were _____

made of _____.

They ate _____ and _____.

They _____.

They _____.

For Thanksgiving:

I am a Pilgrim.

I _____ and _____.

I am an Indian.

I _____ and _____.

On Thanksgiving

we _____ together.

For expository writing:

I have a _____.

It is _____, _____, and _____.

It can _____ and _____.

I can not _____ or _____.

Drafting/Conferencing

When students are ready to write their rough draft, it is helpful if the teacher models this process over and over again during mini-lessons. After the mini-lesson, young authors need uninterrupted time to write. Writing workshop in a primary classroom is a busy time. Expect a constant buzz of activity while students draft their thoughts and ideas. As Dorothy Strickland and Joan Feeley (2003) observed, "writers in the primary years are active, noisy, risk takers, internalizing the rules of written language as they use it to construct meaning in social situations" (p. 346). While students are drafting, teachers meet with individuals to assist them with their pieces.

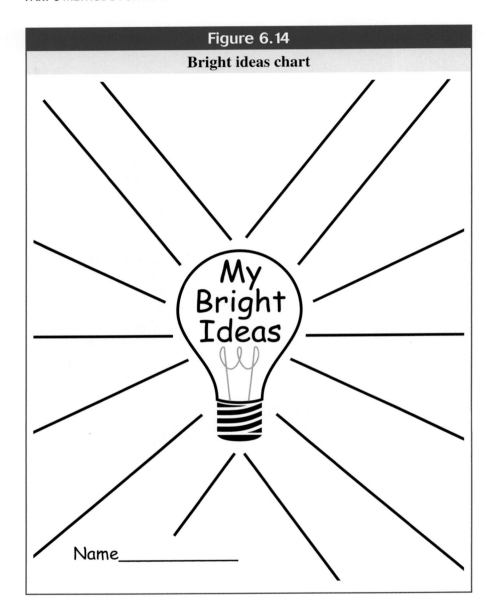

Figure 6.14
Bright ideas chart

My Bright Ideas

Name_____

Revision and Editing

Students then revise and edit their completed drafts. It is very important that students are given clear guidelines for revision and editing. In the early grades teachers may want to guide students by providing them with revision and editing checklists. Again, before students are expected to be proficient at these skills on their own, many mini-lessons using sample stories are needed to demonstrate the process.

A young author shares her finished piece with the class.

Publishing

After revision and editing, stories are ready for publication. The teacher can have the students rewrite or, because this is very tedious for young learners, she can enlist the help of adult or upper elementary grade volunteers to word process the stories and correct the other mechanical and spelling errors that the students were not developmentally ready to correct themselves.

Sharing

Young authors love to illustrate their published pieces and share them with the class in the author's chair.

Figure 6.15 contains a list of picture books to motivate young writers and share with them the process of writing picture books for children.

Independent Writing

Each time a teacher models the writing process for a young child, he edges that child closer to becoming an independent writer. Shared and interactive writing lessons provide a foundation as teachers and students work together to compose meaningful texts. Patterned writing supports the novice as he composes texts on his own. The mini-lessons and support given during writing workshop create an environment for authors to flourish. Teachers of emergent writers also provide time during the day for youngsters to hone their skills on their own. Two opportunities for independent writing occur when students are recording thoughts and ideas in a journal and spending time in a writing center.

Figure 6.15

Picture books to motivate young writers

Borden, Louise. (2001). *The Day Eddie Met the Author.* New York: McElderry.

Brown, Marc. (1996). *Arthur Writes a Story.* Boston: Little, Brown and Company.

Christelow, Eileen. (1995). *What Do Authors Do?* New York: Clarion Books.

Cronin, Doreen. (2000). *Click, Clack, Moo: Cows That Type.* New York: Simon & Schuster.

Duke, Kate. (1992). *Aunt Isabel Tells a Good One.* New York: Dutton Children's Books.

Ehlert, Lois. (1996). *Under My Nose.* Katonah, NY: Richart Owen.

Harris, Wayne. (1994). *Judy and the Volcano.* New York: Scholastic.

Lester, Helen. (1997). *Author: A True Story.* Boston: Houghton Mifflin.

Lyon, George Ella. (1998). *A Sign.* New York: Orchard Books.

Stevens, Janet. (1995). *From Pictures to Words: A Book About Making a Book.* New York: Holiday House.

Teaching Strategy for the Classroom

AN ACTIVITY FOR INTRODUCING THE COMPONENTS OF WRITING WORKSHOP: WRITING WORKSHOP IN FIRST GRADE: OFF TO A GREAT START!

DAY 1

1. Enthusiastically introduce writing workshop. You may want to read a book about writing. *Arthur Writes a Story* (1996) by Marc Brown is a good one!

2. Briefly introduce the basic rules and procedures that you want your students to follow.

3. Begin with a "Driting" (Cunningham, Hall, & Sigmon, 1999) mini-lesson. Place a large sheet of chart paper on the board. Using crayons, draw a picture and write a few words to go with it. Say: "Each day during writing workshop, I am going to begin by drawing or writing something I want to tell you." Tell your students about the picture and why you drew it.

4. Give students a blank sheet of paper and encourage them to do the same. Say: "Use your crayons to draw something you want to share with the rest of the class. You may draw and write whatever you like. I will give you about ten minutes to draw and write and then we will share."

If most children in your class have had writing experiences in kindergarten and at home, you will probably only do one to three "Driting" mini-lessons. Then move on to model how to draw a picture and write on writing lines.

Note: The following lesson plan is one way (not the only way!!) to provide a bit of structure to writing workshop at the beginning of the year. By choosing a topic students are familiar with you can use your mini-lessons to model the important beginning writing skills. Eventually, students will be moving through the stages of writing at their own individual pace.

DAY 2

Begin "All about Me" book—brainstorm list.

Mini-Lesson

- Read *I Like Me* (1988) by Nancy Carlson.
- Explain to students that they are going to write a book all about themselves.
- Ask student what kinds of things might be in a book all about themselves. Record ideas on "Bright Ideas" chart (see Figure 6.15). Some may include things they like to do, their favorite colors, their favorite foods, their family, where they live, their pets, etc.

Due to the length of the lesson and the attention span of beginning first grades, no writing or sharing today.

DAY 3

Mini-Lesson

- Revisit list. Add any new ideas (tell the students this is revising).
- Model creating the first page of your book, which will include a self-portrait (as detailed and personalized as possible) with your name written under it.

Write
Students draw and write about their self-portraits while you circulate and encourage students.

Share
Students share their self-portrait with a partner.

DAY 4

Mini-Lesson

Revisit list. Model how to choose one topic from the list and draw and write about it. Focus on stretching out words to write.

Write
Circulate and encourage students while they are writing.

Share
Begin sharing groups today.

DAYS 5–7

Continue in the same fashion as Day 4, adding three more pages to the book so that students end up with a five-page book. During your mini-lessons model how you choose a new topic, draw your picture, and stretch out words to write about your picture. On some of the pages you may want to leave off the beginning capital and ending marks so that children can help you fix that later.

The purpose of the following three lessons is simply to *introduce and use the terms* "revise" and "edit." We do not expect students to be able to do this on their own. But the goal is to model what writers do during our mini-lessons, and this gets you off to the right start!

DAY 8

Mini-Lesson

Revision (adding a color word).

- Read *A Beasty Story* (1999) by Bill Martin Jr.
- Model choosing one of your pages and adding a color word to it. For example, if you wrote about your dog: "I have a big dog." You could add, "I have a big, brown dog" or add a sentence that has a color word.

Write

Circulate and assist students in adding a color word to one of their pages.

Share

DAY 9

Editing for capital letters.

Mini-Lesson

Reread your book and add capital letters where needed.

Write

Students edit their pieces fixing capital letters.

Share

DAY 10

Editing for periods.

Mini-Lesson

Reread your book and add periods where needed.

Write

Students edit their pieces adding periods where needed.

Share

Publish stories and begin the process again.

Sources: Burns, Griffin, & Snow. (1999). *Starting out right: A guide to promoting children's reading success.* Washington D.C.: National Academy Press (p. 103); Cunningham, Hall, & Sigmon. (1999). *The teacher's guide to the four blocks.* Greensboro, NC: Carson Dellosa (pp. 87–121).

Journals

Writers of all ages enjoy recording their thoughts in a journal. Young children are always brimming with stories to tell. Every primary teacher knows that the first ten minutes of each day are spent hearing the excited chorus of students as they share their latest adventures. "Guess what, I lost a tooth last night." "My dog ran away." "My dad is coming back from his business trip tomorrow." "My mom is going to have a baby." All of these make great topics to share in a journal. For the youngest writer a journal may simply be a book of blank pages where they draw pictures to represent their ideas. For a list of different types of journals see Chapter 3. Eventually, with careful teacher observation, modeling, and encouragement, students will begin adding words to label their picture. As the year progresses, their words will turn into sentences and sentences into paragraphs. The use of journals helps students to further their independent writing skills and provides teachers with a window into a young child's spelling knowledge (Fresch, 2001). The journal entries students create demonstrate their growing knowledge of the English language. To provide an ongoing record of a student's application of spelling knowledge, teachers collect one journal entry a month from the child. These entries are stored in the child's portfolio and are a boon to teachers, who analyze the entries, determine a child's spelling strengths and weaknesses, and adjust their instruction accordingly.

To modify the daily journal for a child who is unable to clearly communicate his thoughts using his oral language, a paper of familiar picture symbols of his typical nightly activities is sent home to the family. The child, with the support of his family, circles the pictures that represent the activities they did that evening. The next day, the child, with assistance from the teacher, cuts out the picture symbols and glues them in his journal. The child dictates a simple sentence to accompany the picture, and the teacher writes the sentence on a sentence strip. The child cuts apart the sentence and puts it back in order. This sentence serves as reading material for that child during the day and goes home with him at night.

The Writing Center

A well-stocked writing center is an inviting place for children to practice their beginning writing skills. The teacher provides a range of materials that students can use to compose written pieces. The writing center includes different writing tools (pens, pencils, markers, colored pencils, stamps) and different kinds of paper (blank, lined, colored, note pads, postcards, memo pads, etc.). Children go to the writing center to independently practice the writing skills they are learning during shared, interactive, and guided writing lessons.

THE MORNING MESSAGE: A DAILY ACTIVITY THAT COMBINES READING AND WRITING

The morning message is an integral part of the daily routine where a number of skills and concepts are explored. The morning message is simply a sentence or two that the teacher writes on the board each day before her students arrive or writes with her students in the morning. Although the idea is a simple one that does not take much time, it is a powerful teaching tool. The dialogue between the teacher and students during the morning message is what gives it its power. The following conversation was recorded in Mrs. Whalen's first grade classroom in October:

Students are working together to complete the morning message.

The message read:

We will learn about living on the farm today.

Lunch   **11:50**

Music   **1:30**

The reading of the morning message went as follows:

Mrs. W.:	See if you can find a word in the morning message that you know.
Child:	*farm,* I sounded it out.
Child:	*on*
Mrs. W.:	That's one we can sound out.
Child:	*today*
Mrs. W.:	Where have you seen that one before?
Child:	On the calendar chart.
Will:	*my name,* "Will"
Mrs. W.:	Why does your name have a capital and this doesn't?
Will:	Because names always have a capital.
Child:	*living*
Mrs. W.:	Tell me about the *-ing* ending. How do we spell that *-ing* ending?

Class:	i-n-g
Child:	*we*
Mrs. W.:	Why does *we* have a capital?
Child:	It started the sentence . . .

This entire exchange took less than five minutes, but in it the children were able to read words independently and Mrs. Whalen was able to listen to her students' responses and observe their developing knowledge. This routine activity, done on a daily basis, gives a consistent opportunity to teach and review concepts and also to informally assess students' understanding of a multitude of skills.

The morning message is described by Hiebert and Raphael (1998) as "rich with potential in its ability to assist children in making the transition from home to school, while at the same time allowing teachers to model writing processes" (p. 155). There is a wide range of skills that can be taught during the morning message, and the teacher can alter the morning message to meet his instructional needs. The following are some variations to the morning message:

1. In a shared writing format, write the message with your students, where they generate the ideas they want included in the message. This is a great way to model what writers do while composing and drafting.

2. The teacher writes a message about the day's activities and has students raise their hands and individually tell her the words they can read. The teacher underlines each word as the child reads it and also points out letters, sounds, sight words, endings, etc.

3. The teacher writes the beginning of a story. The children help finish the story. This version is used to model a variety of writing skills: story elements, beginning-middle-end of story, suspense, and transitional words. This is an excellent writing workshop mini-lesson.

4. The teacher writes a message and leaves out the vowels they are studying and inserts blanks. Students come up and fill in the missing letters.

5. Write a message and leave out words, leaving only blanks. Have children use the context of the sentence to figure out what the missing word is.

6. Write a letter to students, leaving out proper punctuation, etc. This is a great introduction to the parts of a friendly letter (greeting, body, and closing) and also the punctuation that is involved.

7. Assign each student a day to write the morning message. Have them write it on a piece of paper at home and then put it on the board in the morning.

The morning message greets the students each day and is a versatile tool for the teachers. For a child who needs individual assistance, the teacher can write the morning message on a small dry erase board that the child holds himself and edits with assistance from a teacher's aide or peer. Any skill being introduced or reviewed can easily be incorporated into the morning message. It is a wonderful way to set the stage for a day of learning!

Software Programs for
Young Learners

ENHANCING LEARNING WITH TECHNOLOGY

Teachers can use technology to enhance instruction for emerging readers and writers. Children can interact with CD-ROM books, write simple stories using writing programs, or reinforce the skills and concepts they are learning with other related software.

Summary

There is nothing more exciting than watching an emergent learner uncover the mysteries and discover the joy of reading and writing. Educators of young children have an enormous responsibility to guide their students on this path using meaningful experiences that are developmentally appropriate. Young children go through specific stages of oral language development, and their oral language provides a base for learning to read and write. Through listening to stories read aloud and other interactions with text, children develop concepts of print. Young readers are supported through shared and guided reading lessons and practice their skills when they read independently. Emerging writers develop skills as they use their temporary spelling to tell about their ideas. They experience lessons in shared writing, interactive writing, guided writing, and independent writing. Teachers can combine the teaching of all of these skills into a daily activity called the morning message.

Chapter Review

Go to the Online Learning Center at **www.mhhe.com/farrisreading** to take chapter quizzes, practice with key terms, and review important content.

Main Points

- The emergent literacy perspective assumes that a child's knowledge and skills related to literacy grow from the time he is born to the time he can read and write conventionally.

- A developmentally appropriate approach to literacy teaching provides students with ample time to engage in purposeful reading and writing activities.

- A young child's oral language develops at a rapid rate and serves as a foundation for the other literacy skills he gradually will acquire.

- The enjoyable practice of reading aloud is a vital part of every child's life.

- Both caregivers and educators must carefully select materials and make time for reading every day.

- Educators utilize technology and tutors to support the read-aloud experience in their classroom.

- An at-home reading program helps to strengthen the ties between home and school.

- As children participate in shared reading lessons with big books, they begin to develop their concepts of print.

- Carefully constructed literacy play centers, filled with literacy props, help young learners engage in sociodramatic play.

- Shared reading lessons support young children who are on the verge of reading by demonstrating concepts of print, expanding their vocabulary, and introducing them to the wonderful world of literature.

- Small group guided reading lessons help students utilize strategies to become independent readers.

- A well-stocked and clearly organized classroom library is a must in a balanced literacy classroom.

- Teachers must support and encourage a child's spelling development.

- Children go through five stages as they grow as spellers.

- During shared writing, the teacher acts as a scribe while she and the children work together to write a piece.

- Sharing the pen is the key feature of the interactive writing experiences in a classroom.

- Young children learn the structures of the English language by using language patterns presented in frame sentences.

- During writing workshop, children learn about the process of writing.

- Youngsters write independently in their journals and at the writing center.

- Diverse learners benefit from various instructional approaches.

- Teachers use the morning message to model the reading and writing processes.

Key Terms

big books	250	developmentally	
concept books	244	appropriate	
		practices	234

277

Reflecting and Reviewing

1. Think back to your childhood. What experiences did you have with your family that strengthened your literacy skills? How will you encourage parents to create a literacy rich home environment for their children?

2. How will you encourage students to use their oral language in your classroom? How will you extend their knowledge of oral language into daily reading and writing activities? If we peered into your primary classroom, what would we see?

3. Compare shared reading and reading aloud. What elements of a shared reading lesson make it different than reading aloud? What are the benefits of shared reading? How would you use this strategy in your classroom?

Children's Literature

For annotations of the books listed below, please see Appendix A.

Arnosky, Jim. (1990). *Crinkleroot's Guide to Walking in Wild Places.* New York: Bradbury Press.

———. (1996). *Crinkleroot's Guide to Knowing Butterflies.* New York: Simon and Schuster.

Aylesworth, Jim. (1992). *Old Black Fly.* (S. Gammell, Illus.). New York: Henry Holt.

Berger, Melvin. (2000). *Buzz! A Book About Insects.* New York: Scholastic.

Brown, Marc. (1996). *Arthur Writes a Story.* Boston: Little, Brown.

Brown, Margaret Wise. (1999). *I Like Bugs.* New York: Golden Books.

Browne, Anthony. (1996). *Things I Like.* Boston: Houghton Mifflin.

Bunting, Eve. (1999). *The Butterfly House.* New York: Scholastic.

Carle, Eric. (1977). *The Grouchy Ladybug.* New York: HarperCollins.

———. (1987). *The Very Hungry Caterpillar.* New York: Philomel.

Carlson, Nancy. (1988). *I Like Me.* New York: Viking Penguin.

Christelow, Eileen. (1995). *What Do Authors Do?* New York: Clarion.

Coles, Robert. (1995). *Ruby Bridges.* (G. Ford, Illus.). New York: Scholastic.

Duke, Kate. (1992). *Aunt Isabel Tells a Good One.* New York: Dutton Children's Books.

Egielski, Richard. (1995). *Buz.* New York: A Laura Geringer Book.

Fowler, Allan. (1998). *Inside an Ant Colony.* Danbury, CT: Children's Press.

Fox, Mem. (1986). *Hattie and the Fox.* (P. Mullins, Illus.). New York: Bradbury Press.

Gibbons, Gail. (1991). *From Seed to Plant.* New York: Holiday House.

———. (1992). *Recycle.* New York: Little, Brown.

———. (1993). *Spiders.* New York: Holiday House.

———. (1995). *Planet Earth/Inside Out.* New York: Mulberry Paperback.

———. (1997). *The Moon Book.* New York: Holiday House.

———. (2000). *Apples.* New York: Holiday House.

Hoose, Phillip & Hannah. (1998). *Hey, Little Ant.* Berkeley, CA: Tricycle Press.

Kellogg, Stephen. (1988). *Johnny Appleseed.* New York: Morrow Junior Books.

Lionni, Leo. (1960). *Inch by Inch.* New York: Astor-Honor.

London, Jonathan. (1999). *Wiggle Waggle.* (M. Rex, Illus.). San Diego: Harcourt Brace.

Martin, Bill Jr. (1964). *Brown Bear, Brown Bear, What Do You See?* (E. Carle, Illus.). New York: Holt.

———. (1999). *A Beasty Story.* (S. Kellogg, Illus.). San Diego: Harcourt Brace.

McDonald, Megan. (1995). *Insects Are My Life.* (P.B. Johnson, Illus.). New York: Orchard Books.

Murphy, Stuart. (1997). *Divide and Ride.* New York: HarperCollins.

———. (1997). *Every Buddy Counts.* New York: HarperCollins.

Polacco, Patricia. (1993). *The Bee Tree.* New York: Putnam & Grosset.

Williams, Sue. (1989). *I Went Walking.* (J. Vivas, Illus.). San Diego: Harcourt Brace.

Ziefert, Harriet. (1998). *Bugs, Beetles and Butterflies.* (L. Flather, Illus.). New York: Viking.

Classroom Teaching Resources

Burns, M. S., Griffin, P. & Snow, C. E. (Eds.). (1999). *Starting out right: A guide to promoting children's reading success.* Washington, DC: National Academy Press.

Butler, D. (1998). *Babies need books: Sharing books with children from birth to six* (Rev. ed.). Portsmouth, NH: Heinemann.

Campbell, R. (2001). *Read-alouds with young children.* Newark, DE: International Reading Association.

Fisher, B. & Fisher Medvic, E. (2000). *Perspectives on shared reading: Planning and practice.* Portsmouth, NH: Heinemann.

Fountas, I. C. & Pinnell, G. S. (1996). *Guided reading: Good first teaching for all children.* Portsmouth, NH: Heinemann.

Hoyt, L. (2000). *Snapshots: Literacy minilessons up close.* Portsmouth, NH: Heinemann.

Johnson, B. (1999). *Never too early to write.* Gainesville, FL: Maupin House.

McCarrier, A., Pinnell, G. S. & Fountas, I. C. (2000). *Interactive writing: How language and literacy come together, K–2.* Portsmouth, NH: Heinemann.

Northwest Regional Education Laboratory. (1999). *Seeing with new eyes: A guidebook on teaching and assessing beginning writers* (5th ed.). Portland, OR: Author.

Schulman, M. B. & Payne, C. D. (2000). *Guided reading: Making it work.* New York: Scholastic.

Stead, T. (2002). *Is that a fact? Teaching nonfiction writing K–3.* Portland, ME: Stenhouse.

Strickland, D. S. & Morrow, L. M. (Eds.). (2000). *Beginning reading and writing.* New York: Teachers College Press.

Taberski, S. (2000). *On solid ground.* Portsmouth, NH: Heinemann.

Yopp, R. H. & Yopp, H. K. (2001). *Literature-based reading activities* (3rd ed.). Boston: Allyn and Bacon.

There was a farmer
had a bird,
And Sunny was his name-o.
S-U-N-N-Y
S-U-N-N-Y
S-U-N-N-Y
And Sunny was his name-o.

"Children need some powerful, explicit, meaningful, and interesting instruction in phonics and other principles of how words are constructed."

Gay Su Pinnell and Irene Fountas, authors of the books *Guided Reading* and *Word Matters*

CHAPTER 7

A Balanced Approach to Phonics and Word Study

Key Ideas

- A balanced approach to teaching phonics is achieved when educators make informed choices about the instructional methods they select to satisfy the needs of their learners.
- Successful readers and writers capitalize on **phonics** as a tool.
- Effective teachers offer students a wealth of opportunities to learn about and practice their phonics skills.
- An understanding of the importance of phonological and **phonemic awareness** is essential for early learners.
- Listening to nursery rhymes, poems, and songs helps youngsters develop **phonological awareness.**
- Phonemic awareness activities are designed to condition students to focus on and manipulate spoken sounds.
- A young child's knowledge of the **alphabetic principle** is enhanced by listening to alphabet books, doing alphabet puzzles, and playing simple alphabet games.
- Phonics has a language of its own. A knowledgeable teacher understands and uses phonics terminology appropriately.
- **Word study** is an important component of a balanced literacy classroom.
- A working knowledge of **high-frequency words** adds another piece to a child's reading and writing repertoire.
- The goal of spelling instruction is to help young writers understand how words work.

Questions to Ponder

- What activities will the students be engaged in if a teacher is using a balanced approach to phonics teaching?
- Why are phonological and phonemic awareness important? What kinds of activities cultivate a child's awareness of spoken sounds?
- It is imperative that youngsters understand the alphabetic principle. How is this understanding nurtured?
- How can teachers create phonics lessons that demonstrate the utility of phonics as a reading and writing tool and furnish time for students to practice using this valuable skill?
- What types of word study lessons bolster a student's ability to read and write?
- Why is the study of high-frequency words an important ingredient in a balanced classroom?
- Along with word study, what other types of spelling activities help children learn our complex spelling system?

Peering into the Classroom

Phonics Here, Phonics There, Phonics, Phonics Everywhere

What does a balanced approach to phonics instruction look like? Let's take a walk around Bristol Elementary School and see what we can discover. Upon entering Mrs. Roberts' first grade class we hear her students chanting a tongue twister: "Moriah makes marvelous macaroni, Moriah makes marvelous macaroni." "Faster!" encourages Mrs. Roberts as the class quickly repeats the alliteration. "What sound do you say at the beginning of each word?" she asks. The class replies, "MMMMM." "What is your mouth doing when it says the /m/ sound?" inquires Mrs. Roberts. "My lips are together," replies Isaac. "It kind of tickles," adds Mia. "Tell me some other words that begin with /m/," queries Mrs. Roberts. And the lesson continues as Mrs. Roberts records her students' /m/ words on a large sheet of chart paper. Her young learners will refer to this chart later when they are composing their own tongue twisters.

Down the hall in Ms. Phillips' second grade classroom, the children are making words. We see the book they have just finished reading, *Word Wizard* (Falwell, 1998), sitting on the easel. The youngsters have seven paper letters—*h, c, c, t, a, r,* and *s*—lined up across the top of their desks and Ms. Phillips asks, "O.K., boys and girls are you ready to be word wizards?" "Yes," the class exclaims. Ms.

Phillips begins the lesson, "Take two letters and make the word 'at.'" Each child carefully chooses the /a/ and /t/ to make his or her word. Ms. Phillips continues, "Add one letter to make the word 'sat.'" The "word wizards" search to find the /s/ to add to their word. The lesson continues as the children make the words cat, rat, hat, chat, chart, charts, and so on. While her students are busily making words at their desks, Ms. Phillips is modeling and making the same words with large paper letters on the chalkboard. The word-making portion of the lesson concludes when Ms. Phillips poses the challenge of making one big word using all seven letters. For some this is an easy task, while others need a few hints and a little teacher guidance. Finally, all the students put their letters in order to spell the word "scratch." As we leave, the children are walking to the carpet in front of the pocket chart to sort the words in various ways and transfer their newly acquired word knowledge to reading and writing.

Upstairs in Mr. Garcia's third grade classroom the children are carefully cutting apart words to sort. Mr. Garcia found words to highlight the different long o spelling patterns in the story his class was reading entitled *The 18 Penny Goose* (Walker, 1998). As the third graders complete their cutting, Mr. Garcia gives directions, "Today we will be sorting words from the story *The 18 Penny Goose* by their spelling pattern. The words on your paper have three different patterns: o (as in go), o-e (as in home), and oa (as in road). Work with your 'word study buddy' to sort your words, then glue them in categories on a piece of paper. Don't forget to label your categories." The students pick up their collection of words, find their word study buddy, and begin their assignment.

In each of the classrooms we visited the phonics practice had a different focus, but all three activities had similar components. The phonics exercises focused on examining the common patterns in English words. The children were active and engaged. There was an ongoing interaction between the students and the teacher. And, although we only observed the phonics portion of the lessons, all three activities were woven into a balanced literacy program and had strong ties to reading and writing.

REFLECTION: IRA/NCTE NATIONAL STANDARDS IN THE CLASSROOM

When we peered into Bristol Elementary School classrooms, we observed phonics lessons that were carefully designed to draw a student's attention to the distinct features of text, to expand "their sense of phonological awareness" (IRA/NCTE, 1996, p. 31). These lessons were embedded in a balanced reading and writing curriculum because phonics is just one piece of the puzzle that aids students in the complex process of making sense of text (Savage, 2004). Standard 3 emphasizes that students must learn how to flexibly use all of the available strategies when they are reading. If they are faced with a challenging

Web Link:
Phonics: An IRA
Position Paper

text, they must "pause frequently to search for graphic, phonological, syntactic, and semantic clues" (p. 32). Recall the discussion of the interactive approach in Chapter 1. A reader must synthesize information from all of the sources listed above to accurately read and comprehend text. The graphophonic or letter–sound clues are one of the crucial cueing systems that support a reader. Teachers cannot neglect phonics and word study or they will deprive their students of an important piece of the reading and writing puzzle.

PHONICS: THE TOOL OF READERS AND WRITERS

Before you continue reading, stop for a moment and jot down any thoughts, ideas, or opinions that you have concerning phonics instruction. How were you taught phonics? What role does it play in learning to read? Save these thoughts to review and reflect

STANDARDS for READING PROFESSIONALS

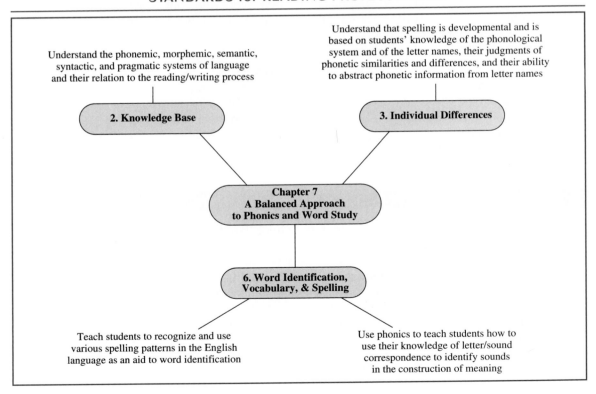

Understand the phonemic, morphemic, semantic, syntactic, and pragmatic systems of language and their relation to the reading/writing process

2. Knowledge Base

Understand that spelling is developmental and is based on students' knowledge of the phonological system and of the letter names, their judgments of phonetic similarities and differences, and their ability to abstract phonetic information from letter names

3. Individual Differences

Chapter 7 A Balanced Approach to Phonics and Word Study

6. Word Identification, Vocabulary, & Spelling

Teach students to recognize and use various spelling patterns in the English language as an aid to word identification

Use phonics to teach students how to use their knowledge of letter/sound correspondence to identify sounds in the construction of meaning on at the end of the chapter. We believe that phonics is a tool for readers and writers. Dorothy Strickland (1998) defines **phonics** as "instruction in the sound–letter relationship used in reading and writing" (p. 5). Strickland (1998, p. 25) conveys the following guidelines for learning and teaching phonics that illustrate our point that phonics is a tool:

1. Teaching phonics is *not* synonymous with teaching reading.
2. Reading and spelling require much more than phonics.
3. Phonics is a means to an end, not the end itself.
4. Phonics is one of several enablers or cueing systems that help us read.
5. Phonics is one of many strategies for spelling.
6. Memorizing phonics rules does not ensure application of those rules.
7. Learners need to see the relevance of phonics for themselves in their own reading and writing.
8. Teaching students to use phonics is different than teaching them *about* phonics.
9. The best context for learning and applying phonics is actual reading and writing.

The reason we spend valuable instructional time teaching phonics is so that children will develop a working knowledge of this powerful tool. This knowledge will assist them on their journey to becoming a skillful reader and writer, but it is not the only knowledge they need. Phonics instruction loses its power if children don't see how it relates directly to their efforts to read and write. This is especially true for diverse learners. They also need systematic instruction in phonics, but this is not enough. Teachers must provide diverse learners with help to apply the word identification skills they are learning to meaningful literacy activities. They must model for these students how to use the knowledge of words when they are reading and writing (Au, 2000). As we look at phonics instruction in this chapter, we will use Strickland's guidelines to steer us in the right direction.

PHONICS: PAST, PRESENT, AND FUTURE

In recent years, there has been a raging controversy about phonics teaching. Articles in the popular press, politicians at their podiums, and even some teachers in their classrooms believe that if we would just teach phonics, phonics, and more phonics all of the children in our country would be proficient readers. But phonics alone does not make a reader, nor does it make a reading program. Phonics is a part of a balanced literacy program. It should focus on the most useful information for identifying words; and it should be systematic, intensive, and completed by third grade (Adams, 1990).

As we have emphasized throughout this textbook, phonics *is* an important *component* in a balanced literacy classroom. The informed voice of Patricia Cunningham (2000) echoes our thoughts: "You don't have to make a choice. You can engage the children's minds and hearts in reading good literature and finding their own voices as authors *and,* at the same time, teach them how our alphabetic language works" (p. viii). When phonics is taught effectively, students transfer and apply the knowledge to authentic reading and writing situations. Part of the confusion and controversy stems from the fact that the phonics lessons of today look much different than they did a generation ago (Strickland, 1998). Let's take a few moments to briefly review the history of phonics teaching and look at the difference between phonics past and phonics future. This historical snapshot illustrates the types of lessons taught in both explicit code or skills emphasis approaches and embedded code or meaning emphasis approaches. Educators who are familiar with the lessons that evolved from these approaches can assess which approach will be the most powerful and meaningful for the students in their classroom and communicate to parents the various ways they are teaching their children the phonics skills used by proficient readers and writers.

Phonics Past

The methods discussed here are "approaches that were in vogue during the 1960s and 1970s but seem to be returning as teachers grapple with how to teach phonics" (Stahl, Duffy-Hester, & Stahl, 1998, p. 344). One group of phonics programs that was popular during that time was the **analytic phonics** programs. In an analytic lesson children locate a phonic element in a preselected group of words that contain that element (Strickland, 1998). "Analytic programs begin by teaching children some words and then helping children to 'analyze' those words and learn phonics rules and generalizations based on those words" (Cunningham, 2000, p. 184). This approach was a component of the basal reading lessons of the 1970s. These lessons have a set pattern of instruction. For instance, each would begin with the teacher introducing a letter sound by writing a word with that sound on the board and telling the children, "This is the word hit, it has the short /i/ sound in the middle." Then the teacher asks her class to listen to other words like bat, pin, fox, and fin to identify whether the short /i/ sound is present. Following this brief auditory practice, the students read a prepared list of words containing the short /i/ sound. Finally, each child completes a few worksheets or workbook pages related to the sound (Stahl et al., 1998).

Synthetic approaches are those that "begin with teaching students individual letters or groups of letters and then showing students how to blend these letters together to form words" (Stahl, et al., 1998, p. 344). During **synthetic phonics** lessons, the teacher introduces a letter/sound (such as short a), writes simple words containing that sound (such as cat, fat, sat), and asks youngsters to blend the sounds together to form a word. The lesson continues by having the entire class read the words together. To practice these words the class reads a story written with a high percentage of words that contain that letter/sound. These texts are called **decodable texts.**

Phonics Present

In the 1990s the emphasis on phonics instruction increased across the United States. Spurred by the publication of Marilyn Adams' (1990) review of phonics and beginning reading instruction research in her book *Beginning to Read: Thinking and*

Learning About Print, administrators, school boards, and parents began putting pressure on teachers to increase the amount of phonics teaching in their classrooms. Two popular misconceptions fueled the increased attention on phonics instruction. First, many people mistakenly believed that teachers who were using the ideas and philosophies related to whole language had abandoned all phonics teaching (Dahl & Scharer, 2000). Second was the assumption that teachers who were no longer teaching phonics using an explicit code or skills emphasis approach were not teaching phonics at all.

In many cases such assumptions were untrue. Teachers were teaching phonics, but they had discovered approaches that were meaning based. These approaches show students how to carefully examine words and word patterns and apply this knowledge when they read and write. Three popular contemporary meaning-based approaches frequently used in the last decade are spelling-based approaches, analogy-based approaches, and embedded phonics approaches (Stahl, Duffy-Hester, & Stahl, 1998).

Spelling-based approaches include **word study** activities like those advocated by the knowledgeable authors of the books *From Phonics to Fluency* (Rasinski & Padak, 2001), *Words Their Way* (Bear, Invernizzi, Templeton, & Johnson, 2000), *Word Matters* (Pinnell & Fountas, 1998), and *Making Words* (Cunningham & Hall, 1994). Some examples of word study activities include sorting words like Mr. Garcia and his third graders were doing and the "making words" lesson we saw in Ms. Phillips' classroom. Word study activities are used to "teach students processes and strategies for examining and thinking about the words they read and write. This knowledge, in turn, is applied to new words students encounter in reading" (Bear & Templeton, 1998, p. 223). Word study activities should increase in difficulty as a student's spelling knowledge develops. See Chapter 6 for a description of this development. Preschool children begin by simply sorting and categorizing objects from their environment. For example, in a preschool literacy play center where the theme is a grocery store, they sort plastic food by its color and food boxes by their size. As they move into kindergarten, they sort pictures that have different beginning sounds, and in the upper grades they sort words with different roots, prefixes, and suffixes (Bear & Templeton, 1998). Word study approaches will be discussed in more detail later in this chapter.

The **making words** (Cunningham & Hall, 1994) lesson we saw at Bristol Elementary School is a multilevel approach to word study. Each student receives six to eight letters and is instructed by the teacher to make a variety of different words by manipulating the letters. As the lesson progresses, the words get gradually more difficult. The challenge of the lesson comes when the students are able to use all of the letters in front of them to make the "mystery" word. Once all of the words are made, they are sorted for different spelling patterns, and there is a brief lesson that demonstrates to students how their word knowledge transfers directly to their reading and writing.

Analogy-based phonics instruction focuses on teaching students to decipher unknown words by looking for spelling patterns and applying those patterns to figure out other words. "In an analogic approach to phonics, children would be taught that

Web Link:
Whole Language
Versus Phonics

if you know how to read and spell cat, you can also read and spell bat, rat, hat, sat and other rhyming words" (Cunningham, 2000, p. 184). The use of **phonograms** or word families in phonics teaching is an example of an analogy-based approach that is explored later in this chapter.

Embedded phonics programs contain lessons that occur in the context of real reading and writing. In their study, Karin Dahl and Patricia Scharer (2000) note three qualities of phonics instruction in context:

1. Teachers assess and respond to the diverse needs of their learners. They make decisions during individual reading and writing conferences that reflect rich knowledge about each student and about their abilities as teachers to provide appropriate instruction for each child in their classroom.

2. Skills are taught in a meaningful context during literacy lessons to enhance children's application of phonics concepts as they read and write.

3. Instruction is not confined to the reading program, but includes an assortment of instructional writing events as children write their own texts, confer with their teacher, and engage in shared writing and writing mini-lessons.

Phonics Future

Web Link:
Questions for Assessing
Phonics Instruction

You, as an aspiring teacher, are the phonics future. You will have to make informed decisions about the type of phonics instruction you want to employ in your classroom. You must keep abreast of the current research and use the knowledge of those who are studying phonics instruction to help guide your decisions. But, more importantly, you must know your students and choose sound instructional techniques that meet their needs. When analyzing the effectiveness of each approach a teacher must ask herself: Were the students active and engaged? Did the lessons demonstrate for students the utility of phonics as a tool for reading and writing? Were the skills learned being directly applied to authentic reading and writing situations? It is important to note that for some students a more explicit code or skills emphasis approach to phonics teaching may be more effective, but it should never overshadow the teaching of reading as a meaning making process.

EXEMPLARY PHONICS INSTRUCTION

In a 1992 article, Steven Stahl outlined nine components of exemplary phonics instruction (pp. 620–624). In a subsequent article (1998), he, along with co-authors Ann Duffy-Hester and Katherine Anne Dougherty Stahl, added to the original list (pp. 339–344). Figure 7.1 is a combination of both lists.

As we continue through the chapter, you will discover how teachers implement the components of good phonics instruction in their classroom. You will find the answers to the following questions: How do teachers cultivate their students' phonological awareness? What types of activities replace the use of worksheets and workbook pages? How do we teach children about onsets, rimes, and spelling patterns? What types of word study activities help children develop automatic word recognition skills? How is phonics integrated into a balanced literacy program?

Figure 7.1
Components of exemplary phonics instruction

Good phonics instruction should:

1. Build on a child's concept of print.
2. Develop the alphabetic principle.
3. Build on and develop phonological awareness.
4. Provide a thorough grounding in the letters.
5. Be clear and direct.
6. *Not* teach rules, not necessarily use worksheets, not dominate instruction, and not have to be boring.
7. Include onsets and rimes.
8. Provide sufficient practice in reading words to develop independent word recognition strategies, focusing attention on the internal structure of words.
9. Lead to automatic word recognition skills so that students can devote their attention to comprehension, not words.
10. Include temporary spelling practice.
11. Be integrated into a total reading program.

Source: Adapted from Stahl, S. (1992). Saying the "p" word: Nine guidelines to exemplary phonics instruction. *The Reading Teacher, 45* (8), 618–625. and Stahl, S., Duffy-Hester, A., & Dougherty Stahl, K. A. (1998). Everything you wanted to know about phonics but were afraid to ask. *Reading Research Quarterly, 33* (3), 338–355.

 ## *PHONICS AND THE DIVERSE LEARNER*

Some students in your classroom may have difficulties with phonics, word study, and spelling for several different reasons. Young learners with poor visual memories frequently have a hard time remembering and recalling the visual images of words. Students who have poor auditory discrimination, the ability to hear the differences of the sounds in words, may struggle when trying to spell words phonetically. Spelling is an arduous task for students with learning disabilities (Shore, 1998). This is due to phonetic processing difficulties that may lead to an inability to remember individual sounds, blend individual sounds into words, and sequence sounds and syllables into words. Because of this these children spell more by sight than by ear and correctly spell words that they can visualize (Henley, Ramsey, & Algozzine, 2002).

If you discover that a student finds phonics a stumbling block rather than a reading and writing tool, begin by getting to know that learner's strengths, weaknesses, and learning style. Using activities that involve multiple modalities will offer students increased opportunities to unlock the sound–symbol code. Many of the lessons and activities discussed in this chapter utilize a variety of learning modes and are helpful for students who struggle to understand how words work. In the section on phonological and phonemic awareness there are appealing lessons that include rhythm, rhyme, movement, and song. Making words and word sorting are excellent activities for tactile/kinesthetic learners. The activities related to the word wall engage both the visual and auditory learner. For other helpful strategies see Figure 7.2.

Portfolio Activity:
Make It Fun!

Figure 7.2

Strategies for learners with diverse abilities

1. Encourage temporary spelling in the primary grades. Don't focus on spelling errors.
2. Be patient and encouraging. Have students chart their progress or keep a list of words they can spell.
3. Have each student develop an individualized spelling list. Words that interest the child or words from his own writing will be more motivating. Words that are not spelled correctly by the end of the week should remain on the list for next week.
4. If you are giving a weekly spelling list, modify it to meet the needs of the child. If the rest of the class is spelling twenty words, have the child work on ten. Have the child only study those words he misspelled on the pretest.
5. Encourage the child to practice his words by writing them.
6. Teach the student about word families and word patterns.
7. Teach the student memory aids. (The princi<u>pal</u> is your <u>pal.</u>)
8. Use a multisensory approach.
9. Use word games such as Boggle, Scrabble, and Hangman.
10. Provide spelling references.

Source: Adapted from Shore, K. (1998). *Special kids problem solver.* Paramus, NJ: Prentice Hall.

Web Link:
Word Study in the
Biliteracy Classroom

In their book *From Phonics to Fluency* (2001), Tim Rasinski and Nancy Padak reinforce the notion that when it comes to teaching diverse learners there are no easy answers or quick fixes. Accomplished teachers have a positive impact on student learning because they focus on getting to know each individual child. When you find yourself faced with the challenge of helping a struggling reader, remember these helpful tips:

1. Focus on a student's individual needs and avoid comparing him to other students in your class.
2. Build on a child's strengths and celebrate her successes.
3. Engage the child in the act of reading on a daily basis.
4. Collaborate with other teachers, specialists, and the child's family members.
5. Utilize volunteers for extra support in school.

Teaching diverse learners is a challenge, but one that comes with great rewards. Giving a child the gift of literacy is one of the many joys of teaching.

DEVELOPMENT OF PHONOLOGICAL AND PHONEMIC AWARENESS

A vast amount of research (Adams, 1990; Griffith & Olson, 1992; Snow, Burns, & Griffin, 1998; Yopp, 1992; Yopp & Yopp, 2000) on the importance of phonological awareness and phonemic awareness is available to educators. It is important that we understand this research and apply it to classroom practice. In order to gain knowl-edge from the research, an informed educator must clearly understand the related vocabulary.

Let's begin by talking about phonological awareness. Most young children begin to develop phonological awareness in their preschool years. Evidence that this knowledge is growing comes from watching the things they do and say. Phonologi-cally aware children love to hear poems and rhyming songs and begin to notice the rhymes. They invent nonsense words and rhymes by substituting one sound for an-other. They can divide long words into syllables or clap each syllable in a phrase. Fi-nally, you hear them say things like "My name starts with B and so does Becky's" when words they hear begin with the same sound. **Phonological awareness** is "a general appreciation of the sounds of speech as distinct from their meaning" (Snow et al., 1998, p. 51). In other words, to be phonologically aware one must begin by un-derstanding that our language is made up of individual words. The next stage is the awareness that these words consist of syllables. The final and most complex stage is the knowledge that the syllables contain individual sounds. These individual sounds are called **phonemes.** And the awareness that words are made up of individual sounds is logically called **phonemic awareness.** One important distinction to make is that phonemic awareness *is not* phonics. Phonics is defined as the instructional techniques that focus on how spellings are related to spoken sounds in systematic ways: letter–sound correspondences.

Why is instructional support for phonemic awareness so important? Because re-search (Adams, 1990) indicates that 25 percent of middle-class first graders lack this vital knowledge, and this number increases substantially for those children who come from less literacy rich backgrounds. Phonemic awareness is difficult for some children because we are asking them to switch their conscious attention away from the meaning of words and tune into the individual sounds. Michael Opitz (2000) of-fers the following best practices for fostering phonological awareness:

- Embed phonological awareness into everyday reading and writing experiences.
- Provide time for children to write and allow for invented spelling.
- Read aloud children's literature that focuses on specific language features.
- Use fun, engaging oral language activities.
- Determine what students need.
- Involve families. (pp. 15–16)

When applying the research on phonological awareness to classroom practice, Opitz' guiding principles will provide a framework for the next section.

Phonological Awareness

As stated earlier, phonological awareness is the awareness that children gain about the sounds of language through linguistic awareness games, nursery rhymes, and rhythmic activities (IRA/NAEYC, 1998). There are many entertaining and engaging activities that teachers can incorporate into their daily lessons to help children

Web Link:
How to Help Your
Children Become
Good Readers

develop phonological awareness. "The activities that are necessary to teach children how to become aware of sounds in language may not seem like real teaching. Instead, they may just seem fun. However, these types of activities are appropriate and necessary for children to learn how to decode words and read independently" (Johns, Lenski, & Elish-Piper, 1999, p. 119). These necessary, but fun, activities include fostering a child's awareness of sounds in the environment, rhyming activities, poetry and chants, simply singing songs, and other phonemic awareness activities.

Fostering an Awareness of Sounds in the Environment

Before we can expect a young child to focus on the sounds of words instead of their meaning, we may have to practice careful listening. Today's children do not have a lot of practice in attending to spoken messages without a visual image. They watch television and movies, play video games, or scan the Internet. They receive a lot more information visually than they do auditorily. The two listening games that follow are part of a phonemic awareness curriculum (Adams, Foorman, Lundberg, & Beeler, 1998) and are designed to "sharpen children's ability to attend selectively to sounds" (p. 11). These activities challenge students to listen attentively:

What Sound Do You Hear?
Play a cassette tape that contains various sounds students are familiar with; have them identify the sounds. An extension of this activity is to have students create their own sound tapes in the listening center.

Listening to Sequences of Sounds
The teacher asks the students to close their eyes while he makes a familiar sound (closing the door, sharpening a pencil, etc.). Students identify the sound, then the teacher makes two sounds in a row, then three, and so on. It is important that students identify the sounds they hear *in sequence*. This will help them later when they are asked to identify the sounds of a word in sequence.

Rhyming Activities

Playing with rhyme helps shift children's attention from the meaning and message of words to their physical form. "Rhyme play is an excellent entry to phonological awareness" (Adams et al., 1998, p. 29). The activities listed below entice students to play with rhymes:

Rhyme Toss
Students stand in a circle around the teacher. They throw the ball to the teacher and say *any* word. When the teacher gets the ball, he says a word that rhymes with the child's word (even if it is a nonsense word) and throws the ball to another student. The game continues in this fashion. Rhyme Toss is designed to be nonthreatening for the students as they only have to provide a word while the teacher provides the rhyme.

Get the Wiggles Out with Rhymes
Have students stand up; explain that when you say a word that rhymes with an action, they are to do that action. Example: "If my word rhymes with jump—jump." "If my word rhymes with hop—hop."

The following is a list of actions and their corresponding rhyming words that the teacher can post in the classroom for easy reference:

clap: cap, tap, gap, zap, lap, trap, map, nap, flap, rap, slap, sap

shake: bake, cake, fake, lake, make, rake, sake, take, wake, flake

spin: bin, din, fin, kin, pin, sin, tin, win, chin, grin, skin, thin, twin

rock: dock, block, hock, flock, lock, crock, mock, knock, sock, shock

hop: bop, crop, cop, drop, prop, mop, shop, pop, stop, top, flop, chop

run: bun, sun, fun, shun, gun, nun, pun, spun, stun

Rhyme in a Line

When students are lining up to go somewhere, give the first child in line a picture card of a simple word (hat, box, net). Ask that child to say the name of the picture and a word that rhymes with it. The card is then passed to the next child in line, who says another rhyming word. Once several rhyming words are given, hand the next child in line a new picture card. The game continues until it is time to leave the room.

Jump Rope Rhymes

Take students outside and teach them one of the many jump rope rhymes. Jump rope rhymes help students with phonological awareness, are entertaining, and are great exercise. If young students are unable to jump rope, the same rhymes work well with bouncing balls or skipping around the room.

Not only are jump rope rhymes fun, but they help strengthen young children's phonological awareness.

Nursery Rhymes

It is truly amazing how many students arrive at the classroom door not knowing any nursery rhymes. For many students this is a missing piece in their development of phonological awareness: "Researchers found that early knowledge of nursery rhymes was strongly and specifically related to development of more abstract phonological skills and of emergent reading abilities" (Adams, 1990, p. 80). Students from other cultures and backgrounds may know rhymes in their own language, but missed out on the traditional English nursery rhymes. The following two rhymes may be familiar to young Hispanic children and are fun to teach to the class in both English and Spanish:

Este minini:	**This One Is Eensy-Weensy**
Starting with the pinkie, touch each finger as you recite this rhyme.	
Este minini.	This one is eensy-weensy.
Este anillado.	This one is Ring Man.
Este espigado.	This one is Tall Man.
Este mininano.	This one is the pointer.
Y este duerme que duerme, todo el verano.	And this one sleeps and sleeps all summer long.
Tortillitas:	**Corn Tortillas**
A Clapping Rhyme.	
Tortillitas de manteca pa' mama que esta contenta.	Corn tortillas, corn tortillas, corn tortillas for my mommy.
Tortillitas de salvado pa' papa que esta enojado.	Flour tortillas, flour tortillas, flour tortillas for my daddy.

Figure 7.3 contains a sampling of some of the nursery rhyme books available to share with your students to develop this early knowledge. Once children know the nursery rhymes, you can play "Chime Right In!" (Opitz, 2000) where students listen carefully while you recite a rhyme and "chime right in" on the missing words. For example, "Little Miss Muffet sat on a _____."

Poetry and Chants

Young children love to hear interesting words roll off their tongues as they chant and recite poems. Short, lively poems enjoyed over and over develop phonological awareness and are great vehicles for shared reading lessons. To share poems with the entire class, teachers often copy them onto a large piece of chart paper or on individual sentence strips for use in the pocket chart.

One facet of phonological awareness is the knowledge that the stream of spoken speech consists of individual words. To illustrate this point to young children the teacher can choose a poem that he and the children are currently working on, pick one line of the poem, and, while the students are watching, cut the words in that line apart. After the line is cut apart, have the students help to reassemble it in the pocket

Figure 7.3
Nursery rhyme books

Bornstein, Harry, & Saulnier, Karen. (1992). *Nursery Rhymes from Mother Goose Told in Signed English.* Gallaudet University Press: Kendall Green Publications.

Cousins, Lucy. (1989). *Wee Willie Winkie and Other Nursery Rhymes.* New York: Dutton Children's Books. (Board Book)

dePaola, Tomie. (1981). *The Comic Adventures of Old Mother Hubbard and Her Dog.* New York: Harcourt, Brace, Jovanovich.

Johnson, David A. (1998). *Old Mother Hubbard.* New York: Margaret K. McElderry Books.

Lansky, Bruce. (1993). *The New Adventures of Mother Goose.* New York: Simon & Schuster.

Long, Sylvia. (1999). *Sylvia Long's Mother Goose.* New York: Chronicle.

Opie, Iona. (1999). *Here Comes Mother Goose.* (R. Wells, Illus.). New York: Candlewick Press.

Stevens, Janet, & Stevens Crummel, Susan. (2001). *And the Dish Ran Away With the Spoon.* New York: Harcourt.

Vail, Rachel. (1998). *Over the Moon.* (S. Nash, Illus.). New York: Orchard.

Ziefert, Harriet. (1997). *Mother Goose Math.* New York: Viking.

chart while counting the number of words in the sentence. This simple lesson repeated a number of times will help children understand that a spoken sentence is divided into words. Other phonological awareness skills that teachers focus on while reading poems are listening for rhyming words, clapping syllables in words, and listening for words that share the same sounds.

Sing, Sing, Sing!

"Singing can be a wonderful vehicle for so many facets of the educational scene. Everything from emotions to academics can be enhanced through music in general and singing in particular" (Wolf, 1994, p. 20). In her article, Jan Wolf (1994) equips teachers with a four-step approach to include songs in the classroom. First, begin with songs that are familiar to the students. Teachers may choose to begin with folk songs like "Mary Had a Little Lamb" and "The Three Blind Mice." Second, proceed with what is comfortable. Using a familiar tune like "Twinkle, Twinkle Little Star" or "Mary Had a Little Lamb" teachers can create songs to go with any situation. The following song was written by Maria Walther for Groundhog's Day to the tune of "I'm a Little Teapot":

> Here's a little groundhog,
>
> furry and brown.
>
> He's coming up to look around.
>
> If he sees his shadow, down he'll go—
>
> Then six more weeks of winter—
>
> oh no!!

Figure 7.4

Song picture books

Adams, Pam. (1973). *There Was An Old Lady Who Swallowed a Fly.* New York: Child's Play.

Clarke, Gus. (1992). *E I E I O.* New York: Lothrop, Lee & Shepard Books.

Goodhart, Pippa. (1997). *Row, Row, Row Your Boat.* (S. Lambert, Illus.). New York: Crown Publishers, Inc.

Hoberman, Mary Ann. (1998). *Miss Mary Mack: A Hand Clapping Rhyme.* (N. Bernard Westcott, Illus.). Boston: Little Brown.

Kellogg, Steven. (1998). *A-Hunting We Will Go!* New York: Morrow Junior Books.

Kovalski, Maryann. (1987). *The Wheels on the Bus.* Boston: Little Brown.

Taylor, Jane. (1992). *Twinkle, Twinkle Little Star.* New York: Scholastic.

Trapani, Iza. (1993). *The Itsy Bitsy Spider.* Boston: Whispering Coyote Press, Inc.

Westcott, Nadine Bernard. (1996). *I've Been Working on the Railroad.* New York: Hyperion.

These songs are generally known as "piggyback" songs and are available in Jean Warren's series *Piggyback Songbooks* (Totline Press, Warren Publishing House, Everett, Washington). Third, teachers move on to what is functional. Teachers use songs for all curricular areas; they are also helpful during transitions from one activity to the next. Finally, reach out beyond singing together with children by providing them opportunities to explore songs on their own. A music center with a cassette recorder and flannel board pieces for acting out songs is one way to do this. See Figure 7.4 for a listing of song picture books.

The Importance of Phonemic Awareness

Web Link:
Phonics Information

Children in a primary grade classroom will enter with different levels of phonemic awareness. Phonemic awareness can be difficult for some children because it is a more advanced form of phonological awareness where children understand "that speech can be broken down into even smaller units (phonemes). This is very important for learning to read, because phonemes are what letters usually stand for. [The idea that letters or groups of letters represent phonemes is called the alphabet principle.]" (Burns et al., 1999, p. 46). Teaching ideas for boosting a student's knowledge of the alphabet principle are described later in the chapter. It is important that teachers expose students to a language-rich environment with a lot of activities that play with sounds. Hallie and Ruth Yopp (2000) make three recommendations for phonemic awareness instruction:

Phonemic awareness instruction should be:

1. Child appropriate.

2. Deliberate and purposeful.

3. Viewed by educators as only one part of a much broader literacy program. (p. 132)

They encourage teachers to plan their instructional sequence by starting with larger units of sound (syllables), continuing with activities that focus on onsets and rimes, then moving to the smallest unit of sound (phonemes). Before this sequence begins, Yopp and Yopp (2000) suggest exposing students to activities that focus on rhyme like those described earlier in this chapter. Activities for fostering phonemic awareness are found in the Teaching Strategy for the Classroom box.

Teaching Strategy for the Classroom

ACTIVITIES FOR PHONEMIC AWARENESS

EYE SPY: ISOLATING BEGINNING SOUNDS

Prepare a basket of objects or picture cards with beginning consonant sounds.

Level 1: Introduce each object by isolating the beginning sound: "This is a b—bear." Have students repeat.
Level 2: Eye spy something in the basket that starts with /b/ :use letter sound, not name.
Level 3: Pick an object and ask: What is this? What is the first sound you hear?

Put objects in the word study center for students to play with and explore. This activity can also be used for segmenting and blending.

SEGMENTING: STRETCHING OUT THE SOUNDS

1. Show students two picture cards. Say, "I'm going to stretch out the sounds of one of these cards; point to the correct card."
2. Stretch sounds out to train the ear to hold a longer chain of sounds. As a visual reminder to children when they are stretching out words, you may want to give them a small Slinky or a rubber band.

ELKONIN SOUND BOXES

1. Prepare a sheet with simple pictures along with a matrix that contains a box for each *sound* in the word. Pass out counters (chips, pennies, beans, etc.).
2. Model the process for the students. Slowly say the sounds of the word and push the counters one sound at a time into the boxes.
3. Encourage students to do the same.

Variation: Move the chip representing a given sound into initial, medial, or final box depending on the sound's position in the word.

LISTEN TO THE SOUNDS: A BLENDING ACTIVITY

Sing the following song to the tune "Frere Jacques" to focus on blending sounds to form a word.

Make these three sounds;
Make these three sounds;
/k/ /a/ /t/ (children repeat /k/ /a/ /t/)
Can you say the word?
Can you say the word for /k/ /a/ /t/? (Children answer—cat.)

BLEND THE PICTURE

Cut assorted pictures out from magazines/clip art. Laminate and cut into the number of sounds in that word. Have students put the picture together while orally blending the sounds.

Assessing Phonemic Awareness

In order to effectively teach we must be involved in assessment that drives our instruction. One way to assess a child's phoneme segmentation skill is by administering Hallie Kay Yopp and Harry Singer's (1995) "Yopp-Singer Test of Phoneme Segmentation" (see Figure 7.5). The purpose of the test is to measure a child's ability to separately articulate the sounds of spoken words. For example, given the orally presented word "fat," the child should respond with three separate sounds: /f/—/a/—/t/. It is important to note that the sounds of the words, not the letter names, are an appropriate response. The test takes about five to ten minutes to individually administer to each child. The following administration and scoring directions may be helpful:

To administer:

1. Read directions on test sheet to child (see Figure 7.5).
2. Assist child with completion of practice items.
3. Give child twenty-two-item test.
4. Feedback is given to the child as he progresses through the list. If the child responds correctly, the examiner nods or says, "That's right." If the child gives an incorrect response, he is corrected.

Scoring:

- A child's score is calculated by counting the number of items correctly segmented into all constituent parts.
- *No partial credit is given.* For example, if a child says /c/—/at/ instead of /c/—/a/—/t/, the response may be noted on the blank following the item but is considered incorrect for purposes of scoring.
- Blends contain two or three phonemes and should be articulated separately: /g/—/r/—/ew/.
- Digraphs are single phonemes: /sh/—/e/ (two phonemes), /th/—/r/—/ee/ (three phonemes).

Figure 7.5

Yopp-Singer test of phoneme segmentation

Student's name _____ Date _____

Score (number correct)_____

Directions: Today we're going to play a word game. I'm going to say a word and I want you to break the word apart. You are going to tell me each sound in the word in order. For example, if I say "old," you should say "/o/-/l/-/d/." (*Administrator: Be sure to say the sounds, not the letters, in the word.*) Let's try a few together.

Practice items: (*Assist the child in segmenting these items as necessary.*) ride, go, man

Test items: (*Circle those items that the student correctly segments; incorrect responses may be recorded on the blank line following the item.*)

1. dog _____
2. keep _____
3. fine _____
4. no _____
5. she _____
6. wave _____
7. grow _____
8. that _____
9. red _____
10. me _____
11. sat _____
12. lay _____
13. race _____
14. zoo _____
15. three _____
16. job _____
17. in _____
18. ice _____
19. at _____
20. top _____
21. by _____
22. do _____

The author Hattie Kay Yopp, California State University, Fullerton, grants permission for this test to be reproduced. The author acknowledges the contribution of the late Harry Singer to the development of this test.

Source: Test from Yopp, Hallie Kay. (1995, September). A test for assessing phonemic awareness in young children. *The Reading Teacher, 49*(1), 20–29.

The Alphabetic Principle

Another valuable piece to the phonics puzzle is a child's understanding of the alphabet principle. Children should be instructed in the **alphabetic principle,** the understanding that there is a systematic relationship between letters and sounds (IRA/NAEYC, 1998). "The best practice is to help children identify letters and numbers in an enjoyable way

Figure 7.6
Popular alphabet books

Bayer, Jane. (1984). *A My Name Is Alice*. New York: Dial Books.

Bender, Robert. (1996). *The A to Z Beastly Jamboree*. New York: Lodestar.

Cleary, Beverly. (1998). *The Hullabaloo ABC*. New York: Morrow Junior Books.

Howland, Naomi. (1994). *ABC Drive*. New York: Clarion Books.

Jahn-Clough, Lisa. (1997). *ABC Yummy*. Boston: Houghton Mifflin.

Kalman, Maira. (2001). *What Pete Ate From A to Z*. New York: Putnam.

Lobel, Arnold. (1981). *On Market Street*. New York: Greenwillow.

Martin, Bill Jr., Archanbault, John. (1989). *Chicka Chicka Boom Boom*. New York: Simon & Schuster.

Rotner, Shelley. (1996). *Action Alphabet*. New York: Atheneum.

Seuss, Dr. (1963). *Dr. Seuss' ABC*. New York: Random House.

Shannon, George. (1996). *Tomorrow's Alphabet*. New York: Greenwillow.

Walton, Rick. (1998). *So Many Bunnies: A Bedtime ABC and Counting Book*. New York: Lothrop, Lee & Shepard.

as they acquire the broader concepts about print and books they will need as a foundation for literacy" (Strickland, 1998, pp. 56–57). Some of the practices Strickland (1998) advocates are teaching the alphabet song, posting alphabet cards in the classroom at eye level, using the children's names to focus on letter concepts, and reading alphabet books. When looking for alphabet books to read to students, it is best to choose simple books with not many words on a page and pictures that most of the children recognize. Some popular alphabet books are listed in Figure 7.6.

In addition to sharing alphabet books with children, there are a number of other simple activities that help children focus on the letters of the alphabet:

Acting Out the ABC Song

When it is time to line up, the teacher randomly passes out one alphabet card to each student. Then the class begins *slowly* singing the ABC song. As the class sings each letter, the child holding that letter lines up. This activity helps students make connections between the alphabet song and the printed letters. Also, by singing slowly, you help the students understand that LMNOP are separate letters.

Alphabet Action Cards

In her book *Phonics They Use* (2000), Patricia Cunningham suggests associating each consonant of the alphabet with an action. To make alphabet action cards the teacher writes a consonant on one side of a card and draws or takes a picture of a student doing an action that begins with that letter for the other side. Once the cards are made, the teacher shows the students the action that matches each consonant. Have fun with it—go outside, use rhythm instruments! Once students know the actions for a few consonants, the class can do the following activities:

1. Have students stand up. Show them a letter; they should do the appropriate action until you put the letter away. Continue by showing them a new letter.

2. Pass out letters and play action charades. Have each student do an action while the class tells what letter matches that action.

3. Play "Follow the Leader." The leader picks a card and does that action; the rest of the class follows.

Possible actions include: bounce, catch, dance, fall, gallop, hop, jump, kick, laugh, march, nod, paint, run, sit, talk, vacuum, walk, yawn, zip.

Making Class Alphabet Books

Students can make alphabet books about almost any topic being studied in the classroom. For example, during Mr. Clyde's animal unit he gave each child a page with a large letter of the alphabet printed on it. Their task was to draw as many animals as they could find that start with that letter. After the pages were complete, he stapled the book together and added a colorful cover to create a "best-seller" for the classroom library. Other alphabet books created in primary classrooms are *An Alphabet of Foods We Like, The ABCs of Outer Space, The Insect Alphabet Book,* and *Things We See at Bristol Elementary School from A to Z.*

Create a Word Study Center

In their book *Word Matters: Teaching Phonics and Spelling in a Reading/Writing Classroom* (1998), Gay Su Pinnell and Irene Fountas suggest creating a word study center. To arrange the center for the study of alphabet letters in a primary classroom:

1. Collect or make various shapes, sizes, and colors of letters (magnetic, cardboard, plastic, etc.).

2. Put the letters in twenty-six boxes (all a's together, all b's together).

3. Model for students different ways to sort the letters.

4. Provide time for the children to use the center. Students use the letters to sort in a variety of ways: letters in their names and letters not in their names, consonants and vowels, letters with straight lines and letters with curved lines.

As young children sing, chant, and actively listen to rhyming text, they begin to attend to the words, syllables, and sounds of our language. Next, with the support of purposeful activities, they fine-tune their ability to hear and manipulate the smallest units of speech. In addition, youngsters must grasp the critical understanding that there is a systematic relationship between these sounds and the letters of our alphabet. The understandings gained through the activities described above serve as a backdrop for the phonics lessons that follow.

PHONICS IN ACTION

When we visited Bristol Elementary School, we found that effective phonics lessons engage students in activities that teach the phonics skills needed to be successful readers and writers. Circling short "a" words on a worksheet does not transfer to reading and spelling. "What seems to work in phonics instruction is direct teacher instruction, not practice on worksheets" (Stahl et al., 1998, p. 342). Through the use of carefully planned lessons, children discover the importance of learning phonics. This direct connection between phonics, reading, and writing is emphasized if the content of their phonics lessons is embedded in and interwoven throughout all literacy events. This does not negate the need for direct instruction in phonics. Direct instruction is needed, but these lessons must be carefully planned in order for the young child to learn. Tim Rasinski and Nancy Padak (2001) remind us that "not any kind of direct instruction and coaching will do however. Word study should be engaging and challenging for all students; it should be enjoyable and nurture a love of the written word among students, and it should be accomplished as authentically as possible so that students can see the application and importance of what they are learning" (p. xv).

The following section showcases three phonics lessons to give a flavor of the type of phonics instruction being advocated by those educators in the field (Bear et al., 2000; Cunningham, 2000; Pinnell & Fountas, 1998; Rasinski & Padak, 2001; Stahl, et al., 1998; Strickland, 1998) who have each researched, written about, and studied phonics instruction for many years. As a precursor to these phonics lessons, it is important to remember that young learners benefit from a strong foundation of phonological and phonemic awareness activities like those described earlier in this chapter. Preschool and primary grade children need to be engaged in activities that introduce and strengthen the alphabetic principle, increase their phonological awareness, and focus on the phonemic awareness skills of segmenting and blending words. Please keep in mind as you read these lessons that they are simply examples of a lesson that would be appropriate for most students at that grade level. Of course, we know that in a classroom all students will be at various levels; therefore, you could use these lessons at any grade level depending on the needs and abilities of your students.

A Kindergarten Phonics Lesson: Focusing on Beginning Sounds

To help kindergartners begin to make connections between letters and sounds Donald Bear and his colleagues (2000) suggest using beginning sound picture sorts. The following helpful hints will assist teachers when they are preparing this activity for their young learners:

1. Choose contrasting sounds from a familiar text like a big book, poem, chant, or rhyme that the class explored during shared reading.
2. Prepare picture cards that represent each of the letters–sounds.
3. Adjust the difficulty of the sort to meet the needs of your students. Begin with two very distinct letters such as "m" and "s," then add one or two more for a total of four categories.
4. Choose a key picture/word for each letter of the alphabet and use it consistently. For this example, use mouse for "m" and sun for "s."
5. Use the key picture/word and the letter as headers for the top of the columns on the sort.
6. Begin with a teacher-directed sort. Discuss the sound, the letter name, and the picture. Model picking up a picture from the pile and placing it under the correct key word. Say, "I put *mmmmm*moon under *mmmmm*mouse because they both start with the /m/ sound."
7. Show children how to check their sorts by naming the pictures in the columns and asking if any are in the wrong column. If they do not notice a picture is

in the wrong column, help them by saying, "There is a picture in this column that needs to be changed. Can you find it?"

8. Provide students with many opportunities to practice sorting.

9. Plan follow-up activities that encourage students to recognize key pictures and letters, recall the letters that they have studied, judge whether other words fit in the categories, and apply their letter knowledge to create something new.

Recall the recommendations (Stahl et al., 1998) shared earlier in the chapter. Good phonics instruction should provide a thorough grounding in the letters and help students develop the alphabetic principle. The word sorting activity does both, and it is a hands-on, manipulative activity that teachers can modify in many ways. After teaching the whole group the sorting activity, the letters and pictures can be placed in the word study center for further exploration. To extend this activity, teachers can photocopy a set of pictures and letters to send home with their students.

A First Grade Phonics Lesson: Finding Words That Rhyme

"Rounding Up the Rhymes" (Cunningham, 2000) is an activity that helps to focus students' attention on the rhyming patterns of words using the authentic context of a book. To prepare this enjoyable rhyming lesson refer to the basal selection in Appendix A entitled *Down by the Bay*:

1. Select a book that has simple rhymes. It should be an "old favorite" book that your students have heard a number of times. You want the book to have rhyming words with different spelling patterns and rhyming words with the same spelling pattern.

2. Read the book. Select a number of pages that have a lot of rhymes with the same spelling patterns.

3. Round up the rhymes: As the children tell you the rhyming words that they hear on each page, write each word on a separate index card.

4. Discard words that do not have the same spelling pattern. Show children each set of words. Explain that you are only going to keep the words that rhyme and have the same spelling pattern (rime/phonogram) at the end. For example, in *Down by the Bay*, you would keep goose/moose, goat/boat, and pig/wig but throw out bear/hair and fly/tie.

5. Transfer (the most important step).
   Reading transfer: Write a word that has the same spelling pattern as the rounded-up rhymes. Without saying the word see if a student can put it under the rhyming word that will help them decode/read the word. Continue with a few more words in this fashion.
   Spelling transfer: Say a word that students might need when they are writing a piece; have students decide which word in the pocket chart would help them spell that word.

"Rounding Up the Rhymes" is an activity that you can do many times throughout the year. It is also important to extend the transfer portion of the lesson into other parts of your daily routine. For example, when you are doing a shared writing lesson and you come to a word that has a common spelling pattern, say, "I'm not sure how to spell cat, but I remember how to spell rat. So if rat is r-a-t, then cat must be c-a-t." The same holds true for shared reading lessons. While reading, point out words in the text that have common spelling patterns.

A Second Grade Phonics Lesson: Looking at Short Vowel Patterns

A second grade teacher has the important task to guarantee that all of her students understand how the alphabet principle works, have phonemic awareness, and know basic letter–sound correspondences. A means to this end is spelling instruction that begins with short, regularly spelled words and gradually extends to more complex spelling patterns (Snow et al., 1998). In early second grade children who are at the within word spelling stage (see Chapters 2 and 6 for a review of spelling stages) benefit from the following activity:

Teaching Feature:
Segmenting Syllables

Begin the lesson using a teaching strategy called "Using Words You Know" (Cunningham, 2000).

1. Pick three or four words with common spelling patterns that your students know how to read and spell.
2. Write the words on the top of a piece of chart paper with a column underneath each one and request that the students do the same on a small piece of paper at their desks. To increase students' interest in the activity, use the singular version of baseball team names such as Cub, Met, Twin, and Red. Simple basketball team names also work: Bull, Laker, Pacer, and Blazer.
3. Show, don't read, the students a word that rhymes and has the same spelling pattern as one of the words heading their papers. Students write the word on their paper in the appropriate column. Once children have written the word, ask them to articulate the strategy they used. "If c-u-b spells cub, then rub is probably spelled r-u-b."
4. The following day, extend this lesson by printing all the words from the chart on a piece of paper and making a copy for each child. The children's job is to cut apart the words and sort them according to spelling pattern. (See Figure 7.7 for a partial and finished chart and a word sorting sheet.)

Reflect for a moment about the three phonics lessons we described. Do the preceding lessons meet the criteria of exemplary phonics instruction proposed earlier in the chapter by Steven Stahl and his colleagues (1998)? Will students who experience these lessons understand that phonics is a tool that is used by readers and writers?

PHONICS TERMINOLOGY

The phonics terminology that appears in Figure 7.8 is a compilation from various sources including *Beginning to Read* (Adams, 1990); *Words Their Way* (Bear et al., 2000); *Phonics They Use* (Cunningham, 2000); *Word Matters* (Pinnell & Fountas,

Figure 7.7

Samples from second grade phonics lesson

Cub	Met	Twin	Laker

Cub	Met	Twin	Laker
rub	get	fin	baker
dub	wet	tin	shaker
	net	shin	maker
	set	spin	

1998); and *Teaching Phonics Today* (Strickland, 1998). Teachers will encounter these terms in many different instructional materials. Knowing these definitions will assist teachers when communicating about their phonics teaching with colleagues, administrators, and parents. Some teachers like to introduce these terms to their students to provide a common language for phonics lessons.

PHONICS GENERALIZATIONS

In a classic study, Theodore Clymer (1963) analyzed phonics generalizations to attempt to find out which generalizations were being taught in the primary grades and "to what extent are these generalizations useful in having a 'reasonable' degree of application to words commonly met in primary grade material" (Clymer, 1996, p. 183). He examined forty-five generalizations like "When two vowels go walking the first one does the talking" and found that only eighteen of the forty-five were useful according to the criteria he established, with the "two vowels go walking" rule only providing a correct pronunciation 50 percent of the time. The message to teachers is that many generalizations taught are of limited value and it is important that we point out the exceptions to the ones we teach. "Teachers should also avoid teaching these generalizations as rules to be memorized; rather, they should be taught as examples of language patterns that may be put to strategic use for reading and spelling" (Strickland, 1998, p. 40). The list in Figure 7.9 includes the eighteen most useful phonics generalizations.

Figure 7.8
Phonics terminology

Consonants—All the letters, except for the vowels.

Consonant blends—Two- or three-letter sequences that are blended together. Although the letter–sounds are blended together quickly, each one is pronounced. There are l-blends (bl, cl, fl, gl, pl, sl), r-blends (br, cr, dr, fr, gr, pr, tr), and s-blends (sc, scr, sk, sp, st, squ, sw).

Consonant digraphs—(th, wh, sh, ch). When two consonant letters represent one sound that is different from either sound alone.

Long vowels—Vowels that say their names and can be spelled various ways. For example, the long "a" can be spelled ay, ai, or a_e.

R-controlled vowels—R-controlled vowels have a sound that is neither short nor long (ar as in car, er as in fern, ir as in bird, or as in cork, and ur as in hurt).

Schwa—The schwa sound like "Uhh" in unaccented syllables (alone, harmony, extra, celebrate, vacation).

Short vowels—The short vowels are produced when the vocal cords are more relaxed. Short vowels make the following sounds: a = apple, i = itchy, e = elephant, o = octopus, u = umbrella.

Vowels—A speech sound produced by the easy passage of air through a relatively open vocal tract. Vowels form the most central sound of a syllable. Every vowel has two sounds, commonly referred to as "short" and "long."

Vowel diphthongs—A combination of two vowels recording a sound unlike that of either vowel. The two vowel sounds glide together. Technically, it is a sound that when made requires a change in mouth position. Some examples include io in boil and ou in shout (au in auto and oo in look are *not* diphthongs).

WORD STUDY

In their book *Word Matters: Teaching Phonics and Spelling in the Reading/Writing Classroom,* Gay Su Pinnell and Irene C. Fountas (1998) define word study as "an instructional process that involves the learner in an investigation of words. The result is 'word solving' in reading and writing" (p. 31). Word solving is "not just word learning. Its power lies in the discovery of the principles underlying the construction of words that make up written language" (p. 23).

Phonograms or Word Families

"Word families offer an easy and appealing way to introduce the issue of vowels. Students are supported in their first efforts to analyze the vowel because the vowel and the ending letters are presented as a chunk or pattern" (Bear et al., 2000, p. 154). These chunks or patterns are also known as **rimes,** and the letter(s) preceding the rime is known as the **onset.** When teaching onsets and rimes, it is important for the young student to begin "to understand that the rime or vowel chunk is a reliable and generative unit for reading and spelling words" (Johnston, 1999, p. 67). The 38 phonograms found in the list in Figure 7.10 can make over 654 different one-syllable

Figure 7.9

Phonics generalizations

	Accuracy in English
1. The r gives the preceding vowel a sound that is neither long nor short.	78%
2. Words having double e usually have a long e sound.	98%
3. In ay the y is silent and gives a its long sound.	98%
4. When y is the final letter in a word, it usually has a vowel sound.	84%
5. When c and h are next to each other, they make only one sound.	100%
6. Ch is usually pronounced as it is in kitchen, catch, and chair, not like sh.	95%
7. When c is followed by e or i, the sound of s is likely to be heard.	96%
8. When the letter c is followed by o or a, the sound of k is likely to be heard.	100%
9. When ght is seen in a word, gh is silent.	100%
10. When two of the same consonants are side by side, only one is heard.	99%
11. When a word ends in ck, it has the same last sound as in *look*.	100%
12. In most two-syllable words, the first syllable is accented.	85%
13. If a, in, re, ex, de, or be is the first syllable in a word, it is usually unaccented.	87%
14. In most two-syllable words that end in a consonant followed by y, the first syllable is accented and the last is unaccented.	96%
15. If the last syllable of a word ends in le, the consonant preceding the le usually begins the last syllable.	97%
16. When the first vowel element in a word is followed by th, ch, or sh, these symbols are not broken when the words are divided into syllables and may go with either the first or second syllable.	100%
17. When there is one e in a word that ends with a consonant, the e usually has a short sound.	76%
18. When the last syllable is the sound r, it is unaccented.	95%

Students refer to this phonogram chart when they are reading and writing.

Figure 7.10

List of most common phonograms

Most Common Phonograms in Rank Order Based on Frequency
(Number of Uses in Monosyllabic Words)*

Frequency	Rime	Example Words
26	-ay	jay say pay day play
26	-ill	hill Bill will fill spill
22	-ip	ship dip tip skip trip
19	-at	cat fat bat rat sat
19	-am	ham jam dam ram Sam
19	-ag	bag rag tag wag sag
19	-ack	back sack Jack black track
19	-ank	bank sank tank blank drank
19	-ick	sick Dick pick quick chick
18	-ell	bell sell fell tell yell
18	-ot	pot not hot dot got
18	-ing	ring sing king wing thing
18	-ap	cap map tap clap trap
18	-unk	sunk junk bunk flunk skunk
17	-ail	pail jail nail sail tail
17	-ain	rain pain main chain plain
17	-eed	feed seed weed need freed
17	-y	my by dry try fly
17	-out	pout trout scout shout spout
17	-ug	rug bug hug dug tug
16	-op	mop cop pop top hop
16	-in	pin tin win chin thin
16	-an	pan man ran tan Dan
16	-est	best nest pest rest test
16	-ink	pink sink rink link drink
16	-ow	low slow grow show snow
16	-ew	new few chew grew blew
16	-ore	more sore tore store score
15	-ed	bed red fed led Ted
15	-ab	cab dab jab lab crab
15	-ob	cob job rob Bob knob
15	-ock	sock rock lock dock block
15	-ake	cake lake make take brake
15	-ine	line nine pine fire shine
14	-ight	knight light right night fight
14	-im	swim him Kim rim brim
14	-uck	duck luck suck truck buck
14	-um	gum bum hum drum plum

*For a complete list of all example words see Fry (1998).

Source: Figure from Fry, Edward B. (1998, April). Teaching reading: The most common phonograms. *The Reading Teacher,* 51(7), 620–622. Used by permission.

words (Fry, 1998). It is important to note that in the Spanish language, syllables do not divide into onsets and rimes. Instead, syllables are the psychological unit of spoken Spanish words. Instruction in Spanish sound–letter correspondences has traditionally been syllabic: teachers who teach Spanish-speaking children to read in Spanish teach groups of syllables that differ by one vowel (such as sa, se, si, so, su) and/or teach children to separate printed words into syllables (for example, casa = ca + sa) and to recombine syllables to make new words (for example, ca + ma = cama; sa + po = sapo) (Moustafa & Maldonado-Colon, 1999). As we have shared in the chapter, there are a variety of methods to teach word families. Another procedure for word building is highlighted in the Teaching Strategy for the Classroom box.

Teaching Strategy for the Classroom

AN ACTIVITY FOR WORD BUILDING

In his article *Word Building: A Strategic Approach to the Teaching of Phonics,* Thomas Gunning (1995) describes a five-step approach to teaching onsets and rimes using word families: for example, teaching the —ay pattern.

STEP 1: BUILD WORDS BY ADDING THE ONSET

Write the phonogram —ay on the chalkboard or large piece of chart paper. Ask your students what letter is needed to make the word bay. As you add the "b," clearly and slowly say b-ay, bay and have your students repeat the word. Then write —ay again and ask what letter is needed to make the word hay. The lesson continues this way until you have a number of words on the board. Ask students to read all the words and identify what is the same about the words, focusing on the two sounds in the rime.

STEP 2: BUILD WORDS BY ADDING THE RIME

Do the same lesson as describe in Step 1 but begin with the onset and have students tell you the rime. For example, write the letter "b" on the board and have students tell you what they need to add to the "b" to make the word bay.

STEP 3: CHOOSE A MODEL WORD FOR THE PATTERN

After teaching the pattern choose a model word that can be displayed in the classroom to help students when they encounter difficult —ay words. It is helpful if the model word is illustrated.

STEP 4: GUIDED PRACTICE

Give students varied opportunities to practice using the pattern. Some might include shared reading of big books with the —ay pattern, interactive writing of stories with a lot of —ay words, and forming —ay words using individual letter cards or blocks.

STEP 5: APPLICATION

Provide opportunities for students to read whole stories and poems that incorporate the pattern.

A primary word wall is ongoing throughout the school year as words are added continually.

Word Sorting

There are two basic types of sorts: picture sorts and word sorts. The kindergarten lesson described earlier was an example of a picture sort. "The basic premise of all sorting tasks in a word study approach is to compare and contrast word elements, separating or categorizing the examples that go together from those that don't" (Bear et al., 2000, p. 60). Teachers vary the type of sorts they want their children to do based on the instructional purpose. Teachers direct the sorts by deciding on the categories and modeling the procedure for the students, or teachers can allow students to sort words and create their own categories. See Figure 7.11 for different ways to sort words.

High-Frequency Words

One effective way to teach students high-frequency words is by posting the most common words on a bulletin board or other large space in the classroom called the word wall and practicing the words on a regular basis in a variety of ways.

The Word Wall in Kindergarten

Janiel Wagstaff (1997/1998) suggests using the word wall in kindergarten as part of the beginning literacy lessons to build phonemic awareness, teach beginning sounds, and assist beginning readers and writers. The way she does this is by introducing a familiar nursery rhyme to her students and then reading and chanting the rhyme a

Figure 7.11

Different ways to sort words

Categories related to sound or letter pattern	Categories related to structure or meaning
Words that begin/end with particular consonants (*mom, mix, or, path, with*)	Words that have prefixes (*redo, unfasten*)
Words that start/end with consonant clusters (*spring, clap, soft*)	Words with endings (*smartest, looking, carried*)
Words with double consonants (*zipper, mitten*)	Words with the same base (*write, reunite, rewriting*)
Words with two consonants that make one sound (*shoe, chimney*)	Words that name people (*brother, friend*)
Words with a vowel sound as in *apple* (*cat, map*)	Words that name places (*home, yard*)
Words with a vowel sound as in *egg* (*pet, then*)	Words that are short or long (*to, remainder*)
Words with a vowel sound as in *igloo* (*sit, lip*)	Words in a category (*carrot, orange*)
Words with a vowel sound as in *octopus* (*hot, top*)	Words that describe (*lovely, green*)
Words with a vowel sound as in *umbrella* (*under, up*)	Words that mean the same (*fight, argument*)
Words with a vowel sound as in *cake* (*late, cape*)	Words that mean the opposite (*hot, cold*)
Words with a vowel sound as in *feet* (*meat, keep*)	Words that can be pronounced two different ways (*live, live*)
Words with a vowel sound as in *kite* (*sign, fight*)	Words that sound the same but are spelled different ways (*to, two*)
Words with a vowel sound as in *goat* (*rope, soap*)	Words that are contractions (*haven't, wasn't*)
Words with a vowel sound as in *mule* (*cute, use*)	Words that are compounds (*someday, cannot*)
Words beginning with a vowel (*under, over*)	Words that have the same part (*fat, fatter, fattest*)
Words ending with a vowel (*tuba, solo*)	Word forms that are singular or plural (*calf, calves*)
Words with the same vowel sound (*play, mail, take*)	
Words with vowel combinations (*cream, boat, soil*)	
Words with a vowel and *r* (*corn, first*)	
Words that rhyme (*mail, sail*)	
Words with a letter that makes a particular sound (the *s* sound in *see* and *bus*, or *was* and *treasure*)	
Words with silent letters (*make, seat*)	
Words that can be paired with another word that sounds the same but means something different (*to, two; sail, sale*)	
Words with one, two, or three syllables (*dog, rab-bit, to-ma-to*)	
Words with an open syllable (*mo-tel, to-ken*)	
Words with a closed syllable (*rob-in, cab-in*)	

Source: Reprinted by permission from *Word Matters: Teaching Phonics and Spelling in the Reading/Writing Classroom* by Irene Fountas and Gay Su Pinnell. Copyright ©1998 by Irene Fountas and Gay Su Pinnell. Published by Heinemann, a division of Reed Elsevier, Inc., Portsmouth, NH.

number of times. Next, she chooses two or three words from the rhyme to add to the word wall. The words are mainly used for identification of beginning sounds. To reinforce the students' knowledge of letters and sounds, Wagstaff suggests using word

A first grade student adds words to his portable word wall.

play activities and daily reading and writing activities. One example of a word play activity is focusing on the beginning sound of one of the words. If the word is hill, the teacher might say, "The word hill begins with an h; listen carefully as I say other words. Give me a 'thumbs up' if it begins with h and 'thumbs down' if it doesn't."

The Word Wall in the Primary Grades

The following are some commonly asked questions and the accompanying answers about the word wall:

Why do we want children to quickly recognize and automatically spell **high-frequency words?**

1. To free their attention to decipher and spell less-frequent words and to focus on the meaning of the text they are reading.
2. Because most high-frequency words are not pronounced or spelled in predictable ways. If children try to use their temporary spelling for these words, they will spell them wrong (Cunningham, 2000).

What are the three principles for teaching high-frequency words?

1. Help students to associate meaning with words.
2. Practice words using a variety of learning modes.
3. If a high-frequency word is easily confused with another word—(of, for, from); (was, saw); (no, on); or (here, there)—teach one first. As soon as that one is learned, teach another and practice both. Then, teach a third and practice all three (Cunningham, 2000).

Figure 7.12

Criteria for choosing word wall words

First Grade

High-frequency words from reading selections
Examples for all beginning sounds
Words with particular spelling patterns

Second Grade

Observations of words children misspell in the writing
Irregularly spelled high-frequency words
Words that represent digraphs and common blends
Less common sounds of c and g
Common vowel patterns
Commonly written contractions (can't, didn't, don't, it's, that's, they're, won't)
Homophones (to, two, too; there, their, they're)
Example words with s, ed, and ing

Third Grade

Most frequently misspelled words (because, they, enough, laugh)
The most commonly confused homophones (to/too/two, write/right, they're/there/their)
The most common contractions
The most common compound words (everybody, everything, sometimes, into, something)
A word beginning with each letter
Common endings and suffixes with common spelling changes
Common prefixes (un, re, dis, im, in)

Source: Adapted from Cunningham, P. M., Hall, D. P., & Sigmon, C. M. (1999). *The teacher's guide to the four blocks*. Greensboro, NC: Carson-Dellosa.

What is a word wall?

> The word wall is a bulletin board or large chart in the classroom with the letters of the alphabet posted where teachers display and *practice* (this is the key) high-frequency words that they expect their students to read and spell automatically. A word wall is *not* just a bulletin board or a place to post words: teachers must work on the words regularly with their students so that they learn, use, and practice them. In addition, powerful instruction related to the word wall transpires during discussions students initiate during reading and writing activities (Brabham & Villaume, 2001). A list of different activities for practicing words is displayed in the Teaching Strategy for the Classroom box on page 314.

How do you select the words?

> Teachers must analyze their students' reading and writing to find words with which they are frequently having difficulty. Teachers can also select words from a sight word list. See Figure 7.12 for criteria for choosing words.

Teaching Strategy for the Classroom

ACTIVITIES FOR PRACTICING WORD WALL WORDS

1. Introduce and write the five new word wall words for the week: Introduce only the five new words. The goal is for you to use each new word in a sentence that is related to something that the children do or know. If it is an abstract word, such as *for, of, from*, use a picture and sentence to help children associate the meaning. Example: This is a can *of* Coke. This is a gift *from* Grandma. These picture/sentence posters can be posted in the room as a reminder to students. After you use the word in a sentence, call on a few students to do the same before you post the word on the chalkboard.

2. Clap, Chant, and Write:
   - Snap and clap the first word three times (snap each letter in each word and end with a final clap when you say the entire word). After the three snaps and claps, write the word on the board modeling the correct handwriting formation of the word.
   - Continue this process by snapping and clapping each word and students writing it on a half sheet of paper.
   - When all words are written, rewrite the words and ask students to check their spelling and handwriting. You may want to have them draw around the shapes of the words.

3. Other rhythmic ways to practice words:
   Pencil Tap: Students need a pencil at their desk and the five new words on the board. Teacher taps the beginning of the word—students tap the end. Sample: *dear* Teacher: d-e- Students: a-r.
   The Ketchup Bottle: Have the students pretend they are shaking a bottle of ketchup each time they say a letter in the word. When they are finished spelling the word, they can eat it!
   Raise the Roof: Students hold their hands above their heads and push them toward the ceiling each time they say a letter in the word.
   Actions: This follows that same procedure as Clap, Chant, and Write, but instead of clapping, students do an action for each letter. Some possible actions include jumping jacks, marching, touching shoulders, waist, knees, and toes, etc. Once students have acted out the word, they write and check it.
   Hand Clapping with a Partner: Student face a partner and clap hands together each time they say a letter in the word.
   The Spelling Cheerleader: Students do actions for each letter as they say each letter. For a top line letter (i.e., l, t, h) they raise both arms for the letter; for a mid-line letter (i.e., m, w, x) they put their arms out to the sides; for a descender line letter (i.e., g, j, y) they bring both arms down to their sides.

4. Read My Mind:
   Using the words already posted on the word wall play "Read My Mind." Choose a word on the word wall. Give students clues to help them locate the word. For this activity the clues are cumulative. After giving a clue, especially in the beginning, the teacher must model and think aloud so that all students understand the procedure. After each clue, students have to write the word that they think matches the clue.
   Rules: They must write one word for each clue. No erasing!

Sample clues:

a. It is a word on the word wall.

b. It is a four-letter word.

c. It starts with a _____.

d. It rhymes with _____.

Source: Adapted from Cunningham, P. M. (2000). *Phonics they use: Words for reading and writing* (3rd ed.). New York: Longman.

How many words do you work on at a time?

Patricia Cunningham (2000) suggests that in first grade you should work on five words every week from the beginning of the year until April 15. Then review and practice until the end of the year. Some teachers choose to work on five words every two weeks to allow for other activities.

Portfolio Activity:
Word Wall

SPELLING INSTRUCTION

"Spelling knowledge is the engine that drives efficient reading as well as writing" (Templeton & Morris, 1999, p. 103). Current instructional emphasis in spelling is on the discovery by students of the patterns or chunks of letters that can be found in sounds, structures, and meanings of words. For kindergarten through first grade, the emphasis is largely on the sounds. As students progress through the grades, structures and meanings of words gain importance and are emphasized. For instance, prefixes and suffixes are introduced in second grade, such as doubling the final consonant when adding "ing" to "run." Upper elementary students learn derivations of words such as "medicine" and discover it has the following derivations: medical, medic, medicate, medicinal, medication, and medicare.

All of the activities and strategies discussed in this chapter are part of a comprehensive spelling curriculum. Students learn to look for patterns in words when they sort words, they learn how to manipulate letters and sounds when they are making words, and they learn and review high-frequency words every time they practice the word wall. These activities help students to build a repertoire of spelling strategies.

Learning Spelling Strategies

For beginning spellers the strategies they use are very basic (Strickland, 1998):

1. Knowledge of letters and sounds. Which letter goes with the sound I hear?
2. Visual memory. I can close my eyes and remember how that word looks.
3. Knowledge of words and word parts. I remember that cat is spelled c-a-t so bat would be spelled b-a-t.

As spellers mature, they begin to use more sophisticated strategies (Tompkins, 2001):

1. Proofread their writing to find and edit spelling errors.
2. Use the references in the room (word wall, charts) to spell words.
3. Break the word into syllables and spell the syllables.

4. Add affixes to root words.

5. Use a dictionary or other reference tool.

Weekly Spelling Tests

Many schools across the country still use a spelling textbook series that mandates that teachers administer weekly spelling tests. The words for these spelling tests are often unrelated to what the children are reading and writing. Typically there is a pretest of the words on Monday. The following day the students review words they missed by spelling them orally to themselves, checking for accuracy, and then writing the words on paper or on a dry erase board and again checking for accuracy (Farris, 2001). As much as possible, teachers should incorporate the activities and spelling strategies discussed in this chapter into their weekly spelling routine.

ENHANCING LEARNING WITH TECHNOLOGY

There are a number of software programs and websites available to help students understand how words work. As the world of instructional technology grows, you will find some wonderful products that help students as well as others that do not meet your students' needs. You need to be an educated consumer of the software products and websites you use in your classroom. There are many software programs on the market today that have been carefully designed by educators and will enrich your existing phonics and word study curriculum. When deciding whether to use a software package with your students, consider the following advantages that Shelley Wepner and Lucinda Ray (2000) share: Well-designed software has unique features that aid children's skill development:

1. Immediacy and predictability of visual and auditory cues.

2. Focused individual feedback.

3. Opportunity for multiple repetitions.

4. Introduction of skills in a predictable sequence.

5. Development of concepts through visual, auditory, and kinesthetic modalities. (p. 170)

Summary

Knowledgeable teachers make informed decisions about the instructional methods they will use to teach phonics to their students. Phonics is a valuable tool in a student's arsenal of reading and writing strategies. A young child's phonemic awareness is cultivated by engaging in activities that strengthen the alphabetic principle, phonological awareness, and specific activities to teach phonemic awareness. Learners benefit from ample opportunities to study and practice phonics skills and apply the skills in the context of real literacy experiences. Word study enhances phonics and spelling instruction by helping students understand how words work.

Chapter Review

Go to the Online Learning Center at **www.mhhe.com/farrisreading** to take chapter quizzes, practice with key terms, and review important content.

Main Points

- Phonics is a tool for readers and writers.

- Phonics is an important component of a balanced literacy program.

- Analytic and synthetic phonics programs were popular in the 1960s and 1970s.

- One approach used today is a spelling-based approach where students are involved in word study activities.

- The analogy-based approach teaches students to look for spelling patterns and apply those patterns to figuring out unknown words.

- In embedded phonics programs, the instruction occurs in the context of real reading and writing.

- Teachers help develop children's phonological awareness by exposing them to rhyming activities, poetry, chants, and songs.

- Phonemic awareness is the ability to hear and manipulate the smallest unit of sound.

- Instruction in the alphabetic principle should take place so that students understand the systematic relationship between letters and sounds.

- Phonics has a language of its own.

- There are eighteen phonics generalizations that are useful to teach, not as rules but as examples of language patterns.

- Word study boosts children's understanding of the underlying structures of words.

- Sorting words offers students the opportunity to compare and contrast the characteristics of words.

- Teachers use the activities related to the word wall to help students read and spell high-frequency words.

- Students should build a bank of spelling strategies.

- There are a number of strategies teachers can employ to assist diverse learners with understanding how words work.

Key Terms

alphabetic principle	299	phoneme	291
analogy-based phonics	287	phonemic awareness	291
analytic phonics	286	phonics	285
decodable texts	286	phonogram	288
embedded phonics	288	phonological awareness	291
high-frequency words	312	rime	306
making words	287	synthetic phonics	286
onset	306	word study	287

Reflecting and Reviewing

1. At the beginning of the chapter you wrote down your thoughts about phonics instruction. Has your view of phonics instruction changed after reading this chapter?

317

2. Review Dorothy Strickland's guidelines for teaching and learning phonics. How will you use these guidelines to help direct your phonics instruction?

3. This chapter was packed with ideas for the classroom. Which of these ideas appeal to you? Which would you like to try out with students? Which will be a part of your teaching repertoire?

Children's Literature

For annotations of the books listed below, please see Appendix A.

Bayer, Jane. (1984). *A My name Is Alice.* New York: Dial Books.

Bender, Robert. (1996). *The A to Z Beastly Jamboree.* New York: Lodestar.

Cleary, Beverly. (1998). *The Hullabaloo ABC.* (T. Rand, Illus.). New York: Morrow Junior Books.

Falwell, Cathryn. (1998). *Word Wizard.* New York: Clarion Books.

Howland, Naomi. (1994). *ABCDrive!* New York: Clarion Books.

Jahn-Clough, Lisa. (1997). *ABC Yummy.* Boston: Houghton Mifflin.

Kalman, Maira. (2001). *What Pete Ate from A to Z.* New York: Putnam.

Lobel, Arnold. (1981). *On Market Street.* New York: Greenwillow.

Martin, Bill, Jr., & Archambault, John. (1989). *Chicka Chicka Boom Boom.* (L. Ehlert, Illus.). New York: Simon & Schuster.

Rotner, Shelley. (1996). *Action Alphabet.* New York: Atheneum.

Seuss, Dr. (1963). *Dr. Seuss' ABC.* New York: Random House.

Shannon, George. (1996). *Tomorrow's Alphabet.* (D. Crews, Illus.). New York: Greenwillow.

Stevens, Janet, & Stevens Crummel, Susan. (2001). *And the Dish Ran Away With the Spoon.* New York: Harcourt.

Walker, Sally M. (1998). *The 18 Penny Goose.* (E. Beier, Illus.). New York: Harper Collins.

Walton, Rick. (1998). *So Many Bunnies: A Bedtime ABC and Counting Book.* (P. Miglio, Illus.). New York: Lothrop, Lee & Shepard.

Classroom Teaching Resources

Adams, M. J., Foorman, B. R., Lundberg, I., & Beeler, T. (1998). *Phonemic awareness in young children.* Baltimore, MD: Paul H. Brookes Publishing Company.

Bear, D. R., Invernizzi, M., Templeton, S., & Johnson, F. (2000). *Words their way: Word study for phonics, vocabulary and spelling instruction* (2nd. ed.). Upper Saddle River, NJ: Merrill.

Cunningham, P. M. (2000). *Phonics they use: Words for reading and writing* (3rd ed.). New York: Longman.

Cunningham, P. M., & Hall, D. P. (1994). *Making words.* Parsippany, NJ: Good Apple, Inc.

————. (1997). *Month-by-month: Phonics for first grade.* Greensboro, NC: Carson-Dellosa Publishing, Inc. (Also available for kindergarten, second, third, and upper grades.)

Dahl, K. L., Scharer, P. L., Lawson, L. L., & Grogan, P. R. (2001). *Rethinking phonics: Making the best teaching decisions.* Portsmouth, NH: Heinemann.

Fitzpatrick, J. (1997). *Phonemic awareness: Playing with sounds to strengthen beginning reading skills.* Cypress, CA: Creative Teaching Press.

Hajdusiewicz, B. B. (1998). *Phonics through poetry: Teaching phonemic awareness using poetry.* Glenview, IL: Goodyear Books.

Jordano, K., & Callella-Jones, T. (1998). *Phonemic awareness songs and rhymes.* Cypress, CA: Creative Teaching Press. (Books available for fall, winter, and spring.)

Pinnell, G. S., & Fountas, I. C. (1998). *Word matters: Teaching phonics and spelling in the reading/writing classroom.* Portsmouth, NH: Heinemann.

Rasinski, T. V., & Padak, N. D. (2001). *From phonics to fluency: Effective teaching of decoding and reading fluency in the elementary school.* New York: Longman.

"*Like writing, reading is an act of composition. When we write, we compose thoughts on paper. When we read, we compose meaning in our minds. Thoughtful, active readers use the text to stimulate their own thinking and to engage with the mind of the writer.*"

Stephanie Harvey and Anne Goudvis, teachers, researchers, and teacher educators

CHAPTER **8**

Reading Comprehension

Key Ideas

- **Reading comprehension** is the process of understanding the message that the author is trying to convey. Very simply, it is making meaning from the text at hand.
- **Activating prior knowledge** is a cornerstone to building comprehension.
- Meaning-making varies somewhat from person to person because it is influenced by individual backgrounds unique to each reader. As a result, multiple interpretations of text must be honored.
- There are a number of strategies that research has proven to be effective in teaching children to comprehend narrative and/or expository text. Knowledge of these strategies is essential for a beginning teacher's reading program.
- In order to add a skill to their personal arsenal of reading strategies, students must see it modeled, and then need ample time to practice it within an appropriate context.
- While it is important to have a command of practical skills and strategies to aid in comprehension, it is time spent in reading itself that makes one a good reader.
- Students who have varying learning needs have practical options available to improve their reading comprehension abilities.
- High-quality technological resources including teacher-monitored Internet sites benefit learners of all abilities in refining their comprehension skills.

Questions to Ponder

- What do we mean when we talk about reading comprehension?
- What skills and strategies are effective in facilitating the growth of comprehension?

- Why are literature circles an important ingredient in a complete reading comprehension program?
- Which strategies can be adapted to meet the needs of diverse learners who face learning challenges?
- How can technology enrich the reading curriculum and strengthen comprehension?

Peering into the Classroom

Piquing and Sustaining Interest in Reading

"The part where Brian ate those turtle eggs," grimaced Ayden, "that was truly gross! I know I've never been as hungry as Brian was, but I just couldn't get those greasy, oily, raw eggs down!" The horrified look on her face underscored her reactions.

"The mosquitoes—that's what would get me," volunteered Tonio. "I mean, they were in his eyes and ears and mouth. You have to listen to this part where Paulsen talks about the 'thick, swarming hordes of mosquitoes that flocked to his body, made a living coat on his exposed skin, clogged his nostrils when he inhaled, poured into his mouth when he opened it to take a breath' (Paulsen, 1987, p. 36). Really, how could you stand that?"

The class has just completed the Newbery Honor book *Hatchet* (Paulsen, 1987), a perennial favorite in the upper elementary grades. Readers are reminiscing together over the experiences they have endured with Brian as they struggled to survive together in the Canadian wilderness. The class worked in literature circles as they read and discussed the book. For their first time experience with a novel, Miss Coleman picked a survival story, one certain to capture their interest and ensure lively, engaged small group discussions. The basal series contained an excerpt from the book, but she opted to use the whole book knowing that the excerpt would not be enough for her readers. It appeared that her class enthusiastically endorsed her decision.

Li Chang raised her hand. "You know what I liked? The way Gary Paulsen writes. He uses words that help you see the story. Sometimes his sentences are just one word or maybe two. Once a sentence was just 'Mistakes,' and another time it was 'Always hungry.' That really emphasized a point for me."

Brow furrowed, another student raises his hand. "I sort of have a problem with the book," critiques Garret. A thoughtful, introspective student, he now turns the attention of the class to what he considers a weakness in the story. "Think about all of the problems Brian faces, some of them so major I sure don't know what I would do in his place. But he always remembers things just at the right time. You know, he remembers something a teacher told him or he gets this idea because of something he saw once on television. I guess I didn't like that. Some solutions seemed too convenient. Maybe we saw how he was a good problem solver, but do you really think that would happen to you?" he queries.

Quiet reigns briefly while the class mulls over this criticism. Suddenly, three hands shoot up and a lively discussion ensues. The book was done, but the class was reluctant to let the story go. This talk time was essential to wrapping up the reading experience, so Miss Coleman was content to let everyone have his or her say. Finally, she directed their attention to a stack of new books designated for the reading corner, three of them extensions of Brian's experiences, and six other titles about other topics penned by this popular author. She expected that they would disappear quickly based upon the enthusiastic response of her class to *Hatchet*. She mused reflectively that, despite her misgivings, this first attempt at literature circles hadn't been so bad after all.

REFLECTION: IRA/NCTE NATIONAL STANDARDS IN THE CLASSROOM

Can you see the Standards at work in this classroom? Standard 3 suggests that students be able to apply a wide range of strategies to comprehend, interpret, evaluate, and appreciate texts, which is clearly supported in Miss Coleman's class. This group of students is engaged in thoughtful discussion, a comprehension **strategy** that enables them to better understand Brian's experiences and his attempts to survive. Garret was drawing on his prior experiences, which led him to question Brian's behavior. Out of that question grew further conversation and additional connections with the story.

Next, Standard 11 advocates participation in a literary community. Don't these young readers appear to be relishing life in their particular literary community? They seem to be comfortable enough with each other to share their ideas and discuss varying points of view in the process of making more sense of events in the story. Then, too, there is evidence that they are thinking like writers. Standard 5 encourages learners to develop the ability to use a variety of writing styles to communicate with their audiences. Li Chang was impressed with the way Paulsen used words to create vivid images. She liked his technique of using one- or two-word sentences to nail down a point. Writers are memorable teachers. It won't be surprising if Li Chang and several of her classmates emulate Paulsen's style in some of their future writing efforts. In Miss Coleman's classroom and others visited throughout this textbook, it is obvious that excellent teachers keep an eye to the Standards and judiciously integrate them into the classroom reading and writing curriculum.

INTRODUCTION

Web Link:

Reading Comprehension

Take a few moments to think about the upcoming topic of **reading comprehension**. What is actually meant by the words "reading comprehension"? Before continuing any further in this chapter, stop and jot down your personal definition of reading comprehension on a piece of scratch paper. Then, as you resume reading, compare your thoughts with those of others who have endeavored to define this involved process:

> Reading means getting meaning from print. Reading is not phonics, vocabulary, syllabication, or other "skills," as useful as these activities may be. The essence of reading is a transaction between the words of an author and the mind of a reader, during which meaning is constructed. This means that the main goal of reading instruction must be comprehension: above all, we want students to understand what is on a page. (Zemelman, Daniels, & Hyde, 1998, p. 30)

Consider the pondering of Diane Bradley, a superb, experienced elementary teacher.

> "Angela could read like the wind. As she glided through the description of the Zuckerman barn in *Charlotte's Web,* her voice manuevered through the difficult vocabulary and landed beautifully at the final punctuation. It was a joy to listen to this third grader. When asked about the text she had read, however, Angela could tell you nothing. She rarely understood anything she read and when she did come up with any connection to her reading, it was usually jumbled and disoriented. How could this be? Don't readers who use fluency and expression in their reading have good comprehension?"

STANDARDS for READING PROFESSIONALS

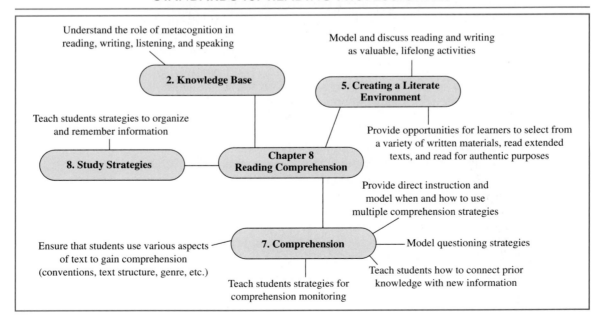

It is clear that reading, as exciting, informative, and magical as it can be, is a decidedly complex process. In *Becoming a Nation of Readers* (Anderson, Hiebert, Scott, & Wilkinson, 1985), the authors draw an analogy between reading and the intricately interconnected, carefully synchronized actions involved in the performance of a symphony orchestra.

Portfolio Activity:
Your Philosophy

> First, like the performance of a symphony, reading is a holistic act. In other words, while reading can be analyzed into subskills such as discriminating letters and identifying words, performing the subskills one at a time does not constitute reading. Reading can be said to take place only when the parts are put together in a smooth, integrated performance. Second, success in reading comes from practice over long periods of time, like skill in playing musical instruments. Indeed, it is a lifelong endeavor. Third, as with a musical score, there may be more than one interpretation of a text. The interpretation depends upon the background of the reader, the purpose for reading, and the context in which reading occurs. (p. 7)

Not mentioned in the analogy, but certainly well understood, are the hours upon hours of practice underlying a superb performance, in respect to the performance of the symphony and also to the performance of the accomplished reader.

Attention does need to be given to the pieces for they are essential to mastering this complex task. In order to teach students to have a command of the multifaceted reading process, there must be carefully orchestrated instruction in word-level skills, the development of background knowledge, and the acquisition of useful comprehension strategies (IRA/NCTE Standards, 1996; Burns, Roe, & Smith, 2002). This chapter will emphasize key strategies, adding further pieces to the comprehension puzzle by building upon the knowledge you gained in Chapter 7 on phonics and word analysis skills. Then, important vocabulary development strategies will be discussed in the following chapter for they are additional essential tools to facilitate comprehension. Although it may not seem to be so initially, these areas will eventually fit together neatly to complete a picture of all that is involved in reading comprehension. It is the fundamental goal of the reading process.

A CLOSER LOOK AT THE COMPREHENSION PROCESS

Stop again for a moment and reflect on yourself as a reader. When you pick up a new novel by a favorite author, you eagerly read the first few pages. If the story line is appealing, you simply slip into the story world. How do you do that? What "inside-your-head" processes kick into gear to enable you to become a part of a book that easily? If you are having difficulty singling out the processes that help you to understand and relate to the author's words, it isn't surprising. Your brain engages in the necessary comprehension steps so effortlessly that you are unaware of the complex interactions taking place.

No doubt what was actually happening is that you were following other able readers who use multiple sources of information while reading to deepen their comprehension of the printed word. They draw on background knowledge, relevant personal experiences, previous literacy experiences with similar books, visual information related to the formation of words, and an understanding of the way language works (Fountas & Pinnell, 2001). The next question to consider is this: How do teachers teach their students to draw from these important reservoirs of information so that they, too, understand an author's message with relative ease?

There are a number of excellent strategies to use to aid readers in their comprehension efforts. A major difficulty, however, is that comprehension strategies take place out of sight, inside one's head. As a result, they are not visible as readers apply them. Unfortunately, they are not visible to students when their teachers apply them, either. Therefore, it is imperative that each comprehension strategy be made visible to learners through activities like modeling, think alouds, and direct or explicit teaching (Allington, 2002; Pearson & Gallager, 1983; Robb, 2003). In that way students will have a clear understanding of how to apply new strategies themselves. Remember, too, that students will acquire comprehension abilities in a developmental process as they become more mature readers. As you read, notice how the strategies highlighted in this chapter and in other places throughout the textbook vary in complexity, some obviously more appropriate for learners in the primary grades while others can be best mastered by middle grade students.

Activating Prior Knowledge: A Cornerstone for Comprehension

Web Link:
Reading Comprehension Connection

One of the first strategies for a teacher to master is that of **activating prior knowledge** or background knowledge in their students. You will find it is an integral part of several teaching strategies in the upcoming pages, including the Directed Reading Activity (DRA), the Directed Reading Thinking Activity (DRTA), and K-W-L-Plus. According to Pearson and Fielding (1996), "Perhaps no other phenomenon has influenced instructional research in the last decade as pervasively as our increased understanding of the powerful role of background knowledge in reading comprehension" (p. 820). It bears scrutiny at this point before delving into other well-researched strategies important in building a reader's understanding of the text in front of him.

When a teacher begins a lesson, he must be aware that there are two components to prior knowledge. The first is general background knowledge made up of a child's personal experiences. Included in these experiences are the variety of books she has had read to her or has read on her own, an understanding of the world and people around her based upon family travel or watching television or movies, and diverse experiences both in school and out (Fountas & Pinnell, 2001). Essentially, a broad background can help readers better connect with the materials to be read.

The second component is knowledge of the topic or theme to be studied in the upcoming story. Research underscores that story comprehension can be influenced by a student's knowledge about and experiences with the materials to be studied. For example, when a reader knows something of the topic, he will generate expectations of what might happen in the upcoming story, a process that facilitates comprehension. If a reader has erroneous ideas about the topic, though, misunderstanding or flawed comprehension is the likely result (Alvermann, Smith, & Readence, 1985). In short, it is knowledge about important story ideas that most adequately facilitates comprehension (Beck, Omanson, & McKeown, 1982).

When beginning the day's reading or content area lesson, it is especially helpful if the teacher can draw out some of these experiences. There are a numerous options for doing so, but several include beginning with a probing question or two, giving a brief overview of the story, using a story map or anticipation guide, or even watching a video snippet to set the stage for reading. Allington (2002) cautions teachers not to spend an inordinate amount of time developing background knowledge. Rather than wasting precious reading time, keep the activity to three to five minutes in length. To better understand the pervasive use of activating prior knowledge, study a teacher's guide in a basal series and note the standard format of a basal reading lesson. So important is addressing the strategy that you will find it is one of the standard components in the majority of basal reading lessons. (See sample basal selections in Appendix B.)

The Role of Schema Theory

During the beginning stage of a reading lesson, the reader's schematic knowledge or background knowledge is being accessed through a teacher's actions. **Schema theory** helps to explain what occurs to facilitate comprehension when that knowledge is tapped. It describes how new learning is integrated into what a reader already knows. This theory delineates the way students learn, change, and then use information gleaned through personal experiences (Heilman, Blair, & Rupley, 2002). When they move through a text, readers are actively engaged as they match their existing knowledge with what they are reading. In the process they may change, elaborate upon, or discard existing **schema,** all the while broadening their knowledge base.

Transforming a story into a play helps build a child's comprehension.

Basically, schema theory tells us that knowledge is arranged in a complex information management system in the brain (Anderson & Pearson, 1984). A simple way to visualize this is to think of a carefully organized filing system. As new knowledge is gathered, it is filed in the appropriate folder containing other previously acquired information on that specific topic. Knowledge within the folder is continually rearranged to be most effective. Care must be taken to be certain that students have a solid understanding of the new information and how it relates to what they already know. Such precautions avoid the possibility of incorrectly filing it, which would result in the formation of misconceptions. As a result, making the appropriate connections is the thrust of attempts to activate prior knowledge and to connect information appropriately as the teacher and students team to broaden comprehension. Consider what this might mean if you have several students in your classrooms from different cultures. Each student brings a different background of life events or schema to the reading situation, leaving room for different interpretations of the printed word. Can you see how important it is to assess background knowledge and correct any misconceptions before beginning a story or nonfiction article?

Moving Beyond Prior Knowledge

It is reassuring to recognize that there are a number of effective methods or formats for teaching a quality reading lesson. Having the knowledge of a variety of ways to help all students become good readers gives the classroom teacher the ability to fine-tune her reading instruction based upon the needs of the particular children in her classroom. She can deftly alter those methods to add variety to the daily fare, to focus on appropriate strategies, and to match learner and materials (Fuhler, 2000). Part of the skill and the challenge in being a quality teacher, then, lies in the ability to make that appropriate match, selecting the strategy that will work the best with the materials to be covered and the specific students who must learn them.

Because the reading process is so complex, let's investigate a little further what good readers do as part of comprehending text. Pressley and Afflerbach (1995) analyzed over forty think-aloud studies of reading in which readers reported what they were doing or thinking as they read. What the researchers learned was that mature readers use a number of processes flexibly as they read, as is demonstrated in Figure 8.1. You are already aware of some of them. Watch for these processes, which are an integral part of several of the effective teaching strategies to be described throughout this chapter. The list in Figure 8.1 is filled with action, with behaviors that reflect readers who are diligently engaged in making sense of text and problem solving in the process. Good readers are busy people.

Obviously, like good readers, good teachers are busy people, too. In fact, the IRA/NCTE Standards or required state standards set their pace. The Standards suggest that teachers use their ingenuity and creativity in teaching all readers "to apply a wide range of strategies to comprehend, interpret, evaluate, and appreciate texts. They draw on their prior knowledge, their interactions with other readers and writers, their knowledge of word meanings and of other texts, their word identification strategies, and their understanding of textual features" (p. 3) as they master meaning

Figure 8.1

A sampling of processes used by good readers

- Being aware of the purpose for reading.
- Previewing the text to determine if it is relevant to the reader's goal.
- Reading selectively with a focus on relevant portions of the text.
- Making associations to ideas from the text based upon personal prior knowledge.
- Evaluating and revising initial hypotheses that were formed during previewing the text and continuing to revise them as needed throughout the reading.
- Figuring out the meaning of new words, particularly those that seem important to grasping the meaning of the text.
- Underlining, taking notes, rereading portions of text, and/or paraphrasing in order to remember important points in the text.
- Interpreting the text, such as having an imaginary conversation with the author.
- Evaluating the quality of the text.
- Reviewing the text after it has been completed.
- Thinking about how to use the information in the text in the future. (Pressley, 2000, pp. 545–550)

in text. There is a great deal for readers to learn and teachers to actively teach. There are excellent skills and strategies to be taught to impel their interactions along.

The teacher strives daily to provide reading instruction that is effective in building each student's comprehension abilities to the extent that her instruction motivates students to process texts as good readers should do (Cambourne, 2001). The following paragraphs describe practical, effective, key strategies based upon a foundation of sound research that will help all readers become adept readers. The strategies are arranged from those that are the most teacher-directed to several that invite more student control. They also involve readers in processing text at different levels, from the basic literal level to those involving higher level thinking skills.

PROMINENT TEACHING STRATEGIES

The following reading strategies have been selected because they are solidly grounded in effective classroom practice and are undergirded by extensive research. It is expected that they will be used flexibly in an effort to help children build their comprehension skills. Some are strongly teacher-directed and closely monitored. Others are carefully modeled by a knowledgeable teacher before the ownership is gradually transferred to the reader (Zemelman et al., 1998). This chapter will present the strategies moving from those that are teacher-directed first, and then to those that readers learn to apply on their own. The teaching of comprehension begins with a supportive technique, that of scaffolding learning.

Web Link:
Reading Comprehension
Instructional Strategies

Scaffolding

When beginning to teach a new reading lesson, the teacher models the expected reading behaviors, offering support and guidance to students so that they will be successful in interpreting the words and grasping the meaning of the story. That support by a knowledgeable adult is referred to as **scaffolding** (Bruner, 1986). It is a temporary teaching process that helps a learner solve a problem, complete a required task, or reach a goal that she might not be able to attain without assistance.

What might scaffolding actually look like? Visualize a young child sitting down to assemble a picture puzzle for the first time. A parent, older sibling, or teacher joins the child and offers assistance as one piece after another is tried, rotated, and rearranged until the puzzle is successfully completed. Throughout the process, suggestions are given to the child like how several colors match between the border of the puzzle and a few of the pieces, or it is pointed out how one unusually notched part fits snugly with a neighboring piece. The learner uses such scaffolded tips as she practices assembling and reassembling the puzzle, continually moving toward independence. Adult support is gradually removed as the task is mastered.

To see scaffolding at work in a classroom, you would note how a teacher provides interesting book introductions at the beginning of a guided reading lesson. In addition, the teacher might take time to clarify and extend the ideas that children have about a story or provide additional information before reading so that they will understand the concepts to be presented (Fountas & Pinnell, 2001). She could point out unfamiliar words so that they don't become stumbling blocks, and then gently nudge readers into thinking at higher levels. In another situation you may find a child who is stuck on a word. The teacher stops to help, pointing out familiar letters or word parts, sounding out the initial letters, and then encourages the learner to sound out the rest of the word on his own. At another time, she might read the beginning of a story aloud, chat briefly about the characters or setting, and then let the class complete the story.

In addition, when a new strategy is being taught, the teacher models its use, **thinking aloud** to demonstrate how she uses the strategy within the context of the story (Cambourne, 2001; Cunningham, Hall, & Cunningham, 2000). Based upon that type of scaffolding, the students are better prepared to try using the strategy themselves. For learners who are struggling with reading, like those with learning disabilities, hearing impairments, or mild mental retardation, the scaffolding process stays in place for a longer period of time. Look for this type of scaf-

Reading involves connecting to previously gained knowledge, pondering how the new information fits.

folding in the upcoming discussions of the Directed Reading Activity and the Directed Reading Thinking Activity.

The concept of scaffolding is validated by the work of a prominent Russian psychologist, Lev Vygotsky (1978). His learning theory has become a cornerstone for instruction in today's classrooms. In his work, he explains the importance of the social interactions between a child and an adult in the construction of meaning and in the process of developing higher level thinking skills. Vygotsky distinguishes between a learner's actual development and her potential development, dubbing the distance between them as the **"zone of proximal development."** He explains that a child's actual development, the ability to function independently, is a measure of what she has learned up to that point. Her potential development is a measure of what the child might be capable of achieving with the assistance of a knowledgeable adult. The zone, then, is:

> the distance between the actual development level as determined by independent problem-solving and the level of potential development as determined through problem-solving under adult guidance or in collaboration with more capable peers. (Vygotsky, 1978, p. 84)

The importance behind Vygotsky's thinking is that he believes instruction should lead a child's development. In his words, "What the child can do in cooperation today, he can do alone tomorrow. Therefore, the only good kind of instruction is that which marches ahead of development and leads it; it must be aimed not so much at the ripe but at the ripening functions" (1962, p. 104).

When this theory is applied to the actual classroom, it appears that teachers must know their students as individual learners in order to scaffold learning and to offer support just a bit ahead of where each one is currently functioning (Robb, 2003). While that sounds like an impossibility when dealing with a class of twenty-five to thirty students, one way it is currently accomplished is by assessing and then building upon a student's prior knowledge, a common thread through numerous structured reading lessons like the Directed Reading Activity.

Directed Reading Activity (DRA)

The Directed Reading Activity (DRA) is a popular instructional procedure that can be used with both fiction and nonfiction text (Burns et al., 1999). Originated by A. Betts in 1946, this carefully structured, teacher-directed approach has long been used by publishers of various basal series. Depending on the needs of their students classroom teachers still tie it into lessons growing from quality children's literature. One way to familiarize yourself with how this method is used is to browse through a teacher's guide, especially from an older basal series. Current series are more likely to be patterned after a revision of the DRA by Stauffer (1969), which he called the Directed Reading-Thinking Activity. Note how the lessons in a DRA follow a prescribed structure involving five basic steps:

1. Preparation: The first step requires that the teacher focus on motivation and development of background, which is essential to understanding the story. At this point he measures and activates students' **prior knowledge** of the content in the story to be read. Additional background information is provided as needed so that all of the children have the same general knowledge of the topic. The reasoning behind this process is that comprehension is strengthened when new knowledge is integrated with previous knowledge. It also provides the opportunity to do as Vygotsky suggests: to lead the child in learning.

Another piece of the presentation segment involves introducing new vocabulary words. In addition, tips for reading the selection might be offered. For example, if the students are reading a newspaper article, they are directed to look for information to answer the questions who, what, where, when, and why, which are commonly associated with newspaper reporting. This quest would also give them a purpose for reading, the point of Step 2. Finally, even though it may not be necessary for every story, the teacher tries to motivate or raise interest in the upcoming material so that readers quickly become engaged in reading. Captivating pictures, music, drawing activities, drama, or knowledge webs draw on current knowledge and are engaging options. All of these preparatory activities can be integrated smoothly into engaging introductory activities.

2. Directed reading: The teacher usually sets the purpose for reading; however, as they gain confidence and ability, the students may come up with their own purposes under the guidance of the teacher. Several ways in which the teacher provides a focus for reading include the use of questions, a graphic organizer, a study guide, or an outline. In the lower grades or with students who need more support, the purpose is framed for shorter, more easily remembered segments of text. After the reading is concluded, students are given an opportunity to respond to the literature by sharing their answers to study guide questions or talking to each other about predictions and corrections they have made. This is a beneficial time because both comprehension and retention of what is being read are strengthened through student talk and teacher-directed activities (Morrow & Gambrell, 2000).

3. Skill/strategy development: Direct instruction on a particular skill or strategy is provided at some point during the lesson. The chosen skill is one that is closely related to the story to be read, growing from the story as a natural extension of learning. It may be presented before reading begins or after the story is completed. Giving the students an opportunity to revisit the text as they practice the new skill, and then providing a thoughtfully developed opportunity for practice, will extend comprehension. For example, this might be the time to present a few critical vocabulary words, practice using them in a semantic web as discussed in the next chapter or in student-generated sentences, and then add them to the current word wall or individual student journals for future reference.

4. Follow-up practice: Strategies and skills are practiced using numerous activities. Teachers who closely follow the suggested format in a basal series might opt for the prepared series practice sheets. Other teachers might offer story maps or other graphic organizers, word study activities, or encourage retellings. In a literature-focused program, the skill can be applied and reinforced while reading an appealing picture book, either individually or in a small group (Fuhler, 2000). In this way, additional practice in reading is provided, the skill is used in an authentic context, and students enjoy another wonderful book.

5. Enrichment: While it is not imperative or even desirable to do so after every story, a number of inviting activities might follow some reading selections to extend the learning experience. During this step, reader response is being emphasized. Here is an opportunity to deepen the contact with a book through creative venues like art, music, drama, or reading another story by the same author or on a similar topic. Linking the language arts including writing, listening, and speaking is another natural way to fine-tune learning. Review the list of possible enrichment activities in Chapter 12 to see the variety that is available to meet the needs of all learners.

In your investigation of the basal series or as you review the previously described steps, you will notice how the teacher plans and paces the lesson. He is building background and vocabulary, activating schema, raising interest, setting the purpose, and providing needed guidance as skills and strategies are taught and practiced. On the surface some of the methods presented in this chapter will look a little different, but that does not mean teachers are any more or any less on top of the teaching process. You will learn how teachers are in control when teaching within a literature-based reading curriculum as well, although the focus might change somewhat depending on the nature of the instruction.

For instance, in middle and upper grades, the reading program might revolve around a reading workshop format where student-selected reading materials and student-paced reading are integral parts of the program. Since Chapter 11 more fully explains the elements of a reading workshop, this is just a brief discussion to highlight the different looks in reading approaches. While the workshop is carefully planned and closely monitored by the teacher, students have more latitude in what they read than when following a basal reading approach. Those students may have to read from all of the genres, complete a certain number of books based on the teacher's assessment of their abilities, and respond to a specified number of them in some way each grading period, but can you see how the process looks different on the surface? The teacher assumes the role of supportive and enthusiastic guide in addition to teaching pertinent mini-lessons on critical reading strategies. Students set their own purposes for reading. They assume the role of predicting and confirming predictions throughout the selection and make additional choices about what they will do after completing the books they are reading (Galda, Cullinan, & Strickland, 1993). They, too, are mastering comprehension skills and abilities but in a less teacher-directed, more student-selected manner. Understand that differences do not mean "better than or worse than." There are just different ways to approach the teaching of comprehension.

Teaching Strategy for the Classroom

DIRECTED READING ACTIVITY LESSON PLAN USING *THE TALKING EGGS* (SAN SOUCI, 1989)

I. OBJECTIVES

The students will make, confirm, and revise their predictions as they analyze and comprehend this award-winning tale.

II. MATERIALS

Copies of the picture book for students in the class (or enough to be shared between two or three readers); recycled file folders to make stand-up vocabulary words or tagboard, folded tent-style so that vocabulary words will stand upright; paper for drawing; crayons or markers; chart paper or overhead transparencies; and a collection of picture book versions of favorite fairy tales. Titles for some you might consider are included later in the lesson.

III. INSTRUCTIONAL APPROACH

A. Motivator

Before the lesson is taught, select vocabulary words or unusual phrases from the text. Look for words that might be unfamiliar to the students or are used in a different context than usual. Using old file folders, trim off the notch on the long edges so that they are even. The folder will then stand up like a tent, with the fold at the top, open edges on the table. Using a dark marker, write the phrase or vocabulary word on one side in letters large enough to be seen easily from the front of the room. Suggested words might include:

putting on airs	trail-train dresses	fetch a bucket of water	backwoods
talking foolishness	got a spirit of do-right	lit into me	tumbledown shack
reckoned	corkscrews	kindling	plaited
underbrush	frock-tail coats	gawked	contrary

Stand the words up on a table at the front of the room or along the chalkboard railing. Put them in place before the reading lesson begins. If words are in place before children enter the classroom for the day, they are sure to grab attention and generate some speculation and conversation before the activity begins. Find enough words so that students can divide into teams of three or four, pick a word, speculate upon its meaning, and then draw a picture illustrating what they think the word means. The group is also to write a sentence using the word or phrase. Then, one by one, the groups present their words, drawings, and sentences to the rest of the class. The class listens, discusses their reactions to what the group has presented, and then agrees or disagrees with the definition and usage. In the role of Word Wizard, you will offer any corrections as needed. This should be fun, will engage children in bringing their prior knowledge to the activity, and will involve the whole class in building vocabulary and background to facilitate comprehension of *The Talking Eggs*. Finally, tell the students to look for these words as they read the story.

B. Teacher/Student Interaction

Hand out copies of the book to the class. Point out the two award designations on the cover of the book, the silver Caldecott Honor symbol and the bronze Coretta Scott King Award symbol. Explain that this book has won two distinguished awards, giving the class a little background on each one. For example, they might like to know that the Coretta Scott King Award is given each year to African American authors and illustrators for books that encourage an understanding and appreciation of people of all cultures. The award also encourages people to pursue the "American dream." Ask the students to discuss the phrase "to pursue the American dream." What does that mean to them personally? Take time to listen to a selection of answers.

Continue by telling the class that this particular award celebrates the life of Dr. Martin Luther King and honors his widow, Coretta Scott King, for her strength in the face of obstacles and her continued work to promote racial equality. As students read this book, suggest that they think about why it may have been selected as the winner of the Coretta Scott King Award. You have just set one purpose for reading.

The second award given to this book was selected as a Caldecott Honor Book. The Caldecott Award is given in memory of an English illustrator, Randolph Caldecott. The award is given to an American illustrator for distinguished art work each year. Often one or two books are selected as Honor Books, or runners-up, as this one was. While students read, encourage them to look carefully at the action-filled illustrations, hypothesizing as to why this might have been an award winner. This is a second purpose for reading.

Building Background

Ask the students to talk about fairy tales. What are a few of their favorites? Invite them to explain the characteristics of a fairy tale. They might mention factors like a contrast between good and evil characters, some items that are magic, animals that talk, or the poor sometimes come out as winners. List these items on the chalkboard or the overhead transparency, if students don't come up with them. They relate directly to this tale. Finally, read the background information on the title page about the tale. Read it aloud while the students follow along or invite a volunteer to read it. Discuss the fact that understanding the Southern setting for the story and knowing that it has its roots in a fairy tale will help them better understand the story.

Directed Reading Activities

- Direct the students' attention to the cover of the book. Have them look at the illustrations and think about the title. What do they think this story will be about? Do they see anything in the illustrations that leads them to believe this is a deserving Caldecott Honor Book winner at this point? Write predictions and comments on the chalkboard, chart paper, or an overhead transparency to be referred to after sampling several pages of reading.
- Tell the students to pay close attention to the way the author uses words. Look at the following sentence as an example: "They lived on a farm so poor, it looked like the tail end of bad luck." What can they learn about the farm from that sentence?
- The students will read to confirm or adjust their predictions. They will also be studying the illustrations to see why Jerry Pinkney's artwork won the attention of the Caldecott Committee. In addition, they will be reading to find the new vocabulary words. That will give them several purposes for reading. Read about half of the book. The students can read silently or read orally in pairs or triads.
- When they are done with the first half, talk about their various predictions. Discuss how close their predictions were to the actual story. Are there some that should be adjusted? Make new predictions and continue reading until the end of the book. Discuss and evaluate predictions. Invite readers to talk about their emerging ideas regarding why they think this book has won two distinguished awards.
- Write the following questions on the chalkboard, an overhead transparency, or chart paper. The use of questions gives the readers a purpose to read, because they are having to look for specific information with which to answer them. When discussing their answers with another student, in small groups, or as a large group, the questions also help to monitor student comprehension.

1. Review some of the unusual things that Blanche saw and experienced on her visit to the aunty's shack. How might they react if they were in Blanche's shoes?
2. What surprised them about the plain eggs?
3. If they could have one of the eggs turn into something special for them, what would it be? Why is that important?
4. What is their reaction to Rose's behavior? Did Rose behave as they anticipated that she would? What clues did the author give about the kind of person she was?
5. What kinds of magic did the author weave into this fairy tale? Can they think of other tales with similar kinds of magic?
6. Why do they think the two sisters were so different?
7. If they were to write their own fairy tale, what elements of a tale would they include? Why?

Discuss the story as a whole group, encouraging as many students to contribute to different parts of the discussion as possible.

C. Gatekeeping

Monitor student understanding as you use the following comprehension questions to direct the discussion, or encourage students to respond to them in their literature response journals:

- Did the story end the way you thought it might?
- Compare and contrast the two sisters as people.
- If the author were trying to teach us a lesson through this story, what might it be?
- Does this story remind you of any other fairy tales you know?
- Provide additional support to students who may need to reread the story, work on vocabulary, or review skills like the ability to sequence events or retell the story based on your observations.

Skill Development

Review some common elements in a fairy tale. List the elements discussed at the beginning of the lesson. Add another one as desired. The students will look for these elements within the context of *The Talking Eggs*. Discuss elements as a whole class after reading this tale.

Follow-Up Practice

Divide the class into triads. Let students choose another fairy tale from a selection gathered ahead of time. List the factors or elements of this tale on the chalkboard or on a student worksheet. The students are to read the new tale, looking for similarities and differences between their new book and *The Talking Eggs* and filling in the sheet upon completion of the book. Each group shares their book and their findings with the rest of the class. In completing this part of the lesson, students are cementing their knowledge of the elements commonly found in a fairy tale.

Additional Titles for Student Practice

Cherry, Lynne. (1995). *The Dragon and the Unicorn*. New York: Harcourt Brace.

dePaola, T. (2002). *Adelita: A Mexican Cinderella Story*. New York: Putnam.

Hoffman, Mary. (1991). *Clever Katya: A Fairy Tale from Old Russia.* (M. Cameron, Illus.). New York: Barefoot Books.

Hooks, William H. (1987). *Moss Gown.* (D. Carrick, Illus.). New York: Clarion.

Jackson, Ellen. (1994). *Cinder Edna.* (K. O'Malley, Illus.). New York: Lothrop, Lee & Shepard.

Louie, Ai-Ling. (1982). *Yeh Shen.* (E. Young, Illus.). New York: Philomel.

Martin, Rafe. (1992). *The Rough-Face Girl.* (D. Shannon, Illus.). New York: G. P. Putnam's Sons.

Paterson, Katherine. (1990). *The Tale of the Mandarin Ducks.* (L. & D. Dillon, Illus.). New York: Lodestar.

San Souci, Robert D. (2000). *Cinderella Skeleton.* (D. Catrow, Illus.). San Diego, CA: Silver Whistle/Harcourt Brace.

———. (1998). *Cendrillon: A Caribbean Cinderella.* (J. Pinkney & D. San Souci, Illus.). New York: Simon & Schuster.

———. (1993). *The Snow Wife.* (S. T. Johnson, Illus.). New York: Dial.

———. (1992). *Sukey and the Mermaid.* (J. Pinkney, Illus.). New York: Aladdin.

Yep, Laurence. (1994). *The Boy Who Swallowed Snakes.* (J. & M. Tseng, Illus.). New York: Scholastic.

IV. EXTENSIONS

- Use the Internet to investigate websites that might have other versions of this tale or to look for other fairy and folktales set in the South. One suggested site is *Tales of Wonder: Folk and Fairy Tales from Around the World* at http://darsie.ucdavies.edu/tales/
  Another option is *The Children's Literature Web Guide,* choosing the Folklore, Myth, and Legend resources at http://www.acs.ucalgary.ca/~dkbrown/storfolk.html
  You might also check *The Cinderella Project: University of Southern Mississippi.* It contains a dozen versions of the Cinderella tale drawn from the de Grummond Children's Literature Research Collection at the University of Southern Mississippi: http://www-dept.usm.edu/~engdept/cinderella/cinderella.html. Finally, investigate *SurLaLune Fairy Tale Pages,* which includes annotated fairy tales, a little information about them, and comparative tales from different cultures: http://members.aol.com/surlalune/frytales/index.htm

- Retell the story visually, creating scenes using crayon batik. Students will draw a favorite scene using sturdy white paper and a heavy application of crayons. Next, cover the entire picture with black or blue tempera paint. The paint will fill in the unwaxed parts of the picture making the colors in the scene stand out against the dark background. Title the picture and put the completed pictures in sequence to retell the story visually.

- Working in teams of four or five, students create a report card for key characters in the story. Draw names of the characters so that all characters are covered. Two groups can grade the same character. First, each group must decide what criteria will be used and what their grading scale might be. Work through an example as a whole group using a character from a previously read story so that all of the students understand the assignment ahead. Share the completed report that has been reproduced on large sheets of tagboard. Display on the wall for the class to enjoy.

- Create a reader's theater production using this fairy tale or another one. The class could divide up into several groups, each one working with a different tale. After presenting the productions to the class, take the show on the road and present it to children in several primary grade classrooms.

- Show a video of Jerry Pinkney so that the children can get to know the illustrator behind a number of award-winning books. Read other books illustrated by this talented man. Search the Web for related information. One practical site is http://www.scils.rutgers.edu/special/kay/author.html. Another excellent resource is http://www.childrenslit.com/lit, and go to the Meet Authors and Illustrators page. Arranged alphabetically, it is easy to locate Jerry Pinkney. Students will learn about the author and read excerpts from a number of his books.

V. ADAPTATIONS/MODIFICATIONS FOR DIVERSE LEARNERS

- Locate folk and fairy tales in several languages to meet the language needs of English language learners (ELLs).
- Read additional tales in buddy teams; a good reader paired with a child with mild retardation or learning disabilities.
- Supply a number of books on tape for the visually impaired and for learning disabled readers.
- Encourage gifted students to search the Internet for different versions of a particular tale to share with the class. The students might write and illustrate their own folk or fairy tale.

Directed Reading Thinking Activity (DRTA)

The **Directed Reading Thinking Activity** (DRTA) developed by Russell G. Stauffer (1969) is a less structured alternative to the DRA. When following this strategy, the control of learning is not characterized as strongly by teacher dominance. Once the steps are modeled and mastered, students assume more of the responsibility for reading stories in the basal text, trade books, or content area materials. Stauffer (1969) explains that the DRTA involves several steps that build on children's natural curiosity, engage them intellectually, and encourage them to think about and to evaluate what they are reading. In the process they are building **metacognitive** abilities, that is, being aware of what they are learning, how they are doing it, and what strategies to use when understanding falters.

To facilitate comprehension of the reading material, the students follow a basic three-step process: sample the text, form hypotheses or make predictions, and read the text to confirm or readjust previous predictions. The process is repeated throughout the story or content area text as students interact with the material, drawing on personal background knowledge, on familiarity with the organization of the text, and engaging in discussion with other students in the class as they confirm or readjust their predictions. When confirming their predictions, they return to the text, locate the specific sentences that support or refute their predictions, and then begin the process once again. One particularly important feature of the DRTA is that of making predictions, an important higher level comprehension strategy. Beck (1989) points out that making predictions based upon clues in the text helps students to see how helpful text information can be when making inferences. When there are no clues to guide them, making predictions encourages creative thinking on the part of the readers.

The DRTA can move across the curriculum to be adapted to both narrative or expository text depending on the wishes of the teacher. See the sample lesson in Figure 8.2 for an illustration of how this strategy might be implemented.

Teaching Strategy for the Classroom

DIRECTED READING THINKING ACTIVITY USING *ZACHARY'S BALL*

STEP 1: MAKING INITIAL PREDICTIONS FROM THE TITLE AND TITLE PAGE ILLUSTRATIONS.

This sample lesson models how the teacher could demonstrate the use of the Directed Reading Thinking Activity, a strategy for future reading lessons. Hold up a copy of the book *Zachary's Ball* (Tavares, 2000) so that all of the class can see the cover. You might even make an overhead copy of the cover to improve visibility. This is a delightful book to introduce in the spring as news of baseball training signals a welcome change of seasons. Ask the students to read the title and to look at the cover illustration. What do they think the story is going to be about? Ask contributors why they think as they do. This will elicit background information including previous experiences attending games or playing ball. Quickly record predictions on the overhead transparency or chalkboard.

STEP 2: READ SEVERAL PAGES. CONFIRM OR ADJUST PREDICTIONS.

Read the first three pages of text and stop. Lead a whole group discussion with questions like "Who correctly predicted what the story was going to be about?" Ask students to support their predictions showing the rest of the class the clues in the title or pictures that lead them to their predictions. Nudge the next predictions by asking "What do you think the story will tell us about what happens next?" Jot down several predictions and continue reading through the next three pages of text.

STEP 3: CONTINUE READING TO THE NEXT STOPPING POINT. CONFIRM OR ADJUST PREDICTIONS.

As the process indicates, adjust previous predictions as necessary. Based on the magic that has happened to this point, invite students to make new predictions. Ask open-ended questions to prompt additional predictions as is necessary. One example is "If it were you, what would you wish would happen based upon the ball's magic? Where would you keep a ball as special as this one? Would you play with this ball?" Tell the students to hold onto their thoughts and compare them with what happens next.

STEP 4: READ THE MATERIAL TO THE NEXT STOPPING POINT, ENDING WITH "ALWAYS HOPING THAT ANOTHER BALL MIGHT COME MY WAY."

Confirm, adjust, discuss, predict. Does the class think that Zachary will ever be that lucky again? Read two more pages and stop for reactions. Query: "Was that Zachary's ball? Did they expect this event to happen? Why or why not? How will this story end?" Have students do a "quick write." They are to take several minutes to write down their predicted ending in just a few thoughts. Then, complete the book.

STEP 5: INVITE REACTIONS.

"Did anyone come up with an ending like the one in the book? What were some of their endings? Did they like the ending? Why or why not?" Chat about the book in the process of wrapping up this reading experience. Explain to the class that they will understand what they are reading much better if they think carefully about their reading. One way to do that is to predict, confirm, or adjust predictions, and then continue reading just like you have done together as a class.

Feature Book: Tavares, M. (2000) *Zachary's Ball.* Boston: Candlewick.

Directed Listening Thinking Activity (DLTA)

Another effective teacher-directed comprehension strategy is an adaptation of the DRTA. In its new form it is called the **Directed Listening Thinking Activity** (DLTA). Adaptable for readers across the grades, it offers a structure for introducing and discussing stories that are read aloud. Morrow (1984) states that the activity can significantly increase children's listening comprehension. With practice, students can apply the process when listening to other stories in the future. The framework that supports listening includes the following steps:

1. Introduce the story to students by showing the cover of the book and discussing the title. Several illustrations might be shown. Then students are invited to make predictions about the story. The teacher may ask specific questions to encourage those predictions and help students to tie in their background knowledge and experiences.

2. Listening, thinking, and predicting follow next. Students listen to confirm or correct their initial predictions. The teacher continues to guide their thinking with questions as the story continues. She stops periodically to talk about important points until the story is completed.

3. The final step involves students in supporting their predictions with evidence from the story. They recall tidbits from the story that either helped them confirm or altered their various predictions.

Because readers must be listeners, too, efforts to strengthen listening comprehension are an integral part of the reading regimen.

Reciprocal Teaching

A third technique that is used in a small group situation and also has the characteristic of being mobile across the curriculum is **reciprocal teaching**. It is teacher-directed initially, until students understand the components and are competent when using them effectively on their own. Developed by Annemarie Palinscar and Ann Brown (1984), reciprocal teaching is one of the most carefully researched, prominent formats for teaching multiple comprehension strategies. In this cooperative-learning procedure, the teacher and the students work together to develop an understanding of the text. There are four thoughtfully integrated comprehension strategies at the core of this approach:

Prediction: As with the DRA and DLTA, this step activates prior knowledge and sets the purpose for reading. Students must review what they have read thus far and develop expectations about what is coming next. When they are beginning a book, students base their predictions on such aspects as the illustrations, headings, and the introduction.

Questioning: Students focus on the main ideas within the reading materials. As a check on the understanding of what they are reading, they pose questions about the content. For instance, during discussion of what has just been read, if a student cannot formulate a question about the content under study, it could be a clue that he or she does not understand the materials well enough. To correct the problem, she would reread a portion of the book or seek clarification from members of her group.

Seeking clarification: This step ensures that readers stay actively engaged with the text and helps them to clear up confusion when it arises. They check their understanding of vocabulary, unusual expressions, concepts, or other information that might be confusing, and they seek clarification during group discussions.

Summarization: This step requires students to pay attention to critical content to determine what is important and what is not. Initially, the teacher, and later, the group leader, summarizes the selection, touching on the main points. If the student has difficulty in the retelling, that is a red flag denoting faulty comprehension. It is a clear warning signal that a review of the material would be a wise decision to make.

When reciprocal teaching is first introduced in the classroom, the teacher demonstrates the process. As group leader, she models each strategy, monitors the students' work, scaffolds experiences as needed, and provides feedback. As soon as possible that leadership role is transferred to students, with each student eventually getting a turn as group leader in their respective groups. As with other cooperative learning efforts, it will take time to learn reciprocal teaching. Careful supervision and practice will help students to master the steps in an educationally interactive dialogue. The benefits of reciprocal teaching in facilitating comprehension are enduring and well worth the effort on everyone's part.

One of the pluses of reciprocal teaching is that it involves all of the students in using sound reading strategies. First graders can learn the rudiments, fine-tuning their skills as they progress through the grades. The strategy works well with science and social studies materials and with fiction and nonfiction selections. Furthermore, the strategy is useful with students who need extra support in their learning. For example, English language learners, students with learning disabilities, and learners with visual impairments are supported within the cooperative learning group, coached in their learning by both classmates and the teacher. Review the four strategies involved in reciprocal teaching as they might look when working with *Steamboat! The Story of Captain Blanche Leathers* (Gilliland, 2000) in Figure 8.2.

Figure 8.2

An example of the reciprocal teaching procedure

The reading lesson begins with the teacher holding up a copy of the day's read-aloud. In this case it is *Steamboat! The Story of Captain Blanche Leathers* (Gilliland, 2000). She reads the title and author, shows the cover and title page, and reads the first page of text, holding the book so that the class can enjoy the unique illustrations. Then she engages the class in the following steps.

1. **Predicting:**

   At the beginning of a book students are activating prior knowledge and setting a purpose for continued reading. Appropriate questions to elicit connections and then several predictions might be, "Has anyone spent any time on the Mississippi River or another river?" "Can you draw any comparisons between your experiences and the description of the Mississippi in this book?" After drawing on what they know, a student might reply, "Rivers aren't what they seem to be on the surface. You just don't know what lies beneath the water, where deep pools might be, or where the bottom has shifted and it is more shallow than you think." To encourage predictions, ask students why Blanche and others might find riverboats so fascinating. Where do they think this fascination will lead Blanche? In longer selections predictions are made throughout the reading. Based upon the segments just read and those that came before it, the group leader or students continue to predict what will happen next.

2. **Questioning:**

   After a segment or a paragraph has been read, the teacher or the students generate pertinent questions. In this case, read to the part of the text where Blanche announces to her husband that she wants to be a steamboat captain. Now the teacher might ask questions like:
   - Do you think it is an occupation for a woman? Why or why not?
   - What makes navigating this river so treacherous?
   - How do you think riverboat pilots navigated the river in the days without sonar?
   - What obstacles does Blanche face in achieving her dream?

3. **Clarifying Issues:**

   When a segment of a book causes confusion for readers, the group leader or other members in the group clarify that confusion. In continuing to read *Steamboat!* readers might wonder about the social occasion that the docking of the ship seems to bring about. Another reader might explain how exciting the arrival of the ship must have been because it wasn't just supplies or a pony for a child that was arriving but news of events on the river as well. They may shudder to learn about the secrets the river hides and wonder aloud why steamboat travel was so dangerous. Someone knowledgeable about how the steamboat generated its power could clarify that part of the issue by discussing the danger of building up too much steam and the resulting explosions, and how the boats were primarily constructed of wood, so the fires that started could quickly destroy a boat. The group might even consult an outside resource to learn about the sandbars and other dangers involved in navigating this river.

4. **Summarizing:**

   Once questions have been cleared up, the teacher summarizes the story. Hitting key points, she will outline how Blanche announces that she wants to be a steamboat captain. First, the task will be difficult because women simply are not riverboat captains. She will certainly have to prove herself to be very capable and overcome a great deal of skepticism on the part of the men on the examination board. She knows the river well, studies extremely hard, and describes the mysteries of the Mississippi thoroughly. During her piloting, she navigates with wisdom. In 1894, Blanche becomes the first female steamboat captain.

Feature Book: Gilliland, J. H. (2000). *Steamboat! The Story of Captain Blanche Leathers.* (H. Meade, Illus.). New York: Dorling Kindersley.

As a final supportive note, in its recent publication, the Report of the National Reading Panel (2000) stated that cooperative learning was one of the more effective approaches to reading instruction, especially when teamed with other strategies as suggested in this chapter. It is a powerful addition to a well-versed teacher's repertoire of comprehension-building tools. Continuing to investigate comprehension options, this time using a combination of whole class and individual work, you can rely upon the well-known K-W-L strategy. It is now available in an improved version, K-W-L-Plus, which integrates the reading and writing processes while it affords solid learning possibilities in both narrative and expository text (Carr & Ogle, 1987).

Working Across the Curriculum: The K-W-L-Plus Strategy

Working in content area classes with expository text that is fact-filled from beginning to end can present comprehension problems to readers who just don't know how to sort out all the information. One way to prepare learners for the changes required to comprehend in this kind of reading material is not new on the reading scene. But it has been adapted. Today teachers use the updated **K-W-L-Plus strategy** to activate students' prior knowledge about a topic to be studied. It is a particularly valuable tool to use before beginning a new unit of study in science or social studies, or to use before beginning an article or a story on a new topic.

This comprehension strategy requires the students to think carefully about what they **(K) know** about the topic, what they **(W) want to learn** about it, and after studying the topic, report what they have **(L) learned**. Lastly, they engage in a selected writing activity to summarize what they have learned **(Plus)**. As you have read, research states that students learn best when prior knowledge is accessed and purposes are set for reading, steps which are addressed directly when using the K-W-L-Plus strategy. The first two areas, *know* and *want to learn,* are covered before the reading begins. They become the motivation for students to investigate a new topic area and try to understand it. After the study is completed, reviewing *what they have learned* becomes an opportune way for the teacher to evaluate comprehension and for students to also do some self-evaluation.

Furthermore, the strategy can be extended by having students research the questions left unanswered by previous work. Then learning can be cemented by an inviting writing activity that facilitates skills in summarization but might also include a creative presentation in written form. Students might work in pairs at this point, drafting and polishing a paragraph, poem, or other writing option to be read aloud to the class upon completion.

See Figure 8.3 for an example of a typical activity sheet that students use when working with the K-W-L-Plus strategy. The sheets are given to the students at the beginning of the day's lesson. The teacher prompts a session of individual brainstorming by asking the students what they know about the specific topic to be studied. After students have had time to quickly record their thoughts, the teacher asks various individuals to contribute a tidbit of knowledge. These are recorded on a large K-W-L-Plus chart at the front of the room. Each point can be elaborated upon briefly by asking students where they learned the information or how they might prove what they know.

	Figure 8.3

An example of a typical K-W-L chart

K-W-L Chart

K What We **K**now	W What We **W**ant to Learn	L What We **L**earned

When misconceptions or disagreements arise, these points might be starred. Students are challenged to look for clarifying or supporting information in the upcoming reading.

In order to better organize contributions from the brainstorming data, the teacher and students try to categorize the previous information. This might be called "Categories of Information We Might Learn More About." The general categories will vary depending upon the topic under study.

Next, students are given a short time to fill in the second column addressing (W), "What They Want to Learn." After adequate thinking time, record all of the students' questions on the large sheet. Additional questions may emerge as students volunteer their interests and curiosities. Just before the reading begins, students are to write two or three questions down on their sheets that particularly interest them. In this way they are establishing a personal purpose for reading.

The final column, (L) "What I Have Learned," is finished after reading and data gathering conclude. This segment can be completed during a general class discussion when talk helps students digest what they have learned (Allington, 2002). Students refer to the answers to their questions, knowledge gained during reading. They share notes on any other information that they thought was particularly interesting, with the class chart being filled in accordingly. If there are still areas to be investigated, questions about them can be included here to promote further independent study.

The K-W-L-Plus technique is an excellent way to begin an interdisciplinary unit as the teacher assesses what her students already know about the subject to be studied. If there are gaps in knowledge, she plans ways to build a foundation of understanding for all learners before serious study ensues. Perhaps there is a short video or a knowledgeable guest speaker at hand. Obviously, this first step is a benefit to learners of varying abilities and backgrounds. Another plus for this group of learners is the opportunity to listen to classmates share what they already know because such discussion provides valuable background information for every learner. Such an interaction is a prime example of scaffolding new learning for all readers in the classroom.

TECHNIQUES TO APPLY TO INDIVIDUAL LESSONS

Sometimes the goal of a reading lesson might be to examine the various pieces of a story in a less teacher-directed manner. In this case, once a skill is taught, the students practice it within the current lesson and then use the skill in specified lessons again and again throughout the year. One such skill for digging into a story to examine its parts is story mapping. Others to be discussed are question-answer relationship (QAR), inferential reading, general questioning suggestions, and the long-used study strategy, SQ3R.

Web Link:
Reading Comprehension
Resources

Story Mapping

As was mentioned earlier in the chapter, when students develop a schema for stories, that is, an internal understanding of the expected pieces that make up a typical story, they are better able to comprehend the narratives that they read. This is true for students who are struggling readers as well as those who are accomplished (Vallecorsa & deBettencort, 1997). One tool to help them recognize those basic pieces is the **story map**, a graphic or semantic visual representation of a story. Two examples of these maps, frequently referred to as graphic organizers, have been provided, a semantic map in Chapter 10 (Figure 10.3) and Figure 8.5 in the current chapter. These maps illustrate two different ways to provide an overview of a story. They typically include brief information about characters, setting, problem, goal, events, and resolution (Beck & McKeown, 1981).

The origin of story maps lies within story grammar research. The term **story grammar** refers to the hierarchical rules or psychological structures that people use to create and remember stories, the skeleton underlying a story, so to speak (Davis & McPherson, 1989; Reutzel, 1985). These "psychological models of comprehension and memory" (p. 821) are used by both adults and children to encode and store information in their long-term memories (Pearson & Fielding, 1996). Put in more simple terms, think about how experienced readers quickly recognize that a story is expected to have a main character and each character is faced with a problem to solve or a crisis to weather. Taking that knowledge one step further and making it visible, one has the beginnings of the story map, a highly effective, practical way to help students organize story content into a coherent whole. Research supports the effectiveness of using story maps with learning disabled and low achieving students in improving comprehension of materials that were above their instructional levels (Idol, 1987). Part of the effectiveness was also due to being able to work in heterogeneous groups with students who could model and explain the process.

Story maps are important tools to teachers and students alike. When created as part of the process of preparing a reading lesson, teachers become more involved in thinking about the structure of the story they are to teach and how each part of the story relates to the others. In other words, completing a story map helps to focus the lesson, leads to more purposeful teaching, and results in a better quality learning experience for the students. Because she has already worked closely with the story, it is easier for the well-versed teacher to show the class its important parts and how they are interrelated.

Students, too, benefit from the use of story maps. Such concrete representations aid readers in visualizing the story. In addition, readers can more easily see how the story pieces mesh, knowledge they continually apply when they predict what might happen next in one story after another. In addition, it appears that mapping enables readers to store information in their personal schema more efficiently and facilitates the recall of story elements more completely and accurately (Reutzel & Cooter, 2000). Not to be overused and thus abused, these maps can be applied to stories in the basal text along with excellent children's literature, particularly the shorter text found in picture books.

The general procedure to follow when preparing a basic story map includes the following steps (Davis & McPherson, 1989; Reutzel, 1985):

1. Read the story. Write a sequenced summary of the main ideas, key events, and characters that make up the plot of the story.

2. Place the title, theme, or topic of the story in the center of the graphic story map in a predominant bubble (Figure 8.4) or at the top of the semantic chart (Figure 10.3).

3. For the graphic organizer, draw enough ties projecting out symmetrically from the center of the map to accommodate the major events of the story's plot. Attach related pieces or second-level information from the summary list to these ties in chronological order, moving clockwise around the center. The semantically organized chart is simply arranged by story elements, so information is transferred to it accordingly.

4. Draw additional ties projecting out symmetrically from each secondary bubble to accommodate the important details associated with the key plot event, adding relevant information from the summary list.

5. Review the final semantic chart or story map for completeness.

These maps can be integrated into instruction in several ways. Use them to introduce the lesson. Put a completed bubble map on a transparency and let the students examine it. Invite predictions based upon the snippets they see on the map. In addition, you can scaffold the comprehension process by filling in only part of the organizer and letting the students complete it during the reading process. Finally, use a blank story map or semantic organizer at the completion of the story to pull students

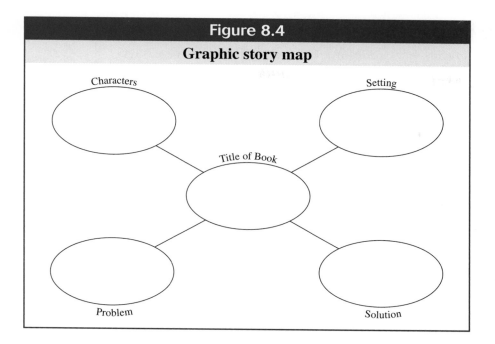

Figure 8.4
Graphic story map

Characters

Setting

Title of Book

Problem

Solution

into analyzing the pieces in preparation for a discussion of the story. In this case, maps may be completed individually or in small groups.

One innovative and particularly effective way to use a mapping technique involves Character Perspective Charting (CPC) (Shanahan & Shanahan, 1997). In this case, the attention is drawn to the characters in the story and the different perspectives each character could have of the events in the story. See the example of the chart in Figure 8.5. Thus, readers have an opportunity to analyze a story from several different perspectives looking beyond just the main character's point of view. Imagine how effective that kind of thinking could be in helping students relate to literature that reflects the experiences of differing racial, ethnic, and linguistic groups. Multicultural novels, picture books, and nonfiction titles do more than just describe characteristics of particular cultural heritages; "they illuminate the difficulties of maintaining positive relationships among those from different backgrounds" (Shanahan et al., 1997, p. 674). Using the CPC as a tool for looking at conflicting goals and/or intentions of various groups could lead to more insightful and memorable learning.

Students from the second grade on up through middle school can master the thinking behind the CPC. As they work within its structure, readers are developing such critical thinking strategies as remembering details, developing vocabulary, drawing inferences and conclusions, and comparing the goals and actions of various characters much more carefully than they would be when only scrutinizing the perspective of the main character.

Figure 8.5

A blank Character Perspective Chart

Main Character: Who is the main character?

Setting: Where and when does the story take place?

Problem: What is the main character's problem?

Goal: What is the main character's goal? What does he want?

Attempt: What does the main character do to solve the problem or get the goal?

Outcome: What happened as a result of the attempt?

Reaction: How does the main character feel about the outcome?

Theme: What point did the author want to make?

Another Character: Who is this character?

Setting: Where and when does the story take place?

Problem: What is the character's problem?

Goal: What is the character's goal? What does he want?

Attempt: What does the character do to solve the problem or get the goal?

Outcome: What happened as a result of the attempt?

Reaction: How does the character feel about the outcome?

Theme: What point did the author want to make?

To integrate the CPC into literature circles or small group use, begin with a demonstration lesson:

1. Read a thought-provoking picture book aloud to the class.
2. Pick two characters to discuss, the main character and one other.
3. Work through the chart with the class, filling in the different areas together, beginning with the main character.
4. Next, refocus on a secondary character and repeat the process, this time probing a different point of view. Then, examine the results. Query the students about why certain parts of the chart changed depending on the character under inspection.
5. Discuss the value of looking at a story from different perspectives, how it pulls a reader into deeper levels of thought and affords a more complete understanding of the story than the standard story map format typically does. See Figure 8.6 for an example of a Character Perspective Chart that has been completed based upon a picture book appealing to older readers, *Shibumi and the Kitemaker* (Mayer, 1999).

Figure 8.6

A completed Character Perspective Chart

Mayer, Mercer. (1999). *Shibumi and the Kitemaker.* New York: Marshall Cavendish.

Summary: Protected from the wretched life outside of the garden wall, the emperor's precious daughter plays in the palace gardens. When she accidentally learns how people in the city live, she is determined to see a change in their surroundings. Enlisting the help of a wise and talented elderly kitemaker, she sets about providing a bit a beauty to the city only to be thwarted by greedy nobles who attempt to kill her. Saved by the brave kitemaker, they fly away to a northern wilderness. Some years later a curious samurai warrior tracks Shibumi down and brings her home to a changed city which she rules following her father's death.

Main Character: Who is the main character?
Shibumi, the emperor's daughter.

Another Character: Who is this character?
The elderly kitemaker.

Setting: Where and when does the story take place?
In a far away kingdom, many years ago.

Setting: Where and when does the story take place?
In a far away kingdom, many years ago.

Problem: What is the main character's problem?
Shibumi tries to make life outside of the palace walls as beautiful as it is inside so that people can enjoy a better quality of life against her father's wishes.

Problem: What is the character's problem?
He must follow the wishes of the princess despite the fact that he will be put to death for it.

Goal: What is the main character's goal? What does he want?
To urge her father to make those changes.

Goal: What is the character's goal? What does he want?
To build a kite strong enough to carry Shibumi high above the city safely.

Attempt: What does the main character do to solve the problem or get the goal?
Requesting the help of the kitemaker, she flies above the city and threatens to stay there until her pleas are granted.

Attempt: What does the character do to solve the problem or get the goal?
He sends the princess aloft, delivers her message, and faces the emperor's wrath.

Outcome: What happened as a result of the attempt?
Greedy nobles plot her death in the face of the emperor's decree to clean up the city, and she and the kitemaker are blown far away.

Outcome: What happened as a result of the attempt?
He courageously risks his life to save Shibumi, and the two of them disappear into the sky to end up in a northern wilderness.

Reaction: How does the main character feel about the outcome?
Sorrowful because she so loves her father and senses that little will change now that she is gone.

Reaction: How does the character feel about the outcome?
Grateful that he could help the princess but perhaps sad because he left someone he cared for behind. The quality of his final days may have been much improved over his life in the city.

Theme: What point did the author want to make?
There is a cost to striving for your ideals, but they can be reached through creativity, thought, and persistence.

Theme: What point did the author want to make?
It takes courage to fight for what you believe in and sacrifice to achieve your goals, but you should never give up.

Source: Used with permission. Shanahan, T., & Shanahan, S. 1997. Character Perspective Charting: Helping children to develop a more complete conception of story. *The Reading Teacher, 50* (8), 668–677.

The Character Perspective Chart is but one alternative to the standard story map format. Other uses include designing maps that will aid in comparison and contrast of story events, or looking at cause and effect in an effort to better understand a piece of text. Used innovatively, the story map is a beneficial comprehension tool. Cunningham, Hall, and Cunningham (2000) have developed an appealing alternative to paper and pencil story maps. They use a real beach ball with selected questions written in the colored stripes with a black, permanent magic marker. Those questions are framed from sections of a typical story map and can be adapted according to the teacher's purpose. Before reading, the students are told that the after-reading activity will be the "Beach Ball." Once they are familiar with the chosen questions, they read to find that information and are prepared for the after-reading circle. When the reading has been completed, the class is seated in the circle. The teacher selects a student and tosses the ball to him. He can answer any question on the ball before picking another student and tossing the ball to that reader. The ball continues back and forth until all questions have been answered and the story is well understood. Without a doubt, these learners are actively involved in reading comprehension.

In continuing to examine other key comprehension strategies, it is important to take some time to examine questioning techniques. Both teacher and student profit from asking the right questions. The following paragraphs discuss practical strategies for generating quality queries.

Question-Answer Relationship (QAR)

Comprehension can be measured at different levels. The most basic level is that of literal understanding. When children read at a literal level, they are reading to "find out" specific information (Cunningham & Allington, 2003). In a whole class or small group lesson, the directions might be, "Everybody read to find out . . . " and give the readers a specific purpose. The answer they are seeking is **explicitly stated** in the book. When students have been raised on a steady diet of literal questions, they are competent in finding the answers that are right there in the story.

It is imperative to move beyond this basic level of comprehension, however. Higher level comprehension is measured by questions that involve connecting to the text at a deeper level. In this case, students are asked to expand the meaning of what they are reading through connections, inferences, summarizing, synthesizing, analyzing, and critiquing, all higher level thinking skills (Fountas & Pinnell, 2001). Finding answers to these kinds of queries requires that readers piece together text information, add a dose of prior knowledge, and do a little speculating in order to come up with a feasible answer. When doing so, they are using more implicit information to reach higher levels of comprehension.

Students can learn to extend their thinking to these higher levels by using a strategy called **question-answer relationship (QAR),** which teaches them to recognize a taxonomy of relationships between specific kinds of questions and their related answers. Using this strategy, students learn how to identify the types of questions they are asked. They also learn how to determine appropriate sources of information to use to answer those questions. Raphael (1986) identified four levels of QARs that are divided into two basic categories (see Figure 8.7):

Figure 8.7

An overview of the question-answer relationship (QAR)

Category One: In the Book	Category Two: In My Head
Right There: Answers to literal level questions can be answered from information *right there* in the text.	*On My Own:* The answer is *not* in the text. The reader uses his own background experiences to answer the question. It is possible to answer the question without even reading the text.
Think and Search: The answer is in the story, but the reader must pull it together from two or more sentences in different parts of the text, *putting the answer together.*	*Author and Me*: The answer is *not* in the story. It is found in the reader's own background knowledge and from what the author offers in the text. Here, the ability to infer, to read between the lines, is a useful skill.

Category One: In the Book

Right There: The answer can be found easily within a single sentence in the story. This is a literal level question that simply requires students to recall explicit information.

Think and Search (Putting It Together): The answer is drawn from several sentences in the story requiring readers to connect different parts of the text.

Category Two: In My Head

On My Own: The answer is found in the student's background experiences, not in the story. It is probable that students could answer these particular questions without even reading the related text.

Author and Me: Now, a combination of information from the text and the reader's own background knowledge is used to answer a question. Students have to move beyond the text because the answer is not in the story.

Based upon her research with QARs, Raphael (1986) recommended that the teacher begin working with students to distinguish between the two basic categories of answers, those that can be located "In the Book" and how those differ from those that are "In My Head." The answers that are "In the Book" coincide with those literal answers that are right there or involve putting it together from different parts of the story. Questions that fall under the category of "In My Head" are those that are "On My Own" and "Author and Me" kinds of answers, inviting readers to go beyond what is so obvious in the text.

To model using the QARs, explain to the class that they typically go to two places to find answers to questions about what they are reading. One is to return to the book and skim through the text to look for the answer. The other is to think about what they already know and find the answer in the storehouse of information in their heads. Demonstrate this concept by selecting several individual text examples including two or three appropriate questions. Place each one on an overhead transparency or chart paper to be read aloud. Following each sample, ask listeners where they would find their answers to the questions you have posed—in the text or in their heads?

Work together until you are comfortable that the students understand the relationship between the kinds of questions being asked and the type of answer those questions require. Once they grasp the idea that sometimes the answer is right in the text while at other times they must search their memory stores, move on to focus on finding information just in the text. Work on sample lessons using examples of "Right There" and "Putting It Together," practicing with several reading selections until students can clearly demonstrate their understanding.

Finally, teach the students to work with the two processes involving questions from "In My Head" using "On My Own" and "Author and Me" with various practice selections until the concepts are grasped. To reinforce their learning and to help them make this information a permanent part of their reading schemata, tell students to develop their own questions as they read, trying to devise questions from each category periodically as an aid to monitoring their own comprehension. Teachers, too, can use QARs to assess their question-asking processes. If they are primarily asking the literal, "Right There" variety, they can modify their behavior accordingly.

An excellent way to assess students' mastery of this strategy is to place all four types of questions together after reading a particular selection and ask students to identify which one is which. Students must be actively engaged in using new skills and strategies if they are going to help them become better readers (Cambourne, 2001). A timely review could be scheduled with students who demonstrate any confusion. From time to time, reinforce students' understanding by having them examine published materials and identify the kinds of questions that are asked. The goal is to achieve automaticity or internalization of this process, rather than overusing it. An understanding of QARs leads naturally to the following explanation of inferential reading, another significant comprehension skill.

Inferential Reading

Teaching Strategy:
Making Inferences

Looking for an answer to an inferential question moves the reader into higher level comprehension as was stated previously. When students make an **inference** related to what they are reading, they are moving past the words on the page and onward to reading between the lines. Like a detective, they are piecing together collected information to get behind the words on the page. In this reasoning process, they are dipping into their schema to activate prior knowledge, combining that information with what the author is telling them explicitly, and coming up with a reasoned assumption about what is happening in the story. Dole, Duffy, Roehler, and Pearson (1991) state that "inference is the heart of the reading process" (p. 245).

Researchers have discovered that readers are more successful in using inference to strengthen comprehension when they are taught directly how to use it (Pearson & Fielding, 1996). Above average readers will grasp this higher level thinking strategy more readily than students with learning difficulties, but with proper instruction, all students can use inferencing successfully. Gordon (1989) outlines a straightforward process for the teacher to follow:

Step 1: Explain what is involved in making an inference: Harvey and Goudvis (2000) explain that "inferring is about reading faces, reading body language, reading expressions, and reading tone as well as reading text" (p. 105). When applied directly to the text, making an inference is taking information that is given to them by an author and thinking about similar experiences they may have had or have heard about. Then readers use those two kinds of information to draw conclusions or inferences about what is happening or may have happened already in the story. They are looking for **implicit meaning**, information that is not directly stated. Remind readers that no author tells the reader everything they need to know, so good readers must fill in the blanks. This process is what is commonly referred to as "reading between the lines." To scaffold students' understanding, illustrate the process using an example from a recently completed story while it is still fresh in readers' minds or connect it to real-world examples. For instance, if your mom looks like she is in a hurry to leave and you are going with her, you infer that it is not a good time to call a friend. Invite other examples from students.

Step 2: Model the process: Put several sentences or a short paragraph on the overhead or the chalkboard. Demonstrate the thinking process you go through as you digest and extend the text. Underline or circle clue words that trigger your thinking as you read the selection aloud. Then say something like, "This paragraph says that . . . Based upon what I know about . . . I inferred that . . . " Explain to the class how the key words helped to reason through to a conclusion. Work through two or three examples as needed.

When students possess effective questioning strategies, it is easier for them to grasp expository text.

Step 3: Share the task: Put the students to work with several examples, completing them as a class. Have the students read a paragraph. Then, ask an inferential question about the selection and listen to answers. Students must support their answers using their background knowledge, explaining how they reasoned their way to the inference.

Step 4: Additional practice: Try asking the students an inferential question. The students come up with an inference. Then the teacher must supply the evidence to justify their inference. For example, after reading the amusing *The True Story of the Three Little Pigs* (Scieszka, 1989), ask the students to examine the character of Alexander T. Wolf. What can they infer about Alexander T. Wolf based upon what they know from the original story, what they know from their experiences with this tale, and knowledge of wolves in general? The students may suggest that the wolf is guilty as charged. Then, the teacher must follow up their inference with his selected evidence: that being a large, strong animal, it is feasible that his sneezes could blow down a house or two, but he didn't stop to try to resuscitate those first two pigs, did he? Fact: Animals are a staple in a wolf's diet, and he wasn't content just eating two but was off to devour the third pig, and so forth. Play with the process a little, reversing roles until it appears that the students understand the steps in drawing an inference and supporting it.

Step 5: Integrate the process into a reading assignment: The teacher includes inferential questions after class assignments to measure how well the students are able to supply both the inference and the evidence to support their thinking. If the teaching, modeling, and practice have been successful, the students will be able to assume control of the strategy.

A final thought on reinforcing the use of inference: To monitor their practice and assimilation of this skill, students might periodically share the way they have inferred knowledge of a story in their literature response journals. Review lessons interspersed throughout the year on any of the reading strategies discussed in this chapter will keep skills fresh in students' minds.

Effective Questioning

Questions. There are those that promote learning and those that keep thinking skimming over the surface of the text. Sometimes the teacher asks them before, during, and after reading in a structured context. At other times they are posed effectively by the students to focus their own reading, keep them engaged, and help them monitor their understanding of what was read. In some instances,

> Curiosity spawns questions. Questions are the master key to understanding. Questions clarify confusion. Questions stimulate research efforts. Questions propel us forward and take us deeper into reading. (Harvey & Goudvis, 2000, p. 81)

Asking the right kinds of questions, authentic questions, is behind quality learning. As tools to reaching higher levels of comprehension, they bear some investigation.

Good questions aid students as they develop important concepts, build critical background information, clarify confusion, and stretch to higher level thinking. In short, the questions asked by the teacher hone comprehension and direct student attention to important aspects of the text (Simpson, 1996). Consider this. If you ask an explicit question, the student simply recalls facts from the text. While there is a place for that type of question, better learning occurs as a result of answering textually implicit questions like those used in the second category of QARs. One way to ensure that you are asking a variety of questions and reaching for higher level thinking is to follow a questioning taxonomy similar to Bloom's (1956) taxonomy of the cognitive domain. Following the steps, the teacher would ask a minimum of questions at the lower levels. Thinking skills then build for middle to upper grade students who are adept at answering questions from the higher levels. The taxonomy looks like this, from highest to lowest levels:

> **Evaluation:** Requires the reader to judge something against a standard.
>
> **Synthesis:** The reader creates or designs something that did not previously exist.
>
> **Analysis:** Requires a reader to break down complex information or ideas into simple parts to see how the parts relate to each other or are organized.
>
> **Application:** Requires the reader to use principles or abstractions to solve novel or real-life situations.
>
> **Comprehension:** The reader is involved in translating, interpreting, or extrapolating.
>
> **Knowledge:** The reader simply recalls information from the text.

In learning to recognize and then to be able to ask these different levels of questions, study the teacher's guides in the basal reading series. Put the questions from several stories into each of the categories to see how the creators of the teacher's guides have aspired to improve question asking beyond the literal level.

It isn't just a matter of asking the right kinds of questions, however. Teachers must teach students how to answer various kinds of questions as is done with the QAR process. Again, modeling how you answer the questions is an appropriate method of teaching. As was suggested in the QAR explanation, it is advisable for students to learn how to generate their own questions about various aspects of the story as a means of assessing their understanding. Then, balance the responsibility for generating good questions by inviting students to write their own to use in discussion groups. Simpson (1996) found that her students clearly enjoyed the challenge of coming up with questions to pose, to then explain, or to have other classmates answer. "By being encouraged to ask questions, direct the focus, and to set the agenda, children were inevitably more interested in the outcomes and the answers" (Simpson, 1996, p. 124).

When teaching students to develop questioning strategies, it is important that they see teachers model such behavior. In addition to the previous suggestions, another way to demonstrate asking questions at different thinking levels is to begin with a read aloud. Then write down teacher-generated questions that relate to the story on an overhead transparency. In this way students can see how questions grow out of a story and lead back to it again in the process of raising the level of thinking. Divide students into groups, pass out other books, and let students apply what they have seen modeled, eventually sharing the results to extend their understanding of this process.

An additional idea is to use two overhead projectors when teaching students to develop questions about a particular piece of writing. One overhead would display a passage from a piece of historical fiction, for example. Students would read through it together and work in pairs or triads to develop pertinent questions related to what they had read. The other overhead project would be used to record the questions that the class creates. Once again, the task is returned to the students who practice the questioning skills within another passage and work to develop probing questions (Harvey & Goudvis, 2000).

Young readers can clearly understand the difference in kinds of questions if you try this approach. Nancy Carnahan, a third-grade teacher, teaches knowledge about questioning by labeling the questions her students ask according to level of difficulty. Those at the literal level are the 25 cent questions while others increase in price as they inspire critical thinking, increasing in value up to the two dollar questions. Students quickly learn that questions that can be found readily in the text are 25 cent questions. Those that require inferential thinking, where there is no clear right or wrong answer, are deemed two dollar questions. This teacher has found a practical and appealing way to get her message across, hasn't she?

While there is no one set of questions that is superior to all others, Pressley (2000) admonishes teachers to teach children to ask questions that answer "why" especially when working with factually dense text. It this instance, learning is longer lasting because students are drawing on prior knowledge to make more sense of the text. Those "why" questions connect with making inferences. Being able to answer these kinds of queries involves more thorough processing of the text and an integration of text ideas with background knowledge, which enhances story understanding (Pearson & Fielding, 1996).

Additional advice is to strive to ask open-ended questions to prompt deeper reader response. Then, be gentle with learners by being accepting and supportive of all answers. Perhaps you can draw on prior knowledge right now and recall a time when you answered a question in class only to give the wrong answer. How did you feel? What behavior did that experience cause? It is probable that you did not answer the next question or the one after that either. Nothing stops thinking and contributing faster than being made an example of because you gave the wrong response. A final thought is offered by Simpson (1996): "But the bottom line is that if the children don't care about the answers, we may as well not bother with the questions" (p. 126). Questioning takes on a different look in the next strategy, another option for students to use independently.

SQ3R: A Tool for Expository Text

This widely taught strategy was developed by Robinson (1946/1961) as a study system for college students. It is also an appropriate study tool for upper elementary students because it is easily adapted to simpler nonfiction text. As students *survey, question, read, recite,* and *review,* they are provided with numerous exposures to the new materials being covered (Moore, Moore, Cunningham, & Cunningham, 2003). As with other new strategies, **SQ3R** is best presented by the teacher, who carefully models it and then engages the whole class in practice. Use it when study begins on a new chapter in social studies or science, work through each of the steps together, and then review it before it is used on the next chapter. This strategy is best maintained if students are reinforced in using it from time to time, but it should not be overly relied upon, and thus abused. Bored students will not be effective learners.

A handy chart posted for review or maintained in a content area journal might remind students to use it on their own when working with future fact-filled, content area text. The steps involve:

> **Survey:** The students quickly skim over the textbook material to be covered. They focus on boldfaced headings, subheadings, and titles to get a general idea of the content. Captions under pictures, graphs, charts, and vocabulary are also noted.
>
> **Question:** Based on that quick survey, students write prediction questions about the material to be covered.
>
> **Read:** Now the students read actively, looking for answers to the questions they posed.
>
> **Recite:** Students put the book aside and try to recall what they have read, talking through the possible answers and testing themselves on the text material. Going over difficult material aloud involves more than one sense, and that auditory feedback is often an effective way to grasp complex materials. Another option is to write down what they have learned. This is a good check on whether the material is clearly understood or not.
>
> **Review:** Students reread parts of the material to confirm the answers previously given. Then they take time to review their notes, their questions, or the material with a classmate. The teacher may also give a short quiz to assess students' comprehension of chapter content.

Be sure to return to this strategy from time to time. It takes practice to make using a new strategy a habit. Students will not use this technique if they are not reinforced in their efforts. It's that scaffolding process once again.

One method for improving comprehension that involves pulling together a number of different strategies and involves large group, small group, and individual work is implementing literature circles as part of the reading program. Intimidating at first, they connect so many of the skills and strategies that augment comprehension, that they should be included as part of the reading curriculum.

FACILITATING RESPONSE TO LITERATURE: LITERATURE CIRCLES

There is a hum in the classroom today. Looking somewhat chaotic, desks have been rearranged into circles or completely abandoned as a small group of students clusters in the corner. One group has actually spilled out into the hall for a little quiet thinking

Portfolio Activity:
Videotape

space. You circulate amidst the talk, talk, talk. **Literature circles** are meeting and these readers have something to say. The value of literature circles as a part of the classroom reading program is that they promote active thinking and engaged learners who are prompted in their efforts to understand a story via small group discussion. If you listen closely, you will recognize how thoughtful discussion is weaving listening, speaking, and thinking together as readers exchange ideas about the book they are reading, respond and react to the text and, then, to the ideas of others in their group. Successful learning involves just this type of social interaction (Allington, 2002; Cambourne, 2001).

Yes, it is noisy. Nearby, one group engages in a lively discussion of *Bud, Not Buddy* (Curtis, 1999), worrying that Bud may never find his father. Another group debates the current dilemma to be handled by *Maniac Magee* (Spinelli, 1990) as he faces prejudice head on. The group in the hall is digging through the layers of story, completely caught up in Stanley's camp life in *Holes* (Sachar, 1998). In the corner, the last group is examining the different characteristics that make for strong friendships and a winning team in *The View from Saturday* (Konigsburg, 1996). True, it may appear to be disorganized. But, in fact, the bottom line is that the ebb and flow of this spirited discussion is essential to quality learning.

Supported by theorists well versed in response theory, literature circles are an excellent method to augment opportunities for discussion (Daniels, 1994; Fountas & Pinnell, 2001). They provide an organizational strategy used to promote response to literature as the teacher and students read an article, story, or novel together. In this curricular structure, children are supported in "exploring their rough draft understanding" (Short, Harste, & Burke, 1996, p. 195) of the text they are reading, moving toward deeper understanding of the material through talk. Whether the primary reading program in the classroom is a basal series, the teacher firmly believes in a literature-based approach to reading, or the readers are exposed to a combination of the two, literature circles can be an integral part of each reading regimen. Regardless of the teacher's instructional preference, however, Cullinan (1987) emphasizes the importance of using literature as a part of it.

> Literature in a reading program does more than merely attract willing readers. Literature educates the imagination, provides language models, and molds the intellect. The heritage of humankind lies in books; we endow students with the key to their legacy when we teach them to read. (p. 6)

With such powerful and delightful reading material available to entice readers, it simply must be a part of the reading program (IRA/NCTE Standards, 1996). Readers should have a plethora of books available for free reading (Allington, 2002; Morrow & Gambrell, 2000). Then, they should use this rich, real literature in discussion groups like literature circles because it offers so much for students to discuss and to discover about themselves and the world around them (Daniels, 1994; Stanovich & Cunningham, 1993).

Within large and small group formats, fueled by student talk, transactions between reader and text are enhanced. It is a well-documented fact that constructing meaning and the use of higher level thinking skills are heightened through social interactions and student collaboration, initiated by a well-written book (Rosenblatt, 1978; Vygotsky, 1978; Zemelman et al., 1998). Talk enriches comprehension, and encouraging it, although it raises the noise level, is time well spent in the reading classroom. Researchers delved into the inner workings of literature circles and learned that:

- Even without direct questioning by their teacher, students' discussions revealed that they recalled information from the text, drew inferences, were able to support those inferences, and read critically (Eeds & Wells, 1989).
- Collaboration within the groups aided readers in constructing meaning and clearing up confusion. Students readily divided up roles, took turns, negotiated leadership responsibilities, and sought out other resources to help interpret the text (Almasi, 1995; Eeds & Wells, 1989).
- Students applied strategic reading behaviors like hypothesizing, interpreting, predicting, confirming, generalizing, and evaluating as they explored different interpretations of literature (McKee, 1992).

In short, literature circles have much to offer both reader and teacher as a critical part of the reading curriculum. They provide an arena for "co-construction of knowledge, advance student learning, and provide opportunities for students to learn important interpersonal skills while conversing, interpreting, and negotiating in active and constructive ways" (Gambrell, 1996, p. 35).

While there is no one best way to use literature circles, there are some general guidelines to follow in preparing students to use them successfully:

1. **Select the literature to be used:** High-quality picture books that will engender lively discussions are perfect choices to begin literature circle work in both primary and upper grades. Upper grade students can practice sharing their responses within a brief text and savor sumptuous art and story at the same time. Primary grade readers will be working comfortably with books already an integral part of their everyday lives. Later, move older readers on to a short novel that is read by the whole class but is discussed in chunks of text in smaller groups of students.

   As students become adept at conversation and collaboration, offer an expanded selection of fine titles. In this case, the teacher book talks a collection of titles. They might revolve around a similar theme but present it from different perspectives, represent award-winning pickings, or the books might highlight a particular genre, including poetry and nonfiction. A memorable tie-in with social studies content can be made when book selections are set during a period of history currently under study (Farris, 2001). Sage advice is to choose a familiar genre as beginning fare. Previous experience with that genre raises the comfort level, while trying this new strategy taps a wealth of prior knowledge and increases the odds that students will have a positive literature circle experience (Wiencek & O'Flahavan, 1994).

2. **Organize the discussion circles:** The size of the group will depend on the size of the class and the number of students interested in a book. Groups may

vary from three to eight students, with five to six as the ideal. The goal is to generate rich discussion, experience a diversity of thinking, and have an opportunity to scrutinize different classmates' perspectives throughout the year (Wiencek & O'Flahavan, 1994). Note that students who rarely speak up in class will be less intimidated in a small group setting and thus be more willing to share their thoughts and reactions. Depending on the purpose for the groups, the teacher may set them up initially herself, selecting for success, and then give students a choice in joining ensuing circles throughout the year. In the latter situation, students benefit additionally because they have more control over their learning. Furthermore, having a personal choice in reading matter increases motivation, could better address individual needs, and certainly taps individual interests. An efficient way to handle student choice when a collection of different books is used is to have them sign up for the respective circles based upon interest. Students write down their first two choices and turn them into the teacher, who makes up the groups based upon student preferences (Short, Harste, & Burke, 1996).

3. **Starting the circles:** To demonstrate how literature circles work, model the format using a picture book read by the whole class. One option is for the teacher to read the book aloud while students follow along in their own texts. A small demonstration circle settles up in front of the class with the teacher as a facilitating member. This group will discuss the picture book with the teacher leading the initial discussion so that the entire class gets a sense of the process. Based upon that scaffolding, the rest of the class is divided into groups, perhaps with one demonstration group member in each group. They continue any additional discussion of the book just read. Then, the group reads another picture book and practices the process within their group. At this point, the teacher becomes the facilitator, moving from group to group to keep conversation flowing, to prompt if the talk stops or gets sidetracked, and to gather student input on how they think the circles are working. Another option for generating student talk during the initial stages of literature circles is "Say Something," more fully explained in the following Teaching Strategy for the Classroom box (Short et al., 1996). Like other strategies being taught to the students, it must be carefully modeled so that they understand how to use it.

Teaching Strategy for the Classroom

SAY SOMETHING

EXPLANATION

"Say Something" involves students working in pairs as they read a selected text aloud, one reader at a time. It is a response strategy that promotes student talk and careful listening, and encourages active involvement in reading. The whole class might break into pairs or triads to read a story in this manner. Once the work has been completed, the class regroups to share thoughts, inspirations, or questions. Using this strategy involves even the quietest of readers and gives everyone a responsive voice. The strategy moves across the curriculum with ease as students take on expository text and digest it carefully two readers at a time. For this to be most effective, teachers should model this strategy a number of times to reinforce appropriate things to say.

MATERIALS

(1) Two copies of the text. It may be fiction or nonfiction depending on student choice or the teacher's request. (2) A brief written direction sheet may be needed to scaffold learning when students try this the first few times. (3) A cassette recorder to record student discussions.

DIRECTIONS

- Find a reading partner.
- Bring the text and directions to a relatively distraction-free spot in the classroom.
- Decide which reader will begin. While she is reading aloud, her partner is following along in the text and listening attentively.
- When the first reader stops at a spot of her choice, both partners say something about the text. They may retell a bit of it, talk about personal connections, ask a question to clarify understanding, predict what might happen next, or other observations.
- The next person takes up the reading while the partner follows along.
- The process is repeated until the text has been completed.
- Summarize the reading session and share with the whole class if desired.

AN ASSESSMENT MEASURE

As students are practicing this strategy and using it from time to time throughout the year, the teacher circulates around the room, monitoring progress and ensuring participation in the process. A hovering teacher has an amazing impact on keeping students focused. A portable cassette recorder is handy to record several conversations. Later, the recordings can be reviewed as an assessment measure to check mastering and responsible participation during the "Say Something" activity.

Source: Adapted from Short, K. G., Harste, J. C., & Burke, C. (1996). *Creating classrooms for authors and inquirers,* (2nd ed). Portsmouth, NH: Heinemann.

Beginning literature circle participants may benefit more fully from their reading and discussing experiences if each member has a particular job or role to help facilitate discussion and purposeful reading. Roles and titles can be adjusted to meet the ages of the readers. Primary grade roles might include:

Discussion Director: Brings questions to the group to help increase the understanding of the story.

Word Wizard: Finds interesting words to share.

Super Summarizer: Writes a summary of assigned reading focusing on main ideas.

Raving Reader: Picks passages to share with the group and explains why those passages were selected.

Checker: Checks that assignments in the group were finished, watches to be sure that everyone in the group participates, and then evaluates the group.

Illustrious Illustrator: Chooses a scene from the day's reading to illustrate, includes important details, and shares the passage that accompanies the illustration.

When students move to shorter novels or longer texts, their personal responsibility increases. They meet in their respective groups to decide how many chapters are to be read before each meeting. Then, they read independently, taking time to note interesting words, phrases, questions, or even to sketch reactions in their literature response journals or on notebook paper set aside for circle work. Notes might be kept on self-sticking notes tacked to key spots in the text for quick reference. Those notes become the fuel for talk in preparation for the next circle meeting.

To encourage the development of multiple perspectives group members might use Character Perspective Charts, with each member taking a different character or working in pairs on a specific character. Refer to the segment on story mapping and the specific example provided in Figure 8.6. Discussions will certainly be lively as circle participants begin to get inside the heads of assorted characters and attempt to present their sides of the story during circle discussions.

If readers with reading problems or language barriers are a part of a group and the text selection seems difficult for them despite the fact that it is the book of their choice, teachers have several alternatives. The student can buddy read with another member of the group, reading the selected pages aloud together. The book can also be audiotaped so that the reader can easily keep up with group members by following along with the tape during independent reading time.

4. **Keeping discussions going:** Group discussion sessions are often ten to twenty minutes in length. The students discuss notes they have taken or work they have done to meet their group goals. The task is to respond to the literature being read. The teacher may scaffold discussions by supplying open-ended questions or prompts initially, and remove them as the groups gain experience and can stay on task with relative ease. Another way to connect reader and text is suggested by Harvey and Goudvis (2000), who teach their students to "leave tracks of their thinking" in the margins of their books, tracking their thinking with sticky notes. These tracks would help students in their group discussions. A teacher might follow those tracks, as well, in the process of monitoring a child's comprehension of a story. Model how to connect with texts by using a think aloud process, making your thinking visible when you show as clearly as possible how you interact with text, what connections you make, what happens when a question arises, and how you infer or predict.

Demonstrate how you leave tracks by using a picture book with which you can connect personally, that taps your prior knowledge. Have a notepad of sticky notes handy as you begin to read the book aloud. Write the following codes on the chalkboard:

T-S: text to self:

These are connections made between myself and the text based on my previous experiences.

T-T: text to text:

These are connections I make between this text and another one I have read. That might even include a poem or a song.

T-W: text to the world:

These are connections I make between what I am reading and current events, world issues, or problems.

Discuss the codes with the class. Tell them that you are going to use the letter codes for appropriate reactions you have as you read, that you will jot a few reminders on the note, and then move on with your reading. Later, you will return to these sticky notes during group discussions as reminders of comments and reactions you want to share in your discussion group.

Begin reading the selected book aloud. Explain to the class why you picked that particular title, how you relate to the story, and that you are going

These students are relating T-S, T-T, and T-W connections as part of the discussion of their assigned reading.

to think aloud as you pause to write out the notes illustrating various connections with the text. This sharing aloud will demonstrate what a good reader does when interacting with text and is a process that students will try later themselves. Thus, when you come to a part of the story that causes a personal reaction, stop briefly and jot down the letter code along with a few words on a sticky note to identify your feelings, thoughts, or connections. Then, attach it to that spot in the text, explain your thinking and reactions to the students, and then continue reading. Upon completion of the story, ask students if they understand the process, answer any questions, and then give them practice time to try it themselves.

Students work in groups of three, reading a story aloud, stopping to add sticky notes as individual members make connections, and then moving on through the text. Rotate from group to group, monitoring progress and supporting as needed. In the future, when students move to individual reading, they are to continue the tracking process. Again, monitor their work in brief conferences. This comprehension monitoring technique can be adapted to include codes for questions, an important idea or theme, or to highlight those "Ah-ha!" moments (Harvey & Goudvis, 2000).

Certainly it would become tedious if one had to stop and code their thinking this way with everything that was read. This is a strategy that can be returned to from time to time for some readers while others may depend on tracking their thinking on a regular basis.

During literature circles there is a concerted effort to move away from the typical teacher-led, teacher-dominated discussions toward a student-centered, literary discussion. As thinkers, students are continually being challenged. As listeners, they are given an opportunity to broaden their personal beliefs as they hear the interpretations and ideas of others (Eeds & Wells, 1989).

5. **Concluding the circle activities:** As circle work ends, students decide if they want to share their book with the entire class in an innovative way. Remember that not all books have to be shared. Students should tackle a creative activity only if they are enthusiastic about their books. Like the dreaded required book reports of years past, extension activities can quickly take on a negative tone if they are continually mandated. Students should take some time to recap the book and their conversations about it, however, before moving on to the next reading activity. This gives them an opportunity for closure and to clear up any lingering confusion.

Do not be lulled into thinking that literature circles are an easy solution to teaching reading. Properly organized and thoughtfully designed, they require a good deal of effort. As such, it would be judicious to use them intermittently throughout the year, rather than as a steady diet. The teacher simply does not relinquish teaching responsibilities when the circles are in progress. Think about the fact that before the circles meet for the day, a mini-lesson on circle procedures can be taught, literary elements might be investigated, ideas for response activities could be suggested, tips for maintaining focused discussions could be offered, and so forth. After circles have met, the class reconvenes for a brief time to share highlights of discussions or raise and examine questions that have emerged.

Furthermore, teacher evaluation and student reflective self-evaluations are ongoing. In this mode, the teacher moves from group to group, writing brief notes on student performance, monitoring the involvement of every student, and watching to see if a few students need the extra support of a short teaching session on a particular skill. Students become a part of the evaluation as the circle concludes and they engage in self-evaluation. What worked? What could have gone better? Why? Personal reflections and individual progress can be discussed in periodic individual conferences with the teacher. Selected information then becomes a part of parent–teacher conferences that highlight each individual's emerging reading skills. While it may not be perceived as such on the surface, there is a tremendous amount of learning going on in a well-organized, carefully modeled literature circle.

SUSTAINED SILENT READING (SSR)

As we end this chapter on comprehension, it is with the admonition that teachers not forget the maxim "Practice makes perfect." Time should be set aside in every class-room day where students read quietly alongside the teacher, who is also engrossed in a captivating book. Honoring the value of reading in this way, modeling its impor-tance as a respected part of the classroom routine, confirms the fact that reading is simply an integral part of life. In the often-quoted text *Becoming a Nation of Read-ers* (Anderson et al., 1985), the authors remark that "reading, like playing a musical instrument, is not something that is mastered once and for all at a certain age. Rather, it is a skill that continues to improve through practice" (p. 16).

Classroom teachers tuned in to the importance of reading as a regular part of the diet have an answer to the amusing query by Richard Allington (1977), who won-dered, "If they don't read much, how they ever gonna get good?" Part of the answer lies in practices like **Sustained Silent Reading**, a time set aside every single day, where everyone in the school in some cases (including the principal, secretaries, custodial staff, cooks—everyone on the premises), or in individual classes in other cases, reads something of their choice (McCracken & McCracken, 1978). One won-derful benefit of this part of the day is that everyone is equal. Good readers and those who are not so adept read side by side with no one checking on reading levels. Read-ers may select information books or fiction, depending on their own personal prefer-ences. Personal choice is the key. Simple steps to follow when setting up SSR are:

1. Designate a time each day for silent reading and stick to it barring fire drills, bloody noses, specials like art and music, and occasional welcomed assemblies. Popular times for independent reading are first thing in the morning, following lunch or recess, or just before leaving school for the day. Very young readers might begin with five minutes, older readers just ten minutes, and work up to twenty to thirty by the end of the year depending on grade level and abilities.

2. Teach the rules and expectations of Sustained Silent Reading during a few mini-lessons. Put class rules on a chart for easy reference. General rules state that children must select their own books, that they take several books or magazines to their seats so that they are not interrupting other readers when they look for something different, and that everyone reads silently with no interruptions. In primary grades students may read in a quiet voice. It seems that one of the most difficult things for children to do is to settle on a book, so one essential mini-lesson should revolve around book selection (Reutzel & Galli, 1998). Model how you find a book. Demonstrate how you look at the book's cover, read the inside blurbs on the cover, sample a few pages, or look at some of the illustrations. If they are in doubt, remind students to take two or three books, especially when they are at the beginning reader stages, to their desks and sample them there.

3. Students are also told that there are no book reports or presentations required for materials read during SSR. A good idea, however, is to have students share what they are reading several times during the week, knowing that talk facilitates comprehension. You might simply give a signal for Chat Time and students have the opportunity to talk to a neighbor for five minutes about their book. The neighbor gets a turn as well, and then transition to the next class activity. This particular step takes SSR beyond the realm of mere practice when you look at it in the light cast by Wilson (1992, p. 163), who reinforces the value of talk.

> Reading becomes something that students do because of friendship, because their friends read. More important, sharing their thoughts and feelings about books becomes part of the intellectual currency of their social relations within the classroom. Reading becomes part of the culture of the classroom.

In addition to building a reading community, reading and then reading some more promotes fluency, builds vocabulary, and expands background knowledge (Pressley, 2000). Automatic word recognition is enhanced based on frequent encounters with words when students practice regularly. Furthermore, reading a variety of literature increases a reader's knowledge about topics of interest (Stanovich & Cunningham, 1993). Without a doubt, independent reading, whether it is done in class or at home, is strongly tied to gains in reading achievement (Allington, 2002; Cunningham & Allington, 2003; Zemelman et al., 1998).

In sum, when teaching reading, the teacher provides the building blocks to bolster reading ability. She continually surrounds her students with a fabulous array of fiction and nonfiction materials. Day in and day out, she teaches and models effective strategies to decipher words and make sense of the author's message. As needed, she motivates children to read in a number of authentic and practical ways. She enthusiastically models her love of reading, talks about books she enjoys, and then adds a dollop of independent reading time. As often as is feasible, she enlists the support of parents and guardians to extend reading practices at home. It is a formula guaranteed to enrich the lives of every reader. With an extra bit of help here, a change in materials there, and care devoted to each individual diet, the reading health of all of the participants will be robust indeed.

 ## COMPREHENSION STRATEGIES FOR DIVERSE LEARNERS

Adaptations for diverse learners have been suggested throughout the chapter. In addition, note that research supports the use of literature circles for students with second language adaptations (Samway & Whang, 1996) and also with other learners with special needs (Giles, 1990). The coaching and support from classmates, the modeling those learners do as they interact with books, and the opportunities to read books aloud together within the literature circle format can make the literary community a friendlier place to be for these readers. Furthermore, more teacher-contact time in the form of short conferences and more frequent opportunities to read with an adult will benefit children with learning disabilities, those with mild mental retardation, and others struggling with attention deficit difficulties (Cunningham et al., 2000). A teacher aide or parent volunteer can add additional adult contact, be certain the student has appropriate reading materials, and can clear up misunderstandings to be sure comprehension is not impaired.

Web Link:
Learning Strategies
Database

A popular way to engage parents and guardians and provide opportunities to practice language is to send home a book bag with a child at least once a week. While this is an excellent activity for all children, students with language processing difficulties or mild mental retardation will particularly benefit from the additional practice it affords. Students select a favorite book to read to someone at home, or the book bags can be prepared by the teacher ahead of time and rotated between readers. As you have already read, a single, interesting activity to extend discussion of the book should be included. Perhaps an inexpensive toy or small puppet might accompany the book to encourage further language use. In second language homes, the parents can even practice their English as they read the book along with their child. The gifted reader can select a challenging book to read as well as to demonstrate his accomplishments to an appreciative audience. A lively discussion following the reading will also extend this reader's comprehension skills.

Readers of all abilities enjoy creating their own books. Students with learning disabilities or mild mental retardation can dictate their stories to a volunteer to eliminate the hurdle of writing. English language learners might dictate their stories in their native language initially. A second copy of the book could be written in English, or the English version can be written below the first text so that the child can read his story in two languages. All writers illustrate their stories. Then, these books can be read aloud to a class partner, shared with the class as a whole, and then taken home to be read to parents and guardians. Students of all abilities are practicing language, learning to follow a story line, and gaining reading fluency at the same time. While the gifted student would not need extensive guidance, he joins his classmates in a creative process, writing and illustrating a creation to share as well.

Poetry is another appealing venue with which to build language skills for students with language deficits and English language learners (Hadaway, Vardell, & Young, 2001). Oral language skills, vocabulary understanding, fluency, and just plain fun with language are scaffolded as students listen to poems read aloud, participate with classmates in chanting poems, and later listen to them again in a listening center. Soon these struggling readers will be reading them aloud on their own. An additional option is to use poems to teach about who the main character is, and this can be accomplished within a narrative poem. Often neglected, poetry is an especially powerful learning tool for students with attention deficit disorders as well because each piece is short and seemingly more manageable as a result. These particular learners do much better with short reading assignments and repetition, familiar characteristics of poetry. A boon to English language learners is that poems are available in several different languages, inviting students to read them in their own language and in the new one. For example, upper grade readers will savor realistic poems in *The Tree Is Older Than You Are* (Nye, 1995), while younger readers might try *Confetti: Poems for Children* (Mora, 1999) or *Around the World in Eighty Poems* (Berry, 2002).

 ## ENHANCING LEARNING WITH TECHNOLOGY

As technology gains a greater toehold in the reading curriculum, teachers have another direction in which to cast their attention. They must extend their planning time to include research into the content of CD-ROM offerings and safe, informative websites to enrich the current curriculum. Another piece of that planning time will be devoted to continued professional development to enrich technical skills because you will be learning to operate a variety of programs. Don't tackle technological development on your own. Instead, form a network of supportive colleagues who can answer questions and troubleshoot frustrating problems along the way (Wepner & Tao, 2002). Be assured that investing in technology is time wisely spent.

One place to begin is to investigate software programs like those suggested throughout this textbook, learn what is available for classroom use in your school, and evaluate their quality using the guidelines in Chapter 3. Some of the interactive books at primary grades are more than entertaining. They have a read aloud, read along feature that will help a visually impaired student, children with reading difficulties, and English language learners learn such skills as sight word vocabulary, use of context, and how to properly pronounce words. A plus is that a number of these programs are in Spanish; therefore, English-speaking children have the opportunity to polish their Spanish skills. An appealing example is *Reader Rabbit's Reading Development Library* (The Learning Company, 2002). The Level 4 Library includes two popular fairy tales, "King Midas" and "The Ugly Duckling." Students can read along with a character, have the tales read aloud to them, and then work with a story map or letter writing skills. They learn about different perspectives because each tale is told from several points of view, the original tale and then from the perspectives of two different characters. Another offering by this company will appeal to young children who love the popular books about Arthur. Now they meet his kid sister in *D. W. the Picky Eater,* which features Arthur's sister in an interactive story that builds reading, vocabulary, and storytelling skills (The Learning Company, 1999).

Software for middle to upper grade readers that works across the curriculum includes two offerings in the *Talking Walls* series (Edmark, 1999). As students read each beautifully illustrated page of text, they are also learning about historical, cultural, and social issues, along with intriguing stories about some of the world's fascinating walls. Another option for improving reading skills across the curriculum is directed at gifted readers and other middle grade science sleuths. They will quickly become engrossed in *The Wreck of the Fortuna Dourada* (Videodiscovery, Inc., 1996), an interactive content area software package that involves humor, problem solving, reading, and science skills. If you are engaged in thematic teaching and the topic is the sea, investigate the appealing *Field Trip to the Sea* (Sunburst Communications, 1999). Adding quality software to your classroom reading curriculum and selections that work across the curriculum is an expensive option. Often school licenses are available that allow you to share copies of the programs between classrooms. This is a prime opportunity to collaborate with colleagues to locate the best software to meet the needs of the school population.

In general, diverse learners who require more repetition to master a skill will profit from the opportunity to work again and again with a story until skills in the software program are mastered. Not quite as personable as an individual tutor, well-conceived, interactive software programs add a helpful dimension to the reading curriculum. While many of the software programs currently available can be adapted to the needs of diverse learners, there is also software especially for special needs students. Primary grade learners with special needs in the areas of fluency, articulation, and/or language disorders will become quickly engaged with *Tiger's Tale* (Laureate Learning Systems, 1998). Students use a microphone and become the voice of an animated tiger who cannot talk. Other story characters ask questions and encourage responses from the child. Eventually, the student can play back the movie and savor the satisfaction of hearing his own voice accompanying the tale.

Excellent Software Options

The Internet

The Internet offerings simply boggle one's mind as they expand continuously. If the classroom has Internet access, a list of safe and educationally sound sites could be developed by the school staff and posted in the classroom computer centers. See the options listed on the Online Learning Center. One choice for furthering comprehension skills could involve daily interaction as a class or individually with education via the Internet. *The World of Reading* brings readers and books together by enabling students to read a "wired book." A wonderful extension is that readers can then write a book review and post it on the Web, an excellent reading-writing-comprehension pairing. *The Alphabet Superhighway* polishes a variety of reading skills as will other Internet sites listed below. Excellent websites exist that celebrate one culture after another. They offer appealing options for readers who are just beginning to make sense of the written word to gifted readers who are questing for content to meet their needs.

Web Links:
Alphabet Superhighway

Cultures of the World

Hot Links to Literature

K–5 Cybertrail:
Multicultural Resources

Child Lit

The World of Reading

NCIP

The Scoop

Be sure to spend some time investigating their riches. In sum, there are excellent learning opportunities proffered by Internet resources, so stay abreast of what is new as another memorable educational option.

Teaching Strategy for the Classroom

TECHNOLOGY AND READER RESPONSE

As discussed throughout this chapter, responding to literature in a thoughtful manner by discussing it with classmates is an effective way to deepen comprehension. A technological twist can be added to a discussion, specifically by engaging in e-mail discussions. These conversations can cross the school, town, city, country, or world. Careful preparations ahead of time will ensure that such long-distance conversations move along with relatively few problems. The realm of technology is not without its glitches, of course, but modeling expectations and giving students time to practice before connecting with other students should eliminate as many problems as possible. Below are the objectives and a sequence of steps that might be followed in moving readers' conversations outside of the classroom.

OBJECTIVES:

- To integrate the language arts (reading, writing, listening, and speaking).
- To motivate readers to reflect upon what they are reading.
- To practice and participate in literature circles in the classroom and further afield.

ORGANIZATION

Locate a teacher who is willing to work with you. The Web addresses below or a willing university professor who teaches reading, children's literature, or language arts methods courses would be a place to start (Sullivan, 1998).

- Select four or five book titles and divide your students into small groups, one group per title. The partner classroom will do the same.
- Teach the students how to look for specific points in the book as part of their regular literature circle process. Suggestions include watching for character development, discussing a possible theme, reviewing points in the plot, and raising personal questions. Partner readers so that students with language deficits or mild mental retardation can read the selected book together with a classmate. A parent volunteer or upper grade student can read the books onto tapes so that these readers can listen to them multiple times to master vocabulary and the story line.

- Have students write a paragraph to introduce themselves to their reflection partner. It would be fun to scan a picture in to accompany the paragraph if possible. The participating class will do the same. Exchange information with the e-mail partner.
- Practice word-processing the responses to be sent to the partner classroom. Before students send them, they are to be checked by the teacher or the classroom aide to be certain they are reflective, cover focus points, and stay on target. Partner students who might need support in writing with accomplished classmates or the classroom aide. Children with visual handicaps or English language learners might dictate their responses to a classmate, which will be checked by the classroom aide.
- Students may be taught to cut and paste their approved responses onto the e-mail site or older students might retype them as a regular e-mail.
- Be sure to print out and to monitor the return e-mails to be certain that the students are replying to their reflective partners' ideas and questions, creating an ongoing dialogue. If the computer has a speech component, the visually impaired student can have responses read to him. Otherwise, assign a partner to relay the responses. Children with hearing difficulties will thrive using this form of technological communication, something they may already rely upon throughout the day.

Note: Sullivan (1998) involved her preservice education majors with an elementary classroom in a successful effort to engage them in using quality literature, to provide an opportunity for them to interact with children, and to teach them about the nature of response. Both children and teachers-in-training found the e-mail journaling to be a valuable experience. This lesson might begin within the school with conversations between classrooms or in the community. Once the process is mastered, e-mail reflections can continue with new friends in faraway places.

WEBSITES TO BE ACCESSED FOR THIS ACTIVITY

ePALS http://www.epals.com *ePALS* is described as the largest online classroom community. It consists of over 2 million students and teachers in 182 countries who are writing back and forth to each other and working on joint projects. Ideas for interactive projects and other teacher resources are also available.

Keypals http://www.keypals.com/p/keypals.html An extensive master list of listservs from different organizations that link teachers to teachers, classrooms to classrooms, and individual students to other students.

Intercultural E-mail Classroom Connections http://www.stolaf.edu/network/iecc If you are looking for e-mail conversations with response partners in other countries, this site has several listservs for teachers looking for partner classrooms.

Rigby/Heinemann Global Keypals http://www.reedbooks.com.au/heinemann/global/global1.html This site is located in Australia. It offers an opportunity for teachers and students to develop keypal correspondence. Keypals are grouped by three different age levels: 5–10, 11–13, and 14–18.

Summary

Reading comprehension refers to a transaction between reader and author as the reader actively makes meaning from the written word. It is a decidedly complex process that becomes more manageable through careful instruction, teacher modeling, and a lifetime of practice. Teacher modeling is especially important when teaching a new strategy to students. Opportunities to actively engage in practicing each newly presented skill solidify learning. Strategies to strengthen comprehension range from those that are teacher-directed to others that can be used independently once they are mastered.

One effective way to practice a number of valuable skills is by participating in literature circles. Carefully organized by the teacher, this learning environment fosters thinking through student talk as they hypothesize, interpret, predict, confirm, generalize, and evaluate literature together. In addition, research reminds us that students who read become better readers, so free choice reading programs like Sustained Silent Reading (SSR) are essential in the literacy curriculum. This is a time when everyone is equal as all children are reading personally selected materials with no grade level issues. Special attention must be devoted to learners with diverse abilities whose needs can also be met in appealing and positive ways. From teacher-directed to student controlled, from large group to individual applications, from real book to technological support, the skills and strategies suggested in this chapter are meant to be employed flexibly to assist and support the growth of comprehension.

Chapter Review

Go to the Online Learning Center at **www.mhhe.com/farrisreading** to take chapter quizzes, practice with key terms, and review important content.

Main Points

- Reading comprehension involves an actively engaged reader making meaning from the text.

- Activating prior knowledge is essential to the comprehension process. Each person brings different background experiences to a reading situation that can enrich a reading experience when books are discussed in large or small groups.

- Knowledge of a number of different strategies to build comprehension is essential for every reading teacher. Strategies range from those that are more teacher-directed to those that can be used independently.

- When a new skill or strategy is taught, learners benefit from scaffolding support by the teacher.

- Thinking aloud makes the thought process visible so students can understand how they might work with a new comprehension strategy themselves.

- The Directed Reading Activity (DRA) involves five steps: preparation, directed reading, skill or strategy development, follow-up practice, and enrichment.

- The Directed Reading Thinking Activity (DRTA) actively involves readers in building metacognitive abilities by sampling text, making predictions, and confirming or readjusting those predictions in a repetitive process.

- Reciprocal teaching is an interactive group process that facilitates comprehension through predicting, questioning, seeking clarification, and summarization.

- The K-W-L-Plus strategy engages the whole class in learning about a topic, recording knowledge on individual or a class chart, and then summarizing their learning through writing.

- When students use a story map, they are working with their schema for stories. Story maps can take on different forms. One type of map, the Character Perspective Chart, focuses on the characters and their different viewpoints.

- When using the question-answer relationship (QAR) students learn to recognize the different kinds of questions they ask themselves as they read, including literal and inferential questions. They also learn where to go for the answers to those questions.

- Inferential reading involves the reader in moving beyond the words on the page to gathering meaning by reading between the lines.

- Asking the right kinds of questions can facilitate comprehension. Good questions aid learners in developing important concepts. Aim for higher level questions, especially as students move into the middle grades.

- Literature circles actively involve readers as they read to fulfill a particular role in their small group and learn from each other through dialoguing about a book. The teacher puts a great deal of effort in the preparation, organization, and continued teaching during literature circles.

- Students improve in their reading abilities through practice, and that means reading.

Time must be set aside during the school day for independent reading through activities like Sustained Silent Reading.

- Diverse learners benefit from support from classmates, extra time with the teacher or an aide, literature circle work, making their own books, reading at home, and reading and writing on the computer using interactive software or Internet sites.

- Carefully selected software and previously previewed Internet sites can extend and enrich the reading comprehension program in your classroom.

Key Terms

Reflecting and Reviewing

1. Think back over your experiences in school. How do you remember being taught reading comprehension strategies? Does anything stand out in your mind as being particularly effective? Is there a strategy in this chapter that you are eager to try? Why?

2. Would you say that you are a good reader? Do you like to read? Why or why not? How do you feel about reading a book on the computer? What might be the advantages or disadvantages of such an experience?

3. The strategies sampled in this chapter range from clearly teacher-directed to those that are more student-directed. Which strategies will you be the most comfortable working with? Are you willing to use literature circles in your classroom? How would you prepare yourself and the students for their first experience with these interactive sessions?

Children's Literature

For annotations of the books listed below, please see Appendix A.

Berry, James (ed.). (2002). *Around the World in Eighty Poems*. (K. Lucas, Illus.). New York: Chronicle.

Curtis, Paul C. (1999). *Bud, Not Buddy*. New York: Delacorte.

Gilliland, Judith H. (2000). *Steamboat! The Story of Captain Blanche Leathers.* (H. Meade, Illus.). New York: Dorling Kindersley.

Konigsburg, E. L. (1996). *The View from Saturday.* New York: Atheneum.

Mayer, Mercer. (1999). *Shibumi and the Kitemaker.* New York: Marshall Cavendish.

Mora, Pat. (1999). *Confetti: Poems for Children.* New York: Lee & Low.

Nye, Naomi Shihab. (1995). *The Tree Is Older Than You Are: A Bilingual Gathering of Stories and Poems from Mexico with Paintings by Mexican Artists.* New York: Simon and Schuster.

Paulsen, Gary. (1987). *Hatchet.* New York: Macmillan.

Sachar, Louis. (1998). *Holes.* New York: Delacorte.)

San Souci, Robert D. (1989). *The Talking Eggs: A Folktale from the American South.* (J. Pinkney, Illus.). New York: Dial Books.

Scieszka, Jon. (1989). *The True Story of the 3 Little Pigs!* (L. Smith, Illus.). New York: Viking.

Spinelli, Jerry. (1990). *Maniac Magee.* Boston: Little Brown.

Tavares, Matt. (2000). *Zachary's Ball.* Cambridge, MA: Candlewick Press.

Classroom Teaching Resources

Cunningham, P. M., Hall, D. P., & Cunningham, J. W. (2000). *Guided reading: The four-blocks way (with building blocks and big blocks variations).* Greensboro, NC: Carson-Dellosa.

Miller, W. (2000). *Strategies for developing emergent literacy.* Dubuque, IA: McGraw Hill.

Robb, L. (1995). *Reading strategies that work: Teaching your students to become better readers.* New York: Scholastic.

"If you were to speak a small language (and there are such languages) where there is no word for blue, you could not think about the color blue. So in our language, if I do not know the meaning of words like subtle, incisive, touchy, crass, then I will not know what these things are in life and my thoughts and intelligence are diminished. Every word in our language has a meaning and a place all its own. Every word I do not know is a thought and an understanding I cannot have."

Rosemary Wells, award-winning author of children's books

CHAPTER 9

Vocabulary Instruction in a Balanced Literacy Program

Key Ideas

- There is more than one kind of vocabulary.
- Increasing word recognition ability, expanding vocabulary, and improving comprehension are three closely related, essential ingredients in a balanced reading program.
- Vocabulary acquisition is a complex process that cannot be left to chance.
- While there is no one "best" way to teach vocabulary skills, there are effective methods for helping children to increase their word knowledge.
- Children's vocabulary knowledge closely reflects their background of real-life and vicarious experiences.
- Children must be actively engaged in learning new words in order for them to become a permanent part of their personal vocabularies.
- There is no replacement for **wide reading** as it facilitates vocabulary growth, language development, and broadens one's general understanding of the world.

Questions to Ponder

- What do we mean when we talk about one's vocabulary?
- What is the relationship between vocabulary and reading comprehension?
- What classroom methods are the most productive in helping students of varying abilities increase their vocabularies?
- How can educators help diverse learners to increase their word knowledge?
- What options does technology provide to increase students' word knowledge?

Peering into the Classroom

Words! Words! Words!

There is always something innovative going on in Mrs. Osmundson's sixth grade classroom. Let's stop in for a few minutes and see what the students are involved with today. We slip into a room filled with the quiet murmur of conversation, the rustling of newspaper pages, and the snip, snip, snip of scissors. The students have been challenged to find words from past issues of the newspaper that describe themselves. Then they are to search for other words that identify items they do not like. Each student has a brown paper lunch bag in front of them. They have used markers to write their names clearly in the center of one side of the bag. Armed with glue sticks, they are busily covering every inch of outside space with choice words, words, words. The items that find their way inside the bag are loose, reflecting those least favorite items. It is obvious that these students are totally engaged in the process of word collection. You almost want to take a paper bag and start a quest for words yourself, don't you?

Mrs. O comes over to discuss the vocabulary work and explain her rationale for the assignment. Once the bags are completed, the students will take turns sharing their personal word descriptors with the rest of the class. As they do so, they are introducing themselves to the class in a memorable way, are using a wonderful array of vocabulary, and are practicing valuable communication skills. At a later date they will revisit these words to identify the various parts of speech that they might represent depending on how they are used in a sentence. We learn that when a student shares her collection of words, she empties out the words from inside the bag, reads them to the class, and emphatically replaces them inside the bag where they belong! Then she goes on to read the words that describe who she is and what she likes. The activity is packed with learning possibilities, isn't it? We promise to return one day later in the week to listen to a few students present their bag of words because Mrs. O assures us that we are in for a treat. The facial expressions and body language that go into individual presentations as students react to various words are simply delightful.

REFLECTION: IRA/NCTE NATIONAL STANDARDS IN THE CLASSROOM

While it is apparent that a great deal more was involved than simply focusing on vocabulary development in Mrs. O's classroom, the sixth graders could not have completed this activity without word knowledge and a variety of words at their disposal. If we return periodically, we will see that the continued attention to vocabulary growth is interspersed throughout the curriculum all year long in Mrs. O's classroom. This work is clearly supported by Standard 4 in relation to the students' expressive vocabularies (IRA/NCTE, 1996, p. 3):

Students adjust their use of spoken, written, and visual language (e.g., conventions, style, vocabulary) to communicate with a variety of audiences for different purposes.

Then, the sharing of the collection of personal descriptors is undergirded by the closely related Standard 12, which states that:

Students use spoken, written, and visual language to accomplish their own purposes (e.g., for learning, enjoyment, persuasion, and the exchange of information).

Today the students were creating their own unusual paper bag "texts," but as we spend more time in this classroom, we will see how written texts of all kinds fill the classroom hours. They spill over into time outside of class as students tie their two worlds together. We will drop into this classroom later in the week to see other instances of memorable teaching and learning so naturally supported by the National Standards. Throughout their days as part of Mrs. O's sixth grade "family" much of the fare involves the medium of words crafted with care by author, writer, student, and learner.

INTRODUCTION

A painter faces a blank canvas preparing to reproduce the scene before him or one from his imagination. He selects his palette of colors with care, for it is with these colors that he forms the images that will communicate with his audience. Applied in feather-light strokes or in vivid, broad splashes, it is through color that he makes his statement. A sculptor, on the other hand, begins with a clump of clay. She smoothes, shapes, pinches, adds, and eliminates bits of clay to mold the creation in her mind. Fired, glazed, or bronzed to completion, it is through the medium of clay that she

STANDARDS for READING PROFESSIONALS

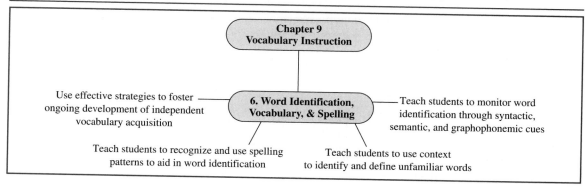

communicates with an appreciative audience or prospective buyer. Writers turn to a different medium, that of words, to ply their craft. Long and short, simple, or complex, writers pick just the right words and assemble them in exactly the right order to connect with the reader (Rupley, Logan, & Nichols, 1998/1999). Flavored by the reader's experiences, a product is created that is unique from reader to reader to reader. That product begins with words.

This chapter will focus on words and on the skills necessary to acquire an ever growing repository that will facilitate communication between writer and reader, speaker and listener, actor and audience. Words used with a deft touch can amuse, tug at the heart strings, inform, offer escape, or incite to action. They are crucial to building personal knowledge, deepening reading comprehension, and exchanging thoughts. The first part of the chapter will explain how words are used in various ways as a part of different kinds of vocabularies. Next, the stages of learning words will be discussed. Finally, strategies based upon serious research will be suggested in an effort to support students as they learn more and more indispensable words. From the beginning to the end of these pages, however, it will be reinforced that wide reading on a regular basis from a variety of materials is undoubtedly the best way for children to expand their vocabularies (Allington, 2001; Anderson, Wilson, & Fielding, 1988; Nagy, Anderson, & Herman, 1987). Teachers could not possibly teach children all of the words they acquire during their school years. Let us begin, then, with a look at the four commonly used kinds of meaningful vocabulary.

VOCABULARY: THERE IS MORE THAN ONE KIND

Visualize a chubby one-year-old, unsteadily toddling across the room focused on the steaming cup of coffee dangerously within reach. The observant parent quickly admonishes the child with a, "No—no! Hot!" and moves the cup safely out of reach. The grinning toddler responds with "No! No!" mimicking words he hears repeatedly throughout his day of busily investigating the world around him. He understands these words for they are a part of his **listening vocabulary**, the first type of vocabulary a young child acquires. It will become the largest of his vocabularies, made up of words he hears and understands but might not actually use in his everyday speech or his writing. Nursery rhymes, names of family members, cherished pets, favorite television characters, and daily foods are the beginnings of this vocabulary.

In time that listening vocabulary becomes the starter set for the second kind of vocabulary, a child's **speaking vocabulary**. Words are learned initially by imitating the modeling done by family members and other adults in the child's life (Miller, 2000). Think back to some of the prized expressions used by your younger brother or sister, niece or nephew. There is nothing quite as delightful as listening to a young child diligently attempting new words, is there? The amusing picture of my one-year-old granddaughter pointing her tiny index finger at the neighbor's two large wriggling dogs and officiously telling them to "Sit!" is etched permanently in my mind. She was trying a new word on for size and doing so quite effectively. A child's speaking vocabulary, then, includes words that she hears, understands, and uses in her speech. Throughout life, it remains somewhat smaller than one's listening vocabulary.

As the child grows, he gathers words from the environment that he can recognize and read. This is the foundation of his **reading vocabulary**. His first name, a stop sign, a favorite brand of cereal, or the Pizza Hut in a nearby shopping center serve as the kindling. This meager vocabulary expands rapidly when the young learner goes to school and begins to gather sight words and to master simple phonetically spelled words. If a child is an early reader, he will bring the beginnings of this expanded vocabulary with him when he enters kindergarten. That is just a start, however. This particular vocabulary continues to grow to include all those words a child can read and understand.

As children learn to read, they are also learning to write. **Writing vocabulary** is learned primarily in school where children are exposed to an increasing variety of words. Those words are accessed throughout the day for different assignments and in efforts to practice written communication. It is interesting to note that this particular vocabulary remains the smallest of the four types because a person doesn't use the same number of words in writing that are utilized in speaking, listening, or when reading.

An additional type of vocabulary could be added to the preceding list, that of the **potential marginal vocabulary** (Miller, 2000). It is composed of all of the words that a child may be able to determine the meaning of by using context clues, examining word parts, or knowing the derivations of words. As you can imagine, this particular vocabulary has more importance in the middle to upper grades than it does in the primary grades because students have expanded cognitive abilities and more strategies to apply to the task of word learning.

Cooter and Flynt (1996) group one's listening and reading vocabularies into a larger category identified as the **receptive vocabulary**. Writing and speaking vocabularies are categorized as the **expressive vocabulary**. These designations make sense when you realize how they illustrate the way a child processes and uses the words, either in a receptive mode or as a spoken or written language producer.

WHAT DOES IT MEAN TO "KNOW" A WORD?

In the opening quote to this chapter, Rosemary Wells (1994) explains how vital word knowledge is because it directly influences comprehension and general understanding. If you follow her logic into the academic world, do you see how the size of a child's vocabulary can correlate positively or negatively with her success in school? Because one needs the words to generate the concepts, it seems obvious that opportunities to acquire vocabulary simply cannot be left to chance alone.

When a teacher makes a conscious decision to devote a part of every classroom day to expanding vocabulary knowledge, she must plan carefully. Current research in the area of vocabulary underscores the complexity in acquiring new words and adding them to one's vocabulary (Moore, Moore, Cunningham, & Cunningham, 2003). The process involves "establishing relationships between concepts, organization of concepts, and expansion and refinement of knowledge about individual words" (Beck & McKeown, 1996, p. 790). Thus, the teaching and learning go beyond the mere reading of words if a word is truly to become a part of one's personal knowledge. While teaching and learning vocabulary is a complex process, it can be broken down into manageable steps for both teacher and learner as will be demonstrated throughout the chapter.

A legitimate question to ask at this point is what does it mean to "know" a word? Actually, the knowing appears to be more related to a degree of understanding. The highest degree involves the child's ability to use the word appropriately. Dale (1965) suggests that the extent to which one knows a word can be thought of by these degrees:

> **Stage 1:** never saw the word before
>
> **Stage 2:** have heard it but do not know what it means
>
> **Stage 3:** recognizes it in context and knows it has something to do with . . .
>
> **Stage 4:** knows the word well

Following the same line of thinking, that perhaps "knowing" a word falls along a continuum of knowledge, Graves (1987) suggests that there are six stages involved in learning words. They are as follows:

> **Task 1:** Learning to read known words.
>
> **Task 2:** Learning new meanings for known words.
>
> **Task 3:** Learning new words that represent known concepts.
>
> **Task 4:** Learning new words that represent new concepts.
>
> **Task 5:** Classifying and enriching the meanings of known words.
>
> **Task 6:** Moving words from the receptive to the expressive vocabulary.

These stages depict the importance of using words, of moving from the "never having seen it before" to having numerous opportunities to meet words and being able to use them again and again in appropriately rich contextual settings (Rupley et al., 1998/1999). It is through active processing involving engaging activities, then, that children build connections between the words that they already know and those that are new to them. All the while they are continually expanding their relationships with words. Think back to the comprehension chapter and draw a corollary between learning a new word and adding new knowledge to one's schema to extend the understanding of a topic or concept. Both new words and new knowledge are integrated into existing schema in the same way, deepening and broadening each one.

Reflect for a moment about how many words you know. Take a wild guess and write that number down. Speculate about how many words an average first grader might know. Jot that guess next to your personal number and then read on. When it comes to specific numbers, there is quite a discrepancy in the estimated number of words a child might know at various grade levels. Part of the confusion lies in what earlier researchers thought constituted a word, what they thought it meant to actually know a word, and what body of words they drew from when developing their testing samples (Johnson, 2001). After reviewing previous research, Beck and McKeown (1996, p. 794) state that "about as precise an estimate as can be given is to place vocabulary size for 5- to 6-year olds at between 2,500 and 5,000 words." Additional review of the research seems to support the fact that children add about seven new words per day, quite a rapid growth in word knowledge. That number must be tempered by the understanding that teachers are always working with individual differences, of course. For example, English language learners and children with learning difficulties might actually be learning only a word or two each day.

In concluding the discussion of the number of words a child might be expected to know, here is one final, sensible thought. It might be more realistic to say that children are aware of as many as seven new words a day, but they have quite a bit of work to do before each word becomes a part of their personal vocabularies (Carey, 1978). If word learning continues at a consistent pace, however, it is estimated that students entering college will have a vocabulary of between 40,000 and 50,000 words, and upon graduation, that might have expanded to close to 200,000 depending on the individual (Graves, 2000; Johnson, 2001). By building on the natural fascination children have with words, personal vocabularies have nowhere to go but upwards, expanding reading, writing, listening, speaking, and thinking skills in the process.

SUCCESSFUL STRATEGIES FOR TEACHING VOCABULARY ACQUISITION

Sage advice from those well-versed in teaching vocabulary agrees that there is no one best way to increase word knowledge. While **wide reading** is promoted as a means to gather new words, one cannot expect children to learn all new words without any instruction. Timely instruction is important, and having a variety of methods at one's disposal to teach and to learn new words appears to be the most beneficial for learners (Beck & McKeown, 1996; Graves, 1986). After reviewing a number of research studies since the 1980s, Blachowicz and Fisher (2000, p. 504) suggest four guiding principles for classroom instruction, placing much of the responsibility upon the students:

1. Students should be active in developing their understanding of words and the ways to learn them.
2. Students should personalize word learning.
3. Students should be immersed in words.
4. Students should build on multiple sources of information to learn words through repeated exposures.

Graves (2000) highlights the close connection between building vocabulary and improving comprehension. He suggests that a successful vocabulary program should involve wide reading, direct teaching of individual words, teaching some specific word-learning strategies to the students, and then fostering a continually growing level of word consciousness in students. Once again the connection between word knowledge and comprehension is reinforced. A sound place to begin looking at ways to learn vocabulary, it seems, is with the admonition to have students read extensively.

Encouraging Vocabulary Growth Through Wide Reading

As students begin to log in the miles on their vocabulary journey, it must seem that reaching a destination of 40,000 to 50,000 words by high school graduation is a rather impossible task. Certainly a teacher cannot be the sole source of any particular child's vocabulary knowledge. Instead, advocating wide reading is one avenue to follow to reach one's goal. Pressley (2000, p. 556) explains that "once children can decode, they are empowered to read, read, and read, with greater fluency, vocabulary, and world knowledge by-products of such reading, all of which contribute to comprehension skills." Therefore, students must spend time reading a variety of materials covering diverse topics presented in numerous kinds of texts during their journey. This applies to children with learning disabilities and other at-risk learners along with regular classroom readers. The caution is that materials must be on their particular levels to avoid frustration resulting from word recognition problems. Reading, even as little as ten minutes a day, ensures progress along the way to word acquisition, general language development, increased understanding of the world around them, while also reinforcing the goal of becoming lifelong readers (Allen, 2000; Beck & McKeown, 1996; IRA/NCTE, 1996). Doubling that investment time to twenty minutes a day could yield rich results indeed.

Resources for encouraging reading permeate this text. Obviously, as enticing a classroom collection as can be gathered is the first place to begin because, unfortunately, many students do not read much outside of the classroom. A program like Sustained Silent Reading as explained in earlier chapters makes reading an essential part of the classroom routine, vastly benefiting those students who use it wisely. Telling the students to read and then not doing it yourself is taking the power from behind your words. It is essential that teachers read right alongside their students day after day after day.

All readers, especially struggling and reluctant readers, need access to a wide variety of reading materials to develop their vocabularies.

Make reading aloud another classroom institution (Allington, 2001). Even those diverse students who struggle with reading can learn new words when the teacher reads aloud every day, a gift to all students in the classroom. Reading from both fiction and nonfiction titles, sharing your love of reading, and stopping to chat about an unusual word from time to time are easy and enjoyable strategies to use to extend vocabulary (Allington & Cunningham, 2003). Dip into poetry to reinforce the wonder of words. One poem to advertise the value of words and to make a pleasing connection with culture is from *Confetti: Poems for Children* (Mora, 1996).

Words Free as Confetti

Come, words, come in your every color.
I'll toss you in storm or breeze
I'll say, say, say you,
taste you sweet as plump plums
bitter as old lemons.
I'll sniff you, words, warm
as almonds or tart as apple-red
feel you green
and soft as new grass,
lightwhite as dandelion plumes,
or thorngray as cactus,
heavy as black cement,
cold as blue icicles,
warm as *abuelita's* yellowlap
I'll hear you, words, loud as searoar's
purple crash, hushed
as *gatitos* curled in sleep,
as the last goldlullaby.
I'll see you long and dark as tunnels,
bright as rainbows,
playful as chestnutwind.
I'll watch you, words, rise and dance, and spin.
I'll say, say, say you
in English,
in Spanish
I'll find you.
Hold you.
Toss you.
I'm free too.
I say *yo soy libre,*
I am free
free, free
free as confetti.

Pat Mora. (1996).
Confetti: Poems for Children. New York: Scholastic. Used by permission.

Promoting wide reading does not fall into that "silver bullet" category, unfortunately. It will certainly benefit those students who love to read and have strong reading skills. Struggling readers who find reading an uphill battle will have to be motivated and supported along their trek, for they will be less likely to embrace the dictate to read, and read more. As with any other learning situation, learners will tackle the vocabulary journey in their own way, at their own pace, with some requiring more maintenance when impeded by major obstacles while others breeze along smoothly. Isn't it frequently said that it is not the destination, however, but the journey that counts? So it can be with vocabulary.

Building a Bank of Sight Words

A natural outgrowth of wide reading is the opportunity to develop a growing bank of **sight words**, words that are recognized and understood quickly as students scan the page. (See Figure 9.1.) Repeated practice with a variety of reading materials ensures that many words will be met again and again. In addition, familiarity with sight words or others deemed as high-frequency words helps the reader to become more fluent. Adams (1990) notes that only 109 words account for nearly 50 percent of all words in students' textbooks and about 5,000 words account for close to 90 percent of words in students' reading materials (Allington & Cunningham, 1996).

Web Link:
Merriam-Webster's
Vocabulary Builder

When teaching sight words to students, children's literature is an attractive resource. Predictable books, books with simple captions, or books with labels corresponding to the illustrations provide appealing learning fare. These books can be read over and over as young students and/or ELLs practice the words. A simple sight word lesson that can be adapted to other words like high-frequency words might follow the steps listed in the following teaching idea.

Teaching Strategy for the Classroom

BUILDING A BANK OF SIGHT/HIGH-FREQUENCY WORDS

1. Begin by using a predictable book like *Do Like a Duck Does* (Hindley, 2002), which has only a few words per page. The sight words to learn might include commonly used numbers and the names of several animals.
2. Gather students around you so that they can all see the book and pictures. A big book version would be ideal for a lesson like this one.
3. Read through the text, stopping to discuss appropriate parts and students' reactions at the end.
4. Now, reread the text, pointing out unfamiliar words. Those words might be rewritten on the chalkboard or lined cards that fit neatly into a pocket chart. Take a little time to analyze the words, looking for any distinguishing features that will aid the child in recognizing it in the future. Continue reading, encouraging students to join in refrains or on easy sentences like, "Do like a duck does! Do like me!" in this book.

5. Return to the new words, read them together, and then ask a student to find each one as you revisit the text one more time. Pass out the new words written on tagboard to individual listeners. When they hear and see their word, participants come up and hold their word next to the text word, one more beneficial visual encounter.

6. The following day read through the text together as a group. Then, give children a reproduced copy of the text without illustrations or rewrite the sentences from the story and place them in a pocket chart, reading through the pocket chart together. Now the students are focusing on the words alone without the aid of the pictures to help them "read" the text.

7. To measure comprehension and assess whether students have mastered the new sight words, duplicate the story and cut the story into sentences. Students can work in pairs to reassemble the sentences into the correct order. Break the task down one more time, this time cutting sentences into words. Various groups can work to put the sentences into meaningful order, checking with the big book when they are done to be certain they are correct.

8. Finally, whenever possible, put several copies of the book in the reading center to be read and reread by students eager to practice their new words and to revel in the delightful illustrations.

Another way to build word knowledge puts students in the role of word collectors. As students gather words, they are to copy them down to be used for future activities. A simple but effective way to collect sight words or high-frequency words is by using word banks, a place where students can keep their words and use them for word sorts, writing activities, or creative word play. In this case, words are printed on 3″ by 5″ index cards, with the word on one side and a simple corresponding sentence and/or picture on the other side. Words can be filed in alphabetical order in a small personal file box, punched in the upper left-hand corner, and collected on a metal ring, or organized in several sturdy resealable bags. As collections grow, students can be given time during the day to work with their words in a number of ways. They might try to create simple sentences with them, writing each sentence down as it is devised. Another time they can work with a partner, quizzing each other on their words or playing a concentration game with a selection of words. They can sort words according to vowel sounds or combinations, endings, beginnings, or parts of speech (Gunning, 2001). Obviously, repeated practice that involves students who think about their words will improve access to sight words for students of all abilities.

ADAPTATIONS/MODIFICATIONS FOR DIVERSE LEARNERS

One option is to adapt this activity for a visually impaired child by providing him with 5″ by 8″ white index cards or segments of sentence strips with the words written with a dark black marker. The teacher can write the words or they can be printed out on the computer in a large, clear font and glued to cards. Encourage independence by providing a supply of blank cards or strips and markers so the student can add words as he discovers them. If possible, provide extra light in the area where the student

Figure 9.1

A list of common sight words

The first 10 words make up about 24 percent of all written material, the first 100 words about 50 percent of all written material, and the first 300 about 65 percent.

1. the	44. each	87. who	130. through	173. home	216. never	259. walked
2. of	45. which	88. oil	131. much	174. us	217. started	260. white
3. and	46. she	89. its	132. before	175. move	218. city	261. sea
4. a	47. do	90. now	133. line	176. try	219. earth	262. began
5. to	48. how	91. find	134. right	177. kind	220. eyes	263. grow
6. in	49. their	92. long	135. too	178. hand	221. light	264. took
7. is	50. if	93. down	136. means	179. picture	222. thought	265. river
8. you	51. will	94. day	137. old	180. again	223. head	266. four
9. that	52. up	95. did	138. any	181. change	224. under	267. carry
10. it	53. other	96. get	139. same	182. off	225. story	268. state
11. he	54. about	97. come	140. tell	183. play	226. saw	269. once
12. was	55. out	98. made	141. boy	184. spell	227. left	270. book
13. for	56. many	99. may	142. following	185. air	228. don't	271. hear
14. on	57. then	100. part	143. came	186. away	229. few	272. stop
15. are	58. them	101. over	144. want	187. animals	230. while	273. without
16. as	59. these	102. new	145. show	188. house	231. along	274. second
17. with	60. so	103. sound	146. also	189. point	232. might	275. later
18. his	61. some	104. take	147. around	190. page	233. close	276. miss
19. they	62. her	105. only	148. form	191. letters	234. something	277. idea
20. I	63. would	106. little	149. three	192. mother	235. seemed	278. enough
21. at	64. make	107. work	150. small	193. answer	236. next	279. eat
22. be	65. like	108. know	151. set	194. found	237. hard	280. face
23. this	66. him	109. place	152. put	195. study	238. open	281. watch
24. have	67. into	110. years	153. end	196. still	239. example	282. far
25. from	68. time	111. live	154. does	197. learn	240. beginning	283. Indians
26. or	69. has	112. me	155. another	198. should	241. life	284. really
27. one	70. look	113. back	156. well	199. American	242. always	285. almost
28. had	71. two	114. give	157. large	200. world	243. those	286. let
29. by	72. more	115. most	158. must	201. high	244. both	287. above
30. words	73. write	116. very	159. big	202. every	245. paper	288. girl
31. but	74. go	117. after	160. even	203. near	246. together	289. sometimes
32. not	75. see	118. things	161. such	204. add	247. got	290. mountains
33. what	76. number	119. our	162. because	205. food	248. group	291. cut
34. all	77. no	120. just	163. turned	206. between	249. often	292. young
35. were	78. way	121. name	164. here	207. own	250. run	293. talk
36. we	79. could	122. good	165. why	208. below	251. important	294. soon
37. when	80. people	123. sentence	166. asked	209. country	252. until	295. list
38. your	81. my	124. man	167. went	210. plants	253. children	296. song
39. can	82. than	125. think	168. men	211. last	254. side	297. being
40. said	83. first	126. say	169. read	212. school	255. feet	298. leave
41. there	84. water	127. great	170. need	213. father	256. car	299. family
42. use	85. been	128. where	171. land	214. keep	257. miles	300. it's
43. an	86. called	129. help	172. different	215. trees	258. night	

Source: From Edward Fry, The new instant word list, *The Reading Teacher.* December 1980, pp. 284–289. Used with permission from Edward Fry and the International Reading Association.

will be working. Depending on the amount of vision the student has, a magnification device to facilitate reading will be handy. Pair this learner with a partner for all word-practice activities.

Using the Context to Teach Vocabulary

Over the years a popular strategy to teach students new words has involved employing **context clues**. Simply put, this strategy requires the use of tidbits of information in the text surrounding an unknown word to try to figure out its meaning. There are reservations about relying too heavily on learning words from context, however (Nagy, Anderson, & Herman, 1987). Basically, researchers do not agree on the degree to which context affects the understanding of unfamiliar words. Beck and McKeown (1996) conclude that,

> Research on the process of acquiring word meaning from a context suggests that learning a word is not simply a matter of lifting the meaning from context. Rather, it is a complex process of developing a meaning in which a series of steps must contribute to achieve a successful outcome. (p. 802)

Web Link:
VoyCabulary

Thus, it is not as simple as it seems. Yet, a vast number of words must be learned from context because there simply isn't time to teach them all. Under the right set of conditions, the use of context can be beneficial (Moore et al., 2003; Sternberg, 1987). Pressley explains (2000, p. 552),

Teaching Strategy:
Enriching Background Knowledge

> Students learn most vocabulary in context, incidentally as a function of experiencing vocabulary words in reading and speaking contexts, and vocabulary words so acquired are going to be better learned and understood than vocabulary taught through explicit instruction because the learner will have been so active and constructive in developing the meaning of the word in the former as compared to the latter situation.

It appears that there are two sides to the context issue, but there can be a meeting of the minds regarding the values of context clues. Sometimes the clues to an unknown word are so strong that students can quite accurately infer its meaning. Consider the following example as you determine the meaning of *gossamer* from the introduction of *Time Windows* (Reiss, 2000):

> Threads of memory, like dreams, tried to weave themselves into a story. But—as with dreams—the harder she thought, face bent in a frown of concentration, the strands fluttered like spider gossamer, broke, and were gone. (no page number)

Drawing on one's background knowledge of spider webs and their fragility, one can surmise that gossamer is a type of material that is web-like, delicate, and easily destroyed. Miranda's memory of some events, then, must also be too fragile to maintain.

That is an example of when using the context can be the most effective. At other times when the context is of little use, the student must resort to other strategies like trying structural analysis, asking a classmate, or using the dictionary to try to determine meaning. When teaching students to use context to ferret out a word's meaning, the best approach is for the teacher to use explicit instruction, model the steps clearly, scaffold learning experiences, and provide adequate practice and feedback (Blachowicz & Fisher, 2000; Robb, 2000).

The process might look like this:

1. In a well-prepared lesson, explain the values of using context to the students. You might say something like, "Context clues are clues and hints that the words and sentences surrounding an unknown word give us about the meaning of the unknown word" (Graves, 2000, p. 124–125). In less obvious cases, students may need to read other sentences too, those that come before and after the word in question. Detective work may involve looking at pictures or studying a graph to get a better understanding of the elusive word meaning.

2. Beginning with relatively easy material, model the way you think through using the context and then give students ample practice and support as they try it over and over again for themselves.

3. Use a variety of different kinds of materials so that students ply their new strategy across the curriculum. Scaffold learning until students have developed a comfort level with the strategy and then gradually turn the responsibility over to the learners.

4. Then, for students who are still struggling with a word, offer them other options. Students with learning difficulties and language barriers will still need help from a teacher, classmate, or the dictionary in many cases.

Laura Robb (2000; 2003) clearly supports the use of modeling using materials with which the students are familiar as she teaches her students to use context clues. She suggests selecting several excerpts from different resources and making a transparency of each of them. Read through one part of text, stopping at the puzzling word. Demonstrate how you might move back a sentence, forward a sentence, and think aloud as you figure out what the word might mean. One example of this thinking process is as follows using several sentences from *Squanto's Journey: The Story of the First Thanksgiving* (Bruchac, 2000, unpaged):

> In the moons that followed, there was much work to do. The Pokanoket freed me to be a guide and interpreter for the English. Not only did I act as <u>envoy</u> between the English and our people, I also had many things to teach the white people about survival.

Following Robb's advice, the teacher would read the passage aloud, stop to think about the word "envoy," wondering aloud what it might mean. Once the sentences have all been read, the thinking aloud process might look like this:

> *Envoy.* I have heard that word before. What information from this page will help me figure that word out? Squanto is talking about being an "envoy" between his tribe and the English. Is that just being an interpreter? I know the Native Americans and early settlers had been at war. Maybe being an envoy also had something to do with keeping the peace. The picture in the book shows Squanto and a man who must be a pilgrim out hunting together. I'm going to guess that envoy means more than being an interpreter. It might be a person who helps smooth out relationships between people from different backgrounds

like the Native Americans and Pilgrims. That seems to fit this context better. But, I'm going to look the word up in the dictionary quickly just to be sure I'm not mistaken . . .

Graves (2000) would reinforce the inference-making process backed up by dictionary use as an even more effective way to learn vocabulary. Another excerpt to try is from *Beautiful Warrior: The Legend of the Nun's Kung Fu* (McCully, 1998, unpaged). Jingyong's father makes an unusual decision to educate his daughter rather than preparing her for a less intellectually stimulating life in the Emperor's court.

Students need to see the word in context and hear it used in the discussion as well as see the word over and over again.

> Instead, he sent her to the tutors as if she were a son. She studied the five pillars of learning: art, literature, music, medicine, and martial arts. Jingyong was a <u>prodigy</u>, excelling especially at martial arts. Kung fu taught her to use her qi, or vital energy. With qi, softness could prevail over hardness, a yielding force master a brute one.

Think through the preceding steps in the previous sample as you mentally practice using the context to infer the meaning of "prodigy." In the classroom, demonstrating thinking aloud via several examples aids the class to understand the way one makes effective use of context.

Take a minute to go back to Chapter 1 and look at the chart that highlights the practices of expert teachers. Notice that the just described practice is one attributed to second grade teachers who as demonstrators "help students climb onto meager or massive prior knowledge by demonstrating literacy processes through masterful think-alouds" (Block, Oakar, & Hurt, 2002, p. 188). Clearly, think-alouds transfer across the grades and facilitate understanding for each student in the classroom.

After the think aloud demonstration, students are given time to practice on a section. They might work with a partner, talking through how they discovered a word's meaning. Such conversation, being able to explain how you do a task, is one way of cementing understanding and revealing when students have gaps in grasping how to apply any strategy. Finally, provide several additional opportunities to practice using context clues throughout the week. To reinforce your teaching, the strategy should be used again over the next few weeks and with materials from across the curriculum. An additional idea is to invite students to write in journals from time to time, sharing how they relied upon the context to understand a word in their personal reading as Robb (2000; 2003) suggests. Common sense dictates that you do not abandon learners until you surmise that it is time to remove the scaffolding process whenever a

Figure 9.2

A decoding strategy for unfamiliar words

1. Recognize that you have encountered an unfamiliar word. Look at all of the letters following a left-to-right sequence.
2. Search your mental file system for information about similar letter patterns and the sounds associated with them.
3. Try a pronunciation that matches that of a real word you already know.
4. Use the context and reread the sentence containing the unfamiliar word. Cross-check your possible pronunciation with meaning. If the meaning makes sense with your pronunciation, resume reading. If it doesn't make sense, try this process again.
5. If the word is long, chunk the word by putting together letters that usually go together in words you already know.

Source: Adapted from Cunningham, P. A., & Allington, R. L. (2003). *Classrooms that work: They can all read and write.* Boston: Allyn & Bacon.

new strategy is directly taught. Certainly, turning the responsibility for using the new skill over to students as they are ready is important, but periodic rechecking is tied with quality instruction. Work independently with diverse learners who continue to need support.

One must listen to the voices of caution that care should be used so teachers do not encourage overreliance on context, especially for diverse learners. Consider the fact that some content area texts do not give enough clues in the text for students to grasp the meaning of a term. Even some narrative texts give the reader little help when encountering a new word. In that case, other strategies are called for, including direct teaching of more difficult words, turning to the dictionary, or developing personal word questing skills, as will be suggested in the remainder of the chapter. See Figure 9.2 to understand how context is used by good readers as they move through a series of steps to decode an unfamiliar word.

THE PARAMETERS OF DIRECT INSTRUCTION

If you have access to a sample teacher's edition from an older basal series, spend a short time browsing through the lessons. It won't take you long to recognize that it was a common strategy for the teacher to directly teach potentially difficult vocabulary words before nearly every story in one lesson after another. It is important to note that research has not supported such extensive use of this particular form of direct instruction. In fact, only a few thousand words usually receive direct instruction in the primary grades (Juel & Minden-Cupp, 1999/2000). That leaves the bulk of vocabulary development in the hands of the readers themselves. Johnson (2001, p. 40) reflectively comments,

> I have come to realize that most children, adolescents, and adults learn most of the words they know through oral and written communication—through listening and reading, speaking and writing. Does that mean words should never be taught directly? Absolutely

not. Every day in school there are words that must be learned if students are to comprehend what they read and hear, to engage in conversations and discussion, and to write and
know what they believe. So the words to teach directly are those the students must learn
to be active participants who can comprehend oral and written text.

For those times when just a few words are singled out for particular focus before
reading or discussion begins, remember these guiding questions (Graves, 2000, p.
121):

1. Is understanding the word important to understanding the selection in which
   it appears?

2. Are students able to use context or structural analysis skills to discover the
   word's meaning?

3. Can working with the word be useful in furthering students' context,
   structural analysis, or dictionary skills?

4. How useful is this word outside of the reading selection being currently taught?

The following paragraphs contain additional ideas for developing one's vocabulary. They are taught using direct instruction and scaffolded until students develop
sufficient expertise to assume responsibility for applying the skills on their own.

A Look at the Vocabulary Possibilities Using Synonyms and Antonyms

Web Link:
Vocabulary University

Vocabulary skills can be augmented by teaching students about synonyms and
antonyms. The main concepts to be taught are that **synonyms** are words that have the
same or similar meaning to the word in question, while words that are **antonyms**
have opposite or almost opposite meanings. When using the synonym/antonym chart
(Figure 9.3), students are involved in a writing-thinking experience that encourages
learning new words. The use of the chart is introduced with a teacher-modeled mini-
lesson using words from the daily reading assignment or a science or social studies
lesson. Continued practice using these charts can be extended as the teacher or student desires. Provide practice through authentic kinds of reading and writing experiences, meaning those that are closely tied to current classroom projects. This is an
ideal opportunity to teach the students the values of using a thesaurus, an invaluable
tool for adding zip and variety to their writing as they search for different words to
replace the tired words they habitually choose. Two popular options are *Roget's Children's Thesaurus* (HarperCollins, 1994) geared for children from eight to twelve
years of age and *Roget's Student Thesaurus* (HarperCollins, 1994), appropriate for
students ages ten through fourteen. Both are alphabetized for ease of use.

To teach a vocabulary enriching lesson, model the use of the synonym/antonym
chart by selecting a passage from the day's read-aloud picture book or a short passage from the novel being read together in class. Copy a section of the text onto the
chalkboard or the overhead transparency. Then, copy the same section again, repro-
ducing it on a student activity sheet. This time leave out selected words, putting a
blank line in their place. The following sentences from *Let It Shine: Stories of Black*

Figure 9.3
Sample synonym/antonym chart

Vocabulary Word	Synonym	Antonym

Name _____

Women Freedom Fighters (Pinkney, 2000) lend themselves to showing how different words can keep the meaning similar while others change the meaning. The story is talking about Harriet Tubman as it relates,

> Harriet's master, Edward Brodas, was one of the <u>meanest</u> slave masters around. As soon as Harriet was old enough to pinch cotton, she was <u>forced</u> to work <u>long</u>, <u>hard</u> days. (p. 18)

Read the original piece on the overhead together and discuss the meaning of the text. What impressions do the words leave with the reader? What other words might be used in place of the four underlined words that are different but still convey the same meaning? Put students to work in pairs with a thesaurus to find words that would be appropriate. List the words students select on the chalkboard. Then, substitute several of them and discuss the results. Point out that there are often different words that can express thoughts in similar ways. Talk about which words were the most effective and analyze why that was so. Point out how using the thesaurus helps add variety to their writing as commonly used words are replaced with others that are more interesting, but still convey the same meaning.

Now switch to antonym study and ask students to locate words in the thesaurus that are opposites from the underlined words. List those suggestions. Try a few of them and query the class on the effects of using antonyms. Replace the underlined words and then read several examples aloud. Discuss how the tone of a passage changes when antonyms are used (Fuhler, 2000). Finally, reflect together upon why an understanding of antonyms is helpful in building one's vocabulary knowledge before moving on to additional practice with these useful words.

At this point, perceptive conversation can deepen students' thinking about how powerful the appropriate words can be. As with all reading skills and strategies, periodically assign work on synonyms and antonyms throughout the year to keep vocabulary skills honed. Invite students to keep an ongoing synonym/antonym chart in their reading or writing journals and to discuss it with you during individual conferences or to share new words with you during a journaling activity.

Semantic Word Maps

Semantic word maps change the method of learning from a simple written process to one where learners create a visual picture of a new word. In the process of completing a semantic map, students tie new words to previously known words, concepts, or words with similar meanings, an activity that enables them to remember the newly acquired word more efficiently (Bear, Invernizzi, Templeton, & Johnston, 2000; Johnson & Pearson, 1984). In brief, semantic maps encourage students to relate new information to schemata in their brains, actively integrating new knowledge with the old (Robb, 2003; Yopp & Yopp, 2001). For some diverse learners, having a different way to relate to the information, that of a visual image, can help connect old and new knowledge (Hatch & Brown, 1995). Another supportive learning tactic is to give a completed semantic map to learners before the lesson begins as a type of blueprint for understanding.

One form of a semantic word map is the **concept of definition map** (Schwartz & Raphael, 1985). Such a map might be used as the class is engaged in the study of mammals. One of the books at their disposal could be *They Walk the Earth: The Extraordinary Travels of Animals on Land* (Simon, 2000). When introducing the book as a possible research resource, the teacher might highlight several unfamiliar words like *migration, lemmings,* and *carnivores,* which are important to understanding various sections of this informational picture book. To model the construction of a semantic word map, the teacher would write one of the words on the chalkboard or an overhead transparency. Read the word to the class and ask them to try to connect that word with other words they know or ideas they might have about the selected word.

On another part of the chalkboard, jot down the students' contributions as they are offered. Then, look at those words as a class and try to group them into categories to answer the questions: What is it like? What are some examples? What is our definition? Using decisions made by the students, complete the word map on the board or overhead. Then, break the class into several groups and have them practice the process together with the remaining words from the story. They might skim a paragraph containing the word in the book for clues to its meaning or consult the dictionary and the book as they learn the word and make connections with what they already know. See Figure 9.4 for an example of what the resulting semantic map might look like.

Word Webbing

Webbing is a version of a word map, a different method to graphically illustrate how to associate different words with each other to build a concept in a meaningful manner. It, too, is a tool to facilitate making connections between what learners know

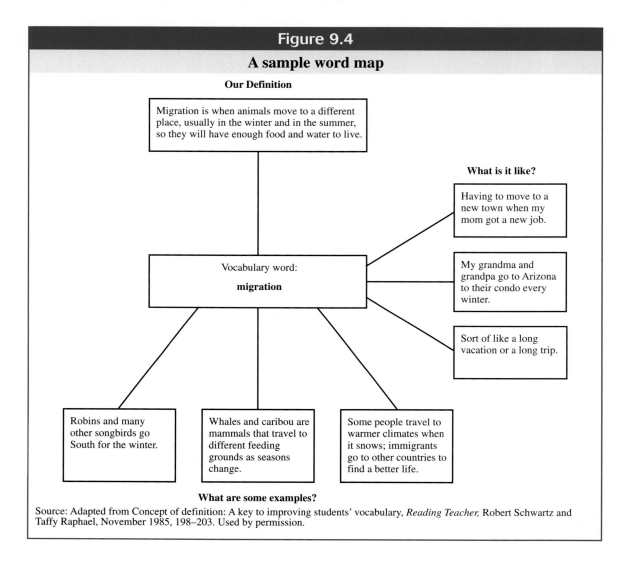

Figure 9.4

A sample word map

Our Definition

Migration is when animals move to a different place, usually in the winter and in the summer, so they will have enough food and water to live.

Vocabulary word:

migration

What is it like?

Having to move to a new town when my mom got a new job.

My grandma and grandpa go to Arizona to their condo every winter.

Sort of like a long vacation or a long trip.

Robins and many other songbirds go South for the winter.

Whales and caribou are mammals that travel to different feeding grounds as seasons change.

Some people travel to warmer climates when it snows; immigrants go to other countries to find a better life.

What are some examples?

Source: Adapted from Concept of definition: A key to improving students' vocabulary, *Reading Teacher,* Robert Schwartz and Taffy Raphael, November 1985, 198–203. Used by permission.

about words and how words are related (Rupley et al., 1998/1999). Johnson (2001) explains that words on a web may be related to the central word or concept in a number of ways. Students might look at synonyms, antonyms, different attributes, examples of the word, or how the word functions. Webs are created as a whole class activity or in teams of learners more frequently than they are used for independent work.

When teaching this strategy, create a sample web ahead of time. Put it on chart paper or on an overhead transparency and talk the children through its construction. A practical guideline to follow is the younger the learners, the more simple the map. Explain how the map shows a relationship between the words you will be learning together. Then, read the related story. Return to the map and review how it is con-

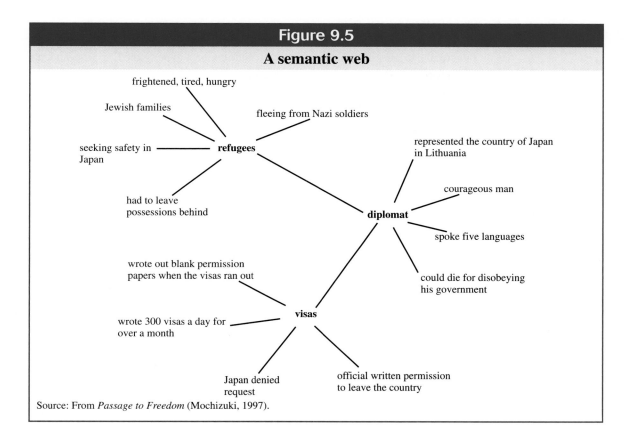

Figure 9.5

A semantic web

Source: From *Passage to Freedom* (Mochizuki, 1997).

structed, tying it to the terms from the story you have just shared. Be sure to talk about the relationship between the words on the map, making certain that students understand the new word and how it ties to information they might already know. In this way you are scaffolding their learning.

As is always good practice allow the students to work in small groups. Select several key words from a second story, write them on the chart paper or overhead, and then read a second short story aloud. Working in groups with a large sheet of chart paper on hand, students create their own maps showing the relationship between the words and ideas in the story. Even with older students, you might begin with a relatively simple picture book text. Remember, it is easier to teach a concept with simple text, assess it to be sure it is understood, and then apply the concept to more difficult text. See the following example of a semantic web (Figure 9.5) based upon *Passage to Freedom: The Sugihara Story* (Mochizuki, 1997).

Semantic Features Analysis

This slightly more complex strategy requires that both words and concepts or features associated with particular words be placed on a grid for closer inspection. In the process of making the grid, learners create a graphic display highlighting features that distinguish words in a particular category. Using a **semantic features analysis chart** or **grid**, the teacher introduces new words or the concept to be studied, and the students fill in their grids by deciding whether the concepts or features are related to each other in a positive or negative manner. By having children actively engaged in thinking about a new concept as they complete the graph, it makes sense that this technique positively affects reading comprehension (Anders, Bos, & Filip, 1984). Johnson and Pearson (1984) suggest the following procedure in teaching students to complete the features analysis grid:

1. The teacher presents a list of words that have some common features to the class. These words, related to a story or current topic of study, are listed down the left-hand side of the grid. Model this process using an overhead projector, chalkboard, or by constructing a large grid on chart paper.

2. List some features of these words across the top of the chart, inviting students to study the words and contribute features that they think might apply.

3. Once the two parameters of the grid have been completed, start with the first vocabulary word on the left and work across the chart, putting a plus sign under the feature if it applies or a negative sign if the feature is missing.

4. Once the grid has been completed, discuss the results with the class. What observations can they make based upon the charted information?

Here, too, is another example of students being involved in recognizing relationships between new words and making connections with knowledge they already possess. This is a strategy that students with learning disabilities, mild mental retardation, or second language hurdles will find challenging. The first two groups of learners may not have the cognitive abilities to understand the relationships between the words. English language learners might not have the background of words necessary to make the connections. These learners should work with classmates and receive additional support from the teacher when learning to use a semantic features grid. See how a sample semantic features analysis grid might look in Figure 9.6.

Learning New Words Through Structural Analysis

By the time students reach the middle grades, they should be actively involved in searching for new and interesting words, being curious and resourceful in broadening their vocabulary. Another tool to provide students to guide their exploration is **structural analysis,** a systematic approach to understanding new words that requires the analysis of word parts (Cooper, 1997; Robb, 2003). For those all too frequent times when context does not provide enough clues to an unfamiliar word, knowledge of word parts can come to one's rescue. In fact, research in vocabulary instruction clearly supports the practicality of having a working knowledge of word parts like prefixes and suffixes and how they combine with base or root words to form new words. Using this tactic, the analysis of word parts leads to "a rich expansion and elaboration of their vocabularies" (Bear et al., 2000, p. 225). During a structural

Figure 9.6

A semantic features analysis grid

	Current frontier	Former frontier	Readily inhabited by man	Naturally supports plant & animal life	Remains largely unexplored
The Oceans	+	−	−	+	+
The Old West—1800s	−	+	+	+	−
Outer Space	+	−	−	−	+
Mars	+	−	−	−	+
The New World—1600s	−	+	+	+	−

What is the criteria to be used to determine whether a place is a frontier or not? Discuss with the class how the definition of a frontier changes as a man learns more about it and makes it his home.

Source: A semantic features analysis grid for *Dive! My Adventures in the Deep Frontier* by Sylvia A. Earle (1999).

analysis activity, students will be working with morphemes. A **morpheme** is simply the smallest unit of meaning in a word. For example, *replaying* contains three morphemes, *re-play-ing*, including a prefix, a base word, and a suffix. With continued application, students will gradually learn the meanings of common prefixes and suffixes, one more usable piece to slip into place in the vocabulary puzzle.

In familiarizing students with the elements of structural analysis, begin with direct teaching. First, explain that structural analysis is the study of the major parts of a word. It requires the reader to dissect the word into morphemes or meaningful chunks, think about the meaning of each bit, and then reassemble the word with a basic understanding of what that word might mean. Then, a reader double-checks the meaning for sense by rereading the sentence or surrounding sentences to see if there is a "goodness of fit." In order to analyze words, students will need to understand the following word parts. As these parts are taught and practiced, they could be added to a reference chart reproduced on tagboard and posted for easy visibility for individual review as needed (Cooper, 1997; Johnson, 2001). See Figure 9.7.

Teach the preceding individual word parts via mini-lessons, providing practice within the materials the students are currently using in reading or language arts. Working with one segment at a time and allowing students to digest that bit before consuming more will aid in the assimilation of new information. When working with prefixes, for example, you might teach the definition and then provide students with

---

Figure 9.7

Reference chart for basic word parts

<u>base words:</u> Meaningful linguistic elements that can stand alone and contain no smaller meaning parts; this is a word to which prefixes and suffixes are added: tie, friend.

<u>root words:</u> These are words from which other words are created; a root word cannot stand alone. It often originates in another language.

<u>prefixes:</u> Units of meaning that can be added to the beginnings of base words or root words, changing the meaning in the process; when they are removed, the base word can stand alone: *un*tie; *be*friend.

<u>suffixes:</u> Small units of meaning that can be added to the ends of base words or root words which change the meaning to some degree; when they are removed, the base word can stand alone: joy*ful*, friend*ly*.

<u>inflectional endings:</u> These word parts can be added to the ends of a base or root word to alter the case, gender, number, tense, or form of the word; sometimes they are also called suffixes.

   <u>possessive case:</u> student's pen, books' covers

   <u>gender:</u> hers, his

   <u>number:</u> readers, singers

   <u>tense:</u> jumped, laughed

   <u>form:</u> happier, happiest

<u>compound words:</u> When two or more base words are combined to form a new word, that word is a compound word. The newly formed word may have a literal, concrete meaning as in an object one can see like *birdbath*; it may be concrete but not touchable as in *afternoon*; or it may have an implied meaning like *brainstorm*.

<u>contractions:</u> Shortened forms of two words in which a letter or letters have been eliminated and replaced by an apostrophe: could not = couldn't; do not = don't.

---

a selection of words including the appropriate prefix adding a mix of "tricksters" (White, Sowell, & Yanagihara, 1989). For example, explain that the prefix "re" means again. Then list the following words:

    renew   register   reheat   reject   relive   remove

Invite students to analyze each word; decide which ones have a prefix and which ones do not. Have them explain each decision. Discuss how vigilant readers must be when breaking words into recognizable pieces because sometimes the "re" is not actually a prefix so it may not always help them decipher a word. Suggest that when in doubt, it is wise to consult the dictionary. This is a point that should be made again with each prefix and suffix because tricksters abound in the English language. An alternative way to approach this lesson is to give the students the selected words, let them discuss their meanings, and then deduce what the prefix might mean. They can check their hypothesis with the dictionary to be certain they are on the right track. Often students remember a rule or skill much longer if they have to work at uncovering the knowledge themselves.

Figure 9.8
Commonly used prefixes and suffixes

Prefixes	Meaning	Examples
un-	means "not"	unable, unreal
re-	means "back" or "again"	review, renew
in-, im-, ir-, il,	means "not"	inevitable, impossible, irresponsible, illiterate
dis-	means "the opposite"	disagree, disobey
en-, em-	means "into" or "within"	encase, encode
non-	means "not" or "impossible"	nonbeliever, nonconformist
over-	means "too much"	overdone, overpower
mis-	means "wrong"	mistake, misbehave
sub-	means "under"	submerge, subtotal

Suffixes	Meaning	Examples
-s/-es	plural	books, boxes
	present tense	sings
-ed	past tense	jumped
-ing	present tense	singing
-ly	means "like"	motherly, friendly
-er, -or	means "more"	wiser, smaller
-ion, -tion, -ation, ition	means "state of being"	creation, elation
-ible, -able	means "capable," "worth"	flexible, peaceable
-al, -ial	means "of" or "like"	comical, parental
-y	means "consisting of" or "inclined toward"	needy, dreamy
-ness	means "state," "quality," "condition," or "degree"	happiness, brightness

Take a few minutes to review Figure 9.8 displaying the chart of common prefixes and suffixes for a sense of direction regarding which ones to teach, at least initially. Research points out that it is a practical approach to concentrate on only this handful of nine prefixes and ten suffixes because they account for 75 to 85 percent of the word beginnings and endings that are most frequently used (White et al., 1989). Then, other prefixes and suffixes can be taught from time to time, discussed within the context of a current assignment.

Once students understand the various word parts, teach a focus lesson in application, providing learners with a handy step-by-step reference chart for their reading folders. Post one in the classroom for quick review until it is apparent that students have mastered the basics of structural analysis. Bear and colleagues (2000, pp. 227–228) suggest the following approach for applying word analysis skills:

1. Examine the word for meaningful parts—base word, prefixes, suffixes.

   a. If there is a prefix, take it off first.

   b. If there is a suffix, take it off second.

   c. Look at the base or root to see if you know it or if you can think of a related word (a word that has the same base or root).

   d. Reassemble the word, thinking about the meaning contributed by the base or root, the suffix, and then the prefix. This should give you a more specific idea of what the word is.

2. Try pronunciation, looking for familiar patterns and trying out pronunciations of syllables.

3. Try out the meaning in the sentence; check if it makes sense in the context of the sentence and the larger context of the text that is being read.

4. If the word still does not make sense, or if you were unable to break the word down into affixes and base or root—and if it is still critical to the meaning of the overall passage—then look it up in the dictionary.

5. Record the word in your writing notebook or on your personal word list for future use.

Armed with strategies they can use independently, readers can unlock the meaning of words they meet both in school and out, enabling them to become adept consumers and users of language.

Let the Students Talk

Students come to school with a fund of words with which to communicate. Through their conversations they build vocabulary. It's such a simple idea, isn't it? Not to be overlooked is this inexpensive, ready-made opportunity to expand vocabulary, which is supported by Dale Johnson (2001) who suggests that teachers let students do what they do naturally and that is to talk. Encouraging numerous opportunities to talk through engaging activities, most of them an integral part of the school curriculum already, is a viable way to build every learner's vocabulary. Johnson states,

> I believe that the best way to help schoolchildren expand their vocabularies so that there is a likelihood of ever-improving communication is to provide plentiful, interactive oral language experiences throughout the elementary and middle school grades. Such development can sustain and expand on the remarkable achievements in oral language usage and vocabulary acquisition made by children before they ever begin their formal education. (p. 19)

Think back over the chapters you have already read in this book. What kinds of activities spring to mind that would increase vocabulary through talk? What might you hear if you eavesdrop on conversations in primary grade literacy play centers? In addition, you can plan specific Center Time over several days during the week. Children rotate from one center to another, practicing several different vocabulary strategies, and the art of collaboration, reading, and writing in the process (Allington,

2002; Fountas & Pinnell, 2001). Listen to their talk as they interact to refine a new skill. Furthermore, imagine the lively conversations in a literature circle, the opportunity to participate in a Reader's Theater production, talking with friends or the class about a book recently completed, or answering questions about content area subjects in large and small groups. These are just a few of the ways conversation is encouraged. Because talk is so important, not only in acquiring vocabulary but in helping students comprehend subject matter, make it an integral part of the learning routine all across the curriculum. Reports in numerous forms in social studies should be read aloud and discussed with the class. If there is a hot topic surfacing in town, put middle and upper grade students to work to learn about both sides, and then organize a debate. Science experiment results can be analyzed between participants as the language of science gains familiarity through use. Quality talk time is essential. Don't short-change it in your classroom.

PROMOTING QUESTS FOR PERSONAL WORD KNOWLEDGE

Filling the Word Jar

Graves (1987) explains that because most vocabulary learning occurs independently, the teacher should make word gathering an interesting and fulfilling activity. In order to develop ownership of new words, students need to use them over and over again. Try a class word jar for a starter activity. To pique interest, read about Donavan whose hobby was collecting words, which he kept in a special jar (DeGross, 1994):

> All kinds of words went into Donavan's collection. He had big words like PROFOUND that made him feel smart. Little words like CUDDLE warmed his heart. Donavan found that soft words like HUSH soothed his fears. Silly words like SQUABBLE slipped off his tongue and tickled his ears. From somewhere he collected HIEROGLYPHIC, a strange word that made him wonder. And just for fun, he added strong words like WARRIOR, words that rang in his ears like thunder. Donavan put mysterious-sounding words like EXTRATERRESTRIAL into his collection. And there were musical-sounding words like ORCHESTRAL.

Read aloud *Donavan's Word Jar* (DeGross, 1994), a short, appealing chapter book for second or third graders, to show the delight and satisfaction Donavan experienced through collecting and sharing his words. Then, decide how you as a class could begin a word collection. You might devote a bulletin board to the word jar with the enlarged shape of a jar in the center. Children write a word they have discovered on a piece of tagboard. At a special time during the day, several words are read aloud and then added to the jar. Challenge classmates to use the daily words throughout the week. After a week or two, the words can be removed and used for charades, integrated into a shared writing story, and then returned to the owners to add to their personal word collections. Then again, the words might be kept in a large plastic jar after they are shared with the class. Periodically throughout the day, a word might be

Word Walls, name charts, science and social studies posters all aid vocabulary development.

drawn from the jar and read aloud, and a volunteer attempts to use it in a sentence. The word jar lends itself to creative extensions, so the teacher and class can return to it off and on throughout the year to boost vocabulary acquisition. Middle grade readers can add wonderful words from the novels they are reading using this readily adaptable strategy.

Personal Word Knowledge Charts

A word knowledge chart is a handy way to encourage the personal quest for words and to keep track of those words as they are encountered during a reading activity. The charts are especially useful in the classroom where students are involved in activities that promote wide reading, an excellent way to expand one's vocabulary. Such charts might be kept in a writing folder in each student's desk for easy access. Figure 9.9 provides an example of a knowledge rating chart that would be appropriate for primary and middle grade students. As students add each word, they must think about it, decide what they know about it, and what to do about making it their own. The charts should be reviewed on a regular basis to keep words fresh in the student's mind. Those that have been added to a personal repertoire of words might be starred, giving the student a sense of satisfaction in seeing his word knowledge increase.

Figure 9.9

An example of a knowledge rating chart

How much do you know about these words? Place a check mark in the appropriate boxes.

Word	Can Define	Have Seen/Heard	Don't Know

Remember, children do not learn words unless they are used and unless connections are made between words they already know and those which are new. It takes learners who are actively involved in gathering vocabulary, and thinking, thinking, thinking about new words in order for vocabulary knowledge to expand. Another option to foster such involvement is getting into the habit of using a second chart, the related words chart, which is particularly appropriate from middle grades on up (Figure 9.10). The chart is relatively easy to use; it encourages students to draw on their previous knowledge, and then add to it with additional information from the dictionary or other reading materials. The teacher can explain how to use the related words chart in small reading groups, modeling its use and helping students as they complete the chart with a word or two from the day's reading. Later in the year students can assume the responsibility of completing the charts themselves, sharing their growing list of words with a classmate or during teacher conferences on a regular basis. It isn't a chart that should be overused or students will come to regard it with disdain. It is just one more way to encourage thinking about new words, broadening one's word knowledge base, and keeping track of personally acquired vocabulary.

Graffiti Word Wall

Set aside a segment of a bulletin board or firmly attach several sheets of newsprint to a prominent place on the wall. Designate this spot as the graffiti word wall (Robb, 1994). During an interdisciplinary unit or perhaps to encourage writing about a current topic like the change of seasons, invite students to write pertinent words on this wall with markers. This activity is supported by research suggesting that students personalize their word learning by selecting some of their own vocabulary words as

Portfolio Activity:
Graffiti

Figure 9.10
A related words chart

Vocabulary Word	Related Words and Phrases

Name

———————————————

they are encouraged to do with this type of word wall (Blachowicz & Fisher, 2000). Review a selection of the words each day, talking about them and how they relate to the unit under study or the changing seasons. Some of these words will come from class readings, the daily read-aloud, or outside sources. Invite students to browse through the words and to integrate them regularly into their writing and their conversations. In addition, the graffiti wall will serve as an excellent and easy reference for invigorating their creative writing. A further idea is that learners take a word a day and write about it in their reading or writing journals. Encourage students to continue to collect personally interesting words in these journals, contributing to the graffiti word wall when appropriate and just enjoying the collection and use of a variety of words at other times.

Fostering Word Consciousness Through Word Play

Web Link:
Word Play

When all is said and done, it is the students who are primarily in charge of their vocabulary growth. It is the teachers who can encourage them to be word conscious learners, however. Being **word conscious** means that,

> students have a disposition toward words that is both cognitive and affective. Students who are word conscious know a lot of words and know them well. They are interested in

words, and they gain enjoyment and satisfaction from using them well and from seeing or hearing them used well by others. (Graves, 2000, p. 127)

While some learners are naturally motivated to use words well and will always be on the lookout for more intriguing words to add to their repertoires, others need to be motivated. Students must use newly discovered words if they are to become a part of a personal word bank from which words are routinely deposited and withdrawn. One way to foster word consciousness is by modeling a personal enjoyment of word gathering, setting the tone for continuous vocabulary growth (Bear et al., 2000). Designating time for word play is another way to make vocabulary growth just plain fun. Use books like *Word Wizard* (Falwell, 1998), which involves students in anagram play, rearranging the letters of one word to form another word. While eating her cereal one morning Anna discovers that she has a job to do. She must use particular words to help a lost little boy return safely home. In order to come to Zack's aid, the *ocean* must become a *canoe* and the *shore* is changed to a *horse*. This motivating text might prompt older readers to try writing anagram adventures of their own once the book is finished.

The brain likes an occasional surprise to keep it focused (Jensen, 1998). Assemble a variety of games in the reading center and have a Word Play Day from time to time just for a change of pace. An hour in the morning or afternoon devoted to Scrabble, Probe, anagrams, or teacher-created bingo games reinforces vocabulary in an upbeat way. Pull in the Internet, trying out sites noted at the end of the chapter. This step might be especially appealing to a gifted child. Get out the personal word collections and create thought-provoking word sorts (Gunning, 2001). Students with second language barriers and learners with language deficits will surely profit from an engaging way to practice and continue to learn. Try repeating the exposure to important words by playing a simple game like bingo. The bingo cards might include words depicting essential skills or words from content area study. No one said learning had to be routine. Practice couched in play will be difficult to resist. No doubt the student with attention deficit hyperactivity disorder (ADHD) will be volunteering to get the games out. Staying focused and on task for lengthy periods is one of the more challenging aspects of the school day. Time to engage in learning in a different way involving varied and interesting tasks should be an integral part of her day. Games that encourage interaction are a natural opportunity for learning while involving a little movement and some important positive peer interactions all at the same time (Carbone, 2001).

Deciphering the Meanings of Homophones and Homographs

Students will enjoy another opportunity for word play through the study and use of **homophones** and **homographs,** which look like decidedly confusing terms. These seemingly similar words can be distinguished from each other by looking at their endings. First, examine the word *homophone*. The morpheme or word part, *phon,* refers to sound. Think of using the "phone" to hear what a friend has to say, and you have a clear connection to what this word means. Homophones, then, are words that have the same sound, but their meanings are quite different. They may or may not be spelled the same way as in the words:

bee   be   toed   toad   knew, new, gnu

Now, look carefully at the word *homograph*. The morphene, *graph*, refers to a written element, as in giving someone your autograph. Homographs are two or more words that have the same spelling, so are written the same way, but they have different meanings and, often, different origins. The confusion that arises with these particular words is that while the words are spelled the same way, they are pronounced differently:

> I *read* the latest chapter about Harry Potter last night.
>
> I plan to *read* the latest Harry Potter book slowly because I just don't want it to end.

or:

> The warm *wind* is a welcome change.
>
> *Wind* the rope tightly around the branch so that the swing does not fall.

Demonstrate the fun one can have when learning to use these words correctly by writing several excerpts from *The Alphabet from Z to A with Much Confusion on the Way* (Viorst, 1994, unpaged) on the board and reading them aloud. Define the words together to reinforce the point that these homophones sound the same but certainly have different meanings.

> V is for VALE and for VEIL
>
> And (I cannot believe this!)
>
> for VANE, VAIN, AND VEIN!
>
> R is for—we're not at R yet.
>
> Now what's your hurry?

or this verse:

> D is for DEW, DO
>
> DYE, DIE
>
> DOE, DOUGH.
>
> Isn't it awful?

An older title that continues to entertain with its delightful foolishness and illustrates homophones at the same time is *A Little Pigeon Toad* (Gwynne, 1988). Encourage students to work at locating words that are homophones or homographs. They can list the words they find on chart paper in a handy viewing spot in the classroom, announcing new additions and their meanings as they are discovered. Put the words to use by encouraging duos of learners to define a pair of words, use them appropriately in sentences, and then illustrate them. The pair can share the polished creation by posting it on an entertaining and informative bulletin board (see Figure 9.11).

When in Doubt, Use the Indispensable Dictionary

While innumerable students have suffered the fate of looking up weekly lists of vocabulary words, writing definitions, and using each word in a sentence, this is definitely

Figure 9.11

A sampling of homophones

Homophones: Words That Sound Alike But Are Spelled Differently

ant—aunt	ate—eight	aisle—isle—I'll	all—awl	be—bee
bear—bare	break—brake	bale—bail	base—bass	bored—board
bow—bough	browse—brows	blue—blew	cell—sell	creek—creak
chord—cord	crews—cruise	choose—chews	days—daze	dear—deer
die—dye	do—due—dew	doe—dough	eye—aye—I	fair—fare
faint—feint	feat—feet	fourth—forth	flew—flu	fir—fur
gait—gate	great—grate	guilt—gilt	grown—groan	guessed—guest
hair—hare	hey—hay	heel—heal	hole—whole	him—hymn
hoarse—horse	here—hear	jeans—genes	know—no	knead—need
knight—night	knew—gnu—new	led—lead	lie—lye	leak—leek
load—lode	loot—lute	mail—male	meet—meat	main—mane
mourn—morn	maize—maze	missed—mist	not—knot	or—ore
pour—pore	passed—past	pray—prey	praise—prays	pale—pail
plain—plane	peer—pier	pole—poll	pause—paws	plumb—plum
peak—peek—pique	rest—wrest	red—read	ring—wring	road—rowed
right—write	rain—rein—reign	seem—seam	sea—see	sail—sale
sleigh—slay	steak—stake	soul—sole	seas—sees	sheer—shear
sown—sewn	some—sum	scents—cents—sense	tax—tacks	tale—tail
team—teem	tide—tied	their—they're—there	tear—tier	threw—through
thrown—throne	to—two—too	you—ewe	wave—waive	wait—weight
wear—ware	weave—we've	won—one	would—wood	wet—whet

not the way to reinforce the values to be found within the pages of a dictionary. Unfortunately, that was the traditional form of vocabulary instruction for many years. In reality, dictionary skills do not have to be deadly. Instead, present the dictionary as the reader's and writer's friend and resource (Moore et al., 2003). When other methods of deciphering a word fail, or even before, the dictionary is there for reference. Encourage its use so that students recognize the wealth of information about words, their roots, various meanings, parts of speech, and more within its cover. In addition, as they refer to the dictionary, students are fine-tuning other valuable skills like alphabetical order, employing guide words, working with the symbols that are clues to pronunciation, and activating their judgment to match the meaning of the word with the text they are reading (Johnson, 2001).

When efforts to infer the meaning of a word from context do not work, one practical application that eventually involves the dictionary is to have the students jot the troublesome word in their reading journal or on a sticky note (Robb, 2000). Include the title of the book and page number as well. At a particular time during the week, students work in pairs or trios to discuss their words, review the way each word was used in context, and then look the word up in the dictionary. To most closely match definition and word, students will need to rely on the book and/or sentence in which it was used. Next, students discuss these words together and note the accurate meaning again on the sticky note or write the words and meaning in a designated section of their journals. In fact, those sticky notes can be transferred directly to a page in their journals for future reference. To keep the vocabulary dialogue growing, invite each group to choose a word they found most interesting and share it with the class from time to time. That way, learning is reinforced and everyone profits, even if it is just from exposure to a new word that they may encounter in the near future in their own reading.

Add humor to dictionary usage by reading *Miss Alaineus: A Vocabulary Disaster* by Debra Frasier (2000). It is a clever tale of a misunderstood vocabulary assignment in Sage's fifth grade classroom. You can see how a problem could develop from this excerpt:

> On Tuesday afternoon I called my best friend, Starr, who is not *a luminous celestial object seen as a point of light in the sky,* but a very smart girl who listens perfectly on Vocabulary Day. She was late for baseball practice so she spelled the first fourteen vocabulary words as fast as she could. I had to scribble them quickly because her mom was calling her to the car. "The last one's 'Miss Alaineus'!" Starr yelled. "I gotta go. I hope you feel better tomorrow, Sage." And she hung up the phone with a crash. (page B)

Quite a misunderstanding occurs as a result of that phone call. Each page in this truly original book is a wealth of information. Page letters are used rather than page numbers. An alliterative sentence stretches from the top page letter to the bottom page letter. It is carefully tied to the story and highlights words beginning with the letter at the same time.

Students can't help but be intrigued with the options a dictionary offers as each page is read and closely inspected. There is a creative writing project in the waiting once this story is completed, for students will be eager to try a tale like this one. Students can choose a letter, develop a page, and assemble a class book revolving around a dilemma like Sage faced. Such a book can help students quickly understand that dictionary work does not have to be dull.

Keep the motivation high for relying upon the dictionary with a creative writing assignment like the one Miss Zittergruen used in a recent fourth grade practicum placement. In preparing for the dictionary poetry lesson she planned to teach, she collected a personal list of fifteen unusual and amusing words. She neatly printed the list and made copies for pairs of students to use. In addition, a copy of the list was printed on an overhead transparency and used to introduce the lesson. As the language arts period began, Miss Z explained the assignment to the class. The day's focus was a creative writing project. Writers were going to begin by locating a dictionary definition of one of the words on the overhead and would rely on its information to develop an imaginary character. That character would be described in a narrative, free-verse poem which integrated information from the definition throughout. Then, Miss Z read the words aloud to the class. Finally, she modeled the assignment. She told the class the word she had chosen and introduced her unusual character by reading her free-verse poetry. The lesson then proceeded as follows:

1. The class was divided into pairs. Miss Z used a simple method to do this, merely assigning students to work with the neighbor next to them, rows one and two and rows three and four pairing up neatly. The one inclusion student was partnered with a classmate, monitored by the classroom aide.

2. As a writing team, the twosome selected a word from the teacher-generated list that they thought looked especially interesting. Armed with dictionaries, paper, and pencils, they went to work. They looked up their word and wrote the definition at the top of their paper.

3. Now they began to brainstorm ideas together to create a rough draft of a free-verse poem patterned after the one Miss Z had written. They had to work information from the actual definition into the description of an imaginary character.

4. During this time, a classroom aide and the young practicum student circulated through the class answering questions and encouraging the young writers. By the time the writing period ended, most pairs had a fairly good rough draft.

5. The following day, the pairs polished their writing. Then it was time to share. Duos volunteered one at a time and came to the front of the room to read their dictionary poem aloud. Quite proud of themselves, Mark and Leala were among the first to volunteer. Grinning from ear to ear, they read the following:

Miss Rhodo Dendron

Definition: rhododendron: any of several bushes, some of which are grown for their evergreen leathery leaves and clusters of showy pink, purple, and white flowers.

Miss Rhodo Dendron is a woman of 59 years.

She is a smelly and leafy person.

Her job is planting flowers.

Her favorite outfit is light pink pants with a dark purple shirt, white hat and lime green shoes.

Miss Rhodo Dendron likes to spend her time picking leaves out of her teeth.

She lives in a flower house and the town is called Flowery Pots.

Her favorite food is wormy leaves.

As you can see, Miss Rhodo Dendron is a leafy character.

A round of applause met each writing team as they concluded their reading. Written work was collected and displayed on the bulletin board for the next week. Students clearly enjoyed the integration of dictionary usage and the paired writing opportunity.

You might even create a word-oriented scavenger hunt through the dictionary several times a year, looking for words that relate to a unit under study or select a list of words so unusual they are difficult to forget. Conveying the belief that this handy resource should be at the tip of the resourceful student's fingers could ensure its daily use as vocabulary continues to grow. Finally, turn to the websites at the end of the chapter for an appealing alternative to typical dictionary skills lessons and for ways to introduce and reinforce dictionary skills.

Teaching Strategy for the Classroom

A SAMPLE VOCABULARY LESSON PLAN

I. OBJECTIVES

To introduce the vocabulary in *The Legend of Freedom Hill* (2000) by Linda Altman.

II. MATERIALS

The Legend of Freedom Hill; 8½ by 11 inch pieces of heavy paper, tagboard, or used file folders, cut in half; dark markers; and vocabulary words written one letter at a time on the paper or tagboard. While specific words have been selected for this lesson, it is important to note that others may be more appropriate depending on the backgrounds of students in the class and/or the grade level of the students using the book. Word suggestions for this lesson: *outsider, boarder, scurried, shackles, thunderstruck.* Because of the nature of this activity, select enough words so that each child can have a letter and be a part of a word group.

III. INSTRUCTIONAL APPROACH

A. Motivator

Ask the class to take out scratch paper and pens or pencils. Tell them they are to think about the following situation and to do a quick-write, a free-flowing few minutes of writing. Use this prompt: You have just acquired a fortune, a great deal of money. Pick an amount that represents a small fortune to you and then explain how you would use it. Ready, set, write!

After four or five minutes, tell the class to stop. Invite three or four students to share what they wrote. Ask the rest of the class to hold onto their thoughts until after the book has been completed, and then there will be additional time to talk about them. Move on to the book, explaining to the class that a small fortune and how to spend it are also a problem for the two main characters they are about to meet.

B. Teacher/Student Interaction

- Introduction of new vocabulary: First, preview the book, *The Legend of Freedom Hill,* by showing the class the cover and reading the title, author, and illustrators. Ask students to speculate about the setting. Gather their initial predictions regarding what this story will be about. Turn to the title page and dedication page, asking for any confirmations or additional predictions. Then set the book aside, telling the class that you want to work with some interesting vocabulary words before reading the story. Tell the listeners that understanding the words will help them to comprehend the story better. In addition, it will give them new words to use in their future reading and writing work.

- From the previously organized stacks of vocabulary words, pick up a pile of letters for the first word you want. In this case, begin with *outsider.* Select one child per letter and have them come up to the front of the room. Hand a letter to each participant, in the right order, keeping the blank side toward the class. Once the students are lined up appropriately, they are to turn their backs to the class. At this point they can turn their letters around. On your cue, one student will turn back around, facing the class, with the letter visible. Eventually the remaining students will follow suit, one at a time, upon your cue, but not yet. Now, give the class their directions.

- Explain that you are going to be playing a guessing game, trying to decide what the new vocabulary words for this story will be, watching the word built one letter at a time by their classmates. Students are to use what they think about the story at this point, tie in thoughts from their motivating activity, and draw on prior knowledge to help them guess the words. One clue that also might help the students is to count all of the letters and think of words that might match as they try to guess the new word. Remind the class that this is not necessarily an easy task because these may be words they do not use frequently.

- On your signal, the first child turns himself around. Give the class a few minutes to think. Students with a guess are to raise their hands and are called upon by a designated classmate or the teacher. If guesses are incorrect, the next student turns around, letter forward, waits a minute or two while students guess, and so forth, until the final letter is revealed or the word is guessed, whichever occurs first. The class then reads the word together.

- Now, tap prior knowledge and ask what that word might mean. Suggest that they try what they know about structural analysis. Is there a prefix or a suffix that they recognize? In this case there is a suffix, "s," so now students might guess that the word means more than one of something. What about root words? Students will note that there are actually two root words; thus this is a compound word. Who or what are *outsiders?* Discuss the contributions, reinforce the right meaning if it is offered, or teach it if it is not. Use the word in a sentence from the story to demonstrate how it can be used. At this point, ask the letter holders to return to their seats with their letters. Their job is done for the moment.

- Repeat the process with the additional words. As you can see, students are definitely actively engaged in learning new words, both as they stand in front of class as a letter holder and as they guess the evolving words and their meanings. Active engagement is one of the keys to remembering new words.

- Once all of the words are guessed you might write a "gift" word up on the board, one that you are giving them because it is quite difficult to understand. Use *abolitionist* for this book and explain its meaning. Students who have studied the issue of slavery will probably connect with this word the best. For others who have not heard the term, a brief explanation will be beneficial as you are building background to better enable readers to understand this story.

- Return to the book. Set the purpose by telling the class to listen for the new vocabulary words once more as you read the story aloud. Suggest that the class listen to discover what kind of fortune is mentioned and how it is used in this instance.

- Read through the story, stopping frequently to confirm and adjust students' predictions. Take a few minutes to discuss reactions as well, keeping the students engrossed in the plot by tapping their feelings.

- Once the story is done, ask for verbal reactions. Note that this is a legend. Go back to the first paragraph of the story, which states, "The story's what you might call local-famous. That's not to say everyone believes it. Knowing's one thing, believing's another." What do the students think? Did the story actually happen? Have the students share their thoughts as partners, giving them each a few minutes to talk. Then, invite class responses. Are there questions they would like answered after reading this story? How might they find out answers to those questions?
- Remind readers to keep their eyes open for other new and interesting words in their own reading. Keep track of them by jotting them down in their reading or writing journals or on personal word lists. Share them with the teacher, use them in their writing, and give one to a friend every once in a while.

C. Gatekeeping

- Invite each vocabulary group to the front of the room. They are to line up their letters on the chalkboard tray or thumbtack them to a bulletin board. Before they sit down, ask them to read the word together and come up with a sentence using it. The remainder of the class should be writing the words in their personal word lists or writing folders, along with the proffered sentence or one of their own. Check for understanding.
- Later in the week, add these words to others and play a bit. Devote a few minutes to review each day by having a student draw a word from a word jar or basket of recently learned words, read it to the class, and challenge a volunteer to use it in a sentence. "Used" words can be tacked to a word wall for future reference.

IV. EXTENSIONS

- Add these words with others from previous stories or personal writing and use an Internet address or software program to create word finds. Students can stump classmates with riddles, too, keeping these kinds of materials in the reading center in a file folder of Vocabulary Fun. Use them during free time or when an assignment is completed early.
- Challenge students, either individually or in small groups, to come up with their own legend about a point of interest in their city or state. Once it is polished, it can be illustrated and bound to be shared with the class first, read to other children in lower grades, and displayed in the learning center for a time.
- Several students might reread the story, noting all of the compound words this time. Using small index cards, each word part can be written on its own card. For example, *everybody* would be written on two cards: *every* on one, *body* on the other. Let the students teach a review lesson on compound words. They might put four or five words on an overhead first, as base words, and challenge the class to make them into sensible compound words. Then the teaching students pass out compound word pieces, one per classmate. Students move about the room to find an appropriate match. On their feet, they may discover more than one option. End the activity by each pair or trio reading the word they created and explaining its meaning.

All of the base words can be kept in a manila envelope or a large resealable bag. Students can work with them as time permits, using them like a word puzzle to see how many compound words they can make. They can list the words in their writing folders, a resource for writing assignments. Review the words with the students to be certain the words are real words.

Suggested Titles for Additional Classroom Use

For students who enjoyed this legend, enjoy reading about fortunes of various kinds, or are in the quest for freedom, these other books might be of interest. While careful additional reading will help students build their vocabulary, sharing any new words they find with classmates is another way to actively involve them in using words.

de Paola, Tomie. (1996). *The Legend of the Bluebonnet: A Tale of Old Texas.* New York: Putnam.

Granfield, Linda. (2001). *The Legend of the Panda.* (S. N. Zhang, Illus.) Plattsburgh, NY: Tundra.

Hopkinson, Deborah. (2003). *Sweet Clara and the Freedom Quilt.* (J. Ransome, Illus.). New York: Knopf. (quest for freedom)

McCully, Emily Arnold. (1998). *Beautiful Warrior: The Legend of the Nun's Kung Fu.* New York: Scholastic.

Mochuzuki, Ken. (1999). *Baseball Saved Us.* (D. Lee, Illus.). New York: Lee & Low. (quest for freedom)

Musgrove, Margaret. (2001). *The Spider Weaver: A Legend of Kente Cloth.* (J. Cairns, Illus.). New York: The Blue Sky Press. (treasure of a different sort)

Provenson, Alice (2001). *The Master Swordsman & The Magic Doorway: Two Legends from Ancient China.* New York: Simon & Schuster.

Winter, Jeanette. (1989). *Follow the Drinking Gourd.* New York: Knopf. (quest for freedom)

V. ADAPTATIONS/MODIFICATIONS FOR DIVERSE LEARNERS

- Locate legends representing the backgrounds of each culture in the classroom. Invite a parent in to share the reading of a legend with their child to enrich the cultural understanding of all of the children in the classroom. This will provide additional reading practice for the English language learner. Videotape the reading session so that students can opt to watch, listen, and follow along in the book at a later time.

- Pair students with learning disabilities, visual handicaps, or mild mental retardation with classmates who can support their learning during the vocabulary activities.

- Continue your professional development by learning some basic sign language so that you can sign some of the vocabulary words to a hearing impaired child. Be certain that such children are in the front of the classroom where they can watch you speak and can use their hearing abilities to the best advantage.

DIVERSE LEARNERS AND VOCABULARY ACQUISITION

Each year when a new class of students enters the room, you are faced with a fresh set of opportunities and challenges. Understanding that you will have learning differences to address, you will ready your materials and strategies as you ready your

Web Link:
English Vocabulary
Generator

classroom, prepared to meet the needs of each unique learner once again. Here are several more ideas to add to your growing repertoire of ways to make every learner feel comfortable, stay motivated, and be successful. Research conducted by Juel and Minden-Cupp (1999/2000) uncovered a strategy that might help a broader range of diverse learners than the students who were focused upon initially in their study. The authors examined four primary grade reading programs. The results of their scrutiny yielded information about an effective method to use with one group of diverse learners, those students who come to first grade with weak knowledge of the alphabet and phonemic awareness. These children progressed using the following good teaching practices:

1. Teachers modeled all word recognition strategies whether it was chunking word parts like finding little words in big ones or working with onsets and rimes.
2. Students developed the technique of finger-pointing as they read.
3. Children manipulated words as they compared and contrasted them using pocket charts, word sorts, and looking at spelling patterns in words.
4. Teachers used small group instruction with a focus on each child's needs.

It makes sense that this approach would be effective with other learners who are slow to develop word knowledge because of varying backgrounds, language or learning deficiencies, not just these particular primary grade learners.

An educationally entertaining book to inspire closer investigation of words is *The Pig in the Spigot* (Wilbur, 2000). Filled with amusing poems that play with words, readers quickly learn that they are to look for little words inside larger ones.

> Because some moths can think of nothing better
>
> Than chewing wool, there is an *eat* in sw*eat*er. (unpaged)

or the slightly longer verse:

> The mother kangaroo makes long, long jumps
>
> And comes to earth with very heavy bumps.
>
> That is the reason why, inside her *pouch*,
>
> Her child is constantly exclaiming, "*Ouch!*"

If several short verses are rewritten on chart paper for the students to see, they can take turns circling little words. Then, give them a list of four or five additional words and let them circle the little words that they find. Choose one and write a silly verse together. Provide time to practice writing their own verses, working with a partner, and celebrate the results. Remind the students to look for little words inside larger words in their reading. Sometimes those little words will help them pronounce a difficult word, but caution learners that they probably won't help them much with meanings. Work with several examples to demonstrate why that might occur. Gifted students will be challenged with a creative activity like this one, writing, illustrating, and sharing their verse.

Teaching Strategy for the Classroom

USING PICTURE BOOKS BASED UPON SONGS TO BOOST VOCABULARY

Another suggestion is to add a supply of books to the reading center that include picture books made from songs. Introduce the book and song by teaching the words to the whole class using an overhead transparency or writing the words on chart paper. Read through them together, sing along with the tape or CD several times throughout the day or the week, and then invite repeated singing later in the reading center. Struggling readers like those with language disabilities, attention deficit problems, and the visually impaired will surely benefit from such engaging practice. They can sing along with the tape, finger-pointing to the words. They are learning through music and repeated exposure to the words in a purely delightful way. The following list of books with corresponding tapes or CDs might be starters (Towel, 1999/2000).

Baby Beluga by Raffi (Crown, 1992)
Butterfly Kisses by Bob Carlisle (Tommy Nelson, Inc., 1997)
Down by the Bay by Raffi (Crown, 1990)
Halley Came to Jackson by Mary Chapin Carpenter (HarperCollins, 1998)
Inch by Inch by David Mallet (HarperCollins, 1975)
The Itsy Bitsy Spider by Iza Trapani (Whispering Coyote Press, 1993)
The Marvelous Toy by Tom Paxton (E. Sayles, Illus.). (Morrow Junior Books, 1996)
Old McDonald Had a Farm (G. Rounds, Illus.). (Holiday House, 1989)
The Teddy Bears' Picnic by Jerry Garcia & David Grisman (HarperCollins, 1996)
What a Wonderful World by George David Weiss and Bob Thiele (F. Cooper, Illus.). (Atheneum, 1996)

A third way to help diverse learners is by using a word wall or building a personal word file of essential vocabulary words. Davis and McDaniel (1998) suggest that there are "essential words" so important to survival and success that everyone should know them and they should be incorporated into literacy programs for readers of all ages. The authors explain that non-English-speaking learners and disabled readers who do not use context or phonetic skills with ease should memorize the following terms to avoid "inconvenience, arrest, embarrassment, serious injury, or even death" (p. 309). See Figure 9.12 for a list that can be adapted depending on the age of the reader.

A wonderfully practical and creative activity for these English language learners or the hearing impaired is to use environmental print in various ways. Rule (2001) devised an alphabetizing idea for her primary students that can be adapted with ease for many learners. The materials for an environmental card set come from cardboard box products like cereal boxes, frozen foods, baking products, snack foods, cleaning items, and the like. Thus, words might include toothpaste, butter, waxed paper, aluminum foil, crackers, rice, soap, soup, candy, and so forth. Each word is cut out from the box or container and mounted on tagboard or matboard rectangles for durability. The tagboard is trimmed neatly leaving a small border around the word. Laminating the words would ensure a longer classroom life. Rule suggests retaining pictures,

Web Link:
Vocabulary Training
Exercises

Figure 9.12

List of essential vocabulary

10 items or less	do not enter	hazardous	no pets	shirt and shoes
30 days same as cash	do not get in eyes	hazardous area	no photographs	required
911	do not ingest	hazardous	permitted	signature
airbags	do not mix	chemicals	no refunds	slippery when wet
alternate route	do not take if	hazardous waste	no returns	slow down
aluminum cans only	allergic to . . .	help wanted	no through traffic	soft shoulders
ambulance	do not take with	hospital	no turn on red	speed limit
asbestos hazard	milk	ID required	no video cameras	stairs (stairway)
automatic	do not use near	if swallowed,	allowed	stop ahead
biohazard	water, fire, etc.	induce vomiting	non-alcoholic	subway
biohazardous waste	don't walk	in case of fire	non-toxic	surgeon general
blasting zone	dosage	incinerate	nuclear waste	warning
bomb threat	drive in	incinerator	one way	take with food
breakable	drive through	infectious area	order here	teller machine
bridge ices before	drive-up window	insert card (ATM)	oxygen in use	through traffic
road	electrical hazard	irritant	pay cashier before	time card
buckle up	Emergency Medical	keep away from	pumping	time clock
bump	Services	water	pay here	tornado warning
business route	enter only	keep frozen	pedestrian crossing	tornado watch
by-pass	escalator	keep out of reach of	polluted area	tow away zone
caffeine	exact change	children	prepare to stop	tow zone
cancerous	(needed or only)	keep refrigerated	quiet please	toxic
cash only	exit only	kerosene	radiation hazard	toxic waste
cellular phones	expect delays	lifeguard on duty	radioactive	turn off cellular
prohibited	expiration	loading zone	materials	phones
chemicals	expires (EXP)	makes wide turns	radioactive waste	turn signal
children at play	explosives	manager	railroad crossing	uneven shoulder
clearance	express line	may cause birth	read directions	use only as directed
construction ahead	evacuate	defects	before using	ventilation required
consult physician	falling rock	may cause dizziness	recyclable	video camera in use
before use	fasten seat belt	may cause	recycle	video monitor in
danger	fax machine	drowsiness	refrigerate	use
dangerous	fire alarm	microwave in use	restricted area	watch for falling
deer crossing	fire exit	microwave safe	restrooms	rocks
delay	flagger ahead	minimum speed	resume safe speed	watch for trucks
deliveries	flush	must be 21 years of	right of way	wear protective eye
detour	for help dial *HP	age	right turn only	gear
diesel fuel	form line here	no jet skis allowed	road closed	wear safety glasses
directions	handicapped	no left turn	school crossing	weight limit
dispose	parking	no littering	school zone	wide load
do not bend	hard hat area	no outlet	service engine	wrong way
do not block	harmful	no pagers	self service	X-ray
intersection	hazard	no parking	shake well	yield

Source: From Davis, A. P., & McDaniel, T. R. (1998). An essential vocabulary: An update. *The Reading Teacher, 52* (3). 308–309. Used by permission. International Reading Association.

icons, or cartoon characters when possible to add visual interest. For these readers, they would also supply clues to the word's meaning.

Word sets can be created from the words to meet varying student needs. Sets are stored in resealable plastic bags with directions for specific language activities tucked inside or taped to the outside of each bag. For example, word sets may be organized to be alphabetized by first, second, or third letters of the alphabet. Another packet may invite students to write a short story using the enclosed words especially supportive for learners who are mildly retarded or whose learning disabilities interfere with language processing. Students might use the words as prompts to think of rhyming words, to divide longer words into syllables, or to make compound words from shorter words. Separate bags can be filled with interesting, more challenging words and directions to engage the gifted learner in higher level, creative thinking. Through this creative strategy, students are polishing a number of vocabulary skills and are also learning to read their environment.

Remember the impact of reading and plenty of it as a natural way to improve all reading skills, including vocabulary. Paired reading and peer tutors offer ready support as students master the printed page (Allington, 2001; Collins, Hendricks, Fetko, & Land, 2002). The more adept reader can help with difficult words, ask questions or prompt to clarify confusion, and just chat about the book at hand. Reach for a variety of materials with which to practice, like short text such as the poetry suggested in the previous chapter, picture books that are appropriate for older readers, and simple chapter books as fare for upper grades. Offer the gifted learner opportunities to team with classmates and other possibilities for working independently. On some occasions

Having students engage in word games will increase vocabulary.

present assignments that involve activities coordinated with her gifted peers. Shape assignments to her particular abilities while focusing at higher levels of comprehension that activate critical thinking and analytic skills. Every child desires to become an accomplished, motivated reader. It is our task to help each one reach that dream.

ENHANCING LEARNING WITH TECHNOLOGY

Portfolio Activity:
School-Home Connection

Software set up in the reading or writing center for ready access is sure to motivate young learners as well as those who are older. In addition, teacher-tested and previewed websites offer engrossing learning opportunities. One of the reminders frequently offered throughout this chapter is that words must be used to be learned. Certainly, one appealing way to provide practice with a variety of words is through technology. One CD-ROM that provides a wealth of information is *The American Heritage Talking Dictionary* (1994). Not only can students of varying abilities hear each of the 200,000 words pronounced correctly, but they have access to complete definitions, parts of speech, examples of the ways in which a word can be used, abbreviations, hyphenation, synonyms, and idioms. Another appealing option is *CD-ROM for Librarians and Educators* (Sorrow & Lumpkin, 1998), which contains 4,000 color illustrations and photographs. Imagine the possibilities of "getting lost in a dictionary" rather than "getting lost in a book." For some students, this just might happen.

Web Links:
5,000 SAT Preparation Words

Hoagies' Gifted Education Package

Consider the options for a gifted student who is able to use technology as a tool for learning. An excellent website for teachers, parents, and gifted learners is *Hoagies' Gifted Education Page*. Each area links teachers, parents, or students, respectively, to hundreds of valuable sites. Teachers will find a myriad of suggestions, professional resources, learning theory, and excellent Internet investigations for students on a wide range of topics. These investigations will challenge and stretch gifted learners in thought-provoking ways. You have to see this site to believe it.

Add success to the learning fare for children with attention deficit hyperactivity disorder (ADHD) when you provide opportunities to do part of their work with this learning tool. They will enjoy the change of pace, essential to keeping them on track, if segments of their day are broken into specific word games that promote learning as suggested in Figure 9.13.

Teaching Strategy for the Classroom

A CENTERS APPROACH: INTEGRATING TECHNOLOGY, VOCABULARY, READING, AND WRITING IN THE MIDDLE GRADES

One effective strategy to provide students with additional practice on a variety of skills is to focus on them during center activities. Center work also provides a wonderfully interactive change of pace to the day. In addition, note that centers offer excellent learning opportunities for diverse learners who gain from the social interactions with their classmates and the small group work as they strengthen skills.

At the beginning of the year, set up a system for working in centers with your class. Walk through the routine and demonstrate expectations before students practice working collaboratively for shorter times initially. Monitor their work and reinforce responsible, independent behavior. Depending on how you set up your classroom, there could be time for one or two rotations per day. Your directions might include:

- A way to signify when the center is "full" so that children know they should choose another center for the time being.
- Stay in the center they choose initially to avoid roving and confusion.
- Logging in: One option for center time is that you work with a small group of students in a center, too. This might be for direct instruction on a skill or strategy, a review of a skill some students are struggling with, or one-on-one time for assessment purposes. You can't be everywhere at once but do need to know which students have been doing what activities. Have students log in at the center, writing their names and the date on lined paper stapled inside an appropriately titled manila folder. That step gives you an opportunity to check what each child did during center time that day when you are catching up on record keeping.
- You might also include a three-minute reflection time as students complete work at one center before moving to another. Those two- to three-sentence reflections can be slipped into the log folder for your scrutiny at a later time.

Whenever you organize a new set of centers, talk about each one briefly with the class as a whole. Read through the activity card that explains the expectations of work to be done, point out the materials at hand, and add any other pertinent information so that center work will proceed smoothly. Review the rules for working independently or collaboratively at the centers and then invite learners to go to work. The following suggestions could be used for activities after several vocabulary strategies have been taught to the class:

TECHNOLOGY CENTER

It would be a boon if there were at least two computers in the classroom so that more students could be involved in the Technology Center at one time. Otherwise the limit for this activity would probably be two children in order for it to be the most beneficial. If there is only one computer available, but you have access to additional computers in the learning center or a technology lab, make arrangements to have a computer available to another pair of students ahead of time. Those students will be under the supervision of the learning center or lab director. If there are two computers available, one pair of students will work with a piece of software like those suggested in the chapter. This option will vary depending on what programs you or the school has purchased.

The second pair of students is to choose a website from those listed below or others that you have thoroughly investigated. They are to select an activity and spend the center time involved in practicing a skill aided by technology. Students are responsible for giving you brief written feedback (several sentences or more depending on ability) on how they spent their time on a half sheet of paper tucked into the log folder before they move to a different site. Excellent sites to explore:

Alphabet Superhighway: www.ash.udel.edu/
Education4Kids: www.edu4kids.com/
Enchanted Learning Dictionary: www.enchantedlearning.com/Dictionary.html
Merriam-Webster Word Central: www.wordcentral.com/
Wacky Web Tales: www.eduplace.com/tales/

When it is possible, schedule time in a computer lab or the learning center where the whole class can have access to software and websites that will appeal to all learners.

READING AND DIALOGUE CENTER

Work in this center is based upon the research that reinforces the fact that wide reading and talk promote vocabulary growth. Provide an appealing selection of three or four book titles, with multiple copies of each title. Book titles should address varied reading levels, reading interests, and diverse backgrounds. Many fine options fill this textbook. If a maximum of six students work at the center, they might work in triads so that you do not have to locate six copies of one title. Students decide upon a book to read together and read it quietly to each other, taking turns reading. Then they discuss it based upon several general questions on the activity card designed to guide their discussion. After that, students may chat back and forth about their books if two groups have read different titles. Center time wraps up with brief reflection for the log folder.

VOCABULARY STRATEGY—FOCUS ON COMPOUND WORDS

Locate several books that have a number of compound words in them. On the activity card, review what compound words are. Then, students are to read independently or in pairs, jotting down any compound words they discover in their reading. Next, they are to decide if their words fit into categories of concrete (doghouse), concrete but not touchable (moonlight), or abstract (brainstorm) and list words accordingly. Then, students are to illustrate several of the words using 5 by 8 inch index cards or appropriately sized pieces of tagboard. On one side of the card they are to neatly print their word. On the other side they are to draw a picture of each part of the word, connecting the two pictures with a plus (+) sign to show that they go together. For example, for doghouse, a student would draw a dog + a house (Fuhler, 2000). At a later time, each center participant can show the picture side of the card to the class and have them respond with the compound word. Pictures can be taped up near the classroom (compound word) door for students to review as they wait in line for lunch, recess, or dismissal. Rotate the books so each center group has new materials with which to work.

Suggested Titles

Bahous, Sally. (1997). *Sitti and the Cats.* (N. Malick, Illus.). Boulder, CO: Roberts Rinehart.

Bartone, Elisa. (1996). *American Too.* (T. Lewin, Illus.). New York: Lothrop, Lee & Shepard.

Bunting, Eve. (1999). *The Butterfly House.* New York: Scholastic.

Casler, Leigh. (1994). *The Boy Who Dreamed of an Acorn.* (S. Begay, Illus.). New York: Philomel.

Cowley, Joy. (1998). *Big Moon Tortilla.* (D. Strongbow, Illus.). Honesdale, PA: Boyds Mills Press.

Kerley, Barbara. (2001). *The Dinosaurs of Waterhouse Hawkins.* (B. Selznick, Illus.). New York: Scholastic.

Lewin, Ted. (1998). *The Storytellers.* New York: Lothrop, Lee & Shepard.

Spaulding, Andrea. (1999). *Me and Mr. Mah.* (J. Wilson, Illus.). New York: Orca.

Stevens, Jan Romero. (1995). *Carlos and the Squash Plant.* (J. Arnold, Illus.). Flagstaff, AZ: Northland.

Surat, Michele Maria. (1983). *Angel Child, Dragon Child*. (V. Mai, Illus.). New York: Scholastic.

VOCABULARY STRATEGY—PERSONAL WORD COLLECTIONS

Students involved in this center are to use their file boxes or personal word lists. They work in pairs or triads to complete the designated activity on the center activity card. They might make sentences from their words, working with one student's words at a time. Another option is to provide several categories and students must search through their words to find words that will match, recording their finds on paper provided in the center. Categories could be parts of speech like nouns (people, places, and things), words that rhyme, words that contain a silent letter, words with consonant blends, and so forth. Students are building familiarity with how words work and practicing structural analysis depending on the focus of their work.

VOCABULARY STRATEGY—INTERACTING WITH WORDS THROUGH POETRY

Place a selection of appealing poetry books at this center. Another option is to print a number of poems on index cards or on laminated photocopy paper, but it is always more tantalizing to have a book in hand, if possible. Learners are to spend some time browsing through the poetry, reading a few of the poems to each other, and enjoying the sounds of the rhymes, the flow of words, or the preposterous words coined by the poets. Then, they are to select one of their favorite silly words, or a particularly appealing phrase, draw a picture illustrating what it means, and finish their work with a sentence in which the word is used. At an appropriate time these creations will be shared with the class as a whole. Posting them for appreciation on a bulletin board would heighten the fun. If there is access to an available computer, the sentence can be word processed and attached to the picture.

Center time is popular with students. Wrap up these sessions with some sharing of insights or new knowledge from the class. Carefully prepared ahead of time, centers are an excellent opportunity to cement learning and celebrate the acquisition of new skills.

ADAPTATIONS/MODIFICATIONS FOR DIVERSE LEARNERS

- In addition to the modifications suggested in the above lesson, use this time to work one-on-one with struggling readers. Students with learning disabilities, the hearing impaired, and visually impaired learners will learn from modeling and direct teaching. While classmates are engrossed in center work, pull one learner aside at a time to reteach, model, or assess word knowledge. Conference with gifted students to plan and monitor individually challenging Internet activities or coordinated work with other gifted students.
- Supplement lessons in vocabulary building with the hearing impaired learner or the English language learner with visual aids whenever possible. Simple pictures of the words being learned or small items representing a selection of words help these learners make quick connections between items and language.
- Center work will facilitate learning for students who have an attention deficit disorder (ADD) because the activities offer variety to help hold their interest. Working in small groups with focused classmates will provide these learners with models to emulate. Monitor work closely to intervene if the less structured work is hampering the ability to concentrate.

Software to Bolster
Vocabulary Acquisition

Web Links:
Education 4Kids

Davis ESL Cafe

Discovery Channel
School

Enchanted Learning
Dictionary

Linguistic Fun Page

Merriam-Webster Word
Central

Thesaurus.com

A Wordo Puzzle Strategy

Wacky Web Tales

Summary

Vocabulary instruction is aimed at teaching actively involved, critically thinking students a number of strategies for learning additional words so that they are continually building word knowledge. While it is crucial to teach students how to acquire new words, it is also important to motivate them to improve their vocabularies on their own. One of the best ways to do so is to encourage wide reading. Often relied upon, the use of context clues is not always the best way to figure out the meaning of a new word. Other strategies, presented by an enthusiastic teacher who demonstrates her curiosity about learning new words, enable students to embark upon a lifelong quest for new, interesting, and useful words. In this way they will deepen their understanding of what they read, write, hear, and express. Becoming adept at using key vocabulary strategies that can be applied responsibly and independently across the curriculum and outside of the classroom is a goal well worth achieving. It is especially important in an era when it is nearly impossible to keep up with the ballooning world of knowledge. Appealing strategies to learn and then practice new words include word play, daily conversations, and excellent children's literature. In addition, well-conceived software programs and interacting on quality websites both in the classroom and at home are motivating technological options.

Chapter Review

Go to the Online Learning Center at **www.mhhe.com/farrisreading** to take chapter quizzes, practice with key terms, and review important content.

Main Points

- There is more than one kind of vocabulary. They include listening, speaking, reading, and written vocabularies. Middle grade students deal with potential marginal vocabulary.

- One's receptive vocabulary includes listening and reading vocabularies, while the expressive vocabulary involves writing and speaking vocabularies.

- Knowing a word involves understanding it in different degrees from being totally unfamiliar with it to knowing and using the word with ease.

- Wide reading is one of the best strategies for increasing one's vocabulary.

- Conversation, both reflection and content-oriented, is a natural way to build vocabulary usage.

- It is efficient to build a bank of sight words or high-frequency words for beginning readers and readers who have language barriers.

- The use of context clues has received mixed reviews from authorities in the field, but it is still a useful vocabulary strategy when combined with other strategies.

- Direct instruction is but one way to teach vocabulary.

- Graphic organizers like word maps and webs help a learner match new words and concepts with information he already knows.

- Using structural analysis, trying to understand a new word based upon its key parts, is a practical strategy to add to one's vocabulary

skills along with developing word charts, using word walls in the classroom, and fostering word consciousness through engaging word play activities.

- Never abandon the dictionary because it is a boon to building word knowledge when used appropriately.

- Diverse learners will benefit from individual and small group work to build their repertoire of words.

- Technology in the form of motivating software and interactive websites provides additional practice and further opportunities to expand one's vocabulary.

Key Terms

antonym	393
concept of definition map	395
context clues	389
expressive vocabulary	381
homograph	407
homophone	407
listening vocabulary	380
morphemes	399
potential marginal vocabulary	381
reading vocabulary	381
receptive vocabulary	381
semantic features analysis chart or grid	398
semantic word map	395
sight words	386
speaking vocabulary	380
structural analysis	398
synonym	393
webbing	395
wide reading	383
word consciousness	406
writing vocabulary	381

425

Reflecting and Reviewing

1. When you come across a word you do not recognize in your reading, either recreational or academic, what do you do? Have you developed your own personal strategy for learning new words? Is it built upon any of the strategies suggested in this chapter?

2. Pick one of the websites and spend some time investigating it. What are the options available to users of the site? Do you see value in integrating the site into a possible vocabulary lesson in your classroom? Why or why not? How do you visualize using technology to teach words to your current or future students?

3. Think about the strategies suggested in the chapter. How do you plan to balance those that are more teacher-directed with motivating your learners to look for new words on their own?

4. Have you had an opportunity to work with children with special learning needs? What techniques were suggested to you or did you use to help the child or children with the task at hand? Be sure to talk with your teachers during practicum placements to find out what strategies work the best for them.

Children's Literature

For annotations of the books listed below, please see Appendix A.

Altman, Linda. (2000). *The Legend of Freedom Hill*. (C. Van Wright & Y-H Hu, Illus.). New York: Lee & Low.

Bruchac, Joseph. (2000). *Squanto's Journey: The Story of the First Thanksgiving*. (G. Shedd, Illus.). San Diego, CA: Silver Whistle/Harcourt Brace.

DeGross, Monalisa. (1994). *Donavan's Word Jar*. New York: Scholastic.

Falwell, Cathryn. (1998). *Word Wizard*. New York: Clarion.

Frasier, Debra. (2000). *Miss Alaineus: A Vocabulary Disaster*. San Diego, CA: Harcourt Brace.

Gwynne, Fred. (1988). *A Little Pigeon Toed*. New York: Simon & Schuster.

Hindley, Judy. (2002). *Do Like a Duck Does!* (I. Bates, Illus.). Cambridge, MA: Candlewick Press.

Levitt, P. M., Burger, D. A., & Guralnick, E. S. (1990). *The Weighty Word Book*. (J. Stevens, Illus.). Boulder, CO: Manuscripts, Ltd.

McCully, Emily Arnold. (1998). *Beautiful Warrior: The Legend of the Nun's Kung Fu*. New York: Scholastic.

Mochizuki, Ken. (1997). *Passage to Freedom: The Sugihara Story*. (D. Lee, Illus.). New York: Lee & Low.

Mora, Pat. (1996). *Confetti: Poems for Children*. (E. O. Sanchez, Illus.). New York: Lee & Low.

Pinkney, Andrea Davis. (2000). *Let It Shine: Stories of Black Women Freedom Fighters*. (S. Alcorn, Illus.). San Diego, CA: Gulliver/Harcourt Brace.

Reiss, Kathryn. (2000). *Time Windows*. San Diego, CA: Harcourt Brace.

Simon, Seymour. (2000). *They Walk the Earth: The Extraordinary Travels of Animals on Land*. (E. Warnick, Illus.). San Diego, CA: Browndeer/Harcourt Brace.

Viorst, Judith. (1994). *The Alphabet from Z to A with Much Confusion on the Way*. (R. Hull, Illus.). New York: Atheneum.

Wilbur, Richard. (2000). *The Pig in the Spigot*. (J. O. Seibold, Illus.). San Diego, CA: Harcourt Brace.

Classroom Teaching Resources

Bear, D. R., Invernizzi, M., Templeton, S. and Johnston, F. (2000). *Words their way: Word study for phonics, vocabulary, and spelling instruction* (2nd ed.). Upper Saddle River, NJ: Merrill.

Gunning, T. G. (2001). *Building words: A resource manual for teaching word analysis and spelling strategies.* Boston, MA: Allyn & Bacon.

Irwin, J. L. (1990). *Vocabulary knowledge: Guidelines for instruction. What research says to the teacher.* Washington, D. C.: National Education Association (ERIC Document Reproduction Service No. ED 319 001).

Kipfer, B. A. (1997, 1998). *The order of things: How everything in the world is organized into hierarchies, structures, and pecking orders.* New York: Random House.

An excellent publisher with valuable classroom resources. Contact them for copies of "Connections: Book News for Teachers and Librarians," an appealing four-page pamphlet packed with teaching ideas.

Teacher-Focused Web sites:
connections@boydsmillspress.com or
www.boydsmillspress.com

Highlights TeacherNet for K-8 Educators

www.teachernet.com

The teacher will find lesson plans, teaching ideas from across America, bulletin board ideas, a children's literature Web guide, and more at this helpful site.

Awesome Library

http://www.neat-schoolhouse.org/awesome.html

Here is an amazing teacher resource of over 15,000 reviewed online resources for teachers, librarians, children, teenagers, and parents.

"All literature—the stories we read as well as those we tell—provides us with a way to imagine human potential. In its best sense, literature is intellectually provocative as well as humanizing, allowing us to use various angles of vision to examine thoughts, beliefs, and actions."

Judith Langer, educator and co-director of the National Research Center on Literature Teaching and Learning

CHAPTER 10

Children's Literature in a Balanced Literacy Program

Key Ideas

- For all children regardless of their abilities or backgrounds, reading on a regular basis is simply the best practice for learning to read well. A variety of fine **children's literature** can motivate children to practice with pleasure.

- Knowledgeable teachers understand the domain of children's literature and its potential for enhancing the reading and writing experience for each learner in today's diverse classrooms.

- The different **genres** within real literature contain appealing titles to invite readers of differing ages and abilities to sample each one.

- Response theory underscores the importance of an individual's interaction with what is being read. There are a variety of activities available to extend a student's personal response to a book.

- **Multicultural literature** in the form of picture books, novels, and nonfiction titles can be used to broaden students' understanding of people from diverse cultures.

- Support for integrating fine literature into the reading/writing classroom and onward across the curriculum is offered in the *IRA/NCTE Standards for the English Language Arts* (IRA/NCTE, 1996).

- In a balanced literacy program, involvement with children's literature complements teacher-directed, skills-based teaching as it invites students to broaden and deepen their thinking about what they read and, as a result, how they view themselves and the world around them.

Questions to Ponder

- What is children's literature?
- What is the rationale for integrating this literature into the reading and writing curriculum?
- Why is it important to give students time to respond to literature in various ways?
- How does a teacher begin to organize the myriad of children's books that are available?
- What role does multicultural literature play in the reading curriculum and beyond?
- What kinds of resources are available for researching quality literature for readers from kindergarten through sixth grade?

Peering into the Classroom

Expanding Students' Worlds Through Literature

Ramon taps his pencil against his head as he peers off into space. His thoughts are on Tep, a boy about his age who is the protagonist, the main character, in a book he's reading. Will Hobbs (1995), the author of *Kokopelli's Flute,* is one of Ramon's favorite writers. Now Ramon is lost in his thoughts about Tep's dilemma.

Ramon loves history. He teased his teacher, Miss Bartelone, when she introduced the "Westward Movement" in social studies class. According to Ramon, "My ancestors were part of the 'Northward Movement.'" Miss Bartelone grinned as she acknowledged that the Spanish did settle much of the west before English-speaking pioneers ventured in large numbers across the plains and Rocky Mountains.

The close ties that Hobbs makes with history in his novels appeal to Ramon. In *Kokopelli's Flute,* Hobbs combines fantasy with information about the cliff dwellers of the Four Corners area of the United States (Colorado, Arizona, New Mexico, and Utah). In his reading, Ramon has reached the part where Tep has climbed into an ancient cliff dwelling called Picture House. Tep believes that by viewing a total eclipse of the moon from this site, he will better understand the secrets and mysteries of the Ancient Ones, or Anasazi Indians. As Tep waits for the eclipse, he discovers robbers stealing the treasures of the cliff dwellings, leaving behind ruined ancient cave pictures and a small bone flute. When Tep tries out the flute, he discovers it is magical.

Tap! Tap! Tap! Ramon ponders what he would do if he was in Tep's situation. How can a boy his age deter robbers? What effect will playing the flute have on

Tep's life? Can the magical spell be undone or is it lasting and permanent? Hastily, Ramon scratches out his thoughts as he writes in a spiral notebook that serves as his literature response journal. Ramon questions whether Tep should take on the thieves and then boldly makes up a plan for Tep to trap them. He pauses to reread what he has just written in his journal. Then he jots down another idea before returning to the book.

From her desk, Miss Bartelone makes a quick observation of Ramon's and her other students' behavior. Then she, too, engages in reading a book and writing her own responses. She is reading *Harry Potter and the Goblet of Fire* (Rowland, 2000). Not a fan of fantasy, Miss Bartelone was persuaded to read the book by its popularity among her sixth graders. Now, like her students, she is deep in thought about the main character in her book.

Literature response engages the reader and evokes emotions. For her students, Miss Bartelone is modeling the behavior of reading and reacting to the author's words. Like her students, she has a favorite genre, or type, of literature she prefers to read. Since she encourages her students to try reading a variety of genres, Miss Bartelone is following her own advice by reading a book from a genre that is not her first choice—or even second or third choice. Her students know this and have encouraged her to join them in reading about their beloved Harry Potter. As Miss Bartelone admits, "If you want kids to eat broccoli, you better show them that you eat broccoli. And if it takes a bit of cheese sauce on the broccoli to accomplish it, so be it!"

REFLECTION: IRA/NCTE NATIONAL STANDARDS IN THE CLASSROOM

Reading that includes quality time spent with children's literature as is demonstrated in Miss Bartelone's classroom is a fine example of what the *IRA/English Standards* advocate in part. Standard 1 is explicitly supported as we see students and teacher reading for personal fulfillment and sampling texts that in this particular instance are contemporary fiction. The Standard proposes that:

> Students read a wide range of print and nonprint texts to build an understanding of texts, of themselves, and of the cultures of the United States and the world; to acquire new information; to respond to the needs and demands of society and the workplace; and for personal fulfillment. Among these texts are fiction and nonfiction, classic and contemporary works. (IRA/NCTE, p. 3)

As Ramon ponders Tep's dilemma and how he might handle the situation, he jots his thoughts in his literature response journal. Miss Bartelone also reads and reacts in her journal. These two readers are demonstrating what it is like to be a "knowledgeable, reflective, creative, and critical member" of a literacy community suggested by Standard 11 (IRA/NCTE, 1996, p. 3). While both of the books being savored happen to be fantasy selections, it is mentioned that Miss Bartelone encourages her students to sample a wide range of literature as is supported by Standard 3. Modeling her expectations for students, she is meeting an original character in an unexplored genre, Harry Potter and his irresistible world of reality and fantasy. With an eye to the general guidelines provided in the Standards and sound knowledge of her individual students, this teacher and others like her can fill the classroom day with sound literacy experiences.

INTRODUCTION

Web Link:
Children's Literature

If you ask a child to tell you about one of his favorite books, it is highly likely that it will not be the latest story in the basal reader. More often than not, the choice will be the teacher's recent read-aloud title, a new picture book discovery, a tattered, nearly memorized book, or a tantalizing novel. Settle in for an enthusiastic retelling for there is nothing quite like a wonderful book, is there? Children who have discovered a fascinating tidbit of information or have traveled to new places to make the acquaintance of amazing characters will be quick to share those experiences with classmates, parent volunteers, the teacher, and family at home.

STANDARDS for READING PROFESSIONALS

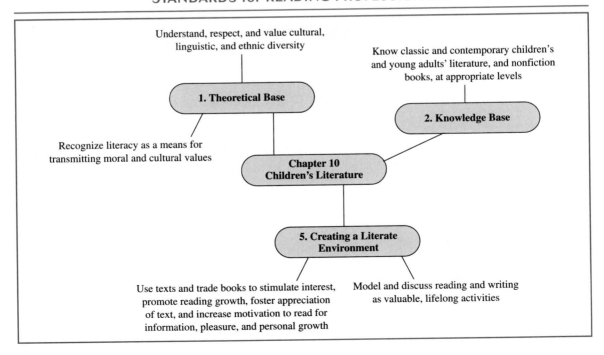

If you extend the conversation to intermediate grade readers, you will find their reading tastes varied and unique to each reader. When allowed to choose their own fare, and they very much appreciate the opportunity to do so, they will reach for magazines, comic books, mysteries or books with scary themes, humorous stories, titles in a series, and books with pertinent characters and themes (Worthy, 2002). A teacher is better able to meet individual differences and to match book and reader across the grades when they have a sound understanding of all that children's literature has to offer.

The realm of children's literature is a wonder to receptive readers of all ages. As such it has much to offer as an integral part of a well-balanced reading and writing classroom. Finely crafted books can become a summons to knowledge and adventure both in the classroom and outside its doors. Coupled with teacher-scaffolded talk time, this body of reading material can so influence attitudes and values, because books enable readers to:

> envision and explore possible selves, roles, and responsibilities through the lives of story characters, both real and fictional; to describe or remember personal experiences or interests in their lives; and to objectify and reflect upon certain problematic emotions and circumstances as they related to important moral and ethical dilemmas in their lives. (McGinley, Kamberelis, Mahoney, Madigan, Rybicki, & Oliver, 1997)

Fortunate are those readers when their efforts are supported and stretched by an enthusiastic and knowledgeable teacher and interested parents or caretakers (Anderson, Hiebert, Scott, & Wilkinson, 1985).

This chapter is an invitation into the irresistible domain of children's literature. It is a primer on children's books that includes a rationale for using literature in a balanced literacy classroom, a short discussion of the role of personal response to a book, a brief explanation of the different genres, suggestions for superb titles, and a sampling of ideas for integrating literature across the curriculum. While the basal reading series might be the core of a reading program, this chapter serves as a reminder that there is still an abundance of room in the curriculum for those quality books that truly excite a reader. As Bernice Cullinan so aptly stated:

> There is no substitute for real books. They are rarely boring or sanitized or squeezed into a reading system that children can smell a mile off. So logic says if we want real readers, we must give them real books; give our young people good literature, good art, and surprisingly, these young people may do the rest. (1987, p. vi)

Please join us as we travel through this primer, then, urged on by the knowledge that we need to know about books, so that we can accept the following poetic invitation and then extend it to the readers in our classrooms:

> A book is something I couldn't do without,
>
> I think they are cool without a doubt.
>
> Books of fantasy, facts, fiction, and war,
>
> A book always has something in store.

Damsels in distress and heroes in planes,

Explore outer space and adventure in trains,

Forests of magic and mysteries galore,

Between the pages there's always something in store.

Books you can read again and again

About sly foxes, fast rabbits, and a little red hen.

Books are great on days with nothing to do,

When it's too hot for baseball and too cold for the zoo.

I think I'll start a good book—don't you?

Erika Sager, 2001. (Used with permission.)

CHILDREN'S LITERATURE DEFINED

Portfolio Activity:
Recommended Reading

Children's literature encompasses a body of fiction, nonfiction, and poetry that is written especially for young people up to the age of fourteen (Mikkelsen, 2000). Rebecca Lukens (1999) explains that this literature varies from adult fare in that the stories are more directly told with more obvious relationships between the characters and their actions. Lukens goes on to explain that "words are merely words, but real literature for any age is words chosen with skill and artistry to give the readers pleasure and to help them understand themselves and others" (p. 10).

Because there are books within this extensive body of literature that are not particularly distinctive, teachers will want to balance some of the best with other materials that may fall short of perfection but rank high in student appeal. Such selections include cartoon collections and comic books or series titles like the Babysitters' Club and Goosebumps selections. Remembering that the best way to improve their skills is to keep readers reading, all kinds of fare, from junk food to gourmet, might be considered essential to their diets. Guiding readers to be discriminating remains an important skill, however. Thus, the American Library Association suggests that quality books should introduce carefully defined characters, represent fine examples of various writing styles, include exemplary interpretations of the theme, and clearly present information in a well-organized fashion. In looking at fictional offerings specifically, Judith Hillman (1995, p. 3) recommends that quality literature for students meet the following parameters:

Web Link:
American Library
Association

- Evoke strong emotions while engaging the intellect
- Empower readers with a will to act
- Express a feeling or an act in beautiful language
- Reveal deep and subtle human motives
- Allow readers to experience vicariously a different time, place, and character

In brief, real books become vehicles that move beyond basic comprehension and skills lessons because each one asks far more than performance from a reader (Turner

& Paris, 1995). When students read and discuss books together, they are broadened as learners who:

> explore new horizons of possibilities. Such explorations help students see from various angles of vision, providing them with increasing sensitivity to the complexities in life as well as in literature. And from this comes their growing ability to understand the options people seem to have before them in literature and life—as well as the ability to explore and find new ones. (Langer, 1995, p. 53)

Web Link:
Carol Hurst's Children's
Literature Site

Thus, literature helps to educate the whole child. Good books captivate the heart and nourish the mind, their impact felt long after "The End" has been reached.

Packaged in an abundance of shapes and sizes one can easily find books that are appropriate for emergent readers, reluctant readers, children with learning difficulties, classmates from varying ethnic backgrounds, and those who are grappling with a second language. Classroom diversity is not an unmanageable issue when fine literature is integrated into the curriculum. In fact, books actually create mind-broadening opportunities for readers to discover the realities of lives of people in one culture after another (Hinchey, 2001). Be assured that there is something for every reader regardless of ability, level of motivation, or personal interests (Worthy, 1996). What fun it can be for the informed teacher and eager student as they join in the quest for just the right book.

WHY USE LITERATURE?

To build upon the quote that opens the chapter, what Bernice Cullinan states, and what the IRA/NCTE Standards advocate, there are a number of other authorities who voice arguments for using quality books as part of the reading and writing curriculum. In their position statement on Excellent Reading Teachers, the Board of Directors (2000) of the International Reading Association states:

> Excellent reading teachers include a variety of reading materials in their classrooms. Sometimes they rely on one or several reading series as the anchor of their reading program, but they also have supplemental materials and rich classroom libraries that contain at least seven books per child. They read to their students, and they provide time in class for children to read independently. (p. 238)

Then, in *Best Practice: New Standards for Teaching and Learning in America's Schools* (Zemelman, Daniels, & Hyde, 1998), the authors have carefully scrutinized numerous suggested reform measures and standards projects from across the United States as noted in Chapter 1. Encapsulating their findings, the authors reinforce "MORE reading of real texts: whole books, primary sources, and nonfiction materials" (p. 5) echoing the IRA/NCTE Standards. In addition, they support providing time for silent reading every day, reading for different purposes, and looking at creative ways to respond to literature. Such efforts are part of an effective reading program that exposes students to a "wide and rich array of print and goes beyond the use of the basal" (p. 31). Finally, they remind the nation's teachers of the impact of modeling, actively reading in their own classrooms right alongside the students.

One cannot argue with these informed voices. They constitute formidable support for promoting children's literature in a balanced literacy classroom and throughout the curriculum. Use books to enrich content area courses. Teach an integrated interdisciplinary unit making exemplary literature the heart of the unit. One could say that real books, authentic resources, and time spent using them wisely are the meganutrients of a healthy curriculum.

THE ISSUE OF RESPONSE

Imagine a classroom filled with students who are engrossed in reading. In looking around the room, you notice several smiles as readers react to what is happening in their books. Another student might look up and gaze off into space, pondering the dilemma facing the main character. Still another might lean over to share a passage with a neighbor. What is happening here? You are observing reader response in action, an absolutely critical event in the life of a reader. If you continue your survey of the room, you will undoubtedly see students who are not involved, who are doodling on a piece of paper, fiddling with a pen, interrupting another classmate, or wandering a bit aimlessly around the room. For them, at that moment, the reading process has been short-circuited. They are an active demonstration of what happens when words are merely "inkspots on paper until a reader transforms them into a set of meaningful symbols" (Rosenblatt, 1978, p. 25).

In order for students to connect with what they are reading, to activate personal reader response, there must be a **transaction** between reader and text (Rosenblatt, 1978). This is a unique experience to every reader because they each bring their particular backgrounds to the reading situation. Meanings are also flavored by personal experiences, feelings, the context in which reading occurs, and the reasons for reading (Huck, Hepler, Hickman, & Kiefer, 2004).

Judith Langer (1995) describes this process of getting into a book as an **"envisionment"** (p. 9), building a text world in the reader's mind. Envisionments are subject to change, growing and becoming enriched over time through continued thought and additional life experiences. Langer explains that readers respond to literature based upon the following factors:

- The level of engagement with the text
- Personal conceptions or perceptions of the text
- Connections with related experiences or similar texts
- Their strengths in asking questions or problem solving to make sense of what they are reading
- Explanations of personal responses through discussion or journaling
- Individual interpretations of texts and responses
- Ability to make critical judgments about the text

Rosenblatt's **response theory** supports the concept of envisionments but explains the process in a little different way. As mentioned in Chapter 1, she suggests that readers' responses are affected by the reasons or particular stances that they are in as they read. For example, they may be reading in the aesthetic stance where getting lost in the book is the focus. They become a part of the world inhabited by the characters assessing events and characters in light of how they might act in similar circumstances (Bond, 2001). When the story is done, these readers still linger in that story world, reluctant to let the shared experiences go. They are actively demonstrating that "in a literary experience there are no ends, only pauses—and future possibilities" (Langer, 1995, p. 5). Because of the "live current" (Rosenblatt, 1978, p. 25) created between the author's words and their personal worlds, they have had a rich experience with reading.

On the other hand, if the teacher has set a specific task connected with the reading experience or if students are seeking pertinent information or examining an idea, the reading experience finds them in the efferent stance. Realistically, this is not an either-or situation. Readers may be moving between the two stances if they are involved in an enjoyable quest for knowledge. Rosenblatt (1991) explains,

> We read for information, but we are conscious of emotions about it and feel pleasure when the words we call up arouse vivid images and are rhythmic to the inner ear. (p. 445)

A basic premise in reader response theory, then, suggests that the reader plays a key role in the construction of meaning from a text. The theory reminds teachers that meaning is not just in the text or within the reader separately; instead it is created in the relationship or transaction between the two. Because the connections between book and reader are so important to the comprehension process, teachers need to facilitate the process of forming them. (See Figure 10.1.)

Facilitating Personal Response

Fortunately, there are a number of ways in which book relationships can be forged. Students may opt to use reader response journals where they react to a specific question posed by the teacher. At other times, a journal becomes a place to share their feelings about what is currently happening in their novel as Ramon and Miss Bartelone were doing in the opening of this chapter. In addition, readers may participate in literature circles previously described in Chapter 8. The social interaction that occurs when readers think together about what they have read is essential to the reading process, and it is inherent in literature circles (Gambrell & Almasi, 1996; Short, Harste, & Burke, 1996; Bond, 2001).

Teachers need to know their students' interests and abilities to help them select books.

Figure 10.1

Dialogue journals and individualized response

A dialogue journal is typically a spiral-bound notebook that becomes a place to share personal connections to books and reactions between classmates and the teacher about those books. When the dialogue is between student and teacher, the journal is a place to hold a "living conversation" (Werderich, 2002, p. 748), an example of real communication in response to what the student is currently reading. Such journals provide an opportunity to differentiate the instruction and to focus on the individual reader and her particular background, abilities, and interests. As such they are a powerful learning tool in an intermediate or upper grade inclusion classroom. For example, journals enable a teacher to carefully scaffold instruction for the struggling reader and to challenge the gifted reader to stretch into books and ponder them in a thoughtful manner.

The following steps provide suggestions for using a dialogue journal:

- At the beginning of the year, provide an overview of journal usage to each student. Explain the format for entries (perhaps a friendly letter or paragraph responses), dating each entry, turn-in procedures, and sample responses.
- Read a book aloud and then model different kinds of responses over a several-day period so that students can understand the connection between reading and responding.
- Provide a series of prompts to encourage response such as the following (Werderich, 2002, p. 748):

    Tell what you noticed about how the author wrote.
    Tell why you think he or she wrote that way.
    Tell what a book said and meant to you.
    Tell what it reminded you of or what surprised you.
    Tell how you read a book and why.
    These suggested responses along with others could be duplicated and stapled inside each reader's journal for easy reference.

- At designated turn-in times, the teacher reads a student's entries and responds to each one personally based upon knowledge of the learner and a desire to encourage meaningful interactions in their dialogues together. Responses might urge the student to think a little further, to make connections to other books, to give reassurance and support, or to offer suggestions for future reading.

Dialoguing with their teacher on a one-to-one basis via a dialogue journal is motivating to readers and enjoyable for the teacher. It is a special opportunity during busy classroom life to connect in a personal way with each student in the classroom.

Teaching Strategy:
Combining Word Sorts
with Story Impressions

For a change of pace, give students an opportunity to respond by easing into drama using reader's theater described in Chapter 3. This is not an intimidating experience since there are no elaborate costumes or fancy scenery demanded. No memorization of parts is required because the readers simply read carefully practiced parts from a script while they stand or sit in front of the class. To start, try the Reader's Theater script from *Young Mouse and Elephant: An East African Folktale* (Farris, 1996) included at the end of the chapter. Students can work with the teacher to create their own scripts from other favorite picture books or from powerful segments of a novel, performing the plays for their own classmates or for children in the lower grades.

    Finally, readers may choose from numerous art, drama, and writing activities as suggested in Figure 10.2's potential response projects. Students who have difficulty with the English language benefit from opportunities to use an interactive journal much like the dialogue journals described in Figure 10.1. Often bilingual students who receive special education services can draw and write simple responses in a journal for immediate peer or teacher response (Ruiz, Vargas, & Beltran, 2002). When a learner is at an emergent literacy level with communication barriers to overcome, encouraging him to draw to construct meaning is a positive starting point. Another option is to act out a story because this type of play with ideas helps them to get at the meaning behind the words through gestures, intonation, and simple sentences (Au, 1993; Larkin, 2001). Regardless of abilities, personal choice is a critical element when children look for ways to deepen their responses to what they are reading. However, every book does not demand a project. If that were the case, students would quickly lose interest in reading and in response. Then, no matter how interesting the options are, the activity becomes like one book report after another, an unhealthy environment in which readers and personal response will cease to flourish.

Portfolio Activity:
Reflection

A LOOK AT THE GENRES

In order to make the discussion of literature more manageable, it is sensible to view these books of prose and poetry by categories or genres. **Genre** is a French word that simply means a type of literature with similar characteristics (Lukens, 1999). Thus, when one understands a particular genre, she can anticipate what type of content will be found within a volume in that category. Whether reading poetry or prose, readers will notice that literature selections are divided into one of two large general genres, that of fiction or nonfiction. Each of these can be further divided into other more specific genres. For instance, under the umbrella of fiction is the broad category of fantasy. Within fantasy one finds titles designated as traditional literature, which includes folktales and fairy tales, modern fantasy, and, a close relative, science fiction. Aside from the numerous kinds of traditional literature, readers will find that both realistic fiction and historical fiction are a part of the broad genre of fiction as well. Interwoven within the entire fiction genre the reader finds inviting multicultural and poetry options. Poetry, too, is a special genre in itself. It runs through the previous genres with fine examples to be interspersed throughout the curriculum as it illuminates people, places, and things in its own unique way. In an effort to keep this primer at a sensible length, examples of both multicultural titles and poetry have been integrated throughout the other genres (see Figure 10.3).

    A close look at the other branch of poetry and prose, that of nonfiction, reveals that it can also be broken down into two more manageable pieces. Each has its own distinctive characteristics. Here the reader is able to examine biographies and autobiographies of people both famous and infamous. In addition one finds the ever popular, continually burgeoning field of informational books. Whether seeking information for

Web Link:
A Celebration of Poets

Figure 10.2

Suggestions for response projects

Writing Focus

- Rewrite one part of the story, telling it from the perspective of a different character.
- Write an advertisement to promote book sales. Identify where the advertisement will be placed to be most effective.
- Write a poem in reaction to the book.
- Write down a passage or quote from the book that was especially appealing to you. Explain why you selected it.
- Rewrite part of the story as a newspaper article.
- Write an opening chapter or one that extends the story.
- Make a list of long-term predictions for the characters in the story.
- Write a letter to the main character. Give advice, express your concern, or ask questions of the character.
- Write a letter from a book character to someone in your class.
- Write several diary entries in the role of the main character to explain what the person might be thinking or feeling after key events in the story.
- Write a letter to the author in care of the publisher explaining your feelings about the book.
- Rewrite part of the story as a reader's theater presentation.
- Write a short autobiography or autobiographical poem about the main character.
- Journal with another classmate who is reading the same book. Write about your reactions, make predictions, and evaluate the book through written dialogue.

Creative Art Activities

- Draw a mural that highlights main events in the story.
- Make a picture and word collage using materials from magazines.
- Make a poster to promote the book.
- Illustrate what you think was the most important part of the book.
- Make an illustrated time line focusing on key events.
- Tell the story in pictures using your own art or pictures from magazines or computer graphics.
- If it is appropriate content, turn the story into a picture book for children in lower grades.
- Practice cartoon art and depict a part of the novel or nonfiction book as a cartoon.
- Make transparencies or a PowerPoint presentation of scenes and quotes to use when you present a book talk on the book.
- Make an author display featuring a short author biography from Internet resources, pictures, quotes, snippets of reviews, and a collection of other books written by the author.
- Make felt board characters and retell part of the story using them as props.
- Make puppets and put on a play based upon the story.
- Create a scale model or diorama of a place or significant event in the story.

Figure 10.2
(concluded)

Oral Presentations

- Give an inspired, enthusiastic book talk to get classmates interested in the book.
- Extend your learning about the topic in the book by doing some research and presenting it to the class as you discuss your book.
- Select several passages from the book to read to the class and discuss briefly.
- Arrange a display of artifacts that represent the book, sharing why you chose them.
- Dress up as the main character in your book and retell part of the story from your point of view.
- Construct a game for two to four players based upon the book.
- Interview the main character working with another student who has read the book.
- Present a reader's theater with several classmates.
- Make up a story bag using a paper lunch bag or a small shopping bag holding key items from the story. Hold up the items as you retell parts of the story.
- If you have read a picture book, take it to the lower grades and read it to a reading buddy or small group of children. Discuss it with them once it is completed.
- Read several biographies including picture book versions about a famous person. Present the person to your classmates telling why the individual was chosen, give a brief synopsis of his or her life, and critique the books used in the project.

a school report or questing for facts to feed one's curiosity, informational books draw an amazingly large audience (Cullinan & Galda, 1998).

If you query a classroom of readers, it will quickly become obvious that each genre has its devoted followers. An important goal for the teacher is to ensure that students are exposed to commendable titles in every genre (IRA/NCTE, 1996). One way to accomplish this is to use book talks and short mini-lessons about the characteristics of the different genres throughout the year. Then, set goals for each reader as a challenge to expand his reading horizons periodically by dipping into the different genres.

Web Links:
Booktalks

The Pura Belpré Award
Coretta Scott King Award
Discussion Guide

 ## MULTICULTURAL LITERATURE

Multicultural literature has grown slowly over the last few decades into a genre all its own. It is unfortunate that only 5 to 6 percent of the 8,000 children's books published annually are multicultural titles. However, good books in this genre are invaluable when they realistically portray characters real and fictional who represent different social, cultural, and ethnic groups. In the process, titles might illuminate socioeconomic, gender, and religious differences and responsibly investigate varying values, beliefs, and standards that are shared by a group of people (Hinchey, 2001).

In recent years there has been a more concerted effort to reflect those ethnic variations within the each broad cultural band. For example, where once all literature

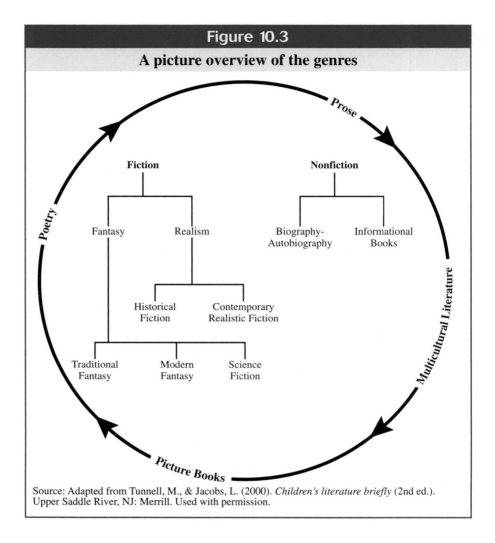

Figure 10.3
A picture overview of the genres

Source: Adapted from Tunnell, M., & Jacobs, L. (2000). *Children's literature briefly* (2nd ed.). Upper Saddle River, NJ: Merrill. Used with permission.

about Native Americans depicted a rather generic Native American, today discerning teachers can find literature that highlights distinctions among the numerous Indian Nations (Reese & Caldwell-Wood, 1997). This is heralded as a positive move toward what Harris (1997) describes as culturally conscious literature. Finally, some authorities in the field include the culture of the physically and mentally challenged under a broad umbrella of multicultural literature (Cullinan & Galda, 1998; Mikkelsen, 2000; Tunnell & Jacobs, 2000). Referred to as the "Alphabet Kids" (Miller, 2001, p. 820) because their labels are abbreviated to LD, EMH, or ADHD, they are included in many of the nation's classrooms, but often excluded because their "culture" continues to be misunderstood.

In this primer an effort has been made to include an assortment of titles to celebrate the stories and people of various cultures in the preceding genre explanations. Thus, multicultural literature is interwoven throughout the chapter as it should be interwoven throughout the classroom reading and writing curriculum (Bieger, 1995/1996; Huck et al., 2004). In this way, children of all nationalities see their faces and their families realistically reflected in the stories and illustrations at their fingertips. As often as possible, classroom teachers must give all children this opportunity because of potential far-reaching possibilities:

> For through multicultural literature, children will be afforded opportunities to look at themselves, study their similarities and differences, enter new worlds of meaning, explore new knowledge, examine their histories, entertain their futures, negotiate their identities, and ponder how to make the world a better place for everybody. Teaching with multicultural literature is every teacher's responsibility. (Barrera et al., 1997, p. xxi)

While it is a small piece of the picture, one sound reason beyond the satisfaction of being able to read a story about yourself is that it is possible to gain insight into another culture via literature (Cullinan & Galda, 1998; Temple et al., 2003; Young et al., 1995). When the classroom teacher consciously offers quality titles free from stereotypes, tokenism, and inaccurate information, filled with diverse representations within a particular culture to read, discuss, and respond to, the door is opened a little further for broadening cultural understanding (IRA/NCTE, 1996; Lukens, 1999.) Refer to Chapter 3 for timely guidelines for selecting exceptional multicultural books.

One way to initiate cultural understanding is to begin with traditional literature, by far the most plentiful of offerings available in the multicultural realm. "Folktales are good vehicles for promoting multicultural understanding because they give insight into the dreams, customs, and philosophy of a group" (Bieger, 1996, p. 309). Any of the folktales previously mentioned could be used to begin lessons in multicultural understanding. Invite the librarian into your classroom to book talk the latest titles that celebrate cultural diversity.

Through reading folktales and other literature, readers get a chance to briefly share in the lives and feelings of the character rather than dealing only with facts. In this way it is possible to understand that people are more alike than they are different, that no matter what the cultural background, people are people. It is apparent that books may be used as agents for change, are a means of introducing cultural concepts, and have the potential for becoming catalysts for opening minds to considering a variety of viewpoints (Hinchey, 2001).

A look at life in contemporary times from culture to culture is available in picture books and in novels. A lovely example of the former is *Tea with Milk* (Say, 1999), which compares and contrasts bits of the Japanese culture with that of American beliefs and practices. *Mama Provi and the Pot of Rice* (Rosa-Casanova, 2001) touches lightly on a number of cultures as Mama Provi trades bits of her delicious casserole for delicacies from her multicultural neighbors. She moves floor by floor up through the apartment building to her granddaughter's apartment and arrives with a mouthwatering feast. Then there is the story of Pablo, who can't decide what he should take to school for International Day. Should it be a delicacy that his Mexican mother prepares

Web Link:
Christopher Award
Winners

in the family bakery, or a specialty that his Jewish father bakes? The decision is surprising in *Jalapeno Bagels* (Wing, 1996).

Middle schoolers might select *Seedfolks* (Fleischman, 1997), a book explaining how neighbors from different racial and ethnic backgrounds come to understand each other as they work on a neighborhood project. *Together in Pine Cone Patch* (Yezerski, 1998) is a love story about a girl from Ireland and a boy from Poland who overcome the prejudices in a small American town. With guidance from the librarian and a keen eye toward fair representation of diverse cultures, today's classroom teacher can find exceptional multicultural titles for interested readers across grade levels.

Poetry reflects the rhythms of a culture through books like *Brown Angels: An Album of Pictures and Verse* (Myer, 1993) based upon antique photos of children as wonderful to look at as the verses are to read. Here they meet smiling Jeannie with an amusing problem:

> Jeannie had a giggle just beneath her toes
> She gave a little wiggle and up her leg it rose
> She tried to grab the giggle as it shimmied past her knees
>
> But it slid right past her fingers with a "'scuse me if you please"
> It slipped around her middle, it made her jump and shout
> Jeannie wanted that giggle in, that giggle wanted out! . . . .

(Myers, 1993, unpaged)

On a more somber note older students can learn from *The Space Between Our Footsteps: Poems and Paintings from the Middle East* (Nye, 1998), which reveals issues and concerns of over 100 poets from nineteen Middle Eastern countries. Children who appreciate Japanese haiku will be interested in *Cool Melons—Turn to Frogs! The Life and Poems of Issa* (Gollub, 1998). Lovers of riddles won't be able to resist *Touching the Distance: Native American Riddle Poems* (Swann, 1998), stumping classmates with delight. For those in need of a mini-vacation, *Under the Moon & Over the Sea* (Agard & Nichols, 2002) offers tantalizing tastes, sights, and rhythms from the vibrant Caribbean. Sometimes painfully depicting the more difficult times in everyone's lives, at other times eliciting an understanding smile, poetry readily illuminates the similarities between people despite varying cultural roots.

There is more to be accepted and understood than cultural or religious differences, of course. It is possible to learn about children who are set apart from the mainstream because they must cope with disabilities; thus these diverse learners become a culture of their own. Books written with sensitivity can begin illuminating conversations of understanding among classmates. Finely done picture book options include *Thank You, Mister Falker* (Polacco, 1998), which recounts the embarrassment of students being taunted because of dyslexia. *Be Good to Eddie Lee* (Fleming, 1997) gives readers much to think about when Eddie demonstrates his goodness to thoughtless neighborhood children. In *Ian's Walk: A Story About Autism* (Lears, 1998), an older sister is humiliated when her autistic younger brother is put into her care. When she loses her brother in the park, however, she learns more than one lesson.

Web Link:
700 Great Sites for
Kids' Books

In addition, there is Cindy in *Just Kids: Visiting a Class for Children with Special Needs* (Senisi, 1998), who spends time daily in a classroom with students with special needs because of a careless and cruel remark she made. As a result, she meets some truly special friends. Readers can extend the understanding that grew from Cindy's experiences by reading the novel *Bluish* (Hamilton, 1999) about overcoming the fear of "catching" another child's disability. What an excellent novel to begin discussions on personal fears and worries connected with interacting with classmates who may be different for one reason or another (Miller, 2001).

Without a doubt, there is tremendous wealth awaiting the readers of multicultural literature. Consult *Multicultural Literature for Children and Adults: A Selected Listing of Books by and about People of Color, Volume Two, 1991–1996* (Kruse, Horning, & Schliesman, 1997) as one option for superb suggestions for classroom use. *Kaleidoscope: A Multicultural Booklist for Grades K-8* (Barrera, Thompson, & Dressman, 1997) or the third edition by Junko Yokota (2001) are other fine resources of carefully previewed titles. Review the websites on the Online Learning Center for excellent teacher support and additional multicultural resources. Clearly, everyone has a culture to celebrate, roots to examine, and horizons to broaden. It can all begin with a good book.

Teaching Strategy for the Classroom

TEACHING STRATEGIES THROUGH LITERATURE: A LESSON PLAN TO TEACH DRAWING CONCLUSIONS

Focus Book: Kurtz, Jane. (2000). *Faraway Home*. (E. B. Lewis, Illus.). San Diego, CA: Gulliver/Harcourt Brace.

I. OBJECTIVES

The students will:

- Learn how to use the reading strategy of drawing conclusions as modeled by the teacher.
- Apply the strategy as they investigate common cultural values in small groups.
- Deduce that one common value across cultures is respect for one's elders.
- Practice the strategy during small group work as they read other multicultural picture books, continuing to investigate cultural values.

II. MATERIALS

The above mentioned book, a collection of multicultural books that underscore the value of respecting one's elders, scratch paper and pens/pencils, chart paper.

III. INSTRUCTIONAL APPROACH

A. Motivator

Write the word "value" on the chalkboard in vibrant colored chalk. Give students two minutes to brainstorm the meaning of this word and an example together with a neighbor. When the time has elapsed, begin a sharing session. Invite four pairs of learners to come up to the board and write their definitions and examples. Let each pair present their thinking, and then ask the class for input. Did they come up with similar thoughts? Different examples? Condense the class's thinking into a web revolving around values; a visual overview of related definitions and corresponding examples.

Hand out a 5 by 8 inch lined index card to each student along with a note to parents or guardians explaining that you are investigating values across cultures. Ask the adults to list three to five values that are a part of their family's life. Request that the cards be returned promptly the next day. Students are to put the cards in their backpacks or with materials that will be going home that afternoon. Tell the students that the lesson will continue as you read a book together and draw conclusions from the story about some values in this particular family.

B. Teacher/Student Interaction

Day 1

Explain to the class that the reading strategy you will be working with is drawing conclusions. This is an important comprehension skill that they can use to better help them understand stories that they read. On the overhead transparency or chalkboard, write the term and a list of simple steps to help the students come to a conclusion. When drawing conclusions, students:

1. Become detectives.
2. Begin by gathering evidence like specific details from the illustrations or text of the story.
3. Apply their knowledge of the topic or situation based upon their prior experiences.
4. Put it all together to arrive at a conclusion.

The challenge in drawing conclusions is that students need to read between the lines, to look for information that the author doesn't explain thoroughly. Explain that this is a challenging but important skill that students will find themselves using in other subject areas and outside of the classroom in daily life as well.

- Take time to model how you draw conclusions selecting a few paragraphs from a story you have used previously in class. Read the segment and talk through what kinds of information you thought might help you, what you can draw from personal knowledge, and the resulting conclusions you reached. Ask the students if they agree or disagree with your detective work. Explain that it is possible for readers to come to different conclusions. Ask them why that might happen. They may suggest that readers could choose different details to support their thinking and that everyone has a little different background or amount of knowledge about a particular topic that they can use. Check to see if students understand the steps in drawing conclusions, clarify or practice as needed, and then introduce the day's read aloud.
- Set a purpose for reading by explaining that students will have an opportunity to draw conclusions in this book. As they listen to the story, what kinds of values are important to the characters in the story? They will have to draw conclusions to come up with their answers.
- Show the book, *Faraway Home,* to the class reading the title, author, and illustrator. Ask the students to predict just from the cover (open it so they can see the entire cover) what the story might be about. Next, read and display the title page and the dedication page. Any more predictions? Adjustments to original predictions?

- Read the first two pages and stop to discuss what has happened in the story. Were students' predictions on the right track? If not, adjust them, make new predictions, and continue reading. You might take a few minutes at this point to locate Ethiopia on the globe or world map so that students have a sense of where this country is. Then, continue reading.
- Stop after three or four pages and ask students if they have ever had similar experiences as these characters have had. There may be several children from other countries in the class who can relate to Desta's father's life as a child. Why do the children think that Desta offered her father her night-light to take on the trip?
- Read through the page where Desta looks at her locket. Ask for student reactions. How do they think Desta feels about her grandmother? What might happen next in the story?
- Complete the book. Invite student reactions. Now, tell them to put on their thinking caps. Using scratch paper, they are to take a few minutes to write down what they think is important in this family. What do they value? Next to their ideas, they are to jot down details and tidbits of their own experiences to support their ideas. Next, work with two other classmates to discuss each other's conclusions, learning how others practiced this new skill.
- Open the discussion to the whole class. Ask students to contribute their conclusions, and you record the values they deduced on the overhead transparency, chart paper, or chalkboard. One important value that will be followed into other books representing different cultural groups is that of respect and love for your elders. Desta demonstrated her respect and love as she listened to her father talk of his homeland and adjusted to the fact that he had to go home for a while. Father demonstrated those values in making the decision to leave his family for a short time and travel far away to his homeland to be with his ailing mother.
- Remind students to get their index cards completed at home that night and bring them back for a continuation of the lesson on family values the following day.

Day 2

- As students arrive in class, gather their family values cards and review them quickly. Once the class is settled, point out the five or six sheets of lined chart paper or blank newsprint taped up around the room. As time permits, one student at a time per sheet records their values neatly before the reading lesson begins. Post the sheets for easy viewing when this task is done.
- Before reading begins, review the values charts together. Quickly go around the room letting each student read their values. Using a colored marker, put a star by values that reoccur, one color per value. Talk about the fact that even though children are from different families and those families have different backgrounds, there are some values that are the same (hopefully!).
- Divide students into groups of three or four to read another multicultural title. They are to discuss the book as they read it together, taking turns reading aloud for those who are comfortable doing so. Then they are to practice drawing conclusions, brainstorming together about the values presented in the book. Each student who has drawn a conclusion is to share how he came to that point.
- Once groups are done, each one briefly presents their book. They are to read the title and author, tell the class the culture represented, and give a four- or five-sentence synopsis of the story. Finally, they are to discuss their discovered values.

- On a long length of butcher paper, divided into categories ahead of time (title, author, culture, values), a scribe from each group records the information. Once the work is done, sit back and study the chart. What conclusions can be drawn by the class about cultural values?
- Because all of the books selected focus on respecting one's elders, one conclusion will be that valuing and respecting one's elders is common across cultures. Additional values will be noted, of course. Talk about those. Discuss the fact that no matter where one's roots are or how cultures differ, we often value many of the same things. Extend the thinking by inviting students to discuss the impact of having different values.
- Practice the strategy of drawing conclusions within a few days in another content area to reinforce the skill and to demonstrate how it works across the curriculum as well as in reading lessons. Review it from time to time throughout the year.

C. Gatekeeping

Students are to take some time during this day to reflect in their writing journals or literature response journals on what they have learned. In addition, ask them to review how they draw conclusions. As you read the journals, you will quickly see what has been absorbed from this reading experience and whether students understand the concept of drawing conclusions.

IV. EXTENSIONS

- Use one of the websites suggested in the preceding chapter like *Kay Vandergrift's Learning about the Author and Illustrator Pages*. Students look on the Internet to find an author or illustrator from their cultural background or from a culture of interest. Read one of that individual's books. Decide what value(s) are depicted in the book. Share the book, culture represented, and values in a short book talk.
- Make a word wall of basic words and their English translations to represent the different cultural backgrounds of class members. Learn the words and proper pronunciations together.
- Divide into pairs and interview each other. The teacher takes a digital camera photo, scans it into the computer, and students word process a short biography of their classmate. Each member of the pair introduces the other to the class, tells a few interesting tidbits, and invites the class to read more about their classmate in the class book where all bios are assembled for continuous enjoyment.
- Read two folktales from a particular culture, listing the values discovered. Discuss the findings with a classmate. Record the information on a handy chart in the reading corner, a pleasant way to continue celebrating cultural similarities and differences together.

V. ADAPTATIONS/MODIFICATIONS FOR DIVERSE LEARNERS

- Adaptations are built right into this lesson. Students who require extra support in understanding the language in the books can rely on classmates in their groups who will be reading the text aloud. Within those groups the stories are discussed, facilitating comprehension for each learner.
- Students have an opportunity to highlight and share values from their respective cultures as they discuss the books they are reading, comparing and contrasting the values represented with their own.

- When recording their values on chart paper, students can work in pairs. In that way, spelling and writing support is provided by a peer partner.
- By using a laptop, the classroom computer, or a handheld computer with the capacity to beam responses to the printer nearby, a student with a hearing impairment can be an active part of the discussion segment of the lesson. The student should also have a copy of the story being read aloud by the teacher so that he can follow along as segments are read and discussed.
- Whenever possible provide a copy of books being used in braille or on tape for the visually impaired student. Check with support staff for other materials to have on hand to enable this inclusion student to be an integral part of classroom activities.

Suggested Titles for Classroom Use

Altman, Linda Jacobs. (2002). *Singing with Momma Lou.* (L. Johnston, Illus.). New York: Lee & Low. (African American)

Belton, Sandra. (1994). *May'naise Sandwiches & Sunshine Tea.* (G. G. Carter, Illus.). Four Winds Press. (African American)

Boyden, Linda. (2002). *The Blue Roses.* (A. Cordova, Illus.). New York: Lee & Low. (Native American)

Castañada, Omar S. (1993). *Abuela's Weave.* (E. O. Sanchez, Illus.). New York: Lee & Low. (Spanish; book is available in Spanish)

Cooper, Melrose. (1999). *Gettin' through Thursday.* (N. Bennett, Illus.). New York: Lee & Low. (African American)

Cowley, Joy. (1998). *Big Moon Tortilla.* (S. Strongbow, Illus.). Honesdale, PA: Boyds Mill Press. (Native American: Papago)

Dengler, Marianna. (1996). *The Worry Stone.* (S. G. Gerig, Illus.). Flagstaff, AZ: Northland. (Native American: Chumash)

Doner, Kim. (1999). *Buffalo Dreams.* Portland, OR: West Winds Press. (Native American)

Dorros, Arthur. (1999). *Isla.* (E. Kleven, Illus.). New York: Dutton. (Mexican American)

Guback, Georgia. (1994). *Luka's Quilt.* New York: Greenwillow. (Polynesian)

Luenn, Nancy. (1998). *A Gift for Abuelita: Celebrating the Day of the Dead.* (R. Chapman, Illus.). Flagstaff, AZ: Rising Moon. (Mexican American; book is available in Spanish)

McCay, Lawrence, Jr. (2001). *Journey Home.* (K. Lee, Illus.). New York: Lee & Low. (Asian American)

Melmed, Laura Krauss. (1997). *Little Oh.* (J. LaMarche, Illus.). New York: Lothrop. (Asian)

Michelson, Richard. (1999). *Grandpa's Gamble.* (B. Moser, Illus.). Tarrytown, NJ: Marshall Cavendish. (Jewish American)

Miller, William. (2001). *Rent Party Jazz.* (C. Riley-Webb, Illus.). New York: Lee & Low. (African American)

Polacco, Patricia. (1992). *Mrs. Katz and Tush.* New York: Dell/Yearling (Jewish/African American)

A Picture Book Overview

Picture books past and present command attention because of their fluid movement across the genres. They are to be prized as invaluable additions in every content area as well. Picture books are unique in that they include imaginative tales, realistic stories, captivating poetry, historical fiction, and carefully gleaned information about innumerable topics. In recent years they have become welcome venues for savoring snippets of one culture after another, graciously celebrating cultural diversity. What makes fictional picture books unusual is that in most of them both the illustrations and the text interact to tell the story. That interplay could be described as a marriage of words and pictures that creates a distinctive end product.

There are some exceptions to the rule to be noted, however. Some illustrators choose to tell their stories without words enabling the reader to write the narrative in her mind. The Caldecott Honor Books *Time Flies* (Rohman, 1994) and *Tuesday* (Wiesner, 1991) entice readers to devise a personal version of the unfolding tale, an excellent strategy to help beginning readers to develop a sense of story. Other picture books have a simple story line with a word or two or a sentence per page. Young readers cast a delighted eye at the unfolding picture story in *The Very Lonely Firefly* (Carle, 1995) or quickly memorize the repetitive text in *We're Going on a Bear Hunt* (Rosen, 1989). While they are starting fare for toddlers and beginning readers, picture books also belong in the hands of students in the upper grades.

Middle grade readers will chuckle over the dilemma faced in *The Math Curse* (Scieszka, 1995). Readers of all ages are inspired to experiment with reflective poetry and art after journeying through *This Place I Know: Poems of Comfort* (Heard, 2002). Picture books for older readers often have more extensive text and an increasingly complex story line. One excellent choice is *Pink and Say* (Polacco, 1994), which relates the friendship that develops between two boys caught behind enemy lines during the Civil War. Another exemplary title is *When Jessie Came across the Sea* (Hest, 1997), a memorable story about a courageous young Jewish girl emigrating to the United States. Both books happen to fit wonderfully into the social studies curriculum. In fact, enterprising teachers will find that picture books travel across the curriculum to introduce a science or social studies concept, add a little humor to the math class, and serve as teachers of distinctive writing styles. That is not the end of ideas, however, because there are a myriad of uses for the amazingly versatile picture book.

Another suggestion for using picture books in any grade is as excellent sources for read-alouds. Their length is ideal for a short reading session or two. As such, they are superb devices to strengthen listening skills, ignite imaginations, and demonstrate the pleasures of reading by "awakening the sounds and rhythms of our language" (Combs, 2003, p. 84) in the process. Furthermore, titles are to be savored for the artwork and story, simply for the joy of the book.

Finally, carefully selected titles can become the impetus for a lesson on a particular reading strategy. Try *Anansi and the Moss-Covered Rock* (Kimmel, 1988) as a title to meet a number of the preceding suggestions. It is a delightful read-aloud that encourages audience participation as Anansi goes "walking, walking, walking" throughout the story. The illustrations are cleverly done inviting closer inspection once the tale has been completed. The story lends itself beautifully to a reading lesson on sequencing as listeners put events in the proper order after a read-aloud session. Whatever the appropriate skill to be taught or reviewed, it is done within the context of this West African tale, supporting the use of real books for real readers. To cement the acquisition of the new skill, students reach for other previously selected picture books for engaging practice (Fuhler, 2000). In conclusion, it should be reinforced that picture books reach out to readers of all ages, levels of motivation, and varying reading abilities (Turner & Paris, 1995). They truly are treasured packages bound into thirty-two to forty-eight pages.

A Quick Walk through the Genres: Focus on Fiction

Fantasy: Traditional Literature

One type of fantasy that children enjoy is **traditional literature.** It is represented by a number of different formats including folktales, fairy tales, myths, epics, and legends. All of the offerings defined as traditional literature share common distinctions that of emerging from a period oft referred to as "Once upon a time . . ." Consider **folktales** and **fairy tales,** for example. What is unique about folktales is that they are deeply rooted in the oral tradition. Their original authors remain unknown. They emerged from a time when tales were told around the fire to while away a long winter evening, to entertain at a family gathering, to instruct young children about the ways of nature, and to share the wisdom and attitudes of the elders (Huck et al., 2004; Tunnell & Jacobs, 2000). Adults passed the tales on to their children, who retold them to their children in an intergenerational chain of storytelling that extends into today's classrooms.

Web Link:
Children's Book Awards
and Other Literary Prizes

With an eye to preserving what could so easily be lost, 19th-century grammarians like Jacob and Wilhelm Grimm captured numerous German tales in writing. English folktales were collected by linguists including Joseph Jacobs and Andrew Lang, while Perrault is one person credited for preserving French tales (Cullinan & Galda, 1998; Huck et al., 2004). The trend continues as 20th-century anthropologists and linguists seek out authentic sources for Native American tales from the elders who still recall these generations-old stories (Temple, Martinez, Yokota, & Naylor, 2003).

Folktales with unusual cultural variants and contemporary retellings afford an inviting reading opportunity. Engrossing literary units have been developed around the innumerable versions of the Cinderella tales. It is amazing to note that the earliest recorded version is of Chinese origin, over 1,000 years older than the earliest Western version of the tale. One fascinating retelling is *Yeh Shen: A Cinderella Story from China* (Louie, 1996) illustrated by Ed Young. Another with a much different presentation is *Little Gold Star: A Spanish American Cinderella Tale* (San Souci, 2000).

Students might investigate the intriguing variants of the popular "Three Little Pigs" beginning with its English version as retold by Paul Galdone (1989). A must read is a clever version, *Nacho, Tito and Miguel* (Salinas, 1998), written in both English and Spanish. Don't miss the ingenious Caldecott Winner, *The Three Pigs* (Wiesner, 2002). Because an impressive number of well-wrought books in this genre grace the shelves of bookstores and libraries today, teachers can easily add traditional literature to the classroom reading program. To do so is a simple but rich way to celebrate one's cultural beginnings (Barrera et al., 1997; Young & Ferguson, 1995).

Because the offerings are numerous within the genre of traditional literature, there seems to be something for everyone. Beginning readers can recite and quickly memorize nursery rhymes and chants from Mother Goose, finding some of their favorites in *Head, Shoulders, Knees, and Toes* (Newcome, 2002) They can jump rope to catchy jump rope jingles, a natural lesson in phonemic awareness. Students of varying ages enjoy the short, impressive **fables** as told by Aesop in which the animal characters teach a moral or lesson in life. No one should remain unacquainted with the amusing **trickster tales,** whose stories and characters emerge from diverse cultures. Fortunately, a growing number of these stories of trickery and being tricked in return have been recaptured and retold much to the pleasure of their readers. Sometimes naughty, sometimes clever, characters such as Anansi the Spider, Raven, Coyote, lktomi, and Brer Rabbit and his companions have become popular main characters of these particular selections. From Mother Goose to clever coyote, there are surprises galore for readers and listeners of folklore.

Not to be overlooked as a segment of traditional literature are **tall tales.** It is difficult to resist these far-fetched yarns as readers go adventuring with long-loved Paul Bunyan, outrageous Pecos Bill, gentle Johnny Appleseed, or the memorable heroine *Sally Ann Thunder Ann Whirlwind Crockett* (Cohen, 1985). By reading a collection of these tales teachers and students will find excellent examples illustrating the use of exaggeration as one way to tell a story. Try a lesson in Roulette Writing (Farris, 1988) suggested in Teaching Strategy for the Classroom as one way to ignite creativity while reinforcing the reading–writing connection.

Teaching Strategy for the Classroom

Activities for Connecting Reading and Writing Using Folktales

Try these activities to strengthen the reading–writing connection in your classroom:

ROULETTE WRITING

Have the class become familiar with legendary characters by reading several versions of tall tales like *Pecos Bill* (Kellogg, 1986), *Johnny Appleseed* (Kellogg, 1988), *Paul Bunyan* (Kellogg, 1994), *Mike Fink* (Kellogg, 1998), and *Swamp Angel* (Issacs, 1994). As a whole class, examine and discuss the characteristics that make these characters legendary. Then divide into groups of four or five. Every student needs notebook paper and a pen or pencil. Within the group each person quickly develops a legendary character in about five minutes of writing time. The teacher indicates when that creating time is up, and writers pass their paper to the person to the right in their group.

The next person reads what has been written and extends the tale, writing for three or four minutes, or until the teacher says to pass the paper to the right again. The process is repeated as the story builds until it is the last person's turn. That student reads the emerging tale and wraps it up with a suitable ending stopping when the teacher calls time. The papers are returned to the original writer, who reads through the final tale. Then it is time to celebrate creativity and reveal a new tall tale. Volunteers read those stories that they think evolved particularly well. Students might select the versions they like the best, illustrate them, and create a bulletin board that applauds the reading–writing–tale tall connection (Farris, 1988).

IT'S IN THE NEWS

Write a news-breaking story, a front-page newspaper story telling the who, what, where, when, and how involving a tall tale, folktale, or fairy tale character and his or her most recent adventure.

FOLKTALES RETOLD

Study several versions of a popular folktale such as Cinderella or Sleeping Beauty. Begin with a classic version *Cinderella* (Perrault, 1997), with Caldecott winning illustrations by Marcia Brown. Then read three other more contemporary retellings. With the new twists on the old, work with a partner in a collaborative writing activity. Write a unique retelling. *Cinder-Elly* (Minters, 1994), *Cinderella Skeleton* (San Souci, 2000), *Cinder Edna* (Jackson, 1994), and *Adelita: A Mexican Cinderella Story* (dePaola, 2002) are just a few contemporary retellings to review. An excellent resource for a dozen more general variants is *Cinderella: An International Collection* (Sierra, 1992).

ADAPTATIONS/MODIFICATIONS FOR DIVERSE LEARNERS

Pair up students to read a folktale together. In the case of language differences, any troublesome English words can be explained to the English language learner to ensure comprehension. To facilitate comprehension for these students or those with different processing difficulties, teammates might take turns reading the pages, talking about them at the conclusion of several pages. Use the illustrations to help strengthen comprehension. Discussion or retellings are good comprehension strategies. When the activity is done, ELL students and learners who need more time to comprehend materials will benefit from repeated readings of the book to practice the language involved.

For a student with learning disabilities that relate to language processing, try software that has a speech-feedback component. Some computers have a built-in speech feature that can be activated. The school district might already have appropriate software for the classroom computer. Two suggestions are *Write:Out Loud* or *Co:Writer,* computer software available from Don Johnson Inc., Wauconda, Illinois. In addition, this type of software will be practical for the visually impaired student.

Finally, pairs share ideas and write together. In Roulette Writing, the more able student serves as scribe, recording the classmate's ideas along with their own so that the timed writing is not a hindrance.

Here, too, are **myths, legends, epics,** and **ballads.** Because of their complexity, many of these ancient tales like *Beowulf* or *The Iliad* and *The Odyssey* are most appropriate for upper grade learners. Myths appeal to a wider range of readers, however. They have been used to tell the complex workings of the world and how things were created. They include **pourquoi tales** for younger readers that suggest such puzzlements as *How Jackrabbit Got His Very Long Ears* (Irbinskas, 1994), or *The Legend of the Panda* (Granfield, 2001), which explains why pandas have such distinctive coloring. Imagine the narrative writing that could be sparked by these tales. Finally, mythology is a common theme in middle school and high school anthologies. Through these stories more mature readers enter the mythical realm of Apollo and Zeus and other Roman and Greek gods and goddesses.

Upper grade readers can examine legends that often reflect bits of actual historical events. For example, an engrossed reader might learn about the deeds attributed to heroes like Robin Hood and King Arthur and his famous Knights of the Round Table through legendary fare. *Sword of the Rightful King* (Yolen, 2003) is an imaginative option here. Whether folktale or legend, tall tale or myth, traditional literature in its numerous guises has much to offer in the balanced reading and writing curriculum.

Fortunately, stories from the genre of traditional literature lend themselves to retelling in the popular picture book format. Not only can they take pleasure in the story, but readers will find that each title contains innovative artwork to savor. Some books are so beautifully illustrated that they have gained the Caldecott Committee's attention. Every year this renowned committee meets to scrutinize the previous year's picture books with special attention directed toward the artistic interpretation of a story. A sampling of selected winners from the traditional literature genre includes:

> *Mufaro's Beautiful Daughters: An African Tale* (Steptoe, 1987)
> *Lon Po Po: A Red-Riding Hood Story from China* (Young, 1989)
> *The Talking Eggs: A Folktale from the American South* (San Souci, 1989)
> *Puss in Boots* (Perrault, 1990)
> *The Stinky Cheese Man and Other Fairly Stupid Tales* (Scieszka, 1992)
> *John Henry* (Lester, 1994)
> *Rapunzel* (Zelinsky, 1997)
> *The Three Pigs* (Wiesner, 2002)

Other Types of Traditional Literature: Modern Fantasy

When readers wish to immerse themselves in purely imaginative worlds, in let's pretend and in make-believe, they turn to the genre of **modern fantasy.** One characteristic that sets these stories apart from the folklore previously discussed is that the authors can be identified. For example, one renowned author is Hans Christian Andersen, remembered for his collection of tales including "The Ugly Duckling," "The Tin Soldier," and "The Emperor's New Clothes." A lovely retelling from this genre is an adaptation of *The Ugly Duckling* by Jerry Pinkney (1999). Older readers will appreciate the richly illustrated version of *The Nightingale* retold by Stephen Mitchell (2002).

In modern fantasy selections anything is possible: animals talk, little people like the Borrowers live their lives right alongside humankind, and magic happens. Stories are often set in Secondary Worlds presented so cleverly that one believes they are real. A reader adventures with the Hobbit in Tolkien's Middle World or battles evil forces with Taran in Prydain. Tad, a twelve-year-old youngling of the Fisher Tribe, leads middle school readers on a heart-wrenching quest to retrieve the precious Waterstone (Rupp, 2002). Author Brian Jacques transports readers to Mossflower Woods to live briefly amongst the personable animals who inhabit fabulous Redwall Abbey, starting place of a growing number of Redwall novels:

It was the start of the Summer of the Late Rose. Mossflower country shimmered gently in a peaceful haze, bathing delicately at each dew-laden dawn, blossoming through high sunny noon-tides, languishing in each crimson-tinted twilight that heralded the soft darkness of June nights.

Redwall stood foursquare along the marches of the old south border, flanked on two sides by Mossflower Wood's shaded depths. The other half of the Abbey overlooked undulating sweeps of meadowland, its ancient gate facing the long dusty road on the western perimeter. (Jacques, 1998, no page number)

Here are different worlds, magic, and more, for the characters are often remarkably unique in modern fantasy.

While some of the characters in fantasy stories are quite realistic, like a classmate across the room or the neighbor down the street, other characters simply could not exist. Long-remembered favorites are Beatrix Potter's Peter Rabbit or the Tin Man, Cowardly Lion, and Scarecrow from Frank Baum's *The Wizard of Oz* series. Alice and the amazing characters she encounters in Wonderland after her mishap of falling down the rabbit hole have moved from the printed page to the movie screen. A contemporary phenomenon is Harry Potter, Wizard-in-training at Hogwarts, a school of witchcraft. While he could hardly be called normal, Harry is a real boy enmeshed in a fascinating world of fantasy. Poetry, too, presents memorable beings through long popular offerings such as A. A. Milne's (1998) lovable Pooh and down-and-out Eeyore and other almost-alive characters in *The World of Christopher Robin*.

In a mix of genres, fantasy and historical fiction intermingle through time travel novels. The option of time travel captivates readers who wonder what it was like in another time and place. Most frequently children in contemporary time travel back into other times and places to meet real or imaginary people. *The Ancient One* (Barron, 1992) begins with a current crisis, the destruction of an old growth forest, but takes readers back to meet the native peoples who once lived in the area in an effort to shed light on a resolution to the heroine's problem. Other readers can safely experience the events of the Holocaust through *The Devil's Arithmetic* (Yolen, 1990), a riveting tale with a realistic, powerful ending.

Poetry offerings that ring with an element of fantasy include selections by the late Shel Silverstein and the ever-popular Jack Prelutsky. A clever alphabet book that tugs at the imagination is *The Disappearing Alphabet* (Wilbur, 2001), which includes an inventive poem for each letter of the alphabet and speculates about possible changes if one part of a letter is missing. Lewis Carroll's (1989) beautifully interpreted "Jabberwocky" delights many a reader, while more contemporary poets like John Ciardi, Ruth Heller, James Marshall, and Barbara Esbensen amuse with imaginative verse and nonsense. Students can be challenged to find other titles of poetry or picture books that fit into modern fantasy.

While many a reader relishes the realm of fantasy and its close cousin, science fiction, there are controversial titles in both genres that raise the ire of some parents. The extremely popular Harry Potter series has been banned from some households where parents fear the possible Satanic overtones that they detect within these imaginative battles between good and evil. Rather than seeing the books as providing hours of fun-filled reading as one side of this issue, other parents worry that they are proponents of witchcraft (Gish, 2000). Lois Lowry's (1993) Newbery Award winner *The Giver* has elicited some of the same types of responses from parents who feel that it advocates euthanasia for one thing, and they decry the roles of the women, whose job it is to only be birth mothers, among other concerns. The best policy for teachers to take is to read these controversial books in order to be aware of the content that might ignite parent concerns. If a title seems that it might be a potential problem, invite parents to borrow a copy of the book early in the year and read it from cover to cover themselves. Then, learn the school district policy for handling book complaints from parents in preparation for any queries or emotional responses about a book from a distressed parent. The American Library Association is an excellent resource for material on preserving intellectual freedom and contains a process to be used to deter censorship (American Library Association, 1996). (See Figure 10.4.) It is best to be prepared for challenges to reading materials, to hear both sides of an argument for or against a book, and to know that the possibility of having such a conversation is a reality.

Fantasy in the Future: Science Fiction

The final genre, fantasy with a forward focus, is **science fiction.** This particular genre takes readers to other worlds, too, but they exist in the future. Readers are invited to become wrapped up in possibilities posed by technological advances that could change the lives of people in upcoming societies. The authors of science fiction take existing physical laws and scientific principles and extend them to what might be a logical outcome in the years to come (Lukens, 1999; Tunnell & Jacobs, 2000). There is a message in these books that urges the readers to be aware of the destructive potential of science and technology if it develops unchecked (Huck et al., 2004). Readers of science fiction can engage in a dialogue about "What if?" They stretch their minds as they examine possibilities and alternative solutions, problem solving in collaboration with an author and book characters, an invaluable life skill.

It seems that this genre has totally devoted followers and a large number of readers who are just not so certain. One way to hook the latter is to read aloud several riveting snippets from a book. For instance, try reading the first few pages of *Eva* (Dickinson, 1989) to upper grade readers. You will need more than one copy of the book because listeners probably cannot resist picking up the book on their own. Lois Lowry's (2000) *Gathering Blue* is a thought-provoking choice for use in literature circles. The discussions about the future world she creates and the greed and cruelty within it will be lively indeed. For those who would enjoy a suspenseful story set in 2194, *The Ear, the Eye and the Arm: A Novel* (Farmer, 1994) is a page-turning option. To conclude, science fiction provides students an imaginative yet thought-provoking glimpse into the future and enables them to speculate upon what life might be like if technology gains an upper hand.

Final Thoughts about Traditional Literature

Despite the fact that this has only been a brief overview of the innumerable selections within the traditional literature area, it is important to focus on the values for using

Figure 10.4

Building a background in technology and children's literature

There should probably be a maxim stating that the time spent in direct contact with Internet exploration has a direct correlation to an increase in professional knowledge and greater opportunities to integrate technology into the classroom. It seems that as teachers we tend to implement practices into our classrooms that we ourselves have experienced. If both of the above suppositions are correct, plan to begin a technology trek to learn more about the connections between technology and children's literature. A suggested itinerary might be:

1. Start small and gradually expand your knowledge base. This takes time.
2. Make it a habit. Set aside a specific time period each week to continue your technology trek.
3. Record your observations, descriptions of key sites that address topics in your curriculum, and sites that students can use for reference. Use index cards and create a usable file system of sites, descriptions, and their potential. Perhaps a notebook or binder divided into content areas would be more practical for you. Just don't lose the information you collect along the way.
4. Share what you learn with a colleague. It is often more motivating to trek with a friend.

Begin with one of the following sites. You will be astounded at where your exploration may take you.

Doucette Index

http://www.educ.ucalgary.ca/litindex/

The Internet Public Library

http://www.ipl.org/

New York Public Library: On-Lion for Kids!

http://www2.nypl.org/home/branch/kids/

Peggy Sharp's Web Site

http://www.peggysharp.com

Vandergrift's Literature Page

http://www.scils.rutgers.edu/%7Ekvander/ChildrenLit/index.html

traditional literature in the classroom. Certainly, children who are exposed to wonderfully imaginative writing are afforded a pleasurable and entertaining reading and listening experience. In addition to that, however, Mike Tunnell and Leland Jacobs (2000) explain that its use:

- Exercises a natural gift, the imagination
- Encourages children to do what they do so well anyway, to invent and retell fantasy stories
- Enables children to explore conflict and sorrow within a story, possibly gaining personal hope and the ability to believe things will improve (as with other genres)

- Is a useful way in which to explore solutions to cultural, social, or philosophical issues like good versus evil

There is much to be taught and to be thought about, then, in traditional tales.

Continuing through the Genres: Another Kind of Fiction

A Reflection of Life: Realistic Fiction

Reading a novel that is **realistic fiction** has been equated to looking into a mirror to see life reflected as it really is or what it might be like for someone somewhere in the world today (Cullinan & Galda, 1998). Whether the story is within a picture book, told in sparse poetry, or written in novel format, the people and places depicted seem hometown real. Readers are quickly caught up in events that could happen and characters who might be their best friends (or worst enemies) if they actually existed. Riveting mysteries are a part of this genre as are stories about seemingly insurmountable problems so much a part of life, including divorce, AIDS, Alzheimer's disease, teen pregnancy, drugs, sexual abuse, and gang pressures.

While the titles are offered as a brief look into the sometimes grim realities of fictional lives from the safety of the real world, they are not all supported in these efforts. A number of these books also raise the ire of censors who consider them to be almost too real and, as a result, a danger to the readers. Consider Katherine Paterson's (1987) *The Great Gilly Hopkins,* an eye-opening story about a tough, needy foster child who says "damn" occasionally. It makes the banned books list because of language issues and anti-Christian themes. Her popular *Bridge to Terabithia* (1987) has faced censorship because it deals with death and with imaginary worlds. Picture books are not without critics as both *Daddy's Roommate* (Wilhoite, 1993) and *Heather Has Two Mommies* (Newman, 2000) have been frequently challenged because they deal with nontraditional families made up of gay and lesbian parents. The American Library Association's website and local librarian are excellent resources for other titles that have made the censorship list.

Picture book titles abound as fine examples of realistic fiction. One award-winning example is *Owl Moon* (Yolen, 1987), a quiet story about a father and his young child going owling on a winter night. A connection to a painful period in history is revisited in *So Far from the Sea* (Bunting, 1998) as a family visits Grandfather's grave in Manzanar, a war relocation center for Japanese Americans. There is comfort and understanding about being new as Marianthe shares her life story with new classmates in *Painted Words and Spoken Memories* (Aliki, 1998), a clever presentation of two books within one.

Excellent books in a series provide younger readers with growing reading skills the opportunity to meet realistic and memorable characters. They surely will become fast friends with Henry and Mudge and empathize with their lifelike experiences in the popular series by Cynthia Rylant. Readers may shake their heads but can probably relate all too well to the much read Ramona series by Beverly Cleary. Older readers can examine the experience of being a foster child in pairings by different authors with *The Pinballs* (Byars, 1993) and *The Great Gilly Hopkins* (Paterson, 1987). Upper grade readers might read *Hatchet* (Paulsen, 1999) and its two sequels, *The River* (1991), and *Brian's Winter* (Paulsen, 1996). They can compare Brian's experiences with those related by Will Hobbs, who pens two suspenseful tales of survival for older readers in *Far North* (1996) and *Wild Man Island* (2002). Followers of Konigsburg will enjoy the friendships between some very diverse people in *The View from Saturday* (1996). Readers who have chuckled over Barbara Park's rib-tickling books like *Skinnybones* (1997) will find smiles watered with tears when they read *Mick Harte Was Here* (1999), a young girl's testament of love for a younger brother killed in a bicycle accident:

> Just let me say right off the bat, it was a bike accident.
>
> It was about as "accidental" as you can get, too.
>
> Like Mick wasn't riding crazy. Or dodging in and out of traffic. And both of his hands were on the handlebars and all that.
>
> His tire just hit a rock. And he skidded into the back of a passing truck. And that was that. There wasn't a scratch on him. It was a head injury. Period.
>
> So this isn't the kind of book where you meet the main character and you get to like him real well and then he dies at the end. I hate those kind of books. And besides, I can't think of anything worse than using my brother's accident as a tear-jerking climax to some tragic story.
>
> I don't want to make you cry.
>
> I just want to tell you about Mick. (Park, 1995, pp. 3–4)

Providing suggestions of titles or even sending home books for parents to read with their children creates a vital school-home link.

In addition, those readers who must refocus in an effort to start their lives anew for one reason or the other might choose from titles like *Hawk Hill Hattie* (Clark, 2003) or *Maniac Magee* (Spinelli, 1990). *Holes* (Sachar, 1998) will ignite the social interaction so important to the reading process as students discuss the unusual characters and uncover layer upon layer of the story together. A memorable poetry connection is achieved in *Harlem* (Myers, 1997), which teaches the reader about the culture and spirit of this area. Then try *Canto Familiar* (Soto, 1995) and look for similarities and differences between the Mexican American experience and that described as a part of life in Harlem. There is a world of quality reading and thinking experiences just waiting in the genre of realistic fiction.

Teaching Strategy for the Classroom

Review of the Literary Elements Using a Story Map Concept

A practical teaching activity to strengthen reading comprehension involves teaching or reviewing the literary elements. Focus on the basic elements: setting, plot, characters, major events, the resolution or solution of a problem, and an exploration of the theme or author's message. Initially, each element could be taught individually or two paired together when working with a picture book as a teaching device. Practice can be extended through other picture books or the novel that students are currently reading to ensure understanding.

At the conclusion of the review of literary elements, group the students into learning triads to read a picture book of their choice from a collection compiled ahead of time. Individuals practice their understanding of the elements by completing the activity sheet, Review of the Literary Elements Using a Story Map Concept, before comparing their answers with triad members. The opportunity for collaboration gives readers a chance to assess their understanding of the story and of each of the elements. Completed forms are reviewed by the teacher to ascertain each learner's understanding of the elements. Form a small skills group and reteach as is necessary. This lesson is an effective way to measure students' understanding of the basic elements, which will become a part of their literary conversations year after year.

ADAPTATIONS/MODIFICATIONS FOR DIVERSE LEARNERS

Students who need extra support with reading will benefit from working in triads or small groups. Moral support and modeling from classmates is motivating and reassuring. They will profit from hearing other classmates discuss the book in the process. In addition, a classmate can buddy read the text with the student and assist in completing the Story Map as needed. In preparation for this lesson, parent volunteers or upper grade students might read a selection of picture books onto audiotapes to supplement those that have been commercially prepared. Then, students needing practice with the English language or who need repetition in order to comprehend materials can listen to a particular tape in the reading center. They are able to reread the book as often as necessary to master its content, to build their understanding of story structure, and/or to practice the language involved. To monitor comprehension, have students retell the story to note mastery of the story elements.

When planning for students with mild mental retardation, scaffold the learning situation carefully. Set up the learning task based upon what the student already knows, the competencies she is developing, geared to the current ability levels. Thus, the book to be read and the group with whom she will read will help her achieve success and allow her to be like everyone else in the classroom.

Activity Sheet for Teaching Strategy: Review of the Literary Elements Using a Story Map Concept

After reading your book, fill in the chart below. Use the back of the sheet as needed. You can draw a story map with corresponding information on it to get a visual picture of the literary elements. Either the chart or the story map can be used when discussing the book or retelling the story.

Title of the book: _____

Author: _____

Setting: (Briefly describe when and where the story takes place.)

Characters: (Who were the main characters in this story? Write a concise description of each one.)

Conflict or challenge: (What is the main conflict, challenge, or problem faced by the character(s) in the story?)

Key events: (Summarize the major events in the story in the proper sequence as the character tries to resolve the conflict or problem.)

Solution/resolution: (How was the challenge or problem resolved?)

Theme: (In your opinion, what do you think the author was trying to say through this story?)

Fiction from Times Past: Historical Fiction

Novels and picture books that represent **historical fiction** are set in the historical past. They are realistic enough that it seems they could have happened. Well-selected titles enable students to sense what it might have been like to live in another place in another time, experiencing the emotions and turmoil of the times through the imagination of the authors. In fact, if the titles chosen "demonstrate scholarly integrity through the accurate portrayal of people and places, past and present" (Fuhler, 1998, p. xviii), they can be eye-opening additions to the social studies curriculum. The key to finding the best in this genre is to seek out authors who carefully research events so that stories seem authentic. In the process, some authors include real people, places, items that were a part of daily life, and actual historical events. Obviously, a textbook can relate the facts surrounding an event in history. A poem, novel, or picture book about the same event can bring the heart and soul of a time period to interplay with the facts, presenting a reader with a clearer picture as a result (Cullinan & Galda, 1998; Huck et al., 2004).

Web Link:
Scott O'Dell Historical Fiction Award

   Wonderful picture books live within historical fiction. Noteworthy titles allow readers to sample a *Medieval Feast* (Aliki, 1986) or dine with the Taino Indians who welcomed Columbus and his men in a disastrous *Encounter* (Yolen, 1992). They might follow in the footsteps of an escaping slave in *Barefoot: Escape Underground Railroad* (Edwards, 1997) or move onward to a different time when a slave family, struggles for freedom in *Freedom's Wings: Corey's Diary, Kentucky to Ohio, 1857* (Wyeth, 2001). They can bump across the prairie in *Grandma Essie's Covered Wagon* (Williams, 1993), stopping to experience life without trees on the prairie with Emily in *Prairie Willow* (Trottier, 2001). Walking the streets and lighting the gas lamps with *Peppe the Lamplighter* (Bartone, 1993) offers a glimpse of the life of one immigrant family in World War II can be experienced from a distance along with Monique, who inadvertently reveals a Jewish family's hiding place in *The Butterfly* (Polacco, 2000); in *Rose Blanche* (Galaz & Innocenti, 1996) while befriending the starving children in a concentration camp; when hiding in *The Lily Cupboard* (Oppenheim, 1999) to escape German soldiers; or while trying to keep hope alive before being captured by the Germans by painting *Flowers on the Wall* (Nerlove, 1996).

Novels abound and fill a reader's head with the sights and sounds of another time. Readers of *Lyddie* (Paterson, 1991) work in the textile mills and learn of the deplorable working conditions. Selected by the Newbery Committee as its 1998 winner, *Out of the Dust* (Hesse, 1998) is written in journal entry free-verse format that leaves an indelible impression on the mind of the tragedies one family endured during the Depression in Oklahoma. Consider the family "Rules of Dining";

> Ma has rules for setting the table.
> I place plates upside down,
> glasses bottom side up,
> napkins folded over forks, knives, and spoons.
>
> When dinner is ready,
> we sit down together
> and Ma says,
> "Now."
>
> We shake out our napkins,
> spread them on our laps,
> and flip over our glasses and plates,
> exposing neat circles,
> round comments
> on what life would be like without dust.
>
> Daddy says,
> "The potatoes are peppered plenty tonight, Polly,"
> and
> "Chocolate milk for dinner, aren't we in clover!"
> when really all our pepper and chocolate,
> it's nothing but dust. (Hesse, 1997, p. 21)

A view of sacrifices and growing up during the Depression is memorably presented in *A Year Down Yonder* (Peck, 2000), a chuckle-out-loud Newbery winner. While it does not make light of the difficulties of the times, it applauds the survivors who came to the top using their wits and plenty of humor. *The Birchbark House* (Erdrich, 1999) immerses the reader in an Ojibwa tribe in the mid-19th century and could be tied to other quality titles to form the foundation for a unit of study on different Native American tribes. *Witch Child* (Rees, 2001) touches on intense feelings of fear and desperation in the mid-1600s when witch-hunts reached a frenzied pitch. Readers can continue this tale into the engrossing sequel, *Sorceress* (Rees, 2002). Well-conceived historical fiction presents numerous options for extending readers' vicarious experiences in another time and place through fine opportunities for reading. (See Figure 10.5.)

Figure 10.5

Promoting critical reading through evaluation: A closer look at novels

The following questions can be addressed individually after completing an especially compelling novel, in pairs, if students have read the same novel together, or by a literature circle upon completion of their novel.

1. Story summary: Briefly, in no more than two paragraphs, summarize this story. What is the plot line?
2. Story analysis using literary elements:
   a. Genre
   b. Plot: Was it believable? Did it have an identifiable beginning, peak, and resolution? How did the author let you know time was passing? When does the story take place? What is the conflict or tension in the story? How is that tension resolved?
   c. Characterization: Identify main characters and secondary characters. What are the main qualities of the main character? Do you see strengths and weaknesses in the character? Does the main character change or grow in some way in the story?
   d. Setting: Location and time period. Realistic, historical fiction, or fantasy? Give a little background on the setting.
   e. Theme: In your opinion, what is the main reason the author wrote this story? Were any values taught?
   f. Mood: What is the prevailing mood of the story?
   g. Style: How is the mood or shifts in mood indicated by the author's style of writing? Illustrate with examples of dialogue, vocabulary, imagery, descriptions, similes, or metaphors.
   h. Point of view: From whose point of view is the story told?
3. Book review:
   a. Would you recommend this book to a classmate? Why or why not?
   b. Option: Present this book to the class in an engaging manner. You might write a lively book review, give an enthusiastic book talk, create an advertisement, or "interview" the author in a talk show format, for example.

THE NONFICTION GENRES

Biography/Autobiography

Whether it is an **autobiography,** penned by a living person about his or her own life, or an authentic or fictionalized **biography** written by someone else about the life of an individual who may or may not be living, the plot and theme of this nonfiction genre center upon a real person's life. A biography may cover an entire person's life or focus on just a part of it. It may be based completely on carefully researched facts as in authentic biography, or it may be enlivened by some fictional conversation or dramatized, attention-grabbing events in a fictionalized biography (Huck et al., 2004; Lukens, 1999). Offerings come in a number of formats including picture books, chapter books, collective biographies, and biographical series.

Books in this genre shed light on history as does historical fiction, because they often illuminate one person's effect on events in another time period. A special value of biographies and autobiographies is that these stories of real people's lives provide role models for contemporary students to emulate. In addition, the books give all students an opportunity to reflect upon the fact that all people have the same needs and desires regardless of the period of history in which they lived or the cultural background they claim as their own (Barrera et al., 1997; Cullinan & Galda, 1998).

Students can be challenged to read more than one biography on the person of their choice. This is one way to get a more complete picture of the individual, but is also an opportunity to do some critical thinking. Students then ask themselves if the information presented in the various books is consistent or if any segments conflict. If there are discrepancies, they can seek the accurate information from additional sources.

Picture book biographies are an excellent beginning whether the readers are young or in the upper grades. Jean Fritz and David Adler highlight leaders from early American history for young readers. Middle grade students will enjoy *A Boy Called Slow: The True Story of Sitting Bull* (Bruchac, 1995). It is an appealing beginning to learning about this compassionate Native American leader. Readers can then pick *Sitting Bull and His World* (Marrin, 2000), a richly researched opportunity for a more in-depth reading. Students might select *Coming Home: From the Life of Langston Hughes* (Cooper, 1994) and couple it with Meltzer's (1998) fine work, *Langston Hughes,* to learn more about this eminent poet's life. *Women of Hope: African Americans Who Made a Difference* (Hansen, 1998) tells about twelve exceptional African American women and their important contributions. An excellent pairing for this book would be *Princess of the Press: The Story of Ida B. Wells-Barnett* (Medearis, 1997), which presents a lively account of the life of a black journalist who used her pen to battle for equality. The sports world, engrossing to readers of all ages, comes to life through books like *America's Champion Swimmer: Gertrude Ederle* (Adler, 2000) and *Hank Aaron: Brave in Every Way* (Golenbock, 2001). These titles are just a taste of the appealing fare available in this genre.

Teachers can pull poetry into this genre with a selection like *Carver: A Life in Poems* (Nelson, 2001) or *Grass Sandals: The Travels of Basho* (Spivak, 1997). *A Humble Life: Plain Poems* (High, 2001) highlights the lives of Amish and Menonite peoples who have settled in the Pennsylvania Dutch Country. Angela Johnson (1998) describes her childhood in a small, African American, Alabama town in a not-to-be forgotten *The Other Side*. Don't stop with these titles for there are many others from which to choose. Both picture book–novel pairings and the rhythms of poetry are an enticing ways to enter the world of biography and autobiography and become engrossed enough to stay there for a while.

Letters, memoirs, diaries, journals, and autobiographies enrich the curriculum offerings in this genre. In fact, they are often some of the primary resources that authors use to write their books. Segments of them actually become a part of the completed text. *Pioneer Girl The Story of Laura Ingalls Wilder* (Anderson, 1998) will lead interested readers to *A Little House Reader: A Collection of Writings by Laura Ingalls Wilder* (Anderson, 1998) to learn more about the author of the distinctive Little House series through her own writings. Topics take on a more serious tone in some books. For instance, readers who want more information on the Holocaust after reading the picture book titles suggested previously in this chapter have a growing collection of riveting reading from which to choose. *No Pretty Pictures: A Child of War* (Lobel, 1998) presents a Holocaust survivor's tale from a child's viewpoint. Award-winning author and illustrator Anita Lobel was only five years old when her gripping account begins. Continuing from a child's viewpoint, readers might follow up with *Hiding to Survive: Stories of Jewish Children Rescued from the Holocaust* (Rosenberg, 1994). This book contains the stories of fourteen children and the gentiles who saved them. A superb photoessay to complement these titles is *My Secret Camera: Life in the Lodz Ghetto* (Smith, 2000).

Boys, often dubbed as reluctant readers, especially need to read such texts (Brozo, 2002). Factual accounts of accomplishments of Galileo, Pelé, and Nelson Mandela will, according to Brozo, help students discover "the goodness in real life men" (p. 18). These books also have the potential to help young men carve out values on which to base their lives. What boy wouldn't be enamored with the life of Admiral David Glasgow Farragut in *Take Command, Captain Farragut!* (Roop & Roop, 2002)? At the tender age of nine he became a midshipman and captained his own ship by the time he was twelve. During the Civil War, Farragut boldly sailed his ships up the Mississippi River and took the port of New Orleans. He was the first admiral in the history of the United States, and his memorable "Damn the torpedoes and full speed ahead!" has echoed through the years. Farragut is but one of the compelling potential role models for boys to study.

Brent Ashabranner, Russell Freedman, Milton Meltzer, and Diane Stanley are names that surface when seeking some of the best in biographers. But they are only a few of the talented authors who apply their artistry to capturing the lives of people past and present. A genre once considered to be rather dull, biographies have come a long way in recent years.

Informational Books

This particular genre offers books filled with facts, facts, facts about people's occupations, fascinating places, geologic discoveries, and a myriad of things that make up the real world and the heavens that surround it. **Informational books** explain a simple concept or delve into a subject for an in-depth study. Specific titles can be collected for student use to extend the information in the science, social studies, or math textbooks. They are as influential in extending comprehension as are choices from the fiction genres, especially when listeners have an opportunity to discuss the book and connect it with content area texts (Oyler & Barry, 1996). Furthermore, they can become an integral part of the classroom reading center because they offer fascinating reading. Information seems to stick better when readers have a particular interest in it, so a variety of books and advice on where to find others like them is important to keep in mind when promoting the use of informational books.

In selecting books for classroom use, keep an eye out for those that are fine examples of expository writing. It might be from those examples that students in the class learn to refine their own expository writing (Cullinan & Galda, 1998; Mikkelsen, 2000). Books must contain information that is factual and dependable so teachers are able to choose them with the conviction that the author has done his or her homework (Tunnell & Jacobs, 2000). From gerbils to whales, ships to castles, to the sources of milk and peanut butter sandwiches, well-researched picture books and more extensive volumes are available to fill the inquisitive mind.

A Drop of Water (Wick, 1997) pulls scientists and nonscientists alike into the world of water with short, interesting text and wondrous photography. Learning can be extended through *The Drop in My Drink: The Story of Water on Our Planet* (Hooper, 1998). Future aviators will be inspired by the brief biography of a famous pilot when reading *Flight: The Journey of Charles Lindbergh* (Burleigh, 1991) or *Sky Pioneer: A Photobiography of Amelia Earhart* (Szabo, 1997). They will delight in the celebration of two strong women in *Amelia and Eleanor Go for a Ride: Based on a True Story* (Ryan, 1999) soaring through the night skies with Amelia Earhart and her friend, Eleanor Roosevelt. Readers can get a detailed look at flying machines via *Cross-Sections Planes* (Johnstone, 1999).

Students who read Hesse's (1998) *Out of the Dust* might want more information, which can be found in *Children of the Dust: The True Story of the School at Weedpatch Camp* (Stanley, 1993). Betsy Maestro's (1996) *Coming to America: The Story of Immigration* might be the perfect follow-up after reading about Peppe and his job of lighting the gas lamps to help his immigrant family or about a Russian Jewish family's flight to safety in *The Memory Coat* (Woodruff, 1999). Another thought is to continue learning about a culture after starting with several representative folktales like the three Chinese folktales suggested previously in the chapter. A nonfiction resource is *Celebrating Chinese New Year* (Hoyt-Goldsmith, 1998), which tells of the preparations a San Francisco boy and his family make for the upcoming festival.

For a completely different change of pace, try poetry. *Cactus Poems* (Asch, 1998) and *This Big Sky* (Mora, 1998) take readers to the desert Southwest. *Flicker Flash* (Graham, 1999) treats them to light in different forms, and *Home to Me: Poems Across America* (Hopkins, 2002) explores the diverse places within America that people call home. All three books can be the beginnings of further investigations of geographic locations across the United States, giving students an idea of what it is really like in a place quite different from their own (Fuhler, 1998; Lempke, 2001). *To the*

Gleaning their information from books, these students are sharing their science reports with the class.

Top: The Story of Everest (Venables, 2003) will take adventurers farther afield to the breathtaking Himalayas. Finally, check poetry anthologies for appropriate single poems to work into every subject across the curriculum.

Seymour Simon's books about the planets, animals, or his series about the human body are excellent reading. Joanna Cole's Magic School Bus series, written in both English and Spanish, presents facts about a variety of science topics in a delightfully appealing way. Gail Gibbons' books are excellent choices for the younger reader. Gibbons investigates the inner workings of lighthouses, the post office, an undersea dive, trucks, bats, farming, and bees, just to mention a few. The fascinating Eye Witness books published by Dorling Kindersley are bound to put some zip into the science and social studies curriculum. Packed to the brim with bright illustrations, a multitude of photographs, and facts galore, these books just beg to be investigated.

Topics covered in the informational books genre range from interesting to amusing to some quite serious in nature. Students can take an exciting journey back in time carefully following a fact-filled travel guide as they learn about the Mayan civilization in *Your Travel Guide to Ancient Mayan Civilization* (Day, 2001). They can examine the touchy issue of interment during World War II as discussed in *The Children of Topaz: The Story of a Japanese-American Interment Camp Based on a Classroom Diary* (Tunnell & Chilcoat, 1996), building fact upon the fictional story *So Far from the Sea* by Eve Bunting (1998). The options go on and on. It is difficult to imagine that a curious reader could not find a number of intriguing books on a topic of personal interest from the innumerable selections in this genre.

Teaching Strategy for the Classroom

READER'S THEATER SCRIPT FOR *YOUNG MOUSE AND ELEPHANT: AN EAST AFRICAN FOLKTALE*

Adapted by Pamela J. Farris. (1996). *Young Mouse and Elephant.* (V. Gorbachev, Illus.). Boston, MA: Houghton Mifflin. Used with permission.

Cast of Characters

Narrator, Young Mouse, Grandfather, Elephant, the lizard, the zebra, and the giraffe.

Narrator: In the lush grass of the African savannah, there lived a village of mice. One mouse in the village was very strong and very proud. His name was Young Mouse. No other mouse could throw farther, run faster, or out-wrestle him. One day Young Mouse was sitting by his old, wise grandfather's hut crushing dried grass in his paws.

Young Mouse: You know, Grandfather, I'm very strong. Why, I'm the strongest mouse in the whole village.

Grandfather: That's true.

Young Mouse: Why, I'm so strong, I must be the strongest animal on the plains.

Grandfather: You are indeed strong. But Elephant is the strongest animal on the plains. She might not like to hear you bragging.

Young Mouse: Elephant! Why, I can break Elephant apart and stomp her to bits, for I am the strongest animal on the plains!

Narrator: With that, Young Mouse marched off to find Elephant.

Grandfather: (smiling to himself) Well, come back soon, Young Mouse, for a storm is coming.

Narrator: The first animal Young Mouse meets is a lizard basking in the last of the sun.

Young Mouse: Hey! Are you Elephant?

Lizard: No, I'm just a lizard.

Young Mouse: In that case, consider yourself fortunate, for if you had been Elephant, I would have broken you apart and stomped you to bits.

Narrator: The lizard gave a great sigh, for he had seen Elephant. When Young Mouse saw him sigh, he stomped his paw on the ground. Just at that moment came a roaring clap of thunder.

Lizard: The little mouse made the sky tremble!

Narrator: The lizard lumbered away to hide under a bush. Satisfied, Young Mouse puffed out his chest and continued his journey. He sees a zebra resting lazily and marches right up.

Young Mouse: Hey! Are you Elephant?

Zebra: No, I'm a zebra.

Young Mouse: In that case, consider yourself fortunate, for if you had been Elephant, I would have broken you apart and stomped you to bits.

Narrator: The zebra snorted because she knew Elephant. When Young Mouse heard her, he glared. Just at that moment a bolt of lightning flashed across the sky.

Zebra: (bellowing) The small mouse made the sky break into pieces!

Narrator: The zebra anxiously galloped off. Young Mouse was pleased that the zebra had run to the herd for protection. He puffed out his chest and continued on his way. He sees giraffe busy nibbling leaves and marches right up.

Young Mouse: Hey! Are you Elephant?

Giraffe: (lowering his head) They call me a giraffe.

Young Mouse: In that case consider yourself fortunate, for if you had been Elephant, I would have broken you apart and stomped you to bits.

Narrator: The giraffe merely shrugged and flicked his ears. When Young Mouse saw that, he shook his paw. At that exact moment, a large rain cloud darkened the entire sky.

Giraffe: (shouting) The tiny mouse caused the sun to leave the sky!

Narrator: The giraffe raced off in fear. The other animals saw him running and they started running, too.

Young Mouse: (puffing out his chest) They are all afraid of me.

Narrator: Soon Young Mouse came upon an enormous animal with legs as big as tree trunks. It had two tails, a small one in back and a large one in front. It was the biggest animal he had ever seen. Young Mouse marched right up.

Young Mouse: Hey! Are you Elephant?

Narrator: Elephant turned to see who was talking. She looked and looked but only saw trees, bushes, and rocks.

Young Mouse: Hey! Are you Elephant?

Narrator: Elephant looked around once more. Squinting her eyes, she spotted a small speck. It was Young Mouse. She leaned down to hear better.

Young Mouse: (yelling) Are you Elephant?

Elephant: Yes, Elephant is my name.

Young Mouse: (puffing out his chest) Well, I've been looking for you. I'm the strongest animal on the plains. Just what do you think of that?

Narrator: Elephant stood a moment, then she slowly filled her trunk with water. WHOOSH! A great flood of water hit Young Mouse. He tumbled head over heels across the savannah. Soon, rain began to fall, first in droplets and later much harder. When the storm had passed, Young Mouse woke up and looked around. Elephant was nowhere to be seen.

Young Mouse: Hump! The storm must have washed Elephant away. In that case Elephant should consider herself fortunate, for I would have broken her apart and stomped her to bits!

DIVERSE LEARNERS AND LITERATURE

Throughout the chapter it has been noted that teaching with children's literature affords every child in the classroom something to read, whether for pleasure, for simple research purposes, or as the source of a reading lesson. Sometimes they offer readers from varying cultures a chance to define and to find themselves (Hefflin & Barksdale-Ladd, 2001). Furthermore, because reading is the best practice for becoming a better reader, a print-rich environment will surely benefit readers of all abilities. For English language learners and others seeking to strengthen their skills, a teacher might select from picture books available in varying degrees of complexity and covering a wide range of topics. With such a plethora of materials, he is sure to be able to match book and student.

As noted in chapter after chapter, there are numerous strategies to help diverse learners become successful, and the use of children's literature can be an aid in

Web Link:
Online Reference Desk

What better way to read than with friends?

 implementing some of them. For example, ample opportunity for practice by rereading a book is suggested for English language learners (Au, 1993), a practice that will scaffold learning for students who need repetition to grasp a concept. Then, too, books that reflect different backgrounds surely motivate a segment of students because they are better able to relate to the materials to be learned through personal connections. For that reason, it is heartening to find a growing number of picture books available in dual languages, although the predominant option continues to be Spanish. Reading a book in their first language, and then in English, will be a boon to these learners. In addition, try working together in pairs or in teams, retelling the story or listening to books on tape as suggested in the Teaching Strategy for the Classroom lessons. Such efforts will offer encouragement to a population of students who may learn a little differently for one reason or another or just need additional assistance when mastering a new language in a different culture.

Web Links:

The Children's Lit Web Guide

Fairrose Cyber Library

deGrummond Children's Literature Collection

 ## *ENHANCING LEARNING WITH TECHNOLOGY*

While series books usually cause connoisseurs of children's literature to raise their eyebrows a little, they have been an appealing part of growing up with books for many readers. The Hardy Boys and Nancy Drew intermingle with the Goosebumps series and the Babysitter's Club, one title after another willingly devoured by eager readers. Three award-winning software programs for middle to upper grade readers draw on the continuing popularity of the famous sleuth Nancy Drew. *Nancy Drew:*

Secrets Can Kill, Nancy Drew: Stay Tuned for Danger, and a more recent title, *Nancy Drew: Message in a Haunted Mansion,* are sure to hold one's interest and activate problem-solving skills in the process.

Young readers will delight in Bill Martin Jr.'s rhythmic *Chicka Chicka Boom Boom* (Davidson, 1995), a poetic review of the alphabet. Aesop's often told tale of *The Tortoise and the Hare* (Broderbund/Living Books, 1999) is another appealing CD-ROM option for early and middle grade readers. Check through earlier chapters for additional positively reviewed software titles. In addition, spend time browsing through journals like *Technology & Learning* for current reviews of promising software.

The Internet provides a wealth of options for locating and using children's literature. There is little doubt that it is affecting the way we think about local literacy, that which takes place within our classroom walls. In a phenomenon termed "The Miss Rumphius Effect" (Leu, Karchmer, & Leu, 1999), the spread of ideas via the Internet is equated to the way *Miss Rumphius* (Cooney, 1982) made the world a better place by spreading lupines wherever she went. Instead of lupine seeds, teachers and students are planting ideas, completed projects, and invitations for collaborations in literacy from one classroom to another, around the world. From teachers' guides to lists of wonderful titles and even opportunities to read a book on the Web, whole new horizons can be opened with a few strokes on the keyboard. Try some of the following websites and share with others what you discover with your colleagues and students.

Summary

A balanced literacy program and fine children's literature are powerful partners. This chapter presented a primer of children's literature in an effort to acquaint some teachers or to remind others of the kinds of books that could become valuable reading and writing resources. Certainly they afford readers hours upon hours of engaging opportunities to be caught up in real books while reading their way to proficiency.

Children's literature includes fiction, nonfiction, and poetry presented in volumes of varying sizes and lengths, on topics that appeal to readers of different interests, abilities, and backgrounds. Such materials facilitate reader response, promoting engagement with both fiction and nonfiction titles. That response strengthens comprehension and deepens connections with reading materials across the genres. While readers tend to have a favorite genre, it is good practice to sample from all of them. A wealth of multicultural literature is available from mythology and folktales to reflections on the lives of heroes and heroines across cultures. Reading such fine fare is a step toward extending multicultural understanding.

With a key stroke or two and adequate time, teachers can expand their personal knowledge of children's literature via the Internet. Children, too, can use this vast resource as they connect with authors and illustrators, submit their own creative stories, and find information to extend nonfiction reading. This resource dissolves walls and distance boundaries and provides enticing learning opportunities where readers and writers become learners together.

Web Links:

Barahona Center for the Study of Spanish for Children and Adolescents

Doucette Index

Drama in the Classroom

KIDLIT-L

Kidzsing Garden of Songs

Myths and Legends

Peggy Sharp's Website

Reader's Theatre Editions

SCORE Cyberguides

Kay Vandergrift's Author and Illustrator Pages

Vandergrift's Literature Page

Web-Travelers ToolKit

Chapter Review

Go to the Online Learning Center at **www.mhhe.com/farrisreading** to take chapter quizzes, practice with key terms, and review important content.

Main Points

- Children's literature encompasses a body of fiction, nonfiction, and poetry that is less complex than that written for adults. It is directed at an audience of young people up to the age of about fourteen.

- The realm of children's books is divided into genres or categories that include traditional literature, fantasy, folktales, fairy tales, science fiction, realistic fiction, historical fiction, biography or autobiography, and informational books. Picture books and poetry are represented across the genres.

- Theorists abound in support of integrating real books into the reading and writing curriculum in an effort to strike a balance between different approaches to teaching reading.

- Depending on how they are used, books can balance the locus of control between teacher and learners. They also provide materials that prompt readers to think carefully about story events and those in real life as they examine others' thoughts, beliefs, and actions, broadening their world views in the process.

- Selections of children's literature serve as wonderful models for students to emulate in their own writing.

- Picture books are written for readers young and old. They are versatile in that they can be read for pleasure, are fine read-loud options, can introduce a lesson or unit of study on a particular topic, and are excellent venues for teaching a reading skill or strategy.

- Picture books can be excellent tools for readers of varying abilities. These children can be successful with books in which brief text and simple concepts make reading less challenging than basal text or other grade level materials.

- Reader response theory explains how readers connect with books when a unique transaction occurs between reader and book. A student's personal response to a book is a key to facilitating comprehension.

- Response can be extended through a variety of creative activities that appeal to readers of varying interests, backgrounds, and abilities.

- A growing number of multicultural books for classroom use means that every child in the classroom will be able to find a book to relate to, to see a face reflected back that resembles theirs, and to read about values or daily practices that mirror their lives.

- When every reader in the classroom has access to fine multicultural titles, there is the added possibility for strengthening an appreciation for and understanding of the similarities and differences between all people regardless of their ethnic roots or academic prowess.

- Access to the Internet provides an exceptional resource for materials related to the world of children's literature and sensible ways to integrate it into the balanced reading and writing curriculum.

- While knowledge of a multitude of titles is important, the most critical piece to infusing literature throughout the curriculum is the informed and enthusiastic teacher.

Key Terms

autobiography	464	fable	452	informational books	465	response theory	436
ballad	453	fairy tales	451	legend	453	science fiction	456
biography	464	fantasy/modern		multicultural		tall tales	452
children's		fantasy	454	literature	441	traditional	
literature	434	folktales	451	myth	453	literature	451
envisionment	436	genre	439	pourquoi tale	453	transaction	436
epic	453	historical fiction	461	realistic fiction	458	trickster tales	452

Reflecting and Reviewing

1. Based upon what you have read in this chapter and the preceding chapters, generate at least six arguments for integrating children's literature into the reading–writing curriculum. Support each argument.

2. Do you have a favorite genre that you tend to reach for almost without thinking? Which genre have you explored the least? Make a concerted effort to read several books from that genre, using titles suggested in the chapter or others deemed popular choices by the local librarian. Share your reactions with a friend.

3. How would you rate your knowledge of multicultural literature titles? Set aside some time to browse through titles new to you from the library collection or those on display in a local bookstore. Keep a growing list of possible books for your classroom library.

4. In reflecting on your reading experiences in school, how was response to literature encouraged? Pick a favorite book from your past reading or this chapter and brainstorm different ways that you might invite children's response to the book. Develop of habit of thinking this way: how can I best use this book in my reading and writing curriculum, and how can I help children connect with it?

5. Dedicate some time to exploring the Internet for useful websites that support children's literature. Browse through several author and illustrator sites to learn about these creative people. Follow several links from one site to another. How could you integrate this technology effectively in your own?

Children's Literature

Due to the vast number of children's literature selections mentioned in this chapter, the annotated bibliography has been moved to Appendix A.

Software

Broderbund/Living Books. (1999). *The Tortoise and the Hare.* (CD-ROM). Novato, CA: Broderbund.

Davidson & Associates. (1995). *Chicka Chicka Boom Boom.* (CD-ROM). Torrence, CA: Davidson & Associates/Simon & Schuster.

HerInteractive. (2000). *Nancy Drew: Message in a Haunted Mansion.* (CD-ROM). Bellevue, WA: HerInteractive. (www.herinteractive.com)

———. (1999). *Nancy Drew: Stay Tuned for Danger.* (CD-ROM). Bellevue, WA: HerInteractive.

———. (1997). *Nancy Drew: Secrets Can Kill* (CD-ROM). Bellevue, WA: HerInteractive.

Classroom Teaching Resources

In addition to the rich resources available on the Internet, the following catalogs, journals, and materials might be useful in your classroom:

Barefoot Books
37 W. 17th Street, 4th Floor East
New York, New York 10010
website: www.barefoot-books.com
Send for a catalog of fine picture books for readers of all ages. This company specializes in the work of artists and writers from many different cultures.

Book Links
American Library Association
50 E. Huron Street
Chicago, IL 60611
For subscription information: 434 W. Downer
Aurora, IL 60506
Highlighting children's literature and retrospective reviews of books appropriate for children from preschool through eighth grade.

Bauer, C. F. (1995). *The Poetry Break, an Annotated Anthology for Introducing Children to Poetry.* New York: H. W. Wilson.
An invaluable volume that contains over 240 poems and suggestions for using them in the classroom.

Brady, Martha. (1994). *Dancing Hearts: Creative Arts with Books Kids Love.* Golden, CO: Fulcrum.
Twenty well-known children's books are a foundation for opportunities for expression. It is an excellent resource for addressing the different ways in which children learn.

CBC Features
The Children's Book Council
568 Broadway, Suite 404
New York, NY 10012
Website: www.cbcbooks.org
The official sponsor of national Children's Book Week, this is a non-profit organization that encourages the use and enjoyment of children's literature and literacy-related materials for young people.

Hamilton, M. & Weiss, M. (1998). *Stories in my Pocket: Tales Kids Can Tell.* Golden, CO: Fulcrum.
Thirty stories from simple to more complex can be mastered by children who want to learn the art of storytelling, an excellent activity to promote sequencing skills and strengthen comprehension.

National Geographic Society. (1994). *Storytelling Live!: Stories of North America.* National Geographic Society: Washington D.C.
This videotape contains five engaging stories told by professional storytellers. It is sure to be a hit as you enjoy tales from different cultures and will serve as a model for students who want to try storytelling on their own.

National Council for the Social Studies-Children's Book Council
Attention: Social Studies
568 Broadway, Suite 404
New York, New York 10012-5497
In a special supplement to the May/June issue of *Social Education,* the Notable Social Studies Trade Books for Young People is published. This annotated list of fine books appeals to children in grades K–8.

Rising Moon/Northland Publishing
P.O. Box 1389
Flagstaff, AZ 86002
Telephone: 800-346-3257
Order a catalog to review the excellent selection of multicultural picture books and novels, many with a Southwest flavor.

Storycart Press: A Readers Theater Subscription Service
P.O. Box 740519
Arvada, CO 80006-0519
www.storycart.com
Send for information and a sample script from this service. Subscribers receive three scripts each month appropriate for grades 1–6. Scripts reflect curricular themes, holidays, and literary genres.

Parts of a Computer

AUTHORS NEED A
WRITING PLAN
First Draft - ideas on paper
Second Draft - self-editing
· peer conference
Third Draft - proofreading
· peer experts
Final Draft - perfect copy
· share

"Reading and writing help the brain achieve what the brain does best—the creation of worlds. Imagination is the essence of mental life—including comprehension, learning, remembering, and reasoning—in public and in private. Reading and writing both provide opportunities to exercise the imagination in manners and to extents no other way possible."

Frank Smith, renowned expert in literacy education

Connecting Reading and Writing: Narrative and Poetry

Key Ideas

- Reading narrative text is often referred to as aesthetic reading because one reads it for enjoyment and pleasure.
- Reading strategies can be taught effectively within the context of quality narrative text.
- Gender preferences influence students' reading selections with girls preferring narrative while boys are less apt to read narrative text for pleasure.
- Narrative text enables readers to make connections: personal, textual, and with the world.
- Reading and writing workshops are important in teaching narrative reading and writing as well as in writing poetry.
- Good writing has six traits: ideas, organization, word choice, sentence fluency, voice, and conventions.
- Children need to learn how to make visual images as they read narrative text.
- One appealing type of text is poetry, a popular choice for pleasurable reading.
- There are several forms of poetry that are enticing to children as readers and writers.
- Reading fluency can be augmented through poetry readings and reader's theater activities.

Questions to Ponder

- How does the aesthetic reading of narrative and poetry selections differ from efferent reading of expository text?
- What skills/strategies enhance narrative text reading?

- How does a teacher set up and use reading and writing workshops with narrative text? With poetry?
- In what ways can readers question the author of the text they are reading?
- In what ways does creating visual images while reading narrative text enhance comprehension?
- What role does fluency play in reading development? How can it be improved?

Peering into the Classroom

Linking Reading and Writing

"Really engaging adolescents in their reading and writing activities can be the toughest part of a teacher's day! No matter how hard we struggle to find a way to make things 'fun' or 'exciting,' many students simply go through the motions of reading or writing and take, little, if anything, away from the effort" write Karen L. Ford and Cynthia A. Bowman (1999, p. 31) of their struggles in teaching middle schoolers. No doubt about it, young adolescents are a tough group to motivate. While Ford and Bowman encountered what some teachers refer to as the "reading and writing blues," that wasn't enough to stifle their creativity as they designed a Literacy Fair composed of "fast-paced, entertaining, literacy-based, learning activities" (Ford & Bowman, 1999, p. 31).

Taking a page from the ever successful Science Fair, Ford and Bowman came up with a twist—the Literacy Fair. Based upon the theme of the famous Iditarod Dogsled Race, students read one of three young adult novels about dogsled racing: *Dogsong* and *Woodsong* by popular young adult author Gary Paulsen (1985; 1990), himself a veteran of the Iditarod Race in Alaska, and *Black Star, Bright Dawn* by Scott O'Dell (1988). Students were encouraged to read an informational book, *Winterdance: The Fine Madness of Running the Iditarod* also by Paulsen (1994), to discover additional background information about the preparation for and actual running of the dogsled race.

Upon finishing their choice of novels, students spent a week participating in the Literacy Fair. To some extent, the fair was a kind of three-ring circus engaging all students in short, motivating activities—reading, writing, and interdisciplinary—that required each of them to draw upon information they had encountered in their reading. Below is the weeklong schedule of events Ford and Bowman established:

Iditarod Literacy Fair Time Line

Day 1—The Writing Prompt

During a two-hour period, in the booklet their teachers provided them, students were to write a first draft response to the following prompt:

> Many of the characters in all three novels showed considerable courage. Discuss how you would explain the idea of courage and use examples from the books to help us understand what you mean. (Ford & Bowman, 1999, p. 31)

During day 4, students were encouraged to revisit their draft, revising and polishing until it was ready to be included as part of a class book entitled *Tales of Courage from the Trail.*

Days 2 and 3—Engaging in Fast-Paced Activities

Students were divided into groups and given twenty minutes to complete nine activities. Since the Iditarod has checkpoints for its mushers, completion of each task was considered a "checkpoint" for the students. The activities included:

- *Going the Distance:* Students were provided with tools (compass, protractor, ruler, string, and calculator) to use to find the length of the Iditarod trail Bright Dawn followed in the novel *Black Star, Bright Dawn* (O'Dell, 1988).

- *Scavenger Hunt:* Working together in teams, students answered multiple choice questions based upon their novel readings to locate clues and find the prize.

- *Iditarod Jeopardy:* Played just like the television version, the students had to develop the questions to the answers given (i.e., "The city where this year's Iditarod began"). Students with the highest scores were given special prizes at the conclusion of the fair.

- *Iditarod Pictionary:* Like Jeopardy, this game was modeled after the popular pictionary game to help students review information and vocabulary. Playing in teams, they were timed in the competition to make it more like the actual game.

- *Dog Rhythm:* Teamwork and music were the focus of this activity as students had to create a human machine of movements and sounds to convey the emotions of the mushers racing in the Iditarod.

- *CyberSearch:* In this twenty-minute segment, students used the Internet to find (1) interesting (or just fun) facts about the Iditarod, (2) historical information about the race, (3) other fiction books about the Iditarod, and (4) nonfiction books about the Iditarod. Information gleaned was then word-processed or handwritten on a prepared activity sheet.

- *Iditarod Haiku:* This checkpoint gave students the format and samples of haiku poetry, a brief three-line poem with seventeen syllables (line 1: five syllables; line 2: seven syllables; and line 3: five syllables) about the seasons or nature. The students then worked as a group to create their own haiku poem based on the Iditarod race and the seasonal elements that the mushers and their dogs encounter.

- *Panther Trail:* Two teams of students ran an obstacle course.

- *Iditarod Survival:* Students were asked to imagine that they were left stranded on the Iditarod Trail. Given a list of limited supplies, they were to select two items from their supply list and write an explanation as to why those two items would be the most important to them to survive in the wilderness of Alaska.

Day 4—Draft, Revision, and Editing

In this two-hour period, students returned to their initial response to the writing prompt they were given on day 1. Upon making revisions and editing modifications for content and mechanics, they then shared their work with peer partners who used a checklist to critique the pieces as well as help in revising their partner's paper.

Day 5—Publishing and Awards

Time was provided for final corrections as well as an Awards Ceremony. Prizes were given for each checkpoint activity with a certificate presented to all students who participated.

End of the Race

All of the student responses to the initial writing prompt were word processed and compiled into a class book entitled *Tales of Courage from the Trail*. Names of individuals who had received special awards, student artwork, and maps were also included in the book.

Clearly Ford and Bowman found an appealing way to entice middle schoolers to read in the depths of winter. They planned carefully and thoughtfully to come up with a workable theme that young adolescents could relate to easily based upon intriguing novels and motivated their learning through engaging activities. The time line they set was realistic as it gave students a sufficient amount of time to complete all of the tasks and kept them moving at a lively pace. They even made certain there was an interval available to set up and dismantle props, astutely sharing the workload by enlisting the help of students and parents to assist with this aspect of the Literacy Fair.

REFLECTION: IRA/NCTE NATIONAL STANDARDS IN THE CLASSROOM

There is no question about it, Karen L. Ford and Cynthia A. Bowman planned a terrific unit that enlivened the normally dismal, dreary winter months. Based upon the three novels selected, they were able to incorporate numerous activities that would be applauded by the authors of *Standards for the English Language Arts* (IRA/NCTE, 1996). They linked their unit to the standards via having their students "read a wide range of print and nonprint texts to build an understanding of texts, of themselves, and of the cultures of the United States and the world; to acquire new information; to respond to the needs. . . of society" (IRA/NCTE, 1996, p. 27) as the students first read fiction, then nonfiction contemporary works. By reading one of the three novels, students learned about the great peril that originated the Iditarod race, and of the challenge to dog mushers to deliver the serum that would save the lives of many ill Alaskan children. In addition, they learned about other cultures, having an opportunity to reflect on the similarities and differences between their own culture and others. Reflection was encouraged when they had to write about their beliefs of what constitutes a courageous act and support their thoughts with ideas from the text they read and the checkpoint activities.

The second standard, "students read a wide range of literature from many periods in many genres to build an understanding of the many dimensions. . . of human experience" (IRA/NCTE, 1996, p. 29), was likewise addressed. Scott O'Dell was one of the finest young adult authors of all time. His compassion for the environment and for Native American cultures is evident in all of his works. As a result of reading *Black Star, Bright Dawn* (O'Dell, 1988), students gained a greater appreciation of the environment and Inuit people.

In addition to the above, Ford and Bowman also had their middle school students "employ a wide range of strategies as they write and use different writing process elements appropriately to communicate with different audiences and for different purposes" (IRA/NCTE, 1996, p. 35). Students were asked to write on a number of occasions throughout the weeklong Literacy Fair. They had to respond to a prompt and come up with their own interpretations of what they believed was an act of courage, explaining why each act selected met their established criteria. Ford and Bowman also provided their students with samples of haiku poetry, which was created in 13th-century Japan as a means of sharing thoughts and feelings about the seasons and nature. From those samples and their reading of one of the unit's novels, students worked together to create a haiku poem. Finally, Ford and Bowman had students write persuasively when they were to select two items they would need if they would be stranded out on the Iditarod trail, giving reasons why each item would be important in their survival out in the wilderness.

Technology was also incorporated by Ford and Bowman in a purposeful, practical way adding to the students' opportunity to learn more in depth about their topic of study. Recall that the students were required to use the Internet to locate four different pieces of information as part of one checkpoint activity. Can you imagine the excited conversations and high levels of interest as classmates read and discovered one tidbit after another during the Internet exploration?

The entire unit encompassed having students "participate as knowledgeable, reflective, creative, and critical members of a variety of literacy communities" (IRA/NCTE, 1996, p. 44). Certainly the middle schoolers had ample opportunities throughout the unit to work with others in groups, albeit the "dogsled team," the obstacle race, or as a peer editing partner in addition to other chances as part of the various checkpoints. The unit also enabled the students to "use spoken, written, and visual language to accomplish their own purposes (e.g., for learning, enjoyment, persuasion, and the exchange of information)" (IRA/NCTE, 1996, p. 45). Whether they were creating haiku poetry, informing readers about their conception of courage, participating in *Pictionary*, or creating a human machine, these students were totally involved in the many uses of language.

Buoyant by completing what they considered a monumental task that turned out to be extremely successful, Ford and Bowman managed to keep their feet adhered securely to the floor as they began to contemplate sequel Literacy Fairs. First and foremost, they believe that pulling off a major instructional unit such as the Iditarod Literacy Fair requires lots of time and effort on any teacher's part. In their case, they were able to work together as a team and include other teachers of their middle school staff to aid in the coordination of the event. This team effort is crucial to the success of any large event. Secondly, detailed planning and a willingness to be flexible helped to make the Literacy Fair an enriching experience for their students.

STANDARDS for READING PROFESSIONALS

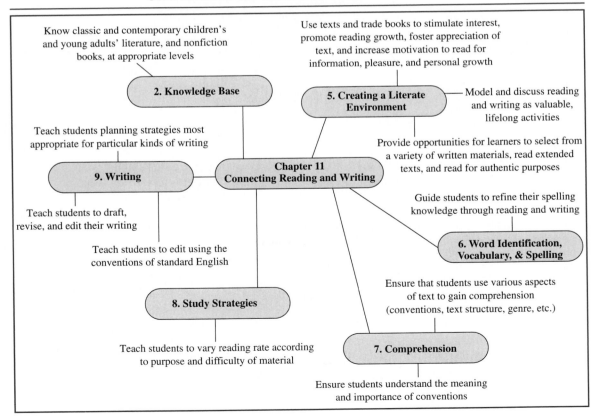

Know classic and contemporary children's and young adults' literature, and nonfiction books, at appropriate levels

2. Knowledge Base

Use texts and trade books to stimulate interest, promote reading growth, foster appreciation of text, and increase motivation to read for information, pleasure, and personal growth

5. Creating a Literate Environment

Model and discuss reading and writing as valuable, lifelong activities

Teach students planning strategies most appropriate for particular kinds of writing

9. Writing

**Chapter 11
Connecting Reading and Writing**

Provide opportunities for learners to select from a variety of written materials, read extended texts, and read for authentic purposes

Teach students to draft, revise, and edit their writing

Guide students to refine their spelling knowledge through reading and writing

6. Word Identification, Vocabulary, & Spelling

Teach students to edit using the conventions of standard English

8. Study Strategies

Ensure that students use various aspects of text to gain comprehension (conventions, text structure, genre, etc.)

Teach students to vary reading rate according to purpose and difficulty of material

7. Comprehension

Ensure students understand the meaning and importance of conventions

INTRODUCTION

You might be scratching your head right about now as you think about the title of this chapter. Why put narrative reading and poetry together in the same chapter? In reality, both **narrative** and **poetic text** offer **aesthetic** literacy experiences for children. An added bonus is that students often gain bits of expository information along the way. Whether they discover the twists and turns of a plot through a good piece of fiction, immerse themselves into a slowly babbling brook of rhythm, rhyme, and language of a poem, or attempt to use similes to describe a character in their writing, all the while they are growing as readers and writers. As lifelong readers and writers, we want them to continue to reach into the world of aesthetic reading and writing especially in the light of the fact that roughly 90 percent of our reading as adults is expository. Likewise, much of our writing is expository primarily because as adults we often have to develop, read, and write informational materials for our jobs.

Competition is stiff for the time once devoted to the pleasures of aesthetic reading and writing. Today television satellite systems capable of tuning in up to 999 channels and the Internet's literally endless sites to check out are tough competition for students' time. A quick reflection on life in our present-day society would find it characterized in the following mode: get things done now, keep the kids involved in a bazillion after-school activities, and stay afloat in an instant gratification society. This frantic lifestyle actually discourages children from curling up in a comfortable chair or sprawling across their beds with a refreshingly enjoyable piece of fiction. Struggling readers may have little desire to open a book and read it for pleasure. However, miracles do happen. For example, look at the repercussions when that scrawny little British imp with horn-rimmed glasses appeared on the scene and, TAH DAH!!!! Millions of American youngsters were caught reading the Harry Potter series. Reading on their way to soccer games. Reading on the school bus. Reading as they eat their hamburgers and french fries. Reading in the tub. Reading ever so quietly under the covers by the light of a small flashlight. Reading. READING. READING!!!!

Aesthetic reading offers students not only pleasure but a means to discover new knowledge by introducing us to new people, exploring other cultures, and expanding our world. Reading has been described by novelist John Gardner (1983) as creating

> for us a kind of dream, a rich and vivid play in the mind. We read a few words at the beginning of the book or the particular story and suddenly we find ourselves seeing not words on a page but a train moving through Russia, an old Italian crying, or a farmhouse battered by rain. We read on—dream on—not passively but actively, worrying about the choices the characters have to make, listening in panic for some sound behind the fictional door, exalting in characters' successes, bemoaning their failures . . . we sympathize, think, and judge. (p. 41)

In our role as teachers, we can foster lifelong connections to books when we use children's literature to enhance the entire curriculum. One way to highlight that literature is to take the opportunity to read aloud daily to students at every grade level from preschool through middle school as mentioned repeatedly throughout this book. Clearly, such read-alouds must include informational text to enhance student understanding of concepts presented in content areas. This is especially critical for average and below average ability readers. Equally important are narrative and poetry texts inasmuch as they both provide rich language and enable students to develop their own meaning based upon their lives and dreams. While all students benefit from listening to read-alouds, such exposure to literature is especially needed by struggling readers and writers.

There is another value that grows from this reading experience. By listening to the teacher read aloud as well as reading such literature on their own, students not only become more adept in their comprehension as readers but are influenced as budding writers. Hearing well-phrased and fully developed texts from quality literature serves as models for future writing attempts. As listeners and readers of narrative and poetic texts, students better understand how words are woven together in a tapestry that holds the audience captive from beginning to the end. Syndicated writer James Kilpatrick (2000, p. 5A) expressed that "they are all a writer has to work with—adjectives, adverbs and verbs, and conjunctions, prepositions, and nouns. They are at once our building materials and our tools. Words are nails. We hammer them into place. Words have ragged edges. We sand them down. Our structures are usually plain and simple, the works of elementary carpentry."

As teachers we must help our "apprentice carpenters" discover more about the way authors convey messages as they "show" rather than "tell" the plot of a story or the theme of a poem. Reading narrative and poetry texts also helps children to better understand the world around them. "As children search for meaning in books, they naturally link what they are reading to their own lives. . . . We want to encourage children to discover personal meaning in books in order to better understand their lives and to extend their perceptions of other lives" (Huck, Hepler, Hickman, & Kiefer, 2004). The challenge is to encourage all readers to partake of the wealth of narrative offerings available to them. See Figure 11.5 later in this chapter for a listing of books to support apprentice writers who might want to scaffold their writing by patterning it after the "pro's." The next section provides suggestions on motivating students to read on their own as part of a strong reading program.

Web Link:
Best Practices in Literacy
Instruction

ENGAGING STUDENTS THROUGH INDEPENDENT READING

Practice makes perfect. It may be an old adage but it is certainly true when it comes to children and reading. "Just reading is a powerful contributor to the development of accurate, fluent, high-comprehension reading" (Allington, 2001, p. 24). As teachers, we encourage our students to read a variety of books during their free reading time. In the beginning of the school year this may be as little as a period of uninterrupted reading time of five minutes at the primary level (K–2), ten at the intermediate (3–5), and fifteen in middle school (6–8) with the times tripling by the end of the first four weeks of school to establish the remainder of the school year free reading time per setting—fifteen minutes at the primary level, thirty at intermediate, and forty-five at middle school. Like someone starting out to jog, readers need to build stamina. Summer and holiday vacations make for antsy readers who lack the attention span and, in some cases, physical demands of sitting still for a period of time just reading.

One successful way to encourage students to select particular books is to hook them by reading aloud only the first chapter just before independent reading time. The initial chapter in a fiction book usually is the strongest as it must possess the "hook" that entices the reader to delve deeper and read chapter two, then three, and on and on, chapter after chapter. Read the first chapter to your class and then glance at your watch and announce, "Girls and boys, I can't believe that we're running short on time. And this is such a great book! So, I'm going to place _____ (share the title at this point) on the free reading table in case you want to know how the story turns out. There are a couple of other copies there already." You'll find that many a reader just can't resist such bait.

Still another approach to encourage students to read is by reading aloud one book by a well-known author and making other titles by the same author readily available. Some authors that primary children love include Jan Brett, Tomie de Paola, Kevin Henkes, Steven Kellogg, Cynthia Rylant, Dr. Seuss, and Janet Stevens. Intermediate students enjoy the works of Sharon Creech, Roald Dahl, Paula Danzinger, Phyllis Reynolds Naylor, Patricia Polacco, Gary Paulsen, and Jerry Spinelli, among other writers. Middle schoolers favor Robert Cormier, Lois Duncan, Will Hobbs, Norma Mazer, Walter Dean Myers, Richard Peck, and other authors who can touch the preadolescents' and young teenagers' world.

Boys are often lured by biographies of heroes. Sharing quality narrative adventure stories with them can lead to increased reading pleasure.

As you read in Chapter 10, students develop preferences for certain genres (Baumann, Hooten, & White, 1999). Given free reading time, they pick up books they find most pleasurable to read. Narrative text tends to be the most popular with elementary students as they tend to relate to certain characters—Arthur, the glasses-wearing aardvark; Clifford, the big red dog; Henry and his enormous dog, Mudge; the curious Ramona Quimby; the eventful Junie B. Jones; the confident Amber Brown; honest and sincere Harry Potter; or courageous Brian's struggle to survive in the wilderness. However, it is not unusual if a student only reads informational books and biographies during free reading while being oblivious to chapter books, historical, or contemporary novels. Another classmate in the same room may avoid reading informational books but devour the latest fantasy book. The key is to encourage all readers to sample the different genres from time to time while still honoring the fact that favorites are fine.

Book Talks

"This is just the greatest book!" "This book is sooooooo cool!!!" "You've just got to read this book. It's the best!" Such comments often blurted out by enthusiastic readers of narrative books. These students are the teacher's best promoters of books because they are giving their peers firsthand critiques. Building on this natural enthusiasm, opportunities must be given for students as well as yourself to give class **book talks**, brief "plugs" about the book they just read. Taking ten to twelve books of varying reading levels and topics, and promoting each book, can be a good Monday, Let's Get the Week Off to a Good Start activity. After giving your brief, focused insights as to the "goodness" of each book, give students access by letting them peruse the books by placing them in a book corner, a classroom library area, or on a table out of the line of traffic. This can be done prior to independent, free reading time. Ideally you'll have multiple copies available for some of the titles you share. When you give such book talks, you are serving as a model for your students to follow later as well as attempting to build enthusiasm for each book. Thus, you have to be a model salesperson—know your product and convey to your customer that you really do believe in it.

Web Link:
Booktalks

A great website of already prepared book talks that teachers may use is entitled "Booktalks" and is located at www.concord.k12.nh.us/schools/rundlett/booktalks. Set the tone for student book talks by modeling the process. Suggestions in Figure 11.1 offer helpful pointers for a polished performance for both teachers and students.

Book Clubs

Student book talk is important in creating contagious enthusiasm for reading. Options that promote talk include literature circles and book clubs, which permit students to discuss their insights and opinions about a book in a community of readers who are interested in discovering more. Many schools encourage children to join book clubs that meet during the lunch period in the library, where everyone reads the book of their own choosing or students with similar interests can read the same title and discuss it at length (Raphael & Hiebert, 1996). Such book clubs need not be limited to one genre, but rather students may read the book of their choice on the same topic. For instance, a topic such as the pioneer movement or immigration might find a student reading picture books (both informational and fiction pieces) while another reads a novel and yet another reads an informational text. Yet, all three students can share and elaborate on the topic in a meaningful discussion.

When children are permitted to express their opinions about the book they are reading, their appreciation for reading and literature grows (Baumann, Hooten, & White, 1999). Likewise, "without high quality literature, it's difficult to sustain an engaging conversation about a book. Genuine discussions arise most often when books are read that contain memorable language, realistic plots, and characters to whom children can relate" (Schlick Noe, 1995, pp. 44–45). Discussions are further enhanced "when readers meet characters of complexity, substance, and familiarity. . . . It does not matter

Figure 11.1

Pointers for polished book talks

To invite students to read and then read even more, practice the art of enticing them into books by giving book talks. Usually such book talks are given early in the week on ten to twelve books from the classroom and school library. The following suggestions will make you adept at promoting fine books:

- Always read the book yourself before trying to promote it. However, as a new teacher you may not be able to do this due to time constraints; hence, either skim the book (highly recommended) or go to the website mentioned earlier and check for a book talk on that specific title. Using someone else's book talk or an annotation of a book will not ring true with potential readers unless you have also read that book.

- Choose a variety of books. Include those that you especially like and then look into others recommended by the librarian, learning center director, or a fellow teacher. Read them and then share them with enthusiasm.

- Prepare an entrance to the book talk. Try bringing the books in a picnic basket, titles and covers hidden from view. Go to a garage sale and buy an old choir or commencement robe. Add a wand and a cone-shaped hat and you've become the "book wizard." If you are promoting an ocean theme, wear a Hawaiian shirt. If you have an adventure theme, dress in a hiker's vest and chinos. Mysteries call for dark glasses, a scarf, and a trench coat. Pretty campy ideas? But they do grab students' attention and help you lure them into reading a previously unknown book.

- Present your book talk with the product in hand. Seeing is part of the sales pitch. Even better is having an extra copy or two so that more than one student can dive into the book immediately after the book talk session ends. While students should be cautioned not to always judge a book by its cover (or, for that matter, author), thereby discarding it too quickly, appealing covers are invitations to read, too. Some students might also want to know how long the book is before they tackle it. Finally, if intrigued, they will certainly want to browse through it once the book talks are over.

- Look at all of the students as you talk. Eye contact encourages students to pay attention. It also lets students know you are thinking about their particular interests as you speak about books on a regular basis.

- Practice brevity, keeping book talks to a few minutes in length. Speak clearly and pace yourself so that you don't have to move through books so quickly that students don't have time to make connections.

- Tell just enough to rouse curiosity, rather than telling too much of the story. A guideline to follow is to use about five to seven sentences per book. You might even write down the book talk on a 5″ by 8″ index card when you first begin doing them so that you won't forget what you want to highlight. Storing such cards for the next year helps to make you more efficient as well.

- What should you highlight? Talk about the main character, an exciting scene, or a funny incident. Ask a question that might tie readers to the character. Do not get involved in the plot or you might find yourself inadvertently giving the ending away.

- Another way to sell a book is to read a page or two from the beginning of the book or an exciting scene. This is particularly true when sharing chapter books or novels. In

Figure 11.1
(concluded)

this way, the students get a sense of the author's style as well as being lured to read the book in its entirety.

- Try connecting the book to others that students have read or that you might have read together in literature circles. Feature a new book by a favorite author or, in case of a picture book, illustrator. Another time focus on books from a particular genre under study. Point out similarities between the character in this book and another with whom students are familiar. From time to time, highlight some of the best-sellers—books that simply don't stay on the shelves.
- Share your own response to the book occasionally. What particular connection did you make with the book? Is the author's style of writing pleasing to you? What situation made you laugh out loud? Students are interested in teachers' reactions. Be certain to invite readers to talk about a shared book when they complete it. Such book conversations often involve a lively exchange of ideas resulting in more students taking the plunge and diving into another book.
- Make a concerted effort to include nonfiction titles including informational books in your talks. There are wonderful offerings available that may get overlooked if you don't single them out as superb reading materials. Keep in mind many boys and some girls prefer informational, factual text to read.
- Finally, place the books on a shelf or table for easy access once the book talks are completed. If you have done your job well, the offerings will disappear into eager hands in no time at all.

Sources: Farris, 2001; Fountas & Pinnell, 2001; Tomlinson & Lynch-Brown, 2002.

whether characters exist during another time period, in another place, or only in myths and legends. What does matter is that they are believable" (Johnson & Giorgis, 2000, p. 106). Thus, a large portion of the classroom library needs to contain quality fiction covering a breadth of reading abilities so that the most and least proficient readers can readily locate a book that appeals to them.

Book Reviews

Besides having students discuss books with friends, in small groups, or with the entire class, students should be permitted to do mini–book reviews. Using sticky notes, students can leave brief reviews inside the front cover of a book as a means of sharing their opinions with classmates. This can be extended to having an occasional sticky note elsewhere. Calkins (2001) found that this activity provides a way for young readers to both recommend and counsel fellow readers as well as give strategies about reading a particular book. For instance, students guided future readers to:

Pay close attention to the cover and the chapter titles because *everything* turns out to be important.

This is part of a series but you can skip about, reading them in no special order, because it makes no difference. (pp. 38–39)

Other suggestions Calkins (2001) found on sticky notes left at key passages:

Read the next page closely because there is a twist.

The part ahead was confusing to me. Watch out.

Alert! Time jumps backwards. (p. 39)

In writing such informal mini-reviews, students are serving as reading guides for their peers as well as assisting you as the teacher in promoting books.

Classroom Library

As we saw in Chapter 4, good readers need access to books—LOTS OF BOOKS! Providing numerous titles of books that are both interesting and understandable for all students in your classroom—avid readers, learning disabled students, English language learners, struggling readers—can be a challenge. This means having an ample classroom library of between five and seven titles per student with reading levels ranging from two grades below to two grades above the actual grade level.

Brand new fourth grade teacher Amy Chura has twenty-four students and will need books ranging from second grade through sixth grade reading level with a total of between 120 and 168 books for her classroom library. That's an incredible amount of books, and it's just the recommended number for the most meager of libraries. Now consider that Amy just graduated from college in May and has expenses including student loans, housing, and a new wardrobe for teaching to cover. Ouch! Being thrifty, Amy finds very inexpensive paperback books at Scholastic book warehouse sales to accompany those purchased through Scholastic, Troll, and Trumpet book clubs when she was taking reading courses. More books will be added during the year from book club bonus points. Hopefully she can buy another ten books a month (a cost of about $35 to $60 depending on hardcover versus softbound). Amy will be seeking out teachers who recently retired from the school district to see if they might be willing to sell part of their classroom collections. Amy's family gave her money and gift certificates to bookstores as graduation presents thanks to her suggestions. Knowing that many diverse learners lack reading resources in their homes, Amy is aware that her classroom must be well-stocked with appealing children's literature. According to Richard Allington (2001), a child living in poverty may have one or two books in the home while a middle-class child will have nearly 300 books to peruse at home.

Purposeful Reading Choices

Let's examine a few ways to promote your classroom library and support your students as readers, even the most reluctant ones. The classroom library itself must be an inviting area (see Chapter 4). Carpet, shelves upon shelves of neatly organized books, along with puppets for the younger students and artifacts for the older students make an appealing setting to read. Toss in a "husband"—a reading chair for the bed—and perhaps a couple of bean bags with three or four big pillows and you have a ready made "reading lounge" for your classroom.

You may want to start out by setting aside time each week to visit the school's library by yourself with ample time to quietly browse and perhaps chat with the school librarian. This may be one morning before school begins each week or while your students have art or music. Bringing books of interest and various reading levels to meet the needs of your students into your classroom and sharing them through book talks as mentioned earlier in this chapter can pay off with huge rewards.

Another tip is to code your classroom library books using colored stickers or a number code to indicate reading level so that students will be able to easily find material at their reading ability. Some teachers prefer to color code by topic as well (red for mysteries, blue for adventure books, etc.). Put the books in bins by their color code. Also encourage students to reread the books you share as read-alouds. And don't get upset when a proficient reader decides to revisit an old favorite title by rereading it even if the book is below the student's reading ability. From time to time, all of us as readers feel comforted by revisiting books we've read before; it's like striking up a conversation with an old friend.

Providing ample independent reading opportunities is critical because "the very act of reading can help children compensate for modest levels of cognitive ability by building their vocabulary and general knowledge . . . those who read a lot will enhance their verbal intelligence; that is, reading will make them smarter" (Cunningham & Stanovich, 1998, p. 14). Indeed, a survey of research findings indicates that reading accounts for up to two-thirds of children's vocabulary growth and the amount of reading children do plays a critical role in intellectual growth (Anderson, 1996). This extremely important research finding makes it essential for us as teachers to find books for our diverse learners that they are motivated to read, particularly English language learners and struggling readers.

As reinforced throughout this book, it is critical that the teacher read aloud quality literature from a variety of genre to broaden the scope and perspective of students. Certainly quality narrative text, including well-written picture storybooks, fantasy, contemporary fiction, and historical fiction as well as poetry that appeals to students offers new paths for budding and competent elementary and middle school readers.

Once frowned upon by teachers, books in a series are superb for classroom libraries. Short, Harste, and Burke (1996) point out that once children have read one book in a series, they are familiar with the main characters and the same structure and characteristics of the other books in the series. This sense of groundedness with one series makes for easier reading than jumping from one novel to another written by yet another author. Popular series include tales about *Strega Nona* by Tomie de Paola, *Frog and Toad* by Arnold Lobel, *Junie B. Jones* by Debbie Dailey, *Ramona* by Beverly Cleary, the *Boxcar* books (popular first in the 1950s and now brought into the new millennium in a contemporary version), *The Little House* books by Laura Ingalls Wilder, *The Magic Treehouse* series, *Encyclopedia Brown* adventures by Donald Sobol, *Wayside School* stories by Louis Sachar, and *Anastasia* books by Lois Lowry. Other series may include historical fiction such as the *American Girls* and

Dear America, a diary series written for girls. The *My Name Is America* series features fictional boys' reports of significant events during America's history.

Some series are questioned by teachers as to the quality of literature they provide. While Mercer Mayer's *Little Critter* series and the ever popular *Babysitters Club* may not go down in the annals of literary history as great texts, they do engage students in interesting plots involving common personal and social problems children face. Then, whenever a movie targeted at youngsters comes out, many times an accompanying narrative text also arrives to be purchased. It is read as part of the moviegoers' fervor that often accompanies a film. Typically such books lack depth but have popular appeal with some students. Many struggling readers gravitate to such books as they already grasp the plot and are familiar with the characters and the setting. While these types of books fail to represent stellar literature, the point is that these students *are* reading and are improving their reading skills.

 ## GENDER AND READING

Gender preferences in reading occur earlier than one might think. Even as young as kindergarten and first grade, some boys are riveted to informational books about dinosaurs, insects, knights, or robots. Like the famous television detective Joe Friday, they want to know "just the facts"—how and why things work, who did what in history and science. They may not give a hoot about what Junie B. Jones or Arthur are up to despite the interest exhibited by their classmates.

Considering gender as one aspect of reading instruction is critical inasmuch as boys read far less than girls at all age levels (Hall & Coles, 1997). By the adolescent years, 85 percent of girls read for pleasure while only 65 percent of boys do (Moffit & Wartella, 1992). As they move from elementary to middle school and beyond, a sexual division of literacy occurs. Research suggests that girls find it easier to lose themselves in a narrative while boys tend to resist such imaginative thoughts, preferring instead books with visual narratives based on television shows and movies (Newkirk, 2000). Many boys devote hours upon hours reading code books for video games. By middle school, reading preferences are well established with scary stories, sports books, adventure stories, comics, and magazines being preferred by boys and fiction with its emphasis on personal feelings and relationships being the favorite choice of girls (Ivey & Broaddus, 2000). Boys tend to be flexible readers of expository, informational texts with the emphasis on ideas and factual information and tend to have a lesser desire to read novels (Luke, 1994; Simpson, 1996b). It has even been argued that because males have a greater familiarity with informational texts, they succeed over their female counterparts in the areas of educational and economic power (Simpson, 1996b).

According to William Brozo (2002), "garnering . . . boys' interest in reading, keeping them reading, and channeling this reading ability into academic mastery must be a priority" (p. 19). Believing that boys are turned off by fiction books, Brozo writes that whenever boys are given nonfiction and informational books to read during free reading time, they "shift their postures from complacency and disengagement to

Portfolio Activity:
Gender Issues

involvement and curiosity" (p. 17). Brozo goes on to point out that what boys prefer to read in fiction is politically incorrect—books with male protagonists with action and adventure plots—but should be permitted if they are going to become competent, lifelong readers. Isn't it far better that they be reading such material than devoting their free time to watching television or playing XBOX games?

Unmotivated students, especially preteenagers and teenagers, frequently find themselves in "a downward spiral of declining academic achievement, diminishing self-esteem, [and] further disinterest outside of school" (Brozo, 2002, p. 16). We must promote books that appeal to our students if we are to nurture a lifelong habit of reading, especially with boys (Young & Brozo, 2001) and girls who are struggling or reluctant readers. Hence as teachers, we need to create a positive learning environment, thereby reducing behavior problems while boosting self-esteem and increasing learning involvement (Filozof, Albertin, Jones, Steme, Myers, & McDermott, 1998). In particular, we must carefully look at our students' interests, particularly boys in our classroom. Research indicates that when reading preferences and interests are matched with books, the depth of students' thinking processes is enhanced and learning is internalized (Guthrie, Alao, & Rinehart, 1997). Devoting time to finding those matches is essential for our average and struggling readers if they are to be successful in the reading arena.

As reinforced throughout this book, it is critical that the teacher read aloud quality literature from a variety of genre to broaden the scope and perspective of students of all age levels. Certainly quality narrative text such as well-written picture storybooks, fantasy, contemporary fiction, and historical fiction as well as poetry that appeals to students offers new paths for budding and competent elementary and middle school readers.

READING STRATEGIES AND NARRATIVE TEXT: MAKING CONNECTIONS

Web Link:
Reading Comprehension
Instructional Strategies

Think about the fact that reading narrative and poetry text is a cooperative venture between the author and the reader. Considering this, Katherine Paterson (1989), noted Newbery Award–winning author, believes that the text that we read "will never become complete until a reader of whatever age takes that book [or poem] and brings to it his or her own story. . . . It is only when the deepest sound going further from my heart meets the deepest sound coming further from yours—it is only in this encounter that the true music begins" (p. 34). As teachers, we need to model how we make such ties as well as assist students in making their own ties.

As mentioned in Chapter 8, both narrative text and poetry enable students to make connections as they read in three different ways. First, they may see similarities between the text and their own lives. A second connection is making links between the text they are presently reading and another text they have previously read. Lastly, students may see connections between the text and the real world.

Readers need to develop background knowledge for literary elements in order to make connections. Students reading narrative text need to become familiar with the previously reviewed literary elements of character, setting, problem and solution, theme, and writing style (see Chapter 8). Words within text, like literary elements, can aid readers in comprehension. By learning to identify cue words, they can determine the "reading road signs" such words point out. For example, *but* suggests a coming change, *most important* means a critical main point is being identified, *perhaps* implies something is questionable, and *in other words* signals a definition follows. Some words are used to show time: *after, about, before, tomorrow, until, meantime,* or *soon.* In addition to literary elements and cue words, textual connections assist readers in comprehending.

Connecting Text and Self

First graders sat intent on the carpet as their teacher read *Quiet, Wyatt* (Maynard, 1999), a story about the dilemma of a child who is repeatedly told he is too small. But in the end, Wyatt saves the day. After sharing the book with her class as a read-aloud, Jennifer Oster modeled a time when she was growing up when she had been told she was too small to ride a roller coaster at an amusement park. As Jennifer talked about being unable to conceal her disappointment as tears flowed down her cheeks, her students nodded in empathy. Next, she had students share their experiences. As part of their discussion, they generated a list that Jennifer wrote on a chart. Here are a few of the first graders' ideas:

Too small to:

- Make cookies
- Play football
- Go trick or treating alone
- Build a tree house
- Stay up until 9:30
- Mow the lawn
- Ride the Metro alone

Next, Jennifer had the students generate a list of things they can do but a smaller child could not.

Big enough to:

- Take care of pets
- Help wash the car
- Play four square
- Tie shoes
- Use a computer
- Change a baby

After the discussion, Jennifer scurried her students off to write about their experiences. Later that same morning, they gathered once more as students shared their writing. The next day, Jennifer followed up with *Olivia* (Falconer, 2000), the upbeat story of a young energetic pig who dreams of being a dancer, a diva, and a painter—

truly a renaissance pig. On this day, the theme was what talents the students possess and what they would like to become. *Olivia* was followed up by *Some Things Are Scary* (Heide, 2000). The class probed things they found frightening such as swinging too high, racing out of control down the street on roller blades, getting separated from their family and being lost in a large store, or finding out that their best friend has another "best friend."

 According to Lisa Haapoja, a third grade teacher, "The key to textual connections is to keep the students making connections that are meaningful and on task—not going off on some tangent in a completely different direction." When the teacher first models appropriate connections, this helps students understand the task. Whenever a student offers a connection that is off-base, the teacher can nudge them in the right direction by asking guiding questions or dropping a hint. Oftentimes ADD, ADHD, and gifted students tend to try to "bolt" the discussion to another topic—usually one they are interested in discussing. A gentle reining in is necessary on such occasions.

As children read quality narrative books, they naturally become involved with the characters who may possess similar feelings or find themselves in like situations. Getting into an argument with your best friend, parents getting a divorce, having an annoying older or younger sibling, being pressured to do something by peers, falling in love—these are but a few of the experiences students may encounter in both real life and the books they read. Students should be encouraged to react to such connections through discussions or journal writing. Making a T chart or Venn diagram comparing their own lives and problems with those of the character can help students to resolve some of life's difficult moments. Questioning the character's views and motives can aid students as they learn how to figure out how to solve personal problems. In short, connections between text and self enhance understanding.

Connecting Text with Text

Web Link:
Text Comprehension
Instruction

Picking up on commonalities between two books helps students deepen their understanding. First graders may compare the differences and similarities between Gloria, the police dog, and Clifford, the gigantic red pooch after reading *Officer Buckle and Gloria* (Rathmann, 1995) and *Clifford, the Big Red Dog* (Bridwell, 1986). Older children become aware of personal and social problems when they read novels that portray youngsters dealing with difficult situations as they pass from childhood to adolescence. Books ten- to twelve-year-olds might compare are *Because of Winn-Dixie* (DiCamillo, 2000), *Shiloh* (Naylor, 1991), and *Where the Red Fern Grows* (Rawls, 1961). Less proficient readers might be encouraged to read *Because of Winn-Dixie,* a warm, easy-to-read story of a ten-year-old girl who finds a dog in the local supermarket. *Shiloh* tells of young Marty, who yearns for the abused beagle puppy owned by an abusive neighbor. In contrast, *Where the Red Fern Grows*, a book for more proficient readers, is the tale of young Billy, who trains his two coon dogs, Little Ann and Old Dan, to be the finest hunting team in the Ozarks. After winning $300 for Billy in a hunting contest, Little Ann is killed by a cougar while protecting her master. Comparing how these two different characters face problems gives students insight into a variety of perspectives people can take.

Just like coming of age novels assist students in viewing and dealing with personal and social issues, historical novels can aid students in seeing two sides to a historical event such as the Civil War. Consider *Bright Freedom's Song: A Story of the Underground Railroad* (Houston, 1998) in which a young girl helps her family hide and assist escaped slaves in the Blue Ridge Mountains and compare it with the Virginia boy who supports the Confederacy in *With Every Drop of Blood* (Collier & Collier, 1992) but gets captured by a young black Union soldier. Likewise, other major historical events such as the Revolutionary War, the Westward Movement, and World War II have a number of quality children's historical novels that may be used in this fashion.

Text-to-text connections require readers to identify commonalities in stories and books. The level of sophistication can increase as students move from sharing obvious story elements such as character traits or problems revealed in plots to comparing plot lines, common themes, or authors' writing styles. The following are text to text connections students can make:

Characters:
- Personalities
- Actions
- Backgrounds

Comparing plots:
- Events
- Plot lines

Comparing works of one author:
- Themes
- Writing style
- Characters
- Plot lines

Comparing works of two or more authors:
- Themes
- Writing style
- Characters
- Plot line

As mentioned previously, the teacher must model linkages so students can determine expectations. Moving from presenting an example of a text-to-text connection to opening up the discussion for the entire class, the teacher can still question or nudge when needed to keep students on task.

Connecting Text to the World

Many narrative texts can be related to real life. They may be as simple for young readers as the story of *The Little Red Hen* with one individual doing the work and others wanting to benefit. Intermediate grade students will pause and give thought to Jerry Spinelli's *Loser* (2002), the story of Zinkoff's school years. Clumsy, offbeat, Zinkoff is ridiculed by other boys until he searches for a missing child and becomes the town's hero. A theme may be as complex as the *Lord of the Rings* series or as simple as a loyal companion accompanying Lewis and Clark on their expedition of the Louisiana Territory in *The Captain's Dog* (Smith, 1999), something middle schoolers may ponder.

As reinforced in Chapter 8, Reading Comprehension, when new concepts or issues are introduced, students may have problems if they lack background knowledge in the area. For struggling readers, this can be a problem because of lack of experiential background. Narrative text often requires a content background for understanding. Reading a narrative set in a historical period or related to a scientific finding usually necessitates having some related knowledge in that specific area. Thus, it can be helpful linking expository text with narrative text. Frequently as part of social studies units, students are required to read a narrative text—picture book, chapter book, or novel—on the same topic being studied. Low ability readers may be given magazine articles with accompanying pictures or illustrations that have relatively brief captions to aid them in gaining background information in terms of facts and concepts. Thus, students are gaining the background knowledge through their expository reading that they apply in their narrative reading as they make connections between text and the world.

 Appropriate children's literature for relating text to self, to other text, or to the world may be found on the Online Learning Center at www.mhhe.com/farrisreading.

THE WORKSHOP APPROACH: READERS AND WRITERS IN CHARGE!

Close your eyes and drift off to a classroom where students are abuzz with energy and ideas and you are their teacher. Four magic words drift from your mouth, "Time for reading workshop." Immediately (yes, without a second to be lost), students begin gathering on the rug near the Author's Chair. After they are situated, you begin reading the first chapter of *Our Only May Amelia* (Holm, 1999), in which the twelve-year-old female protagonist has to keep up with her seven—all older—brothers and deal with a downright shrewish grandmother. Midway through page 4, you glance briefly over the top of the page at the enthralled listeners—each of whom is hooked on this story set in the late 1890s.

At the end of the first chapter, you ask some pertinent questions—Why is everyone concerned about May Amelia? What are her brothers like? Pick one and describe him to us. What is the grandmother like? How would you describe her? What role do you think she'll have in the book? What is May Amelia like? How do you know that? Do you like her as a person? Is she like you or someone you know? As the students respond, you record information on an overhead transparency chart, character by character. You have moved effortlessly from a read-aloud to a mini-lesson about character development. After discussing character development for ten minutes, you change gears as the class prepares for independent reading of books they have self-selected. Now take out a clipboard and roam around the room as you record each student's reading selection for reading workshop—a process called "status of the class."

While they read, you remind them to make at least two references in their literature response journals to how the characters are being developed by the author.

During this stage of reading workshop, each student will have at least forty minutes to read, usually sandwiched around individual or small group instruction. This time is also used as you work with a select group of readers to develop related reading strategies and skills. By rotating through small and large groups and individual students, you address the needs of all students in the class.

Fifty minutes have passed since you announced, "Time for reading workshop." Now you have returned to the overhead transparency you made earlier with your students. With the class, you recall the attributes of the various characters in *Our Only May Amelia* (Holm, 1999). Next you have students share ways the author of the novel they are reading developed that particular main character. As before, you note these aspects by writing them down on another overhead transparency. In rapid-fire fashion, students point out various ways characters were developed—dialogue, description by the narrator, thoughts of the main character, and so on. Again, you have moved to a mini-lesson format, this time for writing workshop. Each of the various ways is modeled by having the students find the passage in the book and reading it out loud. Then you probe, did that develop the character? What do you know now that you didn't know before hearing that portion of the book read? How was the story enriched by this passage? (See Figure 11.2.)

After that you announce to the class that they are going to develop their own character as they pretend to be a new child moving to live near May Amelia. They can come up with an invented name and age as well as other characteristics of this new-found friend—or enemy—of May Amelia. They are reminded to use dialogue, description, and so forth, to develop themselves as a new character in the book. The class disperses to their desks to write. You rove around the room assisting where needed before moving back to a table where you, yourself, write to the same assignment that you just presented to your students. After fifteen minutes, you observe that a few students are getting restless. At this point some students are moving off into peer-conferencing corners to share and discuss their pieces. Another ten minutes pass by before the sharing of writing begins in which the entire class gathers once more. This final gathering brings closure to the workshop and underscores the skill presented that day.

Reading and writing workshops help teachers efficiently introduce and model new skills while giving students freedom to read and write on their own, with a partner, in a group, or as part of the entire class. Through a workshop approach the teacher creates a supportive classroom atmosphere for reading and writing for all students— even those who struggle as readers and writers or who are shy about sharing their thoughts and ideas.

Kindergarten through third graders are "active, noisy, risk takers, internalizing the rules of written language as they use it to construct meaning in social situations" (Strickland & Feeley, 2003, p. 346). As such they need exposure to lots of quality literature written by outstanding authors. Good literature models good writing. When first graders begin to write, their initial narrative pieces tend to be "all about" or attribute books in which they tell or list everything they know about the topic. By the

Web Link:
Effects of Two Types of
Prereading Instruction

Figure 11.2

Questioning to promote reading and writing connections

The following questions are easily adapted for narrative selections to encourage students to think more carefully about what they read. As they do so, not only will they understand the story better, but they will be scrutinizing the author's craft. If they see how it works for this author, then it just might work for them in their own writing.

You might duplicate an assortment of questions to be kept in the student journals to prompt reflection or in writing folders as an aid to developing parts of students' own writing.

- How does the title connect with the book?
- Leads are important because they pull you into the story. How effective was the lead in your book? Why did it work for you?
- If there were illustrations in the story, what was their role?
- What important ideas do you think the author was trying to get across?
- Did you connect personally with any of the characters? Explain how and why you did so.
- What made specific parts of this book stand out? Were they humorous, sad, uplifting, depressing? What words, phrases, or particular actions by the character did the author use to create the moods you experienced?
- Were you satisfied with the ending of the story? Would you have changed it in any way? If yes, how would you have concluded it?
- Does the protagonist make sound decisions to solve the problems he or she faces? Discuss these.
- How would you have acted if you were the protagonist? Did you learn anything from this particular main character?
- How do events in the story or interactions with other characters change the protagonist? Is the change realistic?
- What do you think the author's main message (theme) was in the story? Discuss why you came to this conclusion and if you agree or not.
- Do the setting, plot, conflicts, problems, or characters remind you of other books you have read? In what ways?
- Do the relationships, conflicts, feelings, or dialogue between characters remind you of similar experiences you have had with classmates, friends, siblings, or parents?
- Are the issues presented in the book similar to those you see people dealing with in the news or in real life? If they are difficult issues, how does the author present them in an acceptable way?
- Can you find parts of the story that help you see what a place or character is like? What words does the author use to help you see, smell, hear, and feel?
- If you set this story in another time or place, would it change? If so, in what ways?
- What does this story make you think or wonder about?
- What surprised you as you read the story? Was any of the language particularly interesting, riveting, or surprising?
- Have you read other books by this author? What does this author do to make you want to read other books he or she has written?

Sources: Robb, 2000; Tomlinson & Lynch-Brown, 2002.

end of the year, their narrative pieces are more storylike with a beginning, middle, and end, organized chronologically. At this point their revising of the writing adds more information and details. In second grade, children drift away from the "all about" books to "bed to bed" stories in which they chronologically order every event that took place during the day, giving all events equal weight in their writing (Strickland & Feeley, 2003). For instance, the narrative piece may be about spending a day at a theme park such as Disneyland, but the child may include getting up, eating breakfast, dressing, driving to the theme park, riding a favorite ride, driving home, eating, and going to bed.

By third grade, students are independent readers and writers who still need reassurance and guidance. Intermediate level and middle school students still need lots of ideas and refining of skills to become proficient writers. Mini-lessons are the vehicle we can use to help them become wordsmiths.

By becoming familiar with well-written text such as the Newbery Award winner described earlier, students gain not only in reading but in writing as well. Research suggests that good writers have knowledge of narrative structures and are able to fluently generate text both orally and in their writing. The more efficient language processes and richer linguistic knowledge of skilled readers allow them to generate more complex sentences when they speak and write. Hence, the teacher must include lots of examples of language-rich text to serve as models for students in their own writing and speaking (McCutchen, 2000). For those students who have difficulty with reading and writing, the sharing of literature through read-alouds provides them with a base from which they can scaffold their own reading and writing skills. (See Figure 11.3.)

The act of writing itself has been described as a juggling game much as the busy switchboard operator of the early days of telephones—taking multiple calls, making connections and disconnections, and solving problems all while presenting an outward voice of composure and control (Flower & Hayes, 1980). The writer needs to make a myriad of decisions and keep tapping his short- and long-term memory banks while the pen is frantically moving across the paper. The teacher must find ways to assist him in this juggling game. Certainly one approach is via reading and writing workshop. Organization and planning ahead are keys to holding a successful reading and writing workshop. A teacher has to organize and reorganize the classroom and herself to "support writing, reading, learning, and teaching" (Atwell, 1998, p. 90). The teacher creates a predictable setting taking the time to discover what her learners need as readers and writers.

Below is a sample framework for readers' and writers' workshop during a sixty- to ninety-minute uninterrupted language arts instructional period:

1. Read-aloud by teacher
2. Mini-lesson by teacher
3. Modeling of skill introduced in mini-lesson by teacher
4. Examples shared by students
5. Independent reading by students (teacher conducts–conferences)
6. Review and extension of mini-lesson

> ### Figure 11.3
> ## Steps to follow when teaching a mini-lesson
>
> 1. Select a pertinent strategy or skill based upon students' needs or that ties naturally into the current reading or writing work.
> 2. Introduce the strategy or skill explaining why it is a handy one to have at one's fingertips. Share examples of how and when the strategy is most effective.
> 3. Use the overhead projector so you'll be able to see the faces of your students as you demonstrate the strategy or skill, explaining the steps involved in using it and modeling how to used it when reading or writing.
> 4. Provide ample time for guided practice. Students put the strategy or skill to use immediately while the teacher circulates around the room offering guidance and support. Provide feedback to students about the way they are integrating the new skill with others they already know. Encourage students to make notes about the skill or strategy in their reading or writing notebooks. Notes might be recorded on a poster to be placed on the wall at the end of the session for all to see and refer back to as needed.
> 5. Review the strategy or skill. Ask students to reflect on what they learned and how they can use the newly acquired strategy or skill in future reading/writing activities. Reinforce the learning by showing other examples of its use from time to time as they arise in classroom activities.
> 6. Apply the strategy or skill in upcoming reading/writing activities. The teacher becomes a coach at this point, urging students to use the new strategy or skill and reinforcing the good work as students apply this knowledge in independent reading and writing activities.
>
> Sources: Adapted from Farris, P. J. (2001). *Language Arts: Process, product, and assessment.* 3rd ed. Boston: McGraw-Hill; and Tompkins, G. (2000). *Teaching writing: Balancing process and product.* 3rd ed. Upper Saddle River, NJ: Merrill.

7. Modeling by teacher
8. Examples by teacher
9. Independent writing by students (teacher moves around room conferencing)
10. Peer conferencing
11. Whole class sharing
12. Teacher brings closure to topic of mini-lesson and the workshop

The structure of the workshop varies little each day, thus providing students with the security of knowing what to expect.

6 Traits of Writing

Writers rely upon 6 traits or characteristics to convey their thoughts (Spandel, 2003). These traits of writing are:

Ideas: Having Interesting Things to Say in Your Writing

• The piece must all make sense.

- The writing must demonstrate that the writer knows the topic.
- Interesting details are included.
- The paper has a purpose.
- Once the reader starts reading the piece, she won't want to stop until the very last word that the writer has written.

Organization: The Way the Piece of Writing Fits Together

- It starts out with a hook that attracts the reader to read on.
- Everything ties together well.
- It builds to the good parts.
- There are transitions from one paragraph to the next.
- The reader can easily follow it.
- At the end, it feels finished and makes the reader think.

Word Choice: The Best Words for the Ideas Presented

- The writer's words are the best way to share the message.
- The writer's words create pictures in your mind.
- The writer uses words that are new ways to say everyday things.
- The verbs the writer includes are powerful.
- The nouns and adjectives are specific and precise.
- Some of the words linger in the reader's mind after the piece has been read.

Quality literature should be shared as examples of good writing.

Sentence Fluency: The Way the Piece Sounds When You Read It Aloud

- The writer's sentences begin in different ways.
- Sentences vary in length. Some are long and others are short.
- The piece sounds good when you read it out loud.
- The writer's sentences have power, punch, and sometimes pizzazz.
- The writing flows easily from one sentence to the next.

Voice: The Piece of Writing Sounds Like You Are Talking about the Subject or Sharing the Story

- The piece sounds like a real person wrote it.
- As you read the piece, the reader can tell that the writer cares about the topic.

- There is a feeling that the writer wants others to read the piece and express their emotions about the topic.
- The reader can tell that the writer was aware of the audience for the piece.

Conventions: The Mechanics of Writing Include Spelling, Punctuation, Grammar, Capitalization, and Usage—All the Things That Make Reading the Piece Easier for the Reader

- The writer uses capitals correctly.
- Almost every word in the final draft is spelled correctly (for second semester first and second graders); every word in the final draft of third through eighth graders is spelled correctly.
- Periods, commas, exclamation marks, and quotation marks are in the correct places.
- Each paragraph is indented.
- The writer's spelling, punctuation, grammar, and capitalization make the piece easy to read and understand.

In teaching the six writing traits, it is best to do so in a cyclical manner; that is, to introduce the writing trait in a mini-lesson and model how it is used. Then have the students address it in their own writing. Each writing trait should be revisited three to four times each month in mini-lessons. After introducing the trait, the teacher from time to time reminds, or gently nags, students to apply the trait—that is, capitalizing the days of the week (Monday, Thursday) or proper names of languages (French, Spanish) in their own writings. Examples from quality literature are excellent for modeling writing traits. After modeling a trait, have the students search to locate examples of that specific trait in books they are reading for SSR or in their content area textbook chapter reading assignment.

Perhaps the most critical trait is the first one—ideas. Without ideas, students flounder around like fish on a boat deck, gasping for ideas to share with others before their supply of oxygen runs out. Ideas tend to come from students' own interests and experiences. Avid readers are more apt to develop ideas than struggling readers. To aid students, at the beginning of the year model creating your own list of possible writing topics that you would enjoy developing in your own writing—the first time you gave your golden retriever a bath, the day you got lost at an amusement park, the recipe you used to make your grandpa's favorite chocolate chip cookies, how you broke your collarbone playing soccer. Next, have the students go through the same process. If necessary, brainstorm with your struggling readers and writers. You may want to phone the parent of a student who can't seem to come up with any ideas and get some suggestions from home.

Word choice for older students is aided by computer thesaurus programs. First through fourth graders can make their own personal thesauruses. First graders can make lists of words they frequently use: happy, sad, run, play, etc. By second grade, the words should be placed on pages using alphabetical order for the primary synonym with the book having 26 pages. The "r" page could have "run," "road," "rough," "race," for example. Below is a sample of entries from a personal thesaurus of a fourth grader.

Personal Thesaurus

thing	walk	smile	like	happy
item	step	laugh	enjoy	glad
object	hike	beam	admire	joyful
material	stroll	grin	treasure	lucky
tool	stride	smirk	relish	fortunate
utensil	plod	glow		content
	trample			carefree
	stomp			

river	forest	fun	red	mountain
stream	woodland	play	rust	hill
creek	woods	frolic	maroon	peak
brook	pine tree forest	romp	raspberry	butte
branch	timberland	delight	candy apple	mesa
	grove	revel	cranberry	volcano
		exhilarate	crimson	

Organization is important as it sequences events in the story. A rubric used to evaluate the writing trait of "organization" is found in Figure 11.4.

Writing Workshop and Narrative Writing

In essence, the workshop approach in regard to narrative reading and writing enables students in a semi-structured environment to see what good writing by an author is and then attempt to emulate it in some fashion. Sharing picture books at the kindergarten through fourth grade level, and middle readers through novels with intermediate through middle school level students, has proved to be an effective means of introducing budding writers to exemplary and eloquent writing (McElvenn & Dierking, 2000/2001). See Figure 11.5 for a list of books with the type of writing skill or trait modeled in the book.

Conventions of Language

Mini-lessons offer a good opportunity to teach the conventions of language such as commas, quotation marks for dialogue, semicolons, subject–verb agreement, appositives, and so on, by pointing out how an author uses them. Consider having students locate dialogue and the accompanying quotation marks. Next, direct them to find dialogue in a book they are reading or in a narrative piece they have written themselves. This is good teaching as you are making what is not relevant suddenly relevant and meaningful to your students. Making grammar and punctuation "concrete" and using direct instruction particularly aids learning disabled and low ability readers and writers by making conventions "visible."

Figure 11.4

Organization rubric for fifth grade narrative writing

Six Points

- Narrative structure of the paper is clear—sequence of episodes moves through time with a beginning, middle, and ending without noticeable gaps
- Major episodes are appropriately paragraphed (single-sentence opening and closing are acceptable)
- Coherence and cohesion demonstrated with effective devices (e.g., transitions, pronouns, parallel structure, etc.)
- Varied sentence structure produces cohesion

Five Points

- Narrative structure is evident—sequence of episodes moves through time with a beginning, middle, and ending
- Most major episodes are appropriately paragraphed
- Coherence and cohesion demonstrated with most transitional devices appropriate (not redundant or intrusive)
- Coherence may depend on holistic structure (e.g., chronology)
- If present, transitions may be simplistic, but not intrusive
- May include minor digressions
- Some varied sentence structure produces cohesion

Four Points

- Narrative structure is evident—sequence of episodes moves through time with a beginning, middle, and ending (there are few gaps)
- Some appropriate paragraphing
- Some evidence of coherence (paragraph to paragraph) and cohesion (sentence to sentence); may depend on holistic structure (e.g., chronology)
- If present, transitions may be simplistic, but not intrusive
- May include minor digressions

Three Points

- Noticeable narrative structure, but the reader must infer it; movement through time with gaps
- May evidence some inappropriate paragraphing
- May include inappropriate transitions that disrupt progression of ideas
- May have major digressions
- Lacks sufficiency to demonstrate developed organization

Two Points

- Narrative structure is attempted, but the reader must infer it
- Limited evidence of understanding paragraphing
- Lacks purposeful ordering of sentences (e.g., sentences could be arranged in almost any order)
- Insufficient writing to determine that organization must be sustained

One Point

- Little or no attempt at narrative structure
- Little or no evidence of understanding paragraphing
- Insufficient writing to show that criteria are met

Source: Illinois State Board of Education, 2000.

Figure 11.5

Children's literature books that model writing skills for budding writers

Beil, Karen M. (1992). *Grandma According to Me*. New York: Dell. (Ideas—Describing a person.)

Blume, Judy. (1974). *The Pain and the Great One*. New York: Dell. (Ideas—Comparing and contrasting two people.)

Brett, Jan. (1996). *Comet's Nine Lives*. New York: Putnam. (Organization—Using cause and effect and strong transitions to sequence a story.)

Brown, Margaret Wise. (1949). *The Important Book*. (W. Hurd, Illus.). New York: HarperCollins. (Ideas—Focusing on a topic using strong details.)

Bruss, Deborah. (2001). *Book! Book! Book!* (T. Beeke, Illus.). New York: Arthur A. Levine Books. (Organization—Sequencing a story; Word Choice—Effective use of alliteration.)

Cooney, Barbara. (1982). *Miss Rumphius*. New York: Dial. (Ideas and Word Choice—Developing a strong character.)

Cowley, Joy. (1998). *Big Moon Tortilla*. (D. Strongbow, Illus.). Honesdale, PA: Boyds Mill Press. (Conventions—Vibrant verbs; Word Choice—Wonderful use of metaphors.)

Crews, Donald. (1991). *Big Mama's*. New York: Mulberry. (Organization—Organizing with a clear beginning, middle, and end.)

Curtis, Jamie Lee. (1993). *When I Was Little*. New York: HarperCollins. (Ideas—Brainstorming personal topics to write about.)

Fox, Mem. (1985). *Wilfred Gordon McDonald Partridge*. (J. Vivas, Illus.). New York: Dial. (Sentence Fluency—Using effective lead sentences.)

Himmelman, John. (1997). *A Slug's Life*. Danbury, CN: Children's Press. (Word Choice—Describing an animal.)

Houston, Gloria. (1992). *My Great Aunt Arizona*. (S. Lambe, Illus.). New York: HarperCollins. (Ideas and Word Choice—Developing a strong character; Voice—sense of author's voice.)

Johnson, Angela. (1989). *Tell Me a Story, Mama*. New York: Orchard. (Ideas—Brainstorming personal topics to write about.)

Johnson, D. B. (2000). *Henry Hikes to Fitchburg*. Boston: Houghton Mifflin. (Ideas—Clever ways of problem solving.)

McDonald, Megan. (1999). *The Bone Keeper*. (B. Karas, Illus). New York: Orchard. (Ideas and word choice—Details and problem solving.)

————. (1999). *The Night Iguana Left Home*. (P. Goembel, Illus.). New York: DK Ink. (Organization—Sequence of events)

Tomlinson, Jill. (2001). *The Owl Who Was Afraid of the Dark*. (P. Howard, Illus.). Cambridge, MA: Candlewick. (Ideas—Developing a main character; Organization—Demonstrating story resolution.)

Students as young as first grade should learn the techniques of revising. Here are symbols writers' use.

Writer's Symbols

When revising:

Caret (^):   Use to insert a word, phrase, or sentence.

Arrow (→):   Use when you run out of space to show the writing continues on the back of the page or into the margin.

Circle: Circle words, phrases, or lines that need to be revised later. Could be for spelling, clarity, grammar, etc.

Colored Pens: Use another color pen for each revision. If you start with a pencil, then use a black pen, then a blue pen for example.

Keep in mind that grammar is largely an abstract concept for young children as they enter kindergarten and move up through third grade. They use it when they communicate but can't precisely point out why a sentence works or doesn't. All six parts of speech—nouns, pronouns, verbs, adjectives, adverbs, and conjunctions—are a natural part of their conversation even at this young age. Through reading and writing, children become aware of some of their own grammatical errors. During kindergarten through second grade, grammar instruction should focus on the use of words in both reading and writing (Farris, 2001). Children love descriptive words, so they should be encouraged to find such words in their own reading and writing and share them during a descriptive words mini-lesson. Later they should learn that such words are also called adjectives. To get students to become familiar with adjectives, read a favorite story that the class enjoys and have them identify the words used to describe the main character. Since they already know the story, it will be easy for them to locate the descriptive words as you write them down on chart paper for them to view.

Third graders and older students need to consider how language is used effectively and powerfully by authors and how they, too, can use it likewise. Have students examine sentences from quality writing that you have selected as examples. Here are some examples of sentences students can consider in relation to their own writing:

* Using adverbs by having students suggest substitute words for those in italics below:

    When the swan had laid five eggs, she felt *satisfied*. She gazed at them *proudly*. (From *Trumpet of the Swan* by E. B. White, 1970, p. 18)

* In combining sentences:

    I stood up, squeezed the stiffness from the back of my neck, and gave my brother a parting frown that I hoped would leave him very worried. (From *Morning Girl* by Michael Dorris, 1992, p. 5)

* In the use of relative clauses:

    She clung to the saddle and gave herself up to the astonishing fact that, though her heart was pounding and her backbone felt like a pipe full of cold running water, her head was fiercely calm. (From *Tuck Everlasting* by Natalie Babbitt, 1975, p. 32)

Picture books that lend themselves to grammar mini-lessons include the following:

- Use of verbs for description:

  Baylor, Byrd. (1986). *I'm in Charge of Celebrations.* (P. Parnell, Illus.). New York: Scribner's.

  Ehlert, Lois. (2000). *Market Day.* San Diego: Harcourt Brace.

  Heller, Ruth. (1989). *Many Luscious Lollipops.* New York: Grosset & Dunlap.

  Yolen, Jane. (1996). *Welcome to the Sea of Sand.* New York: Scholastic.

- Writing in first person:

  Krauss, Ruth. (1945). *The Carrot Seed.* New York: Harper & Row.

Each mini-lesson on a specific aspect of grammar, usage, or the conventions of writing such as punctuation, dialogue, and so on, should be followed up by the teacher by encouraging students to point out how they have incorporated these in their own writing. While the teacher needs to be organized so that reading and writing workshops are efficient instructional sessions, it is equally important that students be organized, each keeping a binder or folder in which they write down the mini-lesson components and store any handouts. This is essential if students are to be able to refer to their notes or information shared via handouts. You may need to closely supervise and guide those students who have organizational problems (i.e., ADD, ADHD, learning disabled, and some gifted students).

Enriching their writing with lively, vivid words is a critical mini-lesson to teach. With an eye to authors who model the careful use of words to create just the right character or to establish the perfect setting, students are off to a good start. They need specific instruction as well. Consider the lesson crafted by Linda Carver and Kyra Wilcox-Conley for students in grades five through eight. Concerned with the dull, mundane words so commonly appearing in students' writing, they went to work to dramatically improve the building materials—those critical nail-like words—used in the construction of stories and poetry. The teachers developed a list of attributes of descriptive words so that students understood what they were seeking.

Descriptive words are:

- Words that are original or used originally
- Lengthy words—more letters, more syllables
- Creative—aim for the highest of high
- Words that describe in detail
- More explanatory
- More precise
- Higher level words
- Grade level words rather than first or second grade words

With these parameters in mind, look at the variety of words Carver and Wilcox-Conley unearthed as displayed in Figure 11.6. Stored in their students' writing folders for easy access, these sheets became handy tools used again and again to bolster their daily writing.

Figure 11.6

"Beyond cool" word list

Expanded "Beyond Cool"
Word List

Adjectives

Overused	Superior Synonyms	Spectacular Synonyms
bad	depressed corrupt	doleful sinister vile
colorful	multicolor	vivid full color offbeat impressive weird striking
cute	cherished adorable dear	precious delightful
good	righteous exemplary	conscientious virtuous
happy	joyous gay merry	contented gladden
large	gigantic	enormous
old	elderly aged olden	patriarchal wintry
pretty	beautiful fair	enchanting candid
rough	jagged	serrated craggy
sad	downhearted	melancholy despondent

This activity was created by Linda Carver and Kyra Wilcox-Conley.

Adverbs

Overused	Superior Synonyms	Spectacular Synonyms
happily	happy-go-lucky	fortunately satisfactorily
loudly	rudely roughly	abruptly brutally
quietly	silently speechlessly	peacefully
slowly	gradually sluggishly	cautiously deliberately

Figure 11.6		
(continued)		
Verbs		
Overused	Superior Synonyms	Spectacular Synonyms
ask	request	inquire
	demand	interrogate
carry	transport	sustain
	support	convey
decide	resolve	terminate
	conclude	adjudicate
eat	feast	partake
	sup	devour
	dine	consume
fly	soar	hover
	flutter	decamp
go	depart	flee
	vanish	
jump	leap	bound
	hop	caper
	skip	vault
look	gaze	discern
	scan	behold
	view	
run	race	scurry
	dash	scamper

Teachers as Writers and Role Models

Teachers need to make a commitment to writing by being writers themselves. Donald Graves (1990) believes that by squeezing in as little as ten minutes a day of time for our own writing, we begin to see ourselves as writers. He suggests "piggybacking writing" into our daily routines both inside and outside of school. Once a week open the writing workshop with a ten-minute sustained silent writing time for everyone, or return from lunch ten minutes early to jot down some thoughts about a topic or write in a journal just before going to bed each evening.

Many teachers believe they don't have anything to say. Others are afraid to share anything personal with their students. Rubbish!!! Students love to learn more about their teachers—their likes, dislikes, experiences as children, and so on. Capturing daily life situations on paper—something Graves refers to as "literate occasions"—can be enriching writing experiences. Consider writing about how you felt during difficult moments in your own life—when you saw the police car with its red lights flashing in your rearview mirror only to pass you by, guarding the opposing team's worst player who scores an easy lay up for the winning points, or how you felt when you were the only one in swim class who never learned how to swim.

By sharing our own experiences, we also aid our students as they hone the writing craft. If in our writing we "show not tell," then students will discover some of the subtle nuances of writing. For example, rather than writing, "Mary said, 'You are in my way!'" use "Mary said, 'Get out of my way!'" Or, instead of "David was saddened by the news" write "David slumped over at the news." Graves (1999) suggests that we write about people we know well and list ways that person reveals himself (i.e., talks to himself, taps his foot on the floor keeping time with music, leans against things—the wall, a car, a tree—wears his favorite team's hat whenever watching the game on TV, chuckles to himself when he reads the comics). We can also write—and discover things—about ourselves. What habits do we have? Favorite things to do? Things we avoid? Students always enjoy discovering having something in common with the teacher. They also love knowing the teacher has a hidden quirk they can talk about—being a Britney Spears fan, feeding the dog vegetables under the table until the dog burped, forgetting your lunch tickets were in your pocket and washing your pants, or dying your hair another color that didn't quite work out.

Checking Instruction

As discussed in Chapter 5, we need to constantly review our instructional goals and check our instructional practices as we monitor student achievement. Each quarter, we can objectively measure each writing criterion during a two-day period as we teach writing. This ensures our own progress as we grow as teachers of writing. The OnLine Learning Center has a checklist that allows us to not only self-evaluate our teaching, but monitor the writing curriculum as well.

In the early part of the year there will likely be a number of Ns coded, but by midyear, we should have incorporated all of these writing practices into our teaching.

QUESTIONING THE AUTHOR

An instructional strategy that models the need to question what you read while you are reading is called Questioning the Author (QtA). Successful readers act on the author's message. Thus, the premise of QtA is that if what they are reading doesn't make sense, readers should raise questions about what the author says and means (Beck, McKeown, Hamilton, & Kucan, 1997).

Using QtA requires students to be thoughtful readers who develop quality questions that probe into the author's intent. Students are taught to ask certain questions as they monitor the message of the author.

- What does the author mean?
- How is this significant or important?
- What is the author trying to say here?
- Does what the author says make sense with what was presented earlier in the book?
- Does the author explain this clearly?

These questions assist students as they examine and challenge narrative text. If a student fails to understand a narrative piece, it may not be the fault of the student but rather the author who failed to convey the message in a manner the student could understand. Beck, McKeown, Hamilton, and Kucam (1997) refer to this as "grappling with the text" as readers attempt to make sense out of what may not make sense in the first place.

Your responsibility as the teacher for QtA lessons for narrative texts necessitates that you break the lesson down into three steps. First, identify major understandings and potential problems with a narrative piece you plan to use with your students. As you read the selection, were there places where you stopped and reread to grasp the meaning? If so, mark those spots. The next step is to divide the narrative text into logical stopping points for class or small group discussion. You can use sticky notes to do this. Lastly, develop questions, or queries as Beck et al. (1997) refer to them, that model and demonstrate how to question the author.

Queries are critical in using the QtA and should be thought provoking to stimulate meaningful classroom discussion. Beck et al. (1997) suggest the following "classroom moves" by the teacher to assist in guiding the class in discussing, exploring, and clarifying meaning of a narrative selection as you move from one portion of the text to another:

> **Marking:** Drawing attention to certain ideas by using either a comment ("Nice idea," "That's an insightful observation," "Yes, that's the point," etc.) or repeating what a student said by paraphrasing it.
>
> **Turning back:** Making students responsible for what they share in the discussion by going to the specific location within the text for clarification.
>
> **Revoicing:** Filtering to get the most important information.
>
> **Modeling:** Thinking out loud about an issue that is difficult for your students to understand and grasp.
>
> **Annotating:** Providing additional information that is *not* in the text so that students can fully understand the concepts presented.
>
> **Recapping:** Summarizing the main ideas. If a student does this (or you have to step in and do it), use this as a signal to your students to move on in the lesson.

QtA is particularly helpful when using historical novels because it provides opportunities for students to delve into the historical setting—time and place—of the novel. This format and structure assist diverse learners, especially English language learners who may be unfamiliar with historical events of the period in which the novel is set, by giving them a cognitive framework to aid their concept development.

VISUALIZING THE STORY: MAKING A MOVIE IN THE MIND

Have you ever read a John Grisham novel or Stephen King thriller, and then gone to the movie version at a later time? Was your assessment that the visual pictures you created inside your head were superior to Hollywood's version? If so, you are not alone. Narrative text allows readers to visualize the story as the characters, action, and setting come to life in the mind's eye. What appears to be such a natural process for many readers is actually an excellent comprehension strategy. In short, imagining what the book would be like through mental imagery enhances comprehension.

When younger children create scenarios and pictures in their heads, they are more involved in the stories as they may be living through the story or even pretending to be a part of it than if they simply read the book. Older children become increasingly engaged and attentive when they formulate mental pictures. This is probably why children don't hesitate to tackle large thick books of modern fantasy such as Brian Jacques's *Redwall* (Jacques, 1987) series or J. K. Rowling's Harry Potter books. According to Brian Jacques (2000), "A good book can never be too thick." In short, readers never want a good book to end as a part of them becomes attached to the characters and the plot as well as the magnificent, resplendent, and detailed images created in their own imaginations.

One cannot assume that all children will access this comprehension strategy or understand its importance. Therefore, children need to be taught how to construct or refine their own mental images. Visualizing:

- Allows readers to create mental images from words in the text
- Enhances meaning with mental imagery
- Links past experience to the words and ideas in the text
- Enables readers to place themselves in the story
- Strengthens a reader's relationship to the text
- Stimulates the imaginative thinking
- Heightens engagement with text
- Brings joy to reading (Harvey & Goudvis, 1998, p. 23)

Teachers can help young students or older diverse learners acquire this reading strategy by reading aloud rich, quality text of narrative picture books before letting the students see the illustrations and having students close their eyes as they create the mental images. Some examples of rich language books for emergent and beginning readers include Denise Fleming's (1993) book for emergent readers about life in a pond, *In the Small, Small Pond*, Peggy Rathmann's (1999) book about delaying going to bed, *Ten Minutes Till Bedtime*, Mary Ann Hoberman's (2001) book of short stories, *You Read to Me, I'll Read to You*, Audrey Wood's (1984) classic, *The Napping House*, and Nancy Shaw's (1986) rollicking *Sheep in a Jeep*. Chapter books are effective with second and third grade students, such as Avi's *Poppy* (1995), Beverly Cleary's (1965) *The Mouse and the Motorcycle*, and Deborah and James Howe's (1983) *Bunnicula*. Fourth graders and up can benefit from making visual images as the teacher reads aloud such books as Kevin Henkes's (1999) *The Birthday Room*, Brian Jacques's (2000) *The Legend of Luke*, and Katherine Paterson's (1977) Newbery Award–winning book, *Bridge to Terabithia*. You might ask these readers to make these mental movies visible on occasion. As a response option they might illustrate a favorite scene or work on a mural with friends who have also read the same book.

DIVERSE LEARNERS AND NARRATIVE AND POETRY TEXT

Some diverse learners may need additional time and assistance as they try to grasp information presented during a mini-lesson. Clear examples are critical inasmuch as they are less confusing for all students, particularly students with learning disabilities or struggling readers and writers. Small group mini-lessons allow for closer monitoring as we teach plus provide more opportunities for interacting and questioning. Administering running records (see Chapter 5) on a different struggling reader each day of the week can help you monitor each child's progress and target instruction for that child. You may find two or more students lacking the same skill, thereby enabling you to create a small group for instructional purposes and disbanding it afterwards.

Web Link:

Integrating Reading and Writing for Students with Learning Disabilities

For those students who tend to read and write more slowly than their peers, provide a cassette recorder to record their stories and then later that day or the next morning have an aide or classroom volunteer word process the story for the student to reread or edit. Even a few good readers and writers seemingly are snail-like in doing such tasks and may need extra time to accomplish what other students do in less time. Keep in mind that the work pace of students varies greatly and only *rarely* do they all finish at close to the same time. Therefore, have extension activities for those who finish early so they can still keep learning while the others complete the assigned reading or writing task.

Gifted readers and writers may need to focus on a specific skill before they gallop off at their fast pace learning. For instance, many gifted students overlook the importance of writing conventions as they are more interested in getting their thoughts down and moving on to another writing project. Punctuation and spelling may need to be given additional attention to ensure that such learners possess the basic tools of writing to be effective.

Often learning disabled students and struggling readers find it more difficult to see linkages between their reading and writing. Having them see a pattern of writing and then trying to emulate it can be successful for beginning readers and writers. For instance, having students read a simple pattern book or a song such as "Over in the Meadow Where the Green Grass Grows" that has been written on chart paper for them to easily view while they read can help them understand the structure of our language. Reading the same story or song over and over again until they have actually memorized it and then writing their own versions provides a scaffold for their own literacy development. Older students can benefit from seeing examples from quality literature. Putting examples on a transparency of sentences from a book just shared as a read-aloud makes a great mini-lesson for sentence development. Did the author combine sentences? Which sentences are combined? Where is a short sentence used for effect? What makes the passage interesting? Did the sentences all have the same structure? Why not? Such questions as these are timely reminders to all students including diverse learners to think about how sentences work. Sharing examples from various authors over the course of the school year will lead to enhanced sentence development in your students' writing.

Students need to be aware of how their writing sounds on the ear. That is, rereading their piece of writing aloud can help them with organization, conventions, ideas, sentence structure, and so on.

In the case of English language learners, their comprehension may be a problem while their decoding may be quite good. Just being able to correctly pronounce a word does not mean that the child understands its meaning. Vocabulary acquisition and use of cognates are very important in working with second language learners. For instance, there are hundreds of words in English that are also in Spanish. Below is a list of cognates in both English and Spanish that have the same meanings.

English and Spanish Cognates

Frequently Used Words

English	Spanish
family	familia
group	grupo
popular	popular
program	programa

Animals

English	Spanish
animal(s)	animal(es)
dinosaur	dinosaurio
elephant	elefante
human	humano

Science

English	Spanish
acid	ácido
hypothesis	hipótesis
metal	metal
ozone	ozono

Math

English	Spanish
circle	circulo
decimal	decimal
equal	igual
fraction	fracción

Web Link:
Hearing-Impaired
Children and Story
Structure

With autistic, learning disabled, and English language learners, keeping concepts at the concrete level makes it easier for them to understand and incorporate into their thinking processes. Reading and writing activities need to be structured to be context rich in order to scaffold both English language development and academic development (Truscott & Watts-Taffe, 2000). It is important that you constantly activate such students' prior knowledge and add to that knowledge. Use lots of pictures, objects, demonstrations, and graphic organizers (Williams, 2001). If you have access to closed captioned TV programs or videos, include them as extension activities so students can see and hear the language at the same time. Breaking things down into smaller tasks helps them achieve and feel good about their reading and writing accomplishments. The more opportunities to actually successfully complete an activity and having the positive feeling of closure will encourage such students to engage more readily in other literacy tasks.

Reading and writing narrative and poetic text make for relevant reading and writing for children who represent a variety of cultural backgrounds, typical of most elementary and middle school classrooms. Teachers need to be knowledgeable about multicultural children's literature.

POETRY: THE FLAVOR AND ZEST OF LANGUAGE

Multicultural Children's Literature Book List

To paraphrase Charles Dickens, poetry can be the "best of times and the worst of times" for elementary and middle school students. One of America's best-known poets, Robert Frost, was often quoted saying that a poem goes from "delight to wisdom." Care must be taken that poetry be presented in a manner that *appeals* to students. Poetry offers children the richness of language, for each carefully selected word of a poem contributes both sound and meaning. Poetry "has the power to evoke in its hearers rich sensory images and deep emotional responses. Poetry demands total response from the individual—all the intellect, senses, emotion, and imagination. It does not tell *about* an experience as much as it invites its hearers to *participate in* the experience" (Huck, Hepler, Hickman, & Kiefer, 2004). An added bonus is that at the elementary and middle school level, poetry levels the playing field as all students can enjoy reading and writing poetry.

Elements of Poetry

As students explore the literary world of poetry, through both reading and composing their own poems, they discover the importance of word choice. Selecting the precise word is more important in poetry than in narrative, expository, and persuasive writing because each word in the poem must be the "right" word. Searching for the right word aids students in expanding their writing, reading, and speaking vocabularies.

Poetry has several elements including rhyme, alliteration, rhythm, meter, simile, and metaphor. These elements are often found in narrative text as well. **Rhyme** is the use of words with similar sounds such as the infamous "cat in the hat." Rhyming poems are very popular with elementary students. A good rhyme is almost like a piece of music—natural and unforced. **Alliteration** is the constant repetition of the first sound in a series of words such as "spic and span." **Rhythm** is the pattern or beat of the poem, sometimes referred to as the poem's cadence. When the cadence or rhythm is predictable, it is referred to as **meter**. Perfect meter has almost a singsong verse. For example, most greeting card verses possess perfect meter. **Simile** compares one thing to another using the words *as* or *like* such as "big as a barn" or "crazy like a loon." A **metaphor** is when the writer refers to something as being another thing altogether such as an old car being "an extinct dinosaur."

By reading and writing different forms of poetry using these elements, students hone their reading and writing skills for narrative and expository writing.

Sharing Poetry

Web Link:
Poetry on the Internet

Narrative text and poetry go hand in hand as they are both aesthetic. One way to share poetry every day is to relate children's favorite stories, or narrative text, with poetry. There are unlimited ways to share this link. Consider sharing color poems from *Hailstones and Halibut Bones* (O'Neill, 1989) along with *Color Farm* (Ehlert, 1990) and *Color Zoo* (Ehlert, 1989), both concept books for five- and six-year-olds. "Running Away," a poem by Karla Kuskin (1975) in her collection *Near the Window Tree* fits

Consider buddy poetry reading and writing with older students assisting younger students. Poetry can be enjoyed by both the reader and the listener.

Teaching Strategy:
Choral Reading

perfectly with *When Sophie Gets Angry, Really, Really Angry* (Bang, 1999). As a teacher, poetry that appropriately accompanies specific picture books, middle grade novels, or historical fiction should be copied and filed away for later use. Don't overlook another form of poetry, music lyrics such as those from a particular period of time: for example, "Dixie" and "The Battle Hymn of the Republic" and, for struggling readers, "When Johnny Comes Marching Home" to accompany Civil War novels; "Brother, Can You Spare a Dime?" and, for learning disabled or struggling readers, "You Are My Sunshine" or "Big Rock Candy Mountain" from the CD, *O' Brother Where Art Thou?* with books with Depression era settings such as *Bud, Not Buddy* (Curtis, 1999), *Out of the Dust* (Hesse, 1997), or *A Year Down Yonder* (Peck, 2001).

Delight awaits those who read or listen to humorous poetry—the most popular choice of poetry by elementary students. Thus Shel Silverstein's *Where the Sidewalk Ends* (1974), *A Light in the Attic* (1984), and *Falling Up* (1996) should be part of every elementary classroom library. Another popular book is Douglas Florian's (1999) *Laugh-eteria,* which contains over 150 funny poems on everything including ogres, fear, pizza, school, dragons, trees, and hair. A favorite poet of middle schoolers is Paul Janeczko as his poems focus on the here and now—pet dogs, playing baseball, friendships, and that all important question, why do girls go to the bathroom in groups?

While all children can relate to humor, poetry can also be a verbal vehicle to share the common aspects of our lives as well as how we differ. *Confetti* by Pat Mora (1996) contains perky, rhythmic narrative free verses that convey both the flavor of Mexican American culture and the uniqueness of southwestern United States. Such collections as *Home: A Journey through America* (Locker, 1998) and *In Daddy's Arms I Am Tall: African Americans Celebrating Fathers* (Steptoe, 1997) share the warmth, humor, and grace of verse written by several famous writers. Middle school students enjoy *The Tree Is Older Than You Are* (Nye, 1995), a collection of poems in both English and Spanish.

Many poets have recordings of their own poetry, which always pleases students as they hear the "real poet read their stuff," as one third grader put it. Listening to the gravelly voice of Shel Silverstein encourages students to seek out his poetry collections. The smooth, honey-rich flowing voice of Ashley Bryan is a stark contrast to the indescribable, off-key singing of Jack Prelutsky.

A number of Internet sites offer audio versions of poetry, including experimental poetry. Diverse learners often greatly benefit from such sites because the short lines and length of poetry make the reading more manageable and less intimidating (Hadaway, Vardell, & Young, 2001).

- www.wings.buffalo.edu/epc Electronic Poetry Center Home Page
- www.poetrymagazine.com Poetry Magazine
- www.pw.org Poets and Writers, Inc

Web Links:
Electronic Poetry Center Home Page

Poetry Magazine

Poets and Writers, Inc.

Establishing a poetry listening center will motivate students. Have students from the upper elementary grades or high school record poems and put the cassette and accompanying pieces of poetry in a plastic bag or brown envelope in the listening center for your students to enjoy and read along.

List Poems

List poems offer young children an introduction to poetry and older children an opportunity to create a poem without pressure. All student responses are accepted for a list poem. For instance, a first grade class made this list poem about autumn.

Autumn
Falling leaves
Red
Yellow
Brown
Jump in piles of leaves
Pumpkins
Scarecrows
Jack-o'-lanterns
Witches
Ghosts
Candy
Apples
Raking leaves
Running
Frost
Cold

Poetry Starters

When students find it difficult to write a poem, teachers may choose to have them use poetry starters. Here are a few suggestions:

My pet _____.

____ is my favorite color.

When I go to bed, I dream about _____.

When _____ was alive. (fill in the blank with a name of a historical figure)

Can _____ (athlete's name) ever play _____ (person's sport)!

"I Used to Think That _____ But Now I Know That _____" Poetry

Students can be encouraged to think about their own metacognition and intellectual as well as physical growth when they write "I Used to _____ But Now I _____" poems. What their perceptions were when they were younger or even before a unit of study about a topic and then afterthoughts can make for very deep, informative poetry. Consider the following poem by a gifted student.

I Used to Think That Friendship Was Forever
I used to think that friendship was forever
I played with my friends every day at childcare
Keith Busse, Sara, Richard, and Tony
On the climbing fort
On the swings
Playing with clay
When I was four, things changed
Keith Busse went to school
Tony moved away
Sara went to live in Japan
Now I know friendship may not last
When I was four, I had a midlife crisis

Kurtis, age 8

Acrostic Poems

Students have fun making acrostic poems using their name and transforming it into a poem such as the one below:

ERIC
Energetic
Rich (NOT!!!!!!)
Intelligent
Confident

A variation is using names of famous people with students coming up with their character traits or accomplishments.

Rhyming Poems

Many children believe rhyming poems are the only kind of poetry that exists. Whether this childhood myth is a carryover from learning Mother Goose rhymes or some other reason, it is important for teachers to share rhyming poems along with other types of poetry.

Here is an example of how a fourth grade teacher engages her students in a reading and writing workshop with rhyming poetry. Jeanne Ferenbach begins by reading to her students "A Frog, A Stick," by one of children's most popular poets, Jack Prelutsky (1996). As she shares the poem, Jeanne places each of the items on an overhead projector for her students to view:

A Frog, A Stick

by Jack Prelutsky

A frog, a stick,
a shell, a stone,
a paper clip,
a chicken bone.
A feather quill,
a piece of string,
a ladybug,
a beetle wing.

A greenish wad
of bubble gum,
assorted keys,
and cookie crumbs.
A maple leaf,
a candy bar,
a rubber band,
a model car.

Potato chips
and soggy fries,
plus something
I can't recognize.
A broken watch,
a plastic cow . . .
that's what's inside
my pockets now.

From Prelutsky, Jack. (1995).
A Pizza the Size of the Sun. New York: HarperCollins,
pp. 12–13. Used by permission.

As her students giggle with delight, Jeanne covers up the objects with a towel and turns off the overhead projector. Prior to her reading the poem out loud, each of Jeanne's students was given a sheet of paper. Now Jeanne asks them to try to remember everything that was in the pocket by listing the items on their paper. Students frantically begin to write. The easiest items are those mentioned first and last in the poem. The middle items are more difficult for them to recall. By sharing this enjoyable poem in this way, Jeanne is demonstrating that poetry can be fun to share and an equally pleasant way to encourage her students to listen for details, something all good readers and writers need to do. Next she has her students write their own poems of what someone might find under their beds. Here is a poem that aptly describes what lies under this ten-year-old's bed:

My Hidden Secrets
A dirty sock,
a brown rock,
a blue marble,
an empty
water bottle.

A big dust
bunny,
last Sunday's
funnies,
A piece from a
go cart throttle.

Candy bar
wrapper,
a CD by a rapper,
a ratty eared baseball card
of an unknown player.

A box of wafers,
old homework papers,
a red Lego,
discarded underwear.

SIGH!!!!
I'm not a
house cleaner
Just an
everything saver!!!

Richard, age 10

Clerihews

Clerihews feature a description of a person in four lines. Invented by Edmund Clerihew Bentley, a British detective writer, this type of poetry gives voice to story characters, historical figures, as well as the students themselves (Tompkins, 2001). The first line gives the person's name. Line 2 rhymes with the first line. This is followed by lines 3 and 4, which rhyme with each other. Here is an example based on a book character, Leigh, from *Strider* (Cleary, 1989):

Leigh
Runs like the breeze
In races he flies like the wind
Only to be passed by and fail to win

Teaching Strategy for the Classroom

A SAMPLE POETRY LESSON PLAN

Focus poem: "My Parents Have the Flu Today" from Prelutsky, Jack. (2000). *It's Raining Pigs and Noodles* (J. Stevenson, Illus.). New York: HarperCollins.

I. OBJECTIVES

The students will listen attentively to a poem.
The students will demonstrate understanding of the elements of a rhyming poem.
The students will generate and organize ideas as part of writing a poem.

II. MATERIALS

Poem (see below), scratch paper, construction paper.

My Parents Have the Flu Today

by Jack Prelutsky

My parents have the flu today,
They both are sick in bed,
and thoughts of things to do today
are swimming through my head.
My nimble brain is burgeoning
with ways to misbehave,
I'll give my brother's Teddy Bear
a haircut and a shave.

Perhaps I'll make a mud pie
in my sister's stupid hat,
attach my mother's earrings
to the puppy and the cat,
hang carrots from the ceiling,
stuff bananas into shoes,
then set the clocks to different times,
it's certain to confuse.

I'll switch the salt and sugar,
scatter meatballs on the rugs,
hide spaghetti in a closet,
and refrigerate some bugs.
I'll paint my father's underwear
an iridescent blue.
My options are unlimited. . .
my parents have the flu.

Source: From Prelutsky, Jack. (2000). *It's Raining Pigs and Noodles.* (J. Stevenson, Illus.). New York: HarperCollins. Used by permission.

III. INSTRUCTIONAL APPROACH

A. Motivator

Tell the students that all of the teachers have the flu. What would they do? What would that child do? Have them brainstorm possibilities on their scratch paper. After about three or four minutes, let five or six students share with the class, then have all students share their best idea with their neighbor.

B. Teacher/Student Interaction

Share the poem "My Parents Have the Flu Today" with the class. Ask the students to speculate about the behavior of the child on other days. Have the students recall the things the child was thinking about doing. As they do this, jot them down on the overhead or chalkboard.

- Next have the students write their own poem about being mischievous. The setting may be anywhere they choose—their home, school, the grocery store, and so on.
- Remind the students that the child's actions can't hurt someone, only play tricks on the other people around them.
- Have the students edit their poems on day 2.
- After editing their poems, they may write and illustrate it on the construction paper.

C. Gatekeeping

Gather students in a large circle on the floor and invite each student to read their poem. Share your own version as well. After everyone has shared, ask what elements, content, or lines stood out that piqued their interest.

IV. EXTENSIONS

Over a three- or four-week period, share other forms of poetry. Provide several examples of each to serve as models for the students. Have students create their own book of poems that they write and illustrate.

V. ADAPTATIONS/MODIFICATIONS FOR DIVERSE LEARNERS

Select some brief rhyming poems such as four-line poems by Shel Silverstein or Jack Prelutsky and share with the students. Have them work together in groups of two or three to create a group poem. Provide them with a rhyming dictionary book for children such as *Time to Rhyme* (Terban, 1994).

English language learners may write a poem using a combination of English words and words from their own language: for example, using the Spanish words for soccer, kick, ball, and goal to write a poem about playing soccer.

Terban, Marvin. (1994). *Time to Rhyme.* (C. L. Demarest, Illus.). Honesdale, PA: Boyds Mill Press.

Free Verse

Free verse is often rejected by students as "not poetry" since it lacks rhyme and rhythm. Yet, once such poetry is introduced to students, they typically embrace it as anyone can write a good free-verse poem by merely jotting down a stream of thoughts that pass through one's mind.

If you are introducing free verse to third through sixth graders, you might want to share the experience of Anastasia, the ten-year-old main character in Lois Lowry's (1979) *Anastasia Krupnik,* who was told by her teacher to write a poem as a class assignment. After devoting eight long evenings to writing, editing, and refining her poem, Anastasia reads it to the class:

> hush hush the sea-soft night is aswim
>   with winklesquirm creatures
>   listen(!)
>
> to them move smooth in the moistly dark
> here in the whisperwarm wet. (pp. 11–12)

Despite Anastasia's effort, her teacher rejects the poem as it has no capital letters, the lines fail to rhyme, and there are made up words (winklesquirm and whisperwarm) giving Anastasia's poem an F because it didn't follow a rhyming format. This fictional experience helps students gain insight as to the nature of free verse, reassuring them that this type of poetry has no boundaries—only their own imagination.

Shape Poems

Arranging words on a page can be an eloquent combination of poetry and art. Children love to see a poem in the shape of an object they readily recognize. Students still use the elements of poetry including rhythm, rhyme, and precise word choice as they create their own shape poems. Figure 11.7 has two shape poems by Kurt, a sixth grader.

Haiku

Haiku is a short three-line poem that means "beginning" in Japanese. The first and third lines contain five syllables, and the second line contains seven syllables. The topic of this kind of poetry is nature and the seasons. Here is an example of haiku:

> Silent, snowflakes fall
> Covering grass and tree limbs
> Winter's chill descends.

One of the more famous Japanese haiku poets was Issa, whose life and poetry are contained in *Cool Melons Turn to Frogs* (Gollub, 1998). After sharing this book with students, they can create their own haiku, writing it on heavy stock paper accompanied by their own watercolor paintings, or give them colored tissue and have them tear it into small pieces and glue it with laundry starch onto white paper.

Figure 11.7
Shape Poems

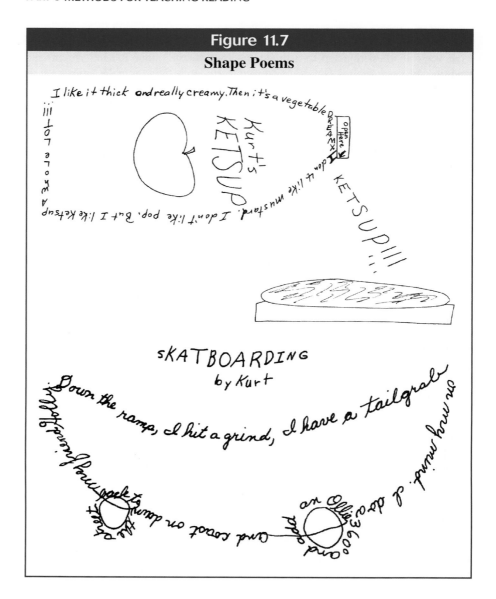

Cinquain

Another type of poetry is cinquain, a five-line poem with two syllables in the first line, four in the second line, six in the third line, eight in the fourth line, and two again in the fifth line. "Puppy" is a cinquain poem by a fifth grade diverse learner:

Puppy

Soft fur
Wiggling body
Licking my cheek and nose
Warm, cuddly, happy, lovable
Puppy.

POETRY WEBSITES

There are a number of poetry websites for elementary and middle school students. Students may share their poetry and read the works of other children at http://www. inkspot.com/young. The Internet Poetry Archive is located at http://www.sunsite. unc.edu/dykki/poetry/home.html. Two other websites devoted to poetry for youngsters are http://www.poetry4kids.com/ and http://www.nesbitt. com/poetry. Some poets have their own websites, for instance Kristine O'Connell George (http://home. earthlink.net/~froggie1/).

Go to the Online Learning Center at www.mhhe.com/farrisreading to link to the above and additional sites.

DEVELOPING FLUENCY IN READING

Slow readers. They are a dilemma. Teachers patiently wait for them while occasionally peers engage in boorish behavior by sighing deeply. Being able to read at a moderate or faster pace while comprehending the text is a strength of good readers. Those who fail to do so are likely to make inadequate or poor progress in learning to read. We do know that by having regular opportunities to read materials of their own choosing, students build reading **fluency** (Rasinski & Padak, 2001). Often they will select books that are relatively easy for them to read. This, too, builds fluency as they are increasing their reading speed. They are routinely practicing using the reading strategies they possess, honing them with each subsequent text they open and dive into.

Students who read slowly are often considered inefficient or even poor readers by teachers. Such students are more likely to be recommended for reading services such as Title I offered within their school. How quickly a student can read a passage with comprehension does matter as word-by-word readers are met with frustration and an inability to understand what they have just read (Rasinski & Padak, 2001). Narrative and poetry text can aid fluency when students share selections orally after devoting time to practice and rehearse prior to going before an audience of their peers or students in lower grades to present their interpretations. The reading and rereading of poetry through read-aloud and choral reading activities promotes fluency (Gasparro & Falletta, 1994). Each student or a small group of students can select a poem to read expressively with the entire class sharing during Poetry Day. Poetry offers children the richness of language, for each word of a poem contributes both sound and meaning. When students listen to poetry read by the teacher, rich sensory images as well as strong, deep emotional responses can be evoked as their imagination, senses, and feelings are piqued. Then, by sharing poetry they have selected and rehearsed, they, too, can stir emotions and create vivid images in the minds of others.

Having students read poems for two or three voices in which they engage in taking turns reading solo then suddenly reading lines together as part of the poem's design aids in fluency as students must practice their lines and make certain their timing is perfect. Sharing poems for two voices or more can be done with several selections such as those from Paul Fleischman's (1988) Newbery Award–winning book *Joyful Noise: Poems for Two Voices*, which offers rich rhyme and rhythm against a backdrop of nature's insect world.

Portfolio Activity:
Reader's Theater

Reader's theater is yet another way to enhance oral fluency as students develop a script from a narrative book, usually a major scene, rehearse it as part of a small group, then present it in an engaging, meaningful manner (Padak & Rasinski, 2001). Reading narrative text and performing it via reader's theater, a developed and performed scripted drama, or selecting and interpreting text segments for an oral performance have been found to improve students' ability to decode and comprehend (Wolfe, 1998; Ivey & Broaddus, 2000). Likewise their self-confidence increases (Martinez, Roser, & Strecker, 1998/1999).

Web Link:
Aaron Shepard's Readers
Theater Editions

While reviewing the scene and preparing the written script, students are noting important dialogue in terms of both the author's intent and the reader's interpretation. As such reader's theater offers a valuable opportunity to point out during minilessons ways writers use to convey meaning. For instance, a mini-lesson by the teacher can model how various authors show actions of a story through the dialogue they include—or fail to include. Scripts of reader's theater are available from Aaron Shepard's Readers Theater Editions located at www.aaronshep.com/rt/RTE.

Teaching Strategy for the Classroom

WRITING A READER'S THEATER SCRIPT

Students need to participate in several reader's theater presentations before they sit down to write their own script. Using poetry, scripts you have written, or those previously published is the best way to scaffold the reading/writing experience. Participants learn that it is the reader who interprets the story using voice and a simple prop or two to make the story come alive. Often speaking parts vary in length and difficulty so every student can participate, regardless of their reading ability. Then invite students to try their hand at writing their own scripts.

- Begin with text that is relatively easy. Picture books including folktales with an interesting plot and lively dialogue are excellent choices. Provide a variety of books for students to read and ample time to read them as they look for materials to develop into a reader's theater production.

- Have readers select three of their favorites and write the titles on a slip of paper along with their own name. Divide students into small writing groups by matching their choices in books. Groups will vary in size depending on how many parts there are and the book choices. Now students are ready to go to work; they have their teammates and their materials in place.

- Guide the students in the writing process. Remind them that much of the text is eliminated when presenting a reader's theater.
  1. Words like "he said" and "she replied" are examples of words to leave out.
  2. Longer text can be summarized.
  3. As they revise the text, students will include the dialogue that each character will speak.
  4. They will also provide information for the narrator to share with the audience, just enough to set the scene and fill in necessary spots between dialogue so that the story flows nicely.
  5. Add a brief introduction, and the rough draft of the script should be ready for teacher review.
- Once the script has been completed and approved by the teacher, it is time to select parts and begin to rehearse. If possible, students should decide who does which part on their own. The teacher can troubleshoot any difficulties.
- Students do not memorize their lines but read them with zest and vitality, bringing the characters and the story to life through their interpretations. This is a time for interpreting moods and feelings and deciding how best to portray them.
- Finally, plan a day of presentations. Students might all put their scripts in the same colored folders, which looks nice from the perspective of the audience. They also might wear T-shirts that are similar or add a crazy hat if that is appropriate to the character. The focus is on the dialogue, of course, but some coordination ahead of time makes for a more polished performance.
- Present and wait for the resounding applause!

ADAPTATIONS/MODIFICATIONS FOR DIVERSE LEARNERS

Learning disabled students, struggling readers, and English language learners can benefit from echo reading in which the teacher reads aloud a paragraph and, in turn, students in small groups read it aloud. This practice enables students to hear the passage being read by a good oral reader. For students whose first language is other than English, the proper enunciation of the words as modeled by the teacher plays an important role in their acquisition of English.

 ## TECHNOLOGY AND NARRATIVE AND POETRY WRITING

Computers in the classroom linked to the Internet make it easy for students to share their narrative writing and poetry with pen pals in another school, in another state, or country. Consider Rod Moore's second graders who write stories and scan in their illustrations as part of a PowerPoint program. With one click, ZIP! The stories sail across the Internet as e-mail attachments to a computer located in another second grade classroom in a school 200 or 2,000 miles away where their pen pals, or "e-pals," anxiously await.

The Internet also makes access to authors possible as students click on the websites of their favorite authors. Here are some websites your students may want to investigate:

Author	Website
Avi	www.aiv-writer.com
Jan Brett	www.janbrett.com
Marc Brown	www.mbrown.com
Tomie dePaola	www.tomie.com
Brian Jacques	www.redwall.org/dave/jacques
Cynthia Rylant	www.rylant.com

Web Links:
Fairrosa Cyber Library

Index to Author and
Illustrator Sites

The Fairrosa Cyber Library website contains several direct links to websites of authors and illustrators of children's books.

Another site that teachers find useful because of its teaching resource files and curriculum resources is the Internet School Library Media Center's Index to Author and Illustrator Internet Sites.

The Internet offers websites for poetry such as *The Young Authors Magazine* at www.yam.regulus.com/ where students can both read and submit poetry to be added to the website. A popular website is Jon Eaves *Magnetic Poetry* located at www.aba. net.au/people/jon/poetry/animate.html where students can find an animated magnetic poetry board.

MAKING CONNECTIONS: INTERDISCIPLINARY INSTRUCTIONAL UNITS

There are numerous interdisciplinary instructional units, or thematic units, that can be created using narrative books along with poetry. By integrating literacy with science, social studies, math, art, physical education, and music, or a combination of these content areas, teaching becomes more efficient. Topics of family, friendship, growing up, sports, historical periods, and more can be featured in interdisciplinary units. Weather is a very common unit in science throughout the various grade levels and makes for a great interdisciplinary unit of study. At the end of this chapter is a weather unit that combines both narrative and expository texts. There are suggestions for the various grade levels as well as for diverse learners. For each activity there is an assessment suggestion to aid with the evaluation process.

One excellent source of ideas and lists of appropriate children's literature for interdisciplinary instructional units is *The Complete Guide to Thematic Units: Creating the Integrated Curriculum* (2nd ed.) (Meinbach, Rothlein, & Fredericks, 2000).

Thematic units are helpful in working with diverse learners who have different strengths, interests, as well as weaknesses. By choosing a variety of novels on the same topic at varying reading levels, all students can participate without becoming frustrated by being asked to read material that is too difficult. Group work assists diverse learners in engaging in discussions and cooperative learning activities. Moving from group work to independent activities helps students to become self-reliant and independent learners.

Thematic Unit

WEATHER: INCORPORATING EXPOSITORY AND NARRATIVE READING AND WRITING

Weather is a typical science unit, and there are numerous narrative books that are based around weather as a setting. Generally weather is a subject covered throughout the elementary and middle school levels. Teachers can adapt this unit to their needs as the activities are indicated by level of difficulty. Thus if you teach middle school students, see the MS, indicating the book, material, and the like, are suitable for middle school students. If you have diverse learners, look for the DL next to activities for such students.

Key: P–Primary Students   I–Intermediate Students
MS–Middle School Students   DL–Diverse Learners

READ-ALOUDS INVOLVING RAINSTORMS

Hershenhorn, Esther. (1998). *There Goes Lowell's Party.* (J. Rogers, Illus.). New York: Holiday House. (P/I/MS–Fiction)
A narrative picture book based on weather folklore. This book is scientifically accurate. Lowell is optimistic as he plans his birthday party all the while a rainstorm develops.

Follow-up Activities:
P/I—Have students write their version of Lowell's birthday party with a different weather setting (i.e., snowstorm, hurricane, tornado). Students must change Lowell's birthday to a date when the weather would be appropriate (i.e., February 5 for a snowstorm). (DL–MS activity) [Assessment: Does the weather event impact the birthday party?]

DL–P/I—Have students write about an event that was affected by the weather (i.e., wedding on a rainy day; an ice storm that prevented them to get to see relatives for Thanksgiving; a football or soccer game played in the snow). (DL–P/I) [Assessment: Have students as a class create a rubric for evaluating the final product.)

I/MS—Have the students classify the weather proverbs in the back of the book as follows:

Which proverbs:

- Pertain to animal behavior? Human behavior? Plant behavior?
- Can be observed by seeing? Hearing? Tasting? Touching? Smelling?
- Can be explained by changes in barometric pressure? By changes in the wind? By changes in water? By changes in temperature?

P/I—Have the students locate the 28 Ozark rain proverbs that are illustrated in *There Goes Lowell's Party.* [Assessment: Do as a class activity with each student needing to come up with one proverb. Nudge DL students to find a proverb if need be by giving hints.]

P/I (DL–MS)—Let students illustrate the weather proverbs. Upper grade students may do a compare and contrast illustration. For example, "Earthworms multiply" could result in a drawing of worms increasing in number as compared with earthworms doing multiplication facts on the chalkboard. [Assessment: Does the portrayal make sense? Is the proverb written legibly?]

P/I (DL)—Ask students to discuss other ways Lowell's relatives might have come to his birthday party. [Assessment: Call on DL students early so they will have a chance to share. Note students who contribute to the discussion.]

P/I/MS–DL—Ask students to name the bodies of water and land mentioned in the book. As a class, have them list other terms for bodies of water and land as a vocabulary extension. Be certain to call on diverse learners first particularly if they have difficulty coming up with suggestions in class discussions. This allows them to participate successfully and feel good about themselves. Primary children might come up with pond, lake, creek, stream, falls, and so forth. Intermediate children who have increased vocabulary might include the above plus such terms as swamp, brook, spring, bay, bayou, rapids, and the like. Middle schoolers might suggest gulf, marsh, bog, fen, and so forth. Land words may include hill, mountain, valley, island, forest, hollow, bluff, peak, cliff, woods, forest, ridge, valley, slough, gully, gulch, prairie, savannah, rain forest, and the like. [Assessment: Note words each student volunteers.]

DL—Have English language learners list weather words in English and their own language (i.e., Spanish and English words for rain, storm, tornado, hurricane). Are any true cognates (same meaning in both languages and spelled the same)?

DL–MS—Have students review the list of weather proverbs from folklore listed in the back of Hershenhorn's book. Then let them research local folklore by interviewing relatives and neighbors and write about which are legends, superstitions, or actual facts. Diverse learners may record their interviews. [Assessment: Put the interviews together in a book as a whole class activity.]

MS—Share weather proverbs from other geographic and/or cultural groups, such as southern farmers and New England fishermen. Are the proverbs similar in content and accuracy? A good source for this activity is Eric Sloane, *Folklore of American Weather*, www.almanac.com. Read aloud other books based on weather settings.

READ-ALOUD BASED ON RAIN

Farris, Pamela J. (1996). *Young Mouse and Elephant: An East African Folktale.* (V. Gorbachev, Illus.). Boston: Houghton Mifflin. (P/I/MS–F)

Follow-up Activities:

P/I—Have students do a reader's theater on the book (see Chapter 10). Struggling readers can repeat the phrases, "Hey, are you elephant?" and "In that case, consider yourself fortunate. . . " [Assessment: Note use of intonation—pitch, stress, juncture—by individual students.]

P–DL—Give the students lunch bags and let them make puppets of the characters and reenact the story. [Assessment: Which puppets are the most creative? Colorful?]

I—Have the students compare this folktale with other folktales. [Assessment: Was the comparison accurate?]

DL–P—Have students list the elements of a rainstorm. [Assessment: Were the elements accurate?]

I/MS—Have the class generate a list of books where plots depend on weather as a setting (i.e., *The Wizard of Oz, Holes, Woodsong*). Have them write a fiction story in which weather influences the plot of the story. [Assessment: Does the story plot hinge on weather? Are the six traits of writing done well?]

READ-ALOUDS INVOLVING TORNADOES

Sloat, Teri. (1999). *Farmer Brown Goes Round and Round.* New York: HarperCollins. (P–F)
   The farm is turned upside down when a tornado hits.
   P—Model narrative writing as you work with your students to write a story about a tornado hitting a zoo. Use an overhead projector and transparencies so students can see as the story develops.
   DL—Have diverse learners record their own version of the story on a cassette recorder. [Assessment: Note use of interesting vocabulary.]
Ruckman, Ivy. (1984). *The Night of the Twisters.* New York: HarperCollins. (I–N)
   A gripping story of the dangers of and devastation caused by tornadoes. Great for intermediate students and low ability middle school readers to read on their own or as a read-aloud.
   I/MS—If you live in a state where tornadoes occur, have students interview relatives or neighbors who have seen a tornado and write up the interview to share with the class. [Assessment: Evaluate the questions asked and quality of description.]
   DL—Have students view a video of a tornado and write a story about a tornado hitting their town. [Assessment: Evaluate quality of ideas and organization of piece.]
   P/I/MS—As a class, visit the FEMA website to learn appropriate safety measures for dangerous weather. (FEMA for Kids—www.fema.gov/kids)

POETRY AND CHORAL READING

Adoff, Arnold. (1977). *Tornado! Poems.* (R. Himler, Illus.). New York: Delacorte. (P/I/MS–Poetry)
Hopkins, Lee Bennett. (1994). *Weather.* (M. Hall, Illus.). New York: HarperCollins. (P/I/MS–Poetry)
Activities involving poetry:

P/I/MS/DL

- Have the class create a list poem of weather terms (grades K–3), or have individual students write cinquain (grades 2 and up) and other types of poetry (grades 3 and up) based on weather. [Assessment: Evaluate only by considering whether the poem meets the specific criteria for poetry by type (i.e., cinquain).]

P/I/MS/DL

- Have students find weather poems and share during poetry readings as part of the unit. [Assessment: Done as enrichment without being evaluated.]

INTERVIEWS

P–DL—Invite a television weather announcer to visit the class and talk about weather forecasting. Prior to the visit, model questions that the students might ask and write them on the chalkboard or overhead. Then have the students work in groups of three to develop appropriate questions. Float between groups and assist when needed. Listen for themes. Use a K-W-L chart for the activity. [Assessment: Evaluate each group's questions.]
   I/MS–DL—Have students interview a person in the community whose job is influenced by weather (i.e., delivery personnel such as UPS and FedEX drivers, soda pop and bread truck drivers, postal workers; airline pilots; police officers; firefighters; meteorologist). Have them work in pairs to develop appropriate questions. You may need to give additional attention to the questions developed by diverse learners. [Assessment: Evaluate final written interview by using six traits of writing.]

THEMATIC WORD WALL WORDS

Primary: rain, sun, cloud, thunder, lightning, snow, tornado, hurricane, blizzard, thermometer, rain gauge, water cycle, condensation, evaporation, predict, ice crystals, precipitation, thunderstorms, etc.

Intermediate: air mass, cumulus, cirrus, stratus, stratocumulus, cumulonimbus, cumulocirrus, cumulostratus, cold front, warm front, barometer, hygrometer, humidity, accumulation, hail, sleet, Fahrenheit, Celsius, high pressure, low pressure, wind chill factor, psychometer, anemometer, etc. [DL—Use the primary level words.]

Middle School: altostratus, altocumulus, nimbostratus, hexagonal snow crystal, turbulence, etc. [DL—Use the primary and intermediate level words.]

LEARNING LOG

During the thematic unit of study, have students write an entry each day in their science or weather learning log. Have them include new weather terms, new information, and concepts they have acquired through the unit of study; the current temperature outside; cloud formations; and any predictions they have about a change in the weather. [Assessment: Note number and accuracy of entries. Have students correct any misspellings.]

EXPOSITORY WRITING ASSIGNMENT

I/MS—Have the students write a descriptive or explanatory piece about some aspect of weather after they have done some research on their topic. Some example topics include:

What is a tornado?—Student could make a tornado out of a 2-liter soda container, water, and food coloring to share as a demonstration along with the research paper.

What is the water cycle?
What causes lightning?
How do oceans affect weather?
What affect does low pressure have on weather conditions?
What are the different types of clouds and what do they mean?
What is wind sheer?
What conditions must be present for a blizzard to occur?
How does humidity impact humans and animals?

[Assessment: Have the class work with you to create an appropriate rubric based on the six traits of writing.]

BIBLIOGRAPHY INFORMATIONAL BOOKS

Barrett, N. (1989). *Picture Library: Hurricanes and Tornadoes.* New York: Watts. (P/I/MS–NF)
Bramwell, M. (1994). *Earth Science Library: Weather.* (C. Forsey, Illus.). New York: Watts. (I/MS–NF)
Branley, F.M. (1983). *Rain and Hail.* (H. Barton, Illus.). New York: HarperCollins. (P/I–NF–PB)
———. (1985). *Flash, Crash, Rumble, and Roll* (B. & E. Emberly, Illus.). New York: HarperCollins. (P/I–NF–PB)
———. (1987). *It's Raining Cats and Dogs.* (T. Kelley, Illus.). New York: HarperCollins. (P/I–NF–PB)

————. (1988). *Tornado Alert.* (G. Maestro, Illus.). New York: HarperCollins. (P/I–NF–PB)

Cole, J. (1986). *Magic School Bus at the Waterworks.* (B. Degen, Illus.). New York: Scholastic. (P/I–F/NF–PB)

Day, J. A. (1998). *Peterson First Guide to Clouds and Weather.* Boston: Houghton Mifflin. (MS)

de Paola, T. (1985). *The Cloud Book.* New York: Holiday House. (P–NF–PB)

Freier, G. (1992). *Weather Proverbs.* New York: Fisher. (I/MS–NF)

Gibbons, G. (1987). *Weather Forecasting.* New York: Four Winds. (P–NF–PB)

Grazullis, T. P. (2001). *The Tornado: Nature's Ultimate Windstorm.* Norman, OK: University of Oklahoma. (MS–NF)

Lehr, P. E. (2001). *Weather.* New York: St. Martin's Press. (MS–NF)

Lockhart, G. (1988). *The Weather Companion.* New York: Wiley. (MS–NF)

Martin, J. B. (1998). *Snowflake Bentley.* (M. Aazarian, Illus.). Boston: Houghton Mifflin. (P/I/MS–NF–PB)

Murphy, J. (2000). *Blizzard: The Storm That Changed America.* New York: Scholastic. (I/MS–NF)

Simon, S. (1989). *Storms.* New York: Scholastic. (I/MS–NF–PB)

————. (1999). *Lightning.* New York: Scholastic. (I/MS–NF–PB)

————. (1999). *Tornadoes.* New York: Scholastic. (I/MS–NF–PB)

————. (2000). *Weather.* New York: Scholastic. (I/MS–NF–PB)

Singer, M. (2000). *On the Same Day in March: A Tour of the World's Weather.* (F. Lessac, Illus.). New York: HarperCollins. (P–NF–PB)

Spier, P. (1997). *Peter Spier's Rain.* New York: Yearling. (P–NF–PB)

Stojic, M. (2000). *Rain.* New York: Crown. (P–NF–PB)

Vasquez, T. (1996). *Weather Forecasting Handbook,* 4th ed. New York: Weather Graphic Technologies.

Ward, A. (1992). *Project Science: Sky and Weather.* (A. Pang & R. Turvey, Illus.). New York: Watts. (I/MS–NF)

Webster, V. (1982). *A New True Book: Weather Experiments.* Chicago: Children's Press. (P/I–NF)

Williams, J. (1997). *The Weather Book,* 2nd ed. New York: Vintage. (MS–NF)

MAGAZINES

National Geographic (MS)
National Geographic World (P/I)
Weatherwise (I/MS)

WEBSITES

AccuWeather (life radar)	www.nws.noaa/gov
Bill Nye the Science Guy	www.nyelabs.kcts.org
The Exploratorium	www.exploratorium.edu
Farmer's Almanac	www.almanac.com
FEMA for Kids	www.fema.gov/kids
National Severe Storms Laboratory	www.nssl.noaa.gov/edu

Science Fair Project Resource Guide	www.ipl.org/youth/project
Storm Fax	www.stormfax.com
Weatherbug	www.weatherbug.com
Weather Here and There	www.ncsa.uiuc.edu/eduRSE
Weatherwise	www.weatherwise.org
The Weather Channel	www.weather.com

Summary

Narrative and poetic text opens the door to imaginative worlds for students. Readers make connections between text and self, text and text, and text and the world as they gain new understandings. As teachers, we need to help all students—boys and girls, good readers and struggling readers—find books they enjoy reading for pleasure. This is the key to lifelong reading.

Reading and writing workshops enable students to apply narrative and poetic reading and writing strategies as well as appreciate and incorporate the writing styles of favorite authors and poets. Through such workshops, mini-lessons also develop students' writing tools, including the six traits of writing (ideas, organization, word choice, sentence fluency, voice, and conventions).

Poetry adds to the richness of language. Students gain vocabulary and learn the importance of word choice through the sharing of poetry. Through oral interpretation, students can also gain reading fluency skills.

Chapter Review

Go to the Online Learning Center at **www.mhhe.com/farrisreading** to take chapter quizzes, practice with key terms, and review important content.

Main Points:

- Narrative and poetic text offers aesthetic reading experiences for children as well as often providing expository information.

- Girls prefer to read narrative text (chapter books, novels) for pleasure more frequently than boys.

- Connections can be made as students perceive links between text and their own lives, text and text, and text and the world at large.

- Hearing well-phrased quality literature read aloud by the teacher serves as models for future writing attempts by students.

- Students are the best promoters of books as they offer candid, enthusiastic critiques to their peers.

- Students develop preferences for certain genres, so the teacher must try to meet student interests as well as broaden those interests by doing book talks and read-alouds of fine literature from all genre.

- There are six writing traits: ideas, organization, word choice, sentence fluency, voice, and conventions.

- Organization and careful planning ahead are key ingredients to holding a successful reader's and writer's workshop.

- If what they are reading doesn't make sense, readers should raise questions about what the author says and means. This is the Questioning the Author (QtA) technique for gaining comprehension.

- When readers create scenarios and pictures in their heads, they are more involved in the stories as they may be living through the story or even pretending to be a part of it than if they simply read the book.

- Poetry demands total response from the individual—all the intellect, senses, emotion, and imagination. It does not tell *about* an experience as much as it invites its hearers to *participate in* the experience.

- The ability to read at a moderate or faster pace while comprehending the text is a strength of good readers. This ability is referred to as reading fluency.

Key Terms

alliteration	515	narrative text	483
aesthetic	483	poetic text	483
book talk	486	reader's theater	526
fluency	525	rhyme	515
gender	491	rhythm	515
metaphor	515	simile	515
meter	515		

Reflecting and Reviewing

1. What children's books are best to have your students read and make connections to their own lives? To other books? To the world?

2. What mini-lessons can be created to aid students to teach them the conventions of writing?

535

3. What are your strengths in the knowledge of children's literature as it relates to other texts and to the world? How can you develop a plan to become more familiar with children's literature?

4. What narrative books are good to share to promote cultural fairness and equity in the classroom?

5. In what ways can reading and writing of narrative text be combined with poetry?

Children's Literature

For annotations of the books listed below, please see Appendix A.

Avi. (1995). *Poppy.* (B. Floca, Illus.). New York: Orchard.

Babbitt, Natalie. (1975). *Tuck Everlasting.* New York: Farrar, Straus, and Giroux.

Bang, Molly. (1999). *When Sophie Gets Angry, Really, Really, Angry.* New York: Scholastic.

Bridwell, Norman. (1986). *Clifford, the Big Red Dog.* New York: Scholastic.

Christopher, Christopher, & Christopher, James. (1992). *With Every Drop of Blood.* New York: Delacorte.

Cleary, Beverly. (1965). *The Mouse and the Motorcycle.* (L. Darling, Illus.). New York: Morrow.

———. (1989). *Strider.* New York: Morrow.

DiCamillo, Kate. (2000). *Because of Winn-Dixie.* New York: Candlewick.

Dorris, Michael. (1992). *Morning Girl.* New York: Hyperion.

Ehlert, Lois. (1989). *Color Zoo.* New York: Lippincott.

———. (1990). *Color Farm.* New York: Lippincott.

Fleischman, Paul. (1988). *Joyful Noise: Poems for Two Voices.* New York: Harper and Row.

Fleming, Denise. (1993). *In the Small, Small Pond.* New York: Holt.

Florian, Douglas. (1999). *Laugh-eteria.* Orlando: Harcourt Brace.

George, Kristine O'Connell. (1997). *The Great Frog Race and Other Poems.* (K. Kiesler, Illus.). Boston: Clarion Books/Houghton Mifflin.

Gollub, Matthew. (1998). *The Life and Poems of Issa* (K. G. Stone, Illus.). New York: Lee and Low.

Henkes, Kevin. (1999). *The Birthday Room.* New York: Greenwillow.

Hoberman, M. (2001). *You Read to Me, I'll Read to You.* New York: HarperCollins.

Holm, Jennifer. (1999). *Our Only May Amelia.* New York: HarperCollins.

Houston, Gloria. (1998). *Bright Freedom's Song: A Story of the Underground Railroad.* San Diego: Harcourt Brace.

Howe, Deborah, & Howe, James. (1983). *Bunnicula.* (L. Morrill, Illus.). New York: Atheneum.

Jacques, Brian. (1987). *Redwall.* (G. Chalk, Illus.). New York: Philomel.

———. (2000). *The Legend of Luke.* New York: Philomel.

Jarrell, R. (1964). *The Bat-Poet.* (M. Sendak, Illus.). New York: MacMillan.

Kirk, D. (1994). *Miss Spider's Tea Party.* New York: Scholastic.

———. (1995). *Miss Spider's Wedding.* New York: Scholastic.

Kuskin, Karla. (1975). *Near the Window Tree.* New York: Harper & Row.

Locker, Thomas. (1998). *Home: A Journey through America.* Orlando: Harcourt Brace.

Mora, Pat. (1996). *Confetti.* (E. O. Sanchez, Illus.). New York: Lee and Low.

Naylor, Phyllis R. (1991). *Shiloh.* New York: Atheneum.

Nye, Naomi Shihab. (1995). *The Tree Is Older Than You Are.* New York: Simon & Schuster.

O'Dell, Scott. (1988). *Black Star, Bright Dawn.* New York: Fawcett.

O'Neill, Mary. (1989). *Hailstones and Halibut Bones* (J. Waller, Illus.). New York: Doubleday.

Paterson, Katherine. (1977). *Bridge to Terabithia.* New York: Crowell.

Paulsen, Gary. (1985). *Dogsong.* New York: Simon & Schuster.

———. (1990). *Woodsong.* New York: Scholastic.

———. (1994). *Winterdance: The Fine Madness of Running the Iditarod.* New York: Harcourt Brace.

Prelutsky, Jack. (1995). *A Pizza the Size of the Sun.* (J. Stevenson, Illus.). New York: HarperCollins.

Prelutsky, J. (2000). *It's Raining Pigs and Noodles* (J. Stevenson, Illus.). New York: Greenwillow.

Rathmann, Peggy. (1995). *Officer Buckle and Gloria.* New York: Putnam.

———. (1999). *Ten Minutes Till Bedtime.* New York: Putnam.

Rawls, Wilson. (1961). *Where the Red Fern Grows.* New York: Doubleday.

Shaw, Nancy. (1985). *Sheep in a Jeep.* (M. Shaw, Illus.). Boston: Houghton Mifflin.

Silverstein, Shel. (1974). *Where the Sidewalk Ends.* New York: HarperCollins.

———. (1981). *A Light in the Attic.* New York: HarperCollins.

———. (1996). *Falling Up.* New York: HarperCollins.

Smith, Roland. (1999). *The Captain's Dog: My Journey with the Lewis and Clark Tribe.* San Diego: Harcourt.

Steptoe, Javaka. (1997). *In Daddy's Arms I Am Tall: African Americans Celebrating Fathers.* New York: Lee and Low.

White, E. B. (1970). *Trumpet of the Swan.* New York: Harper Row.

Wood, A. (1984). *The Napping House.* New York: Harcourt Brace.

Classroom Teaching Resources

Day, F. (1999). *Multicultural voices in contemporary literature.* Portsmouth, NH: Heinemann.

Harvey, S., & Goudvis, A. (2000). *Strategies that work: Teaching comprehension to enhance understanding.* York, ME: Stenhouse.

Heard, G. (1999). *Awakening the heart: Exploring poetry in elementary and middle school.* Portsmouth, NH: Heinemann.

———. (2002). *The revision toolbox: Teaching Techniques that Work.* Portsmouth, NH: Heinemann.

Hopkins, L. B. (1998). *Pass the poetry, please* (rev. ed.). New York: HarperCollins.

Huck, C. S., Hepler, S., Hickman, J., & Kiefer, B. Z. (2004). *Children's literature in the elementary school.* Boston: McGraw-Hill.

Janeczko, P. (1999). *How to write poetry.* New York: Scholastic.

Meinbach, A. M., Rothlein, L., & Fredericks, A. D. (2000). *The complete guide to thematic units: Creating the integrated curriculum* (2nd ed.). Norwood, MA: Christopher-Gordon.

Monahan, M. B. (2003). "On the lookout for language": Children as language detectives. *Language Arts, 80* (3), 206–214.

Routman, R. (2000). *Kids' poems: Teaching first graders to love writing poetry.* New York: Scholastic.

———. (2000). *Kids' poems: Teaching fourth graders to love writing poetry.* New York: Scholastic.

———. (2000). *Kids' poems: Teaching kindergartners to love writing poetry.* New York: Scholastic.

———. (2000). *Kids' poems: Teaching second graders to love writing poetry.* New York: Scholastic.

———. (2000). *Kids' poems: Teaching third graders to love writing poetry.* New York: Scholastic.

"Nonfiction books keep us as enthusiastic, excited, and involved in learning as they do our students. We learn little and are challenged less when we use texts and workbooks that are, no matter how their titles or publishers change, virtually the same each year—someone else's plan for Everychild. In all my years of teaching, I have yet to meet Everychild."

Beverly Kobrin, educator of parents and children who advocates using nonfiction books in the classroom

CHAPTER 12

Connecting Reading and Writing: Expository Text

Key Ideas

- **Expository text** is different from narrative text. Readers benefit from applying specific strategies to better help them understand this fact-filled, informational text.

- Expository text is one of the "survival tools" students can use to try to stay on top of the burgeoning information that is inherent in the current Information Age.

- Writing is a tool for learning. Students can utilize this tool when they are working in journals, creating an original work, or taking the words of others and rethinking them on paper as they write reports and develop content area presentations across curriculum.

- Children's literature can be used to introduce the world of expository reading and writing. It also serves as a model for young writers to follow as they learn how to use expository writing themselves.

- Cognitive psychologists support interdisciplinary teaching as the best way to facilitate a broad understanding of topics for students. A bonus of this approach is that integrating subjects is a wise use of class time.

- Because interdisciplinary teaching invites the use of a variety of materials at different levels of difficulty, it offers more opportunities for success for learners with diverse needs.

- Technology opens the door to the most current knowledge in the content subjects and provides appealing opportunities to learn across the miles or to publish polished works.

Questions to Ponder

- How does expository reading and writing differ from narrative reading and writing?
- How do you build a schema or cognitive foundation for expository writing?
- Why might expository text present a challenge for most students in general and for those with differing learning needs in particular?
- What are some specific suggestions for making learning within expository materials engaging and memorable?
- What tools can students use when writing their own expository pieces?
- How can writing skills be expanded using expository materials?
- What is interdisciplinary teaching and how is it accomplished?
- How might one aid readers with diverse learning needs as they interact with expository materials?
- How does technology expand the opportunities for learning in content area subjects?

Peering into the Classroom

Getting to Know You

There is a hint of fall in the air, and the energy level is high in the sixth grade classroom we will be visiting today. Mrs. O initiates the day's lesson by saying, "Today we are going to begin the process of getting to know each other much better, and we're going to do that in an interesting and unusual way. We are going to play Human Bingo." Smiling at the surprised faces and a few raised eyebrows from the students surrounding her, she continues, "Take the two sheets of 8½ by 11 inch white paper that the student helpers have just passed out and follow along carefully as I show you how to fold your bingo playing card. This, by the way, is a great lesson in listening and being able to follow my directions."

Beginning with the first sheet, the students fold their papers in half, crosswise, once and then again. They open them and refold their papers in half lengthwise, and then refold them lengthwise one more time. Opening them and spreading them flat, they now have two sheets neatly divided into thirty-two squares, one to be designated for each student in the class. Quickly surveying the group, Mrs. O sees that everyone has completed the first step with ease.

As she turns to the overhead transparency and prepares to write, she explains that it is time to do some brainstorming. Mrs. O queries, "If you wanted to get to know someone better, what three questions would you ask them? Take a few minutes to record your questions on a piece of notebook paper. Then we'll share your ideas." Quiet ensues while some students stare thoughtfully off into space and others immediately begin to write. After three or four minutes, the teacher asks for suggestions. Volunteers readily recite their questions, and Mrs. O notes key ideas on the overhead. Next, she asks willing students to come up to the chalkboard and neatly write their favorite question down. Before long quite an interesting list has been completed. By scanning ideas on both the overhead and the chalkboard, students refocus on their particular questions, polishing them up for the following step.

Mrs. O continues, "For the next part of our preparations, you are to pick three questions you like best, those that you came up with on your own or some that other classmates have contributed. Write all three neatly on the 5 by 8 index card I am passing out to each of you. These will be the questions you will ask as you interview sixteen of your classmates over the next week, filling in one per square on your bingo sheets. Remember, you do not have much space in which to write the answers. Take advantage of short phrases and select key words that will really capture the person on paper."

When the questions have been prepared, Mrs. O reminds her sixth grade students to employ good interviewing techniques, including staying on task, and of the importance of giving the person being interviewed your undivided attention. The students are directed to pick a classmate and begin their initial interview. The remaining class time today is spent on two interviews before time runs out and the class must regroup and prepare for P. E. It was a busy and productive morning. These were certainly engaged students, weren't they?

While the students are gone, we have a few minutes to talk to Mrs. O. She explains that this is one of her favorite projects. Year after year the students quickly become involved, and the resulting appreciation for their classmates lasts throughout the year and beyond. We learn that over the next week or so, time will be devoted to completing the Human Bingo sheets. Eventually two students will pair up, and the interviews become the roots of an introductory presentation to the class. To make the process fair and to ensure that no one's feelings get hurt, students draw numbers from a crazy hat, part of Mrs. O's collection of unique hats that pop up now and again for various activities throughout the year. Students match their numbers and a pair is formed. Each pair's interview is fleshed out in writing, no more than several paragraphs in length, before students present each other to the class.

At interview time, the students sit in a large circle, with the day's first pair of interviewers seated together. Several children are introduced in front of the class per day until each student has had time in the spotlight. This is where the Bingo aspect comes in. As a student is interviewed, the other students quickly check their sheets. If they, too, asked a similar question about that person, they put a small X in the appropriate square. As the interviews proceed, they continue to X such squares until they have a column or row filled with Xs. At that point they raise their hands and say, "Bingo!" There is one more piece to note. When one person has completed his interview, the class goes around the circle and each one adds another new tidbit from his or her Bingo sheet about that person. Isn't this a great way to meet your classmates?

Eventually a selection of written interviews, snapshots of each student, and a sampling of Bingo Cards are displayed on a bulletin board of personalities to be reviewed and enjoyed at one's leisure. What a gem of an idea to build a sense of community in this classroom, to strengthen interpersonal skills, and to build writing and vocabulary learning in an authentic multilayered learning activity.

REFLECTION: IRA/NCTE NATIONAL STANDARDS IN THE CLASSROOM

While the research involved in the particular activity is not of the type that requires reading various textbooks and consulting a variety of additional resources, in a sense, these researchers are reading each other. They are gathering data from a living resource, using their language skills to capsulize data into concise bits to be fleshed out later in a paragraph about one person they interviewed. One of the standards illustrated through this classroom visit is Standard 4 as it relates to the expressive vocabularies of these learners (IRA/NCTE, 1996, p. 3):

> Students adjust their use of spoken, written, and visual language (e.g., conventions, style, vocabulary) to communicate with a variety of audiences for different purposes.

This interviewing process is also undergirded by the closely related Standard 12, which states that:

> Students use spoken, written, and visual language to accomplish their own purposes (e.g., for learning, enjoyment, persuasion, and the exchange of information).

In addition, depending on the diversity in the classroom, Standard 9 might come into play, as students learn about different cultures and ethnic backgrounds on a personal basis from a classmate:

> Students develop an understanding of and respect for diversity in language use, patterns, and dialects across cultures, ethnic groups, geographic regions, and social roles.

In this case, students were creating their own "texts," but as we spend more time in this classroom, we will see how written texts of all kinds fill the classroom hours and spill over into time outside of class as students tie those two worlds together. Whenever we drop in on this classroom and interact with these sixth graders, we are guaranteed to learn from a master teacher and intellectually absorbed learners. It is an exciting place to be as an authentic learning activity grows out of flesh-and-blood resources carried forth by motivated sixth graders. Throughout their days much of the work in Mrs. O's class involves the integration of fiction and nonfiction along with the daily events of life. Can you see how this memorable learning experience is supported by the National Standards?

INTRODUCTION

When faced with reading a chapter in a social studies or science textbook, numerous students in upper elementary and middle school react with dismay. This material does not resemble the picture book or novel they just completed reading. It doesn't have that familiar ease of flow, the recognizable plot and main character, or an imaginary setting. Instead, this information is presented in chunks separated by headings in boldfaced type. There are illustrations of a sort, but they are in the form of photographs, charts, graphs, sketches, diagrams, maps, and the like. The vocabulary is more technical and often unfamiliar. In addition, the concept load or number of new

STANDARDS for READING PROFESSIONALS

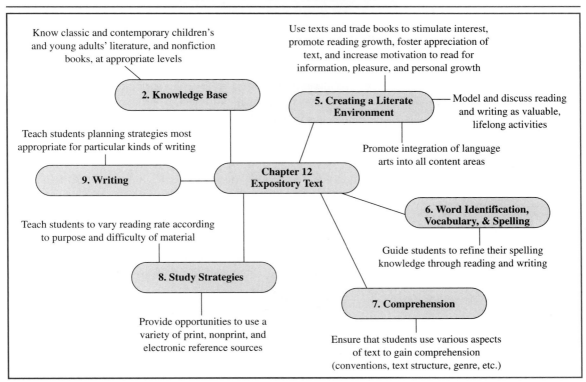

ideas presented to the reader has increased (Atwell, 1990). For many a child, getting through this text with a satisfactory level of comprehension can be tough.

To add to the difficulties, there may be a summary of what was just presented in the chapter followed by vocabulary words to identify and specific questions to answer in place of a neatly resolved conclusion to a fast-paced story. Students simply don't find the same type of coherence in expository textbooks as they do in their narrative reading experiences. Compounding the level of difficulty is the fact that content area textbooks assume that all readers have ready access to an unrealistic level of background knowledge, a challenging problem considering the wide range of diversity in today's classrooms (Good & Brophy, 2000; McKeown, Beck, & North, 1993).

What a different experience for readers as they enter the domain of **expository text**. It needn't be an overwhelming, anxiety-producing experience, however. The following chapter presents strategies to unlock what is initially a puzzling format, offers ideas for connecting reading and writing in this domain, briefly explores interdisciplinary teaching, and includes a variety of suggestions for nonfiction literature to motivate even the most resistant reader and writer.

BUILDING AN EXPOSITORY TEXT SCHEMA

Perhaps part of the difficulty with understanding expository text and its learning potential lies in the fact that it is not what children have been brought up on from kindergarten onward. Instead, narrative reading pervades the elementary school curriculum (Campbell, Kapinus, & Beatty, 1995; Read, 2001; Worthy, 2001). However, with the continual demand for more information about a multitude of topics, the time is ripe for a change in that practice. There is such a wealth of engrossing, attractive expository material available for readers from kindergarten through adulthood. To make reading it as natural as it is to read narrative text, infuse it into the curriculum. Model numerous ways to use it, and conscientiously teach the skills inherent in understanding this type of text (IRA/NCTE, 1996). It seems logical that if children are to even have a hope at keeping in touch with the explosion of information inherent in the Information Age, they must become supremely comfortable with the realm of expository text (Moss, Leone, & Dipillo, 1997). Not only could the initial knowledge gained be a key to unlock doors for future opportunities, but seeking out additional informational resources expands the content presented in textbooks by updating it and adding depth. Finally, well-written text quenches individual curiosities and provides fascinating fodder for research, reports, and required writing assignments.

Not every nonfiction trade book is appropriate for classroom use, however. Diana Rice (2002) cautions teachers to select content area trade books with care. While she focuses her comments on books for use in teaching science, the suggestions hold true for other content area courses. Rice explains that it is possible to select titles that are appealingly written but contain misinformation. Thus, books selected to introduce a unit in science must be carefully scrutinized for accuracy in addition to current content and appeal to readers. To be precise,

Web Links:
Expository Paragraph Frames

Expository Text K–6

Trade books should supplement, not supplant quality science texts; they should be picked with care, not swept en mass from the library shelf. Teachers must have a clear idea of their objectives and the specifics of how a particular trade book will be used with instruction. (Rice, 2002, p. 563)

A teacher's work is not done yet. In addition, he must ensure that students make correct connections between their prior knowledge and the new knowledge offered in the book in order that misconceptions do not occur. Assuredly, superb titles strengthen the science curriculum as they allow students to build literacy skills like predicting and organizing right alongside science activities including hypothesizing, gathering and organizing data, and drawing conclusions.

It is important to teach students that expository text has a job to do. When it is well done, they can expect such text to (Piazza, 2003),

- inform, report, or explain
- be precise and accurate in its explanations
- give examples to clarify concepts
- define unfamiliar concepts and vocabulary
- clearly differentiate between facts and opinions
- emphasize important points
- provide technically sound information
- pose clear and relevant questions
- explain and support any legitimate differences in information that arise

One simple but effective tactic to broaden the exposure to expository text and to build a schema, or cognitive foundation, for understanding it is by introducing books as part of the classroom read-aloud routine on a regular basis (Brozo & Simpson, 1995; Kobrin, 1995; Worthy, 2002). In this way you will be developing a familiarity with fact-filled text. Furthermore, you will be "reading different authors aloud . . . which provides different voices and topics for the children to sample" (Graves, 1983, p. 29). That in itself is a sound reason to share these books aloud because you are providing excellent models for learners to emulate in future writing projects. Real writers—what masterful teachers for us to follow (McElveen & Dierking, 2000/2001).

The chosen read-aloud for the day might be something that is just for fun. *Eye Count: A Book of Counting Puzzles* (Bourke, 1995) takes readers from the numbers one to twelve while hunting for uniquely related treasures within the illustrations. The reader must match the number on the double-page spread to words that are homophones or homonyms. How many kinds of jacks can the reader find in the illustrations? Are there really twelve "eyes" on the last two pages? You may find that this unique book presents an irresistible opportunity for just a quick review of homophones or homonyms in the process.

At another time, the selection might be a nonfiction title that ties into a current unit of study. Primary grade students who often engage in units of study about dinosaurs will enjoy *The News about Dinosaurs* (Lauber, 1989). Just read a few snippets of information comparing what was once believed with what has more recently been discovered and get ready for questions, questions, questions. Inquisitive learners will be compelled to find out the truth, so be certain to have the materials and ideas for directions in which to focus student research efforts close at hand.

Next, have other interesting titles or unit-related books available for students to choose in the classroom reading center. As many as one-fourth to one-half of the books in every classroom's reading center should be expository text (Moss et al., 1997). Book talk those titles and change them periodically in an effort to encourage students to read some nonfiction every day (Dreher, 1998/1999). When reading these books aloud, they should be read a little differently than a narrative selection. Depending on the density of information, read a page or two or a paragraph or two, and then show students how you think about what you have read. Think aloud about how interesting a fact might be to you and wonder aloud where you could learn more, how that information was discovered, or how you might use it in some way (Worthy, 2001). Explain a particularly interesting graph or demonstrate how a book lends itself to problem-solving skills. In this manner, you are demonstrating how one interacts differently with expository text and the steps you can take to make sense of it.

Web Link:
Expository Text

Do not ignore magazines (see magazines listed later in the chapter in Figure 12.8 on page 564). These periodicals offer short, informative articles on a vast array of topics. They appeal to learners with a variety of reading abilities and interests, providing practice in reading nonfiction in an unintimidating format. In fact, after reviewing research on what intermediate-grade students prefer to read, Jo Worthy (2002) found magazines high on their list of favorites. Magazines provide you with an opportunity to examine different viewpoints on a particular topic, a fine way to hone students' critical thinking skills as they evaluate who is right. Selected articles can be provided for additional practice with the graphic organizers discussed in this chapter. Not to be overlooked is that often the information is extended through superb photographs, a subtle way to polish visual literacy skills at the same time students are developing a comfort level with expository text.

Finally, periodically review students' reading records to monitor the balance between fiction and nonfiction. When necessary, remind readers to explore expository materials during their free reading time in addition to using them as resources for research. If a reading interest inventory has been completed by the students at the beginning of the year, it is easy to direct a reader to a nonfiction topic of personal interest (see Figure 12.1). A trip to the learning center or library to discover where nonfiction materials are shelved is a wise use of class time. Once there, you will be in for a pleasant surprise because nearly 60 to 70 percent of the materials in most libraries fall under the nonfiction umbrella (Cullinan & Galda, 1998). With so much to choose from, it is not difficult to infuse the curriculum with contemporary, high-quality expository reading materials. For guidance in selecting the best titles, see the evaluation criteria developed by Sudol and King (1996) at the end of the chapter (Figure 12.14). By following the preceding suggestions, you begin to create an atmosphere of interest and familiarity with informational text, providing the schema or foundation upon which to teach new strategies for reading, writing, and learning (Jensen, 1998).

Figure 12.1

A sample reading interest inventory:
What are your special interests?

Name _____   Date _____

Please answer the following questions on notebook paper and staple your work to this form. Place the completed Interest Inventory in your reading folder.

1. What do you like to do in your free time?
2. Are you involved in any sports activities?
3. How much time do you spend watching television? What are your favorite shows?
   a. Playing video or computer games?
   b. Which games are your favorites and why?
4. Do you have access to a computer and the Internet? If so, which sites do you enjoy?
5. If you could have three wishes, what would they be?
6. Who is your favorite person? Explain why.
7. If you could travel anywhere you wanted to go, where would that be? Why?
8. Which classes are your favorite in school?
9. Do you ever read the newspaper? If you do, which parts do you read?
10. Do you read magazines? Which magazines are the most enjoyable?
11. Name three of your favorite movies.
12. What kinds of books have you especially enjoyed reading?
13. What kinds of books would you like to try in the future?
14. Do you read to younger brothers or sisters? Do you have a family member who reads to you? If either case is true, what kinds of books do you like to read or to hear?
15. If one of your friends needed help in learning to read, how would you help them?

A LOOK AT THE BASIC ORGANIZATION OF EXPOSITORY TEXT

In order to learn to make sense of various kinds of expository text, students need to develop "content literacy" (p. 400), which according to Fountas and Pinnell (2001) includes the following abilities:

- Knowing what to expect from a text based upon its organizational structure
- Understanding various graphic features like those mentioned earlier in the chapter
- Realizing that the vocabulary is different and must be understood to grasp the concepts being taught
- Using critical thinking skills to analyze, organize, and relate new information to what is already known

Therefore, to be able to read, comprehend, and write expository text, specific skills must be taught and modeled.

Web Link:
Multi-Paragraph
Segmentation of
Expository Text

In addition, provide a scaffold or mental framework for future reading and writing by teaching elementary and middle school students that informational text has five basic **organizational patterns**: description, sequence, comparison and contrast, cause and effect, and problem and solution (Piccolo, 1987; Richardson & Morgan, 1997). Once the organizational patterns are understood, students will be able to locate and use information from text and be able to transfer that learning to their personal expository writing (Armbruster, Anderson, & Ostertag, 1989; McGee & Richgels, 1985; Tiedt, Tiedt, & Tiedt, 2001). Each pattern is explained in the following paragraphs. Because research supports the use of graphic organizers as one method for helping learners understand and recall expository text, a commonly used **graphic organizer** is presented for each pattern (Griffin & Tulbert, 1995; Merkley & Jeffries, 2000/2001). Students who profit from the visual presentation of information will particularly benefit from the use of graphic organizers. Useful to learners in general, graphic organizers are of particular help to students with learning disabilities and hearing impairments. These learners benefit from having information presented in several different ways so that they can better process it. Students with visual impairments work well with graphic organizers that have been enlarged. If the organizers are available on an enlarged computer screen, the student can readily type related information in a large, easily visible dark type (Cox & Dykes, 2001; Heilman, Blair, & Rupley, 2002).

A suggested practical sequence useful in teaching each organizational structure would include the following steps (Armbruster et al., 1989; Merkley & Jeffries, 2000/2001; Tompkins, 2000):

1. Identify and discuss the graphic organizer along with key words that signal which pattern is being used.

2. Teach students to identify the pattern by using examples of appropriate text from a textbook and a literature selection to demonstrate how the pattern appears in both kinds of books.

3. Model the process of using the corresponding graphic organizer on the overhead transparency or chalkboard with each text sample, students working right along with you on their own copies. Discuss the relationships between concepts presented in the graphic organizers to help students see connections between key points that are pulled from the text and duly noted on the graphic organizer. Invite students to tie these concepts to what they already know to strengthen comprehension.

4. Provide adequate time for independent practice, which is carefully monitored by the teacher. Students can work in pairs or triads with an additional informational book of their own, reading, discussing, looking for signal words, and completing the graphic organizer appropriately. Once the work is finished, groups can volunteer to share their learning with the rest of the class, reinforcing skills in the process. Student input is vital to the learning process.

5. An extension of this learning would be to have the students write an expository paragraph from content area subject matter currently under study. This provides personal practice in applying the newly gleaned knowledge of the particular structure to expository writing skills.

Expository text includes math, science, and social studies as well as art and music.

As with strengthening any other skill, time to practice each organizational pattern after it has been carefully modeled by the teacher will enable students to develop a facility in recognizing it and in making it their own. This time is not to be short-changed (Robb, 2003). Depending on the class, the modeling and practice sessions could extend from several days to a week. For students who need more guided practice, fill in pieces of the organizers so that they only have to focus on a few segments at a time. When it is appropriate, provide a small picture clue to help the learner with language processing difficulties or a hearing impairment pick the right tidbit of information. Whenever possible, encourage them to work with student buddies to discuss and practice each new graphic organizer.

Being surrounded by opportunities to learn benefits every learner. For English language learners, in particular, structuring learning activities that provide opportunities for listening, speaking, reading, and writing supported by teacher and classmates ensures the greatest academic development (Williams, 2001). Thus, organizers and conversation make a good learning partnership. Once all of the organizers have been taught, student understanding can be assessed by letting pairs or triads select an informational picture book from titles gathered ahead of time, read the book, look for the clues that denote the pattern being used, and complete the appropriate organizer. Writing a summary of the book tops off this assessment.

Description

An easy pattern with which to begin is **description**, a prominent information structure found in both textbooks and children's literature. (See Figure 12.2.) In this case,

Figure 12.2

A graphic organizer modeling description

Read the following segment about bats:

Night Fliers

After a day of resting, a bat wakes up and looks around. As it extends its limbs, the thin skin between the bones stretches tight to form the broad flight surface of the bat's wings. Despite their delicate appearance, the wings are strong and flexible and enable the bat to be an expert flier. Soon the bat will take off into the night, swooping and diving like an aerial acrobat as it searches for the insects that are its food. (Arnold, 1996, p. 4)

Look back through the paragraph for the words that describe the following items. Write those words in the blanks below:

the bat's limbs in sentence two:

(skin) _____

(wings) _____

more about wings in sentence three:

(appearance) _____

three facts about the wings

1. _____

2. _____

3. _____

describe how the bat flies from sentence four: _____

_____

What is the bat doing as it flies? _____

When you read nonfiction books, look for the ways an author describes his topic. Those words help you to visualize the topic, which helps you to better understand the text. Sometimes an author will give you a clue that a description is coming by using cue words like: for example, most important, or the following characteristics are . . .

Text Excerpt:

Arnold, Caroline. (1996). *Bats.* (R. Hewett, Photographer). New York: Morrow Junior Books.

the author points out specific characteristics, details, or features and provides examples for the reader. In the picture book by Seymour Simon (1998), *They Swim the Seas: The Mystery of Animal Migration,* Simon presents numerous descriptions of what tides, fish, sea turtles, and plant life are like in the ocean. For instance, the author describes sea turtles as having the characteristics of being green, feeding on seaweed and sea grasses, weighing up to 800 pounds, and living solitary lives. Tuna are portrayed as streamlined oceanic fish that can reach speeds of over 50 miles an hour. They live in large schools that hunt smaller fish and squid as daily fare. All of these details are scientifically accurate and presented in an interesting manner that is appealing to the reader. Key words to watch for or to use in student writing could include "for example," " most important," or "the following characteristics are . . . "

Look at how effectively a seventh grade writer used description as he explained one of the reasons the Vikings' conquering quests took them far from home. The secret was in their ability to construct seaworthy vessels:

> The Vikings were excellent at building ships and were considered to be the best ship builders of their time. Using wood cut from the vast forests of Scandinavia, their ships were very durable. Vikings developed the concept of a keel, a long, narrow piece of wood attached to the underside of the ship. The keel extended down into the water and ran along the entire length of the ship. The keel reduced a ship's rolling motion and so increased its speed and handling. Because of the use of keels in their ships, the Vikings could travel farther distances faster and did not need to stop as often for food and other supplies.

An author might use the following cue words to tell a reader that the text uses description to relate its information (Piazza, 2003):

a number of	as an example	characteristics are
features are	for example	for instance
several	small sized, medium sized,	
types of	or large sized	

Sequence

A second commonly used expository text structure involves information presented in a **sequence.** (See Figure 12.3). Learners should already have a solid schema for applying this organizational pattern based upon previous opportunities to put a narrative story into its proper sequence. In this instance, items or events are placed in an appropriate order. For example, in *Soaring with the Wind: The Bald Eagle,* Gail Gibbons (1998) outlines the mating habits of bald eagles from the initial high-pitched call of the courtship ritual to the building of a nest for the young. She uses words like "before," "after," and "finally" in her work. Other commonly used words include:

first	second	third	fourth	to begin with
then	later	not long after	next	also
at last	now	at the same time	following	since

Such signal words should be posted on a chart in the classroom for students to use in their own writing of sequential events such as in science experiments and observations as well as for biographies and reports in social studies. A poster might be created that includes key words useful in each of the expository writing structures.

Comparison and Contrast

Comparison and contrast is a third important text structure for students to recognize. (See Figure 12.4.) In using it, the author explains how two or more things may be alike or different. The easiest way to introduce this concept to young children is to make a Venn diagram from two hula hoops. Read about two things that are alike and

Figure 12.3

A graphic organizer to use with sequence

Text Sample:

The Underground Railroad

Leaving behind her family, Tubman headed for freedom. She hid in the woods during the day and traveled during the night. Follow her route on the map.

After many days and nights, Tubman found her way to Wilmington, Delaware. There she went to the home of Thomas Garrett.

Thomas Garrett was part of the *Underground Railroad.* This was not really a railroad, but a group of people who helped slaves escape to freedom. Often these people hid slaves in their homes. Garrett helped Tubman cross the border into Pennsylvania. Here slavery was against the law. Tubman was free!

Put the events above in order below using the cue words given. Then practice this pattern on another paragraph that lists events in a sequence. What other cue words could you use?

Event 1

(*First*) Tubman left her family and headed for freedom.

Event 2

(*Second*) She hid during the day and traveled by night.

Event 3

(*Third*) She reached Wilmington, Delaware.

Event 4

(*Next*) She went to the home of Thomas Garrett who helped slaves escape on the Underground Railway.

Event 5

(*Then*) Garret helped Tubman cross the border into Pennsylvania, a free state.

Event 6

(*Finally*) Tubman was free!

Now, tell a reading buddy how Harriet Tubman escaped to freedom using your cue words and the sequence pattern. A second option is to write a short summary in your learning log.

Excerpt from:

McGraw-Hill/National Geographic Society. (2000). *Regions: Adventures in Time and Place.* New York: McGraw-Hill School Division. p. 120.

have some differences, such as a comparison of sharks and dolphins after reading *Do You Know the Difference?* (Bischhoff-Miersch & Bischhoff-Miersch, 1995). Using yellow tagboard cards, write how the sharks and dolphins are alike and put the cards where the two hula hoops intersect. Write the differences between the animals using red tagboard cards for sharks and blue tagboard cards for dolphins. Put the red cards in the left hula hoop and the blue cards in the right hula hoop. The result is a clearly

Figure 12.4

A graphic organizer to use with comparison and contrast

When using the Venn diagram to compare and contrast a time period, regions, cultures, or other choices, list the differences in the outer circles. The similarities are to be written in the area where the circles overlap.

Teaching Strategy:
Venn Diagram

visual comparison and contrast of sharks and dolphins or a multitude of other items of choice. This initial information can be backed up by reading additional expository books such as *Whales and Dolphins* (Parker, 1994) or *Sharks* (Simon, 1995).

An easily visible chart of words to use when writing and discussing comparison and contrast could include words such as:

alike	the same as	different	in contrast
opposite	however	either . . . or	unlike
but	rather	on the other hand	as well as
although	likewise	nevertheless	yet
while	similarly		

Primary grade learners might also use the format illustrated in the example in Figure 12.5. The teacher and students read several books about bees and butterflies together. They made charts of the information they learned after reading. The facts were reviewed to be certain students understood the words and ideas. Then, they completed the data sheets shown. From that information, they wrote a simple summary of the similarities and differences between a bee and a butterfly. Listen for the author's voice already so prevalent in these young children's writing.

Figure 12.5

Logan's graph and expository writing

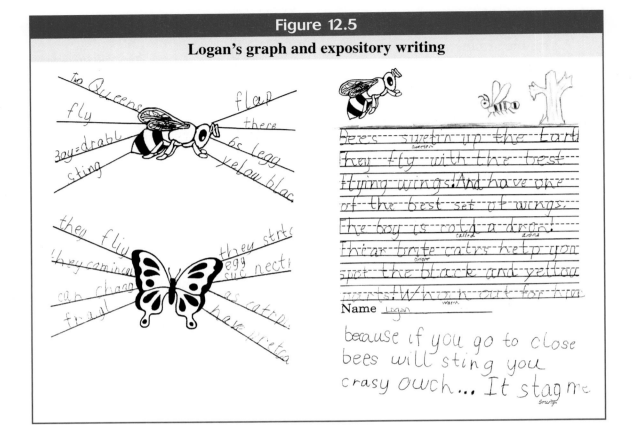

Teaching Strategy for the Classroom

USING A VENN DIAGRAM TO STUDY GEOGRAPHIC REGIONS IN THE MIDDLE GRADES

Older students can use a Venn diagram to focus their content area work. For example, in social studies they might be comparing and contrasting two different geographic regions in the United States such as deserts and the rich region in the Midwest known as the Heartland (Fuhler, 1998).

1. To begin the work, divide into two groups. Group 1 begins their fact-finding with *Mojave* (Siebert, 1988). Group 2 reads *Heartland* (Siebert, 1989). The books are written in poetic verse and rounded out with informative illustrations so that students can quickly get a sense of what it is like there. This is an essential part of the process of building geographic background visually and factually.

2. One student in each group reads the story aloud while classmates jot down pertinent characteristics.

3. Next, each group discusses what they have discovered together. They circle or star key descriptions of their area and prepare to share with the class as a whole.

4. The class gathers together. One group at a time gives an overview of their book and highlights main characteristics of their region. Students listen to each other, writing down any similarities between the two regions on scratch paper.

5. Next, a member from the first group writes "Mojave Desert" on one side of a large Venn diagram drawn on the chalkboard or on chart paper previously prepared for this lesson. One by one, main features of the region are named by group participants. If that same feature exists in the Heartland as well, it goes in the overlapping area.

6. Once all points are covered, a representative from the second group repeats the procedure, beginning with writing "The Heartland" in the other large segment of the Venn diagram. When this activity is finished, the teacher guides the discussion on the obvious similarities and differences between the areas. She then directs the two groups to additional reading to confirm and/or expand their knowledge of the two regions.

7. Additional resources include *A Desert Scrapbook: Dawn to Dusk in the Sonoran Desert* (Wright-Frierson, 1996) and *The Desert Alphabet Book* (Pallotta, 1994). Other views of the Heartland are proffered in *A Walk on the Prairie* (Johnson, 2001) and *If You're Not from the Prairie* (Bouchard, 1995). Once they get started, searchers will find a wealth of information to augment their understanding of two very different regions.

8. Upon completion of the reading students again share the wealth, recording additional information on the Venn diagram. Different colored ink or chalk might be used to denote the different resources, a corresponding key coded in one corner of the diagram.

9. Finally, students check their comprehension by summarizing what they have learned in a brief paragraph. For a more in-depth project, a natural writing extension might be an illustrated report on these regions, comparing and contrasting the areas and highlighting points with vivid illustrations. Students might opt to develop a slide presentation of a project they have researched using Kid Pix Studio where students illustrate their ideas using the computer.

10. One way to reinforce learning is by viewing segments of a video like *The Southwest* (Macmillan/McGraw-Hill, 1997) to understand a little more about the desert and *The Middle West* (Macmillan/McGraw-Hill, 1997) to view the prairies. These videos are available in both English and Spanish.

11. Extend learning by creating a travel brochure that highlights one of the states in this area. Students might focus on one or two destinations that include time to investigate a desert or prairie setting. They can begin gathering information from Excite Travel: Regions, picking a state and then clicking on "Explore the Area" to choose several interesting vacation stops. Using this site, airfares and car rental information can be added to the brochure along with pertinent scanned pictures. Select Online Adventures. The "Flight over Four Corners" will offer pictures and text about this stunning area, while "Underdogs: Prairie Dogs at Home" will provide a different perspective of the prairie. When research and brochures are complete, hold a Travel Fair and promote travel in these regions.

RESOURCES

Fuhler, C. J. (1998). *Discovering geography of North America with books kids love.* (Audra Loyal, Illus.). Golden, CO: Fulcrum.

Macmillan/McGraw-Hill. (1997). *Social studies videotapes: The Southwest.* New York: Macmillan/McGraw-Hill.

————. (1997). *Social studies videotapes: The Middle West.* New York: Macmillan/McGraw-Hill.

PICTURE BOOKS CITED

Bouchard, David. (1999). *If You're Not from the Prairie.* (H. Ripplinger, Illus.). New York: Atheneum.
    A view of life on the rural prairie is described in verse by someone who loves its beauty and extremes.

Johnson, Rebecca. (2001). *A Walk in the Prairie.* Minneapolis, MN: Carolroda Books.
    Plants, animals, and climate are described. Information is extended through color photos and simple sketches.

Pallotta, Jerry. (1994). *The Desert Alphabet Book.* (M. Astrella, Illus.). Watertown, MA: Charlesbridge Press.

Siebert, Diane. (1989). *Heartland.* (W. Minor, Illus.). New York: HarperTrophy.
    The bounty of the nation's Heartland where both author and illustrator have lived is depicted through verse and artwork.

————. (1992). *Mojave.* (W. Minor, Illus.). New York: HarperTrophy.
    The land and the animals that live in the Mohave Desert are described through poetry and lovely illustrations.

Wright-Frierson, Virginia. (1996). *A Desert Scrapbook: Dawn to Dusk in the Sonoran Desert.* New York: Simon & Schuster.
    The author, also an artist, describes a number of native plants and animals along with their surroundings.

ADAPTATIONS/MODIFICATIONS FOR DIVERSE LEARNERS

- Let students with ADD/ADHD type their responses on a Venn diagram on the computer using the website Create a Venn Diagram. If possible, enlarge the diagram so that a visually impaired child has clear access to it via computer as well.
- Invite the interested gifted student to research the areas. He can write and illustrate a travel brochure or book. Encourage the student to use multiple resources, assessing those that appear to be most accurate.
- Be aware that students with learning disabilities, mental retardation, or English language learners will need more scaffolding as they learn how to pull pertinent information for appropriate leveled text and how to place it in a Venn diagram.

Figure 12.6

A graphic organizer to use with cause and effect

Text Sample:

Crowding in the Desert

For a community such as Phoenix, growth can cause problems. Concrete sidewalks absorb more heat than the desert soil. As the city expands, it also grows hotter! The sidewalks can get as hot as 140° F.

Higher temperatures mean more air conditioners. Air conditioners use a lot of electricity. This can put a strain on the city's electricity supply. Most electricity is made from natural resources such as coal or water. When it's hot people also use more water— a precious resource.

To save water, some Phoenix citizens have stopped growing lawns. Instead they have planted cactus gardens in their yards. Perhaps they hope to learn a lesson about using resources from these desert plants!

Examine the paragraph above for the causes of the problems noted and the resulting effects. Then practice this pattern on another paragraph arranged to show cause and effect.

Cause: growth in Phoenix	*Effect 1:* more concrete sidewalks needed
Cause 2: concrete absorbs more heat than the desert soil	*Effect 2:* sidewalks get as hot as 140° F
Cause 3: increased temperatures	*Effect 3:* more air conditioners used, which strains the city's electric supply
Cause 4: need for electricity	*Effect 4:* depletes natural resources used to create electricity like coal and water
Cause 5: the need to preserve water	*Effect 5:* people grow cactus gardens instead of lawns that require watering

Now, write a summary paragraph showing cause and effect at work. Note the following cue words that help you organize your paragraph.

(Cause 1) Growth in Phoenix is leading to problems. *As a result* of this growth (effect 1), _____. *Because* (cause 2) _____ (effect 2) _____. *If* the temperatures increase, *then,* (effect 3) _____. The need for electricity (cause 4) *results* in (effect 4) _____. *This explains why* (effect 5) _____.

Excerpt from McGraw-Hill/National Geographic Society. (2000). *Regions: Adventures in Time and Place.* New York: McGraw-Hill School Division. p. 332.

Cause and Effect

Cause and effect is a slightly more complicated expository text pattern found frequently in intermediate and middle school level text, particularly in social studies and science content materials. (See Figure 12.6.) The writer describes a cause, or sometimes more than one cause, and the resulting effects. A possible introduction to this pattern is the topic of ecology and recycling. If people do not carefully dispose of their waste (cause), then the earth and its air and water will become polluted (effect), a message expertly depicted in *A River Ran Wild* (Cherry, 1992). Through text and detailed pictures readers learn the history of the Nashua River in New England. Because of man's relentless carelessness it gradually changed from a thing of beauty over the years to a mire of pollution. Fortunately, through concerted efforts and renewed wisdom (causes) about taking care of what earth provides, the river once again flows cleanly (effect). Words typically used for cause and effect writing include:

if/then	consequently	therefore	as a result
because	since	so that	the reasons why
hence	accordingly	thus	nevertheless

An excellent picture book to augment the science curriculum and to illustrate this pattern is *Summer of Fire: Yellowstone, 1988* (Lawber, 1991). What happens to start a forest fire? What is the effect of fire upon the forestland? Readers quickly recognize that fire (cause) brings about welcome change, facilitates diversity, and provides opportunity for new life (effects). In learning this organizational structure, begin with concrete examples that are easily visualized. They become stepping-stones to tackling more abstract examples that appear in content area texts on a regular basis.

Problem and Solution

Web Link:
Building Reading
Proficiency at the
Secondary Level

Finally, writers use **problem and solution** as another organizational pattern. (See Figure 12.7.) The writer describes a problem and then presents a solution or solutions. This may be in the form of a question/answer format as in *I See Animals Hiding* (Arnosky, 2000), which illustrates how camouflage (solution) aids in survival from day to day (problem). The pattern might be focused on a specific historical problem and suggested solutions as in *Amistad Rising: A Story of Freedom* (Chambers, 1998), which recounts how John Quincy Adams and Joseph Cinques aligned themselves to fight against racial injustice. This pattern of writing is used by students when they write about why the ice cream cone was invented during the St. Louis World's Fair; why Clara Barton, a nurse, went into the battlefields during the Civil War; or the need to carefully preserve beaches for current and future public use.

Portfolio Activity:
Graphic Organizers on
PowerPoint

Another topic to be broached in upper grades to build skills using the problem–solution format is the continued need to foster multicultural understanding. Using the newspaper or current periodicals as educational tools, students can bring in examples of problem–solution relationships that promote or impede interconnections between cultures. The roots of continuing misunderstandings might then be traced through history, again highlighting problems and the ensuing solutions. Taking thinking one step further, students could break into groups and analyze why the solutions were or were not effective, looking at alternatives as well. Commonly used words for this pattern include "the problem is . . . ," "the puzzle is solved," "the question is," "the answer is," or "the solution involved . . . "

In sum, whether students are identifying a problem–solution organizational structure or the others previously described, training in using text structure, graphic orga-

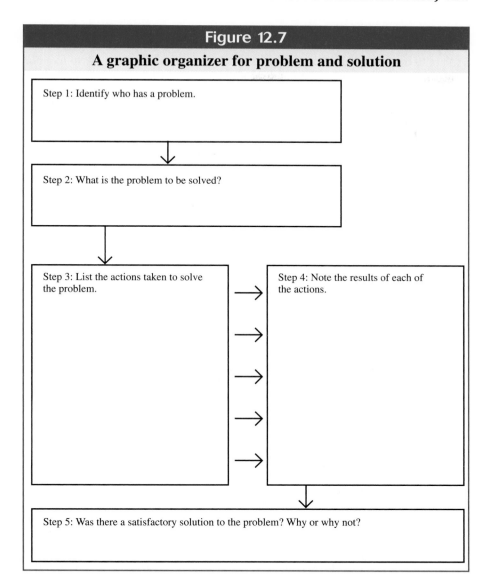

Figure 12.7

A graphic organizer for problem and solution

Step 1: Identify who has a problem.

Step 2: What is the problem to be solved?

Step 3: List the actions taken to solve the problem.

Step 4: Note the results of each of the actions.

Step 5: Was there a satisfactory solution to the problem? Why or why not?

nizers, and key signal words will improve both reading comprehension and student writing within expository text.

ADDITIONAL STRATEGIES FOR DISSECTING EXPOSITORY TEXT

While other practical strategies useful in aiding text comprehension were discussed in Chapter 8 on reading comprehension, there is a **metacognitive practice** that aids

Web Link:
Content, Domain, and
Word Knowledge

understanding of dense expository text which deserves special attention. Place the following steps on a classroom chart easily visible to all learners in the classroom. Explain to the class that you are going to teach them a technique to use to monitor their own understanding, to help them learn how to think about how well they are thinking (Fountas & Pinnell, 2001). Work through each step with the class, modeling aloud what thinking processes are going on in your head as you work through a sample text and each step (Combs, 2003):

- Before I read this text, what do I think it is going to be about?
- After looking over the text, what do I already know about the topic?
- Can I tell by skimming over the text what I might need to be thinking about in order to understand the author's message?
- As I read, am I finding important details?
- Which ideas seem to be the most important?
- Do these ideas fit with anything I already know?
- Should I readjust my thinking based upon what I have just learned?
- Now that I have completed the reading, what was it about?
- What parts of this text do I really need to remember?
- How can I further use these ideas?

Teaching Strategy:
Topic Word Board

It will take practice to make this metacognitive process a habit. Don't leave the acquisition of metacognition to chance alone. Ask students to check themselves from time to time, having them report how they are mastering the steps in a learning log or journal entry. Work through the process as a group periodically for several weeks in a row, then review it after a week or two in order to keep the self-monitoring process active and students personally connected to expository text as a result.

Finally, a simple strategy for conquering the meaning of expository text is to adjust one's reading rate. Model aloud for students how you might quickly read through narrative text, using a segment of the current class read-aloud or the book you have personally selected to read during independent reading time. Then, read a sample from an expository text, slowing down the reading, going back to reread a section that is more difficult, and then resuming the slower pace. This verbal demonstration will help students realize that it is all right to read some materials slowly in case they harbor the misconception that only poor readers are slow readers. An important comprehension strategy, altering reading rates depending on the demands of the text, is a relatively easy one to add to a reader's repertoire of skills.

THE READING–WRITING PARTNERSHIP

Once students are familiar with the different organizational patterns of expository text, and have several useful strategies to monitor their comprehension, take a different tack to be certain that students understand the text they are reading. Activate the closely related process of writing. Sylvia Read (2001, p. 334) remarks, "By providing opportunities to read and write using information texts, educators can strengthen students' understanding of the content they are researching *and* make the language arts an integral part of the learning process." Thus, content areas are tied together and interaction with the content is deepened. Perkins and Blythe (1993) underscore such interaction and reinforce the need to move beyond merely presenting students with information in content areas. That is not enough. Instead, you extend learning opportunities further to ensure that students:

- Retain important information
- Understand topics deeply rather than superficially
- Actively use the knowledge they gain on a regular basis

The writing process enables students to master all three as pointed out by Zinsser (1988) who notes,

> We write to find out what we know and want to say. I thought of how often as a writer I made clear to myself some subject I had previously known nothing about by just putting one sentence after another—by reasoning my way in sequential steps to its meaning. (pp. viii–ix)

When the focus turns to integrating the reading and writing of expository text, a variety of options to facilitate semantic processing are available. They include using the previously described graphic organizers in paragraph and report writing, and journaling or using learning logs. Students might also try paraphrasing materials in writing, outlining material to organize it, or developing time lines to get a sense of the progression of history. Using the previously described Venn diagrams and engaging in a variety of creative activities like those suggested in the interdisciplinary instructional unit at the end of the chapter offer still more reading–writing connections. A popular option for altering the classroom pace is to actively involve students in learning through role playing or engaging in class debates. A learner with ADD/ADHD might especially enjoy the opportunity to role-play a scenario in social studies. Capitalizing on the change of pace that helps to keep her focused and motivated plus the opportunity to move a little makes this mode of demonstrating learning most appealing (Carbone, 2001). In addition, gifted learners can excel in role playing or participate in carefully planned debates about issues in science or social studies. Here is a chance for this group of learners to engage in analysis and problem-solving abilities and to be creative at the same time. The next section takes a closer look at a selection of these reading–writing, information-processing strategies.

Possibilities for Expository Text: Informal Writing

After studying the traditional formats of expository text, students will feel more confident when tackling the writing of it themselves, because a familiarity and a comfort level have been established. Sage advice from Marilee Springer (1999, p. 29) reminds teachers that "the brain desires a safe environment in which to seek new information and experiences." By providing students with strategies for reading and then basing writing upon a better understanding of informational text, many a student will relish the different challenges posed by expository reading and writing within that comfort range.

When the quest becomes information gathering for reports, presentations, or projects of personal interest within fact-filled text, the requisite writing skills vary from the familiar narrative format. As students research and then pen a biography about an influential scientist, a famous statesman, or a leader in a country from afar, for example, they are immersed in expository text. The raw material for nonfiction writing is facts. When moving from reading to writing in content areas, those facts must be rethought, paraphrased, and presented in the students' own words.

Students begin rough-draft thinking on paper, gradually building their knowledge as they convert facts into their own words and connect new information with what they already know. This is an invaluable learning experience, as noted, because writing is a powerful tool for active learning no matter what the subject (Fulwiler, 1987; Moss et al., 1997; Robb, 1994). Janet Emig (1977) reinforces the writing–learning connection noting that writing in one's own words rather than copying directly from a resource demands the use of higher order thinking skills and results in deeper understanding and internalization of learning. The writing–learning connection may take the form of informal writing as well as polished reports or products on topics of interest.

 Students with language processing difficulties or the learner with mild mental retardation will need the expository reading–writing process carefully explained, demonstrated, and scaffolded (Ruiz, Vargas, & Beltrán, 2002). For example, the nonfiction books the students read about the topic under study might be picture books at their individual levels. Those books should be read several times because in the process of repeated reading, students are both understanding the information in the text and becoming familiar with the way it is written. Next, the writing connection should be modeled by the teacher. In sharing what they have learned from their reading, students might have the goal of writing a simple sentence or two initially. As skills grow, those sentences can be grouped together into a paragraph with a topic sentence to start them off. New vocabulary can be mastered at the same time within the context of what the students are reading, and then by using the new words in the follow-up writing (Heilman et al., 2002). Through this process, the learners are actively involved in the classroom study and are contributing successfully within the realm of their abilities.

Learning Logs across the Curriculum

When students write to record or react to what they are learning in art, math, music, physical education, science, or social studies in notebooks or journals, they are using **learning logs** (Atwell, 1990; Fulwiler, 1985). This is a fine example of informal expository writing. One important function of these logs is to enable students to select, connect, and organize information to help them better understand what they read (Koziol, Minnick, & Riddell, 1996). As they write in a content area subject, then, they are actually writing to learn. To be used effectively, students need to take the entries seriously, becoming active observers, thinkers, and writers. Not to be over-used, work in the logs is not required on a daily basis although students may choose to write in them that often.

Eliciting informal writing using logs gives teachers several options. They may use the logs to ask questions that tap prior knowledge, to encourage learners to interact closely with the text as they read, or to respond at the end of a particular class period by asking questions like the following:

- What did you learn today?
- What interested you?
- Is there something that confused you?
- What did you like about the lesson?
- How might you use the information you learned today?
- What connections can you make between today's lesson and what you already know?

A teacher might even ask students to write about a learning problem in one of their subject areas that they recently solved as a way of reinforcing the learning successes of students (Graves, 1989). The value of learning logs is not just that they require writing about a topic, of course. Within the pages of these journals or logs learners are able to "retain, re-collect, re-create, and reconstruct their thinking" through informal writing, a powerful connection between nonfiction text and the reader (Combs, 2003, p. 259).

Logs are a particularly effective tool for the gifted learner who can be encouraged to pose his own questions in the pages of the journal and begin a quest to find data to answer those questions, a tactic used by expert literacy teachers (Block, Oaker, & Hurt, 2002). Learners are often more motivated to dig for answers to some of their own questions than those that are routinely teacher-generated.

Learning logs help students to select, connect, and organize information.

Aside from probes by the teacher, this type of learning tool may include diagrams, vocabulary words and definitions, notes on how to accomplish a specific task, examples of concepts, and relationships between what the students are currently learning and their previous experiences in that content area. Students might pose questions, record interesting information, or summarize the day's learning within these pages. As you can see, these logs are excellent for data collection, but they have other uses.

Furthermore, learning logs become authentic assessment measures as teachers peruse them to assess student learning. They can be used to track students' questions, feelings, the strategies they try, and their reflection (Piazza, 2003). For example, after instructing students in a lesson, the teacher can request that students do a "quick write" in which they spend three to five minutes writing in their learning logs about the concept presented to demonstrate their understanding of it (Zemelman, Daniels, & Hyde, 1998). Later, when reading through the class logs, the teacher can readily pinpoint areas of confusion or misunderstanding to be clarified in the next lesson before instruction continues.

Figure 12.8

Classroom teaching resources: A sampling of children's magazines

Chickadee

For primary grades, this magazine teaches young children about the environment through appealing articles and superb illustrations.

Cobblestone

Geared for intermediate and middle school readers, the magazine is a must for social studies exploration.

ContactKids

An award-winning magazine for middle grade readers who are interested in science, nature, technology, tidbits and amazing facts, and brain-stretching games.

Faces

For intermediate and middle school students this magazine focuses on people from around the world. It is written and published in cooperation with the American Museum of Natural History in New York City.

National Geographic World

Students from age 8–13 will be interested in articles about nature and science coupled with illustrations that are so typical of the *National Geographic Magazine* for adults.

Odyssey

For intermediate and middle school readers who have an interest in astronomy and space science.

Owl

For readers in the intermediate and middle grades, this magazine teaches about the environment with well-written articles and excellent photography.

Ranger Rick

This popular magazine appeals to primary and intermediate grade readers and is filled with interesting articles about nature.

Sports Illustrated for Kids

Upper intermediate and middle school readers will enjoy the sports-oriented articles.

3-2-1 Contact

Students in intermediate and middle school grades will find articles and activities involving science and technology in this magazine.

Your Big Backyard

For primary grade readers who will enjoy wonderful photography and articles in this nature magazine.

Web Link:

Reading Instruction for ESL Students

For those diverse learners who may need additional explanation or opportunities to work with text before it is assimilated, journal responses can signal the need for small group or one-on-one review. At the same time, student attitudes toward a specific subject can be monitored. While the versatile logs can be used in all curricular areas with ease, the following examples will illustrate several appealing possibilities.

Social Studies Learning Logs

Charts, conceptual understandings, graphs, maps, time lines, Venn diagrams, and vocabulary may all be found in a social studies learning log. A chart, for example, may compare the size of the British Army in the colonies with that of the Continental Army during the Revolutionary War. Details about the primary leaders of the two sides may be displayed on another type of chart. Conceptual understandings might include specific British laws such as the Stamp Act or what kind of person would be a member of the Sons of Liberty. Reading *Paul Revere's Ride* (Longfellow, 1996), including its informative end note, provides a taste of this period of history. A Venn diagram might compare viewpoints of the rebels with those of the loyalists, or Tories. Insights here could begin with *A Young Patriot: The American Revolution as Experienced by One Boy* (Murphy, 1996). This particular book is based upon Joseph Plumb Martin's first-person description of his involvement in the Revolutionary War. It is carefully fleshed out with additional information and period photographs, making it a valuable addition to the study of the war.

A graph might depict the population of each of the thirteen colonies in 1776. A map of the locations of major battles during the Revolutionary War along with the dates and which side won would give students a geographical background. Vocabulary terms might include words of the period that are rarely used today. Other information in a social studies learning log might include famous quotes of Revolutionary War leaders. Thumbnail biographies are also appropriate in that the student writes a short sketch of a person's life. Here is one by a fifth grader:

> Paul Revere was a silversmith in Boston. He was A member of the secret group called the Sons of Liberty. When he saw the lantern hung in the Old North Church Towr, he got on his horse and rode to warn the peopel. The British capturred him.

It is through such learning log entries that students can begin to develop a better understanding of the social, historical, and economic events of a period and the resulting ramifications on society.

Remember that students who are challenged with translating thoughts into written words can draw their reactions to what they are reading. Often these learners can use a simple label to better identify their thought processes. Conferencing periodically with the language-delayed learner or the English language learner about their journal responses will help you better understand what each child knows. In the discussion process, the talk often aids children in deepening their comprehension. Thus, journals and talk facilitate learning for the inclusion students in the classroom community.

Beyond the Learning Log

Double Entry Journals

In this variation of journals and learning logs, the students are encouraged to move beyond mere data gathering and to think about the content under study in a slightly different format (Barone, 1990; Robb, 2003). **Double entry journals** can be used interchangeably with learning logs, appropriate in all subject areas. The pages of this type of journal are set up so that the left-hand page is for the fact-including notes, pictures, lists, drawings, ideas, maps, and so forth. Primary grade children might label this section "What I Read." The right-hand side is for reflection, summaries, hypotheses, explanations, critiques, opinions, feelings, and conclusions. These would be aptly designated "What I Think." On this side one finds student ideas in written form. This type of journal could also facilitate inquiry across the curriculum during an interdisciplinary unit while encouraging learners to engage in careful, systematic thinking about the relationships between the subjects under study.

In the area of science, for instance, double entry journals may include labels, concepts, observations, graphs, lists, descriptions, explanations, and vocabulary on one side of the notebook and growing conceptual thinking on the other side (Combs, 2003). Observations may be as basic as a daily chart of the weather by kindergartners or first graders using simple symbols to represent the sun, clouds, rain, or snow on one side of the journal. A picture and simple reaction to the day's weather would be found on the opposite page. Third graders may chart how much they would weigh on each of the planets of the Earth's solar system after recording information on gravity on one side, speculations on the other. Eighth graders may predict the speed and location of a NASA space shuttle during a flight based upon data gathered and ponder the significance of what they are learning for life in the future. Obviously, the complexity of reactions is tied directly to the conceptual abilities of the students involved.

To build upon information recorded in the double entry journal or learning log, Scarnati and Weller (1992) suggest using four different styles of writing in science class, an excellent way to reinforce writing skills in general. They ask students to write about current or historical science events in a narrative style, attempt to describe scientific instruments using descriptive writing, or try to explain a recent experiment by what was seen, heard, and smelled. Finally, simple charts or graphs could be used to persuade a reader to see an outcome in a certain way. This work integrates reading, writing, and thoughtful responding about expository text in a challenging manner.

Describing what takes place during an experiment is another type of observation to be entered in a double entry journal. Denise Levine (1985) explains that her students did some of their best writing in their journals when discussing recent lab work and hands-on activities, rather than responding verbally to class lectures or text readings. This type of writing requires that students be specific and have a large repertoire of descriptive words to explain various properties. They must be able to pinpoint color, shape, size, sound, and texture. A chart listing appropriate descriptive words can be developed during a class discussion and expanded as new words are discovered. The chart should be in a location for easy student reference for future writing assignments.

Other Kinds of Expository Writing Experiences

Aside from writing in logs and journals, students use a myriad of other **informal** kinds of **expository writing** during their days in the classroom. Informal writing is commonplace outside of logs as students list, cluster, and brainstorm; make charts and story maps; jot down notes and explanations; record events; and write descriptions (Combs, 2003). Rough-draft notes for an upcoming debate, scripts for a

Reader's Theater presentation, or typed interviews with people contemporary or historical, might be other forms selected by learners (Tiedt et al., 2001). Two other suggestions include the following:

Bull's-Eye Writing

Bull's-eye writing is a way for students to gather the essential elements of a topic and then jot down that information in a few sentences. Like the center of a target, bull's-eye writing captures the essence of a concept or idea without any extra extraneous details. Below is an example of bull's-eye writing by a ten-year-old fifth grader:

> **Contedents**
> There are many Contedents. First, there is North Amarica. Second, there is Asia. Finally, there is Africa.
>
> First, there is North Amarica. North Aaric has 50 stats. It is canected to South Amarica. North Amarica is north of eqater.
>
> Second, ther is Asia. Asia is the bigest contedent. Asia is north of the eqater. Asia is close to the nort pole.
>
> Finally, there is Africa. Africa has thousands of anamals. Africa is south of the eqater.
>
> There are many Contedents. First, there is North Amarica Second, there is Asia. Finally, there is Africa.

The Herringbone Technique or Fishbone Writing

The **Herringbone technique,** or fishbone writing, is a useful strategy to aid readers in organizing the information they read and then recalling it to write or summarize their reading (see Figure 12.9). It is a bare-bones sort of approach in that only the

Teaching Strategy:
Herringbone

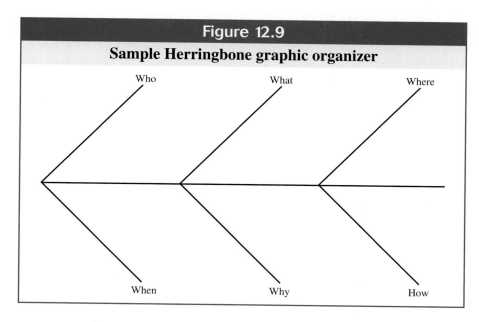

Figure 12.9
Sample Herringbone graphic organizer

Who   What   Where

When   Why   How

basic facts are mined from an article or chapter and then summarized to show understanding. Focus points include who, what, where, when, and why. Teach the technique based upon the reading of a nonfiction magazine article, modeling it with the class first, and then let students choose articles of their own to read and reflect upon using this writing tool. Once they pull the salient facts from the article, students work on a summary of the article based upon their Herringbone information.

Teaching Strategy for the Classroom

USING THE HERRINGBONE GRAPHIC ORGANIZER TO SUMMARIZE A MAGAZINE ARTICLE: AN INTERNET OPTION

The following lesson involves the use of the Herringbone graphic organizer and a magazine article. It focuses on the skills of locating pertinent facts and then using them to write a summary.

- Assemble an interesting array of magazines at the appropriate reading and interest levels of your students. You might also use the Internet as the following lesson illustrates.
- The magazine to be used is an issue from *Time For Kids.*
- Select the grade level that best fits your readers. The articles are available in English and in Spanish. One exciting option for English language learners or for students who need additional time to process information is that the Big Picture Edition has a sound feature. Each bit of text that explains the related picture is read aloud. Try "Now Hear This! Welcome Pandas!" It is an engaging way to demonstrate finding the basic facts needed to complete a simple Herringbone graphic organizer.
- Listen to the story all the way through once. Then play it again. Fill in the who, what, where, when, why, and how facts as the story is read via the computer.
- Model how you would summarize the article based upon the facts you recorded. Point out to the students that summarizing takes careful thinking and involves using just the important facts.
- Work through the process again the following day and again throughout the upcoming weeks to give students an opportunity to internalize this organizer, finding the facts and composing a simple summary.
(Issue: January 29, 2001, Vol. 1, #9)

STUDENTS IN GRADES 4–6

- Read the Top Story: "A Sticky Situation" about a recent fuel spill near the Galapagos Islands. (By Andrea Dorfman. February 2, 2001, Vol. 6, #16)
- In a large group demonstration, read the article aloud first while students follow along. Locate the islands and discuss interesting points of the article.
- Then, invite students to volunteer information from the article to complete the five areas of the organizer. There is no set sequence for answering these points, although the "who" would be a logical starting point if the article is about a person. In this case, you might start the article by answering the "what" portion:

What happened? the Jessica, a fuel tanker, ran aground

Where was the accident? near the Galapagos Islands off the coast of Ecuador

When did this happen? two weeks ago, in mid-January

Why is this a problem? 240,000 gallons of fuel spilled into the ocean in an area where a number of unique animals live.

Who is involved? concerned workers who are desperately fighting to save animals endangered by the spill

How are they working with the animals? Animals that have been affected are being captured, cleaned, and checked carefully to be certain they have not been harmed.

- Working in pairs, ask the students to practice writing a summary. They are to take the facts and organize them, writing a rough draft of their efforts. There will probably be several versions suggested.
- Discuss the resulting offerings, and pick the one that seems to work best.
- Invite students to select another article of interest from magazines on hand and repeat the lesson in writing pairs. Circulate and offer aid as needed.
- Share in a large group once more to reinforce learning.
- Return to the organizer from time to time for future assignments in order that students can refine their skills at finding the facts and in summarizing.

ADAPTATIONS/MODIFICATIONS FOR DIVERSE LEARNERS

- Provide an enlarged screen for visually impaired learners or partner these learners with a classroom learning pal.
- Give explanations and directions clearly and in simple enough terms so that learning disabled students can process the language during the modeling session. Reteach and model again individually or with several students to ensure understanding.
- Maintain eye contact with the ADD/ADHD student to help him focus his attention on the lesson. Be certain this student understands the directions before students begin to write the summary.

Formal Expository Writing

More **formal expository writing** grows from reading expository text and then presenting information gleaned on a topic in a variety of ways as noted in Figure 12.10. One option is that students may create a book that is an innovation on one they have just read together in class. McElveen and Dierking (2000/2001) discovered that it wasn't enough for them to model a writing skill for primary and intermediate grade students. The learners needed "a bridge to link the model to students' ability to write independently and confidently" (p. 362). That bridge became a picture book read and discussed together to support teacher modeling. One of their suggested books is *Welcome to the Sea of Sand* (Yolen, 1996), which informs readers about animals that live in the desert using strong verbs to make the writing interesting.

Figure 12.10

Chart of possibilities: Suggestions for writing in the content areas

Journals or diaries (real or imaginary)

Anecdotes from experience

Thumbnail sketches:
- of famous people
- of places
- of historical events

Applications

Summaries

Plays, skits, Reader's Theater

Fact sheets

Poster displays

Science notes and observations

Interviews of older adults

Directions to go somewhere or to make something

Written notes for debates

Puzzles or word searches

Essay tests

Messages from phone or on the computer

Announcements

Cartoon strips

Flip books with scripts

Biographical sketches

Requests for information/items

Letters
- personal reactions
- observations
- to the editor or public officials
- to imaginary people

Poetry

Children's books/big books

School newspapers

Book, music, or film reviews

Math story problems or solutions to problems

Content-specific dictionaries/ illustrated glossaries

Captions for photos in a display

Word collages or mobiles

Lists

Signs

Postcards

Ads for the newspaper

Pamphlets

Sources: Combs, 2003; Fountas & Pinnell, 2001; Tiedt et al., 2001.

Another option is to create informational ABC books that are rich resources for learning and are inspiring examples to replicate using the topic or theme currently under study (Moss et al., 1997; Yopp & Yopp, 2000). They can be used as an introduction to a new topic, to begin research on a topic of interest, and even to advance multicultural awareness when a particular culture is the focus of an alphabetic overview (Chaney, 1993). One beautiful example is *Antelope, Bison, Cougar: A National Park Wildlife Alphabet Book* (Medley, 2001), an excellent addition to the study of animal habitats, regions of the United States, or a study of national parks. Another title to pull students into a lesson in the science curriculum is *Q Is for Quark: A Science Alphabet Book* (Schwartz, 2001). A variety of science related vocabulary is presented with humor while relating vital facts. See Chapter 7 for other possible titles. The learning center director or local librarian can be a help in locating numerous other titles that would tie into areas under study.

A popular unit in the primary grades involves learning about neighborhoods and communities. Two alphabet books that would support the learning and provide models for writing at the end of the unit are *Alphabet City* (Johnson, 1995) and *A Is for America* (Scillian, 2001). Not only are reading, writing, and learning reinforced via these volumes, but so is working with the structure of sequence since the alphabet proceeds in sequential order (Tompkins, 2000). A change-of-pace activity in the upper grades is to invite students to study a collection of alphabet books and then create their autobiography modeled after one of the books that they particularly liked. They may simply entitle their autobiographical book *The ABC's of Me* or strive for a title more reflective of their personality. Once student text and illustrations are completed, books are "published" by reading them aloud to the rest of the class. If they are displayed in the classroom reading center for several weeks, they are sure to be popular expository reading materials.

A more common kind of formal expository writing involves penning reports, projects, or making presentations. This perfected work presented at the conclusion of a unit of study is one often associated with social studies or science projects. Such a project may wrap up interdisciplinary study. The goal is to tie learning together, deepen understanding of a topic, and engage the brain when the work is chosen by the curious and interested student, rather than being assigned by the efficient and diligent teacher (Tiedt et al., 2001). Time is well spent on expository writing in this vein, as supported by the *Standards for the English Language Arts* (IRA/NCTE, 1996). Standard 7 (p. 38) states:

> Students conduct research on issues and interests by generating ideas and questions, and by posing problems. They gather, evaluate, and synthesize data from a variety of sources (e.g., print and nonprint texts, artifacts, people) to communicate their discoveries in ways that suit their purpose and audience.

Thus, projects are personally chosen by students, facilitated by the teacher, and carried to completion following the writing process described in Chapter 11 on narrative writing. As a quick review of the writing process, the student would follow steps similar to these (Combs, 2003; Tompkins, 2000; Zemelmen et al., 1998):

- Getting started with an idea through memory searches, group brainstorming, or free writes to probe thinking
- Exploring the idea to find a focus through listing, charting, webbing, and clustering of raw ideas
- Composing ideas in sustained writing
- Revising for meaning, discussing work in small groups or with a writing partner
- Editing for conventions
- Sharing the new thinking that has emerged as a result of the writing process by publishing it in an appealing and appropriate way

Obviously, writing like this takes time to develop, so students need to be supported and guided in their efforts. This is valuable application time since writing is an important way for students to discover, recall, organize, classify, connect, generalize, or evaluate. One way to facilitate project progress and encourage completion is via individual conferences during which you discuss, support, monitor, and advise as needed. After reading *Bats* (Gibbons, 1999) an interested third grade researcher began the following report:

> Bats eat insects. Some bats eat fruit. Vampire bats eat cow's blood. Bats have thumbs. Baby bats are calld pups. Bats use echolocation. Bats hibernate. Some bats live in caves.

Then, too, small writing teams or groups of students can be formed as support groups as work proceeds (Tiedt et al., 2001). Jensen (1998) states that the brain functions more optimally when it receives feedback, so maximize the opportunities for specific feedback as learners work toward completion of their various projects.

Student products can extend beyond the typical report-on-a-state format and take the form of any of the items in Figure 12.10. This polished and perfected writing, whether part of a report, poster display, debate, or drama, is supported by the *Standards for the English Language Arts* (1996), which advocates that students learn to "adjust their use of spoken, written, and visual language (e.g., conventions, style, vocabulary) to communicate effectively with a variety of audiences and for different purposes" (p. 3). Such work is often an outgrowth of interdisciplinary teaching, which is spotlighted in the next section.

Concept Muraling

Concept muraling is a technique that Pamela Farris (2004) uses as an effective direct instruction strategy. It is an important technique for all learners but even more so for diverse learners. They have been found to learn more effectively and are better able to retain what they have learned through direct instruction. Muraling relies upon presenting a pictorial overview of concepts to be covered in a content area such as science or social studies. Since pictures offer a pattern that the brain interprets with wholistic meaning, struggling readers, English language learners, and students with learning disadvantages or disabilities are better able to grasp and understand new information and concepts.

Muraling begins with the teacher providing students with a mnemonic devise such as a label for the topic being studied and then presenting an accompanying set of organized, orchestrated illustrations. The combination of the mnemonic clue and pictures provides a "hook," or scaffold, for the brain to recall at a later time. As the teacher gives an oral presentation to accompany the visual, the students are using two modalities to encode the information, aural (hearing) and visual (seeing). After the presentation, the students write down everything they learned from the teacher's presentation on the topic. This adds another learning dimension as the students must put down on paper what they understood and interpreted. Below is a description of how Pam uses muraling in social studies for the topic of China. See Figure 12.11 for the murals she shares with the class.

To prepare for the lesson Pam reads the chapter and accompanying assessment measure from the sixth grade social studies textbook. In this way she determines the major concepts about China that the students will be required to learn. She also reviews the state standards and benchmarks for expository reading and writing along with the content standards and benchmarks for social studies. Next, Pam locates six

Figure 12.11
Concept Mural for China

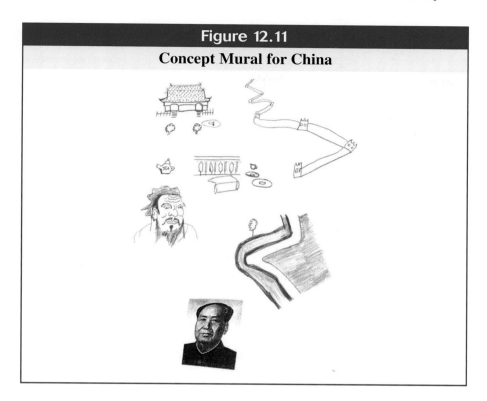

to eight illustrations to represent the major concepts. These may be photocopies of pictures from the textbook or other text, clip art, or illustrations she draws herself. Oftentimes it is a combination of all of these. Then she develops a flow map starting with the top left-hand corner of a page. The other pictures are added, creating a pathway by which the pictures flow. She personally describes this as a "babbling brook that meanders in an orderly fashion through a meadow." The flow map is then made into a single overhead transparency or a one-slide PowerPoint presentation. Let's go into the classroom and observe Pam as she presents the lesson.

"Boys and girls, put a sheet of paper and a pencil on the floor next to you. Now clear your desks."

Surveying the classroom, Pam makes eye contact with a child who is poking along, locks eyes with the student, and delivers a silent "time to get with it" message. José grins and speeds up his pace. In short order, all of the students are attentive with all eyes up front, hands in laps, feet on the floor.

"Our next social studies unit is on China, one of the most interesting countries and cultures in our world. We can remember that we are studying about China because here is a picture of the Great Wall of China, an amazing piece of architecture. (Pam points to a poster at the front of the room.) Let's look at some of the major features of China's history and culture."

Turning on the overhead projector, she uses a pencil to point to the picture at the top of the transparency as she describes the importance and relevance of each illustration. Deliberately, Pam progresses until she reaches the bottom of the transparency.

The remainder of the lesson is filled with fascinating facts about the ruling families, life in the Forbidden City, the Great Wall, farming practices, and the products like silk, tea, and rice for which China is known. Leaders past and present are discussed as is the change in government over time resulting in Communist control.

Turning off the projector, Pam tells the class, "China has lots of history and culture for us to explore. Close your eyes and visualize in your head the pictures on the transparency. Think about what was portrayed at the top, what came next, and so on." She pauses and waits five seconds. Next she has students open their eyes as she reviews what was presented by its location in the illustration. Then she asks the students to pick up their pencils and paper and write down or draw what they remember in the sequence just presented as a part of their social studies learning log. If necessary, students may work in pairs to recreate the information presented.

With the projector turned on once more, Pam follows up with a class discussion about the contents of the mural and what each symbol or picture represented. The discussion begins with Pam asking a struggling learner to provide the main topic and moves on from there, probing for more information. Giving cues to those students who find the task challenging, she is content to provide wait time before a student responds. Academically talented learners are stretched to provide interpretations and cause-and-effect responses where appropriate. After this thirty- to forty-minute muraling session and discussion, students are given fifteen minutes to begin reading the China chapter in their textbook. They are told to jot down additional information in their learning logs as they read. The remainder of the chapter will be read the next day. As a result of this lesson, the way has been thoughtfully paved for effective learning.

Concept muraling moves across the curriculum and involves different kinds of texts. Using a biography, the concept mural might include references to highlights of the person's life. In science a frog concept mural connected to a related read-aloud might include pictures of the life cycle of a frog. Finally, this adaptable strategy can be used for group work, another way to support diverse learners in the classroom. In a cooperative learning or group project, students would select different research topics. Each student can focus on one aspect of the topic with the group relying upon concept muraling for chronicling their findings and sharing their initial ideas with the entire class. Then, the research can extend learning, resulting in a quality collaborative product.

ORGANIZING LEARNING THROUGH INTERDISCIPLINARY UNITS

The commonly heard wail from across the nation's classrooms involves variations on a theme that sound something like this, "Don't ask me to teach another thing! If I taught twenty-four hours a day, I couldn't cover all that I am supposed to do. Honestly, I don't have time to cover the district curriculum as it is." Many teachers are overwhelmed as they face the daunting task of trying to teach basic skills and strategies while encouraging students to become lifelong learners. There is no denying the fact that with so much to learn, it is virtually impossible to sandwich it into a K–12 educational career.

One suggestion to add a measure of sanity to a teacher's life is to use class time as wisely as possible by integrating subject matter and teaching across the curriculum whenever it is feasible. For example, when you combine reading, writing, listening, and speaking within content areas, you maximize learning during the packed instructional day. You are taking advantage of every learning opportunity to facilitate making connections across curricular lines (Barton & Smith, 2000; Good & Brophy, 2000; Zemelman et al., 1998). In addition, you are making the curriculum more relevant and contemporary if you tie learning to real-life issues and the skills to problem-solve those issues, an invaluable way to teach.

An **interdisciplinary teaching unit** designed to integrate the curriculum is defined as (Smith & Johnson, 1994, p. 200)

Portfolio Activity:
Interdisciplinary
Teaching Unit

> a comprehensive learning experience that combines content areas by incorporating concepts, skills, and questions from more than one discipline to examine a central theme, issue, situation, inquiry, or topic. The interdisciplinary model may involve two or more disciplines; for example, language arts and social studies may be organized around a theme, or all content disciplines may be involved. The interweaving of content and skills within the unit is based upon authentic learning tasks that tie the theme and content subject together while also reinforcing the interrelation among subjects.

By integrating the curriculum through several units each year, this provides "whole learning," which is a way of balancing content and chosen instructional strategies to nurture and nudge the whole learner toward self-realization and self-actualization (Lindquist, 1995).

Be forewarned but not dismayed. Developing an interdisciplinary unit is a time-consuming process. While exciting, it is demanding. Often two minds are better than one, so good advice is to work with a colleague or small team of teachers to develop and teach the unit. Troubleshoot and refine along the way based upon collective experiences. Learners together, you, your colleagues, and the students will be much the richer for it.

The basic steps in the process of developing an interdisciplinary unit are as follows and can be adapted to individual class needs accordingly (Combs, 1997; Meinbach, Rothlein, & Fredericks, 1995):

1. Study the required district curriculum, matching objectives and specific topics that must be taught at your grade level. Examine the basal reader and content area textbooks for subject matter that can be naturally integrated. Narrow the focus to several topics or themes that would be of interest to your students.

2. Review the district curriculum again, selecting the skills and objectives from each subject area that will work well together, enhancing learning and covering the curriculum at the same time.

3. Examine your students and consciously choose learning experiences and activities that enhance and extend their individual growth and ability to learn.

Newspapers and magazines are excellent sources of expository text.

4. Look through available materials and children's literature, matching appropriate resources to theme of interest. Consider people in the community who might serve as resources and speakers as well.

5. Organize ideas and activities to meet district learning objectives and the needs of your learners, providing them "hands-on, minds-on" learning (Meinback et al., 1995, p. 20). Brainstorm possible research activities and creative projects that could evolve from the unit of study.

6. Decide on a key motivating activity to kick off the unit.

7. Decide on an approximate length of time in which to teach the unit knowing that flexibility is inherent in its success. Use the students as your teaching barometer. Stretch the unit out a little longer if students are totally engrossed. Review key learning and wrap it up earlier if interest is generally dwindling.

8. Select appropriate assessment strategies to monitor progress and assess what students are actually learning.

9. Upon its completion, evaluate the success of the unit using student input along with your own critiques.

10. Celebrate the unit's conclusion with an event involving a way to share the learning, perhaps inviting parents in for an evening program or taking the learning on the road to another classroom with highlights from the unit.

Another organizational strategy is offered by Deborah Burns (2002). She has pertinent advice for teachers who are working with one eye on particular standards and another on their unique classrooms of learners for whom they want to differentiate instruction. She suggests drawing a picture of a ladder and labeling the rungs from bottom to top with information pertaining to the following questions as it is tied to the topic to be studied (p. 3):

- What is it that *all* of the kids in my room already know?
- What is it that *some* of them already know?
- What is it that a *few* of them already know?
- What is it that *none* of the kids knows going into this unit?

Before beginning the unit, be certain to take time to assess prior knowledge to clearly understand where each learner is and how best to meet their needs. Burns explains that each learner, despite a broad range of classroom abilities, should at least be able to move up one rung of the ladder as the unit is taught.

As the unit concludes and individual papers or projects are submitted to demonstrate what has been learned, assess them to see how effectively you have taught them. Did students organize their thoughts well? Did students grow in the ability to explore and learn on their own? Could you say definitively that students "autographed their work with excellence?" (Block et al., 2002). If so, you are clearly developing exemplary literacy expertise.

An added strength of teaching using several interdisciplinary units per year is that this is an excellent way to reach all learners in your classroom regardless of diverse backgrounds and varying ability levels (Good & Brophy, 2000). If resources and learners are carefully considered, all learners will find materials at their reading and interest levels and can pursue projects and activities within their areas of strength (Barton & Smith, 2000). A checklist to help you select the best nonfiction titles for students' use is available in Figure 12.14. Consider the following text sets, collections of books at varied levels, that might spark a unit of study on the oceans in lower elementary grades or the Civil War in sixth grade or middle school (see Figures 12.12 and 12.13). See the Online Center for an extended version of Figures 12.12 and 12.13, complete with annotations. The suggested books demonstrate how key concepts can be afforded learners with diverse abilities because reading levels and concept loads have been taken into consideration. These titles also reflect the number of invaluable books available to tantalize readers about a topic of study (Kobrin, 1995).

A sample interdisciplinary unit entitled *Heroes and Heroines Past and Present: Lessons to Live By* is included later in this chapter as a model of how a unit might be developed for learners in grades 5 and 6. It can be adapted to fit other grades, of course. Included is a visual overview with ideas illustrating how the curriculum can be integrated, extension ideas, and suggested titles of books to spark learning. Because children from all cultures need people in their lives to emulate, this particular theme should be readily adaptable to many a classroom.

To conclude this brief discussion on interdisciplinary teaching, Nancie Atwell (1990) highlights its benefits beautifully even though she is focusing primarily on the ideal reading–writing, cross-curricular environment. In extending her thinking to the topic of interdisciplinary teaching, consider her words:

Figure 12.12

A starter set of informational books to supplement content area text topic: Oceans (elementary grades)

For annotations of these books, go to the Online Learning Center at www.mhhe.com/farrisreading, choose Chapter 12, and click "Figure 12.12: Oceans".

Cole, Joanna. (1993). *Magic School Bus Explores the Ocean Floor.* (B. Degen, Illus.). New York: Scholastic.

Davies, Nicola. (1997). *Big Blue Whale.* (N. Maland, Illus.). Cambridge, MA: Candlewick Press.

Earle, Sylvia A. (1999). *Dive! My Adventures in the Deep Frontier.* (W. Henry, Illus. with photographs). Washington, DC: National Geographic.

———. (1999). *Hello Fish! Visiting the Coral Reef.* (W. Henry, Illus. with photographs). Washington, DC: National Geographic Society.

Fredericks, Anthony. (2002). *In One Tidepool: Crabs, Snails, and Salty Tails.* (J. Dirubbio, Illus.). New York: Dawn Publishers.

Ganeri, Anita. (1994). *The Ocean Atlas.* (L. Corbella, Illus.). New York: Dorling Kindersley.

Lasky, Kathryn. (2001). *Interrupted Journey: Saving Endangered Sea Turtles.* (C. G. Knight, Photographer). Cambridge, MA: Candlewick Press.

Livingston, Myra Cohn. (1986). *Sea Songs.* (L. E. Fisher, Illus.). New York: Holiday.

London, Jonathan. (1999). *Baby Whale's Journey.* (J. Van Zyke, Illus.). San Francisco, CA: Chronicle.

Pringle, Laurence. (1995). *Coral Reefs: Earth's Undersea Treasures.* New York: Simon & Schuster.

Schuch, Steve. (1999). *A Symphony of Whales.* (P. Sylvada, Illus.). San Diego, CA: Harcourt Brace.

Shahan, Sherry. (1996). *Barnacles Eat with Their Feet: Delicious Facts about the Tide Pool Food Chain.* Brookfield, CT: Millbrook Press.

Simon, Seymour. (1996). *Sharks.* New York: HarperCollins.

———. (1997). *Oceans.* New York: Morrow.

Swanson, Diane. (1996). *Safari Beneath the Sea: The Wonder World of the North Pacific Coast.* San Francisco, CA: Sierra Club Books.

Yolen, Jane. (1996). *Sea Watch: A Book of Poetry.* (T. Lewin, Illus.). New York: Philomel.

In the best of all possible worlds, language study might no longer be isolated as a separate subject in our curricula. Writing and reading workshop would become redundant because students and teachers would be writing and reading everything all day long: poems, plays, stories, essays, lists, articles, autobiographical sketches, and journals about math, literature, history, the sciences, *life*. In the best possible of all worlds, teachers of all subjects might become not English teachers, but experts in the process of reading and writing,

Figure 12.13

A starter set of informational books to supplement content area text topic: The Civil War (middle grades)

 For annotations of these books, go to the Online Learning Center at www.mhhe.com/farrisreading, choose Chapter 12, and click "Figure 12.13: The Civil War."

Adler, David A. (1996). *A Picture Book of Sojourner Truth.* (G. Griffith, Illus.). New York: Holiday House.

Bial, Raymond. (1995). *The Underground Railroad.* New York: Houghton Mifflin.

Bolotin, Norman. (2002). *Civil War A to Z: A Young Reader's Guide to Over 100 People, Places, and Points of Interest.* New York: Dutton.

Chang, Ian. (1996). *A Separate Battle: Women and the Civil War.* New York: Dutton.

Cox, Clinton. (1993). *Undying Glory: The Story of the Massachusetts 54th Regiment.* New York: Scholastic.

Doif, Sylviane A. (2001). *Growing Up in Slavery.* Brookside, CT: Millbrook Press.

Dolan, Edward F. (1997). *The American Civil War: A House Divided.* Brookfield, CT: Millbrook.

Fleischman, Paul. (1995). *Bull Run.* (D. Frampton, Illus.). New York: HarperCollins.

Fleischner, Jennifer. (1997). *I Was Born a Slave: The Story of Harriet Jacobs.* (M. K. Reim, Illus.). Brookfield, CT: Millbrook.

Freedman, Russell. (1989). *Lincoln: A Photobiography.* New York: Clarion.

Haskins, Jim. (1997). *Get on Board: The Story of the Underground Railroad.* New York: Scholastic.

Lincoln, Abraham. (1995). *The Gettysburg Address.* (M. McCurdy, Illus.). New York: Houghton Mifflin.

Lyons, Mary E. (1996). *Letters from a Slave Girl: The Story of Harriet Jacobs.* New York: Pocket Books.

McKissack, Patricia C., & McKissack, Frederick L. (1994). *Christmas in the Big House: Christmas in the Quarters.* (J. Thompson, Illus.). New York: Scholastic.

McLoone, Margo. (1997). *Harriet Tubman: A Photo Illustrated Biography.* Mankato, MN: Bridgestone Books.

Moore, Kay. (1994). *If You Lived at the Time of the Civil War.* (A. Matskick, Illus.). New York: Scholastic.

Murphy, Jim. (1992). *The Long Road to Gettysburg.* New York: Clarion.

———. (1993). *The Boys' War: Confederate and Union Soldiers Talk about the Civil War.* New York: Clarion.

Rappaport, Doreen. (1999). *Escape from Slavery: Five Journeys to Freedom.* (C. Lilly, Illus.). New York: HarperCollins.

Schomp, Virginia. (2002). *Letters from the Homefront: The Civil War.* New York: Benchmark Books/Marshall Cavendish.

Schroeder, Alan. (1996). *Minty.* (J. Pinkney, Illus.). New York: Dial.

Van Steenwyck, Elizabeth. (1997). *Mathew Brady: Civil War Photographer.* New York: Franklin Watts.

Wroble, Lisa. (1998). *Kids during the American Civil War.* (D. Primiceri, Illus.). New York: PowerKids Press.

about literature appropriate to the various disciplines, and about students—who they are, what they can do, and what they know and need to know. Then the child's day might become a learning workshop in which writing and reading are learned in the richest possible context and appreciated as tools of the highest quality for helping children come to know about the world. (xxi–xxiii)

Figure 12.14

A checklist for evaluating nonfiction trade books

Theme: _____ Price: _____

Author: _____ Call no.: _____

Title: _____

Publisher and date: _____

Series: _____ ISBN: _____

Total score: _____ Recommend? _____ For whom? _____

3 = meets all or most criteria   2 = meets some criteria   1 = meets few criteria

_____ **Accuracy**

information about author expertise/experience given
information about photo credits given
references cited throughout text or bibliography provided
information is current and accurate

_____ **Organization & Layout**

table of contents	chapter and section headings	summaries
index	glossary	charts
graphs	maps	illustrations

predominant pattern of organization: cause and effect, comparison/contrast,
problem/solution, time order description

_____ **Cohesion of ideas**

major ideas are logically connected throughout text
sentence level ideas are logically connected to each other
  (i.e., do not require reader to make a lot of inferences)
respects reader's probable background knowledge
appropriate conceptual load
avoids irrelevant details
provides good model of expository writing

_____ **Specialized vocabulary**

defined as it is introduced
defined in pictures, captions, labels, or clarified visually
defined in glossary

_____ **Reader interest**

has aesthetic appeal
has colorful illustrations or photos
uses appropriate format (i.e., page and print size)
has positive role models with respect to gender and ethnicity
activities and/or experiments within the text are motivating

Annotation:

Thematic Unit

AN INTERDISCIPLINARY INSTRUCTIONAL UNIT: HEROES AND HEROINES PAST AND PRESENT: LESSONS TO LIVE BY

Idea Extensions

- Divide into two groups. Each group writes and illustrates a Big Book of Heroes and Heroines based upon the research and reading done for the unit. Take the finished books to the lower grades to read and discuss together.
- Based upon criteria established in class, identify "Everyday Heroes and Heroines" in the community. Invite them in to tell their stories and then celebrate their accomplishments together.
- Dialogue with e-pals who are also learning about heroes/heroines. e-PALS http://www.epal.com

Science
- Research heroes/heroines in this field. Explain the impact of their work on the world of science today.
- Log onto Heroes for the Planet www.time.com/time/reports/ environments/heroes. Learn about contemporary heroes who are working to protect the environment.

Math
- Where appropriate, examine how the actions or contributions of a hero or heroine affected economics.
- Develop a math lesson based upon a concept in one of the books you read. You might use graphing, write word problems, map distances, or use other measurements.

Social Studies
- Make an illustrated time line including key characters from folk tales, expository and fictional texts, and periodicals. Note general era and a key accomplishment or feat plus a simple illustration.
- Use the problem-solution graphic organizer to record how a hero/heroine of choice reached appropriate solutions.
- Map your heroes/heroines on a world map. Where did they live or do they currently live? Record brief pertinent data on a 3×5 index card and tack to the location.

Read Other Books—Novels and Nonfiction
- *The Birchbark House* (Erdrich, 1999)
- *Freedom's Sons: The Story of the Amistad Mutiny* (Jumain, 1998)
- *Greater Than Angels* (Matas, 1998)
- *Basher Five–Two: The True Story of F-16 Fighter Pilot Captain Scott O'Grady* (O'Grady, Captian Scott 1997)
- *Keeper of the Light* (Pfitsch, 1997)
- *Mary on Horseback* (Wells, 1998)

Note: See the related bibliography of appropriate picture books.

Heroes/Heroines Past and Present: Lessons to Live By

Language Arts
- Brainstorm qualities of a hero/heroine; write a definition based upon qualifications.
- After reading a selected text, write a poem or reflective essay on a hero/heroine.
- Write a news article about a hero, past or present, real or fictional, telling who, what, where, when, how, and why.
- Write a job description for a hero/heroine based on a book you have read.

Related Arts
- Create a poster of a hero or heroine. One option is to use pictures and words from magazines to design a character collage.
- Make a Hall of Heroes and Heroines to display various posters made from different kinds of media.
- Hold a Heroes Day. Dress as a favorite hero/heroine and present a bit of your life to the class.
- Present a Story Theater from one of the books. A narrator reads the story aloud while actors pantomine the story. Select appropriate music to play quietly in the background.

Reading
- Work in triads. Read a selection of books about folk heroes; list and discuss traits that made them heroes.
- In literature circles, read different expository texts about real heroes; compare traits with folk heroes. Record reactions in double-entry journals.
- Change literature circles; read a collection of novels about fictional heroes. Use reflection journals to record thoughts as you note what made them heroes.
- Work independently to read newspapers and periodicals to find contemporary heroes. Share.
- Compare results of all your reading in a whole class discussion.

A Bibliography of Related Picture Books

Adler, David A. (2000). *America's Champion Swimmer: Gertrude Ederle.* (T. Widener, Illus.). New York.F

Benét, Rosemary & Stephen. (2000). *Johnny Appleseed.* (S. D. Schindler, Illus.). New York: Margaret McElderry.

Bruchac, Joseph. (2000). *Crazy Horse's Vision.* (S. D. Nelson, Illus.). New York: Lee & Low.

Cooper, Floyd. (2000). *Mandela: From the Life of the South African Statesman.* New York: Puffin.

Cooper, Melrose. (1998). *Gettin' through Thursday.* (N. Bennett, Illus.). New York: Lee & Low.

Davol, Margueritte W. (1997). *The Paper Dragon.* New York: Simon & Schuster.

Harper, Jo. (1998). *The Legend of Mexicatl/La Leyenda de Mexicatl.* (R. Casilla, Illus.). New York: Turtle.

Hopkinson, Deborah. (2001). *Birdie's Lighthouse.* New York: Atheneum.

Kellogg, Steven. (1998). *Mike Fink.* New York: Morrow.

Krull, Kathleen. (2000). *Wilma Unlimited: How Wilma Rudolph Became the World's Fastest Woman.* (D. Diaz, Illus.). New York: Voyager.

McGill, Alice. (1999). *Molly Bannaky.* (C. K. Soentpiet, Illus.). Boston: Houghton Mifflin.

Mochizuki, Ken. (1997). *Passage to Freedom: The Sugihara Story.* (D. Lee, Illus.). New York: Lee & Low.

————. (1997). *Heroes.* (D. Lee, Illus.). New York: Lee & Low.

Poole, Josephine. (2000). *Joan of Arc.* (A. Barrett, Illus.). New York: Dragonfly.

Schroeder, Alan. (1996). *Minty: A Story of Young Harriet Tubman.* (B. Pinkney, Illus.). New York: Dial.

Complete Biography of Novels Listed in the Chart

Blumberg, Rhoda. (2000). *Shipwrecked! The True Adventures of a Japanese Boy.* New York: HarperCollins.

Cummings, Julie. (2000). *Tomboy of the Air: Daredevil Pilot Blanche Stuart Scott.* New York: HarperCollins.

Erdrich, Louise. (1999). *The Birchbark House.* New York: Hyperion.

Jurmain, Suzanne. (1998). *Freedom's Sons: The Story of the Amistad Mutiny.* New York: Lothrop, Lee & Shepard.

Lawlor, Laurie. (2000). *Helen Keller: Rebellious Spirit.* New York: Holiday House.

Matas, Carol. (1998). *Greater Than Angels.* New York: Simon & Schuster.

O'Grady, Captain Scott. (1997). *Basher Five-Two: The True Story of F-16 Pilot Captain Scott O'Grady.* New York: Yearling.

Pfitsch, Patricia. (2002). *Keeper of the Light.* New York: Simon & Schuster.

Well, Rosemary. (2000). *Mary on Horseback: Three Mountain Stories.* New York: Puffin.

DIVERSE LEARNERS AS EXPOSITORY READERS AND WRITERS

Fact-laden expository text is challenging to students with basic reading skills. It is even more so for learners who struggle with the printed word because of learning disabilities or language barriers as English language learners. Williams (2001) explains that it can take between five and ten years for English as Second Language students to develop a competency with this type of cognitively demanding language. Being aware of the demands nonfiction places on these learners helps the teacher to plan accordingly.

For example, one of the benefits of interdisciplinary teaching is that a myriad of materials including informational books at various reading levels is a part of the daily learning fare. The variety will aid this group of readers as the teacher guides them to materials that may interest them and will enable them to learn successfully. There is also the opportunity to draw on a child's talents and expertise because learning projects of all kinds enrich the classroom for each and every learner (Barton & Smith, 2000). Don't forget to talk to these children. Ask students how they might say a word or phrase in their language, which demonstrates your interest and respect for the knowledge they can share with the class (Williams, 2001). Discussing main ideas and clarifying them in light of what the child already knows will be helpful.

Working in small groups with peers to help decipher content will benefit diverse learners. Have them pal up with a learning buddy, changing those buddies from time to time. To take the pressure off of gleaning information via the written text, use guest speakers, pertinent short videos, hands-on artifacts, and field trips. This is also a way to solidify background knowledge, which you know is essential to building comprehension and understanding for a group of learners who are as curious and eager to learn as everyone else. Using parents as speakers to highlight ordinary and not-so-ordinary heroes and heroines as highlighted in the previous thematic unit is one more way to highlight cultural accomplishments. In sum, interdisciplinary teaching, carefully planned with an eye to the interests and abilities in the classroom, will make learning a pleasure for all of the students involved.

This hearing-impaired student has a cochlear implant. Such students benefit from visual clues (pictures and concept muraling).

Furthermore, if the textbook is the backbone of study, have parent volunteers or students who read well tape segments of the textbook. This step will help the visually impaired student and support a student with learning disabilities. Devise a focus question for each segment read so that the listener can test her comprehension by answering that question after careful listening. Caution readers to give the listener clear directions when moving from one page to the next or one segment to the next so that they don't become confused and lose their place. Students might fill in a graphic organizer as they listen to each chunk of material also an aid to those with hearing and visual impairments. Transferring information from text, the mind, and onto paper gives the learner plenty of practice with the content. Remember, however, that this is just one option to support diverse learners, so please do not rely completely on taped books as aids to understanding.

Another way to build the comprehension of expository text is to get students actively involved in related vocabulary acquisition by acting out some of the words that lend themselves to a little drama. As a result, learners will associate the action with the word in a more effective way than memorization typically does. According to research by Fred and Barbara Duffelmeyer (1979), dramatization of words has been more beneficial than the use of the somewhat controversial practice of context clues, trying structural analysis, or reaching for the dictionary. Once acquired, the words will be at the writer's fingertips.

It is probable that the gifted student might be on her feet quickly with actions to "define" a word. The ADD/ADHD student might beat her to it, so eager to be active that he wants to give this a try. In addition, seeing a word defined and getting to try an action definition herself is one more way to make learning effective for the hearing impaired learner. Finally, the student with learning disabilities frequently needs information presented in different ways to assimilate it. A little drama in his vocabulary life might be the most effective way for word knowledge to be remembered.

As work during an interdisciplinary unit is thoughtfully differentiated, set the goals high while collaborating with the gifted students in the classroom. Keeping in mind the individual learner with particular interests and needs, work to design activities and learning opportunities where students are challenged to comprehend at advanced levels and create sophisticated writings or creative projects (Block et al., 2002). In the process, build toward those levels of comprehension by requiring students to question the authenticity, accuracy, and validity of materials they are working with in class and on Internet sites (Heilman et al., 2002). Another option is to partner students with an authority on the topic being studied, perhaps another teacher in the building, the district, or the local business community.

As a unit of study is being developed, look for audiovisual aids that will meet the needs of the visually or hearing impaired inclusion students. For example, support learning for the hearing impaired student with pictures, videotapes, captioned films, or filmstrips. Personal copies of the class notes will fill in gaps that the student might have when trying to follow teacher modeling or a brief lecture on subject matter. Enlarged versions of a semantic web presented on the overhead projector or computer screen that defines a new vocabulary word will aid the visually impaired learner. In addition to other pertinent large print materials, use real objects that are tied to lessons whenever possible. Holding the concrete object and hearing it discussed will facilitate understanding. Finally, it is important for learners to both tie new knowledge with old and strengthen comprehension of expository text in the process.

ENHANCING LEARNING WITH TECHNOLOGY

Software programs appropriate for research to build backgrounds on a variety of topics are growing in number. Several superb programs follow this section, but there are numerous others to be explored. Textbook manufacturers often do some of the legwork for you, so consult the teacher's guides that accompany the reading or other content area series used at your grade level. The school learning center director and local librarians make it their business to purchase the most appropriate programs for the use of young people. Consult them when you are looking for materials to extend the textbook. Their expertise can shorten the time spent in gathering fine materials for interdisciplinary teaching, a wise move when time is such a valuable commodity.

Then, add a catalog from the National Geographic Society to your classroom resource file. In it you will find software and videos to support the themes of oceans and the Civil War mentioned earlier in the chapter. As all learners interact with these resources, it's almost like taking a mini-field trip. The nonfiction materials are simply superb and will tempt both teacher and students with their invitations to learn about a myriad of people and places.

Other content-rich materials can be found in CD-ROMS like *History of the World* (Dorling Kindersley, 1995) or the engrossing *Stowaway!* (Biesty, 1995) where students can learn what life was like on an 18th-century warship. The detailed drawings are authentic, and participants are quickly caught up in time and place because of realistic animation, sound effects, and narration.

Internet options abound. Recognizing today's fascination with the ability to connect with people and places and products around the world via the Internet, students might be highly motivated to ply their expository writing skills beyond pen, pencil, and paper. Conduct mini-lessons introducing appropriate sites for student exploration. There are a myriad of them from which to choose. If students are involved in research as part of an interdisciplinary unit, they might work through the initial phases of the writing process with their classmates. Then, they can turn to experts in another classroom and engage in productive revision conferences through Internet partners located through Keypals sites. What a way to make revision exciting! Always investigate sites thoroughly ahead of time, and then introduce them to the learners. Technology provides the opportunity to grasp the latest learning only a key stroke or two away. Despite a teacher's best efforts, the door to the ever-evolving Information Age is undoubtedly best accessed through one's classroom and home computers.

Software for Expository Writing

Web Links:

Keypals

Amazon.com

Excite Travel

Intercultural E-Mail Classroom Connections

Say Hello to the World Project

Thomas Legislative Information on the Internet

White House for Kids

Teaching Strategy for the Classroom

THE TECHNOLOGY CONNECTION: A LESSON PLAN FOR EXPOSITORY READING AND WRITING

Research Focus: A Legacy—Our National Parks

I. OBJECTIVES

Use Internet resources to acquire information on a specific topic. Integrate Internet facts with related classroom resources. Work collaboratively to create a final product that reflects their learning. Begin with an excerpt from McGraw-Hill/National Geographic Society. (2000). *Legacy—Linking Past and Present: National Parks. In Regions: Adventures in Time and Place.* New York: McGraw-Hill School Division. pp. 16–17.

II. MATERIALS

- Excerpt from a nonfiction resource that introduces national parks and the need to preserve them like the one included in this lesson.
- A nonfiction title that revolves around a national park. Suggestion: George, Jean Craighead. (1995). *Everglades.* (W. Minor, Illus.). New York: HarperCollins.
- Related picture books and nonfiction resources including a selection of pamphlets from national parks to stimulate research.
- Previously researched websites. If you only use one, the following one will keep your students (and you) engaged for hours: http://www.nps.gov/ Not only will you be able to research the nation's national parks, but you can dip into culture and history through Links to the Past, look at natural resources in the parks through Nature Net, and learn about educational options through Park Smart.

III. INSTRUCTIONAL APPROACH

A. Lesson Motivator

Begin with a snippet of tantalizing or thought-provoking information about national parks like the one above. After reading it, ask for students' reactions. As you activate prior knowledge and engage learners, you are also assessing students' backgrounds of experiences. Where will you need to supplement and support? As you wind up this initial discussion, ask students to think about why national parks are important. After several minutes of think time, record their ideas on chart paper for future reference.

B. Teacher/Student Interaction

- Read Jean Craighead George's lovely book, *Everglades,* aloud to the class. Point out the novel way it begins with a storyteller drawing listeners into the story of the birth and near destruction of this legacy. Stop at appropriate spots to discuss student observations and reactions.
- Upon completion of the book, ask students what kinds of questions they would like answered about this park. What else would they like to know? Write those questions down to guide further research.
- Divide students into five groups. Each group will begin to research the Everglades using materials gathered ahead of time. Enlist the aid of the learning center director and computer lab director to facilitate research. Give each group a different graphic organizer that supports one of the five basic organizational strategies of expository text. Once the information has been gathered, they are to reorganize it according to the organizer they have been given.
- Share the reasonably well polished reports with the class as a whole. Analyze the impact of the organization of content upon the way information was presented. Discuss how the reports looked and sounded different depending on the organizational structure used. Did one seem to work better than another? Why or why not?
- Provide a chart of additional national parks and their locations. Suggestions might include the Grand Canyon, Yellowstone, Yosemite, Acadia, Great Smokey Mountains, Mount Rainier, Glacier National Park, Arches National Park among others. Students might pick a state first, and then decide upon the park based upon that location. Students will regroup to research a park of personal interest.

- This time final expository writing can take a variety of forms using suggestions from Figure 12.11. Options might include a magazine article with pictures scanned in from outside resources, a nonfiction picture book, several editorials supporting the care of a particular national park, a "tour" of the park led by a park ranger using posters or slides, and so forth.

C. Gatekeeping

For this practice round, keep the requirements quite simple.

- Reports should be written, proofread, and polished. The point of the lesson is to practice researching numerous resources and presenting findings according to a particular organizational structure.
- For the next round of research, the rubric should be more specific. Provide a rubric for evaluating each project developed in collaboration with the students.

IV. EXTENSIONS

- After sharing projects with the class, take them to another classroom to "share the wealth."
- Display final projects in the local library or in the media center.

V. ADAPTATIONS/MODIFICATIONS FOR DIVERSE LEARNERS

- For English language learners, provide a translator to read the necessary text. Encourage students to use art and simple sentences to express themselves depending on their knowledge of the English language.
- When studying topography or locations, use braille maps to aid the visually impaired learner.
- Allow the gifted student to select a topic of particular interest and develop an individual project outline that will challenge him as a learner.
- Encourage diverse students to draw on their strengths when presenting final projects whenever possible. Perhaps the presentation will be a song, a rap, a poem, or a collage of quotes and pictures.

Summary

Nonfiction books are an exciting way to introduce subject matter, motivate learners of all ages, and expand textbook offerings on a myriad of topics. Because it differs dramatically from familiar narrative text, expository writing in these texts can be challenging, at least initially. A number of strategies were presented throughout the chapter to make reading, comprehending, and writing expository materials manageable to all learners. One particularly effective connection to expository reading is the writing that can grow from it. Using those children's literature nonfiction authors as models, students can learn to write such text well themselves. Interdisciplinary teaching is one way to integrate both fiction and nonfiction across the curriculum, use class time to the best advantage, and meet the needs of a classroom of diverse learners at the same time. The exploding world of technology is an excellent resource to provide backgrounds on nonfiction topics and to provide opportunities for students to read and write about intriguing topics from the realm of the real world.

Chapter Review

Go to the Online Learning Center at **www.mhhe.com/farrisreading** to take chapter quizzes, practice with key terms, and review important content.

Main Points

- The *National Standards for the English Language Arts* urge teachers to provide opportunities for students to master a variety of text and ways to use it. This includes expository text.

- Teachers can build a schema for understanding informational text by making it a part of the daily read-aloud routine and encouraging students to read it on their own.

- Teach the basic organizational patterns of expository text to facilitate comprehension: description, comparison and contrast, cause and effect, problem and solution, and sequence.

- Once students are taught to understand it through graphic organizers, through work with exemplary nonfiction children's literature and periodicals, and in writing of their own, a schema, or cognitive framework for expository text, is established.

- Practice in writing informational text can take many forms including learning logs and double entry journals, informal writing, more formal writing as presented in research papers, and through a variety of other creative products.

- By integrating the curriculum through several interdisciplinary units during the year, teachers can make wise use of class time, help students to integrate ideas together, and foster familiarity with expository text all at the same time. These units best meet the needs of diverse learners in the classroom when materials, backgrounds, and interests are carefully considered.

- When creating an interdisciplinary unit, work with a colleague or two in order to share the workload. Together you can assess the effectiveness of the unit augmented by student input and make improvements accordingly.

- Review strategies for teaching comprehension suggested throughout the book. Many of them will still be appropriate for working with diverse learners and in helping them to comprehend fact-filled text. Texts at their level, reading buddies, and building background knowledge through appropriate software or technology continue to be useful techniques.

- Investigating software options and branching out into the world of the Internet for research, writing, and learning will help teachers and students stay attuned to the exploding knowledge so much a part of the Information Age.

Key Terms

bull's-eye writing	567	learning logs	562
concept muraling	572	metacognitive practices	559
double entry journal	565	organizational patterns	548
expository text	544	cause and effect	557
formal expository writing	569	comparison and contrast	551
graphic organizer	548	description	549
Herringbone technique	567	problem and solution	558
informal expository writing	566	sequence	551
interdisciplinary teaching unit	575		

Reflecting and Reviewing

1. How do the standards encourage you to integrate nonfiction materials into the literacy curriculum?

2. When you are faced with having to read expository text and keep the information organized, what particular strategies work for you? Can you think of a time when you tied something new with knowledge of a topic with which you were already familiar? How did that help you understand the newer information?

3. Pick one of the nonfiction titles suggested in the chapter or find another that particularly appeals to you. Read it carefully. Then, decide which comprehension strategy from the chapter might best be used in helping a young learner from a different cultural background to understand the text. Why did you select that strategy?

4. Think about the reading–writing connection and how it applies to working with expository text. What do you think about using some of the projects suggested to extend learning in the content areas? Which kinds of projects appeal to you as a learner? Why? Can you see any validity in offering different ways of sharing learning or do you think the standard report at the end of a unit is still the most effective way to summarize learning? Why do you feel as you do?

5. Have you had the opportunity to surf the Internet and use it as a resource for your own research or projects? Discuss your experiences with a classmate. How have they used the Internet? Spend some time alone or with a classmate investigating the technology suggested in the chapter.

Children's Literature

For annotations of the books listed below, please see Appendix A.

Aliki. (1998). *Marianthe's Story: Painted Words; Marianthe's Story: Spoken Memories.* New York: Greenwillow.

Arnosky, Jim. (2000). *I See Animals Hiding.* New York: Scholastic.

Bischhoff-Miersch, Andrea, and Michael Bischhoff-Miersch. (1995). *Do You Know the Difference?* (C. Faltermayr, Illus.). New York: North-South.

Bourke, Linda. (1995). *Eye Count: A Book of Counting Puzzles.* San Francisco: Chronicle Books.

Burleigh, Robert. (1998). *Home Run: The Story of Babe Ruth.* (M. Wimmer, Illus.). San Diego, CA: Silver Whistle/Harcourt Brace.

Chambers, Veronica. (1998). *Amistad Rising: A Story of Freedom.* (P. Lee, Illus.). San Diego, CA: Harcourt Brace.

Cherry, Lynne. (1992). *A River Ran Wild.* San Diego, CA: Harcourt.

Gibbons, Gail. (1999). *Bats.* New York: Holiday House.

———. (1998). *Soaring with the Wind: The Bald Eagle.* New York: Morrow.

Johnson, Stephen T. (1996). *Alphabet City.* New York: Viking.

Jonas, Ann. (1989). *Color Dance.* New York: Greenwillow.

Lauber, Patricia. (1989). *The News about Dinosaurs.* New York: Bradbury.

———. (1991). *Summer of Fire: Yellowstone, 1998.* New York: Orchard.

Longfellow, Henry Wadsworth. (1996). *Paul Revere's Ride.* (T. Rand, Illus.). New York: Puffin.

Macy, Sue. (1996). *Winning Ways: A Photohistory of American Women in Sports.* New York: Holt.

Medley, Steven. (2001). *Antelope, Bison, Cougar: A National Park Wildlife Alphabet Book.* (D. San Souci, Illus.). El Portal, CA: Yosemite Association.

Murphy, Jim. (1996). *A Young Patriot: The American Revolution as Experienced by One Boy.* New York: Clarion.

Parker, Steve. (1994). *Whales and Dolphins.* Boston, MA: Sierra.

Schwartz, David. (2001). *Q is for Quark: A Science Alphabet.* (K. Doner, Illus.). Berkeley, CA: Tricycle Press.

Scillian, Devin. (2001). *A is for America.* (P. Carroll). Chelsea, MI: Sleeping Bear Press.

Simon, Seymour. (1998). *They Swim in Seas: The Mystery of Animal Migration* (E. Warnick, Illus.). San Diego: Brown Deer/Harcourt.

———. (1995). *Sharks.* New York: Harper.

Walsh, Ellen. (1989). *Mouse Paint.* San Diego, CA: Harcourt Brace.

Yolen, Jane. (1996). *Welcome to the Sea of Sand.* (L. Regan, Illus.). New York: Scholastic.

Classroom Teaching Resources

Edwards, S. A., Maloy, R. W., & Verock-O'Loughlin. R. (2003). *Ways of writing with young kids: Teaching creativity and conventions unconventionally.* Boston: Allyn & Bacon.

Harvey, S. (1998). *Nonfiction matters: Reading, writing, and research in grades 3–8.* Portland, ME: Stenhouse.

Hoyt, L. (2002). *Make it real: Strategies for success with informational texts.* Portsmouth, NH: Heineman.

Norton, D. E., & Norton, S. E. (2001). *Language arts activities for children* (5th ed.). Upper Saddle River, NJ: Merrill/Prentice Hall.

Appendices

Appendix A

Children's Literature: Annotated Bibliography

Key: P–Primary (K-2)   I–Intermediate (3-5)
M–Middle School (6-8)
PB–Picture Book   CB–Chapter Book
N–Novel   NF–Nonfiction

Aardema, Verna. (1975). *Why Mosquitoes Buzz in People's Ears.* (L. & D. Dillon, Illus.). New York: Dial.
When the young owlet is killed, Lion holds court to find out who killed it. A delightful African folktale with great language use. **(P–PB)**

Adler, David. (1998). *A Picture Book of Amelia Earhart.* New York: Holiday House.
A simple but well-written biography of the famous woman pilot. **(P/I–PB)**

———. (2000). *America's Champion Swimmer: Gertrude Ederle.* (T. Widener, Illus.). New York: Harcourt/Gulliver.
Not satisfied to be an Olympic medal winner, Trudy swims the English Channel. **(P/I–PB)**

Agard, John, & Nichols, Grace. (2002). *Under the Moon & Over the Sea: A Collection of Caribbean Poems.* Cambridge, MA: Candlewick.
Readers will sample what it is like to live on a lush Caribbean island through the more than 50 poems in this book. **(P/I/M–PB)**

Alborough, Jez. (1999). *The Duck in the Truck.* New York: HarperCollins.
Duck and his friends try to get his truck out of the muck. **(P–PB)**

Aliki. (1983). *Medieval Feast.* New York: Harper.
In artwork reflecting that of medieval times, this book shows the flurry of activity in a manor house in preparation for a visit from the king and queen. **(I/M–PB)**.

———. (1986). *Marianthe's Story: Painted Words; Marianthe's Story: Spoken Memories.* New York: Greenwillow.
New to the country, Marianthe goes to school with trepidation, learns a new language, and eventually tells her life story through words and pictures. **(I/M–PB)**

Altman, Linda. (2000). *The Legend of Freedom Hill.* (C. Van Wright & Y-H Hu, Illus.). New York: Lee & Low.
Two young girls from very different backgrounds become best friends in a tale set during the California Gold Rush. **(I/MS–N)**

Andersen, Hans Christian. (1999). *The Ugly Duckling.* (J. Pinkney, Illus.). New York: Morrow Junior Books.
A beautifully illustrated retelling in which an ugly duckling endures ostracism by the other barnyard animals until he matures into a swan. **(P/I–PB)**

———. (2002). *The Nightingale.* Retold by Stephen Mitchell. (B. Ibatoulline, Illus.). Cambridge, MA: Candlewick.
Although banished from the kingdom, the nightingale remains faithful to the emperor and returns to help him when he is near death. **(I/M–PB)**

Anderson, William (Ed.). (1998a). *A Little House Reader: A Collection of*

the Writings of Laura Ingalls Wilder.
(D. Andreason, Illus.). New York:
HarperCollins.
This book contains a collection of
writings that preceded the Little
House books illuminating the
author's early life. **(M–NF)**

———. (1998b). *Pioneer Girl: The
Story of Laura Ingalls Wilder.*
New York: HarperCollins.
Recounted in picture book format,
readers follow Laura's life journey
from the prairies to prominence as an
author.

Anno, Mitsumasa. (1983). *Anno's
Mysterious Multiplying Jar.*
New York: Philomel.
Anno encourages readers to
problem-solve their way through the
book. **(I/M–PB)**

Arnosky, Jim. (1990). *Crinkleroot's
Guide to Walking in Wild Places.*
New York: Bradbury Press.
The wise forest dweller Crinkleroot
offers tips for walking in the wild
and avoiding such hazards as ticks,
poisonous plants, and wild animals.
(P/I–PB)

———. (1995). *I See Animals Hiding.*
New York: Scholastic.
A variety of animals in their natural
habitat and simple text demonstrate
the meaning of camouflage, an
effective solution to one problem of
survival. **(P–PB–NF)**

———. (1996). *Crinkleroot's Guide to
Knowing Butterflies.* New York:
Simon & Schuster.
Crinkleroot introduces readers to the
appearance and habits of various
butterflies and moths. **(P/I–PB)**

Asch, Frank, & Levin, Ted. (1998).
Cactus Poems. (T. Levin, Illus.). San
Diego, CA: Harcourt Brace.
Plants and animals of the American
deserts are depicted in verse and
photographs. **(I/M–NF–Poetry)**

Avi. (1995). *Poppy.* (B. Floca, Illus.).
New York: Orchard.
A mouse bravely challenges the owl
that has terrorized the woods.
(P/I–PB)

———. (2002). *Crispin: The Cross of
Lead.* New York: Hyperion.
A young boy living in a small village
during the Middle Ages faces the
injustices of feudalism. **(I/MS–N)**

Aylesworth, Jim. (1992). *Old Black Fly.*
(S. Gammell, Illus.). New York:
Henry Holt.
The old black fly has a very busy,
very bad day landing where he
should not be. **(P–PB)**

Babbitt, Natalie. (1975). *Tuck
Everlasting.* New York: Farrar,
Straus, and Giroux.
A classic adventure tale of
kidnapping, murder, and a jailbreak
along with the story of a family who
never ages. **(I/M–N)**

Bang, Molly. (1999). *When Sophie Gets
Angry, Really, Really, Angry.*
New York: Scholastic.
Young Sophie becomes upset when
she has to share with her sibling. She
races outside and climbs a tree. After
she calms down, things return to
normalcy in her family. **(P–PB)**

Barron, T. A. (1992). *The Ancient One.*
New York: Philomel.
Readers step back in time to learn
the history of an old growth forest
facing destruction by Oregon
loggers. **(P/I–PB)**

Bartone, Elisa. (1993). *Peppe, the
Lamplighter.* (T. Lewin, Illus.).
New York: Lothrop, Lee & Shepard.
While his job angers his father
because it is so insignificant,
Peppe helps his lost sister find
her way back home because he
has lighted the gas street lamps.
(I/M–PB)

Bayer, Jane. (1984). *A My Name Is Alice.* New York: Dial.
The letters of the alphabet are highlighted in the well-known jump rope rhyme. The illustrations include animals from all over the world. **(P–PB)**

Bender, Robert. (1996). *The A to Z Beastly Jamboree.* New York: Lodestar.
Bender's bright, glowing illustrations are the highlight of this alliterative alphabet book where bats boil Bb and mice mail Mm. **(P–PB)**

Berger, Melvin. (2000). *Buzz! A Book about Insects.* New York: Scholastic.
A photo-illustrated text about the world of insects. **(P–PB)**

Berry, James (Ed.). (2002). *Around the World in Eighty Poems.* (K. Lucas, Illus.). New York: Chronicle Books.
The eighty poems included in this volume represent 51 countries and the Arctic Circle. From lighthearted to serious, there is something for a range of readers and ethnic diversities. **(I–Poetry)**

Birch, David. (1988). *The King's Chessboard.* (D. Grebu, Illus.). New York: Dial.
A wise man decrees that a grain of rice be doubled each day for as many days as there are squares on a chessboard. **(I/M–PB)**

Bischhoff-Miersch, Andrea, & Bischhoff-Miersch, Michael. (1995). *Do You Know the Difference?* (C. Faltermayr, Illus.). New York: North-South.
The similarities and differences between a number of pairs of animals are presented in a text that will interest young readers. **(I/M–PB–NF)**

Blume, Judy. (1970). *Are You There God? It's Me, Margaret.* New York: Bradbury.
When Margaret's first period arrives, she's convinced she's dying. **(I/M–N)**

———. (1972). *Tales of a Fourth-Grade Nothing.* New York: Dial.
Family relationships are the theme of this novel. **(I–N)**

Bouchard, David. (1995). *If You're Not from the Prairie.* (H. Ripplinger, Illus.). New York: Atheneum.
Two intermediate grade children describe life on the rural prairie. **(I/M–PB–NF)**

Bourke, Linda. (1995). *Eye Count: A Book of Counting Puzzles.* San Francisco: Chronicle Books.
An innovative counting book that entices readers to unravel word puzzles involving homophones and homonyms. **(I/M–PB–NF)**

Bradby, Marie. (1995). *More Than Anything Else.* (C. K. Soentpiet, Illus.). New York: Orchard.
A young slave boy desperately wants to learn to read. **(I–PB)**

Bridwell, Norman. (1986). *Clifford, the Big Red Dog.* New York: Scholastic.
Emily Elizabeth has a huge red dog for a pet. **(P–PB)**

Brown, Marc. (1996). *Arthur Writes a Story.* Boston: Little, Brown and Company.
Arthur has a difficult time deciding what to write a story about. **(P–PB)**

Brown, Margaret Wise. (1947). *Goodnight, Moon.* (C. Hurd, Illus.). New York: Harper & Row.
A wonderful bedtime story in patterned, rhythmic language. **(P–PB)**

———. (1999). *I Like Bugs.* New York: Golden Books.
The brief, rhyming text lists all the kinds of bugs the narrator likes. **(P–PB)**

Browne, Anthony. (1996). *Things I Like.* Boston: Houghton Mifflin.

A little monkey lists all the activities that he likes. **(P–PB)**

Bruchac, Joseph. (1995). *A Boy Called Slow: The True Story of Sitting Bull* (R. Baviera, Illus.). New York: Philomel.
The characteristics that made Sitting Bull a great leader are depicted in this overview of his life. **(I/M–PB–NF)**

———. (2000). *Squanto's Journey: The Story of the First Thanksgiving.* (G. Shedd, Illus.). San Diego, CA: Silver Whistle/Harcourt Brace.
Readers learn about the courage and kindness of Squanto and his eventual role in helping the Pilgrims survive in a rugged new land that they knew little about. **(P/I–PB)**

Bruchac, Joseph, & Bruchac, James. (2001). *How Chipmunk Got His Stripes.* (J. Aruego & A. Dewey, Illus.). New York: Dial.
This Native American tale is an appealing read-aloud because it is filled with repetition and supportive illustrations.

Bunting, Eve. (1994). *Smoky Night.* (D. Diaz, Illus.). San Diego, CA: Harcourt.
Cultural differences are overcome during the Los Angeles riots. **(P/I–PB)**

———. (1998). *So Far from the Sea.* (C. Soentpiet, Illus.). New York: Clarion.
Before they move to Massachusetts, Laura and her family visit Grandfather's grave at the Manzanar War Relocation Center where she leaves behind a special gift. **(I/M–PB)**

———. (1999). *The Butterfly House.* (D. Diaz, Illus.). New York: Scholastic.
A little girl and her grandfather make a house for a larva and watch it change before setting it free. **(P/I–PB)**

Burleigh, Robert. (1991). *Flight: The Journey of Charles Lindbergh.* (M. Wimmer, Illus.). New York: Philomel.
Beautiful illustrations and free verse text take the reader along with Lindbergh as he made his historic flight. **(I/M–PB/NF–Poetry)**

———. (1998). *Home Run: The Story of Babe Ruth.* (M. Wimmer, Illus.). San Diego, CA: Silver Whistle/Harcourt Brace.
Realistic illustrations interspersed with baseball cards highlight a brief overview of Babe Ruth's baseball career. **(I/M–PB–NF)**

Byars, Betsy. (1993). *The Pinballs.* New York: Harper & Row.
Three foster children cautiously learn to depend on each other and triumph over life's tragedies. **(I/M–N)**

Carle, Eric. (1969). *The Very Hungry Caterpillar.* New York: Philomel.
A caterpillar eats his way through the days of the week until he forms a cocoon and transforms into a butterfly. **(P–PB)**

———. (1977). *The Grouchy Ladybug.* New York: HarperCollins.
A grouchy ladybug who is looking for a fight challenges all the creatures she meets regardless of their size. **(P–PB)**

———. (1995). *The Very Lonely Firefly.* New York: Philomel.
Eric Carle's collage work may serve as an art lesson for older students while younger students will enjoy the story about friendship. **(P/I–PB)**

Carlson, Nancy. (1988). *I Like Me.* New York: Viking Penguin.
A charming pig shows that the best friend you can have is yourself. **(P–PB)**

Carroll, Lewis. (1989). *Jabberwocky.* (G. Base, Illus.). New York: Harry N. Abrams.
This is a vibrant watercolor interpretation of Carroll's amusing poem. **(I/M–PB)**

Chambers, Veronica. (1998). *Amistad Rising: A Story of Freedom.* (P. Lee, Illus.). San Diego, CA: Harcourt Brace.
Following the brutal kidnapping of fifty-three African Americans to force them into slavery, Joseph Cinques and John Quincy Adams unite efforts to change history. **(M–NF)**

Cherry, Lynne. (1992). *A River Ran Wild.* San Diego, CA: Harcourt.
A group of concerned citizens fight to restore the ecologically dead Nashua River in Massachusetts to its original state after hundreds of years of abuse. **(I/M–PB–NF)**

Christelow, Eileen. (1995). *What Do Authors Do?* New York: Clarion.
The author shares the steps to making a book from idea to publication. **(P–PB)**

Cleary, Beverly. (1965). *The Mouse and the Motorcycle.* (L. Darling, Illus.). New York: Morrow.
An adventuresome mouse uses a boy's toy motorcycle to check out the hotel where he lives. **(I–N)**

———. (1983). *Dear Mr. Henshaw.* (P. O. Zelinsky, Illus.). New York: Morrow.
A boy writes a series of letters to an author and tells of his difficulties when his parents get a divorce. **(I/M–N)**

———. (1991). *Strider.* New York: Morrow.
Leigh's parents are divorced and he finds running track to be an outlet. **(M–N)**

———. (1998). *The Hullabaloo ABC.* (T. Rand, Illus.). New York: Morrow Junior Books.
An alphabet book in which three children make and hear every noise imaginable while frolicking around the farm. **(P–PB)**

Cohen, Caron L. (1985). *Sally Ann Thunder Ann Whirlwind Crockett.* (A. Dewey, Illus.). New York: Greenwillow.
Readers of this tall tale will enjoy meeting the wife of Davey Crockett. **(I/M–PB)**

Cole, Joanna. (1996). *The Magic School Bus Explores inside the Earth.* (B. Degan, Illus.). New York: Scholastic.
Miss Frizzle takes her class on a geological tour of the earth. **(P/I–PB)**

Coles, Robert. (1995). *Ruby Bridges.* (G. Ford, Illus.). New York: Scholastic.
The true story of brave, young Ruby Bridges, the first African American to integrate into Franz Elementary School in New Orleans in 1960. **(P/I–PB)**

Collier, Christopher, & Collier, James. (1992). *With Every Drop of Blood.* New York: Delacorte.
When his father dies, a young Rebel boy must take care of his family, but he is captured by a Yankee soldier. **(I/MS–N)**

Cooney, Barbara. (1982). *Miss Rumphius.* New York: Viking.
This is a quiet story about Miss Rumphius who plants lupine flowers wherever she goes, making the world a prettier place in the process. **(P/I–PB)**

Cooper, Floyd. (1994). *Coming Home: From the Life of Langston Hughes.* New York: Philomel.
Readers get a real understanding of the struggles faced by this

exceptional poet through both text and illustrations. **(I/M–PB–NF)**

Curtis, Christopher Paul. (1997). *The Watsons Go to Birmingham, 1963.* New York: Delacorte.
As Kenny and his family travel from Michigan to Alabama to visit his grandmother, their story reflects the tension and tragedy of the civil rights movement.

———. (1999). *Bud, Not Buddy.* New York: Delacorte.
Winner of the Coretta Scott King award, this book about family and spirit takes readers back to the days of the Great Depression where Bud Caldwell searches for his father. **(I/M–N)**

Day, Nancy. (2001). *Your Travel Guide to Ancient Mayan Civilization.* New York: Lerner.
Readers learn about the ancient Mayan culture in this clever travel guide. **(I/M–NF)**

DeGross, Monalisa. (1994). *Donavan's Word Jar.* New York: Scholastic.
The objects of Donavan's attention are words, all kinds of them. He collects them in a jar until it is simply too full to add any more. Now what should he do? His grandma offers a wonderful solution. **(P/I–CB)**

dePaola, Tomie. (1998). *Big Anthony: His Story.* New York: G. P. Putnam's Sons.
From the day he was born, Big Anthony didn't pay attention! **(P–PB)**

———. (2002). *Adelita—A Mexican Cinderella Story.* New York: Putnam.
A version of the popular tale that is filled with Mexican warmth and humor. A caring nanny and housekeeper replaces the fairy godmother who helps Adelita to a happily-ever-after ending.

DiCamillo, Kate. (2000). *Because of Winn-Dixie.* New York: Candlewick.
A lonely ten-year-old girl moves with her family to a small Florida town where she finds a mongrel dog—and a fast friend—in the supermarket. **(I/M–N)**

Dorris, Michael. (1992). *Morning Girl.* New York: Hyperion.
A novel about a Taino Indian girl and her brother set in 1492 in the Bahamas and how their rich and complex life is threatened by Columbus's exploration. **(I/M–N)**

Duke, Kate. (1992). *Aunt Isabel Tells a Good One.* New York: Dutton Children's Books.
Penelope and her Aunt Isabel create an exciting story with all the right ingredients. **(P/I–PB)**

Dvorak, David Jr. (1994). *A Sea of Grass: The Tallgrass Prairie.* New York: Macmillan.
The readers view the prairie as many a settler might, grass-covered with a variety of native grasses as far as the eye can see. **(I/M–PB–NF)**

Edwards, Pamela D. (1997). *Barefoot.* (H. Cole, Illus.). New York: HarperCollins.
Watching animals help a runaway slave escape his pursuers in a story told from quite a different perspective. **(I/M–PB)**

Egielski, Richard. (1995). *Buz.* New York: A Laura Geringer Book.
When a little boy swallows a bug along with his cereal, pandemonium breaks out as the bug searches for escape. **(P–PB)**

Ehlert, Lois. (1989). *Color Zoo.* New York: Lippincott.
Using colorful collages, Ehlert presents the basic colors as animals found at the zoo. **(P–PB)**

———. (1990). *Color Farm.* New York: Lippincott.

Farm animals are presented in this color concept book for young children. **(P–PB)**

Erdrich, Louise. (1999). *The Birchbark House.* New York: Hyperion. The impact of the white man on the life of an Ojibwa tribe in the Lake Superior area is explained in this engrossing novel. **(I/M–PB)**

Falconer, I. (2000). *Olivia.* New York: Atheneum. This Caldecott winner appeals to younger children. Olivia the pig has a ton of charisma and loads of energy. And she delights in scaring the daylights out of her younger sibling. **(PB–P)**

Falwell, Cathryn. (1993). *Feast for Ten.* New York: Clarion. The bold collage illustrations in this book show an African American family shopping for, preparing, and eating a feast for ten. **(P–PB)**

———. (1998). *Word Wizard.* New York: Clarion. Anna cleverly aids a lost little boy by rearranging letters in her cereal in an anagram adventure. **(P/I–PB)**

Farmer, Nancy. (1994). *The Ear, the Eye, and the Arm: A Novel.* New York: Orchard. In a futuristic setting, detectives with paranormal powers attempt to rescue three kidnapped children. **(M–N)**

Farris, Pamela J. (1996). *Young Mouse and Elephant: An East African Folktale.* (V. Gorbochev, Illus.). Boston: Houghton Mifflin. When boastful Young Mouse is told that Elephant is the strongest animal, he sets out to challenge the huge creature on the African savannah in this humorous folktale. **(P–PB)**

Feelings, Muriel. (1974). *Moja Means One: Swahili Counting Book.* (T. Feelings, Illus.). New York: Dial. A counting book packed with information on South Africa and the Swahili language. **(P/I–PB)**

Fitzhugh, Louise. (1964). *Harriet the Spy.* New York: Harper & Row. The first children's book that emphasized a child keeping a diary. **(I/M–N)**

Fleischman, Paul. (1988). *Joyful Noise: Poems for Two Voices.* (E. Beddows, Illus.). New York: Harper & Row. A Newbery Medal book where all the poems are about insects. **(/MI–Poetry)**

———. (1997). *Seedfolks.* New York: Colter Books. People of varying ethnic backgrounds work together to beautify a neighborhood lot and learn a great deal about each other in the process.

Fleming, Denise. (1993). *In the Small, Small Pond.* New York: Holt. A short verse, counting book with lots of visual images. **(P–PB)**

Fleming, Virginia. (1997). *Be Good to Eddie Lee.* (F. Cooper, Illus.). New York: Philomel. Eddie Lee has a message for readers as he deals with the ridicule of neighborhood children because of his disability, Down's syndrome. **(I/M–PB)**

Florian, Douglas. (1999). *Laugh-Eteria.* San Diego, CA: Harcourt Brace. This book contains 150 humorous poems about many topics including school, trees, and hair. **(P/I–Poetry)**

Fowler, Allan. (1998). *Inside an Ant Colony.* Danbury, CT: Children's Press. Describes how these social insects work and live together in organized communities that are similar to bustling cities. **(P–PB)**

Fox, Mem. (1986). *Hattie and the Fox.* (P. Mullins, Illus.). New York: Bradbury Press.

Hattie the hen spies something in the bushes and tries to warn her barnyard friends, but they are uninterested until they realize it is a fox! **(P–PB)**

———. (1998). *Boo to a Goose.* (D. Miller, Illus.). New York: Dial. A boy lists rhyming alternatives to the saying "BOO!" to a goose. **(P–PB)**

———. (2000). *Harriet, You'll Drive Me Wild!* (M. Frazee, Illus.). San Diego: Harcourt. A cumulative tale about a pesky child who has accidents that stretch her mother's patience to the limit. **(P–PB)**

Frasier, Debra. (2000). *Miss Alaineus: A Vocabulary Distaster.* San Diego, CA: Harcourt Brace. Dictionary definitions have never been so much fun in a story that evolves because Sage misunderstands her homework assignment. **(I/M–PB)**

Freedman, Russell. (1989). *Lincoln: A Photobiography.* New York: Clarion. This book is a photographic biography of the life of Abraham Lincoln. **(I/M–NF)**

Galdone, Paul. (1989). *The Three Little Pigs.* New York: Clarion. This is a traditional retelling of the pursuit of the three little swine by the villainous wolf. **(P/I/M–PB)**

George, Jean Craighead. (1972). *Julie of the Wolves.* (J. Schoenherr, Illus.). New York: Harper & Row. A Newbery Award winner that describes a girl brought up by wolves. **(I/M–N)**

George, Kristine O'Connell. (1997). *The Great Frog Race and Other Poems.* (K. Kiesler, Illus.). Boston: Clarion Books/Houghton Mifflin. A collection of poetry by George including shape poems such as "Egg." **(I–Poetry)**

Gibbons, Gail. (1991). *From Seed to Plant.* New York: Holiday House. Explains the relationship between seeds and the plants they produce. **(P/I–PB)**

———. (1992). *Recycle.* New York: Little, Brown and Company. Describes the process of recycling from start to finish and explains how recyclables are transformed into new products. **(P/I–PB)**

———. (1993). *Spiders.* New York: Holiday House. Gibbons examines a variety of spiders and their individual behaviors and habitats. **(P/I–PB)**

———. (1995). *Planet Earth/Inside Out.* New York: Mulberry Paperback. A detailed look at the internal structure and geology of the earth. **(P/I–PB)**

———. (1997). *The Moon Book.* New York: Holiday House. Explains how man has observed and explored the moon over the years to learn about its movement and phases. **(P/I–PB)**

———. (1998). *Soaring with the Wind: The Bald Eagle.* New York: Morrow. Bald eagles in the wild and their habitats are discussed. **(P/I–PB–NF)**

———. (1999). *Bats.* New York: Holiday House. Youngsters will discover numerous facts about these nocturnal creatures. **(P–PB)**

———. (2000). *Apples.* New York: Holiday House. The story of apples from seed to apple sauce is told. **(P–PB)**

Gilliland, Judith H. (2000). *Steamboat! The Story of Captain Blanche Leathers.* (H. Meade, Illus.). New York: Dorling Kindersley. Courageous and not to be deterred, Blanche studies the Mississippi River thoroughly, enabling her to become the first woman steamboat pilot. **(P/I/M–PB–NF)**

Ginsburg, Mirra. (1972). *The Chick and the Duckling.* (J. Aruego & A. Dewey, Illus.). New York: Macmillan.
The naive chick follows the duckling everywhere, even into the pond. **(P–PB)**

Gollenbock, Peter. (2001). *Hank Aaron: Brave in Every Way.* (P. Lee, Illus.). San Diego, CA: Gulliver/Harcourt.
The inspiring story of a man who battles prejudice to become a great ballplayer. **(P/I–NF)**

Gollub, Matthew. (1998). *Cool Melons Turn to Frogs: The Life and Poems of Issa.* (K. G. Stone, Illus.). New York: Lee & Low.
The haiku poetry of the Japanese poet Issa is presented. **(P/I/MS–Poetry)**

Graham, Joan Bransford. (1999). *Flicker Flash.* Boston: Houghton Mifflin.
Here is a tantalizing book of poetry about all kinds of light. **(I/M–NF–Poetry)**

Granfield, Linda. (2001). *The Legend of the Panda.* (S. N. Zhang, Illus.). Plattsburgh, NY: Tundra.
In a story of sacrifice and love, this ancient tale describes how the panda got its black-and-white coat. **(I/M–PB)**

Grimes, Nikki. (1994). *Meet Danitra Brown.* (F. Cooper, Illus.). New York: Morrow.
An African American child praises friendship and gives the reader insight into other issues in her family and school life. An ALA Notable book and a Coretta Scott King Award Honor Book for illustration. **(I–Poetry)**

———. (1998). *Jazmin's Notebook.* New York: Dial.

An uplifting story about the teenage Jazmin who finds strength in writing poetry and keeping record of the sometimes difficult events in her life. A Coretta Scott King Honor Book. **(I–N)**

Gwyne, Fred. (1988). *A Little Pigeon-Toed.* New York: Simon and Schuster.
A perfect choice for a little word play. **(P/I–NF)**

Hamilton, Virginia. (1999). *Bluish.* New York: Blue Sky Press.
Dreenie wonders about the impact of her friendship with a sickly classmate. **(I/M–N)**

Hanson, J. (1998). *Women of Hope: African Americans Who Made a Difference.* New York: Scholastic.
Twelve courageous and strong women are highlighted in this excellent collection of biographies. **(M–NF)**

Hartman, Gail. (1991). *As the Crow Flies: A First Book of Maps.* (H. Stevenson, Illus.). New York: Bradbury Press.
A look at different geographical areas from the perspectives of an eagle, rabbit, crow, horse, and gull. **(P–PB)**

Heard, Georgia (Ed.). (2002). *This Place I Know: Poems of Comfort.* Cambridge, MA: Candlewick.
This volume offers hope in the form of poetry to those who are sad, angry, or afraid. **(I/M–PB)**

Heide, Florence Parry. (2000). *Some Things Are Scary.* (J. Feiffer, Illus.). New York: Candlewick Press.
A youngster relates everything that is frightening—being hugged by someone you don't like, having people laugh at you and you don't know why, or holding on to what you thought was your mother's hand only to discover it's someone else's hand. **(PB–P)**

Henkes, Kevin. (1993). *Owen.* New York: Greenwillow. Owen has to decide whether to take along his security blanket. His wise mother intercedes with a solution. **(P–PB)**

———. (1999). *The Birthday Room.* New York: Greenwillow. Ben's parents transform the attic into a studio hoping he'll become an artist. But what he really wants is to travel to Oregon to see an uncle the family has all but banned. **(I/M–N)**

Hershenhorn, Esther. (1998). *There Goes Lowell's Party.* (J. Rogers, Illus.). New York: Holiday House. Yahoo! Today is Lowell's birthday and he has quite a party planned. But geese are flying low, floor boards are creaking, and leaves are showing their backs—sure signs of a looming rainstorm. This Ozark tale shares folklore that is scientifically accurate. **(P/I–PB)**

Hesse, Karen. (1998). *Out of the Dust: A Novel.* New York: Scholastic. Told through journal entries and in narrative poetry format, this Newbery winner relates the tragedies faced by a family in Oklahoma during the Great Depression and the Dust Bowl. **(M–N)**

Hest, Amy. (1997a). *The Great Green Notebook of Katie Roberts.* (S. Lamut, Illus.). New York: Candlewick. Twelve-year-old Katie shares her thoughts about the world. **(I–CB)**

———. (1997b). *When Jessie Came Across the Sea.* (P. J. Lynch, Illus.). Cambridge, MA: Candlewick. A courageous young Jewish orphan emigrates to New York City where she sews lace and saves her earnings so that she can eventually bring her grandmother to the United States. **(I/M–PB)**

High, Linda O. (2001). *A Humble Life: Plain Poems.* (B. Farnsworth, Illus.). New York: Eerdmans. A poetic description of people, observations, and events in the daily lives of the Amish and Mennonite peoples in the Pennsylvania Dutch country. **(P/I–NF)**

Hindley, Judy. (2002). *Do Like a Duck Does!* (I. Bates, Illus.). Cambridge, MA: Candlewick. Momma Duck outwits the hairy stranger who claims he is a duck but is really looking for a duck dinner.

Hoban, Russell. (1960). *Bedtime for Frances.* New York: Harper & Row. Frances, a badger, tries to convince her parents not to put her to bed. **(P–PB)**

Hoban, Tana. (1998). *More, Fewer, Less.* New York: Greenwillow. Photographs clearly illustrate groupings of items in smaller and larger numbers. **(P/PB–NF)**

Hobbs, Will. (1995). *Kokopelli's Flute.* New York: Simon & Schuster. When Tep and his dog, Dusty, explore a cliff dwelling while awaiting the total eclipse of the moon, they stumble onto robbers. **(M–N)**

———. (1996). *Far North.* New York: Morrow. A page-turning survival story set in the Northwest Territories in which Gabe Rogers and his roommate, Raymond Providence, learn to respect cultural differences as they struggle to stay alive. **(I/M–N)**

———. (2002). *Wild Man Island.* New York: HarperCollins. Fourteen-year-old Andy is marooned on Admiralty Island, the site of his father's earlier death, leading to adventure and amazing archeological discoveries. **(M–N)**

Hoberman, Mary. (2001). *You Read to Me, I'll Read to You.* New York: HarperCollins.
A delightful book for paired reading of beginning readers. **(P–PB)**

Holm, Jennifer. (1999). *Our Only May Amelia.* New York: HarperCollins.
Set in 1899 in the state of Washington, May Amelia is the youngest of eight children and the only girl. She dreams of going to China, something her strict Finnish family resists. **(I/M–N)**

Hong, Lily Toy. (1993). *Two of Everything.* New York: Whitman.
A Chinese folktale about a couple who finds a magical pot that duplicates everything that is put inside it. **(P–PB)**

Hooper, Meredith. (1998). *The Drop in My Drink: The Story of Water on Our Planet.* (C. Coady, Illus.). New York: Viking.
This informative book explores where water comes from and its importance to all creatures. Both text and illustrations work together to reinforce the importance of this critical resource. **(I/M–NF–PB)**

Hoose, Phillip, & Hoose, Hannah. (1998). *Hey, Little Ant.* Berkeley, CA: Tricycle Press.
A song picture book about the relationship between a boy and an ant. **(P–PB)**

Hopkins, Lee Bennett. (1999). *Spectacular Science: A Book of Poems.* (V. Halstead, Illus.). New York: Simon & Schuster.
A variety of poets provide answers and questions about science-related topics. **(P/I–Poetry)**

———. (2002). *Home to Me: Poems Across America.* (S. Alcorn, Illus.). New York: Orchard.
The varied geography of America attracts different people who settle and call that spot their home be it the prairie, a city, a reservation, or a ranch. **(P/I)**

Houston, Gloria. (1998). *Bright Freedom's Song: A Story of the Underground Railroad.* San Diego: Harcourt Brace.
Bright Freedom and her father help slaves escape in Virginia. **(I/MS–N)**

Howe, Deborah, & Howe, James. (1983). *Bunnicula.* (L. Morrill, Illus.). New York: Atheneum.
The family cat and dog become suspicious when a bunny rabbit comes and suddenly the vegetables start turning white. **(P/I–N)**

Howland, Naomi. (1994). *ABCDrive!* New York: Clarion Books.
A car trip provides the opportunity to see or experience things for every letter of the alphabet, from "ambulance" to "zoom." **(P–PB)**

Hoyt-Goldsmith, Diane. (1998). *Celebrating Chinese New Year.* (L. Migdale, photographer). New York: Holiday House.
A young boy in San Francisco and his family prepare to celebrate Chinese New Year. **(I/M–PB–NF)**

Innocenti, Roberto, & Galaz, Christophe. (1986). *Rose Blanche.* Mankato, MN: Creative Education.
A young girl watches the changes in her community when the Germans arrive. She befriends the children in the concentration camp. **(I/M–PB)**

Irbiniskas, Heather. (1994). *How Jackrabbit Got His Very Long Ears.* (K. J. Spengler, Illus.). Flagstaff, AZ: Northland.
Jackrabbit doesn't listen carefully to what the Great Spirit tells him, and his careless answers to the animals' questions result in much unhappiness. **(P/I/M–PB)**

Issacs, Anne. (1994). *Swamp Angel.* (P. Zelinsky, Illus.). New York: Dutton.

Angelica Longrider, a remarkable female heroine, saves settlers from thundering Tarnation, a terrifying bear creating the Great Smoky Mountains in the process. **(I/M–PB)**

Jackson, Ellen. (1994). *Cinder Edna.* (K. O'Malley, Illus.). New York: Lee & Low.
This feminist version introduces liberated, spunky Cinder Edna and her neighbor, passive Cinderella, in an amusing story of contrasts. **(P/I/M–PB)**

Jacques, Brian. (1987). *Redwall.* (G. Chalk, Illus.). New York: Philomel.
The original Redwall book that begins the series of adventures of good rodents versus evil rodents in the English countryside. **(I/M–N)**

———. (2000). *The Legend of Luke.* New York: Philomel.
When Martin the Warrior seeks information about his father, Luke, medieval adventures abound. **(I/M–N)**

Jahn-Clough, Lisa. (1997). *ABC Yummy.* Boston: Houghton Mifflin.
This alphabetic tour of good things to eat uses alliterative sentences ranging from Alicia's appetizing asparagus to Zoe's zesty zucchini. **(P–PB)**

Jarrell, Randall. (1964). *The Bat-Poet.* (M. Sendak, Illus.). New York: Macmillan.
When a bat can't sleep during the day, he decides to write poems and share them with his friends. **(P–PB)**

Johnson, Angela. (1998). *The Other Side: Shorter Poems.* New York: Orchard.
The author pens her bittersweet memories of Shorter, the town in which she lived when she was young. **(I/M–Poetry–NF)**

Johnson, Stephen T. (1995). *Alphabet City.* New York: Viking.
This innovative Caldecott Honor Book presents common city images with a letter of the alphabet being an integral part of each one. **(P/I/M: PB–NF)**

Johnstone, M. (1999). *Look Inside Cross-Sections Planes.* (H. Jennssen, Illus.). New York: Dorling Kindersley.
Hours of study are afforded plane enthusiasts with this detailed book. **(I/M–NF)**

Jonas, Ann. (1989). *Color Dance.* New York: Greenwillow.
This concept book explores the primary colors and shows how colors mix as three girls dance with sheets of sheer fabric that mix and blend creating new colors. **(P/I–PB)**

Kalan, Robert. (1978). *Rain.* (D. Crews, Illus.). New York: Greenwillow.
Rain falls on a multitude of colorful things. **(P–PB)**

Kalman, Maira. (2001). *What Pete Ate From A to Z.* New York: Putnam.
This dog devours what he shouldn't from A to Z.

Keats, Ezra Jack. (1962). *The Snowy Day.* New York: Viking.
Young Peter enjoys the first snowstorm of the year. This book was the first to utilize collage illustrations. **(P–PB)**

Kellogg, Steven. (1986). *Pecos Bill.* New York: Morrow.
Falling out of his parents' wagon as they moved West didn't phase Pecos Bill, who was raised by the coyotes, tamed the wildest of horses, and won a memorable bride. **(P/I/M–PB)**

———. (1988). *Johnny Appleseed.* New York: Morrow.
A biography of the life and adventures of John Chapman, better known as Johnny Appleseed, friend to man and animal and planter of

thousands of apple trees. **(P/I/M–PB)**

———. (1994). *Paul Bunyan.* New York: Morrow.
A lumberjack from the Northwoods, Paul and his ox, Babe, have been credited with creating the Great Lakes, the St. Lawrence Seaway, and the Grand Canyon. **(P/I/M–PB)**

———. (1998a). *Mike Fink: A Tall Tale.* New York: Morrow.
Mike Fink was a legendary keelboatman on the Ohio and Mississippi Rivers whose fame embellished him and his deeds into a folk hero. **(P/I/M–PB)**

———. (1998b). *A-Hunting We Will Go!* New York: Greenwillow.
Kellogg's detailed illustrations and text give a unique look to this popular rhyming tale. **(P–PB)**

Kimmel, Eric. A. (1988). *Anansi and the Moss Covered Rock.* (J. Stevens, Illus.). New York: Holiday House.
Anansi misuses magical powers to trick the forest animals until Little Bush Deer teaches him a lesson. **(P/I/M–PB)**

Kirk, David. (1994). *Miss Spider's Tea Party.* New York: Scholastic.
In wonderful rhyming verse, Miss Spider invites all the insects to her tea party. **(P–PB/Poetry)**

———. (1995). *Miss Spider's Wedding.* New York: Scholastic.
Gracious Miss Spider finds Mr. Right, but her friends encourage her to marry a more suave spider. **(P–PB/Poetry)**

Konigsburg, E. L. (1996). *The View from Saturday.* New York: Atheneum.
Becoming a winning team takes more than just knowledge but also involves friendships, understanding, and building on differences. **(I/M–N)**

Krauss, Ruth. (1945). *The Carrot Seed.* (C. Johnson, Illus.). New York: Harper Row.
A young boy plants a carrot seed and nurtures it. Shows dedication and commitment to a task. **(P–PB)**

Kurtz, Jane. (2000). *Faraway Home.* (E. B. Lewis, Illus.). San Diego, CA: Harcourt.
Destra worries that her father may not want to return to America when he goes to visit his Ethiopian homeland. **(P/I–PB)**

Kuskin, Karla. (1975). *Near the Window Tree.* New York: Harper & Row.
A collection of poems that will remind children of the warmth home and friends provide. **(P–Poetry)**

Lauber, Patricia. (1989). *The News about Dinosaurs.* New York: Bradbury.
A book that prompts further investigation as Lauber explains new discoveries that challenge what was once believed about dinosaurs. **(I/M–NF)**

———. (1991). *Summer of Fire: Yellowstone, 1988.* New York: Orchard Books.
Readers learn about the number of fires that raged through Yellowstone, leaving both destruction and renewal in their paths. **(I/M–NF)**

Lears, Laurie. (1998). *Ian's Walk: A Story about Autism.* (K. Ritz, Illus.). Morton Grove, IL: Albert Whitman.
Left in his older sister's care, autistic Ian wanders off. **(P/I–PB)**

Lester, Julius. (1994). *John Henry.* (J. Pinkney, Illus.). New York: Dial.
A tall tale about the steel-driving African American man. **(P/I–PB)**

Levitt, Paul M., Burger, D. A., & Gurainick, Elissa S. (1990). *The Weighty Word Book.* (J. Stevens, Illus.). Boulder, CO: Manuscripts, Ltd.

This is an alphabet book of unusual words, each described using a creative story and amusing illustration. **(I/M–NF)**

Lionni, Leo. (1960). *Inch by Inch.* New York: Astor-Honor.
A tiny creature inches his way through his environment. **(P–PB)**

Lobel, Anita. (1998). *No Pretty Pictures: A Child of War.* New York: Greenwillow.
Holocaust survivor and award-winning author Anita Lobel describes her frightening experiences as a child. **(M–NF)**

Lobel, Arnold. (1981). *On Market Street.* New York: Greenwillow.
A youngster buys presents from A to Z in the shops along Market Street. **(P–PB)**

Locker, Thomas. (1998). *Home: A Journey through America.* Orlando: Harcourt Brace.
Poetry by Joseph Bruchac, Robert Frost, Eloise Greenfield, Abraham Lincoln, and Pat Mora among others. **(P/I/MS–Poetry)**

London, Jonathan. (1999). *Wiggle Waggle.* (M. Rex, Illus.). New York: Harcourt Brace.
Describes the sounds they make when different animals walk. **(P–PB)**

Longfellow, Henry Wadsworth. (1990). *Paul Revere's Ride.* (T. Rand, Illus.). New York: Puffin.
A beautifully illustrated version of Paul Revere's ride to warn Boston citizens that the British were coming. **(I/M–PB–Poetry)**

Louie, Ai-Ling. (1996). *Yeh-Shen: A Cinderella Story from China.* (E. Young, Illus.). New York: Philomel.
Reminiscent of the traditional Cinderella story, a young girl overcomes the wickedness of her stepmother and stepsister to marry the prince. **(I/M–PB)**

Lowrey, Janet Sebring. (1942). *The Poky Little Puppy.* (G. Tenggren, Illus.). New York: Golden Books/Simon & Schuster.
A nosy puppy gets into lots of trouble. **(P–PB)**

Lowry, Lois. (1984). *Anastasia Krupnik.* New York: Yearling.
The amusing and engaging Anastasia keeps lists in her green notebook—but only of the most important things. When she discovers her mother is pregnant, she adds parents and babies to her "things I hate" list. **(N–I)**

———. (1989). *Number the Stars.* Boston: Houghton Mifflin.
A young girl's family helps her Jewish friend's family escape to Sweden during World War II. **(I/M–N)**

———. (1993). *The Giver.* Boston: Houghton Mifflin.
A boy is given the task of becoming a storyteller for his people in a future society's utopian world. **(MS–N)**

———. (2002). *Gathering Blue.* Boston: Houghton Mifflin.
Set in a futuristic society, orphaned Kira must endure cruelty and taunts from the people around her because she is different. Her vision of becoming an artist transforms the world in which she lives. **(MS–N)**

Lundell, Margo. (1995). *A Girl Named Helen Keller.* New York: Scholastic.
A simple biography of the life of Helen Keller. **(I–NF)**

MacLachlan, Patricia. (1985). *Sarah, Plain and Tall.* New York: HarperCollins.
Two children help their father get a mail order bride during the 1800s. **(I–N)**

MacMillan, Bruce. (1991). *Eating Fractions.* New York: Scholastic.
Children quickly grasp the idea of fractional parts as they study the

mouth-watering photos of children sharing and eating a variety of food. **(P/I–NF)**

Macy, Sue. (1996). *Winning Ways: A Photohistory of American Women in Sports.* New York: Holt.
Young girls who have the love of a sport will find this motivating and fascinating reading. **(I/M–NF)**

Maestro, Betsy. (1996). *Coming to America: The Story of Immigration.* (S. Ryan, Illus.). New York: Scholastic.
The history of immigration to the United States and the diversity of the people hoping to find better lives are highlighted in this book. **(I/M–PB–NF)**

Mahy, Margaret. (1990). *The Seven Chinese Brothers.* (M. & J. Tseng, Illus.). New York: Scholastic.
Seven look-alike brothers use their unique characteristics to free their imprisoned brother. **(P–PB)**

Marrin, Albert. (2000). *Sitting Bull and His World.* New York: Dutton.
The biography of the Lakota Sioux Chief who was a strong leader for his people. **(I/M–NF)**

Martin, Bill Jr. (1967). *Brown Bear, Brown Bear, What Do You See?* (E. Carle, Illus.). New York: Holt.
A classic repetitive book that introduces young children to colors and animals. **(P–PB)**

———. (1999). *A Beasty Story.* (S. Kellogg, Illus.). New York: Harcourt Brace.
A group of mice venture into the dark, dark woods and through a dark, dark house and find a spooky surprise. **(P–PB)**

Martin, Bill Jr., & Archambault, John. (1989). *Chicka Chicka Boom Boom.* (L. Ehlert, Illus.). New York: Simon & Schuster.
An alphabet rhyme that tells the story of when the whole alphabet climbs the coconut tree. **(P–PB)**

Martin, Jacqueline Briggs. (1998). *Snowflake Bentley.* Boston: Houghton Mifflin.
Wilson Bentley loves the snow and wants to capture its beauty with his camera. **(P/I–P)**

Mayer, Mercer. (1999). *Shibumi and the Kitemaker.* New York: Marshall Cavendish.
Stunning illustrations complement this thought-provoking story about a princess who tries to improve the quality of life for people in the city with the help of a wise kitemaker. **(I/M–PB)**

Maynard, Bill. (1999). *Quiet, Wyatt!* (F. Remkiewicz, Illus.). New York: Putnam.
Wyatt wants to do things with the big kids but he is always told, "Quiet, Wyatt." So he rebels—refusing to utter even a single word. Delightful rhyme and repetition that young children will enjoy and imitate. **(PB–P)**

McCully, Emily Arnold. (1998). *Beautiful Warrior: The Legend of the Nun's Kung Fu.* New York: Scholastic.
The reader learns about the martial art of kung fu and of courageous Wu Mei, a legendary character who may actually have existed. **(I/M–PB)**

McDermott, Gerald. (1974). *Arrow to the Sun.* New York: Viking.
A beautifully illustrated Native American folktale about a young boy trying to find his father, the sun god. **(P/I–PB)**

McDonald, Megan. (1995). *Insects Are My Life.* New York: Orchard Books.
No one at home or at school understands Amanda's love of insects until she meets Maggie. **(P–PB)**

Medearis, Angela S. (1997). *Princess of the Press: The Story of Ida B. Wells-Barnett.* New York: Lodestar.
The life story of a distinguished African American journalist and how she fought for equality. **(I/M–NF)**

Medley, Steven P. (2001). *Antelope, Bison, Cougar: A National Park Wildlife Alphabet Book.* (D. San Souci, Illus.). El Portal, CA: Yosemite Association.
This colorful alphabet book introduces readers to the mammals, birds, and other creatures that live in different areas within the national park system. **(P/I/M–PB–NF)**

Meltzer, Milton. (1997). *Langston Hughes.* (S. Alcorn, Illus.). Brookfield, CT: Millbrook Press.
An excellent resource to learn about this poet's life and the difficulties he faced as a black man struggling for acclaim in America. **(I/M–NF)**

Milne, A. A. (1998). *The World of Christopher Robin.* (E. H. Shepard, Illus.). New York: Dutton.
Young Christopher Robin is never without friends with his forest pals Pooh, Eeyore, Piglet, and other memorable characters to keep him company. **(P/I/M–CB)**

Minarik, Else Holmelund. (1957). *Little Bear.* (M. Sendak, Illus.). New York: Harper & Row.
Little Bear's adventures with his friends are shared in this book about relationships. **(P–PB)**

Minters, Frances. (1994). *Cinder-Elly.* (G. B. Karras, Illus.). New York: Viking.
Written in toe-tapping verse, this Cinder-Elly lives in New York, rides a bicycle to the basketball game, and meets her Prince Charming, the star of the team. **(I/M–PB)**

Mochizuki, Ken. (1997). *Passage to Freedom: The Sugihara Story.* (D. Lee, Illus.). New York: Lee & Low.
A true recounting of a diplomat's courage and his determination to help hundreds of Jewish refugees despite Japan's refusal to issue them visas. **(I/M–PB–NF)**

Moore, Lilian. (1995). *I Never Did That Before.* (L. Hoban, Illus.). New York: Atheneum/Simon & Schuster.
Short poems that explore the joys of doing something new. **(P–Poetry)**

Mora, Pat. (1996). *Confetti.* (E. O. Sanchez, Illus.). New York: Lee & Low.
Brightly illustrated and interspersed with Spanish words, these poems celebrate childhood in the sunny Southwest. Good book depicting Spanish American culture. **(P/I–Poetry)**

———. (1998). *This Big Sky.* (S. Jenkins, Illus.). New York: Scholastic Press.
The distinctive nature of the Southwest is highlighted in these fourteen poems and clever paper-cut illustrations. **(P/I–PB)**

Murphy, Jim. (1996). *A Young Patriot: The American Revolution as Experienced by One Boy.* New York: Clarion.
The book is based on a first-person account as primary source material interspersed with additional material about the Revolutionary War. **(M–CB–NF)**

Murphy, Stuart. (1997). *Every Buddy Counts.* New York: HarperCollins.
A young girl goes through the days counting all her "buddies." **(P–PB)**

———. (1997). *Divide and Ride.* New York: HarperCollins.
A group of friends learn division as they go on different carnival rides. **(P/I–PB)**

Myers, Walter Dean. (1997). *Harlem.* (C. Myers, Illus.). New York:

Scholastic.
Through poetry and collage, the richness of Harlem is brought to life. **(I/M–PB)**

———. (1993). *Brown Angels: An Album of Pictures and Verse.* New York: Harper.
A memorable collection of old photographs celebrate children from an era long gone. **(P/I/M–PB)**

Naylor, Phyllis R. (1991). *Shiloh.* New York: Atheneum.
Young Marty longs to own a dog and can't tolerate his mean neighbor mistreating the beagle Marty calls Shiloh. **(I/MS–N)**

Nelson, Marilyn (2001). *Carver: A Life in Poems.* New York: Front Street Books.
Older readers will gain insight into Carver's efforts to improve the lives of others. **(A–NF)**

Nerlove, Miriam. (1996). *Flowers on the Wall.* New York: McElderry.
A picture book for older readers, this is a story of the losses a family experiences when they are branded as Jews and eventually taken to a concentration camp. **(I/M–PB)**

Newcome, Zita. (2002). *Head, Shoulders, Knees, and Toes and Other Action Rhymes.* Cambridge, MA: Candlewick Press.
From nursery rhymes to favorite chants, primary grade children will find rhythm and action in these pages. **(P–PB)**

Newman, Leslea. (2000). *Heather Has Two Mommies.* (D. Souza, Illus.). Boston: Alyson Publishers.
Newman addresses the sensitive topic of lesbian parents. **(M–CB)**

Norworth, Jack. (1999). *Take Me Out to the Ballgame.* New York: Aladdin.
A picture book version of the popular baseball song. **(P–PB)**

Nye, Naomi Shihab. (1995). *The Tree Is Older Than You Are: A Bilingual Gathering of Stories and Poems from Mexico with Paintings by Mexican Artists.* New York: Simon & Schuster.
A collection of literature that reflects daily life in Mexico. This book is written in both English and Spanish. **(I/M–Poetry)**

———. (1998). *The Space between Our Footsteps: Poems and Paintings from the Middle East.* New York: Simon & Schuster.
Over 100 poets and artists representing nineteen countries in the Middle East touch on issues and concerns through poetry and art. **(I/M–Poetry)**

O'Dell, Scott. (1988). *Black Star, Bright Dawn.* New York: Fawcett.
The story of Bright Dawn, an Inuit girl, who travels the Iditarod trail alone except for her dog team. **(I/M–N)**

O'Neill, Mary. (1989). *Hailstones and Halibut Bones.* (J. Waller, Illus.). New York: Doubleday.
First printed in 1961 and reprinted in 1989, this is truly a classic collection of color poems accompanied by contemporary illustrations. **(P/I/M–Poetry)**

Oppenheim, Shulamith L. (1992). *The Lily Cupboard.* (R. Himler, Illus.). New York: HarperCollins.
A Dutch family shelters a little Jewish girl, Lily, during World War II. **(I/M–PB)**

Palotta, Jerry. (1994). *The Desert Alphabet Book.* (M. Astrella, Illus.). Charlesbridge Press.
With wit and research, Palotta's alphabet books enrich a reader's understanding of numerous topics including plants and animals of the desert. **(I/M–PB–NF)**

————. (1999). *The Hershey's Milk Chocolate Fractions Book.* (R. Bolster, Illus.). New York: Scholastic.
What a memorable, tasty, hands-on lesson in understanding fractions as the various sections of a Hershey bar are counted, broken apart, stacked, and restacked. **(I/M–PB–NF)**

Park, Barbara. (1995). *Mick Harte Was Here.* New York: Scholastic.
Phoebe loved her brother and wants everyone to know how special he was. If only he had been wearing his bicycle helmet when he was hit. **(I/M–N)**

————. (1982). *Skinnybones.* New York: Knopf.
Recipient of the class bully's jokes, smallest kid on the Little League team for six years, this sixth grade, wise-cracking hero has quite a story about trying to enter a cat food commercial contest. **(I/M–N)**

Parker, Steve. (1994). *Whales and Dolphins.* Boston, MA: Sierra.
Easily read text and informative charts, diagrams, and gatefolds extend the reader's understanding of unique physical and social characteristics of these marine mammals. **(I/M–NF)**

Paterson, Katherine. (1976). *Bridge to Terabithia.* New York: HarperCollins.
The new girl, Leslie, can outrun any boy in class. She also calls her parents by their first names. Jess becomes her best friend. When she dies in an accident, Jess must deal with the tragedy. **(I/M–N)**

————. (1978). *The Great Gilly Hopkins.* New York: HarperCollins.
Foster child Gilly is arrogant and cocky. She's convinced her mother will return some day and take her away. **(I/M–N)**

————. (1991). *Lyddie.* New York: Dutton, Lodestar.
In order to save her family from starvation, Lyddie takes a job in a Lowell, Massachusetts, mill where working conditions in the 1840s are deplorable.

Paulsen, Gary. (1985). *Dogsong.* New York: Simon & Schuster.
Paulsen's tale of dogsled racing. **(I/M–N)**

————. (1987). *Hatchet.* New York: Macmillan.
This Newbery Honor winner is a perennial favorite as readers join Brian in his attempt to survive in the Canadian wilderness following the crash of his small plane. **(I/M–N)**

————. (1990). *Woodsong.* New York: Scholastic.
Paulsen further details the loneliness and dangers endured in this story of dogsled racing. **(I/M–N)**

————. (1991). *The River.* New York: Delacorte.
Brian returns to a wilderness setting so that scientists can collect data on his survival techniques. A lightning strike makes this another adventure in staying alive. **(I/M–N)**

————. (1994). *Winterdance: The Fine Madness of Running the Iditarod.* New York: Harcourt Brace.
In this book, Paulsen describes some of his own feelings in running the difficult Iditarod race. **(I/M–N)**

————. (1996). *Brian's Winter.* New York: Bantam Doubleday Dell.
Prompted by readers who wanted to know "what if?" Paulsen describes what happened to Brian when he wasn't rescued before winter set in.

————. (1999). *Brian's Return.* New York: Delacorte.
Brian finds he can no longer live in the city and must return to the

wilderness where he really belongs. **(M–N)**

Peck, Richard (1998). *A Long Way from Chicago.* New York: Puffin Books. A young boy describes memorable summers that he and his sister spent with his wily and unusual grandmother in rural Illinois during the Depression. **(M–N)**

———. (2000). *A Year Down Yonder.* New York: Penguin/Putnam. Life with Grandma Dowdel during the Depression is anything but dull. **(M–N)**

Perrault, Charles. (1990). *Puss in Boots.* (F. Marcellino, Illus.). New York: Farrar, Straus & Giroux. This talking beast tale relates the efforts of a very clever cat as he takes his humble owner from miller's son to being king. **(I/M–PB)**

———. (1997). *Cinderella.* (M. Brown, Illus.). New York: Scribner's. This is the Caldecott-winning version of Perrault's popular tale. **(P/I/M–PB)**

Pinkney, Andrea Davis. (2000). *Let It Shine: Stories of Black Women Freedom Fighters.* (S. Alcorn, Illus.). San Diego, CA: Gulliver/Harcourt Brace. Brief biographies of ten influential black American women from past to present are included as well as a section for further reading. **(I/M–NF)**

Polacco, Patricia. (1993). *The Bee Tree.* New York: Putnam & Grosset. To teach his daughter the value of books, a father leads a growing crowd in search of a tree where bees store their honey. **(P–PB)**

———. (1994). *Pink and Say.* New York: Philomel. Recounted by Say Curtis, the story tells of his meeting with Pinkus Aylee, a black soldier, during the

Civil War and their subsequent capture by Southern troops. **(P/I/M–PB–NF)**

———. (1998). *Thank You, Mister Falker.* New York: Philomel. Based upon events in the author's own childhood, Patricia Polacco tells of her agony in learning to read and credits the teacher who made a miracle happen. **(I/M–PB)**

———. (2000). *The Butterfly.* New York: Philomel. Monique's mother hides a Jewish family during the Nazi occupation of France. **(I–PB)**

Pomerantz, Charlotte. (2000). *The Mousery.* (K. Cyrus, Illus.). San Diego, CA: Gulliver/Harcourt. Acceptance and sharing are at the roots of this rhyming tale. **(P–PB)**

Prelutsky, Jack. (1995). *A Pizza the Size of the Sun.* (J. Stevenson, Illus.). New York: HarperCollins. A collection of humorous poetry by one of the most popular children's poets in America. **(P/I–Poetry)**

———. (2000). *It's Raining Pigs and Noodles.* (J. Stevenson, Illus.). New York: Greenwillow. Poetry with silliness children can relate to easily. **(P/I–Poetry)**

Rathmann, Peggy. (1995). *Officer Buckle and Gloria.* New York: Putnam. The Caldecott-winning story of a school policeman and clever dog. **(P–PB)**

———. (1999). *Ten Minutes till Bedtime.* New York: Putnam. Emergent and beginning readers will enjoy the delaying tactics of this child who refuses to go to bed at "bedtime." **(P–PB)**

Rawls, Wilson. (1961). *Where the Red Fern Grows.* New York: Doubleday. A heartwarming story set during the Great Depression of a young boy and his love for two dogs, Little Ann and Old Dan. **(I/MS–N)**

Rees, Celia. (2001). *Witch Child.* Cambridge, MA: Candlewick Press.
Mary Newbury flees when her grandmother is falsely condemned for practicing witchcraft. Unfortunately, the narrowness of people's beliefs follows her to a new home in a new country. **(M–N)**

———. (2002). *Sorceress.* Cambridge, MA: Candlewick Press.
In this engrossing sequel to *The Witch Child,* readers travel back in time through Agnes' trance-like states to learn the fate of Mary Newbury, a seventeenth-century witch. **(M–N)**

Reiss, Kathryn. (2000). *Time Windows.* San Diego, CA: Harcourt Brace.
A dollhouse is a key to events that happened in the past and ties to Miranda's efforts to battle a pervasive evil influence. **(M–N)**

Rohman, Eric. (1994). *Time Flies.* New York: Crown.
An award-winning picture book that will have readers writing their own versions as they interact with the text. **(P/I/M–PB)**

———. (2002). *My Friend Rabbit.* Brookfield, CT: Roaring Book Press.
Trouble follows Rabbit but patient friends help him. **(PB–P)**

Roop, Peter, & Roop, Connie. (2002). *Take Command, Captain Farragut!* (M. McCurdy, Illus.). New York: Simon & Schuster.
Ten-year-old David Glasgow Farragut was captured off his ship and jailed during the War of 1812. He later rose to become the first admiral in the U.S. Navy. **(I/M–PB)**

Rosa-Casanova, S. (2001). *Mama Provi and the Pot of Rice.* (R. Roth, Illus.). New York: Atheneum.
Mama Provi creates her special casserole to take to her granddaughter. After stops at each floor to exchange a portion of casserole for another international delicacy, she arrives at the top floor with a delicious feast. **(P/I–PB)**

Rosen, Michael. (1989). *We're Going on a Bear Hunt.* (H. Oxenbury, Illus.). New York: Margaret K. McElderry Books.
There is a surprise awaiting this family when they go off to hunt for a bear. **(P–PB)**

Rosenburg, M. (1994). *Hiding to Survive: Stories of Jewish Children Rescued from the Holocaust.* New York: Clarion.
The stories of ordinary, courageous people who risked their lives to hide fourteen Jewish children are recounted in this book. **(M–NF)**

Rotner, Shelley. (1996). *Action Alphabet.* New York: Atheneum.
Striking full-color photographs take you through an alphabet filled with children engaged in activity. **(P–PB)**

Rowling, J. K. (2000). *Harry Potter and the Goblet of Fire.* (M. Grandpré, Illus.). New York: Scholastic.
Further adventures of young Harry Potter, in training at Hogwarts School of witchcraft. **(I/M–N)**

Rupp, Rebecca. (2002). *The Waterstone.* Cambridge, MA: Candlewick Press.
Tad is a twelve-year-old youngling of the Fisher Tribe who learns he is the One designated to save his world from evil and return the Waterstone to its rightful owners. **(I/M–N)**

Ryan, Pam Munoz. (1999). *Amelia and Eleanor Go for a Ride: Based on a True Story.* (B. Selznick, Illus.). New York: Scholastic.
Two famous friends go for a memorable flight. **(P/I/M–PB)**

Sachar, Louis. (1998). *Holes.* New York: Delacorte.
Upper elementary and middle school

readers will enjoy this multilayered story about survival, solutions, and, in the end, justice. **(I/M–N)**

Salinas, Bobbi. (1998). *The Three Little Pigs (Los Tres Cerdos): Nacho, Tito, and Miguel.* Alameda, CA: Pinata Publications.
Filled with authentic cultural flavor, this amusing retelling in both English and Spanish is sure to be a hit. **(P/I/M–PB)**

San Souci, Robert D. (1994). *The Talking Eggs: A Folktale from the American South.* (J. Pinkney, Illus.). New York: Dial.
Winner of the Coretta Scott King Award and a Caldecott Honor book, this southern tale tells how kind Blanche is rewarded and her greedy mother and sister are taught a valuable lesson. **(P/I/M–PB)**

————. (2000). *Cinderella Skeleton.* (D. Catrow, Illus.). San Diego, CA: Silver Whistle/Harcourt.
Set in Boneyard Acres and written in rhyme, it is a ghoulish version of the classic love story that ends happily ever after when Cinderella and Prince Charnel are wed. **(I/M–Poetry–PB)**

————. (2000). *Little Gold Star: A Spanish Cinderella.* (S. Martinez, Illus.). New York: HarperCollins.
Selfish stepsisters earn monkey's ears and horns while Cinderella receives a gold star for her forehead. **(P/I/M–PB)**

Say, Allen. (1999). *Tea with Milk.* Boston: Houghton Mifflin.
Based upon the events in the life of Allen Say's mother, the author gives the reader a look at Japanese cultural beliefs. **(I/M–NF)**

Schroeder, Alan. (1996). *Minty: The Story of Harriet Tubman.* (J. Pinkney, Illus.). New York: Dial.
A beautifully illustrated description of the life of Harriet Tubman. **(I–PB–NF)**

Schwartz, David M. (1985). *How Much Is a Million?* (S. Kellogg, Illus.). New York: Lothrop.
Engaging examples are illustrated to teach the concepts of million, billion, and trillion. **(I/M–PB)**

————. (1989). *If You Made a Million.* (S. Kellogg, Illus.). New York: Lothrop.
Various forms of money are explained from coins to paper bills to personal checks. How money can be used for purchases, getting loans, and the concept of interest are also described. **(I/M–PB)**

————. (2001). *Q Is for Quark: A Science Alphabet Book.* (K. Doner, Illus.). Berkeley, CA: Tricycle Press.
Filled with facts and a sense of humor, this engaging introduction into science facts will surely delight middle and upper grade readers. **(I/M–PB–NF)**

Scieszka, Jon. (1989). *The True Story of the Three Little Pigs as Told by A. Wolf.* (L. Smith, Illus.). New York: Viking.
It's all a matter of perspective according to the wrongfully accused Alexander T. Wolf, who tells his version of this popular tale from behind bars. **(P/I/M–PB)**

————. (1992). *The Stinky Cheese Man: And Other Fairly Stupid Tales.* (L. Smith, Illus.). New York: Viking.
A highly popular book that parodies traditional folktales through the retellings and the illustrations. **(P/I/M–PB)**

————. (1995). *Math curse.* (L. Smith, Illus.). New York: Viking.
A witty book about the trials and tribulations one could face with math difficulties on a daily basis. **(I/M–PB)**

Scillian, David. (2001). *A Is for America: An American Alphabet.* (P. Carroll, Illus.). Chelsea, MI: Sleeping Bear Press.
Filled with facts, alliteration, and colorful illustrations, a reader will get a sampling of America from coast to coast and top to bottom. **(P/I–PB)**

Sendak, Maurice. (1963). *Where the Wild Things Are.* New York: Harper & Row.
Max throws a tantrum and journeys with monsters to a fantasy isle. **(P–PB)**

Senisi, E. B. (1998). *Just Kids: Visiting a Class for Children with Special Needs.* New York: Dutton.
Cindy spends time each day in a classroom for children with special needs because her cruel remark showed that she needs to see the unique qualities of each child. **(I–N)**

Seuss, Dr. (1957). *The Cat in the Hat.* New York: Random House.
When two children are left at home alone, interesting things take place when a cat in a hat arrives on the scene. A true classic of children's literature. **(P/I–PB)**

———. (1963). *Dr. Seuss' ABC.* New York: Random House.
A classic alliterative alphabet book. **(P–PB)**

Shannon, George D. (1996). *Tomorrow's Alphabet.* (D. Crews, Illus.). New York: Greenwillow Books.
A new twist on the alphabet, from A is for seed—tomorrow's apple, to Z is for countdown—tomorrow's zero. Children will delight in figuring out the pattern. **(P/I–PB)**

Shaw, Nancy. (1985). *Sheep in a Jeep.* (M. Apple, Illus.). Boston: Houghton Mifflin.
If sheep get in a jeep, look out! Trouble follows in this patterned book, the first of many sheep adventures. **(P–PB)**

Shulevitz, Uri. (1998). *Snow.* New York: Farrar Straus Giroux.
A charming tale of a boy and his small dog who delight in the whimsical changes snow brings to the city. A Caldecott Honor Book. **(P–PB)**

Siebert, Diane. (1988). *Mojave.* (W. Minor, Illus.). New York: HarperTrophy.
The land and the animals that live in the Mojave Desert are described through poetry and lovely illustrations. **(I/M–PB–NF)**

———. (1989). *Heartland.* (W. Minor, Illus.). New York: HarperTrophy.
The bounty of the nation's Heartland where both author and illustrator have lived is depicted through verse and realistic artwork. **(I/M–PB–NF)**

Silverstein, Shel. (1964). *The Giving Tree.* New York: Harper & Row.
A tree gives everything to a boy it loves. **(P/I/M–PB)**

———. (1974). *Where the Sidewalk Ends.* New York: HarperCollins.
Humorous poetry and drawings that are loved by children. **(P/I–Poetry)**

———. (1981). *A Light in the Attic.* New York: HarperCollins.
A wondrous collection of totally funny poems. **(P/I–Poetry)**

———. (1996). *Falling Up.* New York: HarperCollins.
Rip-roaring, tickle your ribs humorous poetry. **(P/I–Poetry)**

Simon, Seymour. (1990). *Deserts.* New York: Mulberry.
Through pictures, diagrams, and text, the nature and characteristics of deserts around the world are explained. **(I/M–PB–NF)**

———. (1995). *Sharks.* New York: Harper.

Clear, direct writing introduces readers to an animal much feared, but, in truth, quite fascinating. **(I/M–PB–NF)**

———. (1998). *They Swim in Seas: The Mystery of Animal Migration.* (E. Warnick, Illus.). San Diego: Brown Deer/Harcourt Brace. Seymour Simon describes how plankton, fish, turtles, whales, and other oceanic creatures migrate in this picture book. **(P/I–PB–NF)**

———. (2000). *They Walk the Earth: The Extraordinary Travels of Animals on Land.* (E. Warnick, Illus.). San Diego, CA: Brown Deer/Harcourt Brace. The migration of lemmings, elephants, caribou, and frogs is explained through interesting text and informative watercolor illustrations. **(I/M–NF–PB)**

Slate, Joseph. (1996). *Miss Bindergarten Gets Ready for Kindergarten.* (A. Wolff, Illus.). New York: Dutton. An alphabet book where Miss Bindergarten and her students get ready for their first day of school. **(P–PB)**

Smith, Frank Dabba. (2000). *My Secret Camera: Life in Lodz Ghetto.* (M. Grossman, Photographer). San Diego, CA: Harcourt Brace. Relatively sparse text accompanies heartbreaking photographs reflecting the hardship and terror experienced by Jewish families in Lodz Ghetto. **(M–NF)**

Smith, Roland. (1999). *The Captain's Dog: My Journey with the Lewis and Clark Tribe.* San Diego: Harcourt. Seaman, the Newfoundland dog that accompanied Lewis and Clark, describes the experiences of the Monticello Corps Expedition. **(I/M–N)**

Spinelli, Jerry. (1990). *Maniac Magee.* Boston: Little Brown. Maniac Magee may be more legend than real, but he has lessons to teach about prejudice and belonging. **(I/M–N)**

———. (2002). *Loser.* New York: Joanna Colter Books. Donald Zinoff is a great kid but he's a loser. He's a flop at everything he does until one day when a child turns up missing. **(I/M–N)**

Spivak, Dawn. (1997). *Grass Sandals: The Travels of Basho.* (Demi, Illus.). New York: Atheneum. This is a stunning book of haiku and art that tells the life of one of the most beloved poets of Japan. **(I/M–NF)**

Soto, Gary. (1995). *Canto Familiar.* (A. Nelson, Illus.). San Diego, CA: Harcourt Brace. This book celebrates childhood and the Mexican American experience with warm humorous poetry. **(I/M–Poetry)**

St. George, Judith. (1996). *To See with the Heart: The Life of Sitting Bull.* New York: Putnam. The courage of a young boy and the wisdom of a fine leader are related in a book rich with detail and quotes from Sitting Bull's contemporaries. **(M–NF)**

Stanley, Jerry. (1993). *Children of the Dust Bowl: The True Story of the School at Weedpatch Camp.* New York: Crown. The heart-wrenching story of children and the Great Depression. **(I/M–NF)**

Steptoe, Javaka. (1997). *In Daddy's Arms I Am Tall: African-Americans Celebrating Fathers.* New York: Lee & Low. A collection of poetry written by African American writers. **(P/I/M–Poetry)**

Steptoe, John. (1987). *Mufaro's Beautiful Daughters*. (J. Pinkney, Illus.). New York: Lothrop, Lee, & Shepard.
This is a version of the Cinderella tale in which kindness overcomes jealousy and greed. **(P/I/M–PB)**

Stevens, Janet, & Stevens Crummel, Susan. (2001). *And the Dish Ran Away with the Spoon*. New York: Harcourt.
The other nursery rhyme characters hunt for the missing dish and spoon. **(P–PB)**

Swann, Brian. (1998). *Touching the Distance: Native American Riddle Poems*. (M. Rendon, Illus.). San Diego, Ca: Brown Deer/Harcourt Brace.
Readers will enjoy trying to stump each other with these clever riddles. **(I/M–NF–Poetry)**

Sweeny, Joan. (1996). *Me on the Map*. (A. Cable, Illus.). New York: Crown.
A young girl discovers her place in our universe, beginning with a map of her bedroom. **(P–PB)**

Szabo, Corrine. (1997). *Sky Pioneer: A Photobiography of Amelia Earhart*. New York: Scholastic.
The courage of a heroine is related in this well-written story. **(I/M–NF)**

Tavares, Matt. (2000). *Zachary's Ball*. Cambridge, MA: Candlewick Press.
There is magic in the air when Dad takes Zachary to his first Boston Red Sox game. **(P/I/M–PB)**

Trottier, Maxine. (2001). *Prairie Willow*. (L. Fernandez & R. Jacobsen, Illus.). New York: Stoddart Kids.
Emily longs for a tree to break up the endless sea of prairie grass. The willow she plants becomes a symbol for all who put down roots in this part of the United States. **(P/I/M–PB)**

Tunnell, Michael O., & Chilcoat, G. W. (1996). *The Children of Topaz: The Story of a Japanese American Internment Camp Based on a Classroom Diary*. New York: Holiday House.
Actual descriptions of life in an internment camp during World War II. **(I/M–NF)**

Turner, Ann. (1997). *Mississippi Mud: Three Prairie Journals*. (R. J. Blake, Illus.). New York: HarperCollins.
Three pioneer children describe the journey from Kentucky to Oregon in their journals. **(PB–I)**

Udry, Janice May. (1956). *A Tree Is Nice*. (M. Simont, Illus.). New York: HarperCollins.
The author shares the many joys and benefits of having trees in our world. **(P–PB)**

Van Allsburg, Chris. (1981). *Jumanji*. Boston: Houghton Mifflin.
A picture book giving a new perspective on viewing toys. **(P/I–PB)**

Venables, Stephen. (2003). *To the Top: The Story of Everest*. Cambridge, MA: Candlewick.
Readers learn of the challenges faced when scaling the world's highest peak. **(M–NF)**

Viorst, Judith. (1994). *The Alphabet from Z to A with Much Confusion on the Way*. (R. Hull, Illus.). New York: Atheneum.
Written in amusing verse, the headaches of trying to make sense of the English language are dealt with while working through the alphabet backwards. **(P/I–PB)**

Walker, Sally M. (1998). *The 18 Penny Goose*. (E. Beier, Illus.). New York: HarperCollins.
Eight-year-old Letty tries to save her pet goose from the British soldiers

during the Revolutionary War.
(P/I–CB)

Walsh, Ellen. (1989). *Mouse Paint.*
San Diego, CA: Harcourt Brace.
Two mice change colors as they
experiment with paint illustrating
how colors are made while teaching
concepts about color. **(P–PB)**

Walton, Rick. (1998). *So Many
Bunnies: A Bedtime ABC and
Counting Book.* (P. Miglio, Illus.).
New York: Lothrop, Lee & Shepard.
Old Mother Rabbit's twenty-six
children, each named for a letter of
the alphabet, are lovingly put to bed.
Each bunny sleeps in their favorite
place that rhymes with their name.
(P–PB)

Waters, Kate, and Solvenz-Low,
Madeline. (1990). *Lion Dancer:
Ernie Wan's Chinese New Year.*
(H. Cooper, Photographer).
New York: HarperCollins.
Chinatown during the new year is
depicted in this colorful book.
(P–PB)

White, E. B. (1952). *Charlotte's Web.*
(G. Williams, Illus.). New York:
Harper & Row.
The classic tale of Wilbur the pig and
his rescue from death by his friend,
Charlotte the spider. **(P/I–N)**

———. (1970). *Trumpet of the Swan.*
New York: Harper Row.
The joy of the spring and the
hatching of young swans are shared.
(I–N)

Wick, Walter. (1997). *A Drop of Water:
A Book of Science and Wonder.*
New York: Scholastic.
The properties of water are simply
amazing when seen through the eyes
of this author. **(I/M PB–NF)**

Wiesner, David. (1991). *Tuesday.*
New York: Clarion.
Readers will be quite intrigued by
floating frogs on the strangest

Tuesday they've ever seen.
(P/I/M–PB)

———. (2001). *The Three Pigs.*
New York: Clarion.
This Caldecott winner takes an
innovative look at the familiar tale of
those pigs and the wolf. The pigs
escape the boundaries of a page and
slip in and out of other tales as they
elude the wolf. **(P/I/M–PB)**

Wilber, R. (2001). *The Disappearing
Alphabet.* (D. Diaz, Illus.).
San Diego, CA: Harcourt Brace.
Silly humor and clever use of words
make this an unusual alphabet book
that poses a poetic question about
what it might mean to a letter if a
piece of it were missing. **(P/I/M–PB)**

Wilbur, Richard. (2000). *The Pig in
the Spigot.* (J. O. Seibold, Illus.).
San Diego, CA: Harcourt Brace.
Silly verses will tickle readers as they
investigate words and look for short
words tucked inside longer words
such as "pig" in the word "spigot"
and "boo" inside "book." **(P/I–PB)**

Wilder, Laura Ingalls. (1953). *Little
House on the Prairie.* (G. Williams,
Illus.). New York: HarperCollins.
The story of frontier life as viewed
from a young girl's eyes. **(P/I–N)**

Wilhoite, Michael. (1990). *Daddy's
Roommate.* Boston: Alyson
Wonderland.
This is a controversial book about
same-sex parents.

Williams, David. (1993). *Grandma
Essie's Covered Wagon.* (W.
Sadowski, Illus.). New York: Knopf.
Based upon childhood stories told by
Grandma Essie, the reader travels
from Missouri by covered wagon to
Kansas looking for a better quality of
life. **(I/M–PB)**

Williams, Sue. (1989). *I Went Walking.*
(J. Vivas, Illus.). San Diego:
Harcourt Brace.

A young boy finds animals of all different colors during his walk. **(P–PB)**

———. (1998). *Let's Go Visiting.* (J. Vivas, Illus.). San Diego, CA: Gulliver/Harcourt Brace. Simple text and bright, appealing illustrations take the reader through numbers and colors on a visit to baby animals on the farm. **(P/PB)**

Wing, Natalie. (1996). *Jalapeno Bagels.* (R. Casilla, Illus.). New York: Atheneum. Pablo has to make a decision on what to take to International Day at school that will reflect both his mother's and father's cultures. **(P/I/M–PB)**

Wisniewski, David. (1996). *The Golem.* New York: Clarion. A powerful Jewish tale with a strong message. **(I/M–PB)**

Wood, Audrey. (1984). *The Napping House.* (D. Wood, Illus.). New York: Harcourt Brace. A cumulative tale where everyone is sleeping until a wakeful flea causes a commotion with just one bite. **(P–PB)**

Woodruff, Elvira. (1999). *The Memory Coat.* (M. Dooling, Illus.). New York: Scholastic. The lives and perils experienced by a Russian Jewish family are recounted. **(P/I–PB)**

Wyeth, Sharon D. (2001). *Freedom's Wings: Corey's Diary, Kentucky to Ohio, 1857.* New York: Scholastic. Written in diary format, the struggle for freedom is clearly depicted as Corey and his mother flee via the Underground Railroad. **(I/M–N)**

Yep, Laurence. (1993). *Dragon's Gate.* New York: HarperCollins. Otter, a young Chinese boy, journeys to America to join his uncle and father who are Chinese laborers building the transcontinental railroad. **(I/N)**

Yezerski, Thomas F. (1998). *Together in Pine Cone Patch.* New York: Farrar, Strauss, & Giroux. Set at the turn of the century, this appealing story tells of two immigrants who fall in love, teaching the small mining community that love can overpower prejudice. **(I/M–PB)**

Yolen, Jane. (1987). *Owl Moon.* (J. Schoenherr, Illus.). New York: Putnam. A child ventures out during a winter night and learns the secret of owls. **(P/I–PB)**

———. (1990). *The Devil's Arithmetic.* New York: Puffin. Young Hannah would rather be with friends than at the family Seder. When she opens the door for Elijah, she steps back in time to become Chaya, a young Jewish girl who endures the horrors of the Holocaust. **(M–N)**

———. (1992). *Encounter.* (D. Shannon, Illus.). San Diego, CA: Harcourt Brace. Told from a young Taino Indian boy's point of view who tried to warn his people against the arrival of Columbus and his men to little avail. **(I/M–PB)**

———. (1996). *Welcome to the Sea of Sand.* (L. Regan, Illus.). New York: Scholastic. Readers are introduced to the wildlife in the desert in a rhythmic cadence and through the use of vivid verbs.

———. (2003). *Sword of the Rightful King.* San Diego, CA: Harcourt. Young King Arthur struggles to establish himself as the king. **(I/M–N)**

Young, Ed. (1989). *Lon Po Po: A Red Riding Hood Story from China.* New York: Philomel.
Despite their mother's warning not to open the door when she is gone, three young girls let in an uninvited guest and must outwit him to save their lives. **(P/I/M–PB)**

Zelinsky, Paul O. (1997). *Rapunzel.* New York: Dutton.
This traditional tale shares the misfortune of a young girl who is locked away in a tower by a witch. A blinded prince and magic tears bring this tale to a happy ending. **(P/I/M–PB)**

Ziefert, Harriet. (1998). *Bugs, Beetles and Butterflies.* (L. Flather, Illus.). New York: Viking.
Readers meet many different kinds of bugs, beetles, and butterflies. **(P–PB)**

Basal Readers and Reading Instruction

As you have learned, a long popular approach to teaching reading involves teaching from a basal reading series. Sample segments from a low level and a middle level grade teacher's guide are included here as examples. These basal reading excerpts appear in their entirety in *Macmillan/McGraw Hill's Spotlight on Literacy 2000* series. Look at the carefully constructed lessons and how they are developed around a key reading skill or strategy. Notice that not only are lessons carefully planned in a quality basal series, but increasingly greater emphasis is being placed on developing appropriate materials to meet the needs of all children in a culturally diverse classroom. This particular series has some of the lessons available in five different languages with supplemental CD-ROMs available.

"Down By the Bay" (*Out and About*)
Illustrated by: Consuelo Udave

"Down By the Bay" comes from the Teacher's Planning Guide for the text *Out and About,* which is a Level 1, Book 2 selection. This humorous, nonsense folk song provides first grade learners with the opportunity to read a repetitive, rhyming text. The pages that follow offer you a brief glimpse into a teacher's guide. You can see the wealth of information that is supplied for teachers to help guide students as they develop comprehension and strategic reading skills. Also, if you refer back into the textbook in Chapter 7 you will find a first grade phonics lesson that utilizes this text.

Comprehension

STRATEGIC READING

PRINT AWARENESS AND COMPREHENSION STRATEGIES

16 NOTICE WORDS, SENTENCES Where should we begin reading? Point to the word we should read first. What's special about the first letter? (It's a capital letter.)

17 What is the goat sitting in? What is the goat doing? Point to the word on the page that tells us. Use your arms to show me what the goat is doing. NONVERBAL RESPONSE

18 USING ILLUSTRATIONS What is unusual about this pig? Can you find the rhyming word that tells what she is wearing? Point to it. NONVERBAL RESPONSE

19 Some of you can probably read this page by now. Go ahead and try to read it on your own.

PHONICS AND DECODING

/i/-*ig* as in *pig*, page 18
See Phonics and Decoding lesson on Short Vowels and Phonograms: /i/-*ig* on pages 146–148.

ONGOING ASSESSMENT

COMPREHENSION

Observe children's familiarity with this patterned text. Fade your voice when they no longer need your support. Make sure children continue to point to the words as they read.

"Did you ever see a goat
Rowing a boat,
Down by the bay?"

16

"Did you ever see a pig
With a curly wig,
Down by the bay?"

18

Skills in Context

PHONICS AND DECODING

Short Vowels and Phonograms: /i/-*id*

INTRODUCE Write the phonogram -*id* on the chalkboard. Invite children to say -*id* aloud. Remind them that many words end with -*id*, including some in *Down by the Bay*.

DEVELOP/APPLY Reread pages 16–18. Emphasize words that end with the letters -*id*. Have children identify the sound /id/. Write *did* on the chalkboard, underlining the short *i*.

CLOSE Encourage children to suggest other words that end with the sound -*id* and write them on the chalkboard (*lid/hid*).

PRACTICE BOOK: page 87

See also RETEACHING BLM, page 51

SKILLS TRACE

SHORT VOWELS AND PHONOGRAMS: /i/-*id*

Tested:	Progress Assessment: Level 2
Introduce:	Level 1: 238
Review:	Level 2: 131
Practice Book:	50, 87
Reteaching BLM:	30, 51

Down by the bay,
Where the watermelons grow,
Back to my home,
I dare not go.
For if I do,
My mother will say,

19

Down by the bay,
Where the watermelons grow,
Back to my home,
I dare not go.
For if I do,
My mother will say,

A-30

Comprehension

STRATEGIC READING

PRINT AWARENESS AND COMPREHENSION STRATEGIES

20 What is the dragon pulling in his wagon? Where do you think the dragon might be going? Who would like to be the dragon? Show us what you are doing and tell us your plans. ROLE-PLAY

21 TRACK PRINT Let's read this page again. Keep track of the words by pointing as you read.

22 USE ILLUSTRATIONS Do you remember what each of these animals was doing? Look at the pictures to help you. Start with the moose and the goose. Point to the words as you say them.

23 Do you remember what the bear was doing? Pretend you are the bear. Act out what he does. ROLE-PLAY

MEETING
INDIVIDUAL NEEDS

Challenge
Invite children to make up silly rhymes about their favorite animals in their native languages. Have them illustrate their rhymes. Display their work in the reading center.

"Did you ever see a dragon
Pulling a wagon,
Down by the bay?"

20

Did you ever see a moose
Kissing a goose?

22

Did you ever see a bear
Combing his hair?

23

Skills in Context

SELF-MONITORING

Look for Picture Clues

Reread **pages 22–23.** Point out to children that these are sentences they've already read.

• Have children look at the first picture on **page 22.** Do they remember these animals and what they were doing? Help them read the text.

• Help children associate the picture and the text.

• Make sure children point to the words as they read them.

SELF-HELP CHART
Look for picture clues. Point out to children that when they need help reading, they can look at the illustrations for clues.

When I need help
reading, I can:
☺ Listen for rhyming
   words.
☺ Look for picture clues.

Down by the bay,
Where the watermelons grow,
Back to my home,
I dare not go.
For if I do,
My mother will say,

21

Did you ever see a fly
Wearing a tie?

Did you ever see a whale
With a polka-dot tail?

22

A-31

"Do Not Disturb: The Mysteries of Animal Hibernation and Sleep" (*Naturally*)
Author: Margery Facklam

The content in the student materials within the fourth grade level book, *Naturally,* is rich with nonfiction materials and lessons to help students better understand the primarily expository text that it contains. Examine the story, "Do Not Disturb: The Mysteries of Animal Hibernation and Sleep." Margery Facklam, the author, is highlighted and several of her other books are mentioned. Here at the beginning of the lesson is a ticket to further reading for students who particularly enjoy this selection. Study the suggested teaching plan that follows. There are a number of lessons that touch various areas of the curriculum to be taught from this one story. A plan is laid out for an entire week's worth of learning. Remember, with a basal series, the teacher is often provided with considerably more materials than can be taught for each lesson. The key strategy for you as a teacher to learn is how to pick and choose from the suggested materials to best meet the needs of the students in your classroom.

Returning to this lesson, review how carefully prior knowledge is tapped and activities for building background are presented in case they are needed. The emphasis placed on helping limited language students is an important one. Note the availability of the ESL/Second-Language Teacher's Guide as part of the complete set of basal materials.

Readers in the sixth grade and higher often move from a basal reader to a literature anthology. In this case there are teacher's guides and teacher support, but reading selections are longer and involve higher level thinking strategies. Many teachers opt to teach novels instead, perhaps using a Literature Circle format, and tying five different novels in five different literature circles to a central theme. Then, too, novels might be interspersed with the basal anthology, using the basal as a core throughout the reading program. A classic like Ray Bradbury's (1953) *Fahrenheit 451* or Theodore Taylor's (1969) *The Cay* might be the reading focus. Other popular options could include such notable books as Karen Hesse's (1997) *Out of the Dust,* Louis Sachar's (1998) *Holes,* Richard Peck's (1999) *A Long Way From Chicago,* Celia Rees' (2001) *Witch Child,* and Avi's (2002) *Crispin: The Cross of Lead.* Such titles are but a sampling of engrossing titles to consider for older readers. In short, while it changes its look over the grade levels, a basal reader or literature anthology can be the backbone of the reading curriculum from kindergarten through middle school. The wise teacher will draw from its wealth of materials, mix and match it with other reading materials, and most effectively meet student needs in the process.

Children's Literature References

Avi. (2002). *Crispin: The Cross of Lead.* New York: Hyperion.

Bradbury, Ray. (1953). *Fahrenheit 451.* New York: Simon & Schuster.

Hesse, Karen. (1997). *Out of the Dust.* New York: Scholastic.

Peck, Richard. (1998). *A Long Way from Chicago.* New York: Puffin Books.

Rees, Celia. (2001). *Witch Child.* Cambridge, MA: Candlewick Press.

Sachar, Louis. (1998). *Holes.* New York: Farrar, Strauss, & Giroux.

Taylor, Theodore. (1969). *The Cay.* New York: Doubleday.

Do Not Disturb: The Mysteries of Animal Hibernation and Sleep

Available on CD-ROM

DO·NOT·DISTURB
The Mysteries of Animal Hibernation and Sleep

BY MARGERY FACKLAM

ILLUSTRATIONS BY PAMELA JOHNSON

SELECTION SUMMARY

The ways of unlocking the secrets of hibernation can be difficult and dangerous. Margery Facklam tells how, with the aid of tranquilizers, radio transmitters, and radio receivers, two scientist brothers track a grizzly bear to its winter den, and study its hibernation.

Linking Skills to Literature

Key Comprehension Strategies/Skills

☑ **EVALUATE FACT AND NONFACT**

FACT AND NONFACT In order to evaluate whether a statement is true—a fact—or false—a nonfact—readers must pay close attention. If a selection such as *"Do Not Disturb"* challenges what a reader believes to be true, a decision has to be made. What is fact, and what is not fact? Readers must evaluate the reliability of the text as a source of factual information, as well as the reliability of their own preconceived ideas about the truth.

INTERACTING WITH THE TEXT

ENGAGE THE READER Students will get the chance to understand the text better by role-playing both human and nonhuman characters.

See **pages 140J** and **140I**, where the story pages begin.

MARGERY FACKLAM

Margery Facklam has always had a special affection for and curiosity about animals. She has worked very closely with animals in a variety of ways. Her desire to understand the mysteries of animals led to jobs in zoos and teaching in museums. Facklam shares what she has learned with children by writing science books that provide clear and interesting information.

In "Do Not Disturb: The Mysteries of Animal Hibernation and Sleep," Facklam explains in a very straightforward and entertaining manner the wonders of hibernation. Her young readers have fun learning about this amazing phenomenon.

Other Books by Margery Facklam

- *But Not Like Mine* (Harcourt Brace Jovanovich, 1988)
- *Who Harnessed the Horse? The Story of Animal Domestication* (Little, 1992)

A-33

Suggested Lesson Planner
With Flexible Grouping Options

Flexible Grouping Options
- Extra Support
- Challenge
- Second-Language Support
- ✓ These core skills are tested in the Unit Progress Assessment.

WEEK AT A GLANCE	PART 1 — DAY 1 FOCUS ON READING	PART 2 — DAY 2 READ THE LITERATURE	DAY 3 READ THE LITERATURE	PART 3 — DAY 4 EXTEND SKILLS IN CONTEXT	DAY 5 EXTEND SKILLS IN CONTEXT
Reading **Writing** **Listening, Speaking, Viewing**	Preview the Selection, 140G Build Background, 140G Graphic Organizer Transparency/BLM 31 Multimedia Literature Background Building Activities Oral Language Activities, 140H See also ESL/Second-Language Teacher's Guide, 40–45 Vocabulary, 140I Instructional Vocabulary grizzly bear potion devoured survive detecting hibernation Vocabulary Transparency/BLM 6 Practice Book, 41 If you wish to have students begin reading the selection at this point, see 140J.	Set Purposes, 140J Journal Writing Suggestions for Reading, 140J • Read Independently • Read Aloud • Read Together • Read and Teach Teach Strategic Reading, 140J–149 ✓ Evaluate Fact and Nonfact Multimedia Literature Illuminated Literature with multimedia annotations 	Respond to Literature Journal Writing, 149A Writing About the Theme, 149A Practice Book, 45 Multimedia Literature: Notebook Comprehension Checkpoint, 149B ✓ Evaluate Fact and Nonfact Graphic Organizer Transparency/BLM 31 Multimedia Literature Applying Strategies: Evaluate Fact and Nonfact Reteaching ✓ Evaluate Fact and Nonfact, 149 Practice Book, 44 Vocabulary Selection Assessment Selection Assessment/Unit Progress Assessment, Level 10	Skills in Context ✓ Unfamiliar Words, 143 Practice Book, 42 ✓ Steps in a Process, 145 Practice Book, 43 • Multilevel Resources, 149D–149F ✓ Vocabulary, 149G Listening, Speaking, Viewing, 149H Across the Curriculum, 149Q Health/Science Language Arts	Skills in Context ✓ Phonics and Decoding /k/ /au/; context clues, 147 ✓ Fact and Nonfact, 149 Practice Book, 44 Multimedia Literature Strategy Lessons Writing Process: Explanatory Paragraph, 149I • Writing Projects, 149J Study Skills/Reading Resources, 149O ✓ Encyclopedia Practice Book, 46 Multicultural Perspectives The Bear in Native American Cultures, 149R Across the Curriculum, 149R Art Health
Spelling	For a detailed 5-day lesson plan for spelling, see 149M–149N. Pretest: Words Ending in *tion*, *ment*, and *ist*, 149M Words in dark type appear in "Do Not Disturb." **turn** **potion** **notion** **question** **addition** **vacation** **apartment** **station** **argument** **department** **statement** **basement** **artist** **enjoyment** **dentist** **tourist** Spelling Activity Book, 30	The Challenge Words in the spelling list, 149M, come from the vocabulary list in "Do Not Disturb," 140. Challenge Words devoured grizzly bear survive hibernation detecting Sort and Spell Words Students sort the spelling list according to each word's ending, 149M Spelling Activity Book, 31	Midweek Test, 149N Working With Suffixes: Use the Dictionary Students make spelling words into nouns by adding suffixes and then find their histories in the dictionary, 149N Spelling Activity Book, 32	Find and Write Words Students write as many short words as they can find by scrambling letters in the spelling words, 149N Spelling Activity Book, 33	Posttest, 149N Spelling Activity Book, 34
Grammar, Mechanics, and Usage	Daily Language Activity: Plural Nouns 1. The grizzly bear has four huge paws. (paws) 2. The grizzly tramps through many bushs. (bushes) 3. It searchs for juicy, red berrys. (berries) • Grammar Practice Book: Plural Nouns, 13–14 See pages 149K–149L.	Daily Language Activity: Plural Nouns 1. Grizzlys must find winter homes. (Grizzlies) 2. They may search for many day. (days) 3. One bear uses branchs for its bed. (branches) 5-Day Grammar Plan: Plural Nouns, 149K–149L Grammar Practice Book: Plural Nouns, 27	Daily Language Activity: Plural Nouns 1. The two Craighead brothers studied a grizzly. (brothers) 2. The bear measured 65 inchs long. (inches) 3. It weighed over 300 pound. (pounds) Writing Application: Letter, 149L Grammar Practice Book: Plural Nouns, 28	Daily Language Activity: Plural Nouns 1. Some librarys have books about bears. (libraries) 2. Native Americans told storys about them. (stories) 3. Other signed were told by trappers. (legends) (See 149L) Quick Write: Description, 149L Grammar Practice Book: Plural Nouns, 29	Daily Language Activity: Plural Nouns 1. Scientists haven't answered all question about grizzlies. (questions) 2. Why are dens made in different ways? (ways) 3. Several mysterys about hibernation still remain. (mysteries) (See 149L) Grammar Practice Book: Plural Nouns, 30 Grammar Practice Book: Answer Key and Grammar Assessment, 26

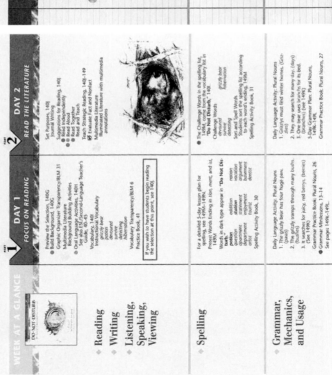

Book Awards

Caldecott Medal and Honor Books (2003–1980)

2003: *My Friend Rabbit* by Eric Rohman
Honor Books: *The Spider and the Fly* by Mary Howitt, illustrated by Tony DiTerlizzi; *Hondo & Fabian* by Peter McCarthy; *Noah's Ark* by Jerry Pinkney

2002: *The Three Pigs* by David Wiesner
Honor Books: *The Dinosaurs of Waterhouse Hawkins* by Barbara Kerley, illustrated by Brian Selznick; *Martin's Big Words: The Life of Dr. Martin Luther King, Jr.* by Doreen Rappaport, illustrated by Bryan Collier; *The Stray Dog* by Marc Simont

2001: *So You Want to Be President?* by Judith St. George, illustrated by David Small
Honor Books: *Casey at the Bat: A Ballad of the Republic Sung in the Year 1888* by Ernest Lawrence Thayer, illustrated by Christopher Bing; *Click, Clack, Moo: Cows That Type* by Doreen Cronin, illustrated by Betsy Lewin; *Olivia* by Ian Falconer

2000: *Joseph Had a Little Overcoat* by Simms Taback
Honor Books: *Sector 7* by David Wiesner; *The Ugly Duckling* by Hans Christian Andersen, illustrated by Jerry Pinkney; *A Child's Calendar* by John Updike, illustrated by Trina Schart Hyman; *When Sophie Gets Angry—Really, Really Angry* by Molly Garret Bang

1999: *Snowflake Bentley* by Jacqueline Briggs Martin, illustrated by Mary Azarian

Honor Books: *Duke Ellington* by Andrea Davis Pinkney, illustrated by Brian Pinkney; *No. David!* by David Shannon; *Snow* by Uri Shulevitz; *Tibet: Through the Red Box* by Peter Sis

1998: *Rapunzel* by Paul O. Zelinsky
Honor Books: *The Gardener* by Sarah Stewart, illustrated by David Small; *Harlem* by Walter Dean Myers, illustrated by Christopher Myers; *There Was an Old Lady Who Swallowed a Fly* by Simms Taback

1997: *Golem* by David Wisniewski
Honor Books: *Hush! A Thai Lullaby* by My Minfong Ho, illustrated by Holly Meade; *The Graphic Alphabet* by Neal Porter, illustrated by David Pelletier; *The Paperboy* by Dav Pilkey; *Starry Messenger: Galileo Galilei* by Peter Sis

1996: *Officer Buckle and Gloria* by Peggy Rathmann
Honor Books: *Alphabet City* by Stephen Johnson; *Zin! Zin! Zin!: A Violin* by Lloyd Moss, illustrated by Marjorie Priceman; *The Faithful Friend* by Robert San Souci, illustrated by Brian Pinkney; *Tops and Bottoms* by Janet Stevens

1995: *Smoky Night* by Eve Bunting, illustrated by David Diaz
Honor Books: *Swamp Angel* by Anne Issacs, illustrated by Paul O. Zelinsky; *John Henry* by Julius Lester, illustrated by Jerry Pinkney; *Time Flies* by Eric Rohmann

1994: *Grandfather's Journey* by Allen Say
Honor Books: *Peppe the Lamplighter*

by Elisa Barton, illustrated by Ted Lewin; *In the Small, Small Pond* by Denise Fleming; *Owen* by Kevin Henkes; *Raven: A Trikster Tale from the Pacific Northwest* by Gerald McDermott; *Yo! Yes?* by Chris Raschka

1993: *Mirette on the Highwire* by Emily Arnold McCully
Honor Books: *Seven Blind Mice* by Ed Young; *The Stinky Cheese Man & Other Fairly Stupid Tales* by Jon Scieszka, illustrated by Lane Smith; *Working Cotton* by Sherley Anne Williams, illustrated by Carole Byard

1992: *Tuesday* by David Wiesner
Honor Book: *Tar Bleach* by Faith Ringgold

1991: *Black and White* by David Macaulay
Honor Books: *Puss in Boots* by Fred Marcellino; *"More, More, More," Said the Baby: Three Love Stories* by Vera B. Williams

1990: *Lon Po Po: A Red-Riding Hood Story from China* translated by Ed Young
Honor Books: *Bill Peet, an Autobiography* by Bill Peet; *Color Zoo* by Lois Ehlert; *Hershel and the Hanukkah Goblins* by Eric Kimmel, illustrated by Trina Schart Hyman; *The Talking Eggs* by Robert D. San Souci, illustrated by Jerry Pinkney

1989: *Song and Dance Man* by Karen Ackerman, illustrated by Stephen Gammell
Honor Books: *The Boy of the Three-Year Nap* by Dianne Snyder, illustrated by Allen Say; *Free Fall* by David Wiesner; *Goldilocks* retold and illustrated by James Marshall; *Mirandy and Brother Wind* by Patricia C. McKissack, illustrated by Jerry Pinkney

1988: *Owl Moon* by Jane Yolen, illustrated by John Schoenherr
Honor Book: *Mufaro's Beautiful Daughters: An African Tale* by John Steptoe

1987: *Hey, Al* by Arthur Yorinks, illustrated by Richard Egielski
Honor Books: *Alphabatics* by Susie MacDonald; *Rumpelstiltskin* retold and illustrated by Paul O. Zelinsky; *The Village of Round and Square Houses* by Ann Grifalconi

1986: *The Polar Express* by Chris Van Allsburg
Honor Books: *King Bidgood's in the Bathtub* by Audrey Wood, illustrated by Don Wood; *The Relatives Came* by Cynthia Rylant, illustrated by Richard Egielski

1985: *St. George and the Dragon* retold by Margaret Hodges, illustrated by Trina Schart Hyman
Honor Book: *Hansel and Gretel* retold by Rika Lesser, illustrated by Paul O. Zelinsky

1984: *The Glorious Flight: Across the Channel with Louis Bleriot* by Alice and Martin Provensen
Honor Books: *Ten, Nine, Eight* by Molly Bang; *Little Red Riding Hood* retold and illustrated by Trina Schart Hyman

1983: *Shadow* by Blaise Cendrars, illustrated by Marcia Brown
Honor Books: *When I Was Young in the Mountains* by Cynthia Rylant, illustrated by Diane Goode; *Chair for My Mother* by Vera B. Williams

1982: *Jumanji* by Chris Van Allsburg
Honor Books: *A Visit to William Blake's Inn: Poems for Innocent and Experienced Travelers* by Nancy Willard, illustrated by Alice and Martin Provensen; *Where the Buffaloes Begin* by Olaf Baker, illustrated by Stephen Gammell; *On Market Street* by Arnold Lobel, illustrated by Anita Lobel; *Outside Over There* by Maurice Sendak

1981: *Fables* by Arnold Lobel
Honor Books: *The Bremen-Town Musicians* by Ilse Plume; *The Grey Lady and the Strawberry Snatcher* by Molly Bang; *Mice Twice* by Joseph Low; *Truck* by Donald Crews

1980: *Ox-Cart Man* by Donald Hall, illustrated by Barbara Cooney
Honor Books: *Ben's Trumpet* by Rachel Isadora; *The Treasure* by Uri Shulevitz; *The Garden of Abdul Gasazi* by Chris Van Allsburg

Newbery Medal and Honor Books (2003–1980)

2003: *Crispin: The Cross of Lead* by Avi
Honor Books: *The House of the Scorpion* by Nancy Farmer; *Pictures of Hollis Woods* by Patricia Reilly Giff; *Hoot* by Carl Hiaasen; *A Corner of the Universe* by Ann M. Martin; *Surviving the Applewhites* by Stephanie S. Tolan

2002: *A Single Shard* by Linda Sue Park
Honor Books: *Carver: A Life in Poems* by Marilyn Nelson; *Everything on a Waffle* by Polly Horvath

2001: *A Year Down Under* by Richard Peck
Honor Books: *Because of Winn-Dixie* by Kate DiCamillo; *Hope Was Here* by Joan Bauer; *Joey Pigza Loses Control* by Jack Gantos

2000: *Bud, Not Buddy* by Paul Curtis
Honor Books: *Getting Near to Baby* by Audrey Couloumbis; *26 Fairmount Avenue* by Tomie dePaola; *Our Only May Amelia* by Jennifer L. Holm

1999: *Holes* by Louis Sachar
Honor Book: *A Long Way from Chicago* by Richard Peck

1998: *Out of the Dust* by Karen Hesse
Honor Books: *Ella Enchanted* by Gail Carson Levine; *Lily's Crossing* by Patricia Reilly Giff; *Wringer* by Jerry Spinelli

1997: *The View from Saturday* by E. L. Konigsburg
Honor Books: *A Girl Named Disaster* by Nancy Farmer; *Moorchild* by Eloise McGraw; *The Thief* by Megan Whalen Turner; *Belle Prater's Boy* by Ruth White

1996: *The Midwife's Apprentice* by Karen Cushman
Honor Books: *What Jamie Saw* by Carolyn Coleman; *The Watsons Go to Birmingham, 1963* by Christopher Paul Curtis; *Yolanda's Genius* by Carol Fenner; *The Great Fire* by Jim Murphy

1995: *Walk Two Moons* by Sharon Creech
Honor Books: *Catherine, Called Birdy* by Karen Cushman; *The Ear, the Eye, and the Arm* by Nancy Farmer

1994: *The Giver* by Lois Lowry
Honor Books: *Crazy Lady* by Jane Leslie Conly; *Eleanor Roosevelt; A Life of Discovery* by Russell Freeman; *Dragon's Gate* by Laurence Yep

1993: *Missing May* by Cynthia Rylant
Honor Books: *What Hearts* by Bruce Brooks; *The Dark-Thirty: Southern Tales of the Supernatural* by Patricia C. McKissack; *Somewhere in the Darkness* by Walter Dean Myers

1992: *Shiloh* by Phyllis Reynolds Naylor
Honor Books: *Nothing But the Truth* by Avi; *The Wright Brothers: How They Invented the Airplane* by Russell Freedman

1991: *Maniac Magee* by Jerry Spinelli
Honor Book: *The True Confessions of Charlotte Doyle* by Avi

1990: *Number the Stars* by Lois Lowry
Honor Books: *Afternoon of the Elves* by Janet Taylor Lisle; *Shabanu,*

Daughter of the Wind by Susan Fisher Staples; *The Winter Room* by Gary Paulsen

1989: *Joyful Noise: Poems for Two Voices* by Paul Fleischman
Honor Books: *In the Beginning: Creation Stories from around the World* by Virginia Hamilton; *Scorpions* by Walter Dean Myers

1988: *Lincoln: A Photobiography* by Russell Freedman
Honor Books: *After the Rain* by Norma Fox Mazer; *Hatchet* by Gary Paulsen

1987: *The Whipping Boy* by Sid Fleischman
Honor Books: *A Fine White Dust* by Cynthia Rylant; *On My Honor* by Marion Dane Bauer; *Volcano: The Eruption and Healing of Mount St. Helens* by Patricia Lauber

1986: *Sarah, Plan and Tall* by Patricia MacLachlan
Honor Books: *Commodore Perry in the Land of the Shogun* by Rhoda Blumberg; *Dogsong* by Gary Paulsen

1985: *The Hero and the Crown* by Robin McKinley
Honor Books: *Like Jake and Me* by Mavis Jukes; *The Moves Make the Man* by Bruce Brooks; *One-Eyed Cat* by Paula Fox

1984: *Dear Mr. Henshaw* by Beverly Cleary
Honor Books: *The Sign of the Beaver* by Elizabeth George Speare; *A Solitary Blue* by Cynthia Voigt; *The Wish Giver* by Bill Brittain

1983: *Dicey's Song* by Cynthia Voigt
Honor Books: *Blue Sword* by Robin McKinley; *Dr. DeSoto* by William Steig; *Graven Images* by Paul Fleischman; *Homesick: My Own Story* by Jean Fritz; *Sweet Whisper, Brother Rush* by Virginia Hamilton

1982: *A Visit to William Blake's Inn: Poems for Innocent and Experienced Travelers* by Nancy Willard
Honor Books: *Ramona Quimby, Age 8* by Beverly Cleary; *Upon the Head of the Goat: A Childhood in Hungary, 1939–1944* by Aranka Siegal

1981: *Jacob Have I Loved* by Katherine Paterson
Honor Books: *The Fledgling* by Jane Langton; *A Ring of Endless Light* by Madeleine L'Engle

1980: *A Gathering of Days: A New England Girl's Journal 1830–32* by Joan Blos

Américas Award Winners

2001: *A Movie in My Pillow* by Jorge Argueta; illustrated by Elizabeth Gómez (Children's Book Press); *Breaking Through* by Francisco Jiménez (Houghton Mifflin Company)

2000: *The Composition* by Antonio Skármeta; illustrated by Alfonso Ruano (Groundwood); *The Color of My Words* by Lynn Joseph (HarperCollins)

1999: *Crashboomlove* by Juan Felipe Herrera (University of New Mexico Press)

1998: *Barrio: José's Neighborhood* by George Ancona (Harcourt Brace); *Mama and Papa Have a Store* by Amelia Lau Carling (Dial)

1997: *The Circuit* by Francisco Jiménez (University of New Mexico Press); *The Face at the Window* by Regina Hanson; illustrated by Linda Saport (Clarion)

1996: *In My Family/En mi familia* by Carmen Lomas Garza (Children's Book Press); *Parrot in the Oven* by Victor Martínez (HarperCollins)

1995: *Tonight, by Sea* by Frances Temple (Orchard)

1994: *The Mermaid's Twin Sister* by Lynn Joseph (Clarion)

1993: *Vejigante Masquerader* by Lulu Delacre (Scholastic)

Pura Belpé Award Winners

This children's book award is given in even years to a Latino/Latina writer (for best narrative) and illustrator whose work best portrays, affirms, and celebrates the Latino cultural experience. The award is named for the first Latina librarian in the New York City Public Library.

2000: Narrative: *Under the Royal Palms* by Alma Flor Ada
Illustration: *Magic Windows* by Carmen Lomas Garza, Harriet Rohmer, and David Schecter, illustrated by Carmen Lomas Garza
Honor Books: Narrative: *From the Bellybutton of the Moon and Other Summer Poems/Del Ombligo De Luna Y Otro Poemas De Verano* by Francisco X. Alarcón; *Laughing Out Loud, I Fly* by Juan Felipe Herrera
Illustration: *Barrio: José's Neighborhood* by George Ancona; *The Secret Stars* by Joseph Slate, illustrated by Felipe Davalos; *Mama and Papa Have a Store* by Amelia Lau Carling

1998: Narrative: *Parrot in the Oven: Mi Vida* by Victor Martinez
Honor Books: *Laughing Tomatoes and Other Spring Poems* (Jitomates Risueños y Otros Poemas de Primavera) by Francisco X. Alarcón, illustrated by Maya Christina Gonzales; *Spirits of the High Mesa* by Floyd Martinez
Illustration: *Snapshots from the Wedding* by Gary Soto, illustrated by Stephanie Garcia
Honor Books: *In My Family/En Mi Familia* by Carmen Lomas Garza; *The Golden Flower: A Taino Myth From Puerto Rico* by Nina Jaffe, illustrated by Enrique O. Sánchez; *Gathering the Sun: An Alphabet in Spanish and English* by Alma Flor Ada, illustrated by Simón Silva

1996: Narrative: *An Island Like You: Stories of the Barrio* by Judith Ortiz Cofer
Honor Book: *Baseball in April and Other Stories* by Gary Soto
Illustration: *Chato's Kitchen* by Gary Soto, illustrated by Susan Guevara
Honor Books: *The Bossy Gallito: A Traditional Cuban Folktale,* retold by Lucia M. Gonzalez, illustrated by Lulu Delacre; *Pablo Remembers: The Fiesta of the Day of the Dead,* written and photographed by George Ancona; *Family Pictures/Cuadros de Familia* by Carmen Lomas Garza

Coretta Scott King Award Winners

2003: *Bronx Masquerade* by Nikki Grimes
Honor Books: *The Red Rose Box* by Brenda Woods; *Talkin' About Bessie: The Story of Aviator Elizabeth Coleman* by Nikki Grimes

Best Illustrated Book: *Talkin' About Bessie: The Story of Aviator Elizabeth Coleman* by Nikki Grimes, illustrated by E. B. Lewis
Honor Books: *Rapa Tap Tap:* by Leo and Diane Dillon; *Visiting Langston* by Bryan Collier

2002: *The Land* by Mildred D. Taylor
Honor Books: *Carver: A Life in Poems* by Marilyn Nelson; *Money-Hungry* by Sharon G. Flake

Best Illustrated Book: *Goin' Someplace Special* by Patricia McKissack, illustrated by Jerry Pinkney
Honor Book: *Martin's Big Words: The Life of Dr. Martin Luther King, Jr.* by

Doreen Rappaport, illustrated by
Bryan Collier

2001: *Miracle's Boys* by Jacqueline
Woodson
Honor Book: *Let It Shine! Stories of
Black Women Freedom Fighters* by
Andrea Davis Pinkney, illustrated by
Stephen Alcorn

Best Illustrated Book: *Uptown* by
Bryan Collier
Honor Book: *Freedom River* by
Doreen Rappaport, illustrated by
Bryan Collier

2000: Narrative: *Bud, Not Buddy* by
Christopher Paul Curtis
Illustration: *In the Time of the Drums*
by Kim L. Siegelson, illustrated by
Brian Pinkney
Honor Books: Narrative: *Black
Hands, White Sails: The Story of
African-American Whalers* by Patricia
C. McKissack and Frederick L.
McKissack; *Monster* by Walter Dean
Myers; *Francie* by Karen English
Illustration: *My Rows and Piles of
Coins* by Tololwa M. Mollel,
illustrated by E. B. Lewis; *Black Cat*
by Christopher Myers

1999: Author: *Heaven* by Angela Johnson
Illustrator: *i see the rhythm* by Toyomi
Igus, illustrated by Michele Wood

1998: Author: *Forged by Fire* by Sharon M.
Draper
Illustrator: *In Daddy's Arms I Am Tall*
by Javaka Steptoe

1997: Author: *Slam!* by Walter Dean Myer
Illustrator: *Minty: A Story of Young
Harriet Tubman* by Alan Schroeder,
illustrated by Jerry Pinkney

1996: Author: *Her Stories: African
American Folktales* by Virginia
Hamilton, illustrated by Leo & Diane
Dillon

Illustrator: *The Middle Passage:
White Ships Black Cargo* by Tom
Feelings

1995: Author: *Christmas in the Big House,
Christmas in the Quarters* by Patricia
McKissack and Frederick McKissack,
illustrated by John Thompson
Illustrator: *The Creation* by James
Weldon Johnson, illustrated by James
Ransome

1994: Author: *Toning the Sweep* by Angela
Johnson
Illustrator: *Soul Looks Back in
Wonder,* compiled and illustrated by
Tom Feelings

1993: Author: *The Dark-Thirty: Southern
Tales of the Supernatural* by Patricia
McKissack
Illustrator: *Origins of Life on Earth:
An African American Creation Myth*
by David A. Anderson, illustrated by
Kathleen Atkins Smith

1992: Author: *Now Is Your Time! The
African-American Struggle for
Freedom* by Walter Dean Myers
Illustrator: *Tar Beach* by Faith
Ringgold

1991: Author: *Road to Memphis* by Mildred
D. Taylor
Illustrator: *Aida,* retold by Leontyne
Price, illustrated by Leo and Diane
Dillon

1990: Author: *A Long Hard Journey* by
Patricia and Frederick McKissack
Illustrator: *Nathaniel Talking* by
Eloise Greenfield, illustrated by Jan
Spivey Gilchrist

1989: Author: *Fallen Angels* by Walter D.
Myers
Illustrator: *Mirandy and Brother Wind*
by Patricia McKissack, illustrated by
Jerry Pinkney

1988: Author: *The Friendship* by Mildred D. Taylor, illustrated by Max Ginsberg
Illustrator: *Mufaro's Beautiful Daughters: An African Tale,* retold and illustrated by John Steptoe

1987: Author: *Justin and the Best Biscuits in the World* by Mildred Pitts Walter
Illustrator: *Half Moon and One Whole Star* by Crescent Dragonwagon, illustrated by Jerry Pinkney

1986: Author: *The People Could Fly: American Black Folktales* by Virginia Hamilton
Illustrator: *Patchwork Quilt* by Valerie Flournoy, illustrated by Jerry Pinkney

1985: Author: *Motown and Didi* by Walter Dean Myers
Illustrator: No award

1984: Author: *Everett Anderson's Good-Bye* by Lucille Clifton
Illustrator: *My Mama Needs Me* by Mildred Pitts Walter, illustrated by Pat Cummings

1983: Author: *Sweet Whispers, Brother Rush* by Virginia Hamilton
Illustrator: *Black Child* by Peter Mugabane

1982: Author: *Let the Circle Be Unbroken* by Mildred D. Taylor
Illustrator: *Mother Crocodile: An Uncle Amadou Tale from Senegal,* adapted by Rosa Guy, illustrated by John Steptoe

1981: Author: *This Life* by Sidney Poitier
Illustrator: *Beat the Story-Drum, Pum-Pum* by Ashley Bryan

1980: *The Young Landlords* by Walter Dean Myers
Illustrator: *Cornrows* by Camille Yarbrough, illustrated by Carole Bayard

Standards for Reading Professionals

Developed by the
Professional Standards and Ethics Committee
of the
International Reading Association

The competencies are rated as follows:

Levels of Proficiency

A—Awareness
> Has awareness of the different aspects for literacy development and related teaching procedures.

B—Basic Understanding
> Has knowledge about specific instructional tasks and has fundamental proficiency in the performance of those tasks for the aspect of literacy development.

C—Comprehensive Understanding
> Is able to apply proficiency broad, in-depth knowledge of the different aspects of literacy development in instructional settings.

O—Not Applicable

Competencies of Teachers	Classroom Professional			
	Early-Childhood Teacher	Elementary School Teacher	Middle and Secondary School Teacher	Special-Education Teacher
KNOWLEDGE AND BELIEFS ABOUT READING				
1.0 THEORETICAL BASE				
The reading professional will:				
1.1 recognize that reading should be taught as a process;	C	C	B	B
1.2 understand, respect, and value cultural, linguistic, and ethnic diversity;	C	C	C	C
1.3 recognize the importance of literacy for personal and social growth;	C	C	C	C
1.4 recognize that literacy can be a means for transmitting moral and cultural values;	C	C	C	C
1.5 perceive reading as the process of constructing meaning through the interaction of the reader's existing knowledge, the information suggested by the written language, and the context of the reading situation;	B	B	B	B
1.6 understand the major theories of language development, cognition, and learning; and	B	B	B	B
1.7 understand the impact of physical, perceptual, emotional, social, cultural, environmental, and intellectual factors on learning, language development, and reading acquisition.	B	B	B	B
2.0 THEORETICAL BASE				
The reading professional will:				
2.1 understand that written language is a symbolic system;	B	B	B	B
2.2 understand the interrelation of language and literacy acquisition;	B	B	B	B
2.3 understand principles of new language and acquisition;	B	B	B	B
2.4 understand the phonemic, morphemic, semantic, syntactic, and pragmatic systems of language and their relation to the reading and writing process;	B	B	B	B
2.5 understand the interrelation of reading and writing, and listening and speaking;	B	B	B	B
2.6 pick up correct 2.6 on map 3 of charts	B	B	B	B

Competencies of Teachers	Classroom Professional			
	Early-Childhood Teacher	Elementary School Teacher	Middle and Secondary School Teacher	Special-Education Teacher
2.7 understand emergent literacy and the experiences that support it;	C	B	A	B
2.8 understand the role of metacognition in reading and writing, and listening and speaking;	B	B	B	B
2.9 understand how contextual factors in the school can influence student learning and reading (e.g., grouping procedures, school programs, and assessment);	C	C	C	C
2.10 know past and present literacy leaders and their contributions to the knowledge base;	A	A	A	A
2.11 know relevant reading research from general education and how it has influenced literacy education;	A	A	A	A
2.12 know classic and contemporary children's and young adults' literature, and easy-reading fiction and nonfiction for adults, at appropriate levels;	B	B	B	B
2.13 recognize the importance of giving learners opportunities in all aspects of literacy (e.g., as readers, writers, thinkers, reactors, or responders); and	B	B	B	B
2.14 understand that goals, instruction, and assessment should be aligned.	B	B	B	B

3.0 INDIVIDUAL DIFFERENCES

The reading professional will:

3.1 recognize how differences among learners influence their literacy development;	B	B	B	C
3.2 understand, respect, and value cultural, linguistic, and ethnic diversity;	C	C	C	C
3.3 understand that spelling is developmental and is based on students' knowledge of the phonological system and of the letter names; their judgments of phonetic similarities and differences, and their ability to abstract phonetic information from letter names;	B	B	B	B
3.4 recognize the importance of creating programs to address the strengths and needs of individual learners; and	C	C	C	C

	Classroom Professional			
Competencies of Teachers	Early-Childhood Teacher	Elementary School Teacher	Middle and Secondary School Teacher	Special-Education Teacher
3.5 know federal, state, and local programs designed to help students with reading and writing problems.	B	B	B	B
4.0 READING DIFFICULTIES The reading professional will:				
4.1 understand the nature and multiple causes of reading and writing difficulties;	B	B	B	B
4.2 know principles for diagnosing reading difficulties;	B	B	B	B
4.3 be well-versed on individualized and group instructional interventions targeted toward those students in greatest need or at low proficiency levels; and	B	B	B	C
4.4 know the instructional implications of research in special education, psychology, and other fields that deal with the treatment of students with reading and learning difficulties.	B	B	B	C
INSTRUCTION AND ASSESSMENT **5.0 CREATING A LITERATE ENVIRONMENT** The reading professional will be able to:				
5.1 create an environment that fosters interest and growth in all aspects of literacy;	C	C	C	C
5.2 use texts and trade books to stimulate interest, promote reading growth, foster appreciation for the written word, and increase the motivation of learners to read widely and independently for information, pleasure, and personal growth;	B	B	B	B
5.3 model and discuss reading and writing as valuable, lifelong activities;	B	B	B	B
5.4 provide opportunities for learners to select from a variety of written materials, to read extended texts, and to read for many authentic purposes;	B	B	B	B
5.5 provide opportunities for creative and personal responses to literature, including storytelling;	B	B	B	B
5.6 promote the integration of language arts in all content areas;	B	B	B	B

| | Classroom Professional | | | |
Competencies of Teachers	Early-Childhood Teacher	Elementary School Teacher	Middle and Secondary School Teacher	Special-Education Teacher
5.7 use instructional and information technologies to support literacy learning; and	B	B	B	B
5.8 implement effective strategies to include parents as partners in the literacy development of their children.	C	C	C	C

6.0 WORD IDENTIFICATION, VOCABULARY, AND SPELLING

The reading professional will be able to:

6.1 teach students to monitor their own word identification through the use of syntactic, semantic, and graphophonemic relations;	C	C	B	C
6.2 use phonics to teach students to use their knowledge of letter/sound correspondence to identify sounds in the construction of meaning;	C	C	B	C
6.3 teach students to use context to identify and define unfamiliar words;	B	B	B	B
6.4 guide students to refine their spelling knowledge through reading and writing;	B	B	B	B
6.5 teach students to recognize and use various spelling patterns in the English language as an aid to word identification; and	B	B	B	B
6.6 employ effective techniques and strategies for the ongoing development of independent vocabulary acquisition.	B	B	B	B

7.0 COMPREHENSION

The reading professional will be able to:

7.1 provide direct instruction and model when and how to use multiple comprehension strategies, including retelling;	B	B	B	B
7.2 model questioning strategies;	B	B	B	B
7.3 teach students to connect prior knowledge with new information;	C	C	C	C
7.4 teach students strategies for monitoring their own comprehension;	B	B	B	B
7.5 ensure that students can use various aspects of text to gain comprehension, including conventions of written English, text structure and genres, figurative language, and intertextual links; and	B	B	B	B

Competencies of Teachers	Classroom Professional			
	Early-Childhood Teacher	Elementary School Teacher	Middle and Secondary School Teacher	Special-Education Teacher
7.6 ensure that students gain understanding of the meaning and importance of the conventions of standard written English (e.g., punctuation or usage).	B	B	B	B
8.0 STUDY STRATEGIES				
The reading professional will be able to:				
8.1 provide opportunities to locate and use a variety of print, nonprint, and electronic reference resources;	B	B	B	B
8.2 teach students to vary reading rate according to the purpose(s) and difficulty of the material;	B	B	C	B
8.3 teach students effective time-management strategies;	B	B	C	B
8.4 teach students strategies to organize and remember information; and	B	B	C	C
8.5 teach test-taking strategies.	B	B	C	C
9.0 WRITING				
The reading professional will be able to:				
9.1 teach students planning strategies most appropriate for particular kinds of writing;	B	B	C	C
9.2 teach students to draft, revise, and edit their writing; and	B	B	C	C
9.3 teach students the conventions of standard written English needed to edit their compositions.	B	B	C	C
10.0 ASSESSMENT				
The reading professional will be able to:				
10.1 develop and conduct assessments that involve multiple indicators of learner progress; and	B	B	B	B
10.2 administer and use information from norm-referenced tests, criterion-referenced tests, formal and informal inventories, constructed response measures, portfolio-based assessments, student self-evaluations, work/performance samples, observations, anecdotal records, journals, and other indicators of student progress to inform instruction and learning.	B	B	B	B

Competencies of Teachers	Classroom Professional			
	Early-Childhood Teacher	Elementary School Teacher	Middle and Secondary School Teacher	Special-Education Teacher
ORGANIZING AND ENHANCING A READING PROGRAM				
11.0 COMMUNICATING INFORMATION ABOUT READING				
The reading professional will be able to:				
11.1 communicate with students about their strengths, areas for improvement, and ways to achieve improvement;	C	C	C	C
11.2 communicate with allied professionals and paraprofessionals in assessing student achievement and planning instruction;	C	C	C	C
11.3 involve parents in cooperative efforts and programs to support students' reading and writing development;	C	C	C	C
11.4 communicate information about literacy and data to administrators, staff members, policymakers, the media, parents, and the community; and	B	B	B	B
11.5 interpret research findings related to the improvement of instruction and communicate these to colleagues and the wider community.	B	B	B	B
12.0 CURRICULUM DEVELOPMENT				
The reading professional will be able to:				
12.1 initiate and participate in ongoing curriculum development and evaluation;	B	B	B	B
12.2 adapt instruction to meet the needs of different learners to accomplish different purposes;	C	C	C	C
12.3 supervise, coordinate, and support all services associated with literacy programs (e.g., needs assessment, program development, budgeting and evaluation, and grant and proposal writing);	A	A	A	A
12.4 select and evaluate instructional materials for literacy, including those that are technology-based;	C	C	C	C
12.5 use multiple indicators to determine effectiveness of the literacy curriculum;	B	B	B	B

	Classroom Professional			
Competencies of Teachers	Early-Childhood Teacher	Elementary School Teacher	Middle and Secondary School Teacher	Special-Education Teacher
12.6 plan and implement programs designed to help students improve their reading and writing including those supported by federal, state, and local funding; and	A	A	A	A
12.7 help develop individual educational plans for students with severe learning problems related to literacy.	B	B	B	C
13.0 PROFESSIONAL DEVELOPMENT The reading professional will be able to:				
13.1 participate in professional-development programs;	C	C	C	C
13.2 initiate, implement, and evaluate professional-development programs;	A	A	A	A
13.3 provide professional-development experiences that help emphasize the dynamic interaction among prior knowledge, experience, and the school context as well as among other aspects of reading development;	A	A	A	A
13.4 provide professional-development experiences that are sensitive to school constraints (e.g., class size or limited resources);	A	A	A	A
13.5 use multiple indicators to judge professional growth; and	B	B	B	B
13.6 model ethical professional behavior.	C	C	C	C
14.0 RESEARCH The reading professional will be able to:				
14.1 apply for improved literacy;	A	A	A	A
14.2 conduct research with a wide range of methodologies (e.g., ethnographic, descriptive, experimental, or historical); and	A	A	A	A
14.3 promote and facilitate teacher- and classroom-based research.	B	B	B	B

	Classroom Professional			
Competencies of Teachers	Early-Childhood Teacher	Elementary School Teacher	Middle and Secondary School Teacher	Special-Education Teacher
15.0 SUPERVISION OF PARAPROFESSIONALS				
The reading professional will be able to:				
15.1 plan lessons for paraprofessionals;	C	C	C	C
15.2 observe and evaluate paraprofessionals interacting with children and provide feedback to them on their performance;	C	C	C	C
15.3 provide professional development and training for paraprofessionals; and	A	A	A	A
15.4 provide emotional and academic support for paraprofessionals.	B	B	B	B
16.0 PROFESSIONALISM				
The reading professional will be able to:				
16.1 pursue knowledge of literacy by reading professional journals and publications, and participating in conferences and other professional activities;	C	C	C	C
16.2 reflect on one's practice to improve on instruction and other services to students;	C	C	C	C
16.3 interact with and participate in decision making with teachers, teacher educators, theoreticians, and researchers;	C	C	C	C
16.4 support and participate in efforts to improve the reading profession by being an advocate for licensing and certification;	B	B	B	B
16.5 participate in local, state, national, and international professional organizations whose mission is the improvement of literacy;	C	C	C	C
16.6 promote collegiality with other literacy professionals through regular conversations, discussions, and consultations about learners, literacy theory, and assessment and instruction;	B	B	B	B
16.7 write for publication; and	A	A	A	A
16.8 make presentations at local, state, regional, and national meetings and conferences.	B	B	B	A

The International Reading Association (IRA) and National Teachers of English (NCTE) Standards for the English Language Arts

The following 12 standards encompass the English language arts:

- Students read a wide range of print and nonprint texts to build an understanding of texts, of themselves, and of the cultures of the United States and the world; to acquire new information, to respond to the needs and demands of society and the workplace; and for personal fulfillment. Among these texts are fiction and nonfiction, classic, and contemporary works.
- Students read a wide range of literature from many periods in many genres to build an understanding of the many dimensions (e.g., philosophical, ethical, aesthetic) of human experience.
- Students apply a wide range of strategies to comprehend, interpret, evaluate, and appreciate texts. They draw on their prior experience, their interactions with other readers and writers, their knowledge of word meaning and of other texts, their word identification strategies, and their understanding of textual features (e.g., sound-letter correspondence, sentence structure, graphics).
- Students adjust their use of spoken, written, and visual language (e.g., conventions, style, vocabulary) to communicate effectively with a variety of audiences and for different purposes.
- Students employ a wide range of strategies as they write and use different writing process elements appropriately to communicate with different audiences for a variety of purposes.
- Students apply knowledge of language structure, language conventions (e.g., spelling and punctuation), media techniques, figurative language, and genre to create, critique, and discuss print and nonprint texts.
- Students conduct research on issues and interests by generating ideas and questions, and by posing problems. They gather, evaluate, and synthesize data from a variety of sources (e.g., print and nonprint texts, artifacts, people) to communicate their discoveries in ways that suit their purpose and audience.
- Students use a variety of technological and informational resources (e.g., libraries, databases, computer networks, video) to gather and synthesize information and to create and communicate knowledge.
- Students develop an understanding of and respect for diversity in language use, patterns, and dialects across cultures, ethnic groups, geographic regions, and social roles.

- Students whose first language is not English make use of their first language to develop competency in the English language arts and to develop understanding of content across the curriculum.
- Students participate as knowledgeable, reflective, creative, and critical members of a variety of literacy communities.
- Students use spoken, written, and visual language to accomplish their own purposes (e.g., for learning, enjoyment, persuasion, and the exchange of information).

Source: IRA/NCTE Standards for the English Language Arts, 1996, p. 3. Used by permission.

References

Adams, M. J. (1990). *Beginning to read: Thinking and learning about print.* Urbana, IL: Center for the Study of Reading.

Adams, M. J., Foorman, B. R., Lundberg, I., & Beeler, Y. (1998). *Phonemic awareness in young children.* Baltimore, MD: Paul H. Brookes Publishing.

Advantage Learning Systems. (2000). *Accelerated reader.* Wisconsin Rapids, WI: Renaissance Learning Systems.

Alleman, J., & Brophy, J. (1999). Current trends and practices in social studies assessment in the early grades. *Social Studies and the Young Learner, 11* (4), 15–17.

Allen, J. (2000). *Words, words, words: Teaching vocabulary in grades 4–12.* York, ME: Stenhouse.

Allen, R. V. (1976). *Language experiences in communication.* Boston: Houghton Mifflin.

Allington, R. L. (1977). If they don't read much, how they ever gonna get good? *Journal of Reading, 21* (2), 57–61.

———. (2001). *What really matters for struggling readers: Designing research-based programs.* New York: Addison Wesley Longman.

———. (2002). What I've learned about effective reading instruction from a decade of exemplary elementary classroom teachers. *Phi Delta Kappan, 83* (10), 740–747.

Allington, R. L., & Cunningham, P. M. (2002). *Schools that work: Where all children read and write* (8th ed.). Boston: Allyn & Bacon.

Almasi, J. F. (1995). The nature of fourth graders sociocognitive conflicts in peer-led and teacher-led discussions of literature. *Reading Research Quarterly, 30* (3), 314–351.

Alvermann, D., Moon, J. S., & Hagood, M. C. (1999). *Popular culture in the classroom.* Newark, DE: International Reading Association.

Alvermann, D. E., Smith, L. C., & Readence, J. E. (1985). Prior knowledge activation and the comprehension of compatible and incompatible text. *Reading Research Quarterly, 20,* 420–436.

American Library Association. (1996). *Intellectual freedom manual* (5th ed.). Chicago: American Library Association.

American Psychiatric Association. (1994). *Diagnostic and statistical manual of mental disorders* (4th ed.). Washington, DC: Author.

Anders, P., Bos, C., & Filip, D. (1984). The effect of semantic feature analysis on reading comprehension of learning-disabled students. In J. A. Niles & L. A. Harris (Eds.), *Changing perspectives on research in reading/language processing and instruction.* Rochester, NY: National Reading Conference.

Anderson, R. C. (1996). Research foundations to support wide reading. In V. Greaney (Ed.), *Promoting reading in developing countries* (pp. 6–21). Newark, DE: International Reading Association.

Anderson, R. C., Hiebert, E. H., Scott, J. A., & Wilkinson, I. A. G. (1985). *Becoming a nation of readers: The report of the Commission on Reading.* Urbana, IL: Center for Study of Reading.

Anderson, R. C., & Pearson, P. D. (1984). A schema-theory view of basic processes in reading, In P. D. Pearson (Ed.), *Handbook of reading research* (pp. 255–291). New York: Longman.

Anderson, R. C., Wilson, P., & Fielding, L. (1988). Growth in reading and how children spend their time outside of school. *Reading Research Quarterly, 23* (3), 285–303.

Apple Education News. (1997). "Technology News," pp. 1–3.

Armbruster, B. B., Anderson, T. H., & Ostertag, J. (1989). Teaching text structure to improve reading and writing. *The Reading Teacher, 39* (2), 130–137.

Aston-Warner, S. (1963). *Teacher.* New York: Simon & Schuster.

Atwell, N. (1987). *In the middle: Reading and writing with adolescents.* Upper Montclair, NJ: Boyton/Cook.

Atwell, N. (Ed.). (1990). *Coming to know: Writing to learn in the intermediate grades.* Portsmouth, NH: Heinemann.

———. (1998). *In the middle: New understandings about writing, reading, and learning.* Portsmouth, NH: Heinemann.

Au, K. H. (1993). *Literacy instruction in multicultural settings.* New York: Harcourt, Brace & Jovanovich.

———. (1997). Literacy for all students: Ten steps toward making a difference. *The Reading Teacher, 51* (3), 186–194.

———. (2000). Literacy instruction for young children of diverse backgrounds. In D. S. Strickland and L. M. Morrow (Eds.), *Beginning reading and writing* (pp. 35–45). New York: Teachers College Press.

Au, K. H., Carroll, J. H., & Scheu, J. A. (2001). *Balanced literacy instruction: A teacher's resource book,* 2nd ed. Norwood, MA: Christopher-Gordon.

Au, K. H., Mason, J. M., & Scheu, J. S. (1995). *Literacy instruction today.* New York: HarperCollins.

Ball, A. F., & Farr, M. (2003). Language varieties, culture and teaching the English language arts. In J. Flood, D. Lapp, J. R. Squires, & J. M. Jensen (Eds.), *Handbook of research on teaching the English language arts* (pp. 435–445). Mahwah, NJ: Lawrence Erlbaum Associates.

Barone, D. (1990). The written response of young children: Beyond comprehension to story understanding. *The New Advocate, 3* (1), 49–56.

Barrentine, S. J. (1999). Introduction. In S. J. Barrentine's (Ed.) *Reading assessment: Principles and practices for elementary teachers.* Newark, DE: International Reading Association.

Barrera, R. B., Thompson, V. D., & Dressman, M. (1997). *Kaleidoscope: A multicultural booklist for grades K–8.* Urbana, IL: National Council of Teachers of English.

Barton, K. C., & Smith, L. A. (2000). Themes or motifs? Aiming for coherence through interdisciplinary outlines. *The Reading Teacher, 54* (1), 54–63.

Baumann, J. F., Hooten, H., & White, P. (1999). Teaching comprehension through literature: A teacher-research project to develop fifth graders' reading strategies and motivation. *The Reading Teacher, 53* (1), 38–51.

Bear, D. R., Invernizzi, M., Templeton, S., & Johnson, F. (2000). *Words their way: Word study for phonics, vocabulary, and spelling instruction.* Upper Saddle River, NJ: Merrill.

Bear, D. R., & Templeton, S. (1998). Explorations in developmental spelling: Foundations for learning and teaching phonics, spelling, and vocabulary. *The Reading Teacher, 54* (7), 700–702.

Beck, I. L. (1989). Reading and reasoning. *The Reading Teacher, 42,* 676–682.

Beck, I. L., & McKeown, M. G. (1981). Developing questions that promote comprehension: The story map. *Language Arts, 58* (9), 913–918.

———. (1996). Conditions of vocabulary acquisition. In R. Barr, M. L. Kamil, P. Mosenthal, & P. D. Pearson (Eds.), *Handbook of reading research, Vol. II.* (pp. 485–597). Mahwah, NJ: Lawrence Erlbaum.

Beck, I. L., McKeown, M. G., Hamilton, R. L., & Kucam, L. (1997). *Questioning the author: An approach for enhancing student engagement with text.* Newark, DE: International Reading Association.

Beck, I. L., Omanson, R. C., & McKeown, M. G. (1982). An instructional redesign of reading lessons: Effects on comprehension. *Reading Research Quarterly, 17*(4), 462–481.

Bieger, E. M. (1995/1996). Promoting multicultural education through a literature-based approach. *The Reading Teacher, 49* (4), 308–312.

Birnbaum, J., Emig, J., & Fisher, D. (2003). Case studies: Placing literacy phenomena within their actual context. In J. Flood, D. Lapp, J. R. Squire, & J. M. Jensen (Eds.), *Handbook of research on teaching the English language arts* (pp. 192–200). Mahwah, NJ: Lawrence Erlbaum Associates.

Bitter, G., & Pierson, M. (2002). *Using technology in the classroom* (5th ed.). Boston: Allyn and Bacon.

Blachowicz, C. L. Z., & Fisher, P. (2000). Vocabulary instruction. In M. L. Kamil, P. B. Mosenthal, P. D. Pearson, & R. Barr (Eds.), *Handbook of reading research, Vol. III* (pp. 503–523).

Black, P., & Wiliam, D. (1998). Inside the black box: Raising standards through classroom assessment. *Phi Delta Kappan, 80* (2), 139–142.

Blake, B. E. (2001). Fruit of the devil: Writing and English language learners. *Language Arts, 78* (5), 435–441.

Block, C. C., Oakar, M., & Hurt, N. (2002). The expertise of literacy teachers: A continuum from preschool to grade 5. *Reading Research Quarterly, 37* (2), 178–206.

Bloom, B. (1956). *Taxonomy of educational objectives.* New York: David McKay.

Board of Directors: IRA. (2000). Excellent reading teachers: A position statement of the International Reading Association. *The Reading Teacher, 42* (1), 91.

Bohler, S. K., Eichenlaub, K. L., Litteken, S. D., & Wallis, D. A. (1996). Identifying and supporting low-literature parents. *The Reading Teacher, 50* (1), 77–79.

Bond, G., & Dykstra, R. (1967). The cooperative research program in first-grade reading instruction. *Reading Research Quarterly,* 2, 5–141.

Bond, T. F. (2001). Giving them free rein: Connections in student-led book groups. *The Reading Teacher, 54* (6), 574–584.

Boston Public Schools. (1998, March 9). High school restructuring. Boston: Author.

Brabham, E. G., & Villaume, S. K. (2001). Building walls of words. *The Reading Teacher, 54* (7), 700–702.

Brassell, D. (1999). Creating a culturally sensitive classroom library. *The Reading Teacher, 52* (6), 651.

Breece, K. A. (1988). Write-Out: A way to teach content and writing too. *Middle School Journal, 20* (1), 14–15.

Brent, R., & Anderson, P. (1993). Developing children's classroom listening strategies. *The Reading Teacher, 47* (2), 122–126.

Brogan, P. (2000). A parent's perspective: Educating the digital generation. *Educational Leadership, 58* (2), 57–59.

Brown, J., Goodman, K., & Marek, A. M. (Eds.). (1996). *Studies in miscue analysis.* Newark, DE: International Reading Association.

Brown, R., El-Dinary, P. B., Pressley, M. (1996). Balanced comprehension instruction: Transactional strategies instruction (pp. 177–192). In E. McIntyre and M. Pressley (Eds.), *Balanced instruction: Strategies and skills in whole language.* Norwood, MA: Christopher-Gordon.

Brown, R., & Fraser, C. (1963). The acquisition of syntax. In C. N. Cofer & B. Musgrave (Eds.), *Verbal behavior and learning: Problems and processes.* New York: McGraw-Hill.

Brozo, W. G. (2002). *To be a boy, to be a reader: Engaging teen and preteen boys in active literacy.* Newark, DE: International Reading Association.

Brozo, W. G., & Simpson, M. L. (1995). *Readers, teachers, learners: Expanding literacy in secondary schools.* Upper Saddle River, NJ: Merrill/Prentice Hall.

Bruner, J. S. (1977). *The progress of education.* Cambridge, MA: Harvard University Press.

———. (1986). *Actual minds, possible worlds.* Cambridge, MA: Harvard University Press.

———. (1991). Introduction. In S. R. Graubard (Ed.), *Literacy: An overview by fourteen experts* (pp. vii–xi). New York: The Noonday Press.

Burden, R., & Williams, M. (1998). Language learners' perceptions of supportive classroom environments. *Language Learning Journal, 17,* 29–32.

Burger, C., Chapman, K., & Christiansen, C. (1998). A balanced writing workshop. *Illinois Reading Council Journal, 26* (2), 8–15.

Burke, E. M. (1999). Literature in a balanced reading program. In S. M. Blair-Larsen and K. A. Williams (Eds.), *The balanced reading program* (pp. 53–71). Newark, DE: International Reading Association.

Burns, D. (2002). Standards and curriculum differentiation. *Education Update, 44* (1), 3.

Burns, M. S., Griffin, P., & Snow, C. E. (Eds.) (1999). *Starting out right: A guide to promoting children's reading success.* Washington, DC: National Academy Press.

Burns, P. C., Roe, B. D., & Smith, S. H. (2002). *Teaching reading in today's elementary schools* (8th ed.). Boston: Houghton Mifflin.

Butler, A., & Turbill, J. (1984). *Towards a reading-writing classroom.* Portsmouth, NH: Heinemann.

Button, K., Johnson, M. J., & Furgerson, P. (1996). Interactive writing in the primary classroom. *The Reading Teacher, 49* (6), 446–454.

Butts, R. F., & Cremin, L. A. (1953). *A history of education in American culture.* New York: Holt, Rinehart, and Winston.

Calkins, L. M. (1994). *The art of teaching writing* (rev. ed.). Portsmouth, NH: Heinemann.

———. (2001). *The art of teaching reading.* New York: Addison Wesley Longman.

Calkins, L. M., Montgomery, K., Santman, D., & Falk, B. (1998). *A teacher's guide to standardized reading tests: Knowledge is power.* Portsmouth, NH: Heinemann.

Cambone, E. (2001). Arranging the classroom with an eye (and ear) to students with ADHD. *Teaching Exceptional Children, 34* (2), 72–81.

Cambourne, B., & Turbill, J. (1990). Assessment in whole-language classrooms: Theory into practice. *Elementary School Journal, 90,* 337–349.

Campbell, J. R., Kapinus, B., & Beatty, A. S. (1995). *Interviewing children about their literacy experiences. Data from NAEP's integrated reading performance record at grade 4.* (223-FR-05). Washington, DC: U.S. Department of Education.

Carey, S. (1978). The child as word learner. In M. Halle, J. Bresman, & G. Miller (Eds.), *Linguistic theory and psychological reality* (pp. 265–293). Cambridge, MA: MIT Press.

Carnine, D., Silbert, J., & Kameenui, E. J. (1990). *Directed instruction in reading.* Columbus, OH: Merrill.

Carr, E., & Ogle, D. M. (1987). K-W-L Plus: A strategy for comprehension and summarization. *Journal of Reading, 30* (7), 626–631.

Carrier, K. (2001, June 23). "Transitioning from Spanish to English: Reading Connections and Disconnections." Northern Illinois Reading Conference, DeKalb, IL.

Cassidy, J., & Cassidy, D. (2001/2002). What's hot, what's not for 2001. *Reading Today, 18* (3), 1, 18.

Cassidy, J., & Wenrich, J. K. (1998/1999). Literacy research and practice: What's hot and what's not. *The Reading Teacher, 52* (4), 402–406.

Castellano, J. A., & Diaz, E. (2002). *Reaching new horizons: Gifted and talented education for culturally and linguistically diverse students.* Boston: Allyn & Bacon.

Chall, J. (1967). *Learning to read: The great debate.* New York: McGraw-Hill.

Chall, J. S., & Curtis, M. E. (2003). Children with reading difficulties. In J. Flood, D. Lapp, J. R. Squire, & J. M. Jensen (Eds.),

Handbook of research on teaching the English language arts (pp. 413–420). Mahwah, NJ: Lawrence Erlbaum Associates.

Chaney, J. H. (1993). Alphabet books: Resources for learning. *The Reading Teacher, 47* (2), 96–105.

Clay, M. M. (1966). *Emergent reading behavior.* Doctoral Dissertation, University of Auckland, New Zealand.

———. (1979). *Reading: The patterning of complex behavior,* (2ⁿᵈ ed.). Portsmouth, NH: Heinemann.

———. (1985). *The early detection of reading difficulties: A diagnostic survey with recovery procedures.* Portsmouth, NH: Heinemann.

———. (1991). *Becoming literate: The construction of inner control.* Auckland, New Zealand: Heinemann.

———. (1993). *Reading recovery: A guidebook for teachers in training.* Portsmouth, NH: Heinemann.

———. (1998). *By different paths to common outcomes.* York, ME: Stenhouse.

———. (2000). *Concepts about print.* Portsmouth, NH: Heinemann.

———. (2000). *Running records for classroom teachers.* Portsmouth, NH: Heinemann.

Clymer, T. (1963/1996). The utility of phonics generalizations in the primary grades. *The Reading Teacher, 50* (3), 182–186.

Combs, M. (2003). *Developing competent readers and writers in the middle grades,* (2ⁿᵈ ed.). Upper Saddle River, NJ: Merrill/Prentice Hall.

Cook, E. (Ed.) (1986). *A guide for curriculum planning reading.* Madison, WI: Wisconsin Department of Public Instruction.

Cooper, J. D. (1997). *Literacy: Helping children construct meaning.* Boston: Houghton Mifflin.

Cooter, R. B., & Flynt, E. S. (1996). *Teaching reading in the content areas: Developing content literacy for all students.* Columbus, OH: Merrill.

Cotterell, A. (1994). *Ancient China.* New York: Alfred Knopf.

Cox, P. R. & Dykes, M. K. (2001). Effective classroom adaptations for students with visual impairments. *Teaching Exceptional Children, 33* (6), 68–74.

Crawford, J. (1997). *Best evidence: Research foundations of the Bilingual Education Act.* Washington, DC: National Clearinghouse for Bilingual Education.

Cuban, L. (1993). Computers meet the classroom: Classroom wins. *Teachers College Record, 95* (2), 185–210.

Cullinan, B. E. (1987). *Children's literature in the reading program.* Newark: DE: International Reading Association.

———. (1992). *Read to me: Raising kids who love to read.* New York: Scholastic.

Cullinan, B. E., & Galda, L. (1998). *Literature and the child,* 4ᵗʰ ed. San Diego: Harcourt Brace.

Cunningham, A. (1990). Explicit versus implicit instruction in phonemic awareness. *Journal of Experimental Child Psychology, 50,* 429–444.

Cunningham, A. E., & Stanovich, K. E. (1998). What reading does for the mind. *American Educator, 22* (1&2), 8–15.

Cunningham, P. M. (2000). *Phonics they use: Words for reading and writing* (3ʳᵈ ed.). Boston: Addison Wesley.

Cunningham, P. M., & Allington, R. L. (2003). *Classrooms that work: They can all read and write* (3ʳᵈ ed.). Boston: Allyn and Bacon.

Cunningham, P. M., & Hall, D. P. (1994). *Making words.* Parsippany, NJ: Good Apple.

Cunningham, P. M., Hall, D. P., & Sigmon, C. M. (1999). *The teacher's guide to the Four-Blocks.* Greensboro, NC: Carson-Dellosa.

Cunningham, P. M., Hall, D. P., & Cunningham, J. W. (2000). *Guided reading the Four-Blocks way.* Greensboro, NC: Carson-Dellosa.

Curtis, M. E., & Longo, A. M. (1998). *When adolescents can't read: Methods and materials that work.* Cambridge, MA: Brookline Books.

Dahl, K. L., & Scharer, P. L. (2000). Phonics teaching and learning in whole language classrooms: New evidence from research. *The Reading Teacher, 53* (7), 584–594.

Dale, E. (1965). Vocabulary measurement: Techniques and major findings. *Elementary English, 42* (9), 895–901, 948.

Daniels, H. (1994). *Literature circles: Voice and choice in the student centered classroom.* York, ME: Stenhouse.

Davis, A. P., & McDaniel, T. R. (1998). An essential vocabulary: An update. *The Reading Teacher, 52* (4), 308–309.

Davis, Z. T., & McPherson, M. D. (1989). Story map instruction: A road map for reading comprehension. *The Reading Teacher, 42* (3), 232–239.

DeFord, D. E. (1985). Validating the construct of theoretical orientation in reading instruction. *Reading Research Quarterly, 20* (3), 351–367.

DeSotell, K. (1998). Strategies for using the new literature anthology basal. *Illinois Reading Council Journal, 26* (4), 8–12.

Dewey, J. (1938). *Experience and education.* New York: Macmillan.

Dole, J. S., Duffy, G. G., Roehler, L. R., & Pearson. P. D. (1991). Moving from the old to the new: Research on reading comprehension. *Review of Educational Research, 61* (2), 239–264.

Dreher, M. J. (1998–1999). Motivating children to read more nonfiction. *The Reading Teacher, 52* (5), 414–416.

Duffelmeyer, F. A., & Duffelmeyer, B. B. (1979). Developing vocabulary through dramatization. *Journal of Reading, 23* (November), 141–143.

Duffy, G. S., & Hoffman, J. V. (1999). In pursuit of an illusion: The flawed search for a perfect method. *The Reading Teacher, 53* (1), 10–16.

Duffy-Hester, A. (1999). Teaching struggling readers in elementary school classrooms: A review of classroom reading programs and principles for instruction. *The Reading Teacher, 52*(5), 480–495.

Durkin, D. (1966). *Children who read early.* New York: Teacher's College Press.

———. (1974–75). A six year study of children who learned to read in school at the age of four. *Reading Research Quarterly, 10,* 9–61.

Eckman, A. (2000a). Among like minds: What's new with networking. *Education Update, 42* (8). Alexandria, VA: Association for Supervision and Curriculum Development.

———. (2000b). Web wonders: Teaching the Internet generation. *Educational Leadership, 58* (2), 96.

Eeds, M., & Wells, D. (1989). Grand conversations: An exploration of meaning construction in literature study groups. *Research in the Teaching of English, 23* (1), 4–29.

Eliot, C. W. (1898). *Education reform.* New York: Century.

Emig, J. (1977). Writing as a mode of learning. *College Composition and Communication, 28,* 122–128.

Farr, R. (1992). Putting it all together: Solving the assessment puzzle. *The Reading Teacher, 45* (1), 9–15.

Farr, R., & Beck, M. D. (2003). Evaluating language development. In J. Flood, D. Lapp, J. R. Squires, & J. M. Jensen (Eds.), *Handbook of research on teaching the English language arts* (pp. 590–599). Mahwah, NJ: Lawrence Erlbaum Associates.

Farris, P. J. (1988). Roulette writing. *The Reading Teacher, 42* (1), 91.

———. (1999). *Teaching bearing the torch* (2nd ed.). Boston: McGraw-Hill.

———. (2001). *Language arts: Process, product, and assessment,* 3rd ed. Boston: McGraw-Hill.

———. (2003). "Concept muraling: A strategy for struggling readers." International Reading Association Conference, Orlando, FL: May 5, 2003.

———. (2004). *Elementary and middle school language arts: An integrated approach,* 4th ed. Boston: McGraw-Hill.

Farris, P. J., & Vespa, P. (2002). "Concept muraling in kindergarten." Unpublished Research Report: DeKalb, IL: Northern Illinois University Honors Research Program.

Feistritzer, E. (1996). *Profile of teachers in the U.S.* Washington, D.C.: Center for Education Information.

Fielding, E. H. (1999). *Learning differences in the classroom.* Newark, DE: International Reading Association.

Filozof, E., Albertin, H., Jones, C., Steme, S., Myers, L., & McDermott, R. (1998). Relationship of adolescent self-esteem to selected academic variables. *Journal of School Health, 68,* 68–77.

Fisher, B., & Fisher Medvic, E. (2000). *Perspectives on shared reading: Planning and practice.* Portsmouth, NH: Heinemann.

Fitzgerald, J. (1999). What is this thing called balance? *The Reading Teacher, 53* (2), 100–107.

Flynt, E. S., & Cooter, R. B. Jr. (1995). *Flynt/Cooter reading inventory for the classroom.* Scottsdale, AZ: Gorsuch Scaribrick Publishers.

Ford, K. L., & Bowman, C. A. (1999). Creating a 'Literacy Fair.' *Indiana Reading Quarterly, 31* (4), 3–12.

Fountas, I. C., & Pinnell, G. S. (1996). *Guided reading: Good first teaching for all children.* Portsmouth, NH: Heinemann.

———. (1999). *Matching books to readers: Using leveled books in guided reading.* Portsmouth, NH: Heinemann.

———. (2001). *Guided readers and writers, grades 3–6: Teaching comprehension, genre and content literacy.* Portsmouth, NH: Heinemann.

Fresch, M. J. (2001). Journal entries as a window on spelling knowledge. *The Reading Teacher, 54* (5), 500–513.

Friend, M., & Bursuck, W. D. (1999). *Including students with special needs: A practical guide for classroom teachers* (2nd ed.). Boston: Allyn and Bacon.

Fry, E. B. (1997). *Elementary reading instruction.* New York: McGraw-Hill.

———. (1998). The most common phonograms. *The Reading Teacher, 51* (7), 620–622.

Fuhler, C. J. (1990). Let's move toward literature-based reading instruction. *The Reading Teacher, 43* (4), 312–315.

———. (1998). *Teaching geography of North America with books kids love.* (A. Loyal, Illus.). Golden, CO: Fulcrum.

———. (2000). *Teaching reading with multicultural books kids love.* Golden, CO: Fulcrum.

Fulwiler, T. (1985). Writing and learning, grade 3. *Language Arts, 62* (1), 55–59.

———. (1987). *The journal book.* Portsmouth, NH: Heinemann.

Galda, L., Cullinan, B. E., & Strickland, D. S. (1993). *Literature, literacy, and the child.* San Diego: Harcourt Brace.

Gallagher, C. (2000). A seat at the table: Teachers reclaiming assessment through rethinking accountability. *Phi Delta Kappan, 81* (7), 502–507.

Gambrell, L. B. (1996a). What research reveals about discussion. In L. B. Gambrell & J. F. Almasi (Eds.), *Lively discussion! Fostering engaged reading* (pp. 8–15). Newark, DE: International Reading Association.

Gambrell, L. B. (1996b). Creating classroom cultures that foster reading motivation. *The Reading Teacher, 50* (1), pp. 14–25.

Gambrell, L. B., & Almasi, J. F. (1996). *Lively discussion! Fostering engaged reading.* Newark, DE: International Reading Association.

Gambrell, L. B., & Mazzoni, S. A. (1999). Principles of best practice: Finding the common ground. In Gambrell, L. B., Morrow, L. M., Neuman, S. B., & Pressley, M. (Eds.), *Best practices in literacy instruction* (pp. 5–14). New York: Guilford.

Garcia, G. E. (2000). Bilingual children's reading. In M. L. Kamil, P. B. Mosenthal, P. D. Pearson, & R. Barr (Eds.). *Handbook of reading research, Vol. III.* (pp. 813–834). Mahwah, NJ: Erlbaum.

Gardner, H. (1993). *Multiple intelligences: The theory into practice.* New York: Basic Books.

Gardner, J. (1983). *The art of fiction.* New York: Random House.

Gasparro, M., & Falletta, B. (1994). *Creating drama with poetry: Teaching English as a second language through dramatization and improvisation.* Washington, DC: ERIC Clearinghouse on Languages and Linguistics. (ERIC Document Reproduction Service No. ED 368 214).

Gentry, J. R. (1981). Learning to spell developmentally. *The Reading Teacher, 34* (4), 378–381.

Giles, C. (1990). Collaborative literacy strategies: "We don't need a circle to have a group." In K. G. Short & K. M. Pierce (Eds.), *Talking about books: Creating literate communities* (pp. 55–68). Portsmouth, NH: Heinemann.

Gilles, C., Dickinson, J., McBride, C., & Vandover, M. (1994). Discussing our questions and questioning our discussions: Growing into literature study. *Literature Arts, 71* (7), 499–508.

Gish, K. W. (2000). Hunting down Harry Potter: An exploration of religious concerns about children's literature. *Horn Book Magazine,* May/June.

Goatley, V., Brock, C., & Raphael, T. (1995). Diverse learners participating in regular education "book clubs." *Reading Research Quarterly, 30* (4), 352–381.

Goldhaber, J., Lipson, M., Sortino, & Daniels, P. (1996). Books in the sand box? Markers in the blocks? Expanding the child's world of literacy. *Childhood Literacy, 73* (2), 88–91.

Good, T. L., & Brophy, J. E. (2000). *Looking in classrooms* (8th ed.). New York: Longman.

Goodman, K. S. (1965). A linguistic study of cues and miscues in reading. *Elementary English, 42* (6), 639–643.

———. (1986). *What's whole in whole language?* Portsmouth, NH: Heinemann.

Goodman, Y. M. (1989). The roots of whole language. *Elementary School Journal, 90* (2), 113–127.

———. (1991). Evaluating language growth: Informal methods of evaluation. In J. Flood, J. Jensen, D. Lapp, and J. Squire (Eds.), *Handbook of research on teaching the English language arts* (pp. 502–509). New York: Macmillan.

Gordon, C. J. (1989). Modeling inference awareness across the curriculum. *Journal of Reading, 28* (5), 444–447.

Graves, D. H. (1981). A new look at research on writing. In S. Haley-James (Ed.). *Perspectives on writing in grades 1–8.* Urbana, IL: National Council of Teachers of English, 93–116.

———. (1983). *Writing: Teachers and children at work.* Portsmouth, NH: Heinemann.

———. (1989). *Investigate nonfiction.* Portsmouth, NH: Heinemann.

———. (1989). *The reading/writing teacher's companion: Investigating nonfiction.* Portsmouth, NH: Heinemann.

———. (1990). *Discover your own literacy.* Portsmouth, NH: Heinemann.

———. (1994). *A fresh look at writing.* Portsmouth, NH: Heinemann.

———. (1999). *Bring life into learning: Create a lasting literacy.* Portsmouth, NH: Heinemann.

Graves, M. F. (1986). *Vocabulary learning and instruction.* In. E. Z. Rothkopf (Ed.), *Review of research in education, Vol. 19* (pp. 91–128). Reston, VA: American Educational Research Association.

———. (1987). Roles of instruction in fostering vocabulary development. In J. G. McKeown

& M. E. Curtis (Eds.), *The nature of vocabulary acquisition* (pp. 165–184). Hillsdale, NJ: Lawrence Erlbaum.

———. (2000). A vocabulary program to complement and bolster a middle-grade comprehension program. In Taylor, B. M., Graves, M. F., and Van Den Broek, P. (Eds.). *Reading for meaning: Fostering comprehension in the middle grades.* Newark, DE: International Reading Association.

Graves, M. F., Juel, C., & Graves, B. B. (2001). *Teaching reading in the 21st century* (2nd ed.). Boston: Allyn and Bacon.

Gray, W. S. (1937). A decade of progress. In G. M. Whipple (Ed.), *The teaching of reading: A second report* (37th Yearbook of the National Society for the Study of Education). Bloomington, IL: Public School Publishing Co.

Griffin, C. C., & Tulbert, B. L. (1995). The effect of graphic organizers on students' comprehension and recall of expository text: A review of the research and implications for practice. *Reading and Writing Quarterly, 11,* 73–89.

Griffith, P. L., & Olson, M. W. (1992). Phonemic awareness helps beginning readers break the code. *The Reading Teacher, 45* (7), 516–523.

Gunning, T. G. (2001). *Building words: A resource manual for teaching word analysis and spelling strategies.* Boston: Allyn & Bacon.

———. (1995). Word building: A strategic approach to the teaching of phonics. *The Reading Teacher, 48* (6), 484–489.

Guthrie, J., Alao, S., & Rinehart, J. (1997). Engagement in reading for young adolescents. *Journal of Adolescent & Adult Literacy, 40* (9), 438–446.

Hadaway, N. L., Vardell, S. M., & Young, T. A. (2001). Scaffolding oral language development through poetry for students learning English. *The Reading Teacher, 48* (6), 796–806.

Hall, C., & Coles, M. (1997). Gendered readings: Helping boys develop as critical readers. *Gender and Education, 9,* 61–68.

Hall, M. (1985). Focus on language experience learning and teaching. *Reading, 19,* 5–12.

Halliday, M. A. K. (1975). *Learning how to mean: Exploration in the development of language.* London: Arnold.

———. (1994). The place of dialogue in children's construction of meaning. In Ruddell, R. B., Ruddell, M. R., & Singer, H. (Eds.). *Theoretical models and processes of reading* (4th ed.), (pp. 70–82). Newark, DE: International Reading Association.

Hancock, M. R. (2000). *A celebration of literature and response.* Upper Saddle River, NJ: Merrill.

Harris, A. J., & Sipay, E. R. (1985). *How to increase reading ability* (8th ed.). New York: Longman.

Harris, V. J. (1997). Children's literature depicting blacks. In V. J. Harris (Ed.), *Using multiethnic literature in the K–8 classroom.* (pp. 21–58). Norwood, MA: Christopher-Gordon.

Harvey, S., & Goudvis, A. (2000). *Strategies that work: Teaching comprehension to enhance understanding.* York, ME: Stenhouse.

Hatch, E., & Brown, C. (1995). *Vocabulary, semantics, and language education.* Cambridge, Great Britain: Cambridge University Press.

Haycock, K. (1985). *Teaching spelling.* Boston: Houghton Mifflin.

———. (2001). Closing the achievement gap. *Educational Leadership, 58* (6), 6–11.

Hefflin, B. R., & Barksdale-Ladd, M. A. (2001). African American children's literature that helps children find themselves: Selection guidelines for grades K–3. *The Reading Teacher, 54* (8), 810–819.

Heilman, A. W., Blair, T. R., & Rupley, W. H. (2002). *Principles and practices of teaching reading* (10th ed.). Upper Saddle River, NJ: Merrill/Prentice Hall.

Henderson, E. (1985). *Teaching spelling.* Boston: Houghton Mifflin.

Henley, M., Ramsey, R. S., & Algozzine, R. F. (2002). *Characteristics of and strategies for teaching students with mild disabilities* (4th ed.). Boston: Allyn and Bacon.

Hicks, K. F., & Simpson, P. L. (1998). *Breaking reading barriers in grades 4–12.* Minneapolis, MN: Jostin Press.

Hiebert, E. H., & Raphael, T. E. (1998). *Early literacy instruction.* Ft. Worth, TX: Harcourt Brace.

Hillman, J. (1995). *Discovering children's literature.* Englewood Cliffs, NJ: Merrill.

Hinchey, P. H. (2001). Learning to read the world: Who and what is missing? *Reading Online, 4* (10).

Hodgkinson, H. (2001). Educational demographics: What teachers should know. *Educational Leadership, 58* (4), 6–11.

Hoffman, J. V., Au, K. H., Harrison, C., Paris, S. G., Pearson, P. D., Santa, C. M., Silver, S. H., & Valencia, S. (1999). High-stakes assessments in reading: Consequences, concerns, and common sense. In S. J. Barrentine (Ed.), *Reading assessment: Principles and practices for elementary teachers* (pp. 247–260). Newark, DE: International Reading Association.

Hohmann, C. B., Carmody, B., McCabe-Branz, C. (1995). *High/scope buyer's guide to children's software.* Ypsilanti, MI: High/Scope Press.

Holdaway, D. (1980). *The foundations of literacy.* Portsmouth, NH: Heinemann.

Hoyt, L. (1992). Many ways of knowing: Using drama, oral interactions, and the visual arts to enhance reading comprehension. *The Reading Teacher, 45* (8), 580–584.

Huck, C. S. (1996). Literature-based reading programs: A retrospective. *The New Advocate, 9* (1), 23–33.

Huck, C. S., Hepler, S., Hickman, J., & Kiefer, B. Z. (2004). *Children's literature in the elementary school* (8th ed.). Boston: McGraw-Hill.

Hudelson, S., Poynor, L., & Wolfe, P. (2003). Teaching bilingual and ESL children and adolescents. In J. Flood, D. Lapp, J. R. Squire, & J. M. Jensen (Eds.), *Handbook of research on teaching the English language arts* (pp. 421–434). Mahwah, NJ: Lawrence Erlbaum Associates.

Huey, E. B. (1908). *The psychology and pedagogy of reading.* New York: Macmillan.

Idol, L. (1987). Group story mapping: A comprehension for both skilled and unskilled readers. *Journal of Learning Disabilities, 20,* 196–205.

International Reading Association. (1998). *Standards for reading professionals* (revised). Newark, DE: Author.

———. (2000). Excellent reading teachers: A position statement of the International Reading Association. *The Reading Teacher, 54* (2), 235–240.

———. (2002). *Integrating literacy and technology in the curriculum.* Newark, DE: International Reading Association.

International Reading Association & National Association for the Education of Young Children. (1998). Learning to reading and write: Developmentally appropriate practices for young children. *The Reading Teacher, 52* (2), 193–215.

International Reading Association/National Council of Teachers of English. (1996). *Standards for the English Language Arts.* Newark, DE & Urbana, IL: International Reading Association/National Council of Teachers of English.

Ivey, G., & Broaddus, K. (2000). Tailoring the fit: Reading instruction and middle school readers. *The Reading Teacher, 54* (1), 68–78.

Jacques, B. (2000, October 8). *CBS Sunday Morning with Charles Osgood.* New York: CBS News.

Jensen, E. (1998). *Teaching with the brain in mind.* Alexandria, VA: Association for Curriculum and Supervision Development.

Johns, J. (2000). *Basic reading inventory.* Dubuque, IA: Kendall-Hunt. (2000). *Basic reading inventory: Spanish version.* Dubuque, IA: Kendall-Hunt.

Johns, J., & Elish-Piper, L. (1997). *Balanced reading instruction: Teachers' vision and voices.* Dubuque, IA: Kendall-Hunt.

Johns, J., Lenski, S. D., & Elish-Piper, L. (1999). *Early literacy assessments and teaching strategies.* Dubuque, IA: Kendall-Hunt.

Johnson, D. (1999). Electronic collaboration: Children's literature in the classroom. *The Reading Teacher, 53* (1), 54–60.

Johnson, D. D. (2001). *Vocabulary in the elementary and middle school.* Boston: Allyn & Bacon.

Johnson, D. D., & Pearson, P. D. (1984). *Teaching reading vocabulary.* New York; Holt, Rinehart, & Winston.

Johnson, N. J., & Giorgis, C. (2000). Promoting discussion. *The Reading Teacher, 54* (1), 106–113.

Johnston, F. R. (1999). The timing and teaching of word families. *The Reading Teacher, 53* (1), 64–75.

Jongsma, K. (2002). Instructional materials: Good beginnings! *The Reading Teacher, 56* (1), 62–65.

Jonson, Kathleen. (1998). The role of independent reading in a "balanced" reading program: Re-thinking California's reading initiative. *Reading Improvement, 35* (2), 90–96.

Juel, C., & Minden-Cupp, C. (1999/2000). One down and 80,000 to go: Word recognition in the primary grades. *The Reading Teacher, 53* (4), 332–335.

Katz, C. A., & Kuby, S. A. (2001). The Fish Bowl: A strategy for assessing independent reading. *Book Links, 10* (6), 28–29.

Keene, E. O., & Zimmerman, S. (1997). *Mosaic of thought: Teaching comprehension in a reader's workshop.* Portsmouth, NH: Heinemann.

Kilpatrick, J. J. (2000, March 19). James J. Kilpatrick Column. *San Antonio Express News,* 5A.

Kleinfeld, J. (1999, Winter). Student performance: Males versus females. *The Public Interest, 134,* 3–20.

Korbin, B. (1995). *Eyeopeners II: Children's books to answer children's questions about the world around them.* New York: Scholastic.

Koskinen, P. S., Blum, I. H., Bisson, S. A., Phillips, S. M., Creamer, T. S., & Baker, T. K. (1999). Shared reading, books, and audiotapes: Supporting diverse students in school and home. *The Reading Teacher, 52* (5), 430–443.

Kozil, S. M., Minnick, J. B., & Riddell, K. (1996). *Journals for active learning: A two-day workshop module for primary teachers in Bosnia.* Pittsburg, PA: University of Pittsburg International Institute for Studies in Education.

Kruse, G. M., Horning, K. T., & Schileman, M. (1997). *Multicultural literature for children and young adults: A selected listing of books by and about people of color, Volume Two, 1991–1996.* Madison, WI: The Cooperative Children's Book Center.

Labbo, L. D. (2000). 12 things young children can do with a talking book in a classroom computer center. *The Reading Teacher, 53* (7), 542–546.

Langer, J. A. (1995). *Envisioning literature: Literary understanding and literature instruction.* New York: Teachers College Press.

Larkin, B. R. (2001). "Can we act it out?" *The Reading Teacher, 54* (5), 478–481.

Latham, A. S. (1999). Computers and achievement. *Educational Leadership, 56* (5), 87–88.

Lemann, N. (1997, November). The reading wars. *The Atlantic Monthly.* pp. 128–134.

Lempke, S. D. (2001). Getting serious about series geography. *Book Links,* 10 (6), 22–25

Leslie, L., & Jett-Simpson, M. (1997). *Authentic literacy assessment: An ecological approach.* New York: Longman.

Leu, D. J. (2000). Our children's future: Changing the focus of literacy and literacy instruction. *The Reading Teacher, 53* (5) 424–429.

Leu, D. J., Karchmer, R. A., & Leu, D. D. (1999). The Miss Rumphius effect: Envisionments for literacy and learning that transform the Internet. *The Reading Teacher, 52* (6), 636–642.

Levine, D. S. (1985). The biggest thing I learned but it really doesn't have to do with science. . . *Language Arts, 62* (1), 43–47.

Lindquist, T. (1995). *Seeing the whole through social studies.* Portsmouth, NH: Heinemann.

Luke, A. (1994). On reading and the sexual division of literacy. *Journal of Curriculum Studies, 26,* 361–381.

Lukens, R. (1999). *A critical handbook of children's literature.* New York: Longman.

Marcus, L. S. (1998). *Dear genius: The letters of Ursula Nordstrom.* New York: HarperCollins.

Martens, P., Goodman, Y., & Flurkey, A. D. (Eds.). (1995). Miscue analysis for classroom teachers. *Primary Voices K–6, 3* (4): pp. 1–3.

Martinez, M., Roser, N., & Strecker, S. (1998–1999). "I never thought I could be a star." A Readers Theatre ticket to fluency. *The Reading Teacher, 52* (4), 326–334.

Mathews, M. M. (1966). *Teaching to read: Historically considered.* Chicago: University of Chicago Press.

Mayer, F. (1960). *A history of educational thought.* Columbus, OH: Merrill.

McCarrier, A., Pinnell, G. S., & Fountas, I. C. (2000). *Interactive writing: How language and literacy come together, K–2.* Portsmouth, NH: Heinemann.

McCracken, R. A., & McCracken, M. J. (1978). Modeling is the key to sustained reading. *The Reading Teacher, 31* (5), 406–408.

———. (1986). *Stories, songs and poetry to teach reading and writing.* Winnipeg, Manitoba, Canada: Portage and Main.

———. (1995). *Reading, writing, and language: A practical guide for primary teachers.* Winnipeg, Manitoba, Canada: Portage and Main.

McCutchen, D. (2000). Knowledge, processing, and working memory: Implications for a theory of writing. *Educational Psychologist, 35* (1), 13–23.

McElveen, S. A., & Dierking, C. C. (2000/2001). Children's books as models to teach writing skills. *The Reading Teacher, 54* (4), 362–364.

McGee, L. A., & Richgels, D. J. (1985). Teaching expository text structure to elementary students. *The Reading Teacher, 39* (8), 739–748.

McGinley, W., Kamberelism G., Mahoney, T., Madigan, D., Rybicki, V., & Oliver, J. (1997). Visioning reading and teaching literature through the lens of narrative theory. In T. Rogers & A. Soter (Eds.), *Reading across cultures* (pp. 42–68). New York: Teachers College Press.

McKee, L. M. (1992). Exploring the literature-based reading revolution: Focus on research. *Language Arts, 69* (7), 529–537.

McKenzie, M. G. (1985). Shared writing: Apprenticeship in writing. *Language Matters, 1* (2), 1–5.

McKeown, M. G., Beck, I. L., & North, M. J. (1993). Grappling with text ideas: Questioning the author. *The Reading Teacher, 46* (6), 560–566.

Means, B. (2000/2001). Technology use in tomorrow's schools. *Educational Leadership, 58* (4), 57–64.

Meinbach, A. M., Rothlein, L., & Fredericks, A. D. (2000). *The complete guide to thematic units: Creating the integrated curriculum.* (2nd ed.). Norwood, MA: Christopher-Gordon.

Merkley, D., & Jefferies, D. (2000/2001). Guidelines for implementing a graphic organizer. *The Reading Teacher, 54* (4), 350–357.

Mikkelsen, N. (2000). *Words & pictures: Lessons in children's literature and literacies.* Boston, MA: McGraw Hill.

Miller, H. M. (2001). Teaching and learning about cultural diversity: Including the "included." *The Reading Teacher, 54* (88), 820–821.

Miller, W. (2000). *Strategies for developing emergent literacy.* Dubuque, IA: Kendall Hunt.

Moats, L. C. (2001). When older students can't read. *Educational Leadership,* 58(6), 36–40.

Moffit, M. A., & Wartella, E. (1992). Youth and reading: A survey of leisure reading pursuits of female and male adolescents. *Reading Research and Instruction, 31,* 1–7.

Moore, D. W., Monaghan, E. J., & Hartman, D. J. (1997). Values of literacy history. *Reading Research Quarterly, 32* (1), 90–101.

Moore, D. W., Moore, S. A., Cunningham, P., & Cunningham, J. W. (2003). *Developing readers and writers in the content areas K–12* (4th ed.). Boston, MA: Allyn & Bacon.

Morrow, L. M. (1984). Reading stories to young children: Effects of story structure and traditional questioning strategies on comprehension. *Journal of Reading Behavior, 16* (3), 273–288.

Morrow, L. M., & Gambrell, L. B. (2000). Literature-based reading instruction. In Kamill, M. L., Mosenthal, P. B., Pearson, P. D., & Barr, R. (Eds.), *Handbook of reading research, Vol. III.* (pp. 563–586). Mahwah, NJ: Lawrence Erlbaum.

Morrow, L. M., & Tracey, D. H. (1997). Strategies used for phonics instruction in early childhood classrooms. *The Reading Teacher, 50* (8), 644–651.

Mosier, R. D. (1947). *Making the American mind: Social and moral ideas in the McGuffey Readers.* New York: King's Crown Press.

Moss, B., Leone, S., & Dipillo, M. L. (1997). Exploring the literature of fact: Linking reading and writing through information trade books. *Language Arts, 74* (6), 418–428.

Moustafa, M., & Maldonado-Colon, E. (1999). Whole parts to instruction: Building on what children know to help them know more. *The Reading Teacher, 52* (5), 448–458.

Murphy, S. (1991). The code, connectionism, and basals. *Language Arts, 68* (3), 199–205.

Murphy, S., & Dudley-Marling, C. (1999). Editors' pages. *Language Arts, 77* (1), 8–9.

Murray, D. (1968). *A writer teaches writing: A practical method of teaching.* Boston: Houghton Mifflin.

Nagy, W. E., Anderson, R. C., & Herman, P. A. (1987). Learning word meanings from context during normal reading. *American Educational Research Journal, 24* (3), 237–270.

Nastase, N. K., & Corbett, F. (1998). Literature-based reading in a basal world: The dilemma of double vision. *Reading Improvement, 35* (2), 50–72.

National Board for Professional Standards. (2001). *What teachers should know and be able to do.* Washington, DC: Author.

National Center for Education Statistics. (1998). *The condition of education, 1998.* Washington, DC: U.S. Department of Education.

———. (2000). *Trends in educational equity of girls and women.* Washington, DC: U.S. Department of Education.

National Center on Education and the Economy and the University of Pittsburgh. (1999). *Reading and writing grade by grade: Primary literacy standards for kindergarten through third grade.* Author.

National Reading Panel. (2000). *Report of the National Reading Panel: Teaching children to read: An evidence-based assessment of the scientific research literature on reading and its implications for reading instruction.* Retrieved from http://www.nichd.nih.gov/publications/nrppubskey.cfm

National Telecommunications and Information Association. (1999). *Falling through the Net: Defining the digital divide.* Retrieved from http://www.ntia.doc.gov/ntiahome/fttn99/contents.html.

Neuman, S. B., & Celano, D. (2001). Books aloud: A campaign to "put books in children's hands." *The Reading Teacher, 54* (6), 550–557.

Newkirk, T. (2000). Misreading masculinity: Speculations on the great gender gap in writing. *Language Arts, 77* (4), 294–300.

Nieto, S. (2000). *Affirming diversity: The sociopolitical context of multicultural education.* New York: Longman.

Norton, D. (1999). *Through the eyes of a child.* (3rd ed.). Upper Saddle River, NJ: Merrill.

Olson, L. (2000). Children of change. *Education Week, 29* (4), 30–41.

Opitz, M. F. (1999). Empowering the reader in every child. *Instructor, 108* (5), 35–38.

———. (2000). *Rhymes and reasons: Literature and language play for phonological awareness.* Portsmouth, NH: Heinemann.

Oyler, C., & Barry, A. (1996). Intertextual connections in read-alouds of information books. *Language Arts, 73* (5), 324–329.

Palinscar, A. M., & Brown, A. L. (1984). Reciprocal teaching of comprehension and monitoring activities. *Cognition and Instruction, 1* (2), 117–175.

Paris, S. G., Lipson, M. Y., & Wixson, K. K. (1983). Becoming a strategic reader. *Contemporary Educational Psychology, 8* (3), 292–316.

Park, B. (1982). The big book trend: A discussion with Don Holdaway. *Language Arts, 59* (8), 815–821.

Paterson, K. (1989). *The spying heart: More thoughts on reading and writing books for children.* New York: Lodestar.

Pearson, P. D., & Fielding, L. (1996). Comprehension instruction. In Barr, R., Kamill, M. L., Mosenthal, P. B., & Pearson, P. D., (Eds.). *Handbook of reading research, Vol. 11.* (pp. 437–479). Mahwah, NJ: Lawrence Erlbaum.

Pearson, P. D., & Gallager, M. C. (1983). The instruction of reading comprehension. *Contemporary Educational Psychology, 8,* 317–344.

Pearson, P. D., & Tierney, R. J. (1984). On becoming a thoughtful reader: Learning to read like a writer. In A. C. Purves and O. Niles (Eds.), *Becoming readers in a complex society. Eighty-third yearbook of the National Society of the Study of Education.* (pp. 144–173). Chicago: University of Chicago Press.

Perkins, D., & Blythe, T. (1993). Putting understanding up front. *Educational Leadership, 51* (5), 4–7.

Piaget, J. (1973). *The language and thought of the child.* New York: World.

Piazza, C. L. (2003). *Journeys: The teaching of writing in elementary classrooms.* Upper Saddle River, NJ: Merrill.

Piccolo, J. A. (1987). Expository structure: Teaching and learning strategies. *The Reading Teacher, 40* (9), 838–847.

Pinnell, G. S., & Fountas, I. C. (1998). *Word matters: Teaching phonics and spelling in the reading/writing classroom.* Portsmouth, NH: Heinemann.

Popham, W. J. (1999). Why standardized tests don't measure educational quality. *Educational Leadership, 56* (6), 8–15.

Pottorff, D. D., Phelps-Zientarsky, D., & Skovera, M. (1996). Gender perceptions of elementary and middle school students about literacy at school and home. *Journal of Research and Development in Education, 29,* 203–211.

Pressley, M. (2000). What should comprehension instruction be the instruction of? In Kamill, M. L., Mosenthal, P. B., Pearson, P. D., &

Barr, R. (Eds.), *Handbook of reading research, Vol. 111.* (pp. 545–562). Mahwah, NJ: Lawrence Erlbaum.

Pressley, M., & Afflerbach, P. (1995). *Verbal protocols of reading: The nature of constructively responsive reading.* Hillsdale, NJ: Lawrence Erlbaum.

Putnam, L. R. (1994–1995). An interview with Noam Chomsky. *The Reading Teacher, 48* (4), 328–333.

Putney, L. G., Wu, Y., & Wink, J. (1999). What can English-dominant teachers do in a multilingual context? Stop, think, and proceed with care. *The California Reader, 32* (2), 10–15.

Raphael, T., & Brock, C. (1993). Mei: Learning the literacy culture in an urban elementary school. In D. Leu & C. J. Kinzer (Eds.), *Examining central issues in literacy research, theory, and practice* (pp. 179–188). Chicago: National Reading Conference.

Raphael, T. E. (1986). Teaching question-answer relationship, revisited. *The Reading Teacher, 39* (6), 516–523.

Raphael, T. E., & Hiebert, E. H. (1996). *Creating an integrated approach to literacy instruction.* Fort Worth, TX: Harcourt Brace.

Raphael, T. E., and Members of the Book Club Plus Group. (1999). What counts as teacher research: An essay. *Language Arts, 77* (1), 48–53.

Rasinski, T. V., & Padak, N. D. (2001). *From phonics to fluency: Effective teaching of decoding and reading fluency in the elementary school.* New York: Longman.

Read, C. (1971). Preschool children's knowledge of English phonology. *Harvard Educational Review, 41* (1), 1–34.

Read, S. (2001). "Kid mice hunt for their selfs": First and second graders writing research. *Language Arts, 78* (4), 333–342.

Reese, D., & Caldwell-Wood, N. (1997). Native Americans in children's literature. In V. J.

Harris (Ed.), *Using multiethnic literature in the K–8 classroom* (pp. 155–192).

Reutzel, D. R. (1985). Story maps improve comprehension. *The Reading Teacher, 38* (4), 400–405.

Reutzel, D. R., & Cooter, R. B. (2000). *Teaching children to read: Putting the pieces together* (3rd ed.). Upper Saddle River, NJ: Merrill.

Reutzel, D. R., & Galli, K. (1998). The art of children's book selection: A labyrinth unexplored. *Reading Psychology, 19* (3), 3–50.

Rhodes, L. K., & Dudley-Marling, C. (1996). *Readers with a difference: A holistic approach to teaching struggling readers and writers.* Portsmouth, NH: Heinemann.

Rhodes, L. K., & Nathenson-Meija, S. (1999). Anecdotal records: A powerful tool for ongoing literacy assessment. In S. J. Barrentine (Eds.), *Reading assessment: Principles and practices for elementary teachers* (pp. 83–90). Newark, DE: International Reading Association.

Rice, D. C. (2002). Using trade books in teaching elementary science: Facts and fallacies. *The Reading Teacher, 55* (6), 552–565.

Richardson, J. S., & Morgan, R. F. (1997). *Reading to learn in the content areas* (3rd ed.). Belmont, CA: Wadsworth Publishing.

Richgels, D. J., Poremba, K. J., & McGee, L. M. (1996). Kindergartners talk about print: Phonemic awareness in meaningful contexts. *The Reading Teacher, 49* (8), 632–642.

Richgels, D. J., & Wold, L. S. (1998). Literacy on the road: Backpacking partnerships between home and school. *The Reading Teacher, 52* (1), 18–29.

Richey, D. D., & Wheeler, J. (2000). *Inclusive early childhood education: Merging positive behavioral supports, activity-based interventions, and developmentally appropriate practice.* Albany, NY: Delmar Thomson Learning.

Robb, L. (1994). *Whole language, whole learners: Creating a literature-centered classroom.* New York: Morrow.

———. (2000). *Teaching reading in middle school: A strategic approach to teaching reading that improves comprehension and thinking.* New York: Scholastic.

———. (2003). *Teaching reading in social studies, science, and math: Practical ways to weave comprehension strategies into your teaching.* New York: Scholastic.

Robinson, F. (1961). *Effective study, revised edition.* New York: Harper & Row.

Roehler, L. R., & Duffy, G. G. (1984). Direct explanation of comprehension processes. In G. G. Duffy, L. R. Roehler, & J. Mason, (Eds.), *Comprehension instruction: Perspectives and suggestions* (pp. 265–280). New York: Longman.

Roget & HarperCollins. (1994). *Roget's children's thesaurus.* New York: HarperCollins.

———. (1994). *Roget's student's thesaurus.* New York: HarperCollins.

Rosenblatt, L. M. (1978). *The reader, the text, and the poem.* Carbondale, IL: Southern Illinois University Press.

———. (1991). Literature—S.O.S! *Language Arts, 68* (6), 444–448.

Roswell, F. G., & Chall, J. S. (1994). *Creating successful readers: A practical guide to testing and teaching at all levels.* Chicago: Riverside.

Routman, R. (1991). *Invitations: Changing as teachers and learners, K–12.* Portsmouth, NH: Heinemann.

———. (1999). *Conversations.* Portsmouth, NH: Heinemann.

Rudman, M. (1995). *Children's literature: An issues approach* (3rd ed.). New York: Longman.

Ruiz, N. T., Vargas, E., & Beltrán, A. (2002). Becoming a reader and a writer in a bilingual special education classroom. *Language Arts, 79* (4), 297–309.

Rule, A. C. (2001). Alphabetizing with environmental print. *The Reading Teacher, 54* (6), 558–562.

Rumelhart, D. E. (1980). Schemata: The building blocks of cognition. In R. J. Spiro, B. C. Bruce, & W. F. Brewer (Eds.), *Theoretical issues in reading comprehension* (pp. 33–58). Hillsdale, NJ: Erlbaum.

Rupley, W. H., Logan, J., & Nichols, W. D. (1998/1999). Vocabulary instruction in a balanced reading program. *The Reading Teacher, 52* (4), 336–344.

Salisbury, C. L., & MacGregor, G. (2002). The administrative climate and context of inclusive elementary classrooms. *Exceptional Children, 68* (2), 259–274.

Samway, K. D., & Whang, J. (1996). *Literature study circles in the multicultural classroom.* York, ME: Stenhouse.

Sanders, W., & Rivers, J. (1996). *Cumulative and residual effects of teachers on future student academic achievement.* Knoxville, TN: University of Tennessee Value-Added Research and Assessment Center.

Sapon-Shevin, M. (2001). Schools for all. *Educational Leadership, 58* (4), 34–39.

Savage, J. F. (2004). *Sound it out: Phonics in a balanced reading program.* Boston: McGraw-Hill.

Scarnati, J. F., & Weller, C. J. (1992). The write stuff. *Science and Children, 29,* 28–29.

Schafer, S. (1997). *Writing effective report card comments.* New York: Scholastic.

Schlick Noe, K. L. (1995). Nurturing response with emergent readers. In B. C. Hill, Johnson, N. J., & Schlick Noe, K. L. (Eds.), *Literature circles and response.* Norwood, MA: Christopher-Gordon.

Schwartz, R. M., & Raphael, T. E. (1985). Concept of definition: A key to improving students' vocabulary. *The Reading Teacher, 39* (3), 198–205.

Scott, Foresman, and Company. (1996). *Fun with Dick and Jane: A commemorative collection of stories.* San Francisco: Collins Publishers.

Shanahan, T., & Shanahan, S. (1997). Character Perspective Charting: Helping children to develop a more complete conception of a story. *The Reading Teacher, 50* (8), 668–677.

Shore, K. (1998). *Special kids problem solver.* Paramus, NJ: Prentice Hall.

Short, K. G., Harste, J. C., & Burke, C. (1996). *Creating classrooms for authors and inquirers,* 2nd ed. Portsmouth, NH: Heinemann.

Shurtleff, N. (1853). *Records of the Governor and Company of the Massachusetts Bay in New England, vol. 2.* Boston: Order of the Legislature.

Sierra, J. (1992). *Cinderella: An international collection.* Phoenix, AZ: Oryx.

Silvaroli, N., & Wheeler, W. (2004). *Classroom reading inventory* (9th ed.). Boston: McGraw-Hill.

Simpson, A. (1996a). Critical questions: Whose questions? *The Reading Teacher, 50* (2), 118–127.

———. (1996b). Fictions and facts: An investigation of the reading practices of girls and boys. *English Education, 28* (4), 268–279.

Smith, F. (1985). *Reading without nonsense* (2nd ed.). New York: Teachers College Press.

———. (1988). *Joining the literacy club.* Portsmouth, NH: Heinemann.

———. (1989). Demonstrations, engagement, and sensitivity. The choice between people and programs. In G. Manning & M. Manning (Eds.), *Whole language beliefs and practices, K–8.* Washington, DC: National Association of Educators.

———. (1989). Overselling literacy. *Phi Delta Kappan, 70,* 353–359.

Smith, J. L., & Johnson, H. (1994). Models for implementing literature into content areas. *The Reading Teacher, 48* (2), 198–209.

Smith, N. B. (1965/1986/2002). *American reading instruction.* Newark, DE: International Reading Association.

Snow, C. E., Burns, M. S., & Griffin, P. (Eds.), (1998). *Preventing reading difficulties in young children.* Washington, DC: National Academy Press.

Sorrow, B. H., & Lumpkin, B. S. (1996). *CD-ROM for librarians and educators* (2nd ed.). Jefferson, NC: McFarland.

Spandel, V. (2003). *6-traits plus writing.* Boston: Pearson Education.

Spandel, V., & Stiggins, R. J. (2000). *Creating writers through 6-trait assessment and instruction* (3rd ed.). New York: Longman.

Spiegel, D. L. (1999). The perspective of the balanced approach. In S. M. Blair-Larsen and K. A. Williams (Eds.), *The balanced reading program* (pp. 8–23). Newark, DE: International Reading Association.

Springer, M. (1999). *Learning and memory: The brain in action.* Alexandria, VA: Association for Supervision and Curriculum.

Stahl, N. A., & King, J. R. (2001). Preserving our professional heritage: A call for oral history projects. *Illinois Reading Council Journal, 28* (2), 40–45.

Stahl, S. A., (1992). Saying the "p" word: Nine guidelines to exemplary phonics instruction. *The Reading Teacher, 45* (8), 618–625.

Stahl, S. A., & Fairbanks, M. M. (1986). The effects of vocabulary instruction: A model-based meta-analysis. *Review of Educational Research, 56* (1), 72–100.

Stahl, S. A., & Kuhn, M. R. (2002). Making it sound like language: Developing fluency. *The Reading Teacher, 55* (6), 582–584.

Stahl, S. A., Duffy-Hester, A. M., & Dougherty Stahl, K. A. (1998). Everything you wanted to know about phonics (but were afraid to ask). *Reading Research Quarterly, 33* (3), 338–355.

Stanovich, K. E., & Cunningham, A. E. (1993). Where does knowledge come from? Specific associations between print exposure and information acquisition. *Journal of Educational Psychology, 85* (3), 211–229.

Stauffer, R. G. (1969). *Direct reading maturity as a cognitive process.* New York: Harper & Row.

Sternberg, R. J. (1987). Most vocabulary is learned from context. In M. G. McKeown & M. E. Curtis (Eds.), *The nature of vocabulary acquisition* (pp. 89–105). Hillsdale, NJ: Erlbaum.

Stiggins, R. J. (2002). Assessment crisis: The absence of assessment FOR learning. *Phi Delta Kappan, 83* (10), 758–765.

Strickland, D. S. (1998). *Teaching phonics today: A primer for educators.* Newark, DE: International Reading Association.

Strickland, D. S., & Feeley, J. T. (2003). Development in the elementary school years. In J. Flood, D. Lapp, J. R. Squire, & J. M. Jensen (Eds.), *Handbook of research on teaching the English language arts* (pp. 339–356). Mahwah, NJ: Lawrence Erlbaum Associates.

Strickland, D. S., & Strickland, M. R. (1997). Language and literacy: The poetry connection. *Language Arts, 74* (3), 210–215.

Strickland, D. S., & Morrow, L. M. (1988). New perspectives on young children learning to read and write. *The Reading Teacher, 42* (1), 70–71.

Strong, R. W., Silver, H. F., & Perrini, M. J. (2001). *What matters most: Standards and strategies for raising student achievement.* Alexandria, VA: Association for Supervision and Curriculum Development.

Sudol, P., & King, C. M. (1996). A checklist for choosing nonfiction trade books. *The Reading Teacher, 49* (5), 422–424.

Sullivan, J. (1998). The electronic journal: Combining literacy and technology. *The Reading Teacher, 52* (2), 90–96.

Taberski, S. (2000). *On solid ground: Strategies for teaching reading K–3.* Portsmouth, NH: Heinemann.

Teale, W. H. (1995). Young children and reading: Trends across the twentieth century. *Journal of Education, 177* (3), 95–127.

Teale, W. H., & Yokota, J. (2000). Beginning reading and writing: Perspectives on instruction. In D. S. Strickland & L. M. Morrow (Eds.), *Beginning reading and writing* (pp. 3–21). New York: Teachers College Press.

Temple, C., Martinez, Yokoto, J., & Naylor, A. (2001). *Children's books in children's hands: An introduction to their literature.* Boston: Allyn and Bacon.

Templeton, S., & Morris, D. (1999). Questions teachers ask about spelling. *Reading Research Quarterly, 34* (1), 102–112.

Thorndike, R. L., & Hagen, E. P. (1977). *Measurement and evaluation in psychology and education* (4th ed.). New York: Wiley.

Tiedt, P. L., Tiedt, I. M., & Tiedt, S. W. (2001). *Language arts activities for the classroom* (3rd ed.). Boston: Allyn & Bacon.

Tierney, R. J. (1998). Literacy assessment reform: Shifting beliefs, principled possibilities, and emerging practices. *The Reading Teacher, 51* (5), 374–390.

Tompkins, G. E. (2000). *Teaching writing* (3rd ed.). Columbus, OH: Merrill.

———. (2001). *Literacy for the 21st century* (2nd ed.). Upper Saddle River, NJ: Merrill Prentice-Hall.

Tomlinson, C. M., & Lynch-Brown, C. (2002). *Essentials of children's literature* (4th ed.). Boston: Allyn & Bacon.

Towel, J. (1999/2000). Motivating students through music and literature. *The Reading Teacher, 53* (3), 284–289.

Tracey, D. H. (2000). Enhancing literacy growth through home-school connections. In Strickland, D. S., and Morrow, L. M. (Eds.), *Beginning reading and writing* (pp. 46–57). New York: Teachers College Press.

Truscott, D., & Watts-Taffe, S. (2000). Using what we know about language and literacy development for ESL students in the mainstream classroom. *Language Arts, 77* (3), 258–265.

Tunnell, M. O., & Jacobs, J. S. (2000). *Children's literature briefly.* (2nd ed.). Englewood Cliffs, NJ: Merrill.

Turner, J., & Paris, S. G. (1995). How literacy tasks influence children's motivation for literacy. *The Reading Teacher, 48* (8), 662–673.

Valencia, S. (1999). A portfolio to classroom reading assessment: The whys, whats, and hows. In S. J. Barrentine (Ed.), *Reading assessment: Principles and practices for elementary teachers,* (pp. 113–117). Newark, DE: International Reading Association.

Vallecorsa, A. L., & deBettencourt, L. U. (1997). Using a mapping procedure to teach reading and writing skills to middle grade students with learning disabilities. *Education and the Treatment of Children, 20* (2), 173–188.

Veatch, J. (1986). Teaching without texts. *Journal of Clinical Reading, 2,* 32–35.

Villaume, S. K., & Brabhamj, E. G. (2002). Comprehensive instruction: Beyond strategies. *The Reading Teacher, 55* (7), 672–675.

Vygotsky, L. S. (E. Hanfmann & G. Vaka, Eds. & Trans.). (1962). *Thought and language.* Cambridge, MA: MIT Press.

———. (M. Cole, V. John-Steiner, S. Scribner, & E. Sounerman, Eds. & Trans.). (1978). *Mind in society.* Cambridge, MA: Harvard University Press.

Wagstaff, J. M. (1997/1998). Building practical knowledge of letter-sound correspondences: A beginner's word wall and beyond. *The Reading Teacher, 51* (4), 298–304.

Walther, M. P. (1994). The development of a first-grade writer: An integrated language arts program. *Illinois Reading Council Journal, 22* (4), 19–33.

———. (2001). Geography: Exploring the whole world through interdisciplinary instruction. In P. J. Farris (Ed.). *Elementary and the middle school social studies: An interdisciplinary instructional approach* (3rd ed.), (pp. 200–228). Boston: McGraw-Hill.

Watson, D. (1989). Defining and describing whole language. *Elementary School Journal, 90* (2), 129–141.

Wells, R. (1994). As I see it. In L. Robb's *Whole language, whole learners: Creating a literature-centered classroom.* New York: Morrow.

Wepner, S. B., & Ray, L. C. (2000). Sign of the times: Technology and early literacy learning. In D. S. Strickland and L. M. Morrow (Eds.), *Beginning reading and writing* (pp. 168–182). New York: Teachers College Press.

Wepner, S. B., & Tao, L. (2002). From master teacher to novice: Shifting responsibilities in technology-infused classrooms. *The Reading Teacher, 55* (7), 642–651.

Werderich, D. E. (2002). Individualized responses: Using journal letters as a vehicle for differentiated reading instruction. *Journal of Adolescent & Adult Literacy, 45* (8), 746–754.

White, T. G., Sowell, J., & Yanagihara, A. (1989). Teaching elementary students to use word part clues. *The Reading Teacher, 42* (4), 302–308.

Wiencek, J., & O'Flahaven, J. F. (1994). From teacher-led to peer discussions about literature: Suggestions for making the shift. *Language Arts, 71* (7), 488–498.

———. (1996). Planning, initiating, and sustaining literature discussion groups: The teacher's role. In L. B. Gambrell & J. F. Almasi, (Eds.), *Lively discussions! Fostering engaged reading* (pp. 49–56). Newark, DE: International Reading Association.

Williams, J. A. (2001). Classroom conversations: opportunities to learn for ESL students in mainstream classrooms. *The Reading Teacher, 54* (8), 750–757.

Wilson, P. (1992). Among nonreaders: Voluntary reading, reading achievement, and the development of reading habits. In C. Temple & P. Collins (Eds.), *Stories and readers:*

New perspectives in literature in the elementary school (pp. 157–169). Norwood, MA: Christopher Gordon.

Wixson, K., & Peters, C. W. (1984). Reading redefined: A Michigan Reading Association position paper. *Michigan Reading Teacher, 17* (1), 4–7.

Wixson, K. L. (1979). Miscue analysis: A critical review: *Journal of Reading Behavior, 11,* 163–175.

Wolf, J. (1994). Singing with children is a cinch. *Young Children, 49* (4), 20–25.

Wolfe, S. (1998). The flight of reading: Shifts in instruction, orchestration, and attitudes through classroom theatre. *Reading Research Quarterly, 33* (3), 382–414.

Wood, D. J., Bruner, J. S., & Ross, G. (1976). The role of tutoring in problem-solving. *Journal of Child Psychology and Psychiatry, 17* (2), 89–100.

Worthy, J. (1996). A matter of interest: Literature that hook reluctant readers and keep them reading. *The Reading Teacher, 50* (3), 204–212.

———. (2001). The intermediate grades: A life of learning and enjoyment from literacy. *The Reading Teacher, 53* (5), 410–423.

———. (2002). What makes intermediate-grade students want to read? *The Reading Teacher, 55* (6), 568–569.

Worthy, J. & Broaddus, K. (2002). Fluency beyond the primary grades: From group performance to silent, independent reading. *The Reading Teacher, 55* (4), 334–342.

Yokota, J. (1993). Issues in selecting multicultural literature. *Language Arts, 70* (2), 156–170.

Yokota, J. (Ed.). (2001). *Kaleidoscope: A multicultural booklist for grades K–8*

(3rd ed.). Urbana, IL: National Council of Teachers of English.

Yopp, H. K. (1992). Developing phonemic awareness in young children. *The Reading Teacher, 45* (7), 696–703.

———. (1995). A test for assessing phonemic awareness in young children. *The Reading Teacher, 49* (1), 20–29.

Yopp, H. K., & Yopp, R. H. (2000). Supporting phonemic awareness development in the classroom. *The Reading Teacher, 54* (2), 130–143.

Yopp, H. K., & Yopp, R. H. (2001). *Literature-based reading activities* (3rd ed.). Needham Heights, MA: Allyn & Bacon.

Yopp, R. H., & Yopp, H. K. (2000). Sharing informational text with young children. *The Reading Teacher, 53* (5), 410–423.

Young, J. P., & Brozo, W. G. (2001). Boys will be boys, or will they? Literacy and masculinities. *Reading Research Quarterly, 36* (3), 316–325.

Young, T. A., & Ferguson, P. M. (1995). From Anansi to Zoo: Trickster tales in the classroom. *The Reading Teacher, 48* (6), 490–503.

Ysseldyke, J. E., Algozzine, B., & Thurlow, M. L. (2000). *Critical issues in special education.* Boston: Houghton Mifflin.

Zemelman, S., Daniels, H., & Hyde, A. (1998). *Best practice: New standards for teaching and learning in America's schools* (2nd ed.). Portsmouth, NH: Heinemann.

Zinsser, V. (1988). *Writing to learn.* New York: Harper & Row.

Glossary

Activating prior knowledge   The knowledge a reader brings to the text based upon background and experiences. Activating this knowledge is an important step in the reading process as readers connect what they already know with what they are learning.

Aesthetic   A type of reading in which attention is focused on the idea and feelings being evoked.

Alliteration   The repetition of the initial sounds in neighboring words or stressed syllables.

Alphabetic principle   The assumption that each speech sound of a language should have its own distinctive letter representation.

Alternative assessment   The use of student work or observation of student behavior to measure student performance on learning tasks.

Analogy-based phonics   Teaching children how to decipher unknown words by looking for patterns in known words and using those patterns to figure out other words.

Analytic phonics   Teaching children the rules and generalizations to help them analyze words.

Anecdotal record   A description of behavior such as notes written by the teacher regarding student performance.

Antonym   A word that is opposite or nearly opposite in meaning from another word.

Assessment   The process of gathering data in order to better understand the strengths and weaknesses of student learning.

Attention deficit disorder (ADD)   A developmental disorder involving one or more of the cognitive processes relating to orienting, focusing, or maintaining attention.

Attention deficit hyperactivity disorder (ADHD)   A student with ADD plus hyperactivity. The child demonstrates inattention, impulsivity, and deficits in rule-governed behavior. Not to be confused with natural squirming of childhood.

Authentic assessment   The use of means of assessment other than standardized tests to measure student performance.

Autistic   A severe developmental disorder in which the individual is so self-centered as to be largely or completely unable to judge reality.

Autobiography   A factual account of someone's life written by that person.

Balanced reading approach   Knowledge and application of a wide variety of reading instructional practices and materials in which the teacher selects and implements the best method for each student in the classroom. It includes the use of phonics with beginning readers along with comprehension strategies based upon student needs and interests.

Ballad   A narrative form of poetry that describes love, courage, or the supernatural and is written in stanzas; may be accompanied by music.

Basal reader   The leveled reading text in a reading program that contains a variety of genre (traditional tales, fantasy, poetry, realistic fiction, historical fiction, biography, and informational selections) of reading material for students.

Basal reading series   A collection of student texts and workbooks, teacher's manuals, and supplemental materials for developmental reading and sometimes writing instruction in the elementary and middle school grades.

Behavior modification   A technique to change behaviors by systematically rewarding desirable behaviors. Undesirable behaviors are either disregarded or punished.

Benchmark The expected achievement level of a reading or writing skill that the typical student at that grade level will be able to successfully reach.

Big book Oversized books that provide an opportunity to share text and illustrations with a large group of children in ways that one might share a standard sized book with an individual child.

Biography A factual account of someone else's life; in an authentic biography almost all of the facts can be documented. If fictionalized biography, facts are interspersed with some fictional material.

Book talk A discussion of a book by a teacher, librarian, or student to introduce it to other potential readers.

Bottom-up approach Theorists supporting this approach suggest that in the reading process, the text is of prime importance. Learning to read begins with the smallest elements—the letters—and moves sequentially to larger and larger pieces until sentences are mastered and text is comprehended. Accurate sequential processing of words is a key factor in this approach.

Bull's-eye writing Like the small center of a target, this type of informal expository writing focuses on the key points or ideas of a topic, capturing them in concise thoughts.

Cause and effect An expository text structure that involves an association between a cause and the resulting effect(s). For example, the text might discuss a decision that resolves a problem and students examine the ensuing effects.

Children's literature A body of fiction, nonfiction, and poetry that is written especially for young people up to the age of fourteen. It also includes titles that were originally written for adults but children have made them their own.

Codeswitching An individual's change from one language to another during oral or written communication such as combining Spanish and English.

Cognitive behavior therapy An approach used with ADD and ADHD students to get them to reward themselves internally for doing desired classroom behaviors.

Common School Movement Trend that occurred during the early and middle 19th century in the United States which established state agencies to control local schools and aimed to use public schools as instruments of government policy to solve social problems. All children had the right to a free, public education. One-room schools were built in rural areas to serve students in grades 1–12.

Comparison and contrast An expository text structure in which an author explains how two items, events, people, or places are alike and different; a useful graphic organizer to use with this text structure is the Venn diagram.

Concept books A child's first informational book, usually describing various dimensions of an object, a class of objects, or an abstract idea. Some concept books include ABC books, color books, counting books, and shape books.

Concept of definition map This is a word map strategy that is most helpful for students in middle grades and above; it is used to illustrate the kinds of information needed to define a word. Background knowledge is activated as a part of learning new words by creating a visual picture of the word that addresses questions like what is it, what is it like, and what are some examples?

Concept muraling Presenting via overhead transparency or PowerPoint presentation a single visual with six to eight illustrations representing different concepts for a unit of study. The concepts represent the most significant objectives to be learned by the students during the unit.

Context clues   Context clues are bits of information collected from the sentence containing an unknown word, or from surrounding sentences in an effort to decipher the meaning. Use of context is most effective when the clues are clear and closely positioned to the word in question.

Criterion referenced tests   The assessment of performance on a test in terms of the kind of behavior expected of a person with a given score (e.g., driver's license exam).

Decodable texts   Stories where the majority of the words are based on clear sound–letter relationships.

Decoding   Breaking down words by the sound–letter relationships.

Description   A prominent expository text structure in which an author points out specific characteristics, details, or features of a topic under study and provides clear examples of each one.

Developmentally appropriate practices   The use of concrete, hands-on, age appropriate activities that meet the individual learning needs of the student. This learning occurs in a carefully prepared environment where student choice, active exploration, individual and small group work are encouraged. Worksheets and workbooks are discouraged.

Developmental reading program   Reading instruction, except for remedial, for elementary and middle school students. Reading these materials is directed by the teacher.

Differentiated instruction   Based on research describing how students learn, differentiated instruction focuses on how students are both alike and different. Teachers study student differences in understanding concepts, learning modalities, and interests, and then plan accordingly to allow for different learning rates and to structure tasks of varying complexity.

Directed Listening-Thinking Activity (DL-TA)   A structure used to build comprehension for students as they listen to a story read aloud, make predictions, and then listen to confirm or correct those predictions.

Directed Reading Activity (DRA)   A teacher directed step-by-step method for facilitating comprehension during a reading lesson. It includes the following sequence of activities: preparation, guided reading, skill development and opportunity to practice, and enrichment activities.

Directed Reading-Listening Activity (DR-LA)   A structure used to build comprehension for students as they listen to a story read aloud, make predictions, and then listen to confirm or correct those predictions.

Directed Reading-Thinking Activity (DR-TA)   An adaptable strategy for teaching reading that involves three key steps: predicting, reading, and confirming or adjusting predictions. It is an effective method for teaching students to predict outcomes and draw conclusions.

Discovery/inquiry learning   A student-directed inquiry approach where students, faced with a relevant question to answer or problem to solve, work in small groups in an inductive process to reach a solution.

Double entry journal   An informal writing tool, this variation on the typical journal requires the students to use two pages or two columns to organize their information. The left-hand side may contain notes, diagrams, ideas, lists, vocabulary, and so forth. The right-hand side is used for reflections on the content, explanations, or even questions to be clarified. These journals work equally well across the curriculum.

Drop Everything and Read (DEAR)   A time during the day where children are given the opportunity to read books they choose at their independent level.

Eclectic teaching   Using a wide variety of instructional strategies depending on student abilities, needs, and interests.

Embedded phonics   Teaching children about sound–symbol relationships in the context of real reading.

Emergent literacy   Development of the association of print with meaning that begins early in a child's life until a child reaches the stage of conventional reading and writing. The focus is on the ongoing development of literate behaviors in real-life settings where the child is engaged in purposeful reading and writing activities.

English language learners   Individuals who are acquiring English and who have another native, first language.

Environmental print   Print and other graphic symbols, in addition to books, that are found in the physical environment, such as street signs, food products, television commercials, and the like.

Envisionment   The process of getting into a book in which a unique textworld is built in the reader's mind based upon that individual's life experiences.

Epic   A long narrative poem about a heroic person whose actions reflect the values of the culture in which the epic originates; may have been passed down by word of mouth originally. The language is often quite sophisticated as in Homer's *Iliad*.

Evaluation   The process of testing, appraising, and judging achievement, growth, product, process, or changes usually relying upon both formal and informal measures.

Explicit meaning   The reader can quickly locate a piece of information because it is directly stated in a sentence of the text he is reading.

Expository text   Nonfiction, informational books or magazines that are written for the purpose of providing information on a topic or an explanation. It is more dense than narrative writing, filled with facts, and may include photographs, maps, graphs, and other visual aids to help readers better understand the text.

Expressive vocabulary   This is a category that includes both speaking and writing vocabularies, those vocabularies that enable an individual to communicate her thoughts to someone else.

Fable   A short narrative or tale told in verse that ends with a clear moral which has been illustrated through the actions of the animal characters.

Fairy tales   A type of folktale that is filled with magic and enchantment. They are based on some fundamental truth like courage and hard work being rewarded while evil is punished.

Fantasy/modern fantasy   A genre of picture books or novels that contains an imaginative, unreal element; may involve magic or the supernatural. In traditional fantasy, the author is unknown, while in modern fantasy, the author can be identified.

First reader   The initial hardback book in a basal reading program.

Flexible grouping   The teacher forms temporary instructional groups based on students' learning needs and concepts that the teacher wants to teach. Types of groups include whole group, teacher facilitated small groups, cooperative groups, partners, and individuals.

Fluency   Freedom from word identification problems that might hinder comprehension in silent reading or the expression of ideas in oral reading.

Folktales   Stories of the oral tradition that have been passed down through the generations; every culture has its tales with similar themes appearing across cultures. Folktales are often well known within a culture because of repeated storytelling.

Formal assessment   The collection of data using standardized tests or procedures under controlled conditions.

Formal expository writing   This writing involves researching a number of sources on a topic of choice. Carefully assembled and condensed information is then polished into a report and presented in a variety of ways in an effort to share the information gleaned.

Formative assessment   The continuing study of the process of change in an instructional program as it moves toward its goals and objectives by monitoring the learning progress of its participants.

FQR   An acronym for a study system that represents the terms fact, question, and response. Can be used with narrative or expository text.

Gender   Sex of individual students; may influence interests, classroom interactions, etc.

Genres   Categories used to classify different types of literature that have a set of similar characteristics (i.e., poetry, fantasy, folktales).

Graphic organizers   Visual pictures or diagrams used to show relationships between ideas in both narrative and expository text. Examples include semantic maps, Venn diagrams, concept murals, and pictorial maps.

Graphophonic clues   The system that deals with letters and the specific sounds those letters make; in our graphophonic system, a grapheme represents a letter, so there are twenty-six letters in the English alphabet. A phoneme is tied to sounds and represents the smallest unit of spoken language. There are forty-four phonemes associated with those twenty-six letters. You can understand this when you think of the fact that vowels make more than one sound depending on how they are used in a word and that a letter like "c" sometimes sounds like a "k" or an "s" in certain words.

Guided reading   The teacher works with a small group of students who are at a similar level in their development as a reader. The teacher introduces a carefully selected story to the students, then assists the children while they read it quietly and independently. The focus of the lesson is to help children develop the independent use of reading strategies.

Head Start   A federally funded educational program that began in the United States in 1965 to assist children from low-income families. Children between the ages of four and six are given support to stimulate their intellectual, physical, and emotional development so that they will have an improved academic and social performance when they enter formal schooling.

Herringbone (Fishbone) technique   A graphic organizer that aids learners in picking out particular information from an article or chapter to answer the questions who, what, when, where, how, and why.

High-frequency words   The words that occur most frequently in reading and writing. For example, the following ten words account for almost one-quarter of all the words we read and write: the, of, and, a, to, in, is, you, that, and it.

Historical fiction   The genre of literature in which story events are set in the historical past. Often the stories are realistic enough that they could have happened. Because some parts of them may actually be true, they give readers a sense of what it might have been like to live in another time and place.

Holistic   Teaching in which subject matter is kept intact rather than separated into parts for instructional purposes.

Holophrase   A single word used to imply a complete sentence. Example: "Juice" rather than saying, "I want more juice."

Homograph   The morpheme or word part "graph" is a clue to the words that fall into this category; it means a written element, so these words are written in the same way but are pronounced differently and have different origins. Example: bow (ribbon), and bow (end of a performance).

Homophone   The important morpheme is "phon," which refers to sound. Thus, these words sound the same but have different meanings; most often their spellings differ as well. Example: see and sea.

Implicit meaning   The reader must read between the lines to understand the author's message. This involves drawing on prior knowledge coupled with information provided by the author to come to a conclusion or draw an inference about the story.

Inclusion   A practice of keeping all children, regardless of their abilities, in the regular classroom, a microcosm of real life. Thus, students identified as having special needs are an integral part of the classroom routine. It is based upon the belief that professionals collaborating and students cooperating can provide the least restrictive learning environment as everyone involved learns together. In some more severe cases, the special needs student may have an adult aide who works with him or her for more individualized instruction.

Individual educational plan (IEP)   A plan created by the classroom teacher, special education teacher, speech therapist, building principal, and other support personnel for a student with special needs. It includes the child's present level of functioning, annual goals, short-term objectives, services needed, strategies for evaluation, the initiation date, and duration of services. The IEP is updated annually.

Inference   Making a reasoned assumption(s) based upon information in the text and a reader's prior knowledge; reading between the lines.

Informal expository writing   Ungraded writing that occurs in journals like learning logs or double entry journals which involves such activities as taking notes, brainstorming, drawing a quick graph, sketching, jotting down key ideas, or posing questions to be answered during the process of reading

expository text or when reflecting upon it after reading.

Informational books   A genre of nonfiction books that contain factual writing about a variety of topics.

Inquiry learning   A student-directed inquiry approach where students, faced with a relevant question to answer or problem to solve, work in small groups in an inductive process to reach a solution. Also known as "discovery learning."

Interactive approach   Theorists support the belief that reading involves processing text, drawing on background knowledge, and applying one's language abilities in order to comprehend what is being read. Thus, both the reader and the text are vital to the comprehension process.

Interactive writing   Teacher and students share the pen to create a preplanned text. The goal of the shared pen is to focus on specific conventions of written language that need to be learned or reviewed.

Interdisciplinary teaching (unit)   The practice of combining all or a portion of the language arts (reading, writing, listening, speaking, viewing, and visually representing) across content areas in an effort to tie learning into a cohesive unit. It replaces the typical subject oriented chunking of a classroom day. Teaching using interdisciplinary units several times throughout the school year is a common practice in most school curricula because it is more efficient in terms of time.

Item analysis   The examination of item difficulty, item discrimination, and any analysis of performance on the various item response options of a test as they relate to the teaching objectives.

Journal writing   An independent writing activity where students record their thoughts and ideas usually in a notebook.

K-W-L Plus   A method that is used to develop comprehension of expository text through activating prior knowledge. It is based upon students answering three questions: What do I Know? What do I Want to Know? and What did I Learn? (K-W-L) This can be enhanced with K-W-L-Plus by summarizing in a paragraph or other writing experience what they have learned after the unit of study is completed.

Language experience approach (LEA) An approach where the teacher acts as a scribe to record children's ideas in a group setting. Emphasis is on children's exact words.

Learning disability (LD) A group of disorders manifested by significant difficulties in the acquisition and use of listening, speaking, reading, writing, or mathematical abilities.

Learning logs Used across content area classes, these logs incorporate informal writing as students focus closely on materials being read and note both responses and reactions, as well as questions, definitions, sketches, and the like, to facilitate their learning. They are an effective record of learning and help students evaluate their progress in understanding a topic, think about their learning, and even plan further learning.

Legend A traditional story of the people often rooted in some bit of historical truth. Part of the oral tradition, it was eventually written down.

Linguistic reader A beginning reading program based on highly regular sound–symbol patterns, temporarily substituted for the term "phonic" in the 1960s.

Listening instruction Direct instruction in specific strategies for effective listening.

Listening vocabulary The first vocabulary acquired by a young child consisting of words heard and reinforced in the environment around him by parents, family members, and caregivers.

Literacy In its simplest terms, it is the ability to read and write. Coupled with that ability, however, is the knowledge of how to use one's skills to communicate effectively in our print-rich society. There is a range or continuum of literacy skills beginning with those who are illiterate and cannot read or write. The next step moves to functional literacy, which refers to the skills or abilities required to use print adequately from day to day. Those with advanced literacy skills display the ability to engage in higher level thinking using reading and writing. Literacy skills can extend into other areas such as math, technology, and the visual arts.

Literacy play centers A carefully designed space where children explore literacy through meaningful situations.

Literature anthology basal A basal reading series that uses real, published literature usually in its original format.

Literature-based instruction A curriculum in which literary works, usually trade books, are the dominant materials for instruction, especially in the language arts.

Literature circles A small discussion group of three to eight students who read selected books or novels independently, then meet to discuss their feelings, reactions, and responses to the text. It is an effective way to increase comprehension and to encourage engagement and responses to literature.

Making words A multilevel activity where children make a variety of words from six to ten individual letters, when arranged correctly to spell a big word. Once the words are made, children sort them based on their spelling features.

Manuscript handwriting Print handwriting.

Metacognition Being aware of one's own mental processes: monitoring one's comprehension, understanding when it is failing, and making appropriate adjustments. Good readers have this ability, while poorer readers are often not aware of their difficulties or how to remediate them.

Metacognitive practices Include a series of steps internalized by learning to monitor their own understanding of materials and to regulate their thinking by taking corrective action when they notice confusion about text materials being read.

Metaphor   Comparing one object to something else without the use of like or as; e.g., "a mountain of a man."

Meter   The cadence or beat of a poem.

Morning meeting   A gathering of all students with the teacher to go over the events that will occur that day.

Morning message   A shared writing experience where the teacher and her students work together to create a short message about the day's events.

Morphemes   Basic units of meaning that make up words; they may be "bound," which means they must be attached to a base word to have meaning (like prefixes or suffixes), or they may be "free," which are words that make sense on their own.

Multicultural literature   A growing body of literature, both fact and fiction, that reflects the diverse values, attitudes, customs, beliefs, and ethics of various cultures who call America their home.

Myth   A story that originated in the folk beliefs of many cultures; it typically shows supernatural forces at work to help explain a natural phenomenon or the mysteries of life.

Narrative text   A story, actual or fictional, expressed in writing.

Norm referenced test   A test that relates the performance of a single individual to that of a specific group usually based on population subgroups.

Onset   The onset of a single syllable or word is the initial consonant(s) sound. Example: The onset of the word man is /m/. The onset of the word green is /gr/.

Organizational patterns   Students can learn to decipher expository (informational) text if they recognize the common structures an author follows to relate the information. Common organizational structures include

description, sequence, comparison/contrast, problem/solution, and cause/effect.

Patterned writing   Students use standard sentence speech patterns of oral English to record ideas. They fill in a sentence or groups of sentences with missing words. These sentences are commonly referred to as frame sentences.

Pedagogy   Examination of teaching methods, materials, and problems.

Phoneme   The smallest unit of speech that corresponds to letter(s) of an alphabetic writing system.

Phonemic awareness   An understanding that spoken language contains a series of individual sounds.

Phonics   A way of teaching reading and spelling that stresses symbol–sound relationships, used especially in beginning instruction.

Phonogram   Also known as word families, phonograms end in high-frequency rimes that require only a beginning consonant to make a word. For example, ay, ill, ot, and ug are all high-frequency phonograms.

Phonological awareness   The appreciation of sounds as well as the meanings of spoken words.

Poetic text   Prose or poetry.

Portfolio   A selected collection of a student's work that may be used to evaluate learning progress.

Potential marginal vocabulary   This type of vocabulary is made up of all the words a child may be able to understand by using context clues or structural analysis; it is difficult to determine the size of this vocabulary because it will vary with each learner and his or her primary grade instruction and the time spent broadening vocabulary through wide reading. This vocabulary is important in upper elementary and middle school learning.

Pourquoi tale   Folktales that attempt to explain why something in nature, like animal behavior or physical event, is the way it is.

Preprimer　In a basal reading program, a booklet used before the first reader to introduce students to features in texts and books.

Primer　The first formal textbook in a basal reading program, usually preceded by a reading readiness book and a preprimer.

Print concepts　The "rules of the road" to reading a book including book orientation and print direction. Which way do you hold a book? Where do you start? Where do you go next? Where do you start to read on a page?

Problem and solution　An expository text structure or organizational pattern used by an author to describe a particular problem and then suggest a probable solution to that problem.

Psycholinguistics　The interdisciplinary field of psychology and linguistics in which language is examined.

Question-answer relationship (QAR)　A comprehension strategy that invites readers to examine questions and the information needed to answer them at four levels in two categories. The "in the book" category includes questions that are "right there" or require "putting it together." The "in my head" category involves questions that are "on my own" and "the author and me."

Read a Book Because It's Terrific (RABBIT)　A time during the day where children are given the opportunity to read books they choose at their instructional level.

Reader's theater　An oral presentation where the text is presented by two or more children reading aloud from a script based upon a picture book or novel.

Reading readiness　The readiness to profit from beginning reading instruction. This term has now been replaced by "emergent literacy."

Reading workshop　A workshop format where reading strategies are taught and practiced in the whole group, in small groups, and independently.

Read-aloud　The teacher reads or rereads a story to the class.

Reading comprehension　The active process of constructing meaning from written texts resulting in a rich, deep, and thoughtful reading experience.

Reading readiness　The belief that a child has to reach a certain level of maturity or possess a certain number of skills to profit from formal reading instruction.

Reading vocabulary　A vocabulary that is developed more rapidly once a child begins school; it may develop simultaneously along with writing vocabulary. Reading vocabulary typically extends both writing and speaking vocabularies.

Realistic fiction　A genre in which the stories mirror real life; the characters and plots are believable and possible.

Receptive vocabulary　This vocabulary includes one's listening and reading vocabularies, the words an individual understands.

Reciprocal teaching　A teaching strategy that includes a type of cooperative learning in which the teacher and small groups of students work together to improve comprehension; four key strategies are used: predicting, questioning, clarifying, and summarizing.

Remedial reading　Specialized reading instruction, usually individualized or in small groups, adjusted to the needs of a student who does not perform satisfactorily with regular reading instruction.

Response theory　The theory that explains how readers interact with text to form a transaction or unique personal connection based upon their own memories, feelings, and thoughts. Both the reasons for reading and the context in which the reading occurs affect this interaction between reader and book.

Rhyme   Identical or very similar recurring final sounds in words usually at the end of lines of a poem.

Rhythm   The pattern or beat of a poem.

Rime   A rime is the unit composed of the vowel and any consonants that follow within the syllable. For example, the rime unit in man is /an/. The rime in green is /een/.

Rubric   A set of criteria used for evaluating a behavior.

Running record   An assessment of the text reading designed to be taken as a child reads orally from any text.

Scaffolding   The support, guidance, and instruction provided by a knowledgeable adult to assist a student in learning a new skill, solving a problem, or carrying out a task that could not be accomplished successfully alone. This support is gradually withdrawn as the child becomes more accomplished at the task.

Schema   A system of abstract structures stored in the memory that represents objects, topics, or relationships; a unit of organized knowledge that could be likened to a file folder on a specific topic. The topic may be broad in nature like "weather" or narrow in scope like "straight line winds." The plural of schema is schemata.

Schema theory   The cognitive learning theory that explains how knowledge is arranged in a complex information management system in the brain. Active readers integrate new knowledge into older, existing knowledge as learning deepens and expands.

Science fiction   A genre of literature in which narrative stories are set in a future time; imaginary technological inventions or extensions of today's technology are an integral part of the story.

Second language learners   Individuals who acquire a second language in addition to their native, first language.

Self-selected independent reading   A time during the day where children are given the opportunity to read books they choose at their independent level.

Semantics   The meaning of language; students often use the context of a sentence to figure out the meaning of an unfamiliar word.

Semantic features analysis grid   A way to connect old and new by gained knowledge of words and related concepts by graphing common or interesting traits of words that fit into the same category on a grid.

Semantic word map   A diagram or a graphic picture of concepts using lines and ovals or boxes containing information related to the word under study; the visual relationship between parts enables some students to see how words related to one another.

Sequence   An expository text structure that is common in narrative text in which an event unfolds in chronological order or in a series of steps; a noted successive order among ideas or events.

Shared reading   A group reading and discussion of a text, generally on a large chart or in a big book, that involves focused teaching of the vital concepts of print, comprehension strategies such as predicting, and other skills related to reading. Students participate and get the feeling of reading.

Shared writing   Similar to the language experience approach (LEA) because the teacher acts as a scribe, but the focus is on the composing process and on creating a text that children can later read. The emphasis is on the message or story.

Sight words   Frequently occurring words that are so familiar to a reader that they are recognized immediately without a need to decode them.

Simile   Making a comparison using "as" or "like."

Speaking vocabulary   The second meaning vocabulary that a child learns; words included in this vocabulary are learned by imitating family members and/or caregivers.

SQ3R   An acronym for a study system that represents the terms survey, question, read, recite, and review. It is especially effective when learners are working with expository text.

Standardized reading test   A reading test with specified tasks and procedures so that comparable measurements may be made by testers working in different geographical areas. Typically, norms are made on a reference group (a large number of students from a region or the entire country) and provided as a comparison group for local test results.

Standardized test   A test with specific tasks and procedures so that comparable measurements may be made by testers working in different geographical areas.

Standards   Specified requirements that must be met.

Story grammar   Hierarchical rules or psychological structures that specify relationships between parts of a story; people use knowledge of story grammars to create and remember stories.

Story map   A visual representation of a story that provides an overview including characters, setting, the problem, and resolution or ending.

Strategic reader   A reader who applies and adapts conscious and flexible plans to particular tasks and texts.

Strategy   A specific activity or procedure used to construct meaning and understand the text. Strategies are typically used before, during, or after reading.

Structural analysis   A way of investigating new words by breaking them into recognizable or meaningful parts (morphemes) to try to grasp their meaning.

Structured writing   Students learn the structure of specific types of writing: narrative, persuasive, and expository. They learn how to organize and develop these pieces, then write on a specific topic or prompt.

Summative assessment   The final evaluation, usually quantitative in nature, of the degree to which goals and objectives of a program have been met.

Sustained Silent Reading (SSR)   A time during the day where children are given the opportunity to read books they choose at an independent level.

Synonym   A word that has nearly the same meaning as another word like coarse/ scratch/rough.

Syntax   The order of language and how language works. Example: the subject of a sentence usually precedes the verb.

Synthetic phonics   Teaching children how to blend individual letters together to form words.

Tall tales   Tales that are included in a country's folklore whose characters are larger than life. North American tales feature characters like Pecos Bill and Paul Bunyan and his ox, Babe, with their daring deeds, humor, and superhuman efforts to tame the West.

Telegraphic speech   The use of short and precise words to communicate. Example: "More juice" rather than "I want more juice."

Text sets   Sets of books related to a common theme that are at varying reading levels.

Think-alouds   A way of modeling for students how you, as the teacher, think as you read selected text. To demonstrate, the teacher talks out loud to make her thinking visible as she reads the text aloud.

Top-down approach   Theorists who support this model or approach to teaching reading believe that the reader is of primary importance rather than the text. Meaning is made by drawing on one's background knowledge, ability to use language, and the expectation of what is going to be read. Teaching from the whole story to its parts.

Traditional literature   A wide range of literature that contains a variety of stories, proverbs, rhymes, and jingles that come from the oral tradition; the original authors are unknown.

Transaction   A key event in reader response; a unique interaction between a reader and the text that is influenced by one's background experiences, personal feelings, the context in which the reading occurs, and the reasons for reading.

Trickster tale   A part of the offerings of folklore; nearly every culture has its share of tricksters who try to outwit others with their cunning. Native American tricksters include Coyote and Raven, for example. Sometimes they succeed, while at other times they are tricked in return.

Webbing   A type of graphic organizer that helps students put words into recognizable categories.

Whole language approach   Reading and writing instructional approach that involves using real, relevant materials. Skills are taught when needed during "teachable moments."

Wide reading   Perhaps the most productive way to build vocabulary; students practice reading and work attack skills as they read a variety of materials including fiction and nonfiction texts both in school and out.

Word consciousness   Refers to an interest level in words that is both cognitive and affective as motivated students continually add to their pool of usable vocabulary.

Word study   An instructional technique that helps a child examine the way words are constructed and apply this knowledge to reading and writing.

Word wall   A space in the classroom with the alphabet posted where the teacher displays and practices (this is the key) the high utility words students need to know in order to read and spell automatically. The words may be outlined with a black marker to emphasize their shape.

Writing workshop   The teacher guides students through mini-lessons as well as individual and small group conferences. Students choose their own writing topics and write independently. The children are encouraged to share their writing with others.

Writing vocabulary   This is the smallest of the four key vocabularies because people tend to use fewer words in writing than they do in speaking or when reading. While it may begin before school, it is developed primarily in school.

Zone of proximal development   The term coined by Vygotsky; this is the difference between what a child can actually do on his own today, determined by his ability to solve problems, and what that same child can do under the guidance of an adult or more capable peer to reach his potential developmental level.

Acknowledgments

Chapter 1

CO 1 ©Michael Newman/Photo Edit   Fig. 1.1 ©Michael Newman/Photo Edit
Fig 1.2 ©Michael Newman/Photo Edit   Fig. 1.3 ©Tony Freeman/Photo Edit
Fig. 1.4 ©Myrleen Ferguson Cate/Photo Edit   Fig 1.5

Chapter 2

CO 2 ©Bettman/Corbis   Fig. 2.2 ©Bettman/Corbis   Fig 2.3 ©Hulton Getty/Stone
Fig. 2.5 ©Tony Freeman/Photo Edit   Fig. 2.6 ©Michael Newman/Photo Edit

Chapter 3

CO 3 ©Will Hart/Photo Edit   Fig. 3.2 ©David Young Wolf/Photo Edit
Fig 3.4 ©Frank Siteman/Photo Edit

Chapter 4

CO 4 ©Michael Newman/Photo Edit

Chapter 5

CO 5 ©Nancy Sheehan/Photo Edit   Fig. 5.1 ©Stephen McBrady/Photo Edit

Chapter 6

CO 6 ©Michelle Bridwell/Photo Edit   Fig. 6.2 ©Myrleen Ferguson Cate/Photo Edit
Fig. 6.3 ©Nancy Sheehan/Photo Edit   Fig. 6.4 ©David Young Wolf/Photo Edit
Fig. 6.6 ©David Young Wolf/Photo Edit

Chapter 7

CO 7 ©Michael Newman/Photo Edit   Fig. 7.1 ©David Young Wolf/Photo Edit
Fig 7.2 ©Myrleen Ferguson Cate/Photo Edit   Fig. 7.3 ©Robert Daemmrich/Stone
Fig. 7.4 ©Jonathan Nourok/Photo Edit

Chapter 8

CO 8 ©Robert Daemmrich/Stone   Fig. 8.1 ©Robert Daemmrich/The Image Works
Fig. 8.2 ©Robert Daemmrich/The Image Works   Fig. 8.3 ©Mary Kate Denny/
Photo Edit   Fig. 8.4 ©Tony Freeman/Photo Edit

Chapter 9

CO 9 ©Robert Daemmrich/The Image Works   Fig. 9.1 ©Tony Freeman/Photo Edit
Fig. 9.2 ©Bill Aron/Photo Edit   Fig. 9.3 ©Bill Aron/Photo Edit
Fig. 9.4 ©James Darrell/Stone

Chapter 10

CO 10 ©Mary Kate Denny/Stone   Fig. 10.1 ©Mary Kate Denny/Stone
Fig. 10.2 ©Mary Kate Denny/Photo Edit   Fig. 10.3 ©Monika Graff/The Image Works
Fig. 10.4 ©Michael Newman/Photo Edit

Chapter 11

CO 11 ©Syracuse Newspapers/The Image Works   Fig. 11.1 ©Tony Freeman/
Photo Edit   Fig. 11.2 ©Will Hart/Photo Edit   Fig. 11.3 ©David Young Wolf/
Photo Edit   Fig. 11.4 ©Kelly Mooney Photographs/Corbis

Chapter 12

CO 12 ©Syracuse Newspapers/The Image Works   Fig. 12.1 ©
Fig. 12.2 ©David Young Wolf/Photo Edit   Fig. 12.3 ©Robert Daemmrich/Stone
Fig. 12.4 ©Arthur Tilley/Stone

Name Index

Aardema, V., 61, 78, 138, A-2, A-35
Aazarian, M., 533, A-33
Abodeeb, T. L., 191, 205
Ackerman, K., 139, 141, A-36
Ada, A. F., 138, A-38
Adams, John Quincy, President, 558
Adams, M. J., 69, 110, 111, 243, 285, 286, 290, 291, 292, 294, 304, 318, 386
Adams, P., 296
Adams, R., 141
Adler, D. A., 104, 128, 139, 180, 464, 579, 582, A-2
Adoff, A., 531
Afflerbach, P., 328
Agard, J., 444, A-2
Ahlberg, J., 138
Alao, S., 195, 492
Alarcón, F. X., A-38
Albertin, H., 492
Alborough, J., 102, 128, A-2
Alcorn, S., 426, A-11, A-16, A-19, A-39
Algozzine, B., 119
Algozzine, R. F., 119, 151, 155, 289
Aliki, 138, 458, 461, 589, A-2
Allard, H., 138
Alleman, J., 192, 202
Allen, J., 384
Allington, R. L., 12, 20, 25, 83, 105, 129, 150, 151, 216, 240, 326, 327, 344, 350, 358, 365, 366, 380, 385, 386, 392, 402, 419, 484, 489
Almasi, J. F., 359, 437
Almond, D., 141
Altman, L. J., 412, 426, 449, A-2
Alvermann, D. E., 7, 326
Ambrosini, M., 182
Ancona, G., A-38
Anders, P., 398
Andersen, H. C., A-2, A-33
Anderson, D. A., A-39
Anderson, J. S., 142

Anderson, P., 108
Anderson, R. C., 7, 67, 68, 77, 105, 325, 328, 365, 380, 389, 433, 465, 490
Anderson, T. H., 548
Anderson, W., A-2, A-3
Andreason, D., A-2
Angelou, M., 142
Anno, M., 139, A-3
Anonymous, 142
Apple, M., 537, A-22
Archambault, J., 318, A-15
Armbruster, B. B., 548
Armstrong, J., 142
Armstrong, L., 42
Armstrong, W. H., A-38
Arnold, C., 550
Arnold, J., 422
Arnosky, J., 139, 141, 246, 278, 558, 589, A-3
Aruego, J., 129, 138, 247, A-5, A-9
Asch, F., 466, A-3
Asimov, I., 142
Astrella, M., 556, A-18
Atwell, N., 66, 101, 118, 182, 499, 544, 562, 577
Au, K. H., 66, 161, 198, 199, 285, 439, 470
Auel, J. M., 142
Avi, 141, 512, 528, 536, A-3, A-32, A-37
Aylesworth, J., 138, 263, 278, A-3
Ayton, R., A-13

Babbitt, N., 141, 506, 536, A-3, A-38
Bahous, S., 422
Bahti, T., A-35
Bailey, P., A-40
Baker, J., A-8
Baker, O., A-34
Baker, T. K., 103
Ball, A. F., 71
Bang, M. G., 138, 139, 516, 536, A-3, A-33, A-35
Banks, C. A., 24
Banks, J. A., 24
Banks, L. R., 141

Barksdale-Ladd, M. A., 469
Barone, D., 565
Barrentine, S. J., 205
Barrera, R. B., 443, 445, 451, 464
Barrett, A., 582
Barrett, J., 139
Barrett, N., 532
Barron, T. A., 142, 455, A-3
Barry, A., 466
Barton, C., 558
Barton, H., 532
Barton, K. C., 575, 577, 583
Bartone, E., 422, 462, A-3, A-33
Base, G., A-5
Baskin, L., A-35
Bates, I., 138, 426
Bauer, C. F., 474
Bauer, J., 142, A-36
Bauer, M. D., A-37
Baumann, J. F., 485, 486
Baviera, R., A-5
Bayard, C., A-40
Bayer, J., 300, 318, A-4
Baylor, B., 138, 507, A-35
Bear, D. R., 65, 114, 260, 287, 302, 305, 306, 310, 318, 395, 398, 401, 407, 426
Beatty, A. S., 544
Beck, I. L., 326, 338, 345, 381, 382, 383, 384, 389, 510, 511, 544
Beck, M. D., 194
Beddows, E., 128, A-8
Beecher, H. W., 55
Beeke, T., 138, 505
Beeler, T., 292, 318
Begay, S., 422
Beier, E., 318, A-24
Beil, K. M., 505
Belton, S., 449
Beltrán, 439, 562
Bender, R., 300, 318, A-4
Benét, R., 582
Benét, S., 582
Bennett, N., 449, 582
Bentley, E. C., 519
Berger, M., 263, 278, A-4
Berry, J., 368, 374, A-4

Subject Index